WE CALLED HIM
RABBI
ABRAHAM

WE CALLED HIM RABBI ABRAHAM

LINCOLN AND AMERICAN JEWRY

A DOCUMENTARY HISTORY
—

EDITED WITH INTRODUCTIONS BY
GARY PHILLIP ZOLA

Southern Illinois University Press
Carbondale

Copyright © 2014 by Gary Phillip Zola
All rights reserved
Printed in the United States of America

"Abraham" by Irving Berlin copyright © 1941 by Irving Berlin;
copyright renewed; International Copyright Secured; all rights
reserved; reprinted in chapter 10 by permission.

Excerpts from *Land of Lincoln*, copyright © 2007 by Andrew
Ferguson; used by permission of Grove/Atlantic, Inc.; any
third-party use of this material, outside this publication, is
prohibited.

17 16 15 14   4 3 2 1

Library of Congress Cataloging-in-Publication Data

    We called him Rabbi Abraham : Lincoln and American
Jewry, a documentary history / edited with introductions by
Gary Phillip Zola.
        pages cm
    Includes bibliographical references and index.
    ISBN-13: 978-0-8093-3292-2 (cloth : alk. paper)
    ISBN-10: 0-8093-3292-2 (cloth : alk. paper)
    ISBN 13: 978-0-8093-3293-9 (ebook)
    ISBN-10: 0-8093-3293-0 (ebook)
    1. Lincoln, Abraham, 1809–1865—Relations with Jews.
2. Lincoln, Abraham, 1809–1865—Influence. 3. Jews—United
States—History—19th century. 4. United States—History—
Civil War, 1861–1865—Jews. I. Zola, Gary Phillip, editor of
compilation. II. Zola, Gary Phillip, editor of
compilation. Abraham Lincoln and American Jewry.
III. Title.
E457.2.W48 2014
973.7089'924—dc23   2013015585

Printed on recycled paper. ♻
The paper used in this publication meets the minimum
requirements of American National Standard for Information
Sciences—Permanence of Paper for Printed Library Materials,
ANSI Z39.48–1992. ∞

To my parents
Roy M. Zola
Estelle C. Zola
Sidney Rothberg
Sylvia Rothberg

"We cannot escape history"
—Abraham Lincoln, second annual message to Congress

∽

To my darlings
Mandi
Jory
Jeremy
Samantha

"The struggle of today . . . is for a vast future also"
—Abraham Lincoln, second annual message to Congress

∽

And to my dearest
Stefi

"Throughout that long period, [s]he has constantly been the most loved"
—Abraham Lincoln's eulogy on Henry Clay, 1852

Contents

List of Illustrations   ix

Acknowledgments   xi

Introduction: Abraham Lincoln and American Jewry   1

1. Immigrants and the Old Northwest: Lincoln's First
   Encounters with American Jewry   9

2. "The Most Favored Family Visitor at the White House": The Enigmatic
   Relationship between Lincoln and Isachar Zacharie, M.D.   44

3. Lincoln and the Chaplaincy Controversy   72

4. Lincoln and the Revocation of General Orders No. 11   91

5. Lincoln and the Movement to Christianize the U.S. Constitution   117

6. "A Great Man in Israel Has Fallen": American Jewry Mourns Lincoln   138

7. Conflicting Obligations: Shavuot and the National
   Day of Humiliation and Mourning   178

8. Criticisms and Commendations: Conflicting
   Views on the Lincoln Presidency   191

9. Memorializing and Judaizing Lincoln   227

10. "His Name Will Ever Be Green in Your Hearts":
    Jews and the Cultural Preservation of Lincoln's Legacy   267

11. "Lincoln! Thou Shouldst Be Living at This Hour!" Lincoln
    as a Moral Compass for American Jews   309

12. Lincoln Miscellany   354

Epilogue   392

Notes   397

Index   443

Illustrations

Samuel G. Alschuler 13

Abraham Jonas 14

Simon Wolf 24

Drawing by Lloyd Ostendorf of Lincoln
    sitting for Alschuler 27

Abraham Lincoln, 1858 27

Charles H. Jonas and Lincoln's note 32

Abraham Kohn 35

Kohn's Hebrew flag 35

Alexander Gardner's "cracked glass" portrait of Lincoln 41

Facsimile of last Lincoln portrait 42

Isachar Zacharie 44

Broadside advertising Zacharie's skill as a podiatrist 58

Max Friedman 73

Michael M. Allen 74

Jacob Frankel 78

Arnold Fischel 84

Isaac Leeser 88

Ulysses S. Grant, circa 1865 92

Petersburg, Va., sutler's tent, Second Division,
    Ninth Corps, November 1864 93

Cesar J. Kaskel 96

Abraham Lincoln, 1863 98

Charles Sumner 118

Abraham Lincoln, 1864 120

Temple Emanu-El on Twelfth Street in New York City, 1854–66 139

Lodge Street temple where Congregation Bene Yeshurun
    of Cincinnati worshipped, 1848–66 143

Abraham Lincoln's railroad funeral car, 1865 173

Jacques Judah Lyons 179

Benjamin Szold 180

Isaac M. Wise 195

Isaac Goldstein's Hebrew "Acrostic" 220

Eleanor H. Cohen 221

Julius E. Francis 229

Emil G. Hirsch 232

Jewish immigrants arriving in the United States, circa 1900 233

David Philipson 234

Isaac Markens 268

Emanuel Hertz 271

Bertram Wallace Korn 274

Solomon Nuñes Carvalho 286

Carvalho's painting *Lincoln and Diogenes* 286

Victor David Brenner 287

Reproduction of Brenner's Lincoln Medal of 1907 288

Lincoln penny featuring Brenner's initials 288

Moses Jacob Ezekiel 289

Ezekiel's studio 290

Max Kalish 291

Kalish's statue of Lincoln at Gettysburg 293

Jo Davidson 294

One of Davidson's portrait busts of Lincoln 295

Cover sheet for *Yente Telebende* 296

Cover sheet of Jacob Weinberg's score of "The Gettysburg Address" 297

Aaron Copland's annotated copy of the speaker's
    part in "Lincoln Portrait" 301

Jacob Salmon Raisin 317

Americanization pageant, Milwaukee, 1919 327

Tehilla Lichtenstein 347

Rav A. Soloff 350

Arthur Szyk's lithographed illumination of Lincoln's
    second inaugural address 357

World War II "good luck ring" advertisement 375

Page from *Little New Angel* by Sadie Rose Weilerstein 378

Acknowledgments

Those who are born and raised in Illinois understand from an early age, almost by osmosis, that they live in the state that claims Abraham Lincoln as its favorite son. There can be little doubt that the root of my interest in Abraham Lincoln comes from the fact that my formative years—the first two decades of my life—were spent in the "Land of Lincoln," where the sixteenth president's name and image are ubiquitous. A number of my friends in junior high school had attended Lincoln Elementary, one of our family's favorite eateries was on Lincoln Avenue, and the synagogue my family attended—Temple Beth El—was adjacent to a suburb known as Lincolnwood.

My earliest recollection of Lincoln and Judaism explicitly intersecting in my life stems from the time that one of my parents' friends gave me a bronze bust of Abraham Lincoln on the occasion of my becoming a Bar Mitzvah on January 30, 1965. My parents gently recommended that I return the bust to Marshall Field's department store and purchase something more "useful"—something more suitable for a thirteen-year-old boy. To my parents' astonishment, I dismissed the suggestion out of hand. I had no intention of returning my Lincoln bust, I told them. One day, it would look very impressive on my desk. Although the bust does not sit on my desk, it remains in my possession to this day.

It was my teacher and mentor, however, the late Jacob Rader Marcus—the dean of American Jewish historians—who first introduced me to Lincoln's singular place in the annals of American Jewish history. I can still see myself sitting in his American Jewish history class at Hebrew Union College–Jewish Institute of Religion (HUC-JIR) in Cincinnati, and, if I close my eyes, I can hear his distinctive voice recounting the details surrounding the promulgation of Ulysses S. Grant's General Orders No. 11, the only time in U.S. history that Jews "as a class" were banished from American soil. Marcus taught us about a Jew named Cesar Kaskel, who had been expelled from his hometown of Paducah, Kentucky. Kaskel traveled to Washington, D.C., to ask President Lincoln to revoke Grant's odious order. Marcus described how Kaskel managed to procure a personal interview with the president, at which time he implored Lincoln to revoke Grant's order and thereby protect American Jewry's rights under the U.S. Constitution. Lincoln immediately rejoined with his often-repeated (though historically undocumented) pledge: "And this protection you shall have at once." Lincoln revoked Grant's order then and there.

I was completely mesmerized.

Years earlier, Marcus had urged his star pupil, Bertram W. Korn, to research the history of American Jewry and the Civil War and, specifically, Abraham Lincoln's relationship with his fellow Jewish citizens. I read Korn's book from cover to cover that year, and I learned that there was much more to the story of Lincoln and the Jews than the revocation of Grant's order. Years later, in my own courses, I taught my students about Lincoln, relying on the knowledge I had acquired from Marcus and Korn. For years, I assumed these scholars had unearthed most of what there was to know about Abraham Lincoln and American Jewry.

All of these experiences may well have played a germinating role in the origination of this particular work, but my decision to write an entirely new book on Lincoln and American Jewry first began to take shape in 2006, the year I was invited to serve on the Academic Advisory Council of the U.S. Abraham Lincoln Bicentennial Commission (ALBC).

As a member of the ALBC's Academic Advisory Council, I had the privilege of meeting some of the nation's most accomplished and distinguished Lincoln scholars. Although I was familiar with their publications, it was overwhelming to see my own name on an academic roster that included people such as Michael Beschloss, Richard N. Current, Eric Foner, John Hope Franklin, Doris Kearns Goodwin, James M. McPherson, and many others. After all, at the time I was appointed to the council, I had not published even one sentence of original research on Abraham Lincoln.

Many of the meetings of the ALBC featured academic colloquia where outstanding Lincoln scholars such as Harold Holzer, Frank J. Williams, and Gabor S. Boritt lectured. I quickly realized how little I knew about Abraham Lincoln in general, and I decided that my own personal contribution as a member of the ALBC's Academic Advisory Council would be to dedicate myself to studying and teaching about Lincoln and American Jewry.

As a specialist in American Jewish history, I was familiar with the major works that had already been published, including Isaac Markens's *Abraham Lincoln and the Jews* (1909), Emanuel Hertz's edited volume *Abraham Lincoln: The Tribute of the Synagogue* (1927), and Bertram W. Korn's *American Jewry and the Civil War* (1951). My studies began with these works and fanned out from there. It did not take long for me to realize that there was much more to say about Lincoln and American Jewry now that more than half a century has passed since Korn first published his meticulously researched volume. With the publication of this book, I have fulfilled a promise I made to myself nearly seven years ago.

My professorial beau ideal, Jacob Rader Marcus, always began his acknowledgments by emphasizing, "No book writes itself."[1] How true! Without the help and encouragement of dozens of individuals and institutions, it would be impossible for any author to produce a publication of this sort. It is no exaggeration to say that this volume in particular would never have appeared had it not been for the unhemmed support and generous assistance I was given by so many men and women. I am grateful for the opportunity to express my genuine gratitude to those who responded so graciously to my many appeals for help in bringing this work to completion.

I am everlastingly indebted to my colleagues at The Jacob Rader Marcus Center of the American Jewish Archives (AJA). No matter how eloquently framed, words cannot possibly express the extent of my appreciation to Dana Herman, the center's academic associate and managing editor of the *American Jewish Archives Journal*. Dana's editorial expertise can be seen on literally every page of this volume. She subjects herself to the highest standards of excellence in her work at The Marcus Center, and her general editorial assistance was invaluable. She cared for this manuscript as if it were her own. To simply say, "Thank you, Dana," seems unforgivably inadequate, but I offer her my earnest gratitude with the deepest sincerity.

Sonja Rethy has checked and rechecked each and every document in this volume in an effort to ensure the highest level of accurate transcription. In doing so, Sonja's close reading of the manuscript has unquestionably resulted in a final product that was significantly improved in both style and content. I am grateful for her meticulous efforts and her exceptionally fine editorial contributions. Phil Reekers, the AJA's talented digitization and graphic design staffer, originally keystroked all of the documents in this volume. His manifold contributions to this project have consistently gone above and beyond the call of duty, and I sincerely appreciate his loyal support and his dedication to every facet of his work at The Marcus Center.

Those who have had the opportunity to conduct research at the AJA, or have ever had an occasion to ask one of the AJA's archival professionals for scholarly assistance, will confirm the assertion that the AJA sets an extremely high bar when it comes to being "research friendly." I believe it is fair to say that I received the same outstanding archival assistance that every AJA patron enjoys, and I am profoundly grateful to the following members of the AJA archival staff for their ongoing commitment to the highest standards of their profession: Kevin Proffitt, senior archivist for Research and Collections; Dorothy Smith, archivist; Nathan Tallman and Elisa Ho, associate archivists; and Camille Servizzi, assistant to the archivists. The Marcus Center's staffers also deserve recognition for their ongoing contributions to my academic and administrative responsibilities: Stacey Roper, Nancy Dowlin, and Al Simandl, as well as those who retired before this volume was ready for publication, namely Eleanor Lawhorn, Ruth Kreimer, and Elise Nienaber.

It is literally impossible for me to express a full measure of my gratitude for the help and support I have received from distinguished Lincoln scholars such as Harold Holzer, one of this nation's leading authorities on Abraham Lincoln. I had the good fortune of meeting Holzer when he served as a cochair of the ALBC. Subsequently, we both participated in a special program on Lincoln and the Jews. Since that time, Holzer has encouraged my research and taken a special interest in this particular project. His scholarly advice and wise counsel have unquestionably resulted in a much-improved publication. Similarly, Jonathan D. Sarna of Brandeis University, my Ph.D. dissertation advisor and an indefatigable mentor, carefully read an earlier version of this manuscript. The same is true of Edward Goldman of Hebrew Union College–Jewish Institute of Religion (HUC-JIR). I benefited greatly from the efforts of these scholarly readers, and their comments unquestionably prevented me from including errors, infelicities, and inaccuracies. Of course, I am entirely responsible for all those that remain.

I also wish to express my deep gratitude for the generous academic support I have received from HUC-JIR. Specifically, I wish to acknowledge David Ellenson, president of the College-Institute, who has been an enthusiastic booster of the school's renowned academic resources—the AJA and the Klau Library, located on the school's historic Cincinnati campus. The Klau Library has been inestimably helpful with this project, as it is with every academic endeavor undertaken by an HUC-JIR faculty member. I am particularly grateful to David Gilner, director of libraries, Laurel Wolfson, administrative librarian, and the library's staff for their ongoing assistance. Many thanks are due to students (and former students) who have served as research assistants over the years: David McKenzie, Alison Schottenstein, Matthew Semler, and Elizabeth Wood.

This volume contains a number of rabbinical sermons, originally written in German, that have never before appeared in English. I wish to thank and recognize Elizabeth Petuchowski, former adjunct associate professor in the German department of the University of Cincinnati, for graciously providing me excellent English renditions of the German originals.

It has been a privilege to work with Southern Illinois University (SIU) Press on this book project. A special word of gratitude is due to Sylvia Frank Rodrigue, executive editor, who has consistently offered wise counsel and unstinting support. Julie Bush's meticulous copyediting and her incisive queries unquestionably resulted in a much improved final product. Thanks are also due to project editor Wayne Larsen and to Barb Martin and Bridget Brown for their dedicated efforts. I have no doubt that the book has been greatly enhanced as a result of my ongoing collaboration with the SIU Press staff.

I now turn to my friend and colleague of nearly three decades, Lisa B. Frankel, director of programs and administration at The Marcus Center. It is literally impossible for me to express all that I owe her. Again, I imitate my own mentor when I thank Lisa "for her years of service, experience, and tolerance!" Thank you, thank you, thank you, Lisa!

There were so many others who lent me their support and assistance as this book took shape over the past seven years but whose names will regrettably go unmentioned. I am deeply grateful to all who have helped me on this particular journey.

The great American orator and politician Robert G. Ingersoll—himself a Civil War veteran—framed beautiful, resonant words that capture my final heartfelt expression of gratitude: "Love is . . . the air and light of every heart—builder of every home, kindler of every fire on every hearth. . . . It is the perfume of that wondrous flower, the heart, and without that sacred passion, that divine swoon, we are less than beasts but with it, earth is heaven."[2]

With these sentiments in mind, I wish to offer my deeply felt appreciation to my own family for their countless sacrifices—always offered up and given with love—that have enabled me to complete this task. To them, I gratefully and lovingly dedicate this work.

WE CALLED HIM
RABBI
ABRAHAM

Introduction: Abraham Lincoln and American Jewry

On Wednesday, April 19, 1865, Lewis Naphtali Dembitz, a prominent lawyer, Jewish communal leader, and longtime activist in the Republican Party, ascended the pulpit of Beth Israel Synagogue on Green Street in Louisville, Kentucky, to participate in the congregation's obsequies for Abraham Lincoln. He began his lament with these remarkable words: "You often called him, jocosely, Rabbi Abraham, as if he were one of our nation—of the seed of Israel; but, in truth, you might have called him 'Abraham, the child of our father Abraham.' For, indeed, of all the Israelites throughout the United States, there was none who more thoroughly filled the ideal of what a true descendant of Abraham ought to be than Abraham Lincoln."[1]

Lincoln's familiar nickname, "Father Abraham," was popularized in the Union army. The country's soldiers enjoyed seeing the president when he visited the camps. He called them "my boys," and they called him "Father Abraham." In doing so, they playfully associated the biblical patriarch Abraham, the father of monotheistic faith, with their American "father," Abraham Lincoln, the nation's president.[2] American Jewish soldiers undoubtedly also referred to Lincoln as "Father Abraham." Yet it is an indisputable fact that some Jews—as Dembitz's eulogy demonstrates—whimsically referred to the president as *Rabbi* Abraham, "as if he were one of our nation."

Over the course of American history, Jews have held many American leaders in high esteem, but American Jewry's emotional bond with Abraham Lincoln can be described only as sui generis. From the time of his presidency to the present day, American Jews have persistently believed that Lincoln was one of their own. They continuously conceived of Lincoln as a Jewish sojourner and, in certain respects, a Jewish role model. But how did Lincoln acquire this exceptional status, and how, over the past century and a half, did this interesting relationship evolve?

One facet of this special bond may be traced back to the fact that Lincoln and his Jewish contemporaries interacted on a personal level. Lincoln knew some American Jews, and some American Jews knew Lincoln. The sixteenth president was arguably the first man to arrive in the White House having long fraternized with a considerable number of Jews prior to assuming the presidency. During the 1850s, Lincoln patronized Jewish businesses, worked shoulder to shoulder with Jews who were actively involved in local politics, and made friends with a noteworthy number of Jews while he traveled across Illinois's Eighth Judicial Circuit. In addition, a considerable number of Jews considered Lincoln to be a personal friend or, at the very least, a personal acquaintance. Jews had had political associations with Lincoln for years, and some took part in helping Lincoln to secure his party's nomination in 1860. After he was chosen to head the Republican ticket, numerous American Jews participated enthusiastically in his election campaign. In short, among Lincoln's many friends, there was a band of Jewish Lincoln loyalists.

Interestingly, had Abraham Lincoln been running for president in 1840 instead of 1860, this relationship might never have been possible. This is because, demographically speaking, American Jewry had become a perceptible communal presence at the very time that Lincoln's political career was unfolding. Between the mid-1830s and the 1860s, thousands of Jews from German-speaking lands, as well as Jews from the Baltic region, immigrated to the United States. A considerable number of these immigrants settled in Illinois, Indiana, Kentucky, Missouri, Ohio, and Wisconsin. Many of them had been activists in the liberal revolutionary movements of their native lands. The failure of these revolutions and the subsequent reactionary political response drove them to emigrate in search of a better life. Economic opportunity, American democracy, and the Constitution's promise of freedom pulled them from across the Atlantic to the New World. It did not take long for many of these seasoned activists to dive headfirst into the pool of local politics.

These Jewish newcomers discovered they were welcome to participate in the hurly-burly world of politics on the American frontier. Many took a keen interest in the intensifying debate over slavery in America. Those who had fought for civic enfranchisement in the Old World identified with the struggle to abolish slavery in the New. Typically, the Jews who were opposed to the institution of slavery did not associate themselves with abolitionist societies; the Christian evangelical rhetoric and the exclusiveness that dominated these associations were off-putting. They needed a way to participate on their own terms. Many immigrant Jews were attracted to the Republican Party and to Lincoln's candidacy for these very reasons.[3]

The interaction between Lincoln and the American Jewish community continued to evolve during his years in office. The president encountered a number of Jewish communal leaders—including many American rabbis—who made personal appeals to him on behalf of their constituents. He also engaged with various Jewish personalities who were soliciting a personal favor. Lincoln invited Jewish citizens to attend social functions held at the White House, and he even developed a personal association with a Jewish chiropodist who cared for his feet and whom he subsequently sent to New Orleans to serve as a special envoy for his administration. During the Lincoln presidency, Jewish newspaper editors reported on these various encounters.

In assessing Lincoln's attitude concerning the African American and civil rights, Mary Frances Berry argues that Lincoln had "no static, dead-hand view of the Constitution. [For Lincoln], the Constitution was a changing, evolving document yielding to necessity."[4] It has been similarly noted that one of Lincoln's most admirable personality traits was his openness to change and his willingness to reassess his principles in the face of changing realities. As the distinguished African American historian Carter G. Woodson observed many years ago, Lincoln "gradually grew into the full stature of democracy."[5] Lincoln's decisive actions in a series of highly publicized controversies concerning Jews and civil rights constitute another useful perspective on his view of the Constitution as well as on his ability to respond to changing social circumstances.

In July 1861, the U.S. Congress adopted a law that permitted each of the Union's regimental commanders, on a vote of his field officers, to appoint a chaplain who was "a regularly ordained minister of some Christian denomination."[6] As the implications of this law dawned on the American Jewish community, an organized protest was brought directly to Lincoln. He immediately understood why this law was exclusionary and unfair, and he subsequently took steps to see that the law was amended so that Jews as well as Christians could become chaplains in the U.S. military. Similarly, his decision to immediately revoke Ulysses S. Grant's infamous General Orders No. 11—an order banishing "Jews as a class" from the military's Department of Tennessee—further enhanced his reputation as a man of fairness who was genuinely concerned about the welfare of the American Jewish community. The rise of an organized effort to install Christianity as the official religion of the United States by amending the Constitution was a particularly worrisome development for American Jewry. Again, Lincoln's skillful management of this movement sheds light on his political acumen as well as on his views on the Constitution.

The aforementioned controversies attracted widespread public attention during the Lincoln administration, and even Jews who had never been Lincoln loyalists would eulogize the fallen president graciously and describe him as a man who was earnestly sympathetic to American Jewry's concerns and interests. Rabbi Morris J. Raphall of New York, for example, was never a Lincoln loyalist. Nevertheless, he did not hesitate to go to Washington and ask the president to grant his son a military promotion. Lincoln acceded to Raphall's request, and the rabbi left the meeting convinced that his request had been granted, in part, because Lincoln knew he "was a Jew."[7] Lincoln made a similar impression on Rabbi Isaac Mayer Wise of Cincinnati. Wise was a loyal member of the Democratic Party and, from time to time, would criticize Lincoln harshly in the pages of his newspaper, the *Israelite*. Yet, after he met Lincoln personally to thank him for revoking Grant's odious order, Wise told readers of the *Israelite* that Lincoln "entertained no prejudices of any kind against any nationality, and especially against Israelites, to whom he manifested a particular attachment."[8]

As president, Lincoln definitely had his share of Jewish detractors and political opponents. In the South, there were those who wanted to assassinate him before he could take his oath of office. One of the most urgent warnings about this plot came from a man who may very well have been Lincoln's oldest Jewish friend, Abraham Jonas from Quincy, Illinois. Jonas had ten children, and some of them lived in New Orleans when Lincoln won the election. The Jonas children knew Lincoln well; he visited their father in Quincy on a number of occasions. They always spoke fondly of Lincoln, and this familial relationship may have prompted at least one of them to notify Jonas in Quincy that there were those in New Orleans who intended to kill Lincoln upon his arrival in Washington in order to prevent him from assuming office. Jonas promptly wrote Lincoln a letter of warning, urging him to take all necessary precaution. The fact that Abraham Jonas's children leaked the plot to their father, however, did not mean they were Lincoln supporters. To the contrary, four of Jonas's sons joined the Confederate army and remained lifelong loyal sons of the South.[9]

The vast majority of southern Jews were Confederate patriots who were ardently opposed to Lincoln's party and his politics. Arguably the most prominent Jewish Confederate of all, Judah P. Benjamin, once described Lincoln as the candidate "who denies me all my rights, openly and fairly."[10] As far as Benjamin and his peers were concerned, the die for secession had been cast once the nation elected a man who carried the banner of the Republican Party. Benjamin was undoubtedly speaking for thousands of fellow southerners—Jewish and non-Jewish—when, on December 31, 1860, he arose in the chambers of the U.S. Senate to defend the right of the southern states to secede from the Union. "An enslaved and servile race you can never make of us," Benjamin defiantly proclaimed; "Never! Never!"[11] Throughout the South, thousands of young Jewish men took up arms to defend their homeland once hostilities erupted.

President Lincoln had Jewish critics in the North, too. Jewish spokesmen like Wise, Raphall, and Isaac Leeser often spoke as though they were formally associated with the Copperheads—northern Democrats who opposed the government's war policy in favor of a negotiated peace settlement with the South. In their newspaper columns and from their pulpits, these men periodically berated the way Lincoln prosecuted the war, criticized his decision to suspend the writ of habeas corpus, and bemoaned his various political missteps. Yet, Lincoln's Jewish critics—whether in the North or the South—were also known to acknowledge his probity and earnestness.

In analyzing the Lincoln-Douglas debates, for example, Judah P. Benjamin concluded that it was "impossible not to admire [Lincoln's] perfect candor and frankness."[12] Similarly, at the very end of the war, when Lincoln made his famous visit to Richmond in April 1865—only days before his death—Gustavus A. Myers, a loyal southerner and one of the city's most prominent Jewish citizens, met with Lincoln in the hope of persuading him to be lenient with the South. Lincoln impressed Myers with his friendly disposition and his "civility and good humor."[13] In the wake of Lincoln's brutal assassination, Jews joined with the rest of the Union in exalting Lincoln and honoring his memory. Although there were a few instances where southern Jews literally celebrated Lincoln's death, most Confederate Jews chose to shun manifest expressions of rejoicing.

Even in death, Lincoln provided members of the Jewish community an opportunity to participate as equals in the affairs of the nation. In every city in the Union where there was a significant Jewish population, Jewish citizens and Jewish organizations figured prominently in the public obsequies held in Lincoln's memory. Jews marched as a collective in Lincoln's various funeral pageants and processions, and rabbis were invited to offer prayers in public memorial ceremonies that were subsequently organized. Eulogies for Lincoln were delivered in practically every Jewish congregation throughout the country. Like the hundreds of eulogies delivered in Christian houses of worship, a noteworthy number of the Jewish eulogies appeared in the community press or were later published in pamphlets for public circulation. In a sense, Lewis Dembitz was speaking for all of American Jewry when he told the Jews of Louisville, "I speak to you on this occasion not as a preacher—I am not a prophet nor a son of a prophet—but I stand before you as the chief mourner, thinking, as I do, that, among this congregation, none thought oftener or more than I did of the great dead, whose fate we today lament."[14]

It was in the context of the Lincoln eulogies that American Jews first began to embrace Lincoln as a Jewish exemplar. Making specific mention of Lincoln's longstanding personal relationship with American Jewry and recollecting the tangible efforts the president made to safeguard Jewry's civil rights, Lincoln was repeatedly eulogized as an adoptive father of the children of Israel. Lincoln, these Jewish leaders explicitly declared, "was like one of us."[15] Rabbi Max Lilienthal of Cincinnati declared, "A great man has fallen in Israel!" Rabbi Wise, also of Cincinnati, assured his people that Lincoln "preserved numerous features of the Hebrew race, both in countenance and character."[16] In Baltimore, Rabbi Benjamin Szold dramatically proclaimed: "Even while [Lincoln] was not flesh of our flesh, he was spirit of our spirit and essence of our essence. His soul and heart, his entire nature . . . are all truly Judaic and truly Jewish in spirit."[17]

The widespread promulgation of these assertions, and others like them, throughout the American Jewish community marked the beginning of a process that might best be called the Judaization of Abraham Lincoln. For American Jewry, this phenomenon incrementally transformed Lincoln from a great American president and national hero into a bona fide American Jewish icon.

Over the past century and a half, the Judaization of Lincoln has gone hand in hand with the Americanization of this country's Jewry. Jews eagerly participated in the process of memorializing and exalting Lincoln together with the rest of the American nation. They contributed funds to erect communal monuments and iconic statues in his honor. They continually played a leading role in the process of gathering and preserving Lincolniana and in publishing books about his life. As the custom of commemorating Lincoln's birthday took root during the last decades of the nineteenth century, American Jews dutifully marked these occasions and paid homage to his life in sermons and orations. In 1909, when the nation celebrated the centennial anniversary of Lincoln's birth, American Jewry produced a torrent of lectures, sermons, essays, and programs in almost every Jewish community throughout the country. All through the twentieth century, Jews participated in the cultural construction of Lincoln's image. They composed music about Lincoln, they sculpted his image, and they painted his likeness. In every conceivable way, American Jews have been active participants in what one rabbi called "the sacred memory of one of [the] true and faithful servants for the common good of all mankind and the honor of our land."[18]

Yet, the image and ideal of Abraham Lincoln in the nation's collective memory has concomitantly influenced the Americanization and acculturation of American Jewry. It was Lincoln, more than any other personality in American history, who spoke to the nation's immigrant newcomers. A sociologist who studied Lincoln's influence on the nation's memory has observed that "beneath the immigrants' diverse experiences of Lincoln was the common belief that he would have understood and respected them in their singularity."[19]

The legacy of Lincoln appealed to the millions of East European Jewish immigrants who poured into this country between 1881 and 1924. There was no one more authentically American than Lincoln, and, by revering Lincoln, immigrants were simultaneously embracing the nation's heritage. Through the world of Yiddish culture—stories, poems, and songs—immigrants learned about Lincoln and, in doing so, made him one of their own. He became meaningful to them as Jews *and* as Americans. Just as the biblical Abraham was a father to all the monotheistic faiths, so too was the memory of Abraham Lincoln an inspiration to all Americans, especially to the immigrant newcomers.

Yet, it has been aptly noted that it is very difficult to "distinguish the sense in which the Jews had assimilated Lincoln from the sense in which Lincoln had assimilated them."[20] The symbiotic relationship linking American Jewry to Abraham Lincoln is particularly apparent in a genre of sermons and speeches that began to appear around the time of the centennial anniversary of Lincoln's birth in 1909. Again and again over the course of the twentieth century, rabbis, educators, and Jewish communal leaders pondered the question, "What would Lincoln do if he were alive today?" The answer was inevitably the assertion that a Jewish lesson could be conveyed by Lincoln's personal example. Jewish liberals and conservatives, Jewish businessmen and laborers, Jewish socialists and capitalists, Jewish religious reformers and traditionalists all insisted that if Lincoln were alive, he would be urging them to pursue their particular mission because they were Americans *and* because they were Jews.

∼

The foregoing generalizations are based on a careful study of the numerous primary source documents that have been assembled in the following chapters as well as on the accompanying secondary literature used to elucidate them. Although other scholars have written on this topic, this work constitutes the first thoroughgoing documentary analysis of Abraham Lincoln's historical relationship with American Jewry from its beginnings nearly two decades before he became a national figure through the first decade of the twenty-first century. Each chapter begins with a concise introduction, which adumbrates its thematic content, and contains a series of illustrative documents. Each item in this section of the chapter is introduced by a headnote that highlights the document's significance and places it in a historical context.

Chapter 1 describes Lincoln's earliest Jewish encounters, which began in the 1840s and continued to evolve up until he assumed the presidency in 1861. Shortly after his inauguration, Lincoln came into contact with one of the most complex and intriguing of his many Jewish associates, Isachar Zacharie. The story of Lincoln's relationship with Zacharie—a podiatrist who was destined to become Lincoln's friend and, ultimately, a furtive envoy for the Lincoln administration—is reconstructed in chapter 2.

Chapters 3, 4, and 5 focus respectively on three significant sociopolitical controversies concerning the Jews that transpired during Lincoln's presidency. Chapter 3 concentrates on the so-called chaplaincy controversy that resulted from a law adopted by the U.S. Congress in July 1861 that permitted each of the Union's regimental commanders, on a vote of his field officers, to appoint a chaplain so long as he was "a regularly ordained minister of some Christian denomination."[21] Lincoln's response to a second crisis, brought on by the promulgation of General Orders No. 11, Ulysses S. Grant's infamous edict expelling "Jews as a class" from the Military Department of Tennessee—the only time in all of U.S. history when Jews were banished from American territory—is the subject of chapter 4. Chapter 5 deals with a third concern that worried the Jewish community during Lincoln's presidency: the rise of an organized effort to install Christianity as the official religion of the United States by amending the Constitution. In each one of these instances, representatives of the Jewish community addressed their complaints to Lincoln and urged him to side with them. He did not disappoint.

Chapter 6 contains a sampling of the many eulogies and obsequies that the Jewish community offered up in the wake of Lincoln's assassination. This is the first time that many of these addresses have been published in English, and they highlight the particularistic way American Jewry mourned the martyred president. Chapter 7 is entirely devoted to a "Shavuot controversy," an interesting situation that relates to the topic of Jewish communal mourning for Lincoln. This episode, which occurred on June 1, 1865—a month and a half after Lincoln's death—created a vexing moral dilemma for American Jewry when President Andrew Johnson proclaimed a national day of mourning on the Festival of Weeks (Shavuot), a day of Jewish rejoicing.

Abraham Lincoln maintained a close association with many Jews, and he also patronized Jewish businesses. Yet, as noted above, Lincoln also had a number of Jewish detractors. Chapter 8 brings these conflicting sentiments into bold relief by examining an assortment of the contesting views that Jews expressed during Lincoln's presidency and at the time of his death.

Chapters 9, 10, 11, and 12 explore the evolution of Lincoln as a unique cultural icon and a historical phenomenon for American Jewry from the time of his death in 1865 to the present day. In Chapter 9, I examine the ways in which American Jews began to Judaize Lincoln and embrace him as a unique amalgam of Americanism and Judaism. Chapter 10 focuses on the story of various American Jews who actively participated in the process of crafting Lincoln's image as well as of preserving his memory in American culture.

As the centennial of Lincoln's birthday approached in 1909, Americans first began asking themselves—in sermons, newspaper articles, addresses, and social commentaries—"What would Lincoln do?" if he were alive today. Chapter 11 explores how American Jews made use of this same rhetorical technique in order to assert that Lincoln would want Jews to embrace their own Jewish heritage and thereby become better Americans. Finally, chapter 12 explores a potpourri of topics, all of which relate to Lincoln's remarkable versatility as an American Jewish lodestar. This chapter concludes with an analysis of a popular Internet rumor maintaining that Abraham Lincoln was literally of Jewish descent.

~

Jewish sociologists have taken note of the fact that in the United States, Jews relate to their religion and their ethnicity in a particularly distinctive manner. As one scholar framed this point many years ago, American Jews "locate the source of their ethic in Judaism," though the "motive power for their making such an identification comes from the general [American] culture." More recently, another scholar has described this particular phenomenon as the coalescence of American and Jewish values. In other words, the practice of Judaism and the content of one's Jewishness in America are shaped by a foundational and immovable presupposition that Americanism and Jewishness are, for all intents and purposes, "almost identical."[22]

It is not always possible to distinguish clearly between the Judaization of Lincoln and Lincoln's role in Americanizing the Jew. This is why one scholar has suggested that in order to understand American Jewish culture, a historian must "negotiate between a dominant culture and a precarious deviation from it." American Jewry's unfolding historical encounter with the life and symbolic image of Abraham Lincoln serves as a fruitful case study shedding light on how the cultural interchange between American ideals and Jewish historical traditions has functioned in the past and, most likely, will continue in the years ahead to influence the dynamics of the American Jewish experience.[23]

1

Immigrants and the Old Northwest:
Lincoln's First Encounters with American Jewry

In the 1830s, dramatic demographic changes transformed American Jewry. The Jewish population began to grow, and prominent centers of Jewish life sprang up west of the Eastern Seaboard. By the 1860s, cities such as Cincinnati, Indianapolis, St. Louis, Chicago, Milwaukee, Louisville, and San Francisco each had between 800 and 2,000 Jewish citizens. Abraham Lincoln's political ascendancy occurred at this very time, when the immigrant population in the territories of the Old Northwest and the population of American Jewry were both undergoing a dramatic growth spurt. The mass immigration of Jews from Central Europe—primarily from present-day Germany and Austria—would come to play, as we will see, an important role in Lincoln's personal and political development.

Lincoln, Politics, Jews, and the Old Northwest

In 1809, the year of Lincoln's birth, there were very few population centers in the territories of the Old Northwest. Yet by the time Lincoln became president in 1861, almost a quarter of the nation's population—approximately 7 million people—resided in that section of the country. Before 1830, the vast majority of new settlers in the Old Northwest hailed from one of the original thirteen states. During the 1840s and 1850s, however, a wave of foreigners swelled that region's population, and by the mid-1840s, immigrants constituted 79 percent of the net migration to the Old Northwest. In the 1850s, that figure jumped to 88 percent. As one historian noted, "Lincoln, even if he would, could not help coming in contact with the few Jewish people in the part of the country which was then the Middle West. They were the same hardy pioneers . . . who trekked along with others to open up the country, ever westward-bound." It would indeed have been difficult for any aspiring politician to ignore the rapidly increasing number of foreigners who migrated to this part of the country during the two decades that preceded the Civil War.[1]

What was it that made the Old Northwest so appealing to newcomers during this period? Even before territories became states, the region drew many settlers because it seemed so full of promise. Many of the vital freedoms enshrined in the U.S. Constitution and the Bill of Rights were safeguarded by the Northwest Ordinance, including freedom of religion, the inviolability of private contracts, and the legal right to convey inheritance to one's heirs. The availability of land for settlement, periodically encour-aged by federal legislation, also attracted newcomers looking for a place to settle in the expanding nation. The Northwest Ordinance's ban on slavery, which was carried over into the states' constitutions, was particularly appealing to European immigrants. Above all, the region of the Old Northwest offered people promising opportunities to earn a dependable livelihood. For instance, many of the German and Irish immigrants who came during the 1830s found reliable work wherever the rivers, the various canal projects, and even the fledgling railroad lines carried them.[2]

As the number of foreign newcomers ballooned during the 1830s and 1840s, the number of Jewish immigrants who settled in the Old Northwest similarly rose. Be-ginning in the 1830s and continuing in waves throughout the course of the nineteenth century, a large number of Jews from Central Europe immigrated to the United States. The political, social, and economic disabilities that plagued Jews in the Old World pushed them to emigrate, and America beckoned them to its shores. Eager to make a reliable living, many of these Jewish immigrants quickly left the East Coast cities where they originally disembarked and followed the settlement patterns of the general American population. To earn their livelihood, these immigrant Jews made use of their business skills and the various trades they had learned in the Old World. They contributed to the region's growing economic infrastructure by establishing shops and businesses or by working as skilled tradesmen. It was at this time that many Jewish immigrants were drawn to the fast-growing cities of the Old Northwest—cities such as Chicago, Cincinnati, Indianapolis, Louisville, Milwaukee, and St. Louis. Others made their way into the smaller communities all across the vast Mississippi River basin, where they settled and remained for many years.

Abraham Lincoln's life unfolded in this region, just as all of these changes tran-spired. He not only was a firsthand witness to these demographic transformations but also was personally affected by them. In 1834, the year that the twenty-five-year-old Lincoln first won a seat in the Illinois General Assembly, there may have been only 5,000 or 6,000 Jews in all of the United States. However, by the time he campaigned for the U.S. Senate in 1858, there were approximately 15,000 Jews living in the states of Illinois, Indiana, and Ohio alone. In 1860, approximately 150,000–200,000 Jews lived in the United States. Lincoln, both as an aspiring politician and as a circuit-riding lawyer, became familiar with immigrants, foreign settlers, and the atmosphere of a rapidly expanding society. During these same transformational years, Lincoln encoun-tered and, in some instances, befriended many of the Jews who settled in the Old Northwest.[3]

Cincinnati represents the most dramatic example of the Jewish population surge that occurred during the two decades that preceded the Civil War. In the early 1820s, there could not have been more than a dozen or so Jews in the town that Henry Wadsworth Longfellow would poetically crown the "Queen of the West" in 1854. By 1855, when Lincoln made his first (and famously unpleasant) visit to Cincinnati, he unquestionably encountered a burgeoning metropolis as well as a Jewish community that was growing so rapidly that it would soon become the second largest Jewish population in the United States. Walking down the streets of Cincinnati in 1855, Lincoln would have seen Jewish shop owners, businessmen, and even some political activists. He would have had a similar experience during this same decade when he visited other cities like Chicago, Indianapolis, Louisville, and Milwaukee, all of which enjoyed a noteworthy rise in their Jewish population as a result of the Jewish migration from Central Europe. In addition to his experience in these large cities, many of which had hundreds of Jewish citizens, Lincoln was unquestionably accustomed to encountering a colorful assortment of foreign immigrants, among them a handful of pioneering Jewish settlers who peddled and settled in many of the small towns he frequented while riding the Eighth Judicial Circuit.[4]

Lincoln's Encounters with Jewish Proprietors

As Lincoln rose to local prominence during the 1840s and 1850s, crowds of curious on-lookers throughout the region of the Old Northwest would gather to hear this familiar local personality speak on issues of the day as he campaigned for party candidates or ran for office himself. It was during this period that Lincoln first established warm personal and professional associations with an array of immigrant Jewish businessmen. Years later, a number of these individuals would write about their contact with Lincoln in their memoirs. Considered collectively, these testimonies—some of which admittedly may have been retrospectively exaggerated—demonstrate that Lincoln frequently patronized Jewish shopkeepers and left them with the impression that he was more than a transient customer; they remembered him as their friend.[5]

Julius Hammerslough (1831–1908) of Springfield, Illinois, owned one of the haberdasheries that Lincoln frequented and also claimed that Lincoln was a close personal friend. Julius immigrated to the United States from Germany with his family when he was a young boy. The Hammersloughs originally lived in Baltimore, but Julius and two of his three brothers, Edward and Samuel, moved to Springfield and opened a haberdashery in the 1850s. One of Hammerslough's two sisters, Augusta, married an immigrant from the city of Bünde in the Herford District of Westphalia named Samuel Rosenwald (1828–99).[6] Augusta and Samuel followed the Hammerslough brothers to Springfield and opened a dry goods store of their own. The Lincolns patronized the Hammersloughs and the Rosenwalds, and, as far as these two families were concerned, Abraham Lincoln was a personal friend.[7]

In 1861, Julius Hammerslough claimed that he traveled to Washington to attend Lincoln's first inaugural, and during Lincoln's term in office he insisted that he visited the White House on a number of occasions. Years later, Hammerslough remembered that the Lincoln family once entrusted him with the duty of escorting Mary Todd Lincoln's sister Elizabeth Porter (née Todd) Edwards from her home in Springfield to Washington.[8] According to Hammerslough, Lincoln always treated him like a friend, invariably greeting him by inquiring, "How are the boys?"—a reference to Hammerslough's brothers back home in Springfield. The bond of friendship between the Lincolns and the Hammersloughs was strong enough that, after Lincoln's assassination, community leaders in Springfield asked Julius Hammerslough to serve on the Springfield citizens' committee that accompanied Lincoln's remains from Chicago to Springfield on his final trip home in 1865.[9] Some months later, when the National Lincoln Monument Association was organized in order to raise the funds needed to erect a fitting memorial for the martyred president, Hammerslough was asked, as an official member of the association, to solicit his coreligionists. On May 30, 1865, he explained why American Jews should donate funds to such a project: "It is above all, fitting in this land where the Hebrews have won so proud a name and are so greatly respected and honored that they should thus show their love and veneration for the fallen chief of the nation, whose wisdom, honesty and purity of purpose were so highly appreciated by foreign nations and who was so beloved at home."[10]

Henry Rice (1834–1914) was another Jewish immigrant who, like Hammerslough, considered Lincoln to be a friend and neighbor. Rice came to the United States from Germany in the late 1840s and by 1853 had established his own store in Jacksonville, Illinois—Henry Rice & Co., a haberdashery. Rice's business in Jacksonville prospered, and in 1861, after the Civil War broke out, Rice served as a military storekeeper—a sutler—for the Union army in Cairo, Illinois. In 1862, Rice relocated to Memphis, where he opened a wholesale dry goods store named Rice, Stix, and Company. Rice subsequently moved to West End, New Jersey, in 1866 and ran the eastern branch of his company, which moved its headquarters to St. Louis in 1879. In New Jersey, Rice remained active in numerous Jewish organizations, including the United Jewish Charities, which he led from 1874 to 1904.[11]

Rice recollected that Lincoln patronized his store whenever he was in Jacksonville and claimed he maintained a casual friendship with the tall country lawyer. Rice must have had confidence in Lincoln's legal abilities, too, for he recommended Lincoln as a "reputable lawyer" to friends who were in need of legal services. After Lincoln became president, Rice managed to persuade his friend, the president, to return the favor: he asked Lincoln to appoint him as the official sutler for the military district near Cairo. The post did come his way, but it seems the appointment may have been a brief one, because the following year, in 1862, Rice moved to Memphis. Later in life, Rice insisted that Lincoln had made a great effort to grant his requests for patronage.[12]

Like Hammerslough and Rice, Louis Salzenstein (1811–84), who hailed from Halsdorf, Hessen, was also a Central European immigrant. He immigrated to the United States around 1831 and lived in Baltimore, Maryland, for a decade before settling in Athens, Illinois, in 1843. Salzenstein, who lived in Athens for nearly forty years, succeeded in business as a general store owner and a livestock trader. According to local legend, Lincoln patronized Salzenstein's store whenever he was visiting Athens. Today, Salzenstein's home houses the Abraham Lincoln Long Nine Museum, wherein visitors still learn about Lincoln's friendship with "Old Salty": "Abraham Lincoln and Louis Salzenstein were close friends and Lincoln often stopped at his store and his residence. Mr. Salzenstein built a sort of bar room where liquors were dispensed. Most of the stores in that age were selling whiskey. It is a tradition that Lincoln stayed in the front part of the store and many times refused to accompany his friends to the bar room for a drink."[13]

Salzenstein's son Myer claimed that Abraham Lincoln once borrowed an ax from his father's store in order to cut down a tree and catch a raccoon! According to Myer, Lincoln never returned the ax, though Honest Abe did offer to pay for the tool.[14]

There were also Jews, like Samuel Huttenbauer (1840?–83) of Cincinnati, who would regale their families with nostalgic reminiscences about their former associations with the famous president. Huttenbauer, who immigrated to the United States in 1857 from Mayence, told his children and grandchildren that when he was an eighteen-year-old peddler selling his wares in central Illinois, a lawyer named Abraham Lincoln made a point of purchasing suspenders and collar buttons from his pushcart.[15]

All of these examples suggest that Lincoln did indeed patronize immigrant Jewish business owners as he traveled along the legal circuit in central Illinois. These warm recollections suggest that Lincoln conducted himself in a manner that convinced Jewish midwesterners like Hammerslough, Rice, Salzenstein, and Huttenbauer that he bore Jews no prejudice; he treated them like any other fellow citizen. One particularly colorful illustration of Lincoln's openness and good nature toward strangers, including immigrant Jews, comes from his encounter with Samuel G. Alschuler (1826–82), an immigrant Jewish photographer from Urbana, Illinois.

Alschuler, who came to the United States in 1848 from Bavaria, opened a photography studio in Urbana in the mid-1850s. In April 1858, when Lincoln was positioning himself to be selected as the U.S. senator from Illinois, he came to Urbana to represent clients at the Champaign Circuit Court. Neophyte photographers were always eager to

Samuel G. Alschuler, a Jewish immigrant who lent Lincoln his own coat prior to photographing him. Courtesy Jean Powers Soman.

13

display photographs of notable figures in the hope of promoting their technical skills to the general public. Lincoln was likely aware that if he allowed Alschuler to take his picture, a copy of the print would undoubtedly be prominently displayed in the immigrant photographer's window for publicity purposes. Perhaps for this reason, or perhaps due to his good nature, Lincoln agreed to let Alschuler take his picture.

Lincoln arrived at Alschuler's place of business wearing a rumpled linen coat—possibly the same unkempt frock coat that Edwin M. Stanton (1814–69) famously lampooned when the two men first met in Cincinnati in 1855.[16] Alschuler politely suggested that the photograph would turn out better if Lincoln wore a black coat, but Lincoln could not fulfill the request, since he had left his black coat at home. Hoping to make the best of the situation, the immigrant photographer offered his own black coat to the future president. Alschuler was much smaller than his subject, so Lincoln's arms extended through the sleeves of his coat "a quarter yard." A fellow attorney, Henry C. Whitney, who had accompanied Lincoln to Alschuler's place of business remembered that Lincoln "was overcome with merriment" when the short coat "proved to be a bad misfit." The awkward incident did not deter Lincoln from sitting for Alschuler again, this time when the immigrant photographer's subject was the president-elect.[17]

Lincoln's Jewish Political Allies

It was during this same period that Lincoln began to encounter Jews who were active in politics. Abraham Jonas (1801–64), a prominent political activist from Quincy, Illinois, appears to have been one of Lincoln's earliest and closest political associates. It is quite likely that Jonas and Lincoln first became acquainted with one another in the early 1840s

Abraham Jonas, Lincoln's political ally and close friend for more than two decades. Courtesy The Jacob Rader Marcus Center of the American Jewish Archives, at the Hebrew Union College–Jewish Institute of Religion, Cincinnati, Ohio.

when the two men were members of the Illinois Whig Party. Jonas was an English Jew who immigrated to the United States on the advice of his older brother, Joseph, who was among the first Jews to settle in Cincinnati. Abraham came to Cincinnati in 1819, but in 1826 he left his brother and moved to Williamstown, Kentucky, where he worked as a shopkeeper. It was in Williamstown that Jonas began to take part in Kentucky politics. In 1837, Jonas moved his business to Quincy, Illinois, where he began to study law, involve himself in local politics, and emerge as a leader in both the Jewish and the general communities. He was one of the founders of the city's first Jewish congregations, B'nai Abraham, which met in a building that Jonas owned during its early years.[18]

It was during this time that Jonas came into contact with a fellow Whig partisan, Abraham Lincoln. Lincoln had settled in Springfield the same year that Jonas came to Quincy and was then representing Sangamon County in the Illinois General Assembly. Jonas had the same aspirations and in 1842 made an unsuccessful bid to represent Adams County in the assembly. Then, in 1844, Jonas tried to win a seat in the Illinois Senate but was again defeated. Although Lincoln's legal work did not bring him to Adams County, the two men must have been together at numerous Whig gatherings because the correspondence that survives from the mid-1850s suggests that when Lincoln visited Quincy for the first time in his career, the two men had already long established a mutual respect and a close political alliance.[19]

Jonas was among those who beckoned Lincoln to Quincy in 1854 so he could endorse the Whigs' congressional candidate, whose Democratic opponent was to benefit from a personal appearance by Stephen Douglas (1813–61). In a letter urging Lincoln to come to Quincy, Jonas is obviously writing to a colleague he knows quite well: "Be assured that nothing will afford greater pleasure to your personal friends and the Whigs generally than you consent to visit us—and the Douglasites would as soon see old nick here as yourself."[20]

In the mid-1850s, Jonas and Lincoln both abandoned the rapidly disintegrating Whig Party and joined the recently established Republican Party. In 1856, the two men took the stump for the Republicans' first presidential candidate, John C. Frémont (1813–90).[21] Evidently, Jonas was himself a compelling orator who was in demand, yet he admired Lincoln's oratorical skill and witnessed his ability to "effect wonders" from the speaker's platform. Jonas was one of Lincoln's earliest and most loyal boosters; he supported Lincoln in his unsuccessful bid to become a U.S. senator in 1858, and he served as the chair of the "Republican Committee of Arrangements" for the Lincoln-Douglas debate in Quincy.[22]

The reminiscences left by one of Jonas's sons, Edward (1844–1918), from the time of the Lincoln-Douglas debate in Quincy leaves one with a sense of Lincoln's playful personality as well as the spirit of friendship he felt for Jonas and his children:

> I saw Mr. Lincoln in my father's home in Quincy during the great Douglas-Lincoln Debates and during the same period, my father, who was taking part in the campaign, took me with him to various points

where Mr. Lincoln was present. I was only thirteen years old and it was I think at August or Newcomb, Illinois. While my father was speaking, I, with a boy's curiosity was strolling about the speaker's platform on a tour of investigation when I suddenly felt a tickling behind my ear. Thinking it a bug or fly I slapped vigorously, but upon its being repeated several times, I became suspicious and turned suddenly and caught the fly. It was Mr. Lincoln with a straw in his hand. He made it all right at once by catching me up with his long arm, drawing me to his side and talking to me very entertainingly until his turn came to address the assemblage.[23]

By the late 1850s, Jonas had become "an influential leader in the Republican Party." He had earned the admiration of Illinois's fledgling Republican machine by distinguishing himself "in all the positions he occupied," and contemporaries testified to the fact that he was "a personal friend of Lincoln." Horace Greeley (1811–72), the well-known publisher of the *New York Tribune* and a Republican Party activist, came to Quincy in December 1858 to deliver a public lecture. Jonas was invited to be among those who would meet with the powerful publisher and strategize about the party's plans for the upcoming 1860 election.[24]

It was Henry Asbury (1810–96), one of Jonas's partners, who suggested that Abraham Lincoln—a man who was, relatively speaking, little known outside of Illinois—deserved serious consideration to head the party's ticket. According to the participants' recollections, most of those in attendance at the meeting, including Greeley, remained awkwardly mute, but Jonas waded into the embarrassing silence by saying, "Gentlemen, there may be more in Asbury's suggestion than any of us now think." Asbury and Jonas understood that by mentioning Lincoln's name to Greeley, they were giving their man's name a hearing that may otherwise not have occurred. As unlikely a presidential candidate as Lincoln may have been in January 1859, twelve months later Abraham Jonas was actively campaigning for Old Abe in the hope of procuring the presidential nomination at the upcoming Republican National Convention, scheduled to convene in Chicago in June 1860. In one of his many letters to Lincoln, Jonas assured his old friend that "we shall be able to carry the day [in Chicago] and in November proclaim *victory* to all the world" (emphasis in original).[25]

Fundamentally, Lincoln and Jonas were political allies, but their correspondence reveals an unmistakable bond of warm personal feelings between them as well. In an oft-quoted letter, Lincoln addresses Jonas as "one of my most valued friends," and this sentiment was unquestionably reciprocal. After Lincoln secured the presidential nomination, Jonas became increasingly protective of his old friend. In July, he warned Lincoln that an arch opponent, Democratic congressman Isaac N. Morris (1812–79), was spreading the word that Lincoln had once been associated with the Know Nothing Party. If a rumor of this sort took hold, they worried, it could erode the precious support that Lincoln needed from foreign-born citizens and, of course, Jewish voters. Lincoln responded promptly to Jonas's letter of concern and provided him with political strategy and the information he needed to combat the rumor.[26]

A letter written by Jonas to President-elect Lincoln on December 30, 1860, reveals the strong bond of loyal friendship that linked these two men. Jonas reminded Lincoln that his six children "and a host of other near relatives" lived in New Orleans and had emotional "connections" to the South. One of these relatives—perhaps one of Jonas's own children—told Jonas that a large number of "desperate characters" from New Orleans planned go to Washington on March 4, 1861, in an effort to prevent the president-elect from taking office. These men were determined to succeed, Jonas wrote, and would even use "violence on the person of Lincoln," if necessary. Jonas was convinced that outgoing President James Buchanan (1791–1868), "the damned old traitor at the head of the Government," would not lift a finger to ensure a safe transition of power and suggested that the governors of all the states in the North that elected Lincoln band together and take collective "precautionary measures" to provide the president-elect with the security he needed. In any event, Jonas wanted Lincoln to have this information, and he conveyed his confidence that his old friend was the best person to decide "what ought to be done."[27]

During Lincoln's trip from Springfield to Washington, D.C., a few months later, the president-elect was once again informed that a plot on his life had been uncovered. Detective Allen Pinkerton (1819–84) and Lincoln's close advisors urged him to heed the warning. They wanted the president-elect to make an unannounced change to his publicized travel route in order to foil the plot of any prospective assassins. At first, Lincoln refused to cooperate, but ultimately he hesitatingly agreed to the plan.[28]

After the inauguration, Lincoln demonstrated his gratitude for Jonas's friendship by reappointing him postmaster of Quincy in 1861, a patronage office that Jonas had previously held from 1849 to 1853. He had wanted the reappointment, though he did not personally pursue the post. Even as president, Lincoln did not hesitate to rely on Jonas's dependability. For example, when he received an onslaught of appeals asking him to release a Missourian incarcerated in Quincy, Union army officers insisted the man was a traitor, but the man's petitioners denied the charge. In a note to Secretary of War Edwin Stanton, Lincoln advised consulting Jonas and Henry Asbury and leaving the final disposition of the matter in their hands: "I know [both men] to be loyal and sensible."[29]

Jonas was firmly dedicated to the Union's cause, and he was devoutly patriotic. Only a few days after the Battle of Fort Sumter in April 1861, a home guard was quickly organized to protect the local population. Volunteer brigades were formed around ethnic groupings, and Jonas organized the Jewish men of Quincy "for the purpose of drilling and making necessary arrangements, to get ready for active service at a moment's notice." Once organized, the Jewish brigade was placed under the leadership of "Colonel" Abraham Jonas. The Jews of Quincy clearly played a prominent role in civic affairs. In February 1862, a notice was circulated inviting the entire community to come to the synagogue on the third floor of the Jonas Building and join them in commemorating George Washington's birthday. Abraham Jonas offered a special reading of Washington's Farewell Address to mark the occasion.[30]

In 1864, Abraham Jonas's health began to decline, and it became clear to his family that death was imminent. These dire circumstances compelled them to do what Jonas typically eschewed doing: they appealed directly to Lincoln for a special favor. Despite Jonas's ardent loyalty to Lincoln and the Union, only one of Jonas's five sons, Edward, joined Jonas in support of the Union's cause. The other four—Benjamin Franklin, Julian, Samuel Alroy, and Charles Henry—had been sent to the South to pursue their education and fought for the Confederacy. Charles had been captured by the Union army and imprisoned, and the family asked Lincoln to intercede on Charles's behalf so that the young man could visit his dying father. Lincoln promptly agreed to the request, and Charles arrived just hours before his father died. The Confederate son was deeply grateful to his father's old friend, and he conveyed these sentiments in a touching thank-you note. Some weeks later, in another display of friendship, Lincoln appointed Jonas's widow to serve out the remainder of her late husband's unexpired term in office.[31]

Lincoln's Jewish Supporters

At the Republican National Convention of 1860, Jonas was one of many Illinois politicians who believed that Lincoln, a dark horse candidate, could ultimately manage to reel in the party's nomination. He was also one of a handful of Jewish politicos from around the country who ultimately lent their support to Lincoln. For example, a Jew named Moritz Pinner (1828–1911) was a member of the Missouri delegation to the 1860 Republican Convention. Pinner had been an outspoken opponent to American slavery since 1856. He worked directly with prominent leaders of the abolitionist movement, including Theodore Parker (1810-60), Wendell Phillips (1811–84), and William Lloyd Garrison (1805-79). In 1859, Pinner established an antislavery newspaper in Kansas City, the *Kansas Post*, and he played an influential role in the Missouri Republican Convention, where he actively opposed those who wanted Edward Bates (1793–1869) to become the Republican Party's presidential candidate. Although he had been a supporter of William H. Seward (1801–72) because of his strong antislavery stance, Pinner subsequently embraced the party's choice, and after Lincoln secured the nomination, Pinner worked diligently to send the Republican candidate to the White House. Pinner later contended that he and Lincoln had become very friendly, and, in return for his dedicated efforts, the president-elect offered to send Pinner to Honduras as the U.S. ambassador. Pinner claimed he declined the opportunity because he wanted to fight in the Union army, and he was appointed to serve as a quartermaster on the staff of Major General Philip Kearney (1815–62) by the Lincoln administration.[32]

Another Jew who played a key role in securing the nomination for Lincoln was Lewis Naphtali Dembitz (1833–1907), a lawyer who would go on to become a leading Jewish communal leader. Dembitz was born in Zirke, a province of Posen in Prussia, and immigrated to the United States in 1849. He studied law at the University of

Cincinnati and then moved to Louisville, Kentucky, to set up his practice. Dembitz joined the fledgling Republican Party shortly after it took shape, and he was elected to occupy a number of Republican Party offices. In 1860, Dembitz served as a delegate to the Republican National Convention in Chicago, where Lincoln became the party's presidential candidate in 1860. In contrast to Pinner, however, Dembitz came to his party's convention as a Lincoln supporter and later maintained that he cast his vote for Old Abe on the first ballot.[33]

After the passage of the Kansas-Nebraska Act of 1854, which reignited Lincoln's interest in government office, the circle of his Jewish political acquaintances began to enlarge. Henry Greenebaum (1834–1914), a prominent Chicago banker who had recently been elected alderman, was introduced to Lincoln in 1855 by John Wentworth (1815–88), mayor of Chicago. Although Greenebaum was an ardent supporter of Stephen A. Douglas, his first exchange with Lincoln left him "greatly impressed."[34] On July 10, 1858, Greenebaum and his young cousin Caroline's husband, Simon Wolf (1836–1923)—a man who would become personally acquainted with Lincoln during his presidency—were both present when Lincoln delivered his famous speech at the Tremont House in Chicago. Wolf's recollection of the occasion testifies to Lincoln's unusual ability to win over new friends and to retain their loyalty:

> Mr. Greenebaum and I were admirers of the "Little Giant of the West," Stephen Douglas, yet like all fair-minded people should ever be, we were open to conviction and concluded to hear Mr. Lincoln. It was the first time I had ever seen the Great Emancipator, and the first impression made was one that has never been obliterated from my memory. Tall, gaunt, with his clothes hanging loosely, solemnity about his features, his eyes beaming with an intensity born of conviction, he looked to me then, as he did many times afterwards, the personification of realism, strength of thought and purpose. We went away from that hall more patriotic than when we entered it, and while our political convictions had not been changed by anything that Mr. Lincoln had said, our love of the Republic was materially increased.[35]

Both Greenebaum and Wolf maintained their contact with Lincoln after the election. In early February 1861, Greenebaum visited with the president-elect in his Springfield home. He and Lincoln's other guests were on hand at the Springfield train depot on the morning of February 11 to bid Lincoln farewell as he began his trip to Washington, D.C.[36]

Lincoln's brief personal encounter with a Jewish immigrant named Abraham Kohn (1819–71) sheds light on Lincoln's artful ability to relate positively to Jews and their biblical heritage. Like so many of Lincoln's Jewish acquaintances, Kohn was a Bavarian-born immigrant who came to the United States in 1842. Following his arrival in New York, Kohn spent his first year as a struggling peddler meandering the states of Massachusetts, New Hampshire, Connecticut, and New York. He moved to Chicago in 1843 and opened a haberdashery. His business flourished quickly, and by 1845 he was able to send for his younger brothers, his sister, and his aged mother. Together with a quorum of Chicago's pioneering Jewish citizens, Kohn helped to establish the city's first synagogue, Kehilath Anshe Ma'ariv (KAM), in 1847.

Kohn possessed a brilliant mind and taught himself to speak and write in English even prior to settling in Chicago. As his business flourished, he immersed himself in community affairs. He was active in the Democratic Party, and in 1860, Chicago mayor John Wentworth appointed Kohn city clerk. In 1860, Isaac Newton Arnold (1815–84), a bitter opponent to slavery who was a Republican candidate for Congress, brought Lincoln to meet Kohn at his store. According to Kohn's daughter Dila Kohn Adler (1850–1918), Arnold and the future president actually went to Kohn's store in order to meet him. Kohn's contemporaries described the city clerk as a man with "a truly religious cast" who vehemently despised slavery. Lincoln must have intuited that the Bible might be the key to Kohn's support. He told the Jewish city clerk that the Bible was "their book" because they were both men of faith and lovers of the American republic. By the time they had parted, Kohn was in Lincoln's corner. "It was this meeting that inspired Kohn with a feeling of admiration for his visitor and a conviction that he was the destined Moses of the slaves and the saviour of his country."[37]

A few weeks later, Kohn sent the president-elect a special gift—a handmade silk American flag with verses from the Hebrew Bible inscribed in Hebrew on the thirteen bars. The biblical injunction he used was a spiritual message to Lincoln that may have been reminiscent of the conversation the two men had when they met in Chicago: "Be strong and of good courage; be not affrighted, neither be thou dismayed: for the LORD thy God is with thee whithersoever thou goest."[38]

It seems that Lincoln had an extraordinary ability to win over new friends and attract loyal political supporters after a meeting or two. His gift for acquiring the confidence of Jewish activists, most of whom were Central European immigrants like Abraham Kohn, manifested itself repeatedly during the late 1850s, when Lincoln was quietly mapping out his plans for a presidential bid. Marcus Otterbourg (1827–93), a well-educated Jewish immigrant with a flair for languages, was introduced to Lincoln at this same time. He, too, would quickly become a Lincoln loyalist.

Otterbourg was born and raised in Landau, Germany. After completing his education, Otterbourg learned the cap-making trade, but he was eager to advance his studies in order to become an educator. In the 1840s, Otterbourg moved to Paris to live with his older brother, Solomon, a devout Jew who had become a respected physician. In Paris, Otterbourg realized he had a knack for acquiring languages. He became fluent in French and began supporting himself as a teacher. A few years later, he moved to England, where he taught French as he honed his fluency in English. He then returned to Germany, where he taught both French and English. In the early 1850s, Otterbourg immigrated to the United States and soon settled in Milwaukee, Wisconsin. After working for a brief time as a distiller of vinegar, Otterbourg began to work as a journalist, specializing in covering political news in Wisconsin. It was at this point in his career that he met Abraham Lincoln.[39]

Later in life, Otterbourg told a newspaper reporter, "I am a Hebrew by birth and belief, but I suppose I am called a liberal one in belief."[40] He was a liberal in politics, too, and while he was working as a political correspondent, he became closely associated with another liberal-minded German immigrant, Carl Christian Schurz (1829–1906), a man who would have an extremely distinguished career as a U.S. ambassador, a U.S. senator and, ultimately, secretary of the interior during the presidency of Rutherford B. Hayes. Like Otterbourg, Schurz had been one of the ardent liberalist activists in Germany who eventually immigrated to the United States in the aftermath of the failed revolutions of 1848. Schurz settled in Watertown, Wisconsin, where he became active in local politics and an outspoken opponent of slavery. In 1855, he joined the fledging Republican Party and, two years later, made an unsuccessful run for the office of Wisconsin lieutenant governor. It was during this period that Schurz and Otterbourg became close personal friends and political allies.[41]

Schurz was one of Lincoln's early supporters. He traveled around the Midwest to give speeches on Lincoln's behalf in German in order to boost his support among the immigrant population. It was Schurz who first introduced Otterbourg to Lincoln, and, deeply impressed by Lincoln's abilities, Otterbourg quickly became a Lincoln partisan. After Lincoln's assassination, Otterbourg described his assessment of Lincoln, saying, "A more kind-hearted, more noble minded, and patriotic man never graced the earth." Like Schurz, Otterbourg worked to elect Lincoln, and after the election, both men received political appointments in return for their support: Schurz became the U.S. minister to Spain, and Otterbourg was appointed U.S. consul in Mexico City. Having obtained his political assignment on August 10, 1861, it is probable that Abraham Jonas and Marcus Otterbourg were the first Jews to receive political appointments from the Lincoln administration.[42]

During the late 1850s, Lincoln won the loyalty of yet another Jewish politico, Abram J. Dittenhoefer (1836–1919). Dittenhoefer, a young New York lawyer, first met Lincoln on the night of February 27, 1860—the night he delivered his famous address at Cooper Union. A native-born son of German-Jewish immigrants, Dittenhoefer recollected that he took note of Lincoln a few years before he ran for the presidency in 1860. Dittenhoefer followed the Lincoln and Douglas debates "with close attention," and Lincoln's performance at Cooper Union in February 1860 enthralled Dittenhoefer and "strengthened" his determination to fight for the abolition of slavery. Many years later, Dittenhoefer recalled that Lincoln impressed him with an unusual charisma that, paradoxically, arose from his ungainly physical appearance: "He was a very homely man," Dittenhoefer wrote many years later, but "after he began to talk he was awkwardness deified."[43]

A few months later, Dittenhoefer was a "looker-on" at the Republican Convention of 1860. He went to Chicago not as a delegate from New York but as "a student of

American politics." Once Lincoln landed his party's nomination, Dittenhoefer traveled to Springfield to meet with him again. The Republican nominee immediately won young Dittenhoefer's loyalty by inviting him to his "modest home" to solicit his counsel. "What are the chances of my election?" Lincoln asked. Dittenhoefer confidently predicted that his candidate would carry the entire North "on account of the Democratic division between [John] Breckenridge and Douglas." Lincoln agreed, but he shrewdly ingratiated himself with the young politico by courteously responding: "I am glad to get the views of everybody of experience in political matters."[44]

Dittenhoefer dedicated all his energy to the Lincoln campaign in New York, and because Lincoln's victory made Dittenhoefer a political insider, he frequently called on Lincoln in the White House. In 1864, he devoted himself to reelecting Lincoln, who, Dittenhoefer noted, feared his party might decide not to renominate him. As he had done four years earlier, Dittenhoefer campaigned vigorously. In an important campaign speech, coincidentally given at Cooper Union, where he first heard Lincoln speak, Dittenhoefer's partisan support for Lincoln was unmistakable. After reminding the audience that Lincoln was the commander-in-chief of the Union forces, he told his listeners that Lincoln's opponent, General George B. McClellan (1826–85), was actually "the leader of the Confederate forces": "Confederate bonds advanced on the announcement of McClellan's nomination. Every Southern sympathizer in the North, passive or active in his devotion to Jefferson Davis, will vote for McClellan. . . . Is it not then true that McClellan heads, in this campaign, the Confederate forces in the North? . . . Lincoln's re-election will banish all hope of triumph for the Confederacy. A firm and everlasting peace will follow, based upon a reconstructed Union and freedom everywhere."[45]

Dittenhoefer's loyalty earned him the privilege of serving as one of the thirty-three members of the electoral college from New York after Lincoln's victory in November 1864. Some time prior to his second inauguration, Lincoln invited Dittenhoefer to the White House to express his appreciation for the work he had done on the reelection campaign. Dittenhoefer took the opportunity to show Lincoln a wooden block that read "President, Abraham Lincoln"; underneath, in brackets, were the words "[Abram J. Dittenhoefer] Elector." The memento touched Lincoln, and he asked his young friend if he would give it to him as a "souvenir," a request that Dittenhoefer fulfilled.[46]

On its way to Washington in 1861, Lincoln's train stopped in New York City. An immigrant lawyer named Sigismund Kaufmann (1825–89), born near Frankfurt-on-the-Main, was on hand to welcome the president-elect upon his arrival. Like so many of his peers, Kaufmann had fled the German states after the failed revolutions of 1848 and made his way to the United States, settling in New York. He studied the practice of law and became increasingly involved in politics. He joined the new Republican Party in 1856, and by 1860 he was prominent enough to be asked to serve as a member of the electoral college, where he would cast his vote for Lincoln. After the 1860 election, Kaufmann was among the many leading citizens who gathered to greet the president-elect. According to Kaufmann, Lincoln's impish sense of humor manifested itself as soon as the two men met. "On [my] being presented to Lincoln, the president remarked, 'I know enough German to know that Kaufmann means merchant.' Then he added, as if to emphasize his linguistic accomplishments, 'And Schneider means tailor. Am I not a good German scholar?'"[47]

Although president-elect Lincoln had a cadre of ardent Jewish supporters in 1860, it is important to note that there were some Jews, even in the northern states, who were among Lincoln's critics. First, many Jews—particularly in New York—had supported Stephen A. Douglas and the Democratic Party during the campaign, believing that the radical antislavery wing of the Republican Party made its candidates unelectable. Newcomers to the country were always eager to support those who would have power and influence in the government, and some Jews chose the Democrats because they appeared to be the party most likely to prevail. One prominent example of this tendency was the New York Jewish financier August Belmont (1813–90), who not only backed Douglas but actually managed the Little Giant's presidential campaign.[48]

Others, like Rabbi Isaac M. Wise (1819–1900) of Cincinnati, believed that a civil war would be unavoidable if the nation elected the Republican candidate. As Lincoln prepared himself to begin his first term in office, Rabbi Wise viewed the president-elect skeptically. Editorializing in his newspaper, the *Israelite*, Wise pointedly noted that it was impossible to determine "what Mr. Lincoln has done for this country in politics, warfares, science or art . . . [so let us] wait till he has done something, then show him the honor due." Wise unquestionably was not alone when he wondered whether or not Lincoln was up to the job. Referring to Lincoln's emotional farewell speech at the train depot in Springfield, Wise remarked: "He wept on leaving Springfield and invited his friends to pray for him; that is exactly the picture of his looks. We have no doubt he is an honest man and, as much as we can learn, also quite an intelligent man; but he will look queer, in the white house, with his primitive manner."[49]

For some Jews, skepticism about Lincoln and his ability to lead the nation was underscored by an infrequently quoted sentence he used in his first inaugural address. In an attempt to convince the South that, despite culturally based ideological differences, commonalities could still overcome the impending crises, Lincoln stated: "If it were admitted that you who are dissatisfied hold the right side in the dispute, there still is no single good reason for precipitate action. Intelligence, patriotism, Christianity, and a firm reliance on Him who has never yet forsaken this favored land are still competent to adjust in the best way all our present difficulty."[50]

Lincoln's rhetoric was nothing unusual, and, as even Wise himself noted in an editorial rejoinder to worried readers, the word "Christianity" was understood by Lincoln and many others to be merely a synonym for the word "religion." Yet the controversy about Lincoln's choice of wording lingered, and some newspapers contended that Lincoln was speaking expressly about Christianity. After all, they reasoned, Christianity was the religious bond that united all Americans. This sentiment infuriated Wise, and when the editors of the *Chicago Tribune* carried an article on this topic, Wise vented his spleen at the new president for "forgetting altogether his Jewish compatriots."[51]

Toward the end of the nineteenth century, many prominent American Jews insisted that they had known Lincoln in their youth. George Schneider (1823–1905), an important Chicago banker and editor of the *Illinois Staats-Zeitung*, later in life claimed he was one of the first organizers of the Republican Party in Illinois and an early advocate of Lincoln's presidential bid. Isador Bush (1822–93), another German-Jewish immigrant, later insisted he was one of Lincoln's first supporters from Missouri. Bush claimed to have met Lincoln on a number of occasions and stated that Lincoln personally appointed him to serve as a captain in the Union army on July 20 and as aide-de-camp to General Frémont during the Civil War. The prominent lawyer and educator Moses Aaron Dropsie (1821–1905) recollected that his first meeting with Lincoln took place at the first Republican National Convention, which was held in Philadelphia. Dropsie later took pride in having been a financial supporter of Lincoln's presidential campaign.

The distinguished lawyer and diplomat Benjamin Peixotto (1834–90) famously backed Stephen Douglas for president in 1860, but he would later insist that he quickly became an ardent Lincoln supporter after the election. The New York banker Joseph Seligman (1819–80) claimed he visited the White House on a variety of occasions to discuss the nation's financial matters with Lincoln. Seligman did compose a written appeal to the president asking that the government provide Mary Todd Lincoln (1818–82) with a pension. Although many of these claims are staked on personal remembrances with little or no corroborative documentary evidence, these testimonies clearly demonstrate that American Jews were convinced that Lincoln maintained a wide variety of Jewish associations during the course of his life.[52]

Two Jewish leaders who lived in Washington, D.C., during the Lincoln administration established a bond with Lincoln after he became president. Their recollections

Simon Wolf, a lawyer and Jewish communal leader who related his interesting encounters with Lincoln in published reminiscences.
Courtesy The Jacob Rader Marcus Center of the American Jewish Archives, at the Hebrew Union College–Jewish Institute of Religion, Cincinnati, Ohio.

of the various encounters they had with Lincoln have been frequently quoted, and their colorful anecdotes have been used to describe Lincoln's personality and character. Adolphus S. Solomons (1826–1910), a Jewish communal leader in Washington, D.C., established his publishing house, Philp and Solomons, in 1859. This firm held printing contracts with the U.S. government for several years. Solomons also owned a bookstore that featured a fine photographic gallery. He later published a number of his most interesting encounters with Lincoln.

Simon Wolf was one of the most distinguished Jewish communal leaders of the late nineteenth and early twentieth centuries. Raised in Uhrichsville, Ohio, Wolf studied law and, after his apprenticeship in Ohio, moved to the nation's capital to establish his own legal practice in 1861. He met Lincoln on a few occasions during those early years, and later in life when Wolf had become one of the most influential Jewish leaders and lobbyists, he flaunted these reminiscences to illustrate that his associations with U.S. presidents dated back to his warm encounters with Abraham Lincoln. Wolf spoke about his meetings with Lincoln on dozens of occasions, and most of them appear in his autobiographical volume, *The Presidents I Have Known from 1860–1918*.[53]

By the time Lincoln began his first term as president of the United States, he had already had numerous personal encounters with a diverse array of American Jews. He had frequented Jewish places of business, fraternized with Jews, and unquestionably considered Jews to be among his friends. Lincoln was arguably the first American president to have had this kind of personal contact with such a large number of Jewish citizens prior to assuming national office. Moreover, the demographic realities of life in the Old Northwest during Lincoln's formative years made him fully cognizant of the influential role that newcomers, immigrants, and social outsiders could potentially play in the world of American politics. Even before he became president, Lincoln had personal contact with "minority status" Americans, and these experiences certainly influenced his thinking when, as president, he was called to respond to a number of political issues that were deeply concerning to American Jewry.

DOCUMENTS

1. Lincoln's Jewish Photographer: Samuel G. Alschuler
2. Jews, Too, Were the Object of Lincoln's Wit: Charles
   Edward Pancoast's Encounter with Lincoln
3. Two Friends Named Abraham: Correspondence between Lincoln and Jonas
4. A Final Act of Friendship
5. Simon Wolf Remembers Lincoln's Mercy
6. Abram J. Dittenhoefer's Impressions of Lincoln
7. Abraham Kohn Presents the President-Elect with a Hebrew Flag
8. "Could Anything Have Given Mr. Lincoln More Cheer?"
   Excerpts from William A. McKinley's Speech
9. Henry Wentworth Monk Visits Lincoln at the White House
10. Adolphus Solomons's Account of the "Cracked Glass" Photograph of Lincoln

1. LINCOLN'S JEWISH PHOTOGRAPHER: SAMUEL G. ALSCHULER

The story behind photographer Samuel Alschuler's familiar photograph of Lincoln comes from Illinois judge J. O. (Joseph Oscar) Cunningham (1830–1917), who recounted the tale in a speech he delivered to the Firelands Pioneer Association in Norwalk, Ohio, on July 4, 1907. The sketch of this humorous encounter was drawn by Lloyd Ostendorf (1921–2000), an American artist devoted to the study of Lincolniana.[54]

The following is a description of the event from the speech "Some Recollections of Abraham Lincoln" and reprinted from the Firelands Pioneer *journal of December 1909.*[55]

During the spring term of our circuit court, 1858, and but a few weeks before Lincoln entered with Douglas upon their celebrated debate, I was one morning in the rooms of an artist in Urbana whose business was to make pictures then known as ambrotypes, before the science of photography had become in general use in our place. Soon, in walked Mr. Lincoln with the remark to Alschuler, the artist, that he had been informed that he, Alschuler, wished him to sit for a portrait. Alschuler said that he had sent such a message to Mr. Lincoln, glancing at his subject, who was attired in a long linen duster, but that he could not take the picture in that coat, and asked if he had not a dark coat in which he could sit. Mr. Lincoln said he had not; that this was the only coat he had brought with him from his home. Alschuler said that he could wear his coat, and gave it to Mr. Lincoln. The arms of Lincoln extended through the sleeves of Alschuler's coat a quarter yard, making him appear quite ludicrous, at which he, Lincoln, laughed immoderately, and sat down for the picture to be taken, with great effort looking sober enough for the occasion.

Drawing, by Lloyd Ostendorf
(1975), of Lincoln sitting for
Alschuler. Most scholars
agree that the Alschuler
photograph of Lincoln was
taken on April 25, 1858, in
Alschuler's studio at 218
West Main Street in Urbana.
Courtesy Abe Lincoln Collectibles
(www.abelincoln.com) and Lloyd
Ostendorf.

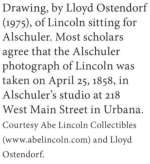

Photo of Lincoln taken in 1858 by Alschuler.
Some suggest that Lincoln's expression
reflects his bemusement in wearing Alschuler's ill-fitting coat while posing for the
photographer. Courtesy Jean Powers Soman.

2. JEWS, TOO, WERE THE OBJECT OF LINCOLN'S WIT:
CHARLES EDWARD PANCOAST'S ENCOUNTER WITH LINCOLN

Charles Edward Pancoast (1818–1906), a Quaker, was one of the thousands of Americans who raced to the West Coast in 1849 on account of "gold fever." In his memoirs he recalls his many adventures along this journey, including a fascinating encounter with a man who, years later, would become the sixteenth president of the United States.

Incidentally, Pancoast's autobiography provides us with a rather unrefined anecdote about Lincoln. Pancoast's tale reminds us that it was not unusual to come into contact with Jews in the Old Northwest and that Jews were not immune from being the target of Lincoln's wit.

About December, 1841, I concluded to take a trip to Illinois to make some collections from delinquent Debtors. I took passage on a Stern Wheel Boat that ran up the Illinois River, for Meredosia (then a small but promising Town) where some money was owing us. I was landed there about twelve o'clock at night, the only Passenger that got off the Boat. Not a soul was to be seen anywhere, and I had no directions in regard to the Town. The extreme cold weather admonished me that I must speedily seek for shelter; so I took up my Valise and proceeded to hunt for a Hotel. I had not wandered far before I discovered a Sign that read "Hotel."

After rapping lustily for some time I succeeded in arousing a disgruntled Landlord, who came to the door with a Candle and in a very uncivil manner invited me into a cold Room. He informed me that he had no Bed for me, and I should have to lie on an old Settee. I could see the light of the Moon through cracks in the unplastered walls. The Room was so cold that my Blanket and Overcoat failed to keep me warm, and I procured but little sleep that night. Yet this was the best Hotel in Meredosia at that time.

In the morning I found a number of Guests in the House and we sat down to a welcome Breakfast of Ham and Eggs and strong Coffee. After I visited our Agent (who settled up with me speedily) we were ready to start. There were four of us in the Party: one, a wandering Jew, to be found everywhere throughout the universe; two Yankees, equally omnipresent wherever it has been my lot to travel; and myself, one of those Jerseymen who are also well scattered throughout the United States. We had expected to find the Steam Cars running to Jacksonville, but learned that the Road was not finished: this, I think, was the first Rail Road in Illinois.[56] As there was no other conveyance to be procured, we were compelled to travel to Jacksonville (about 40 miles from Meredosia) in an open Farm Wagon without Springs, with a full-blooded Illinois "Sucker" for a Driver. With this Rig we started on our Journey, with the Thermometer at Zero. My Clothing was anything but proper for such weather, as I had no Flannel Underwear; but I had a Spanish Cloak, then much worn by City Folks.

We had not travelled far before we struck an immense open Prairie, where the sweeping winds came down upon us with such force that we soon began to feel that they were more than we could endure in our sitting posture; so we proposed to the Driver to run with the Wagon. Three of us got out; the Jew, however, preferred to keep his place in the Wagon; and as my cumbersome Cloak would not permit me to run with ease, I loaned it to him. The Driver, being anxious to terminate his disagreeable Journey as soon as possible, had little mercy on us; he kept his Horses moving at a rapid rate, and we did the best running we had ever done. The Driver was so well wrapped with Buffalo Robes that he did not appear to be much affected by the cold, but the Jew complained very much; but although a young man, physically perfect, and as agile as any of us, he persisted in keeping his place in the Wagon. When we arrived we found his ears frozen stiff and his feet also badly frozen, and we had a sorry time with him that night. When he came to the fire his suffering was intense, and he did not bear it with Christian humility and submission.

We found a comfortable Hotel in Jacksonville, then a pleasant Town with a prosperous appearance, having 2000 inhabitants or more. I met here the Nation's Idol, Abraham Lincoln, then of little note except in that locality, where they spoke of him as their distinguished Attorney and excellent Citizen. The Landlord introduced me to him. He made only a few remarks: asked me where I came from, spoke of our freezing Journey across the Prairie and other commonplace remarks; and also remarked that he thought our Hebrew Companion was fortunate after all, for although his feet and ears were badly damaged he had saved his Stock in Trade. When I asked, "How was that?" he replied, "His Tongue was left intact."[57]

3. TWO FRIENDS NAMED ABRAHAM:
CORRESPONDENCE BETWEEN LINCOLN AND JONAS

The following letters shed light on the friendship that linked Abraham Lincoln and Abraham Jonas of Quincy, Illinois.

In the letter dated February 4, 1860, below, Lincoln refers to Jonas as one of his "most valued friends." In the following letters, dated February 3, February 4, July 20, and July 21, 1860, the intense level of Jonas's involvement in Lincoln's campaign for the presidency in Illinois is readily apparent. Among the many interesting facets of this correspondence, we see that Jonas was genuinely concerned about Lincoln's public image. He informed the candidate that his political opponents were alleging that Lincoln associated with members of the nativist American/Know Nothing Party. Lincoln insisted that he was never in a Know Nothing lodge, but he shrewdly noted that he had more to gain, politically speaking, by ignoring the accusation and leaving it up to friends like Jonas to defend him publicly. The third letter is a hair-raising and touching warning from Jonas that he believed "desperate characters" in the South were plotting to prevent the president-elect's inauguration by perhaps "using violence upon the person of Lincoln."[58]

Quincy Feb 3/60

My dear Sir

I want to get a copy of the book publishing in Ohio containing the speeches of your self and Doug in the Campaign of last year, can you procure me a copy, or advise me, how and where I can get one—

Let me congratulate you on the election of Speaker—and indicators are that with proper exertions and judicious selections at Chicago in June, we shall be able to carry the day and in November proclaim victory to all the World.

Yrs &c A Jonas

Springfield. Feb. 4 1860
Hon: A. Jonas

My dear Sir:

Yours of the 3rd inquiring how you can get a copy of the debates now being published in Ohio, is received. As you are one of my most valued friends, and have complimented me by the expression of a wish for a book, I propose doing myself the honor of presenting you with one, as soon as I can. By the arrangement our Ohio friends have made with the publishers, I am to have one hundred copies gratis. When I shall receive them I will send you one by Express. I understand they will not be out before March, and I probably shall be absent about that time. So that you must not be disappointed if you do not receive yours before about the middle of that month.

Yours very truly,
A. Lincoln

"Confidential"
Quincy Ills. July 20/ 60

My dear Sir

I have just been credibly informed, that *Issac* [sic] *N Morris* is engaged in obtaining affidavits and certificates of certain Irish men that they saw you in Quincy come out of a Know Nothing Lodge—the intention is to send the affidavits to Washington for publication—I do not know if there is any truth in the matter, neither do I care, but thought it best to let you know about it—the object is to work on the Germans—and Morris can get men to swear to any thing—my informant saw one of the affidavits or certificates—

Yrs truely
A Jonas

if it all false, let me know

Confidential
Springfield Ill July 21st 1860.

My Dear Sir—

Yours of the 20th is received. I suppose as good, or even better men than I may have been in American or Know-Nothing lodges; but in point of fact, I never was in one, at Quincy or elsewhere. I was never in Quincy but one day and two nights while Know-Nothing lodges were in existence, and you were with me that day and both those nights. I had never been there before in my life; and never afterwards, till the joint debate with Douglas in 1858. It was in 1854 when I spoke in some hall there, and after the speaking, you with others took me to an oyster saloon, passed an hour there, and you walked with me to, and parted with me at the Quincy House, quite late at night. I left by stage for Naples before day-light in the morning, having come in by the same route, after dark the evening previous to the speaking, when I found you waiting at the Quincy House to meet me. A few days after I was there, Richardson, as I understood, started this same story about my having been in a Know-Nothing lodge. When I heard of the charge, as I did soon after, I taxed my recollection for some incident which could have suggested it; and I remembered that on parting with you the last night, I went to the office of the Hotel, to take my stage passage for the morning, was told that no stage office for that line was kept there, and that I must see the driver before retiring, to insure his calling for me in the morning; and a servant was sent with me to find the driver, who after taking me a square or two, stopped me, and stepped perhaps a dozen steps farther, and in my hearing called to some one, who answered him, apparently from the upper part of a building, and promised to call with the stage for me at the Quincy House. I returned and went to bed, and before day the stage called and took me. This is all.

That I never was in a Know Nothing lodge in Quincy, I should expect could be easily proved, by respectable men who were always in the lodges and never saw me there. An affidavit of one or two such would put the matter at rest.

And now, a word of caution. Our adversaries think they can gain a point if they could force me to openly deny the charge, by which some degree of offence would be given to the Americans. For this reason it must not publicly appear that I am paying any attention to the charge.

Yours Truly
A. Lincoln

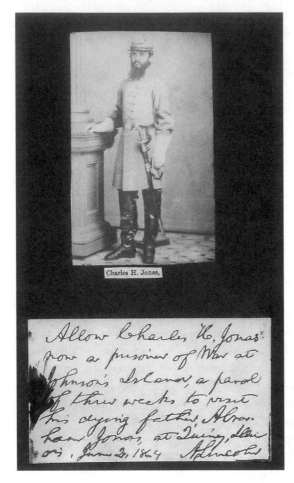

Charles H. Jonas,

Photo of Charles H. Jonas and Lincoln's note. Charles H. Jonas, one of Abraham Jonas's sons, was a captain in the Confederate army. Lincoln granted the imprisoned rebel "a parol [sic] of three weeks to visit his dying father." Courtesy American Jewish Historical Society, New York, N.Y., and Newton Centre, Mass.

4. A FINAL ACT OF FRIENDSHIP

Charles H. Jonas (1831–1910) was a son of Lincoln's longtime friend from Quincy, Illinois, Abraham Jonas. Thanks to Lincoln's short note dated June 2, 1864, the young Charles—then a captain in the Confederate army who had been captured by Union forces and incarcerated—was granted "a parol [sic] of three weeks" to visit his dying father. Over the years, Charles Jonas praised Lincoln for his compassion and the loyal friendship he showed to his father.

5. SIMON WOLF REMEMBERS LINCOLN'S MERCY

Lawyer and Jewish communal leader Simon Wolf took pride in having met every president of the United States from Lincoln through Woodrow Wilson. He enjoyed regaling listeners with his reminiscences of Lincoln, many of which have been cited over the years.

Lincoln's penchant for granting pardons to deserters and disobedient soldiers was well known, even during his lifetime. Wolf's story illustrates this trait. According to Wolf, Lincoln was persuaded to pardon a Jewish soldier once he learned the circumstances that prompted the young man to go AWOL.

I have on several occasions given the history of the Jewish soldier whom he pardoned at two o'clock in the early morning. While seated in my office prior to going to my home I received a telegram from a town in New England asking me to wait for a letter that was coming by express. The letter came, and it stated that a young soldier, American born, of Jewish faith, had been condemned to be shot and the execution was to take place the next morning. It was in the crucial days of the war when every soldier was needed at the front and when Edwin M. Stanton, Secretary of War, had threatened to resign unless the President would stop pardoning deserters. It seemed this soldier could not get a furlough. His mother, who was on her death bed, had begged for his return, to lay her hands lovingly on his head and give him a parting blessing. The filial love was superior to his duty to the flag, and he went home, was arrested, tried and condemned to be shot. For a moment I was dazed and uncertain as to the course to be pursued. Night came on apace, and finally I concluded to call on the Hon. Thomas Corwin of Ohio who was on intimate terms with the President. Mr. Corwin, as ever, was most gracious, but said, "My dear Mr. Wolf, it is impossible to do anything in this direction. The President has been maligned for being too generous and liberal in this respect." But I begged so hard that finally Corwin sent word over to the White House, inquiring whether an interview could be secured. The word came back, "Later in the night," and it was two o'clock in the morning before we reached the President.

The whole scene is as vividly before me as in those early hours of the morning. The President walked up and down with his hands hanging by his side, his face wore that gravity of expression that has been so often described by his historians and biographers, and yet he greeted us as if we were his boon companions and were indulging in an interchange of anecdotes, of which he was a past master. Corwin told him why we had come. He listened with deep attention, and when Corwin had exhausted the subject the president replied, "Impossible to do anything. I have no influence with this administration," and the twinkle in his eye was indescribable: "Stanton has put his foot down and insists upon one of two things, either that I must quit or he will quit." Corwin turned to me and said, "I told you, my dear friend, that it was hopeless," and was about leaving the room. I said, "Mr. President, you will pardon me for a moment. What would you have done under similar circumstances? If your dying mother had summoned you to her bedside to receive her last message before her soul would be summoned to its Maker, would you have been a deserter to her who gave you birth, rather than deserter in law but not in fact

33

to the flag to which you had sworn allegiance?" He stopped, touched the bell; his secretary, John Hay, who time and again spoke of that occurrence, came in; he ordered a telegram to be sent to stop the execution, and that American citizen of Jewish faith led the forlorn hope with the flag of his country in his hands at the battle of Cold Harbor and was shot to death fighting heroically and patriotically for the country of his birth. When months afterward I told the President what had become of that young soldier, he was visibly moved and with great emotion said, "I thank God for having done what I did." It was an impressive scene, one full of pathos and sublime humanity, and is engraved on the tablets of memory as no other incident of my whole life.[59]

6. ABRAM J. DITTENHOEFER'S IMPRESSIONS OF LINCOLN

Abram J. Dittenhoefer, a New York Republican and enthusiastic supporter of Lincoln, played an active role in both of his presidential campaigns. A few years prior to his death, Dittenhoefer published his memoirs, How We Elected Lincoln: Personal Recollections of Lincoln and Men of His Time.

Yet even before he published his own reminiscences, Dittenhoefer shared many of his firsthand impressions of Lincoln in a letter to Isaac Markens (1846–1928), the first independent scholar to reconstruct Lincoln's Jewish associations. Markens published excerpts from Dittenhoefer's letter in his pioneering 1909 publication, Abraham Lincoln and the Jews. *In Dittenhoefer's memory, his friend Abraham Lincoln was a man who was intrinsically "melancholy" and "genial."*

While an air of melancholy seemed always to suffuse his features, I always regarded President Lincoln as the most genial of men. I often found him sitting in the business office of the White House having on a black, threadbare, alpaca coat, out at the elbows and in slippers. I could always notice when he was about to indulge in a jest, which he frequently did in the midst of the most serious conversation; a sort of half suppressed smile would appear on that strong face for a brief interval before the jest was given, as if he was anticipating the pleasure it would give in the hearing of it. I remember distinctly presenting to him the ballot I had cast as one of the Presidential electors for him in the New York college of electors. Looking at it a few minutes, he said, "It represents the power and dignity of the American people and the grandeur of American institutions." In thanking me for giving it to him he said he would leave it to his children as a memento. I saw him in Washington a few days before his death. He seemed then to be in the best of spirits and spoke of the great work that was before him in completing the restoration of harmony and peace between the North and the South.[60]

Abraham Kohn, a prominent civic leader in Chicago who became a Lincoln supporter when the two first met in 1860. Courtesy The Jacob Rader Marcus Center of the American Jewish Archives, at the Hebrew Union College–Jewish Institute of Religion, Cincinnati, Ohio.

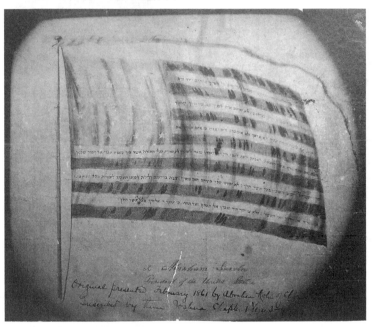

Kohn's Hebrew flag. This print, made from an old glass negative, is the only known image of the flag that Kohn painted for Lincoln in 1861. Courtesy Spertus Institute, Chicago.

7. ABRAHAM KOHN PRESENTS THE PRESIDENT-ELECT WITH A HEBREW FLAG

The picture reproduced above is the only known image of the famous flag with Hebrew letters that Abraham Kohn, also pictured above, painted for President-elect Lincoln. At the bottom of the image, one can discern a dedication: "To Abraham Lincoln, President of the United States." This picture comes from an old glass negative that was found

in the archives of the Kehilath Anshe Ma'ariv Temple by Joseph Levinson (1904–93), chair-
man of the Archives Committee of KAM Temple. Kohn had served as president of KAM,
and when he first met Lincoln, he was the city clerk of Chicago.

Also provided is Isaac Markens's detailed description of the circumstances surround-
ing Kohn's presentation of the extraordinary gift, including a letter of appreciation sent
to Kohn by Lincoln's longtime friend Jonathan Young Scammon (1812–90).[61] *Finally, a*
letter written to Abraham S. Cohen (d. 1867) from Abraham Lincoln's private secretary
John Hay (1838–1905) is reproduced. Cohen, then the editor of New York's Jewish Record,
had written a letter to President Lincoln asking him about the Kohn flag. Hay's response
confirms the fact that Lincoln kept the Kohn flag in the White House.[62]

Isaac Markens on Kohn's Flag

It was during the Presidential campaign of 1860 that Abraham Kohn, City Clerk
of Chicago, first met Lincoln, the acquaintance being formed in the store of
Kohn, at that time a merchant. Kohn was a Bavarian, then in his 42d year, a
man of excellent education, well versed in Hebrew literature and known and
respected as a public-spirited citizen. He had been for several years President
of the Hebrew Congregation Anshe Maariv (Men of the West). In politics Kohn
was described by the Democratic press as "one of the blackest Republicans and
Abolitionists." Kohn's popularity and influence had probably been brought to
Lincoln's attention, and the latter, consummate politician as he was, recognized
in Kohn, presumably, an ally whose acquaintance would prove a valuable asset
in the pending election. Lincoln was introduced by Congressman Isaac N. Arnold who accompanied him and it was this meeting that inspired Kohn with a
feeling of admiration for his visitor and a conviction that he was the destined
Moses of the slaves and the saviour of his country. Thus says his daughter,
Mrs. D[ila] K[ohn] Adler, in a letter to the writer. Lincoln in the course of the
conversation spoke of the Bible as their book and Kohn, being a devout Jew as
well as an ardent patriot, conceived an intense admiration for Lincoln. This
found expression in his sending to the president-elect before his departure for
Washington a silk flag, the work of his own hands, painted in colors, its folds
bearing Hebrew characters exquisitely lettered in black with the third to ninth
verses of the first chapter of Joshua, the last verse being:

> Have I not commanded thee? Be strong and of good courage; be not
> afraid neither be thou dismayed; for the Lord thy God is with thee
> whithersoever thou goest . . .

Mr. Lincoln at once wrote to Mr. Kohn thanking him for his gift. His letter was
sent through a mutual friend, John Young Scammon, a prominent citizen of Chicago,
who delayed its delivery until six months after Lincoln's departure from Springfield,
when he wrote to Mr. Kohn as follows:

Chicago, August 28, 1861

Abraham Kohn, Esq.

My Dear Sir: The enclosed acknowledgment of the receipt of your beautiful painting of the American flag by the President got among my letters or it would have been sent to you before. Regretting the delay, I am,

Truly your friend,

J. Young Scammon[63]

Letter from John Hay to Abraham S. Cohen[64]

Washington. November 28, 1862

My Dear Sir:

The paragraph to which you refer was altogether erroneous.

The "flag" referred to was a small painting of the American banner, inscribed in Hebrew characters with a passage from the 1st Chapter of Joshua, from the 4th to the 9th verse. It was presented to the President in February, 1861, before his departure from Illinois, by Abraham Kohn City Clerk of Chicago, who had himself painted it. It has been in the Executive Mansion ever since the President's inauguration.

Your obt. [obedient] Servant,

John Hay,

Assist. Priv. Sec.

A. S. Cohen & Co.

8. "COULD ANYTHING HAVE GIVEN MR. LINCOLN MORE CHEER?" EXCERPTS FROM WILLIAM A. MCKINLEY'S SPEECH

Although the Hebrew flag that Kohn gave to Lincoln has been lost for over a century, there is no doubt that the flag once existed and was kept in the White House during Lincoln's presidency. Admiral George H. Preble made mention of the Kohn flag in his History of the Flag of the United States.[65] *In his famous volume* The American Jew as Patriot, Soldier, and Citizen, *Simon Wolf claimed that William McKinley (1843–1901) read about the Kohn flag in Preble's book. According to Wolf, the then governor of Ohio and aspiring presidential candidate was inspired by the story of Kohn and the flag, and he often made use of the anecdote when he delivered campaign addresses. Evidently, just prior to the publication of Wolf's book in 1895, the* Reform Advocate *published the text of a speech McKinley gave in Ottawa, Kansas, on June 20, 1895. Wolf cited excerpts from McKinley's speech in which he made special reference to the Hebrew flag. He also cited a few sentences from a letter that McKinley subsequently wrote to Kohn's daughter Dila in response to a letter she had written upon reading that the governor had made reference to her father's famous flag in one of his speeches.*

What more beautiful conception than that which prompted Abraham Kohn, of Chicago, in February, 1861, to send to Mr. Lincoln, on the eve of his starting to Washington, to assume the office of president, a flag of our country, bearing upon its silken folds these words from the first chapter of Joshua: "Have I not commanded thee? Be strong and of good courage. Be not afraid, neither be thou dismayed, for the Lord, thy God is with thee, whithersoever thou goest. There shall not any man be able to stand before thee all the days of thy life. As I was with Moses so shall I be with thee. I will not fail thee nor forsake thee."

Could anything have given Mr. Lincoln more cheer, or been better calculated to sustain his courage or to strengthen his faith in the mighty work before him? Thus commanded, thus assured, Mr. Lincoln journeyed to the capital, where he took the oath of office and registered in heaven an oath to save the Union. And the Lord, our God, was with him, until every obligation of oath and duty was sacredly kept and honored. Not any man was able to stand before him. Liberty was the more firmly enthroned, the Union was saved, and the flag which he carried floated in triumph and glory from every flagstaff of the republic.

In a reply to a letter addressed to him by the daughter of Abraham Kohn, Mrs. Dankmar Adler (whose husband, the architect of the Auditorium building and one of the architects of the Columbian Exposition, had fought through the war and been wounded at Chickamauga), Major McKinley wrote:

The incident deeply impressed me when I first learned of it, and I have taken occasion to use it, as in my speech at Ottawa, to which you refer. I am very glad to have been able to give publicity to this striking incident, and I am sure that the family of Mr. Kohn should feel very proud of his patriotic act.[66]

9. HENRY WENTWORTH MONK VISITS LINCOLN AT THE WHITE HOUSE

It is impossible to verify the facts relating to the unusual encounter between President Lincoln and the highly eccentric Henry Wentworth Monk (1827–96), the Canadian-born mystic and millenarian who was passionately committed to the idea of creating a state for the Jews in the ancient homeland.

To publicly demonstrate his prophetic abilities, Monk, in 1863, agreed to submit to a "test" initiated by the English art critic and social thinker John Ruskin (1819–1900). Ruskin had proposed that Monk travel to Washington to meet with Lincoln and present him with his plan to end the Civil War. Monk claimed to have done so and stated that during his interview he also urged Lincoln to establish a Jewish homeland in Palestine, which was, Monk told him, a necessary precondition for world peace.[67]

Monk's account of Lincoln's response to his recommendation is all the more enthralling in light of Mary Todd Lincoln's firm insistence that her husband had confessed to her his keen desire to visit Jerusalem in the near future.[68]

At the White House, Henry Wentworth Monk wedged himself into a perspiring, chattering, gesticulating queue of soldiers, contractors, news-papermen, officials, sightseers, women and children that filled the ante-room outside the President's office. Some carried papers and petitions; others talked loudly of their grievances, or rehearsed the requests they intended to make. Sometimes a messenger or secretary would enter or leave the President's room, and then everyone would fall silent, and watch him open and shut the door as if it might be possible to peep through. After nearly three hours of waiting some of the visitors grew hungry, and produced sandwiches or cake which they ate in a hurry, as if fearing interruption.

Suddenly at midday there was a stir in the office. The door was flung wide open, and one of the President's secretaries whispered inaudibly to the nearest visitor. All knew the signal; and in a moment the crowd was jostling and elbowing its way into the President's room. Mr. Lincoln was seen completing the signing of some papers; and he did not look up till the room was full. Then, he began brief interviews with visitors chosen more or less at random.

Monk had taken up a position at the back of the crowd, near the door, where he could watch the proceedings and get his bearings. Most of the visitors, he noticed, were seeking favours—a commission, a concession, an appointment or a pardon. He considered that their attitude was mercenary, and that they showed small respect to their President. Lincoln looked care-worn and preoccupied, sometimes almost appearing not to hear what his visitor said. Then suddenly he would "come to." His expression would change, a smile would play on his lips, and he would crack a joke. These rapid transitions in the President's mood from melancholy to humour seem to have fascinated Monk, who now began to press forward a little so as to obtain a better view of Mr. Lincoln. Perhaps in his usual impetuous fashion he made more of a stir than he intended, for he soon became aware that the President was looking squarely at him, with an expression of part amusement, part curiosity. Seeing the direction of the President's stare, the people now parted a little, so that Monk was forced to move forward towards the desk.

According to a letter addressed subsequently by Monk to his friend, Chewett, Mr. Lincoln spoke first, and asked him who he was; and then, on hearing that he was a Canadian, rose and beckoning him forward, shook his hand warmly. He asked Monk how he liked Washington. "I took this as an opportunity to tell him why I had come," wrote Monk. "I explained to the President that I was a friend of Mr. Ruskin and Mr. Hunt, and that many Englishmen and Canadians, like myself, while applauding his Emancipation Proclamation, could not but hope that a way might be found to terminate this terrible war before it was too late, and ruin had overtaken the civilization of North America. The President replied, Amen to that, in a quiet and rather sad manner; then asked me whether I had any plan to propose for bringing peace about. I replied that the South was fighting, not merely for its independence but for its property in slaves. Let the North, which in the past had shared in the profits from slavery, generously compensate the South for emancipating its slaves. 'It will be less expensive,' I added, 'to pay this compensation than to fight the war to a finish.' Mr. Lincoln nodded, but immediately asked me whether I had any reason to suppose that the South would return to the Union on these terms. I assured him that, once slavery were abandoned, secession would die a natural death, particularly if the South would be left to itself for a few years to find out that machinery could do the work which slave labour had done up till now. 'Thus,' I said, 'all the blood and treasure which the war has already cost will not have been spent in vain. For the world will thereby have been led to take a great step forward in social, intellectual and moral progress.' My suggestion appeared to amuse the President, for he now gave our conversation a jocular turn. 'Your plan,' he said, 'reminds me of the outcome of a fight between two friends of my son at school, Bill and Tom. One day I saw Tom with his face bloody, limping along and doubled up as if in pain. I asked him if he had been fighting, and he replied, "Yes, Sir, but I won the victory!" "And how did you do that?" I said. "Why," answered Tom, "when Bill swung a hard right, I stopped it with my nose. When Bill delivered a vicious kick, I stopped it with my stomach. I certainly gave him a trimming." Now it seems to me that your plan is like Tom's victory—it is all self-sacrifice.'

"But to be serious," went on the President, "do not you Canadians consider my Emanclamation Proclamation as a great step forward in the social and moral progress of the world?" "Indeed we do," answered Monk, "only it does not go far enough. Why not follow the emancipation of the Negro by a still more urgent step—the emancipation of the Jew?"

"The Jew—why the Jew? Are they not free already?"

"Certainly, Mr. President, the American Jew is free, and so is the English Jew—but not the European. In America we live so far off that we are blind to what goes on in Russia and Prussia and Turkey. There can be no permanent peace in the world until the civilized nations, led, I hope, by Great Britain and the United States, atone for what they have done to the Jews—for their two thousand years of persecution—by restoring them to their national home in Palestine, and making Jerusalem the capital city of a reunited Christendom."

"That is a noble dream, Mr. Monk," said the President, "and one shared by many Americans. I myself have a regard for the Jews. My chiropodist is a Jew, and he has so many times 'put me upon my feet' that I would have no objection to giving his countrymen 'a leg up.' But the United States is, alas, at this moment a house divided against itself. We must first bring this dreadful war to a victorious conclusion, which no compromise can do—and then, Mr. Monk, we may begin again to see visions, and dream dreams. Then you will see what leadership America will show to the world!"[69]

10. ADOLPHUS SOLOMONS'S ACCOUNT OF THE
"CRACKED GLASS" PHOTOGRAPH OF LINCOLN

Adolphus S. Solomons was a prominent entrepreneur and Jewish communal leader in Washington, D.C., during the Lincoln administration. Born and raised in New York City, Solomons moved to the nation's capital in 1859 and established a publishing firm under the name Philp and Solomons. As a member of Washington's social elite, he received invitations to attend social functions at the White House, and, according to his memoirs, he developed a warm personal association with Lincoln.[70]

According to Solomons, the last images of Lincoln were taken by the photographer Alexander Gardner (1821–82)[71] on the premises of "Philip and Solomons"[72] on "the second Sunday previous to the Friday night" of his assassination—Sunday, April 2, 1865. This data is erroneous since we know from many sources that Lincoln was away from Washington at that time. Traditionally, the last photos of Lincoln were believed to have been taken on Monday, April 10, 1865, so today the Gardner photos can only be called some of the last photographs of Lincoln from life, because research has convinced many scholars that the session with Gardner took place in February 1865, and therefore one or two other photographs of Lincoln were apparently taken subsequently. In any event, Solomons allowed the American Hebrew *to print one of the photographs taken during that sitting.[73]*

Nearly half a century later, Solomons provided the editors of the American Hebrew *with a detailed account of that photographic session. Like the dating of the photo session itself, it is difficult to gauge the accuracy of Solomons's reminiscences. What is beyond question, however, is the fact that Solomons contended that he and Lincoln enjoyed a*

Alexander Gardner's "cracked glass" portrait of Lincoln. Many have insisted that this photograph, taken probably in February 1865, is the last photograph of Lincoln before his death. The crack was later characterized as an ominous sign of impending disaster. Courtesy Library of Congress Prints and Photographs Division, Washington, D.C.

Facsimile of last Lincoln portrait, taken for Mr. Adolphus S. Solomons (owned by Mrs. N. Taylor Phillips). Washington businessman Adolphus S. Solomons insisted that this photo was the last taken of Lincoln before his death. In his reminiscences, Solomons claimed that the picture was taken in his studio by the prominent Civil War photographer Alexander Gardner. *The American Hebrew and Jewish Messenger* 84, no. 15 (February 12, 1909): 387.

very warm and personal association. Solomons explained that the president arrived at his studio in a sorrowful mood, and consequently some of the photographs did not do him justice. Lincoln seemed to sense his friend's disappointment, Solomons recollected, so he asked for "one of [Solomons's] funny stories" in the hope of lightening his mood and producing a more natural photograph. "I complied as best I could," Solomons declared, and the result was the photograph that accompanied the publication of his memories on the pages of the American Hebrew.

As many statements have been made relating to the "last photograph" Mr. Lincoln sat for, I feel assured that the following disposes of the fact.

During the early 60s our bookselling and publishing firm of Philip and Solomons, located at 011 Pennsylvania avenue in this city, had a large photograph branch in the upper part of the building under the charge of Alexander Gardner who was well known for his celebrated Photographic Sketch Book of the war, in two oblong folio volumes, in which Mr. Lincoln was a frequent and conspicuous figure in camp in battle fields.

One day, while in his office, I casually remarked that I would like very much for him to give us another sitting, as those we had been favored with were unsatisfactory to us, and would he permit us to try again, to which he willingly assented.

Not long afterwards he sent word that he could "come on some Sunday," and a date was arranged, which was the second Sunday previous to the Friday night when the assassin, Wilkes Booth, in cold blood shot to death one of the most beloved men God ever created.

At the time named by appointment, he came, and, at my first glance, I saw, with regret, that he wore a troubled expression, which, however, was not unusual at that eventful period of our country's fitful condition, and throwing aside on a chair the gray woolen shawl he was accustomed to wear, Mr. Gardner, after several squints at his general make-up, placed him in an artistic position, and began his work.

After several "snaps" during which the President, while making jocular remarks, had completely upset the operator's calculation, I followed Mr. Gardner into his "darkroom" and learned to my sorrow that he had not succeeded in getting even a *fair* expression of his mobile countenance, and therefore was much discouraged which, however, was but a repetition of former occasions.

I courageously named the result of my investigation to Mr. Lincoln, whereupon he, noticing, perhaps, my disappointment, said to me, "tell Mr. Gardner to come out in the open"—referring to the "dark room,"—"and you, Solomons, tell me one of your funny stories and we will see if I can't do better."

I complied as best I could, and the result was the likeness as reproduced in these memories.[74]

2

"The Most Favored Family Visitor at the White House": The Enigmatic Relationship between Lincoln and Isachar Zacharie, M.D.

One of the most celebrated and intriguing of President Lincoln's many contacts with Jews during his years in the White House was the extraordinary relationship he had with a fascinating chiropodist named Isachar Zacharie (1827–1900).[1] Writing in 1951, Bertram W. Korn, the pioneering scholar of American Jewry and the Civil War, described Zacharie as one of Abraham Lincoln's "most enigmatic intimates."[2] Who *was* Isachar Zacharie? Was Lincoln's chiropodist simply a "patriotic corn doctor," or was he, as some have suggested, a mendacious "rebel spy"?[3]

Zacharie was born in Kent, England, in 1827. There exists evidence that Zacharie was already working as an apprentice to a distinguished medical scholar in 1837. Though he

Isachar Zacharie was Lincoln's chiropodist and covert envoy for the administration.
Courtesy American Jewish Historical Society, New York, N.Y., and Newton Centre, Mass.

would have been only ten or eleven years old at that time, such things often happened in Victorian England. In this capacity, he may have been introduced to chiropody—a burgeoning profession and potentially a lucrative calling.[4]

Zacharie was seventeen or eighteen years old when he, his parents, and his siblings immigrated to the United States in the mid-1840s. Within a few years of his arrival, he was receiving kudos for his exceptional abilities to relieve his patients' discomforts by treating their corns, bunions, and ingrown toenails without inflicting pain or provoking subsequent infection.[5] Zacharie seems to have traveled extensively during his first decade in the United States,[6] and he cared for the feet of some of the most prominent Americans of the antebellum era, including U.S. senators Henry Clay of Kentucky, John C. Calhoun of South Carolina, Lewis Cass of Michigan, Thomas Hart Benton of Missouri, and James A. Bayard of Delaware. At the conclusion of his treatment, Zacharie solicited and received flattering letters of commendation.[7]

Edwin M. Stanton appears to have been the man who first introduced Zacharie to prominent members of the Lincoln administration. Armed with a fistful of highly complimentary professional endorsements, the young foot doctor came to Stanton in 1862 and urged him to create an army corps of chiropodists who would tend to the podiatric needs of battlefield soldiers. Zacharie's proposal did not interest Stanton, but the "doctor's" skill impressed him. Within months, Zacharie's clientele included men like Secretary of State William H. Seward, General Nathaniel P. Banks (1816–94), General Ambrose E. Burnside (1824–81), General George B. McClellan, and many others. By the summer of 1862, Zacharie was trimming the toenails of the nation's first citizen—Abraham Lincoln.[8]

Lincoln, like many other contemporaries, was impressed by Zacharie's skill. He and Seward actually composed a joint letter of endorsement. Whether Lincoln actually came to think of Zacharie as a friend or whether he was merely being courteous to a helpful pedal servant is difficult to determine. We do know that the two men enjoyed a personal association that was neither superficial nor fleeting.

Contemporaries have left conflicting impressions of Zacharie's personality. A correspondent writing for the *New York Herald* described him as a "man of charm and grace": "Dr. Zacharie is distinguished by a splendid Roman nose, fashionable whiskers and eloquent tongue, a dazzling diamond breastpin, great skill in his profession and an ingratiating address, a perfect knowledge of his business, and a plentiful supply of social and moral courage."[9]

In stark contrast, George S. Denison (1833–66), a twenty-seven-year-old treasury agent in New Orleans (and cousin of Salmon P. Chase [1808–73], treasury secretary under Lincoln and later chief justice), characterized the Jewish foot doctor as a fop and a name-dropper: "His vest is flowered velvet—his hair beautifully oiled—and his presence distills continual perfume sweeter than the winds that blow from Araby the blest. In season and out of season, he fails not to announce himself as the *Confidential Agent* or *Correspondent* of the President."[10]

Zacharie's copious correspondence with men like Lincoln, Seward, and Banks testifies to the fact that this man was a colorful personality. He could be obsequious, oleaginous, and painfully solicitous. At other times, he could be self-congratulatory, petty, and critical. His letters bespeak a personality always characterized by passion, energy, and assertiveness.

The true nature of Zacharie's relationship with Abraham Lincoln is genuinely inscrutable. On the one hand, various primary source documents suggest that the chiropodist was a toady, a self-promoter, and a dishonorable phony. In his many letters to Lincoln, Zacharie repeatedly flatters the president. "My desire is to serve you," he wrote, "in such a manner that my services may rebound to your honor." In another note, he insisted that "what I wish to do is for the benefit of yourself & my country." Zacharie even made use of humor in order to reassure Lincoln that he was fundamentally a humble personal friend who wanted to prove he was also a faithful political ally: "Perhaps I'm somewhat like the Irish Biddy who remarked to the lady of the house, 'Shurr Mistress darlent a poor gal that works hard likes to know if she gives satisfaction to youz.'"[11]

Over the years, Zacharie sent a variety of presents to the Lincolns—a barrel of hominy, a box of pineapples, a case of oranges and bananas—but it is difficult to determine whether these gifts came from a shameless opportunist or from a man who genuinely cared about Lincoln and believed him to be a "dear friend." We do know, however, that Zacharie did more for Lincoln than merely trim his toenails. He ultimately became the president's personal envoy and a loyal partisan for Lincoln's reelection campaign.[12]

By the fall of 1862, Zacharie's relationship with the Lincoln administration became a matter of public discourse. He earned a considerable reputation as a powerful Washington insider, and on October 3, an exposé on the president's foot doctor appeared in the pages of the *New York Herald* under the tongue-in-cheek headline "The Head and Feet of the Nation." According to the article, Dr. Zacharie "enjoyed Mr. Lincoln's confidence perhaps more than any other private individual . . . [and was possibly] the most favored family visitor at the White House." Even if the article exaggerated the dimensions of the chiropodist's political clout, Zacharie's remarkable role in a covert diplomatic mission substantiates the fact that Lincoln held him in high regard.[13]

Zacharie's diplomatic duties for the Lincoln administration may very well have had their genesis in a series of political deliberations that culminated in the issuance of the so-called preliminary Emancipation Proclamation by Lincoln on September 22, 1862, a document that gave official notice to the states in rebellion that unless they laid down their arms and rejoined the Union by January 1, 1863, the president would emancipate their slaves.[14]

During the weeks leading up to the issuance of the preliminary Emancipation Proclamation, Zacharie frequently treated the president's feet. Was Lincoln thinking about this important matter while he was receiving pedal therapy? The answer to this question is unknowable, but on the very same day that he signed the preliminary Emancipation Proclamation, Lincoln issued another much less historic missive, this one validating Zacharie's podiatric skills: "Dr. Zacharie has operated on my feet with great success, and considerable addition to my comfort."[15]

The issuance of these two statements on the very same day may very well have been nothing more than an odd historical coincidence. Nevertheless, in light of the covert diplomatic activities that Zacharie would carry out for the Lincoln administration over the coming months, one cannot help but ponder whether the president discussed his plans to emancipate the Confederacy's slaves with his podiatrist and, moreover, whether the two men began to exchange views as to the possibility that the proclamation might spur the South's leadership to give serious consideration to a negotiated peace![16]

The day after Lincoln issued the preliminary Emancipation Proclamation, September 23, 1862, Edwin Stanton gave Zacharie permission "to pass with the lines of the United States forces around Washington and the Potomac for the purpose of operating upon the feet of the soldiers for corns, bunion's etc." Zacharie's efforts to help the Union soldiers must have been a noteworthy success because he soon received a different and much more significant assignment to carry out in New Orleans.[17]

In November 1862, Lincoln ordered General Banks to go to New Orleans and replace the roughshod Major General Benjamin ("Beast") Butler (1818–93) as commander of the Department of the Gulf.[18] Zacharie had already developed a personal bond with Banks, perhaps because Banks had been one of Zacharie's first patients in Washington, D.C. Nevertheless, with Banks's encouragement, Zacharie asked Lincoln and Secretary Seward to send him to New Orleans to work for Banks "in some capacity so as to render some service to the government." Zacharie assured Seward that he could help the government in its efforts to solidify the Union's control over New Orleans, an erstwhile Confederate city.[19]

In an "official and confidential" letter, Banks outlined Zacharie's assignment while in New Orleans. He was to mingle freely with the people of New Orleans—"especially with [his] own countrymen." He was to work as an "informant," assessing the mood of the local citizenry and helping the Union win its loyalty. Banks also directed Zacharie to conduct secretive reconnaissance missions in the Confederate stronghold of neighboring Mississippi in order to ascertain the location, number, and preparedness of the enemy's troops as well as "the extent of their supplies and ammunition and the different organizations of which their army may be composed." Finally, Banks authorized Zacharie to employ qualified informants who could assist him in carrying out these important assignments.[20]

Zacharie arrived in New Orleans in mid-January of 1863, and thus began his brief but well-documented career as a U.S. intelligence official. Zacharie immediately began to establish relations with the Crescent City's social elite, including prominent leaders of the Jewish community. Zacharie gathered reconnaissance information, wrote reports, and worked diligently to curry favor with Jewish leaders by serving as something of a fixer for his coreligionists who may have previously been sympathetic to the Confederacy. According to General Banks, the courtesies that Zacharie showed to some of the key leaders in New Orleans endeared him to "leading men of the Rebel Government . . . and secured for him such endors[e]ments as will enable him to do that which other men cannot do, and which perhaps could not be given to a man of more commanding social or political position." Clearly, Zacharie's community relations campaign pleased and impressed Banks, and he assured Seward that Zacharie was "a zealous supporter of the Government."[21]

While he was in New Orleans, Zacharie worked under Banks, but he sent periodic briefings directly to Lincoln and Seward detailing the progress he was making. "Everywhere Union spirit is gaining in power," he wrote. He eagerly informed Lincoln that the general population in New Orleans—and particularly the Creoles—received him warmly. "I came here" he wrote, "to use my best efforts, humble though they be, in aiding to unite our country. Should I in any way be instrumental in consummating so great a result, my ambition will be gratified. For I shall know full well my name will not be forgotten either by the United States government or the people of Louisiana."[22]

Yet, Zacharie's espionage work for the Union must have annoyed some southern loyalists, and he wrote Lincoln to explain he had "made some enemies" who may have been surreptitiously accusing him of taking graft and profiteering. As for the accuracy of these accusations, Zacharie declared: "I most earnestly deny [them]."[23]

Zacharie's Jewishness became grist for the mill of his ardent detractors. One northern critic remembered him as "the lowest and vulgarest of Jew pedlars [*sic*]," and he expressed shock that "Mr. Lincoln [would] make a friend of such an odious creature." According to this same writer, General John G. Foster's (1823–74) wife refused to sit at the same table with a Jew like Zacharie.[24]

But Banks and Zacharie had a mutual admiration society. Zacharie stoked Banks's presidential ambitions with a steady stream of fawning compliments, though he ultimately supported Lincoln in the 1864 election. Banks told Seward that Zacharie had neither solicited nor received any "favors" for his efforts.

Zacharie's attempt to negotiate a peace treaty between the Union and the Confederacy in 1863 was arguably the most intriguing facet of his short diplomatic career in the Lincoln administration. His desire to become a peacemaker seems to have taken root in May 1863, in the wake of the Union's pivotal victory over the Confederate forces at Vicksburg. Zacharie's Confederate informants told him that most "Southern people earnestly desired to have the war settled without further bother."[25] They told Zacharie they would help him meet with members of the Confederate cabinet if he could persuade Lincoln to pursue a negotiated peace plan.[26]

Banks, too, seems to have believed that the Confederate leadership could be enticed into peace negotiations, and he dispatched Zacharie to Washington, instructing him to deliver special reports and secret memoranda to Lincoln. Ten days later, on the eve of his departure for New Orleans, Zacharie wrote a letter to Lincoln wherein he confessed to being anxious over "the great responsibility" that the administration had given him. Nonetheless, once he was back in New Orleans and under the direction of General Banks, Zacharie began to conduct a series of secret meetings with his southern contacts in the vicinity of New Orleans.[27]

Zacharie believed that repairing the Union should be the administration's top priority and that the only formula for peace would be a plan that brought "*honour* to the *North, . . . without humiliation to the South.*" According to the *New York Herald*, Zacharie thought that the U.S. government should agree to transport Jefferson Davis, the Confederate government, and 150,000 of the Confederacy's most ardent troops to the New Mexican Territory: "With this force [Jefferson Davis would] drive away Napoleon's hordes and proclaim himself President of the new Mexican republic. Simultaneously the seceded Southern States [would] return to the Union with whatever negroes [we]re left in them. This [would] end the war satisfactorily to all concerned."[28]

It was most unlikely that Lincoln, or any other member of his administration for that matter, would give serious consideration to such a plan. However impractical, this idea was based on the established fact that many Confederate leaders considered the New Mexican Territory to be vitally important to an independent southern nation. In fact, after General Robert E. Lee's (1807-70) capitulation, some Confederate troops actually fled to the New Mexican Territory in the hope of keeping Dixie's national flame aglow in the Southwest.[29]

According to Zacharie's correspondence, his initial entreaties were cordially received by the Confederate officials, but he quickly realized that the Lincoln administration was sending him mixed signals about the idea of negotiating a peace settlement with the Confederacy. According to Zacharie, Seward was urging him to continue his furtive conversations with the Confederates. The secretary of state told him, he asserted, that Lincoln was aware of his efforts and that he should continue to negotiate in accordance with his best judgment. Zacharie also reiterated, in a letter to Banks, that Seward continued to encourage his negotiations: "When the time came & all was ready" Zacharie assured Banks, "[Seward told me he] could clintch [*sic*] the matter."[30]

Lincoln's level of interest in Zacharie's plan may be gauged from the fact that silence reigned between the two men for three months during the summer of 1863. Then, inexplicably, Lincoln summoned Zacharie to Washington in early September. After two days of intense conversation, Lincoln gave his chiropodist the green light to go to Richmond and see if the Confederate leadership was truly ready to stop the "effusion of blood" and return to the Union.[31]

On Sunday evening, September 27, 1863, Isachar Zacharie met furtively with four high-ranking Confederate officials on the outskirts of Richmond: Stephen R. Mallory (1813-73), secretary of the navy; James A. Seddon (1815-80), secretary of war; General John H. Winder (1800-1865), provost marshal of Richmond, and, to Zacharie's surprise and delight, Secretary of State Judah P. Benjamin (1811-84).[32]

Until now, very little was known about this gathering. A letter from Zacharie to General Banks, written on October 9, 1863, identified the participants and summarized the meeting by saying "the interview was of the most friendly nature." Thanks to a recently resurfaced piece of correspondence between Zacharie and Benjamin written the day after the meeting, we now know definitively that this meeting occurred, and, more important, we have some indication of what transpired.[33]

Zacharie's tone was effervescent; he was evidently thrilled by his unexpected rendezvous with Benjamin: "I was so excited last night and overcome at the pleasure of meeting *you*, knowing that the confederate flag was waving over my head, that my heart was bursting with joy. I had so *much* to say and so *short* time to say it in, that I fear I have forgotten much, but I hope the day is not far distant when we shall meet again."[34]

Astonishingly, it seems that in addition to discussing the prospect of a negotiated peace, Zacharie opened the meeting by soliciting a personal favor: he asked Benjamin to permit him to travel through the Confederacy in order to visit his elderly father in Savannah. Evidently, Benjamin declined the request on the spot, but Zacharie promised Benjamin in his letter that he would ultimately prove himself "worthy, not only of your confidence, but of the small favour I have asked." Through his future efforts, he assured Benjamin he would convince him he was *not* a secret agent for the Union.[35]

With this personal matter out of the way, Zacharie returned to peace negotiations. He stressed he was not just sympathetic to the South; he portrayed himself to be, at heart, a true Confederate patriot: "I hope I have made a favourable impression—and that you have taken all I said in good part, as it came from a pure heart. I would gladly join the armies of the confederacy if I did not know that I could be of more service to you from where I am, I endeavoured to explain all to you last night, which I hope was satisfactory."[36]

Finally, he assured Benjamin that he would "go immediately to Washington . . . [for] an interview with Mr. Lincoln . . . [and] assure him that no propositions of peace may be expected from the South." Yet Zacharie's letter also implies that the rebel leaders gave him something with which to tantalize Lincoln: "I shall put matters in the right light, and I know [Lincoln] will listen to me, and my word for it. Some good must come out of our *unexpected meeting*. I cannot explain to you why I think so, but I conscientiously believe there will (*time will show*)."[37]

Although nothing more came of this peace initiative, this letter offers us a sense of what transpired. Not only does this document confirm the fact that two Jewish Americans tried to negotiate an end to the Civil War in 1863, it also strongly suggests that if the Union would have proposed a compromise that was framed "in the right light," then the South might well have been receptive.[38]

In all probability, Zacharie tried to convince Seward that the administration should continue to negotiate with Benjamin. Nevertheless, despite Seward's previous promises and the behind-the-scenes encouragement Zacharie believed he had received from Lincoln, by the fall of 1863 it was clear that the administration had no intention of continuing these secretive negotiations with the Confederacy. Zacharie was peeved. In a letter to General Banks, he complained that the Lincoln administration had left him out to dry. The administration's disunity over the idea of pursuing peace negotiations made any ongoing efforts pointless. Zacharie wrote to Banks in exasperation: "Now what is the use of my going to see Benjamin, if we are not ready to do anything?"[39]

Although the Lincoln administration pulled the plug on Zacharie's diplomatic negotiations with Confederate leaders, leaving the podiatrist frustrated and insulted, he continued to try to curry favor with Lincoln. In 1864, Zacharie threw himself whole-heartedly behind the effort to reelect Lincoln. He traveled through Pennsylvania and

New York electioneering for the president, paying special attention to his Jewish coreligionists. "As regards the Isrelites [sic] . . ." Zacharie wrote Lincoln, "I understand them well." He hired campaign workers who registered voters, and he took steps to ensure that the "Israelites" voted for Lincoln in accordance with their promise. In regard to his efforts to sway the Jewish voters of New York, Zacharie assured Lincoln he had been effective. As for his work in Pennsylvania, Zacharie was even more definitive. "If you knew *all*—you and your friends would give me much credit, for I flatter myself I have done one of the sharpest things that has been done in the campaign. Will explain it to you when I see you." Though Lincoln feared he would lose his bid for reelection, Zacharie was confidence incarnate: "I hope to see you after the fun is over," he wrote, "when I hope you will say 'well done, My good and faithful servant.'"[40]

It is important to note that Zacharie's efforts to garner the "Israelite" vote for Lincoln in 1864 constituted an important turning point in the political history of American Jewry. As noted in chapter 1, the mass emigration of Jews from Central Europe during the 1840s and 1850s resulted in the growth of important Jewish communities in key urban centers throughout the states of the Old Northwest and, of course, in the seaboard states of New York and Pennsylvania as well. A large percentage of the Central European Jewish immigrants took an active interest in politics. Many of these migrants—Jews and non-Jews alike—had been ardent supporters of the liberal revolutions of 1830 and 1848, and it was the failures of those movements that had pushed many of these disheartened activists to emigrate. After settling in America, these erstwhile European liberal activists were eager to participate in American politics. The political sentiments of this foreign-born cohort, who described themselves as "Germans in America," were summed up during the election of 1864 by the German American scholar and political philosopher Francis (Franz) Lieber (1800–1872):

> German working men! Why did you leave home, family, the friends of your youth, and seek this distant America? It was because you had heard that in the United States you would find a country wherein you and your children would enjoy all the rights of the free citizen; where skill and industry would surely find their reward, and where your children would never find themselves debarred from any merited attainment by the privileges of others. . . . Do not lend your aid to the party which would give up the Union to the dominion of the Southern landholders. For do you know what this slave-owning, would be oligarchy pretends to aim at? Perhaps you suppose they struggle only to retain possession of their negro slaves. The Southern slaveholders are fighting for that which was for so long a time the prerogative of the owners of the soil, the privilege of using the working man, whether white or black, as the instrument of their power, their pleasure, and their arrogance. The working man is to bear all the burdens of the state, but he is to have no rights in it. It is for him to obey, and for the rich man alone to rule.[41]

Zacharie's open assertion that he could persuade the majority of Jews in the north-ern states to vote as a bloc for Lincoln sparked an intense and interesting controversy. Evidently, Zacharie was not the only Jew seeking to organize a "Jews for Lincoln" campaign. Samuel A. Lewis (1831–1913), a Jewish communal leader from New York, was apparently working with Zacharie on behalf of the Jews for Lincoln's reelection effort in New York. Lewis wrote to Lincoln and warned him to be wary of any "par-ties representing themselves [as] 'a committee from the Jews' . . . [who may] solicit contributions." Lewis emphatically told Lincoln that American Jews had no desire to take money to support his candidacy. To the contrary, Lewis wrote, Jews "propose to give—not to take."[42]

Other Jewish leaders quickly spoke out to discredit the "Jews for Lincoln" idea altogether. Until the election of 1868, when it became necessary to decide whether Ulysses S. Grant (1822–85) was essentially anti-Jewish, the vast majority of American Jews distanced themselves from even a whiff of group politics. Jews were expected to participate in politics as American citizens and certainly not as members of a Jewish caucus or constituency.[43] Zacharie and Lewis may have been Lincoln men, but that did not entitle them to speak for American Jewry as a whole. "The Jews, as a body, have no *politics*," wrote Myer Samuel Isaacs (1841–1904), coeditor of New York's *Jewish Messenger*; ". . . there is no 'Jewish vote.'"[44]

If Zacharie composed a written congratulation to Lincoln when he won reelection in the fall of 1864, a copy of that communication has apparently not survived. He did, however, send a congratulatory telegram to Lincoln on December 26, 1864, only five days after Savannah surrendered to the Union armies. Zacharie, whose father and rel-atives lived in Savannah, declared, "My family are [*sic*]crazy with joy." The following month, Lincoln asked Secretary of War Edwin Stanton to permit Dr. Zacharie to "go to Savannah, remain a week . . . , bringing with him, if he wishes, his father and sisters or any of them." Lincoln candidly explained to Stanton that by obliging him, the secretary would be sparing him from time-consuming appeals, in that Lincoln had "long ago" promised to help Zacharie reunite with his family "whenever Savannah should fall into our hands." For Zacharie's part, he was deeply appreciative. In a brief note to Lincoln written just prior to his departure for Savannah, Zacharie offered one final gesture of support: "If you have any matters that you would have properly attended to, I will con-sider it a favour for [you] to let me attend to it for you."[45] This communication appears to have been the last between the president and his chiropodist.

After Lincoln's death, Zacharie seems to have lost his thirst for public life and lived quietly in New York through the early 1870s. He cut back on his political involvement, though he remained somewhat active in local Republican politics for several years. In 1872, for instance, he was a public supporter of Horace Greeley's hapless attempt to pre-vent President Grant from winning a second term.[46] Two years later, Zacharie attempted to have the U.S. Congress Committee on War Claims pay him $45,000 in fees for the podiatric services he rendered during the Civil War. Even with written support from his friend General Banks, Zacharie's appeal was flatly rejected.[47]

Around 1875, Zacharie returned to his native England, where he continued working as a podiatrist. During the last decades of his life, he became a prominent leader
of English Freemasonry as the founder of an English chapter of an American-based
society called "The Order of the Secret Monitor." In 1887, his Masonic brothers chose
him to be their "Grand Supreme Ruler." To this day, this order respectfully lauds this
Jewish chiropodist and credits him for being a distinguished founder of its fraternity.[48]
He died on September 16, 1900, at the age of 73.[49]

Isachar Zacharie was, as one historian summarized, a multifaceted personality—"a
sycophant, court-jester, politician, spy, and friend." Yet he was no fool. He was a clever
operator—a shrewd and ambitious personality who was ever ready to ingratiate himself
if he thought there might be some benefit to be gained.[50] As he observed in a moment of
frank self-assessment: "You know I lack Education, but I have managed to push smoothy
[sic] thus far through the world, with many true friends who admire my Energy and
true friendship—which I hope I shall always maintain."[51]

Zacharie was unquestionably a sycophant, but the surviving documents lead us to
conclude he was a man of exceptional talent. He was certainly an opportunist, and his
work in New Orleans for the Lincoln administration demonstrated that he possessed
a shrewd cleverness that concomitantly benefited his interests and those of the Union.
Was he working both sides of the aisle—helping the South while working for the North?
The surviving documents strongly suggest that he did whatever he could do to ingratiate
himself with southerners only in order to succeed in his work for the North.

Above all, Zacharie had pride in his own abilities and in the attainments of the
Jewish people. During the Lincoln administration, his activities betokened a belief
that, in America, Jews could assume influential leadership roles that were denied them
in other parts of the world. If the president of the United States selected an immigrant
Jewish chiropodist to fulfill high-level envoy and reconnaissance work for the good
of the nation, then it was self-evident that Jews could achieve a political distinction in
America that was denied them elsewhere. Zacharie asserted this very point in a speech
he delivered at a New York testimonial dinner held in his honor in 1864: "Let us look at
England, France, Russia, Holland, aye, almost every nation in the world, and where do
we find the Israelite? We find them taken into the confidence of Kings and Emperors.
And in this republican and enlightened country, where we know not how soon it may
fall to the lot of any man to be elevated to a high position by this government, why may
it not fall to the lot of an Israelite as well as any other?"[52]

DOCUMENTS

 1. Two Editorials on Isachar Zacharie
 2. Zacharie Briefs Lincoln on Conditions in New Orleans
 3. "Patriotic Corn Doctor" or "Rebel Spy"?
 4. Lincoln Was "Delighted" with Zacharie's Revelations
 5. "I Am Sorry to Say He Lacks Stability"
 6. A Rare Letter from Lincoln to Zacharie
 7. Mr. Lincoln's Unionism and Bunionism
 8. "We Propose to Give—Not to Take"
 9. No Such Thing as a "Jewish Vote"
10. "About Jews"
11. Freaks of Legislation

1. TWO EDITORIALS ON ISACHAR ZACHARIE

Isachar Zacharie became a frequent visitor at the White House in the fall of 1862, when Secretary of State William H. Seward first recommended his services to President Lincoln. Zacharie's skill impressed Lincoln, and he gave the doctor a written testimonial stating, "Dr. Zacharie has operated on my feet with great success, and considerable addition to my comfort."[53]

The New York press took note of Zacharie's impressive list of clients, which, in addition to the president, included the secretary of state, the secretary of war, Generals McClellan, Banks, and Burnside, and an array of Washington's social elite. As the following editorials from the New York Herald *demonstrate, Zacharie's meteoric rise proved to be excellent grist for the satirist's mill.*

The Head and Feet of the Nation

In the certificates furnished to the chiropodist by the President, Secretary Seward and other members of the Cabinet, and by Generals McClellan, Banks and Burnside, we have a cornucopia of information about the secrets of this war. The President has been greatly blamed for not resisting the demands of the radicals; but how could the President put his foot down firmly when he was troubled with corns? There have been rumors of personal animosities and ill-timed bickerings among the members of the Cabinet; but undoubtedly these have been caused by the honorable Secretaries inadvertently treading upon each other's bunions under the council board. Some of our generals have been reproached for their slow movements; but is celerity of motion to be expected of persons whose toe nails are growing into the flesh? No human being could be expected to toe the mark of our expectations under such circumstances.... General Pope, who by a singular paradox placed his head-quarters in the saddle, made a few rapid evolutions, during which he nearly succeeded in using up himself, the enemy, and our army; but Jackson's bare-footed rebels, who do not know the need or the value of a chiropodist, got the better of him at last. . . . It would seem, therefore, that all our past troubles have originated not so much with the head as with the feet of the nation. Dr. Zacharie has shown us precisely where the shoe pinches.[54]

More Important Negotiations for Peace

We have already been favored with a large crop of independent peace negotiators. First there was poor Greeley, who corresponded with Count Mercier and Vallandigham. Then there was J. Wesley Green, who reached Richmond via the penitentiary, and obtained a hundred dollars or so from the War Department. Then there was Chase Barney, who was taken prisoner by the rebels, and subsequently negotiated himself out of captivity and into oblivion. Then there was Louis Napoleon, who could not get the shrewd Palmerston to join him, and was consequently rebuffed by Secretary Seward. Then last, but not least there was the Chevalier Jewett,[55] who turned Colorado, Europe and the rest of the world upside down to find a chance for peace, and who is now cooling himself off under the Falls of Niagara. Indeed, almost the only amateur diplomats who have not negotiated and intrigued for peace are the Chevaliers Weed and Wikoff. They have busied themselves solely with contracts and gunnery and musketry, and the former is now buried under a load of Charleston stone and election matters, while the latter is ornamenting and delighting metropolitan society, as usual.

But a rival to all these distinguished personages has now appeared in the person of the renowned Dr. Zacharie. We remember when the Doctor made his debut upon the national stage. Just after the war was fairly inaugurated Dr. Zacharie went to Washington, resplendent with diamonds and surgical instruments, and cut the corns of the President, the Cabinet, General McClellan and the entire Army of the Potomac. For some time after this the movements of the administration and the soldiers were astonishingly rapid. Now, alas? Both our administration and our armies stick in the mud. The corns have evidently grown again and need cutting. However, Dr. Zacharie did the country a service then, and Mr. Lincoln and Secretary Stanton were not ungrateful. They sent Dr. Zacharie to New Orleans to cut the corns of General Banks and his bravo corps. Zacharie performed this operation with his usual marvelous skill, and the result was the almost immediate capture of Port Hudson. This fact shows Zacharie's value as an ally in the vigorous prosecution of the war. But Dr. Zacharie did more than this. He talked with a great many friends and adherents of Jeff Davis in New Orleans, and he learned that the Southern people earnestly desired to have the war settled without further bother. With this intelligence the acute and diplomatic corn cutter immediately started for Washington, and having escaped the foils of the rebel pirates, whom Rip Van Winkle Welles[56] allows to rule the wave, he arrived safely at the goodly but ungodly city.

Again in Washington, Dr. Zacharie called upon his friend, Secretary Stanton, who, mistaking him for some visionary fellow, like Greel[e]y or Jewett, refused to listen to his story. The Doctor then left Stanton and went to the President. The moment Zacharie entered the President's private reception room, the Chief Executive held out his foot and complained of his corns. Zacharie removed the corns and told his tale at the same time. Old Abe was greatly comforted and interested, and gave Zacharie a pass to go to Richmond. Zacharie took the pass, went to Fortress Monroe and embarked upon the flag of truce boat. At some point near the rebel capital he had interviews with Jeff Davis, Secretary Memminger, of the rebel Treasury, and Secretary Benjamin, of the rebel State Department. He agreed with these rebels upon a plan of peace. It is this:—Davis, the rebel Cabinet and the rebel armies are to go to Mexico. Our government is to furnish them with transportation to that favored land and with rations on the way. Jeff Davis calculates to land in Mexico with one hundred and fifty thousand veteran fire eaters, each of whom can devour a Frenchman at a meal, without salt and without the slightest injury to his digestion. With this force he will drive away Napoleon's hordes and proclaim himself President of the new Mexican republic. Simultaneously the seceded Southern States will return to the Union with whatever negroes are left in them. This will end the war satisfactorily to all concerned. Such is the plan which Dr. Zacharie has arranged with the Southern leaders, and he is not only waiting for the President and the Cabinet to ratify it in order to carry it into instant effect. If he succeeds he will be the greatest man of the age, and neither Talleyrand nor Metternich can be compared to him. Strange as this narrative may appear, there is a great more in it than most people think, and perhaps the skeptical will soon have to acknowledge the corn and the corn doctor.[57]

2. ZACHARIE BRIEFS LINCOLN ON CONDITIONS IN NEW ORLEANS

A fine collection of Isachar Zacharie's correspondence with President Lincoln appears as an appendix to Bertram W. Korn's authoritative volume American Jewry and the Civil War.[58] *The following letters, however, do not appear in Korn.*

Writing on May 9, 1863, from his room at the St. Charles Hotel in New Orleans, Zacharie provided Lincoln with a status report on the attitude of the local citizenry in the occupied Crescent City. This particular missive is exceedingly interesting. Zacharie tells the president that most of the city's "rebels" are despondent over their cause, and were it not for the "female portion of their families," many were ready to declare their loyalty to the Union. He cited Rabbi James K. Gutheim (1817–86) as a case in point. According to Zacharie, it was Gutheim's wife and not the rabbi who refused to pledge loyalty to the Union. Gutheim's decision to leave made him a southern hero when he returned to New Orleans after the South surrendered.

St Charles Hotel
New Orleans May 9th 1863

To his

Excellency A Lincoln

President of the United States

Washington DC
Dear Sir

An intense excitement has pervaded this city for the past few days. First the issuing of General Banks' order notifying "registered enemies" to leave the Department by the 15th inst. Then the arrival of the invincible Illinois Cavalry at Baton Rouge, having performed the most brilliant feat of the war, again the news of [David D.] Porter joining [David G.] Farragut.[59] You can form no idea of the joy which overcomes the hearts of all loyal people.

As for the rebels, I can see their despondency, not only for themselves but their cause, was it not for the female portion of their families, who I fear have become perfect monomaniacs, they would in many instances take the oath.

Rev Doctor Gutheim minister of the Portuguese Israelite Congregation of this city—registered enemy—called yesterday to see me & spoke most feelingly. In his heart he wishes the Union restored for he says under its Government the Israelite has lived and prospered—why then should he leave? It is his wife who influences him. Another thing he took the oath of allegiance to the Confederacy & could not satisfy his own conscience to take it now to the Government, but as I said before at heart his [sic] for the Union & I believe his going out will do good.

Col Gardner commanding the Illinois Cavalry is now here on a few days furlough, he is one of the most modest unassuming gentlemen I have ever seen. You should make him a General as he possesses the true mettle.

A friend with Schooner left here yesterday on mission to Pemberton. I look for him back in ten or fifteen days when I expect to go over. Please inform M. Seward of this fact. While writing Commander Farragut has arrived from above Port Hudson. Porter took possession of Alexandria on the morning of the 6th thus [illegible] the advance column of General Banks reaches them. Thus the work goes bravely on.

Very Respectfully
Your most obd Servt [obedient servant][60]

3. "PATRIOTIC CORN DOCTOR" OR "REBEL SPY"?

Until recently, little was known about Zacharie's September 27, 1863, secret meeting with four prominent Confederate officials: Stephen R. Mallory, James A. Seddon, John H. Winder, and Judah P. Benjamin.[61] Historians have studied a letter from Zacharie to

A broadside (ca. 1862) advertising Zacharie's skill as a podiatrist. Courtesy Collections of Maine Historical Society (www.VintageMaineImages.com).

General Banks, written on October 9, 1863, which identified the names of those who participated in the meeting and summarized the gathering's overall atmosphere by saying "the interview was of the most friendly nature."[62] Thanks to the recent discovery of a letter that Zacharie wrote to Judah P. Benjamin the day after the meeting, we now have a clearer sense of what may have transpired.

confidential

Steam Boat New York aff [off?]
City Point Sept 28th 1863

Dear Sir,

Since my interview with you last night, I have had time to meditate upon what transpired. And now let me again assure you of my sincere friendship towards you and the confederacy.

I was so excited last night and overcome at the pleasure of meeting *you*, knowing that the confederate flag was waving over my head, that my heart was bursting with joy. I had so *much* to say and so *short* time to say it in, that I fear I have forgotten much, but I hope the day is not far distant when we shall meet again.

Should not that—I hope I have made a favourable impression—and that you have taken all I said in good part, as it came from a pure heart. I would gladly join the armies of the confederacy if I did not know that I could be of more service to you from where I am, I endeavoured to explain all to you last night, which I hope was satisfactory.

I am much disappointed at not receiving permission to visit my old father but I am a strong believer in the old adage (*that every thing happens for the best*) and who knows but our meeting may lead to beneficial results. God grant it may; more unlikely things has [*sic*] transpired, one thing is sure that I shall continue to hope and toil on, if not to win, to prove to you that I am worthy, not only of your confidence, but of the small favour I have asked, but unless I can visit the confederacy without the least doubt of my sincerity towards you all, I would rather sacrifice Father Sister and all, in fact my honour is at stake, and without that, man is worth but little, if however you are satisfied of my sincerity towards you all and you can say at any time grant me the permission to visit Savannah or Macon, I shall be under everlasting obligations.

I shall go immediately to Washington from here, shall have an interview with Mr. Lincoln, shall talk to him (as but few can) I shall assure him that no propositions of peace may be expected from the South, I shall put matters in the right light, and I know he will listen to me, and my word for it. Some good must come out of our *unexpected meeting*.

I cannot explain to you why I think so, but I conscientiously believe there will (*time will show.*)

I will write to you immediately all that transpires, but shall have to be very careful how I write. Should any thing important transpire, I shall come myself. So if I write or telegraph to you at this point, come immediately to me. You will know it is of importance.

Should you know any person visiting New York in whom you have im-plicate [implicit] confidence in, write to me and I will post you up on all you wish to know. Be careful not to sign your name. I will know who it comes from. Should I write I will sign (thus,) [Zacharie drew a square box with a dot in the center] unless I return on flag of truce which I can as I know all the officers.

Do not think me to[o] anxious to serve you. *I do it from pure motives* and you I hope, will never regret the interview we had last night. Wishing you every success,

I am with much Respect
Your obt. Servant
I Zacharie MD
760 Broadway
New York

to Hon. J. P. Benjamin

Sec of State

Richmond

V.A.[63]

4. LINCOLN WAS "DELIGHTED" WITH ZACHARIE'S REVELATIONS

In this letter to General Nathaniel P. Banks, dated October 9, 1863, Zacharie reports on his recent activities to his immediate superior, the commander of the Department of the Gulf. He informs Banks that President Lincoln was "delighted" with his report on the top-secret meeting he conducted with various Confederate leaders, including President Jefferson Davis. Zacharie had discovered, much to his astonishment, that Lincoln had kept his mission a secret from Secretary of State William H. Seward. Consequently, the South's openness to discussing a negotiated peace settlement placed Lincoln in an awk-ward spot. If he wished to pursue the matter, what would he say to Seward? According to Zacharie, Lincoln was like a man who won an elephant in a raffle and does not know what to do with it!

Clearly eager to ingratiate himself with his superior, Zacharie assures the general that he had urged Lincoln to select Banks to negotiate a peace treaty with Judah P. Benjamin, secretary of state for the South. The shrewd Lincoln thanked his foot doctor for the "happy thought" and told him he would ponder the matter further. Although Lincoln dropped the idea of negotiating peace with the Confederacy, Zacharie left Lincoln that day entirely convinced that the president was "perfectly delighted with [his] success."

Willard's Hotel
Washington. Oct 9th. 1863

My Dear General

I wrote to you from Fortress Monroe, the day I started South. I now write to inform you of my success. I can write but little as the mail is on the eve of closing. Enough to say that Mr. Benjamin, Mr. Mallory Mr. Siddon [Seddon] & Genl Winder came to City-point to receive me. The interview was of the most friendly nature. Benjamin was anxious for me to return to Washington as it would not be safe for me to pass through the Southern states, unless I could take the oath of allegiance. So I heard all they had to say & returned here, and now comes the rub. It seems that Mr. Lincoln has done everything for me on his own responsibility, and did not say a word to Mr. Seward until I returned, which seems I think to have displeased the Premier, but the President is true and is perfectly delighted with my success. But how to act he does not know. *He reminds me* of the *man* that *won the Elephant* at a *Raffle*. He does not know what to do with it. On my first arrival Mr. Lincoln detained me 2 hours, locking his doors and preventing any person from having access to him. He seemed to be delighted with my revelations. From what I can understand the subject has been brought before the Cabinet and bitterly opposed by Mr. Chase—Mr. Lincoln seemed in my interview with him to be desirous of effecting something, but still unwilling to give me his *proyromise* [sic] but stated, much good would grow out of it. But it required time to give it shape & life. He asked me if I had any thing to suggest, by which something could be effectively done, this gave me an opening to make this suggestion,

Send for Genl Banks, he is your friend and you can trust him with your Confidence in carrying out any negotiation, and let me go down and tell Benjamin that you will be sent to represent the President so soon as you can be got here. He replied that is a happy *thought*. Let me reflect and come and see me tomorrow. Thus the matter stands. I have not time to give you my conclusions.

The Herald to my great surprise yesterday in a leading article, recited that negotiations were being considered by the Cabinet, for a Peaceful termination of our troubles, and that the information could be relied upon. I find that my interview with the Chief of the Confederate Governt. is already known to many, which leads me to believe, that these revelations have been purposely made, with a view of throwing obstructions to prevent the consumption of this most desirable movement.

I will write you more by next mail.

Yours in haste
I. Zacharie. Md

P.S. Much credit is due to Mr. Martin Gordon for paving the way for me.[64]

5. "I AM SORRY TO SAY HE LACKS STABILITY"

On October 16, 1863, one week after informing General Banks that he had urged Lincoln to pursue a negotiated treaty with the South, Zacharie wrote again from the nation's capital. Lincoln's inaction frustrated Zacharie, and he exasperatingly contended that Lincoln "has it in his powers to stop all fighting in 24 hours if he would follow out my program." In his letter to Banks, Zacharie's fawning nature and opportunistic instinct come into sharp focus.

Willards Hotel
Washington Oct 16th 1863

My Dear General,

I wrote you by the last mail. Sent the letter to New York to be mailed, *for certain reasons*. Hope you received it. Since which time nothing has been done. Mr. Lincoln has refused to send for you but has not given me his reasons, but can see through it—it will make you to[o] popular. But my opinion is, that if anything is to be done, that they must send for you as I am determined that no person shall have the Eclaim [Acclaim?] but you. As I remarked to Mr. Lincoln, if it had not been for you, I could have accomplished nothing, I know one thing that no person will be received by Benjamin, except myself, as he pledged his word to me that if any thing was to be done that I should have all the honour. I forgot to mention in my last that both Benjamin & Mallory spoke of you in the *kindest manner*, and Benjamin said that he was under many obligations to you for your kindness towards his *sister*.

I wish you was [*sic*] here to advise me how to act, as I cannot talk to any person. I need not tell you that Mr. Lincoln has done all on his own hook, and has a hard road to travel, as he did not say a word to Seward until I returned. I do not know if anything will be done or not. I should like you to know all, but I am afraid to write for fear the letter will not come to hand. Should of taken a trip to *see you*, but do not know how to act. Mr. Lincoln is in great trouble, fighting is going on in the front, in fact I think matters look bad.

I am sorry to say he *lacks stability*. He has it in his powers to stop all fighting in 24 hours if he would follow out my program, it was a misfortune that I did not see you on my return before I saw the President, you could of arranged everything. However it is not too late. I wish you would advise me how to act. Write to me at my residence 760 Broadway New York. Hoping to hear from you by return of mail.

Yours Respectfully
I. Zacharie. Md

To Major Genl. N. P. Banks
New Orleans[65]

6. A RARE LETTER FROM LINCOLN TO ZACHARIE

Among the Lincoln Papers at the Library of Congress, one finds thirteen letters from Isachar Zacharie to Lincoln, but only one letter from Lincoln to Zacharie, dated September 19, 1864, survives in the collection. At this time, Zacharie was working to reelect Lincoln. Is Lincoln expressing his appreciation for Zacharie's efforts on his behalf and promising Zacharie that his "friend" will be "fully and fairly considered" for a patronage post at the proper time? It is impossible to know for certain, but Zacharie promptly replied to the president and told him his note "had the desired effect, with the friends of the Partie [sic]."[66]

> Executive Mansion
> Washington, Sept. 19, 1864
>
> Dr. Zacharie
> Dear Sir
>   I thank you again for the deep interest you have constantly taken in the Union cause. The personal matter on behalf of your friend, which you mentioned, shall be fully and fairly considered when presented.
>
> Yours truly
A. Lincoln[67]

7. MR. LINCOLN'S UNIONISM AND BUNIONISM

On September 21, 1864, Zacharie informed Lincoln that he planned to leave the following day to visit "the interior of Pennsylvania" and, perhaps, Ohio. He intended to "impress on the minds of [Lincoln's] friends . . . not to be to[o] sure."[68] Presumably, Zacharie was among the many who felt that Lincoln's reelection was far from a certainty. Evidently, the chiropodist never left New York. Newspapers reported he had been shot in a quarrel with his business partner. The violent incident made Zacharie newsworthy, and on September 24, 1864, this highly critical and humorously sarcastic article concerning Zacharie's influence on President Lincoln appeared in the New York World.

> Doctor (?) Isachar Zacharie, the corn-doctor who was shot on Thursday in a quarrel with his partner (the particulars of the fracas were published in our columns yesterday), is a man who has enjoyed Mr. Lincoln's confidence perhaps more than any other private individual. He has visited the conquered cotton districts, armed with autograph letters from the President, by the aid of which he obtained special privileges which have inured greatly to his advantage. (These speculations are usually on joint account with *somebody*.) At New Orleans, soon after its capture, he was courted, feted, flattered, by high officials, because of these autograph missives of Mr. Lincoln. Dr. Zacharie is perhaps the most favored family visitor at the White House, and the President has often left his business-apartment to spend an evening in the parlor with this favored bunionist. The following illustration (one of many) may possibly suggest a reason

for this remarkable intimacy between an obscure toe-nail trimmer and the chief executive of a great nation. About a year ago a Mr. Mordecai and friend, from Charleston, were arrested in Washington for having passed through our military lines. Mr. Mordecai's father is the rich Charlestonian who gave ten thousand dollars to aid the rebellion when it began—the first gift of any magnitude to the confederate cause. Dr. Zacharie and Mr. Mordecai were united in the golden bonds of friendship. Dr. Zacharie asked of the President the release of young Mordecai and it was promptly granted, but his friend (probably not having this golden influence) is still confined in a military prison. The evidence against both is precisely the same; but the President and the Secretary of War have refused the release of Mr. Mordecai's companion. Do the public interests demand such a distinction? Why were not both imprisoned or both released? What consideration had Mr. Lincoln (or his son "Bob") for this favoritism?[69]

8. "WE PROPOSE TO GIVE—NOT TO TAKE"

Samuel A. Lewis was a prominent Jewish communal leader and political activist in New York City. Evidently, Zacharie notified Lewis that "a committee from the Jews" had approached the president to solicit funding in support of their efforts to reelect him. Writing on October 26, 1864, Lewis vehemently assured Lincoln that these individuals did not represent the American Jewish community and had come to Lincoln "against the wish" of Lincoln's Jewish friends. Lewis concludes by categorically insisting that "nothing shall be wanting on the part of your friends here towards carrying the Union Cause."

New York, Oct 26th 1864

His Excellency A. Lincoln

President

Sir

Having understood through our friend Dr Zacharie that some parties representing themselves "a committee from the Jews" had called on you to solicit contributions, I hasten to inform you that it is entirely against the wish of your Jewish friends here to take any money from outside committees or others—

We propose to give—not to take—I would esteem it a favor should any *Jewish committees* call on you or the Union Committee in Washington, if you would send them to me (as Dr Zacharie will be away frequently between now and the election) and I will furnish them such amounts as we see can be used to advantage—

Be assured nothing shall be wanting on the part of your friends here towards carrying the Union Cause,

I Remain, Sir,
Very Respectfully
Your Obdt Servt
Saml. A. Lewis[70]

9. NO SUCH THING AS A "JEWISH VOTE"

Myer Samuel Isaacs, a distinguished Jewish communal leader in New York, worked closely with his father, Samuel Myer Isaacs (1804–78), in the founding and editing of the Jewish Messenger *(established 1857) and also on the Board of Delegates of American Israelites (1859), the first successful attempt at organizing American Jewry in furtherance of the civil and political rights of Jews.*[71]

Isaacs was concerned about Isachar Zacharie and Samuel Lewis's assertion that they would be able to secure the support of the Jewish community on behalf of Abraham Lincoln's reelection in 1864. Although he was a Republican and a firm supporter of the Union, Isaacs was strenuously opposed to the suggestion that there was a "Jewish vote" in America. In his letter to Lincoln, Isaacs noted that most American Jews (in the North) were indeed pro-Lincoln and pro-Union, but this support, he explained, derived from the fact that Jews were—above all else—"advocates of the cherished principles of liberty & justice, and must inevitably support and advocate those who are the exponents of such a platform."

Private

"Jewish Messenger" Office

119 West Houston Street,
New York, October 26th 1864.

Your Excellency:

As a firm and earnest Union-man, I deem it my duty to add a word to those that have doubtless been communicated to you from other sources, with reference to a recent "visitation" on the part of persons claiming to represent the Israelites of New York or the United States and pledging the "Jewish vote" to your support, and, I am informed, succeeding in a deception that resulted to their pecuniary profit.

Having peculiar facilities for obtaining information as to the Israelites of the United States, from my eight years' connection with the Jewish paper of this city and my position as Secretary of their central organization, the "Board of Delegates"—in which capacity I have had the honor heretofore of communicating with yourself and the Departments—I feel authorized to caution you, sir, against any such representations as those understood to have been made.

There are a large number of faithful Unionists among our prominent coreligionists—but there are also supporters of the opposition; and, indeed the Israelites are not, as a body, distinctively Union or democratic in their politics. In the conduct of our Journal for example, while, from the first firing upon our national flag, there has been a steady support of the government in its efforts to maintain the integrity of the Union and crush the unhallowed rebellion, there has also been a studied persistence in the expression of what is an implicit belief, that the Jews, as a body, have no *politics*: and while we have earnestly counselled & implored attachment to the Union at whatever cost, we have refrained from interfering with the private political views of individual readers. This is predicated on our direct knowledge of the character and opinions of our coreligionists.

Therefore, sir, I am pained and mortified to find that you had been imposed upon by irresponsible men, animated, I am sure by mercenary motives; and I wish to inform you with all promptitude, that such acts are discountenanced and condemned most cordially by the community of American Israelites—As an illustration that an influential class of Jewish citizens are warm adherents of the administration, you have the fact that a Hebrew will cast for you the vote of a New York city congressional district. A single Union meeting this week presented these facts: the chairman of the Executive Committee & Committee of Arrangements, the gentlemen who presented the resolutions, two principal speakers and many prominent persons upon the platform, were Jews.—I refer to the German Union Mass Meeting on Monday night.

It is because I sympathize heart and soul with the action of government in using every means to restore the Union and overthrow the machinations of those who seek its disruption, that I ~~am~~ the more regret this attempt to deceive you. There is no "Jewish vote"—if there were, it could not be bought. As a body of intelligent men, we are advocates of the cherished principles of liberty & justice, and must inevitably support and advocate those who are the exponents of such a platform—"liberty & Union, now and forever."

Pardon the liberty I take in thus trespassing on your attention, but I pray that you will attribute it to the sole motive I have, that of undeceiving you and assuring you that there is no necessity for "pledging" the Jewish vote which does not exist—but at the same time that the majority of Israelite citizens must concur in attachment for the Union and a determination to leave no means untried to maintain its honor and integrity.

With the expression of high esteem, I am, sir,

Yours Most Respectfully,

Myer S. Isaacs[72]

10. "ABOUT JEWS"

Historians have wondered why President Lincoln thought to begin his January 25, 1865, memorandum to Secretary of War Edwin M. Stanton with the fragment "About Jews." In this memorandum, Lincoln requests that Dr. Zacharie be granted a pass to visit his family in Savannah. The note also makes reference to Major Leopold Blumenberg (1827–76), a war hero who was "crippled" during the Battle of Antietam and subsequently appointed to serve as provost marshal of the Third Maryland District. Evidently, Blumenberg had been summarily dismissed, having been accused of "cruelty in gagging men to make them confess they were deserters."[73] *Lincoln politely reminds Stanton that Blumenberg had "suffered" for the Union and should not be "dismissed in a way that disgraces and ruins him without a hearing" just "for being our friend."*

Why did Lincoln introduce these two matters with the words "About Jews"? Does this peculiar opening reveal something about Lincoln's attitude toward Jews? The passage from Naphtali J. Rubinger's Abraham Lincoln and the Jews *explicates some of the interpretative difficulties Lincoln's strange remark engendered.[74]*

Executive Mansion
Jan. 25, 1865

Hon. Secretary of War,
My dear Sir,

About Jews. I wish you would give Dr. Zacharie a pass to go to Savannah, remain a week and return, bringing with him, if he wishes, his father and sisters or any of them. This will spare me trouble and oblige me—I promised him long ago that he should be allowed this whenever Savannah should fall into our hands.

Blumenberg, at Baltimore, I think he should have a hearing. He has suffered for us and served us well—had the rope around his neck for being our friend—raised troops—fought, and been wounded. He should not be dismissed in a way that disgraces and ruins him without a hearing.

Yours truly,
A. Lincoln[75]

Lincoln's Strange Remark

Many have been puzzled as to why Lincoln chose such an odd form of reference, "About Jews," for his opening phrase. Was this an indication that Lincoln regarded Jews as a nuisance or that off the record he shared and harbored prejudice against them? Korn, in his analysis of this problem, discounts the possibility of Lincoln being in any way intolerant. He points out the many instances when Lincoln dealt with kindness and justice toward Jews. If there was an intent to be conveyed by the phrase "About Jews," it was intended as a rebuff to those who disliked Zacharie, and perhaps Jews in general. Bertram W. Korn concludes:

It is my personal opinion therefore, that when Lincoln wrote "about Jews" he was in effect saying to Stanton, who disliked Zacharie (perhaps on account of his Jewish origin) and had previously denied him a pass to Savannah: "I know there is prejudice against the Jews. I know that there is intolerance toward them. Therefore, I label these two men as Jews. I want you to know that they are Jews. I anticipate any objection based on their religious affiliation. Just because they are Jews I want to be generous to them."

It should be noted, however, that Lincoln repeats this stylistic oddity at the beginning of the second paragraph of this same letter when he noted, "Blumenberg at Baltimore." Zacharie himself used similar phraseology in one of his letters when he wrote: "As regards the Isrelites [sic]." Possibly Lincoln penned this phrase in conjunction with a personal memo that may have been marked "About Jews," and "Blumenberg at Baltimore." In either case it can not be asserted that the phrase reflects any ill feelings on the part of Lincoln toward the Jew.[76]

11. FREAKS OF LEGISLATION

On January 14, 1896, the New York Times *criticized those who submitted claims to the U.S. Congress requesting financial compensation for "questionable" services. The case at hand involved none other than Dr. Isachar Zacharie, who had presented a petition to Congress requesting payment of $45,000 for the podiatric treatment he provided to "15,000 men" in the Union army during the course of the Civil War.*

The Committee on War Claims, chaired by former congressman Stephen W. Kellogg (1822–1904), was not impressed with Zacharie's claim. Although the aging chiropodist provided letters confirming he had the endorsement and support of Abraham Lincoln, William H. Seward, and Edwin Stanton, the committee concluded that "the claimant was plying his vocation and voluntarily sought to pursue the same in the lines of the Union Army." Not only had the foot doctor failed to substantiate the validity of his appeal, the committee saw no reason to pursue the matter further. The final recommendation was to let Dr. Zacharie's claim "lie upon the table."

Washington, Jan. 13.—The document rooms of the Senate and House of Representatives are mines of the most interesting information if one only has the patience to delve through the indexes of volume upon volume of the claims and bills which have never been reported from the committees. Each Congress furnishes examples of "freak bills," which originate too often with the constituents of members who introduce them in the hope of recompensing the petitioners for the offices they didn't get. There are other classes of bills which are born and presented in a rational manner, but the nature of them and the manner in which the committees to which the bills have been referred have looked upon them in a jocular light, and the reports which have been submitted to the House and Senate are written in a vein of keen humor and satire.

There is, perhaps, no better example of the case of a doubtful claim handled in a summary if amusing manner than that of Issachor Zacharie, a gentleman learned in the profession of extracting corns, who plied his trade during the war of the rebellion. The petition of Issachor was reported from the Committee on War Claims by Mr. [Stephen W.] Kellogg of Connecticut in June, 1874.[77] The report opens with the statement of Zacharie's petition; that he was by profession a chiropodist, practicing his profession in the City of New-York and elsewhere, and that in the year 1862, upon the recommendation of certain Surgeons of the United States Army and citizens of the United States, the claimant alleges that the following letter was written:

Executive Mansion
Washington, D.C., Sept. 23, 1862

From numerous testimonials of the highest character, and from personal experience, we approve the very great success of Dr. I. Zacharie in operating upon corns, bunions, and other troubles of the feet, by which instantaneous relief is afforded, and we desire that the soldiers of our brave army may have the benefit of his surprising skill.

A. Lincoln
William H. Seward

In pursuance of this letter the following order was issued by the Secretary of War:

War Department
Washington, D.C., Sept. 24, 1862

Dr. I. Zacharie has permission to pass within the lines of the United States forces around Washington and on the Potomac for the purpose of operating upon the feet of the soldiers for corns, bunions, &c. this pass to continue for thirty days.

Edwin M. Stanton

Continued for sixty days by the order of Gen. Tucker Blake, Assistant Secretary of War.

Signed Nov. 21. 1862.

It appears that, under the authority conferred by these orders, Zacharie proceeded to Fort Monroe and operated upon the feet of numerous soldiers—according to his own report, at least 5,000 in number—under command of Gen. John A. Dix, with entire satisfaction, according to his own account, to the soldiers as well as to Gen. Dix. A letter was submitted by Zacharie to the committee purporting to have been written by Gen. Dix, the hero of "Shoot him on the spot" memory, but nothing was presented to establish its genuineness, and the evidence of the soldier whose pedal extremities are alleged to have been operated on was not given so that the committee in its consideration of the case reported itself as without that light and information necessary to make a careful analysis of the evidence which the character of the claim—not to mention its peculiarity—entitled it to receive.

Zacharie also alleged that, under a written recommendation from President Lincoln to Gen. Banks, then commanding the Department of the Gulf at

New-Orleans, La., he proceeded to that city, with his assistant, and for a period of nearly ten months remained with the troops and operated upon the suffering members of about 6,000 men; that he then returned to Washington, and during the remainder of the years 1863–[sic] operated upon the feet of troops stationed at or near Washington, Baltimore, and other points, to the number of 4,000, making in all a total of 15,000 men. For these services and for other valuable services incidentally rendered during his connection with the army, the character of which was not stated, Zacharie alleged that he received no compensation. He made what he stated to be the very low and modest charge of $3 for each man operated upon. As he claimed that he had operated upon the feet of 15,000 men, the claim was, therefore, for $45,000.

The report of the committee is amusing.

"Primarily," the report says, "and to commence at the beginning, in order to fairly present the facts, it is not even pretended by Zacharie that the corns and bunions upon the feet of the soldiers of the Army of the Potomac operated upon by him were the results either of active military operations of said army, or that the same did not exist at the time of the enlistment of the soldiers who were the beneficiaries of the skill of the claimant. . . . Other commands, as, for instance, that of Gen. Sherman in his famous march to the sea, which traversed the country from the Mississippi River to the Atlantic Ocean, developing thereby, without doubt, numerous corns and bunions, were equally entitled to have their corns and bunions removed. Aside from the fact that the proof to establish the claimant's statements is wanting, that he did operate upon the number of men of the several commands stated for corns and bunions, is the important fact that the claimant rendered no account whatever to the proper authorities of the several commands as to the disposition of the said corns and bunions secured by him, provided the facts are as stated. Such a collection, supposing the facts to be as claimed by Zacharie, would be so valuable an addition to the Army Medical Museum that in considering this claim your committee feels constrained to consider such loss to the museum in the way of recoupment or setoff as against the claim set up by Zacharie.

"The claimant was plying his vocation and voluntarily sought to pursue the same in the lines of the Union Army. He obtained from the proper authorities the necessary passport, but did not apply to the Quartermaster General—the officer charged with furnishing transportation to the troops, and which, if furnished, would have doubtless nipped, as it were, thousands of incipient corns in the bud—for a contract to do the work alleged by him to have been performed. The word corn is derived from the Latin *cornu*, horn, and is defined to be a hard, horn-like excrescence of induration of the skin on the toes or other part of the feet. The claim partakes somewhat of the character of the corn for whose alleged removal compensation is claimed, and the similarity is so evident that your committee refrains from comment in that respect.

Besides the reasons above set forth, showing why the claimant is not entitled to compensation for the services alleged by him to have been performed,
there is the further consideration that, were Congress to admit the justice of
Zacharie's claim, it would thereby establish the principle that the Government
was bound to remove the corns and bunions from the feet of the soldiers of
its armies during the late war. And then, if soldiers are entitled to relief from
corns and bunions at Government expense, why not sailors? And if sailors,
why not civilian employees? And then the soldiers who suffered with corns and
bunions, and who were not relieved therefrom, would naturally bring claims
for damage thereby, flooding Congress with the same, and necessitation the
appointment of a Standing Committee on Corns and Bunions, or the creation
of a special commission composed of men skilled in chirurgery. Other reasons
might be given for the rejection of this claim, but those above stated are, in the
opinion of your committee, sufficient, and the petition is accordingly reported
back with the recommendation that it do lie upon the table." So it happened
that Issachor Zacharie did not get his claim.[78]

3

Lincoln and the Chaplaincy Controversy

Three significant and highly publicized controversies arose during Lincoln's presidency that captured the attention of American Jewry: the so-called chaplaincy debate; General Ulysses S. Grant's infamous order expelling all Jewish citizens from the Military Department of Tennessee; and the rise of a political movement that hoped to declare the United States a Christian nation by amending the text of the U.S. Constitution. Arguably, the core of American Jewry's solemn admiration for Lincoln may be traced back to the personal role he played in responding to these three hotly debated political issues. Although much has already been written about these important events, a brief review of how Lincoln handled these issues from a diplomatic point of view sheds light on why so many—even people who did not vote for Lincoln—came to regard the sixteenth president as American Jewry's compatriot and benefactor, an ardent defender of "justice and liberality."[1]

After Confederate forces attacked the U.S. military installation at Fort Sumter in South Carolina on April 12, 1861, Lincoln called on Congress to raise a volunteer army from each state. The ninth section of the proposed "Volunteer Bill" authorized regimental commanders to appoint military chaplains for the regiments' soldiers. However, the bill stipulated that all chaplain-appointees must be "regularly ordained minister[s] of some Christian denomination."[2]

It was Clement L. Vallandigham (1820–71), a man who would soon become one of Lincoln's bitterest congressional opponents, who was among the first to note on the floor of the House of Representatives that the bill's chaplaincy provision effectively barred Jewish chaplains from the Union army. On July 12, 1861, in the context of the congressional debate on the "Volunteer Bill," Vallandigham moved an amendment that would have replaced the bill's parochial phraseology (a "minister of some Christian denomination") with more universal terminology: "a member of some religious society." He explained his rationale for amending the bill on the House floor: "There is a large body of men in this country, and one growing continually, of the Hebrew faith whose rabbis and priests are men of great learning and piety, and whose adherents are as good citizens and as true patriots as any in this country."[3]

Insisting that the bill was "without constitutional warrant," Vallandigham proposed that the bill be amended so that Jews in the Union army could be served by their own religious leaders. The amendment failed and the bill became law once it passed the House of Representatives on July 22, 1861, and the U.S. Senate on August 3, 1861.

At this same time, the Sixty-Fifth Regiment in the Fifth Pennsylvania Cavalry (a regiment that was known as "Cameron Dragoons") contained a large number of Jewish volunteers and was led by a Jewish officer, Colonel Max Friedman (1825–1900). The men of this regiment elected one of their fellow enlistees, Michael M. Allen (1830–1907), to serve as their chaplain, a decision that made Allen the first Jew to serve in this capacity in the U.S. Army. It is likely that Friedman was unaware that the U.S. chaplaincy law forbade a Jew from serving as a regimental chaplain. Friedman and his regiment needed a chaplain, and Allen was a knowledgeable layman capable of leading worship services. Once the regiment elected Allen, he began ministering to his comrades as would any military chaplain.[4]

Only a month later, in early September 1861, a zealous YMCA worker from Philadelphia realized that Allen was illegally functioning as a chaplain for the entire regiment, Jew and non-Jew alike. Once the illegality became public, it was almost a certainty that Allen would be dismissed. Before this could occur, though, Allen resigned his post on September 23, 1861, on account of poor health. Yet it seems that Colonel Friedman had no intention of letting the issue drop. He wanted a *Jewish* chaplain to minister to his mostly Jewish regiment, and if Michael Allen did not fit the bill, Friedman planned to find a suitable alternative.[5]

Since the Volunteer Bill approved the appointment of "regularly ordained ministers," Friedman recognized that he would need to identify a Jewish minister who would

Colonel Max Friedman, who led a platoon of Jewish soldiers in the Sixty-Fifth Regiment in the Fifth Pennsylvania Cavalry, invited Michael M. Allen to serve as military chaplain.
Courtesy The Jacob Rader Marcus Center of the American Jewish Archives, at the Hebrew Union College–Jewish Institute of Religion, Cincinnati, Ohio.

The forced resignation of the first unofficial Jewish military chaplain, Michael M. Allen, prompted American Jewry to appeal directly to Lincoln for relief. Courtesy The Jacob Rader Marcus Center of the American Jewish Archives, at the Hebrew Union College–Jewish Institute of Religion, Cincinnati, Ohio.

be willing to take on the duties of a military chaplain and serve as the trial case that would challenge the new law. Most likely, it was Colonel Friedman who first approached the Reverend Arnold Fischel (1830–94), a minister and teacher at New York's highly respected Congregation Shearith Israel, and urged him to submit a formal request to Secretary of War Simon Cameron for a chaplaincy appointment. There are a number of reasons why Friedman considered Fischel a likely prospect for this mission.[6]

First, we know that later in life, Friedman became a prominent broker on Wall Street in New York. Although Friedman and his family immigrated to Philadelphia from Nuremberg when he was a very young boy, it is highly probable that Friedman had heard of Fischel even before the chaplaincy incident occurred. Fischel, a Dutch Jew, served as a lecturer in the Liverpool Old Hebrew Congregation in England before being engaged by New York's Congregation Shearith Israel in 1856. During his tenure in New York, Fischel became a lecturer of some note, and he regularly delivered learned orations to large crowds composed of Jews and non-Jews alike. Interestingly, Fischel seems to have been planning to leave his post at Shearith Israel even before this controversy arose. It appears he was seeking a different occupation that would accommodate his desire to spend more time researching, publishing, and lecturing. The prospect of becoming a chaplain for the U.S. Army might have arisen at just the right time.[7]

Even before his contract with Shearith Israel elapsed on October 31, 1861, Fischel wrote directly to Secretary Cameron on October 17, 1861, soliciting a commission to serve as a chaplain in the U.S. Army. Cameron promptly rejected Fischel's appeal in an apologetic memorandum dated October 23, 1861. The secretary of war explained that on account of legal "impediments," he had no alternative but to decline the Jewish minister's appeal. Were it not for the law, Cameron explained, "the Department would have taken your application into its favorable consideration." The news of this rejection quickly spread to every segment of the American Jewish community, sparking widespread outrage over a chaplaincy law that prohibited Jewish religious leaders, particularly a figure like Fischel, from serving his country together with Christian ministers.[8]

Jewish leaders and Jewish newspapers agitated vociferously, and an onslaught of letters, newspaper editorials, and protest petitions signed by both Jews and non-Jews demanded that the government amend what Rabbi Isaac M. Wise labeled as "that unconstitutional law."[9] Wise printed an array of protest letters and complaints in the pages of his paper, the *Israelite*. One of the most passionate of these appeals was penned by Jacob P. Solomon of Franklin, Indiana, who accused the Republicans of shamelessly pandering to religious abolitionists and suggested that the public vote the party out of office as soon as possible:

> If Catholics are allowed their priests and Methodists their preachers, why in the name of common sense should our congress prohibit Israelites from having a chaplain of their own persuasion to direct the religious services? Are the Jews less patriotic than the Methodists or the Presbyterians, the fact of there being nearly a regiment of them is sufficient evidence to the contrary? . . . Why should they be denied privileges which are granted to other denominations merely to gratify the bigotry and proselytizing proclivities of Abolition preachers? The Jews love this country as well as the Christians; the Constitution protects them as every body in their religion; but if the Republican party will persist in violating the Constitution and infringing upon the sacred rights of the people, we can only offer our protest against such proceedings and bid the people bide their time until the great Democratic party the defenders of the liberties of the people shall again control the affairs of government.[10]

The public outcry continued to snowball. If Jewish chaplains were barred from the field, was this law not tantamount to invalidating Judaism itself? The indignation was only exacerbated by the fact that *Confederate* law did *not* exclude Jews from serving as military chaplains.[11]

By the end of November 1861, the Board of Delegates of American Israelites (BODAI), the first national Jewish civil rights organization in the United States, resolved to assume responsibility for addressing this issue.[12] Since Fischel had already applied for the post, and in light of Cameron's written explanation that Fischel would have been appointed had U.S. law not restricted the appointment of military chaplains to Christian ministers only, the members of the Board of Delegates met and resolved that "Jewish ministers should be present in the camps & hospitals to administer consolation to Jewish soldiers" and, also, that the board should send Reverend Fischel to

Washington to meet with President Lincoln and plead his case on behalf of the board. Fischel would be expected to "report the result" to a subsequent meeting of the Board of Delegates "without delay."[13]

Only a few months after Michael Allen had been forced to resign his commission, Reverend Fischel traveled to the nation's capital in early December 1861 armed with a briefcase full of documents, letters of introduction, and justifications rationalizing the need for his appointment. Fischel's mission may very well have been the first time that a national Jewish organization sent one of its representatives to the White House to submit an appeal for action on behalf of the American Jewish community.

Despite being told in advance that the president would not have time to discuss the matter, Fischel was determined to meet with Lincoln personally. He managed to procure an appointment with Lincoln on December 11. According to Fischel's own detailed reports on this remarkable meeting, once he arrived he was ushered past "hundreds of people [who] were anxiously waiting for admission, some of whom told [him] that they had been for three days waiting their turn." Lincoln greeted Fischel cordially, spoke to him respectfully, read Fischel's documentation, and listened carefully to the rabbi's appeal. Then, according to Fischel, Lincoln unequivocally stated that the rabbi's request was entirely proper. Lincoln maintained that "the exclusion of Jewish chaplains [was] altogether unintentional on the part of Congress, and [he] agreed that something ought to be done to meet this case." He asked Fischel to give him a chance to sleep on the matter and invited the rabbi to return to the White House the following day. "If [I] have five minutes to spare, [I] will receive you and let [you] know [my] views."[14]

Evidently, Lincoln did not have time to meet with Fischel the next day, but on December 15, 1861, Lincoln sent him the following memorandum in which he made known his plan of action: "I find there are several particulars in which the present law in regard to chaplains is supposed to be deficient, all which I now design presenting to the appropriate Committee of Congress. I shall try to have a new law broad enough to cover what is desired by you in behalf of the Israelites."[15]

There is every reason to believe that Lincoln did just as he promised, because the legislative process for revising the status quo pertaining to the military chaplaincy began immediately. A week after Fischel met with Lincoln, on December 20, 1861, Indiana congressman William S. Holman (1822–97) submitted a resolution to the U.S. House of Representatives that called on the Committee of Military Affairs to submit a bill to the House that would enable regularly ordained ministers "of any religious society" to serve as military chaplains.[16]

Throughout the early months of 1862, Congress debated the text of the revised chaplaincy bill. The exact wording of the revision became an extremely important issue because some American citizens had expressed strong opposition to any wording that would suggest that the Jewish religion had parity with Christianity. Isaac M. Wise published a colorful sampling of this opposition in the pages of the *Israelite*. "Jews regard Jesus of Nazareth as an imposter, a deceiver, and one worthy of every term of reproach," wrote the editor of the *Presbyter*, a Cincinnati-based Presbyterian newspaper. Should "this bill become a law ... [the] government would, in effect, say that one might despise and reject the Savior of men, and thus trample under foot the son of God . . . and yet be a fit minister of religion."[17]

Despite these objections, it was clear that Congress was working hard to find wording that would avoid diminishing the prominence of Christian chaplains while opening the door to chaplains from other religious traditions wishing to serve in a similar capacity. In April, however, even before Congress passed a revised version of the law that would legalize the commissioning of rabbinical chaplains, the BODAI informed Fischel that it could no longer afford to compensate him as promised for his activities in Washington. Without a stipend from the Board of Delegates, Fischel had no means of livelihood, and he promptly abandoned his lobbying efforts as well as his ministrations on behalf of the servicemen. He returned to his native Holland within a few months, where he lived out the remainder of his life. Despite his having played a central role in the controversy up to this point—including the important role he assumed as a rabbinical chaplain pro tem in the vicinity of the nation's capital during the first months of 1862—Fischel never received the appointment he worked so hard to obtain.[18]

On July 17, 1862, Congress passed a new law declaring that "no person shall be appointed a chaplain in the United States Army that is not a regularly ordained minister of some religious denomination." As far as the American Jewish community was concerned, Lincoln had made good on his promise, and it was only a matter of time before a Jewish religious leader submitted an application for just such an appointment.[19] Yet the wording of the revised legislation also presented the Jewish community with a small administrative challenge. Not only was it necessary for a U.S. Army chaplain to be "a regularly ordained minister of some religious denomination," but the new law included an additional stipulation: a minister seeking appointment as military chaplain in the U.S. Army had to "present testimonials of his present good standing as such minister with a recommendation for his appointment as an army chaplain from some authorized ecclesiastical body, with not less than five accredited ministers belonging to the said religious denomination."[20]

In order to meet this requirement, Reverend Isaac Leeser (1806–68), a prominent Philadelphia rabbi, editor of the monthly periodical the *Occident and American Jewish Advocate*, and organizer of the Philadelphia Board of Ministers of the Hebrew Congregations, nominated a candidate for chaplain on behalf of the board so as to ensure he was meeting the new law's requirements. On August 21, 1862, Leeser informed Lincoln, in his official capacity as secretary, that the Philadelphia Board of Ministers of the Hebrew Congregations "deemed highly expedient to have a Jewish chaplain appointed by the President of the United States, to be invested with the privileges pertaining to ministers of other persuasions holding the same position."[21]

On September 6, 1862, John Hay, Lincoln's secretary, informed Leeser that the president had considered his request and was resolved to appoint a Jewish chaplain if the Board of Ministers of the Hebrew Congregations designated a candidate. What Leeser and the other members of the board did not know was that on the very day that Lincoln received Leeser's letter, he took concrete steps to fulfill the request. On August 23, 1862, Lincoln directed Hay to send Leeser's letter to Surgeon General William A. Hammond, M.D. (1828–1900), and asked what Hammond thought of the request of the Board of Hebrew Ministers. In order to make sure that the surgeon general knew where Lincoln stood, however, Hay added an important postscript: "If possible," Hay wrote Hammond, "the President would like this to be done." On September 5, 1862, Hammond returned Leeser's letter to Lincoln with a written assurance that he considered the board's request to be "both legal and proper." Having completed the diplomatic groundwork, Lincoln then instructed Hay to communicate with Leeser and ask the board to submit a name for approval.[22]

The Board of Ministers of the Hebrew Congregations wasted no time in nominating Reverend Jacob Frankel (1808–87), minister of Philadelphia's Rodeph Shalom Congregation, for the appointment. On September 18, 1862, Lincoln signed Frankel's commission, making him the first American rabbi to serve as a military chaplain for the U.S. armed forces.[23]

On September 18, 1862, a commission signed by Lincoln made Jacob Frankel the first American rabbi to serve as a military chaplain in the U.S. armed forces. Courtesy The Jacob Rader Marcus Center of the American Jewish Archives, at the Hebrew Union College–Jewish Institute of Religion, Cincinnati, Ohio.

DOCUMENTS

1. The Board of Delegates Resolves to Address the Chaplaincy Controversy
2. The Board of Delegates Adopts Its Plan of Action
3. The Board of Delegates Petitions Both Chambers of Congress
4. Rabbi Fischel's Letters of Recommendation
5. Lincoln's Memorandum to Rabbi Fischel
6. Isaac Leeser Urges Lincoln to Appoint a Jewish Chaplain
7. The Man Who Led the Fight for the Right to Serve Denied Appointment

1. THE BOARD OF DELEGATES RESOLVES TO ADDRESS
THE CHAPLAINCY CONTROVERSY

Myer S. Isaacs, a New York lawyer, jurist, and Jewish communal leader, was only twenty years old when he kept the minutes of the meetings of the Board of Delegates of American Israelites. He carefully documented the BODAI's collective opinion that "Jewish ministers should be present in the camps & hospitals to administer consolation to Jewish soldiers."

Founded in New York City in 1859, the BODAI was the first central organization that sought to defend the rights of American Jews and, also, to work on behalf of Jews abroad. The chaplaincy controversy was one of the first Jewish civil rights issues in America to attract the interest of the BODAI.

The minutes of the BODAI's November 28, 1861, meeting confirm that the board's leadership had resolved to petition Congress to change the law that required Union military chaplains to be bona fide members "of some Christian denomination." Moreover, delegates instructed their president to "enter into communication with Reverend Dr. Fischell"[24] to see if he would be interested in helping them address this controversy.

At a meeting of the Executive committee of the Board of Delegates of American Israelites held at 30 West 28th St., Tuesday Evening, November 28th, 5622/1861.

Present: Henry I. Hart, Esq, President in the chair, Messers B. W. Hart, B. Russak, M. Wolfsohn, S. Wilzinski & M. S. Cohen

The minutes of the last meeting were read and approved.

The Secretary reported the receipt of $10 from each of the following Congregations, B'nai Jeshurun[25] and Beth El of New York, B'nai Jeshurun of Newark, NJ. Report accepted.

The President called the attention of the Committee to the letter published in the N.Y. Tribune from Hon. S. Cameron, Sec'y of War to Rev A. Fischell [clipping pasted into minute book]:

War Department, October 23, 1861

Rev. A. Fischel, Rabbi, Jewish Synagogue, No. 5 Carroll place, New York:

Sir,—Your communication of the 17th inst., enclosing a letter from the Honorable F[rederick] A. Conkling,[26] in reference to the Chaplaincy of the Cameron Dragoons, has been received. In reply, you are respectfully informed that by the 9th section of the Act of Congress approved July 22, 1861, it is provided that the Chaplains appointed by "the vote of the field officers and company commanders must be a regular ordained minister of some Christian denomination." A like provision, also, is made in the 7th section of the Act of Congress, approved August 3, 1861. Were it not for the impediments thus directly created by the provisions of these two acts, the Department would have taken your application into its favorable consideration.

I have the honor to be,

Very respectfully,
Simon Cameron,
Secretary of War

Whereupon it was Moved & Seconded that this Committee shall petition Congress to alter the law limiting the appointment of Chaplains to "ordained ministers of some Christian denomination."

That the framing of the petition be confided to the President & that he is hereby authorized, with the Secretary, to sign the same, affix the seal of the Board thereto & present it in due form to Congress.

Carried

Moved & Seconded that it is desirable that Jewish ministers should be present in the camps & hospitals to administer consolation to Jewish soldiers.

That, with a view of furthering this measure, the President be requested to enter into communication with the Rev. Dr. Fischell, & that he report the result therefore to this Committee without delay.

On motion, Adjourned
Myer S. Isaacs,
Secretary[27]

2. THE BOARD OF DELEGATES ADOPTS ITS PLAN OF ACTION

In the minutes of the BODAI's December 5, 1861, meeting, we learn that the chaplaincy controversy had become a very high priority for the young organization. The man they hoped would lead the charge, Rabbi Arnold Fischel, had been invited to this meeting. Fischel told the board that he was willing "to proceed to Washington & supervise the general welfare of Israelites in the army, if his expenses were paid." At this same meeting, the BODAI adopted five resolutions that related to the steps it would take to address this pressing communal concern. First, the BODAI planned to send Fischel to Washington as its spokesman and representative; second, the BODAI voted to adopt "a Memorial" (a petition) that would be sent to the U.S. Congress requesting the appointment of Jewish chaplains; and third, the BODAI resolved to compose an address "to the Israelites of the United States" that would alert them to this issue and engage them in an effort to identify "suitable persons as Chaplains" who would be ready to assume duty "should the object of memorializing the President be secured."

At a special meeting of the Executive Committee of the Board of Delegates of American Israelites held on Thursday December 5th 1861–5622.

Present: Henry I. Hart, Esq., President in the Chair, Messers B. W. Hart, Ellis Joseph, M. S. Cohen, B. Russak & M. Wolfsohn.

The minutes of the last meeting were read & approved.

The President reported having communicated with Dr. Fischell in accordance with the resolution adopted at last meeting, and that he had asked the Dr. to be present this evening.

Dr. Fischell being called upon, explained the circumstances under which the letter of Genl. Cameron dated Oct. 23, reached him, and expressed his willingness to proceed to Washington & supervise the general welfare of Israelites in the army, if his expenses were paid.

Moved & Seconded that suitable persons be appointed to supervise the general spiritual welfare of our coreligionists in the Military Hospitals of the United States.

Carried

Moved & Seconded that the Rev. Dr. Fischell be invited to proceed to Washington, & take charge of the spiritual welfare of our coreligionists in the Camps & hospitals attached to the Department of the Potomac.

Carried

Moved & Seconded that a committee of Three be appointed, to draw up & issue an address to the Israelites of the United States, on the subject contemplated in the foregoing resolutions, and that communication be had with the Committees of Israelites at the West on the subject of appointing suitable persons as Chaplains to the Departments of Kentucky & the West should the object of memorializing the President be secured.

Carried

Messers B. W. Hart, Wolfsohn, Saroni were appointed Committee on Address.

On motion, resolved that subscriptions in response to the address be received by the President, Vice President & Treasurer of the Board.

Carried.

The President called attention to paragraph 10 of General Orders No. 113 issued from the Adjutant General's office of the State of New York, reading thus: "The Regimental Chaplain, who must be a regular ordained minister of some Christian denomination, shall be appointed, &c."

On motion, the Secretary was instructed to prepare a suitable remonstrance & address the same to Gov. Morgan of N.Y.

On motion, Adjourned.

Myer S. Isaacs,

Secretary[28]

3. THE BOARD OF DELEGATES PETITIONS BOTH CHAMBERS OF CONGRESS

On December 6, 1861, the BODAI prepared a beautiful "Memorial," penned with a fair hand, addressed to the Senate and the House of Representatives. Presumably, Rabbi Fischel would carry this "Memorial" to the nation's capital. The tone of the remonstrance was firm. The document emphasized that the congressional act concerning military chaplains excluded from "the Office of Chaplain in the service of the United States 'regular ordained ministers' of the Jewish faith." The writers insisted that the current law was "prejudicial discrimination against a particular class of citizens, on account of their religious belief." Moreover, the law established a "religious test," which manifestly contravened the protections afforded the nation's citizens by the Constitution of the United States.

The "Memorial" concluded by insisting that the congressional acts relating to military chaplains be amended "so that there shall be no discrimination as against professors of the Jewish faith."

To the Honorable, the Senate and House of Representatives of the United States of America

The Subscribers, your memorialists respectfully show:

That they are the President and Secretary of the "*Board of Delegates of American Israelites*": and that they are duly empowered to submit to your honorable body the facts herein set forth, and to crave, at your hands, that attention to the subject which its importance to American citizens professing the Jewish religion, demands—

Your Memorialists respectfully show:

That by the 9th section of the Act of Congress, approved July 22, 1861, and the 7th section of the Act of Congress approved August 3, 1861, it is provided that "the Chaplain appointed by the vote of the field officers and company commanders, must be a regular ordained minister of some Christian denomination," and, that, as appears by the following letter from the War Department to which your Memorialists beg leave to refer the said sections have been interpreted to exclude from the Office of Chaplain in the service of the United States "regular ordained ministers" of the Jewish faith.

War Department, October 23, 1861

Rev. A. Fischel, Rabbi, Jewish Synagogue, New York

Sir, Your communication of the 17th inst. . . . has been received. In reply, you are respectfully informed that by the 9th section of the Act of Congress approved July 22, 1861, it is provided that the Chaplains appointed by "the vote of the field officers and company commanders must be a regular ordained minister of some Christian denomination." A like provision, also, is made in the 7th section of the Act of Congress, approved August 3, 1861. Were it not for the impediments thus directly created by the provisions of these two acts, the Department would have taken your application into its favorable consideration.

I have the honor to be,

> Very respectfully,
> Simon Cameron,
> Secretary of War

Your Memorialists respectfully submit that the body of citizens of the United States whom your memorialists represent, numbering not less than two hundred thousand, are unexcelled by any other class of citizens in loyalty and devotion to the Union, that thousands of them have volunteered into the Army of the United States, and are, by the provisions of the acts hereinbefore mentioned excluded from the advantages of spiritual advice and consolation provided by Congress for their fellow Citizens professing Christianity.

That the said Acts are oppressive inasmuch as they establish a prejudicial discrimination against a particular class of citizens, on account of their religious belief, and further—

That the said Acts inasmuch as they establish a religious test as a qualification for an office under the United States, are manifestly in contravention of Section 3, Article VI of the Constitution and Article I of Amendments thereto.

Your Memorialists, therefore respectfully pray that your honorable body will take this, their memorial into favorable consideration, and that you will in your wisdom, cause the Acts of Congress approved July 22nd and August 3rd 1861, respectively to be formally amended, so that there shall be no discrimination as against professors of the Jewish faith, in the several laws affecting the appointment of Chaplains in the service of the United States.

And your memorialists will ever pray.

> Henry I. Hart
> President
> Myer S. Isaacs
> Secretary[29]

In 1861 the Board of Delegates of American Israelites sent Arnold Fischel to meet with Lincoln and solicit his support for the appointment of Jewish military chaplains.

Courtesy American Jewish Historical Society, New York, N.Y., and Newton Centre, Mass.

4. RABBI FISCHEL'S LETTERS OF RECOMMENDATION

Rabbi Arnold Fischel departed from New York for the nation's capital on Monday, December 9, 1861. Since he was determined to bring this matter to the personal attention of President Lincoln, Fischel came to Washington armed with letters of introduction and reference. One of these letters was written by E. Delafield Smith (1826–78),[30] a man whom Lincoln had only recently appointed to serve as the U.S. district attorney for New York. Smith assured the president that the "Rev. Dr. A. Fischel" was the official representative of the Board of Delegates of American Israelites and a "gentleman of great worth and intelligence." In addition to his kind words about Fischel's character, Smith also volunteered his own sympathetic opinion on American Jewry. The Jews, he wrote, have "evinced loyalty to the Government and, I need not say, [are] entitled to at least a hearing on this subject."

Moses Hicks Grinnell (1803–77) also composed a letter of reference for Fischel. Grinnell, a former U.S. congressman and a member of New York City's political elite, first met Lincoln personally when the president-elect stopped in New York on his way to Washington, D.C., in February 1860. A politically influential figure, Grinnell subsequently wrote a number of letters to Lincoln.

U. S. District Attorneys Office,
New York, December 9th, 1861

His Excellency,

Abraham Lincoln,

President of the United States,
Sir:

Mindful of the constant pressure upon your strength, I have refrained from obtruding letters of introduction upon you. I depart from this course now, to introduce to you the Rev. Dr. A. Fischel, who had been appointed by the Board of Delegates of The Israelites of the United States to urge the modification of the laws in relation to Chaplains, so far as they effect the practical, though I doubt not unintended, exclusion of clergymen of the Jewish faith from acting in that capacity even in regiments composed of persons of that religion.

The class of our citizens has evinced loyalty to the Government and, I need not say, is entitled to at least a hearing on this subject.

Doctor Fischel is a gentleman of great worth and intelligence, connected with the Jewish Synagogue in 19th Street, in this City. The congregation worshipping there is the oldest and wealthiest in this Country, as I am informed.

Hoping that a brief interview with Doctor Fischel may be agreeable to you and useful,

I am,

Honored Sir,
With great respect and regard,
Your faithful servant,
E. Delafield Smith
U. S. Dist. Atty.[31]

New York, Dec. 10, 1861

To Prst. Lincoln,

Sir, permit me to present to you Rev. Dr. Fischell of this city who visits Washington as a delegate from the Board of Delegates of American Israelites, having been selected as chaplain to the Jews of the army around Washington estimated at about 8000. Dr. Fischell is of high literary abilities and greatly esteemed by distinguished men of all religious denominations. Believe me, etc.

M. A. Grinnell[32]

5. LINCOLN'S MEMORANDUM TO RABBI FISCHEL

Despite reports to the contrary, President Lincoln agreed to see Rabbi Fischel on December 11, 1861. From Fischel's perspective, the meeting went quite well. Lincoln even asked him to return the next day to discuss the matter further. Much to Fischel's disappointment, Lincoln was unable to meet with him the next day, though the overall tenor of the meeting sustained Fischel's hope that Lincoln would, at the very least, agree to ask Congress to modify the law so that Jewish ministers would be able to become chaplains.

On December 15, 1861, Rabbi Fischel received a short but gratifying letter from Abraham Lincoln. He sat down on the spot and penned a buoyant letter to Henry I. Hart (1816–63), president of the BODAI.[33] Fischel wanted Hart and the rest of the BODAI to read Lincoln's words for themselves, so he quoted the entire text of Lincoln's letter verbatim. Had the rabbi not done so, we might never have been able to document Lincoln's personal involvement in the controversy, since the original of Lincoln's note appears to have been lost.[34]

"I think we may congratulate ourselves," Fischel effused in his letter to Hart, "on having gained an important front in our cause." Lincoln told Fischel that he would do more than submit a recommendation to Congress supporting a modification of the current law; the president informed the rabbi that he would actually submit to Congress "a new law broad enough to cover what is desired by you in behalf of the Israelites."

Lincoln kept his word. Five months later, Congress passed new legislation that would enable ministers of the Jewish faith to serve as chaplains in the U.S. military.

> 332 Pennsylvania Ave.
> Washington, Dec. 15, 1861
>
> My dear Sir,
>
> Yr letter of the 13th inst. has reached me, and its contents will be acted upon.
>
> I think we may congratulate ourselves on having gained an important front in our cause. As you will have learned from my letter of the 13th inst. the President has resolved to lay my case before the Cabinet, and accordingly I rec'd on Friday evening the following letter, from which you will perceive that the President has decided not only to recommend to Congress the modification of the law but actually to submit to them a bill which will embrace in general terms all religious denominations:
>
> [Copy of the president's letter]
> Executive Mansion Dec. 15, 1861
>
> Rev. Dr. A. Fischel
> My dear sir
>
> I find there are several particulars in which the present law in regard to chaplains is supposed to be deficient, all which I now design presenting to the appropriate Committee of Congress. I shall try to have a new law broad enough to cover what is desired by you in behalf of the Israelites.
>
> Yours truly,
> (signed) A. Lincoln

Having fully studied the subject, I was prepared to affirm that this is by far the most important step the Pres't could have taken. Had he appointed me under some fictitious title, to evade the act of Congress and merely to pacify the demands of the Jews, it would have been very advantageous to myself, but the Jewish community would have gained nothing by it, since they w[ould]d be actually excluded by law and only admitted by the back door. The great principle the Jews have to contend for is, that the Constitution takes no cognizance of religious sects and that consequently we do not want *special* legislation for the Jews, as is the case in England, but all legislation must be *general* for *all American citizens* without any regard to their faith. Now this is precisely what we need for in undertaking to submit to Congress a bill based on general principles, he virtually throws his entire influence in our favor and with more force than by merely sending a special message on the subject to Congress. The course I shall have to pursue is now self evident. The Committee on Military Affairs will have charge of that bill, and I will make it my business to see its members with the object of forcing on their attention our claims, as well as examining the details in so far as they relate to the religious opinions of the chaplains. As soon as the bill is printed I will send you a copy, and if the Committee report the same favorably to the House, it is sure to pass. Some weeks may elapse before this bill will come before them, and you will, therefore, see the propriety of my abstaining from bringing the matter before Congress, as such a process is sure to injure rather than benefit the cause.

This now is in the best hands, and everything will be done on my part that is likely to promote its success. As You will probably not hear from me again till next week, unless something of importance is to be communicated. I shall pass all my time this week in the camps and hospitals. . . . Whenever you have any suggestions to make, please write me.

Very respectfully yrs,
A. Fischel

Henry I. Hart, Esq.[35]

6. ISAAC LEESER URGES LINCOLN TO APPOINT A JEWISH CHAPLAIN

On July 17, 1862, Congress passed a law that authorized the Jewish ministers to serve as military chaplains in the armed forces. Now the president needed to make the first chaplaincy appointment. Rabbi Isaac Leeser, one of the most distinguished rabbinic figures of the period, was serving as secretary of the Board of Ministers of the Hebrew Congregations of Philadelphia when he urged President Lincoln to "speedily comply" with the Board of Ministers' petition that he approve the appointment of a Jewish chaplain to serve soldiers in military hospitals in and near Philadelphia.

Isaac Leeser of Philadelphia was one of the most significant rabbinical personalities of the nineteenth century. Courtesy The Jacob Rader Marcus Center of the American Jewish Archives, at the Hebrew Union College–Jewish Institute of Religion, Cincinnati, Ohio.

In his letter to the president dated August 21, 1862, Leeser stressed his belief that there was now a moral necessity for Lincoln to take swift action on this matter. Lincoln "recognized the propriety of [Leeser's] suggestion,"³⁶ and on September 18, 1862, Rabbi Jacob Frankel of Congregation Rodeph Shalom in Philadelphia became the first Jewish clergyman in the history of the United States to serve as a military chaplain.

To the Hon. Abraham Lincoln

President of the United States of America

Sir

By order of the Board of Ministers of the Hebrew Congregations of Philadelphia, I take the liberty, as their secretary of addressing you briefly on a subject of great importance to us as a religious body.

Many Israelites are serving in the army of the United States, and this city and vicinity being the locality where numerous hospitals for the sick and wounded soldiers have been established, it is to be expected that not a few persons of our persuasion will be brought hither in a condition to require spiritual no less than bodily care. In fact two at least of our persuasion have already died in the hospitals, one of these had his religious affinities not made known to us till after he had been already buried without an Israelite being present. From the steps taken by us it is not probable that another Israelite will die under similar circumstances without some one of his fellow believers being made cognizant of his case.

Nevertheless it has at our last meeting been deemed highly expedient to have a Jewish chaplain appointed by the President of the United States, to be invested with the privileges pertaining to ministers of other persuasions holding the same position. The act of the last session of Congress having given you full authority to delegate to Israelites this office of mercy, we trust that you will speedily comply with our request.

The object of this being merely a preliminary step, to bring the matter under your notice, it is useless to enlarge, especially as we are well aware that your time is greatly occupied by public concerns of the gravest importance. Still our request is one which should of right receive the kind attention of the chief magistrate of the Union, mainly because the moral effect of the compliance with our request cannot fail of being manifest to yourself.

If an appointment is made, it is suggested that the district for the operation of the chaplain might conveniently include York, Harrisburg, Chester and other towns not at too great a distance, where U.S. hospitals are or may be established.

Please to command my services in whatever way I could convey such information as may be needed by you.

For our trustworthiness, as our board are strangers to you, we may refer to Messrs Biddle, Lehman & Kelly members of the House of Representatives of this city.

Respectfully your obt. sevt.
Isaac Leeser
minister Franklin St. Synagogue
and secry. Board of Heb. mins. of Phila.
Philadelphia
1229 Walnut St
August 21st 1862[37]

7. THE MAN WHO LED THE FIGHT FOR THE RIGHT TO SERVE DENIED APPOINTMENT

Although Jacob Frankel had been appointed to care for Jewish soldiers in the vicinity of Philadelphia, this did not alleviate the need for Jewish chaplains elsewhere. On October 6, 1862, the president of the BODAI, Henry I. Hart, asked Lincoln to appoint Dr. Arnold Fischel a military chaplain so he could tend to the needs of Jewish soldiers in hospitals in and around Washington.

In this case, the surgeon general's office surveyed the military hospitals in the Washington area and, allegedly finding only seven Jewish patients, rejected Hart's request. Evidently, the man who, as one historian noted, "won for American Jewry the first major victory of a specifically Jewish nature . . . in a matter touching the Federal government" never himself received a commission and never served as a military chaplain.[38]

New York, Tishri 12th 5623
October 6th 1862

Sir,

May we not once again call your Excellency's attention to the necessities of the Jewish volunteers? We know your time is fully occupied with the engrossing cares of state, but feel sure you will require no apology for bringing once more to your notice the case of our coreligionists who, expending their life's blood in the noble cause of country, are still, when racked by pain and suffering, debarred the privilege of the ministrations of spiritual advisers of their faith. They are sick and dying in the hospitals—hundreds of them. We beg of you to relieve them.

Congress has empowered you to designate regularly ordained ministers of various religious denominations as chaplains to the army hospitals. In the vicinity of Washington City, we are informed that the 48 hospitals contain nearly 20,000 patients; among them are a fair proportion of Jewish soldiers. May we not earnestly solicit you to confer on the Rev. Dr. Arnold Fischel, a capable & respected minister of our faith, duly ordained, whose testimonial as required by law, was duly forwarded to your Excellency in August last,—or on some other suitable person the appointment of Chaplain to the hospitals in and around Washington, so that the pain of our suffering brethren may be assuaged and their mental agony soothed?

We do not address you in the capacity of seekers after office; but, in the name of humanity and of our Country which Israelites love as dearly as their fellow citizens, ask your speedy compliance with our request.

Fervently trusting that peace and unity may soon be restored to our land, and that you may long be spared to preside over its destinies, I beg to subscribe myself, in behalf of the Executive Committee of this Board, and awaiting your Excellency's reply,

Your Obedient Servant
Henry I. Hart
President
office, 369 Broad Way,
Myer S. Isaacs.
Secretary[39]

4

Lincoln and the Revocation of General Orders No. 11

L ess than three months after Reverend Jacob Frankel's appointment brought the chaplaincy controversy to a satisfactory conclusion for the American Jewish community, and just two days after President Lincoln signed the Emancipation Proclamation, Lincoln adjudicated the most notorious anti-Jewish act in American history. This extraordinary event, known as Grant's "General Orders No. 11," resulted in the first and only time in the nation's history that Jews, "as a class," were expelled from American territory.[1]

On December 17, 1862, General Ulysses S. Grant telegraphed the following order throughout the Military Department under his command:

> The Jews, as a class, violating every regulation of trade established by the Treasury Department and also department orders, are hereby expelled from the department within twenty-four hours from the receipt of this order.
>
> Post commanders will see that all of this class of people be furnished passes and required to leave, and anyone returning after such notification will be arrested and held in confinement until an opportunity occurs of sending them out as prisoners, unless furnished with permit from headquarters. No passes will be given these people to visit headquarters for purpose of making personal application for trade permits.
>
> —By the order of Maj. Gen. U. S. Grant: Jno [John]
> A[aron] Rawlins, Assistant Adjunct General[2]

This order authorized regional commanders to expel all Jewish citizens—men, women, and children—living in the newly created Military Department of the Mississippi, which included the states of Kentucky and Tennessee and parts of Alabama and Mississippi. Understandably, the order has been called "the most sweeping anti-Jewish regulation in all American history."[3]

During the months leading up to the infamous edict's promulgation, Grant had been particularly vexed by the problem of "unprincipled traders" who traveled into the occupied South, both with and without authorized permits, to conduct commercial activity. Many of these profiteers tried to make some fast cash by gathering up cotton crops and other commercial goods from vanquished southerners and then transporting the goods into the Union. By the fall of 1862, illicit trading activities had become a

Ulysses S. Grant, half-length portrait, standing, facing slightly right, wearing uniform, circa 1865. The implementation of Grant's General Orders No. 11 constituted the only time in history that Jews, as a class, were banished from American territory. Courtesy Library of Congress Prints and Photographs Division, Washington, D.C.

serious problem. "Bribery and corruption" were rife, and the demoralizing profiteering was so widespread that Lincoln himself complained that "the army itself is diverted from fighting the rebels to speculating in cotton."[4]

It is not difficult to understand why Grant associated this activity with Jews. First, it is a fact that many, though certainly not all, of those involved in this kind of commercial trading were Jewish. Peddling and trading was a popular livelihood among the Jewish immigrants who had settled in the states of the Old Northwest Territory. The actual number of Jewish tradesmen doing this kind of work was made to appear even larger because of the popular tendency to stereotype the Jew. During this era, the term "Jew" was often unthinkingly used as an epithet to describe anyone—Jew or non-Jew—who behaved in a shrewd, ambitious, and in some instances dishonorable fashion. These factors caused many in the North to stereotype Jewish peddlers and entrepreneurs in the region as being profiteers. Yet Grant's decision to punish Jews *as a class*—men, women, and children—when he issued his infamously bigoted edict remains to this day a truly incomprehensible ruling.[5]

Historians have proffered an array of hypotheses in an attempt to explain Grant's confounding decision to expel Jews "as a class" from the military department in such an indiscriminate manner. Some have asserted that Grant's superiors in Washington directed him to issue the order and then, after the tidal wave of resentment hit, told Grant to abandon the idea and let the longsuffering general take the heat for the decision. Others have suggested that Grant was acceding to the will of his own military

Petersburg, Va., sutler's tent, Second Division, Ninth Corps, November 1864. Civil War sutlers traveled with the armies and sold the soldiers clothing, food, dry goods, and other necessities.
Courtesy Library of Congress Prints and Photographs Division, Washington, D.C.

personnel. Many of the officers in the U.S. Army had been collaborating with profiteers in order to fatten their own wallets. If an unscrupulous trader was unable to procure a legitimate trading permit, he would try to serve as the agent/representative for an army officer who was authorized to grant him permission to travel into southern territory for commercial purposes. Many officers were eager to collaborate with these ambitious traders and sutlers so they could earn a cut of the profits. It has been argued that a number of these officers wanted to eliminate Jewish competition in the hope of gaining more direct control over the enterprise. Therefore, they urged their general to give the Jewish competition the boot.[6]

Another explanation ascribes Grant's decision to an act of displaced anger. Only a short time prior to the issuance of General Orders No. 11, Jesse R. Grant (1794–1873), the general's father, arrived at his son's Mississippi headquarters with three Jewish business partners in tow: Harman, Henry, and Simon Mack of Cincinnati, Ohio. Jesse and his partners approached Grant in an attempt "to procure a permit for them to purchase cotton" in the South and transport it back to the Union for a profitable sale. As one historian summarized, Grant was furious but could not bring himself to punish his own flesh and blood, so he "expelled the Jews rather than his father." A fourth consideration may have contributed, in some measure, to any of the aforementioned explanations:

Grant's well-documented drinking habit may very well have left his mind cloudy on an occasion or two, making him particularly irritable and impulsive. No matter what the actual cause may have been, it is unmistakably clear on the basis of Grant's own dispatches that Grant himself had concluded that the most efficacious way for him to address the vexing problem of illicit trading practices would be to expel all Jewish tradesmen from his department so as to keep them from traveling to the South. This ambition ultimately led him to issue his condemnable order.[7]

By November 1862, it was clear that Grant had had his fill of illegal traders and sutlers—and the Jewish ones had become a particular annoyance. In a dispatch dated November 9, Grant canceled all trading permits for the South and added an additional injunction: "The Israelites especially should be kept out." The next day Grant issued a similar order, which again singled out the Jews for special treatment: "No Jews are to be permitted to travel on the railroad southward from any point. They may go north and be encouraged in it; but they are such an intolerable nuisance that the department *must be purged of them*" (emphasis added). On the very day that Grant promulgated General Orders No. 11, he discussed his decision in a communication to Assistant Secretary of War Christopher Parsons Wolcott (1820–63):

> I have long since believed that in spite of all the vigilance that can be infused into post commanders, the spice regulations of the Treasury Department have been violated, and that mostly by Jews and other unprincipled traders. So well satisfied have I been of this that I instructed the commanding officer at Columbus to refuse all permits to Jews to come South, and I have frequently had them expelled from the department, but they come in with their carpet-sacks in spite of all that can be done to prevent it. The Jews seem to be a privileged class that can travel everywhere. They will land any wood-yard on the river and make their way through the country. If not permitted to buy cotton themselves they will act as agents for some one else, who will be at military post with a Treasury permit to receive cotton and pay for it in Treasury notes which the Jew will buy up at an agreed rate, paying gold. There is but one way that I know of to reach this case; that is, for Government to buy all the cotton at a fixed rate and sent it to Cairo, Saint Louis, or some other point to be sold. Then all traders (they are a curse to the army) might be expelled.
>
> U. S. Grant, Major-General[8]

Was Grant's decision an outgrowth of a fundamentally anti-Jewish disposition? It is impossible to say with certainty. He and his supporters firmly denied the accusation. General Orders No. 11, Grant later insisted, was a misguided effort on his part to address a demoralizing problem of greedy and unpatriotic traders. Years later, during the presidential campaign in 1868, Grant—who tenaciously refused to discuss General

Orders No. 11 publicly—did confess, in private correspondence, that the entire affair was due to the fact that he had acted much too carelessly and precipitously:

> The order was issued and sent without any reflection and without think-
> ing of the Jews as a sect or race to themselves, but simply as persons who
> had successfully (I say successfully instead of persistently because there
> were plenty of others within my lines who envied their success) violated
> an order, which greatly inured to the help of the rebels. . . . I have no
> prejudice against sect or race, but want each individual to be judged by
> his own merit. Order No. 11 does not sustain this statement, I admit, but
> then I do not sustain that order. *It never would have been issued if it had
> not been telegraphed the moment it was penned, and without reflection.*[9]
> (emphasis added)

Fortunately for the Jews, surprise military attacks were disrupting communications between Grant's headquarters and his military commanders, which caused the order, promulgated by telegram, not to reach many of the command posts in a timely fashion. Some of the commanders who did receive the order telegrammed headquarters for additional clarifications: did the general mean for them to expel *all* Jewish merchants and sutlers who provided goods to the soldiers? The order had been revoked by the time headquarters had a chance to consider these queries. It is also interesting to note that Isaac M. Wise contended in his newspaper, the *Israelite*, that General Jeremiah Cutler Sullivan (1830–90) actually refused to carry out the order. Nevertheless, General Orders No. 11 was carried out by some and primarily took effect in two particular regions of Grant's department: northern Mississippi and Paducah, Kentucky.[10]

Northern Mississippi is where Grant was headquartered, and this fact may explain why subordinates in this particular region wasted no time in identifying Jews in the territory and deporting them. Distressing reports to this effect soon began to circulate. Rabbi Wise provided his readers with an alarming exposé on the expulsion of Jews from Holly Springs and Oxford, Mississippi, in the *Israelite*, and in New York, Reverend Samuel M. Isaacs's *Jewish Messenger* carried similar stories. Later in the month, after the order had already been rescinded, hair-raising stories about the mistreatment of Jews in these two cities continued to circulate.[11]

It was in Paducah, Kentucky, however, where the most sensational developments occurred. Captain L. J. Waddell, provost marshal in Paducah, received Grant's edict and acted on it with alacrity. He notified the entire Jewish community—store owners, businessmen, families, law-abiding citizens all—that they had twenty-four hours to leave Paducah. One historian has emphasized that Paducah had been well primed for such bigotry because the then-bustling community had been suffering from rampant political and economic strife, which heightened anti-Jewish fervor in the region. In other words, Waddell and some other local officials were inclined to act promptly because Paducah had become fertile soil for "cupidity, suspicion, and fear."[12]

By the end of the month, the Jews of Paducah—save two ill women—had left on steamships that headed up the Ohio River toward Cincinnati. Although these hapless Jews must have been profoundly stunned by these catastrophic and fast-paced developments, there was one member of the community, Cesar J. Kaskel, who was determined to fight back against the odious order. Kaskel's indignation carried him to Washington, D.C., where he would have a remarkable personal meeting with Abraham Lincoln in the White House.[13]

Thirty-year-old Cesar J. Kaskel (1833–92) and his younger brother, Julius W. Kaskel (1837–1909), the most prominent Jewish activists involved in this upsetting incident, were immigrants from Wiesbaden, Prussia. Very little is known about their lives aside from the courageous role they played in advocating for the revocation of General Orders No. 11. They apparently immigrated to the United States in the early 1850s and settled in the Middle West. Julius lived in Burlington, Iowa, in the late 1850s, and he was listed as one of the city's "clothiers and tailors" in Des Moines's 1859 City Directory. On April 23, 1861, Julius enlisted as a volunteer in the First Iowa Infantry, though he was mustered out a few months later. By the end of 1861, he and Cesar were living in Paducah, Kentucky, where they had opened a clothing business. Some time shortly after the revocation of General Orders No. 11, the Kaskels relocated to New York City, where they opened a haberdashery and lived out the rest of their lives. Historical evidence suggests the two men were also adventurous entrepreneurs. They owned property and had business dealings in Leadville, Colorado, at the height of that city's economic boom in the early 1880s. Although they returned to Germany for a visit now and then, they remained residents of New York City, making a respectable living and participating in communal affairs.[14]

It was their response to General Orders No. 11, however, that has earned the Kaskels a place of honor in the annals of American Jewish history. Evidently, as soon as news of Grant's order arrived in Paducah, the Kaskel brothers, together with two other Jewish

Cesar J. Kaskel traveled from Paducah, Kentucky, to Washington, D.C., in order to ask Lincoln to revoke Grant's order that Jews be expelled from the Military Department of Tennessee. Courtesy The Jacob Rader Marcus Center of the American Jewish Archives, at the Hebrew Union College–Jewish Institute of Religion, Cincinnati, Ohio.

merchants, the Wolff brothers, organized a meeting in Paducah to map out a response to the troubling edict. A written record of these activities, which Julius Kaskel evidently preserved, provides us with much of what we currently know about Cesar Kaskel's astounding activities.[15]

The very first response to Grant's order came in the form of a telegram written by the Kaskel brothers and sent directly to President Lincoln. In the telegram, the Kaskels ask Lincoln for an "immediate interposition." The text of this remarkable communication, preserved in the *Official Records of the Union and Confederate Armies*, is a testament both to the moral courage of these immigrant writers and to their fervent faith in the promise of the U.S. Constitution.

The telegram informed Lincoln that many "good and loyal citizens of the United States," who were longtime residents of Paducah and honorable merchants, had been unjustly expelled from their community. These Jewish citizens felt "greatly insulted and outraged" by Grant's "inhuman order," which constituted "the grossest violation of the Constitution and our rights as good citizens under it." Unless this edict was promptly overturned, the telegram reasoned, then innocent, law-abiding Jewish citizens would be seen as "outlaws before the whole world."[16]

Evidently, the Kaskels and their compatriots did not want to rely solely on the telegram. This was a wise decision, since it seems that Lincoln showed the telegram to his general-in-chief, Henry W. Halleck (1815–72), who told the president he had never heard of this order and could not believe that Grant would have done such a thing.[17] In order to ensure that Lincoln was fully informed of the entire story, Cesar Kaskel decided to go to the nation's capital and seek an audience with the president. He left Paducah by a steamer, which stopped in Cairo, Illinois, where he conveyed a "full account of the affair," in writing, to an Associated Press correspondent who began to disseminate news of the incident. From Cairo, Kaskel traveled to Cincinnati, where he procured letters of introduction from Rabbi Isaac Wise, Rabbi Max Lilienthal (1815–82), and Daniel Wolf (ca. 1819–1904), a political activist and prominent Cincinnati merchant.[18]

On Saturday, January 3, 1863, seventeen days after Grant issued General Orders No. 11 and two days after Lincoln signed the Emancipation Proclamation, Kaskel arrived in Washington, D.C. He immediately made contact with Ohio congressman John A. Gurley (1813–63), a former clergyman and newspaper publisher from Cincinnati, who knew both Rabbis Wise and Lilienthal. Without the help of a loyal Republican and Lincoln partisan like Gurley, it is unlikely that Kaskel, a man who heretofore had no political contacts, would have succeeded in procuring an emergency meeting with Lincoln at the White House.[19]

Gurley and Kaskel arrived at the White House as the sun was setting on the evening of January 3.[20] They apologized for appearing without an appointment but explained that they had come to discuss a matter of some urgency with the president. The two men were told to wait. Soon the president sent word that he would meet with them, noting he was "always glad to see his friends." Although no documentation of Kaskel's meeting with President Lincoln has survived, secondhand accounts have appeared in numerous sources. Kaskel showed the president a copy of his expulsion orders and described the occurrences that had brought him to Washington. The extraordinary exchange that is said to have then occurred between Lincoln and Kaskel constitutes one of the most memorable dialogues in all of American Jewish history. The president wryly observed:

> "So the children of Israel were driven from the happy land of Canaan?"
> Kaskel replied: "Yes, and that is why we have come unto Father Abraham's bosom, asking protection."
> Lincoln responded: "And this protection they shall have at once."
> Then seating himself at a table the President penned an order to General [Henry] Halleck [and] request[ed] his visitors to deliver it at once.[21]

Having concluded their meeting with the president, Kaskel and Gurley went directly to see General Halleck, who once again insisted he knew nothing about Grant's order. Halleck continued to doubt the veracity of Kaskel's story until he was shown a copy of Grant's order, countersigned by Captain Waddell. Kaskel gave the general-in-chief the president's written directive to reverse the order, and Halleck promised he would do so. "You may leave for home at once if you wish," Halleck told Kaskel, "and before you reach there, Grant's order will have been revoked."[22]

In a telegram to Grant sent on January 4, 1863, Halleck wrote: "If such an order has been issued, it will be immediately revoked." Yet in spite of Halleck's directive, General

Abraham Lincoln, August 9, 1863. Courtesy Library of Congress Prints and Photographs Division, Washington, D.C.

Orders No. 11 was not *immediately* revoked. It was not until three days had passed—on January 7, 1863—that General John Rawlins (1831–69) circulated the official revocation from Grant's headquarters. The brief text of the revocation noted clearly that the decision to withdraw the order came directly from the "General-in-Chief of the Army, at Washington"—not from General Grant.[23]

Kaskel left Washington the next morning and returned to Paducah, where, Halleck's promise aside, he was dismayed to learn that Captain Waddell still had not been told that the order had been revoked. As soon as the provost marshal saw Kaskel was back in town, he asked: "By whose orders do you return?" Kaskel rejoined, "By order of the President of the United States."[24]

It was during this interim—that is, between January 4, when Halleck instructed Grant to revoke the order, and January 7, when Grant's office issued the official revocation—that Grant's supporters tried to convince Lincoln to let the order stand. On January 6, 1863, a day before Grant himself had officially revoked the order, Congressman Elihu B. Washburne (1816–87), a fellow Republican from Illinois and an ardent supporter of General Grant, urged Lincoln *not* to rescind the order: "I see a report that you have revoked Grant's order touching the Jews,—I hope not. I consider it the wisest order yet made by a military command, and from my own personal observation, I believe it was necessary. As the friend of that distinguished soldier, General Grant, I want to be heard before the final order of revocation goes out, if it be contemplated to issue such an order. *There are two sides to this question*" (emphasis added).[25]

Washburne was not the only government official who was ambivalent about Lincoln's decision to revoke the order. In conveying to the president a formal resolution of protest about Grant's order that was submitted by the officers of the St. Louis B'nai B'rith Lodge, Attorney General Edward Bates expressed little enthusiasm for Lincoln's decision. "In handing you the papers," he wrote the president, "[I take] no particular interest in the subject."[26] Evidently, even the highest legal authority in the nation was not convinced the president had made the proper decision.

Yet, even after Grant formally revoked his order on January 7, the controversy continued to simmer in Washington. Several members of Congress clashed bitterly over Lincoln's instantaneous decision to order a revocation of General Orders No. 11. Although some congressmen proposed resolutions condemning the order and congratulating Lincoln on the revocation, there were others who expressed little interest in praising the president for publicly countermanding the popular General Grant. Partisanship prevailed, and in the end, Congress refused to act. Lincoln's decision was no less controversial in the press. Some newspaper editorials vigorously condemned the order, while others vociferously defended General Grant as well as the need for the order.[27]

There is no evidence that Lincoln ever paused to reconsider his initial negative reaction to Grant's General Orders No. 11. To the contrary, he seems to have been resolute in his decision and eager to assume responsibility for countermanding Grant. According to Isaac M. Wise, who led a protest delegation to Washington on the heels of Kaskel's visit, Lincoln expressed genuine regret over the issuance of an order like General Orders

No. 11. Originally, Wise's group had planned to protest the order, but upon reading in the press that the order had already been rescinded, the protesters decided to use the occasion to express their appreciation to the president for quickly responding to the crisis. Wise and his entourage met with Lincoln on Wednesday evening, January 7.[28]

According to Wise's account of the group's meeting, Lincoln welcomed his Jewish guests with "a frank cordiality, which . . . becomes men high in office so well." Wise recalled that the president's demeanor was "informal and friendly." Lincoln told his guests that he could not fathom how or why General Grant would have issued such a "ridiculous" order. "To condemn a class," Lincoln told the delegation, "is . . . to wrong the good with the bad. I do not like to hear a class or nationality condemned on account of a few sinners." In describing the meeting, Wise noted that Lincoln was "splendidly eloquent on this occasion," and he effectively "dispelled every doubt" about his sincerity. The president, Wise subsequently testified, "entertained no prejudices of any kind against any nationality, and especially against Israelites, to whom he manifested a particular attachment."[29]

Generally speaking, the story of Grant's General Orders No. 11 illustrates the tremendous undercurrent of "anxiety and conflict" that expressed itself during the Civil War in random acts of "animosity and bigotry."[30] In this kind of atmosphere, American Jewry became a favored target, and this bigotry worried many in the Jewish community. Isaac M. Wise articulated his concern about this hateful spirit, and he reminded his readers that the way America treated its Jews would be a barometer of liberty for the nation's future:

> If the Jew as a nationality may be treated with impunity, where are the guarantees that other nationalities, the Germans, Irish, Dutch, French, etc., will not be treated in the same manner tomorrow? . . . Liberty is represented as a mighty woman, we the people, all of us, are her limbs, bones, muscles, nerves, veins, intestines, heart and soul, and allow the government to be her head and brain; if she is wounded in any one of her members, she is wounded, and requires a careful treatment. . . . Therefore, it is everybody's business to look at this affair.[31]

Lincoln's prompt and resolute response to the abrogation of their rights as American citizens persuaded most American Jews that the president was determined to do something about the inclement social atmosphere that seemed to be darkening the American horizon. Wise himself testified to the fact that Lincoln had "fully illustrated to us and convinced us that he knows of no distinction between Jew and Gentile, that he feels no prejudice against any nationality." Although Lincoln's revocation brought political relief to a very small number of Jews who were affected by Grant's order, Lincoln's action loomed large in Jewish popular opinion during that era. Over the 150 years that have passed since this incident occurred, this episode has repeatedly been cited by Jews as a striking example of Lincoln's remarkable moral compass that guided him to hold fast to the Constitution's fundamental promise to ensure liberty and justice for all.[32]

DOCUMENTS

1. General Orders No. 11 Breaks into the News
2. "Good and Loyal Citizens" Felt "Greatly Insulted and Outraged"
3. Letter from the United Order of B'nai B'rith Protesting Grant's Order
4. From the *New York Times*: Lincoln Relieved Himself of a "Serious Affliction"
5. Rabbi Wise Editorializes on Grant's Order
6. The *Israelite* Reports on Grant's Order: Lincoln's Meeting with the Jewish
   Delegation
7. The *New York Times* Criticizes the Order's "Bad Writing and Worse Logic"
8. Wise Refuses to Vote for Ulysses S. Grant

1. GENERAL ORDERS NO. 11 BREAKS INTO THE NEWS

Soon after the provost marshal of Paducah, Kentucky, Captain L. J. Waddell, received a telegraphed copy of General Grant's General Orders No. 11, he ordered the city's Jewish citizenry to report to his office and ordered them to leave Paducah within twenty-four hours.

Shortly thereafter, the text of Waddell's orders began to appear in newspapers together with a letter to the press from one of the banished Jews, Cesar J. Kaskel. Kaskel wrote his appeal while on board the steamboat Chaley Bowe *that carried him and his fellow Jews upriver to Cincinnati. The texts of Waddell's orders and Kaskel's letter to the press appeared in the* Jewish Record *on December 30, 1862.*

Rabbi Isaac M. Wise of Cincinnati was incensed by Kaskel's report. In his editorial, which appeared in the January 2, 1863, edition of the Israelite, *Wise vented his spleen at this appalling example of "military despotism." Decrying what he called an "outrage without a precedent in American history," Wise urged "every honest friend of the republic" to take action. "It is your duty, the duty of self defence, your duty to bring this matter clearly before the president of the United States and demand redress, the satisfaction due to the citizen thus mortified and offended."*

Justice of Provost Marshal
Paducah, Ky., December 28, 1862

C. J. Kaskel—Sir: You will report to this office immediately, as I wish to see you in relation to General Order No. 11, issued from Major General Grant's headquarters.

L. J. Waddell
Captain and Provost Marshal

[Copy]

Office of Provost Marshal

Paducah, Ky., December 25, 1862

C. J. Kaskel—Sir: In pursuance of General Order No. 11, issued from General Grant's headquarters, you are hereby ordered to leave the city of Paducah, Kentucky, within twenty-four hours after receiving this order.

By order,

L. J. Waddell

On Board Steamboat "Chaley Bowe"

December 30, 1862

The accompanying copies of orders issued respectively by Major General U. S. Grant and Captain Waddell, Provost Marshal at Paducah, Kentucky, will explain easily the cause of my coming before the public.

I, a peaceable, law abiding citizen, pursuing my legitimate business at Paducah, Kentucky, where I have been a resident for nearly four years, have been driven from my home, my business, and all that is dear to me, at the short notice of twenty-four hours; not for any crime committed but simply because I was born of Jewish parents. Nearly thirty other gentlemen, mostly married, all respectable men, and old residents of Paducah, two of whom have served their country in the three months' service, and all loyal to the Government, have suffered the same fate.

On my way to Washington, in order to get this most outrageous and inhuman order of Major General Grant countermanded, I ask you, gentlemen, to lend the powerful aid of the press to the suffering cause of outraged humanity; to blot out as quick as possible this stain on our national honor, and to show the world that the American people, as a nation, brand the author of that infamous order as unworthy of their respect and confidence.

Yours, respectfully,

C. J. Kaskel[33]

The Outrages in Major-General Rosecrans' Army

The order of Colonel [John Van Deusen] Du Bois,[34] reviewed in our last, it appears, was entirely in consonance with orders from head-quarters. The colonel was removed since for other offences and we have no more to say about him.—But gentlemen just arrived from Mississippi and Tennessee communicate facts to us which leave no doubt to our mind, that gentlemen higher in rank than a colonel, are the originators of wrongs which, if reported from Turkey, Russia, Austria or from Morocco, would excite the indignation of every liberal man in this country. It appears that the sacred rights of loyal citizens and the laws of the land are as little regarded by military commanders and their next subordinates in the above mentioned states, as the laws of the Chinese empire.

Gentlemen of undoubted integrity, connected with some of the most highly respectable firms in Cincinnati, New York, Chicago, St. Louis and elsewhere, just returning from Holly Springs, Miss., having footed their way to Memphis, communicate to us, that one evening shortly before Holly Springs was taken by the Confederates, they were apprised by a military officer of the arrival of a general order (No. 29)[35] issued by Major-General U. S. Grant, commanding All Jews (in these very terms) to leave the lines within 24 hours, not even excepting the numerous Jews in the service of the United States whom he certainly did not mean to exile. The gentlemen considered the order spurious, and desired the officer to grant them the privilege of telegraphing General Grant to ask him, whether he issued such an order, which he could not grant, but told them to write down what they wished to ask him, and he promised to telegraph. They went to their lodging and Mr. Silberman of Chicago wrote the dispatch and had it delivered to that officer. Late in the evening an orderly arrived to inquire after the author of the telegram, and being told it was Mr. Silberman, he arrested him, because he doubted the genuineness of the order and kept him imprisoned to 12 M. the next day. Jewish citizens who had resided in Holly Springs for years together with all others were obliged to leave. Our informants next morning went to the Rail Road depot, but being told there that civilians could not be accommodated that day, they footed their way to Memphis.—They could not tell how the others came off, or whether they were not taken prisoners by the Confederates.

Need we comment on this handsome piece of military despotism? We trust not. We expect, every man acquainted with the laws of the country and the principles of the people to regard to political freedom and the rights of citizens;—every man of liberal and just opinions, condemns with indignation this outrage without a precedent in American history.

In the first place we supposed these prejudices are of a religious character and pitied their purblind agents; but the gentlemen informed us different. The next order, after the Jews were banished from the lines was of the same general, that no farmer or planter, under the penalty of confiscation, dare charge or receive more than 25 cents for the pound of cotton, which a day before sold at 40 cents a pound. This let the cat out of the bag. The Jews bought cotton of planters (who before selling must take the oath of allegiance to the U.S.) at 40 cents a pound; the military authorities with their business partners, agents, clerks, portiers, &c., intend to buy that staple at twenty-five cents a pound, it appears, they could sell it in eastern cities just as high as the next man—and the Jews must leave because they interfere with a branch of the military business. So the matter appears to us.

Another fact is this. Jews leaving Nashville, Tenn., who come to Captain [William M.] Wiles[36] for a passport, after standing three or four days at his door, are sent to the chief of police who has a nomenclature of all Israelites coming and going. This dignitarian, for the time being, before granting a permit to leave, demands of every Hebrew to sign a pledge promising *never* to return to Nashville, after which the fellow this tortured receives a peculiar card of clearance. Our informants, two young men of this city, having come to Nashville with pass and permit to sell dry goods, finding, however, that they were not allowed to do their legitimate business, concluded upon returning to this city. On applying to Captain Wiles for a pass, he was sent to the chief of police who tried to exact the same pledge from him as from all other Hebrews: but the gentleman said, he rather would rot in a military prison than do such a thing, notwithstanding his very determination, not to do business in Nashville. After the exchange of hard words, the chief of police had found out that he caught a tartar, he insisted no longer on his terms, sent him back to Captain Wiles who signed his pass. This is the routine of business in Nashville under the very eyes of General Rosecrans.[37] We do not mention names, because we expect these gentlemen and others treated in the same manner will publish lawful affidavits. We request every person who was thus illegally treated, without delay to send us affidavits to this effect made before a justice of the peace or a notary public, or publish them in other papers, and send us the publications.

The Nashville chief of police said to our informant, "the Jews smuggle, therefore they are treated in this manner." Granted they do, why are they not punished? Are the Jews the only smugglers in existence? Are all Jews smugglers? Granted even all the Jews are smugglers and the only persons who carry on this prohibited trade; what right has any military or civil officer to maltreat a whole race or religious denomination, because the few known to him are smugglers? Where is the letter of the law in any code of a civilized nation conferring the authority on a military officer to deprive loyal and peaceable citizens of their well defined rights, because he suspects some of them to be guilty of illegal acts? The evidence, sir, bring us the evidence that the Jews are the only smugglers, punish the guilty ones according to the terms of the law, or expel them from the lines. I, sir, am a Jew who did not smuggle, if I come to Nashville, I, nevertheless, must go to the office of the inquisition and sign a pledge *never* to return. Who is the author of the holy office of the inquisition in the heart of God's only spot of freedom and in the second half of the nineteenth century? Who is responsible for these high-handed outrages, this lawless despotism, spit into the face of a free people and an enlightened age?—General Rosecrans must be able to tell us, for he is responsible for the actions of his subordinate officers. Let him speak, if he thinks it worth while to render account to the offended majesty of freedom and law.

Reviewing closely the orders of General Grant in regard to Jews and cotton, it would strike us by a little reasoning from analogy that there are also in Nashville certain nephews, uncles, cousins, old acquaintances, generous gentlemen and such other non-Jewish merchants who found out that the Jews spoiled the marked by selling too cheap and bringing too large stocks into market. They, it appears, found out they could not get rich fast enough on account of that competition, and the Jews must go to make room to patriotic speculators and valorous companions. We are told, and if true it is, we are bound to have it under oath—yes, we are told that money well applied changes entirely the aspect of things. Permits, they say, are in the market like other commodities. So the thing appears after a cursory inspection.—We can not see how any complaints could justly be raised about demoralization, if superior officers set such examples of lawlessness.

But we do not care for causes. The orders mentioned above do exist, and this suffices to alarm every honest friend of the republic. Are we to be the slaves of military chieftains? Are we playthings in the hands of presumptuous men, to abuse and maltreat us at pleasure? Are we frogs and mice to be trampled under anybody's feet, or are we men who stand by their rights? Is no law in the land, no authority higher than bayonets? If we can stand this, we are unworthy of being citizens of a free country. If we do stand all this, we just not wonder, if one day anybody will treat us like paria[h]s and outcasts of society. Israelites, citizens of the United States, you have been outraged, your rights as men and citizens trampled into dust, your honor disgraced, as a class you have officially been degraded! It is your duty, the duty of self defence, your duty first to bring this matter clearly before the president of the United States and demand redress, the satisfaction due to the citizen this mortified and offended.

It is not only the business of the Jew to look to these matters, it is everybody's affair. If the Jew as a nationality may be treated with impunity, where are the guarantees that other nationalities, the Germans, Irish, Dutch, French, &c., will not be treated in the same manner to-morrow? If the Jews as a religious community are handled thus, how will the Catholics, Unitarians, Universalists or any other religious denomination be treated, if a general or provost officer sees fit to come down on one or the other. Liberty is represented as a mighty woman, we the people, all of us, are her limbs, bones, muscles, nerves, veins, intestines, heart and soul, and allow the government to be her head and brain; if she is wounded in any one of her members, she is wounded, and requires a careful treatment. Wounded in her right arm or her little toe, wounded she is, and the whole body must feel it, and be protected against more serious injuries. Therefore it is everybody's business to look to this affair.[38]

2. "GOOD AND LOYAL CITIZENS" FELT "GREATLY INSULTED AND OUTRAGED"

Before departing from Paducah, Cesar and Julius Kaskel and David Wolff described their circumstances in a telegram they sent to Abraham Lincoln on December 29, 1862. The Jewish businessmen told the president that the "inhuman" order made them and their fellow

Jews into "outlaws before the whole world." General Orders No. 11 was, they insisted, "the grossest violation of the Constitution and our rights as good citizens under it."

Kaskel traveled directly to Washington, D.C., and, with the help of Ohio congressman John A. Gurley, he secured a personal meeting with Lincoln that took place on January 3, 1863. After convincing the president that such an order had actually been issued, Kaskel is said to have told Lincoln that he and his fellow Jews had come to Father Abraham's bosom for protection.

Paducah, Ky., December 29, 1862

Honorable Abraham Lincoln,
President of the United States:
General Orders, Numbers 11, issued by General Grant at Oxford, Miss., December the 17th, commands all post commanders to expel all Jews, without distinction, within twenty-four hours, from his entire department. The undersigned, good and loyal citizens of the United States and residents of this town for many years, engaged in legitimate business as merchants, feel greatly insulted and outraged by this inhuman order, the carrying out of which would be the grossest violation of the Constitution and our rights as good citizens under it, and would place us, besides a large number of other Jewish families of this town, as outlaws before the whole world. We respectfully ask your immediate attention to this enormous outrage on all and humanity and pray for your effectual and immediate interposition. We would respectfully refer you to the post commander and post adjutant as to our loyalty, and all to respectable citizens of this community as to our standing as citizens and merchants. We respectfully ask for immediate instructions to be sent to the commander of this post.

D. Wolff & Bros.
C. F. Kaskell
J. W. Kaskell[39]

3. LETTER FROM THE UNITED ORDER OF B'NAI B'RITH PROTESTING GRANT'S ORDER

Although President Lincoln ordered General Halleck to revoke General Orders No. 11 on January 3, 1863, during his meeting with Cesar Kaskel, it took a few weeks for the revocation to work its way through the military bureaucracy. In the meantime, American Jews remained outraged. Complaints about the odious action appeared in the Jewish press during the first week of January 1863.

On January 5, the United Order B'nai B'rith of Missouri sent the president a remonstrance. Signed by the lodge's president, Rabbi Henry Kuttner (1820–1902), and secretary, Morris Hoffman (1828?–94), the protest decried the immorality and unconstitutionality of Grant's order.[40]

It is interesting to note that the remonstrance was originally received by Attorney General Edward Bates. It was Bates's duty to forward the document to the president, and in doing so, the attorney general affixed a note, saying, "I do not comply with [their] expressed wish, in handing you the papers, myself feeling no particular interest in the subject."[41]

United Order "Bne B'rith" Missouri Loge [*sic*]
St Louis. Jan 5, 1863
Sir

An Order, Expelling and ostracizing all Jews, as a class has been issued by Maj. Genl U. S. Grant and has been enforced at Holly Springs, Trenton, Corinth, Paducah, Jackson and other places.

In the name of that Class of *loyal* citizens of these U.S. which we in part represent. In the name of hundreds, who have been driven from their homes, deprived of their liberty and injured in their property *without* having violated any law or regulation.

In the name of the thousands of our Brethren and our children who have died and are now willingly sacrificing their lives and fortunes for the Union and the Suppression of this rebellion.

In the name of religious liberty, of justice and humanity—we enter our solemn Protest against this Order, and ask of you—the Defendor & Protector of the Constitution—to annull that Order and to protect the liberties even of your humblest Constituents[.]

Henry Kuttner
President
Morris Hoffman
Secy[42]

4. FROM THE *NEW YORK TIMES*: LINCOLN RELIEVED HIMSELF OF A "SERIOUS AFFLICTION"

This terse news item from the New York Times, dated January 5, 1863, reported, in a somewhat peculiar tone, that the Jews of the West had threatened to send "large delegations" to Washington to protest Grant's orders. With tongue in cheek, the writer implies that it was the thought of facing a delegation of "exasperated" Jews, and not the injustice of the orders, that prompted Lincoln to revoke the odious orders with such alacrity.

Gen. Grant and the Jews

The action of General Grant, in ordering all Israelites out of his Department, was today reversed by Gen. Halleck, at the instance of the President. The "Jewish persuasion" throughout the West, according to telegrams received, were greatly excited and exasperated at the order, and were organizing large delegations to visit Washington, for the purpose of having it rescinded. In view of this threatened visitation, the president's action had undoubtedly relieved him from a serious affliction.[43]

5. RABBI WISE EDITORIALIZES ON GRANT'S ORDER

On January 9, 1863, Rabbi Isaac M. Wise published another column on Grant's General Orders No. 11 in the Israelite. *Clearly unaware of the fact that the orders had already been officially revoked, Wise notified his readers that a delegation of citizens from Cincinnati, Louisville, and Paducah planned to "proceed to Washington, to bring this matter to the notice of the administration." The editorial goes on to heap scorn on the many Cincinnati newspapers that failed to publish a condemnation of Grant's order, and in his criticisms, Wise expressed some of his own perhaps illiberal views.*

Steps have been taken to bring this matter in proper shape before the President of the U.S., to see whether a general may with impunity deprive people of their rights which to protect he is sworn and paid for. In Cincinnati the Rev. Doctors Lilienthal and Wise were appointed; in Louisville, Martin Bijur, Esq., and in Paducah, Ky., Mr. Goldsmith[44] were also sent on the same mission, who as one delegation proceed to Washington, to bring this matter to the notice of the administration. Therefore we abstain from any further publication or comment on this subject.

We have only to say one thing more. The Cincinnati newspapers were timely informed of the outrage committed on citizens because they are Jews. In Cincinnati thousands of Israelites live and contribute largely to the wealth of the city, to every benevolent or charitable institution, contributed largely to the military funds of various descriptions, and read the said newspapers, for which they pay, advertise therein and support them otherwise. What do you think these selfsame papers did learning of the outrageous order of General Grant?—Nothing, nothing in the world. Shame on such press!

The *Enquirer* and the *Volksfreund* are the only Cincinnati papers which condemned the order of Grant and had the manliness to speak earnest words against a wrong without precedent in American history.

So we know what we have to expect of the Cincinnati press in case of emergency. So we know with what zeal those gentlemen watch over the rights of white people. So we learned what their pretensions at liberality and their declamations on freedom are actually worth. So we are aware now (and facts speak) of what metal they are made.[45]

6. THE *ISRAELITE* REPORTS ON GRANT'S ORDER: LINCOLN'S MEETING WITH THE JEWISH DELEGATION

Once he arrived in Washington, D.C., Rabbi Wise learned that General Grant's orders had been revoked. Wise and the other members of the delegation decided to meet with

Abraham Lincoln and express their collective appreciation for his decisive action. Wise reported on his visit with Lincoln in the Israelite *of January 16, 1863. He praised Lincoln, who received the contingent cordially and "convinced" them "that he knows of no distinction between Jew and Gentile." This report contains many intriguing details about the controversy, including Wise's bitter condemnation of certain congressmen who defended General Grant's actions and criticized President Lincoln's decision to revoke them.*

The Israelite's *last editorial concerned with Grant's Orders No. 11 appeared on January 23, 1863. The introductory section of the editorial, which follows, reiterates the details of the order and the Jewish community's reaction against it and concludes with another description of Lincoln's conversation with the Jewish delegation from Cincinnati and Louisville.*

Letter from the Editor

The history of General Grant's order and its revocation forms quite an interesting chapter in the annals of the day. Gentlemen from Paducah, Ky., telegraphed to the President, who informed General Halleck instantly; we wrote immediately to Secretary Stanton; but neither the former nor the latter believed that Gen. Grant could have issued an order so absurd and ridiculous, and, therefore, did not do anything in the matter. When Mr. Kaskel came to Washington, January 3, and was introduced to the President, by Mr. Gurley of Cincinnati, the President at once gave order to Gen. Halleck to revoke said order. General Halleck would not believe in the existence of such order, till Mr. Kaskel showed him the official copy. General Halleck instantly and peremptorily revoked the order and telegraphed to Gen. Grant to inform all post commanders instantly, of the will of the government in this matter. The Cincinnati and Louisville delegation came too late.—The order was rescinded. Still we thought proper to see the President to express our thanks for his promptness in this matter.— Mark, however, how democratic things look in Washington. We arrived from Baltimore around 5 P.M. on Wednesday, arrived in the hotel without changing clothes. Rev. Dr. Lilienthal inquired and was informed that Mr. Gurley was in the same house, but was not in at present. Meanwhile Mr. Bijur and myself went to Mr. [George H.] Pendleton of Cincinnati [member of the U.S. House of Representatives] and talked half an hour to him.

On returning to our hotel we met Mr. Gurley, who without bestowing any consideration on our traveling garbs, went with us to the White House and before 8 P.M. we were introduced to the President, who being all alone, received us with that frank cordiality, which, though usually neglected, becomes men high in office so well. Having expressed our thanks for the promptness and dispatch in revoking Gen. Grant's order, the president gave utterance to his surprise that Gen. Grant should have issued so ridiculous an order, and added—"to condemn a class is, to say the least, to wrong the good with the bad. I do not like to hear a class or nationality condemned on account of a few sinners." The President, we must confess, fully illustrated to us and convinced us that he knows of no distinction between Jew and Gentile, that he feels no prejudice against any nationality, and that he by no means will allow that a citizen in any wise be wronged on account of his place of birth or religious confession. He illustrated this point to us in a very happy manner, of which we can only give the substance at present, and promise to give particulars on another occasion. Now then, in our traveling habiliments, we spoke about half an hour to the President of the U.S. in an open and frank manner, and were dismissed in the same simple style.

Sorry we are to say that Congress did not think proper to be as just as the President is. Congress is not now the people's legislative body, it belongs to a party. Senator [Lazarus] Powell of Kentucky, as noted elsewhere, introduced a resolution condemning the unjust order of Gen. Grant, to inform others that orders of this kind must not be issued; but the resolution was tabled to be killed, when called up again. Mr. Pendleton of Cincinnati, attempted in vain on Monday and Tuesday to bring the following resolution before the house. He finally succeeded on Wednesday (yesterday) to propose the following:

Mr. Pendleton offered a preamble setting forth that Major General Grant, on the 17th of December, as the commander of the Department of the Tennessee, did issue an order stating that the Jews, as a class, had violated every regulation of trade established in that department, and for this were to be expelled from the department within twenty-four hours &c., and as in the pursuance of the order General Grant caused many peaceful citizens to be expelled within twenty-four hours without allegation of misconduct, and with no other proof than that they were members of a certain religious denomination; and whereas said sweeping order makes no discrimination between the innocent and the guilty, and is illegal, unjust, tyrannical and cruel, therefore

Resolved, That the said order deserves the sternest condemnation of the House and of the President of the United States as Commander-in-Chief of Army and Navy.

Mr. PENDLETON moved the previous question of the passage of the proposition.

Mr. WASHBURNE (R) moved that it be laid upon the table; and this was agreed to—yeas 56, nays 53.

On motion of Mr. Washburne, the everlasting Mr. Washburne, the resolution was tabled by a vote of 56 yeas to 53 nays. If the Hebrew citizens of the United States were "gentlemen of color," Mr. Washburne would certainly have made a brilliant effort to vindicate their rights and expose a general who committed a gross outrage on them. But being only white men, it would not pay Partisan legislation, that is all we have to expect of this congress. Mr. Pendleton said Washburne's motive was that of friendship for Grant, whom to defend in congress he had several times taken upon himself; but Republican members openly say, it is a rule of the House to vote down every thing coming from the other side, viz: the democratic. How do you like this remarkable impartiality?

Having to see a good many things to-day, we must conclude this, to say more to-morrow.[46]

The Last of General Grant's Order

We do not mean to say that General Grant issued his last order, he may yet issue his farewell order to the army. We simply wish to say that this is the last we write and publish on the notorious persecution order of General Grant. Whether those materially injured by that queer document will bring civil suits for damages against General Grant, wherever and whenever he shall be accessible to the arms of justice and law, as they ought to do—we can not tell, nor is it our business to meddle in that part of the proceedings, this being the lawyer's business. As far as the honor of our co-religionists was involved, we tried to get satisfaction, and we only review the matter for future reference and the benefit of the historian. This is to conclude this affair.

Long before Grant's order was issued, the *Israelite* called attention to the existence of a spirit of dark prejudice in the army against our people. The order of Col. [John Van Deusen] Du Bois, however, was the first official document we obtained, published and censured. Still nobody appeared to care particularly for the matter. Saturday, December 27, two gentlemen coming directly from Holly Springs, Miss., informed us of the publication and enforcement of Grant's order. Monday next we took their affidavits, as well as affidavits of gentlemen who had been offended in Louisville by General [Jeremiah] Boyle, in Bowling Green, Ky., and especially in Nashville by provost-marshals, merely and exclusively on account of their being Jews. We exhibited these papers to several influential gentlemen who, we know not why, did not feel disposed to take the matter in hand. We wrote a letter to Secretary Stanton, and resolved to wait for an answer, before taking any further steps in the matter.

Meanwhile this famous order was put in force in Paducah, Ky., where several Jewish citizens resided for years past. This caused a considerable alarm. One of the Jewish residents of Paducah repaired at once to Washington, published the affair in a Cincinnati paper, and took letters of recommendation by Rev. Dr. Lilienthal to Mr. Gurley, M[ember of] C[ongress], of this city, and by Mr. Daniel Wolf to Mr. Pendleton, M.C., also of this city. Another resident of Paducah, Mr. Wolf, also repaired to Washington in company of an influential citizen. Again another resident of Paducah, Mr. Goldschmit went to Louisville, presented the case to some gentlemen of our persuasion, whereupon a meeting was called, resolutions as the case deserves were adopted, and Martin Bijur,

Esq., a popular lawyer of our persuasion, residing in Louisville, was appointed a delegate to act in conjunction with others appointed to the same purpose, to bring the matter before the President of the U.S.

Thursday, January 1, 1863, some influential merchants of Cincinnati held a meeting, appointed a committee to call a general meeting and prepare the business for it. The committee was to meet again on Saturday evening. Meanwhile Messers. Bijur and Goldschmit came to Cincinnati and gave a new impulse to the matter. Sunday evening, January 4, a large and enthusiastic meeting convened in the hall of the Phoenix; resolutions befitting the occasion were unanimously adopted, and three delegates chosen to act forthwith in conjunction with other delegates. The Cincinnati delegates were Rev. Dr. Lilienthal, Edgar M. Johnson, a popular lawyer of our persuasion, and our humble self. Monday morning the delegation of Louisville and Cincinnati, in company of Mr. Goldschmit started for Washington, provided with sufficient affidavits to substantiate our case.

We intended to go to Philadelphia and Baltimore, meet there delegates from these cities and New York, and act in conjunction with them; but it appears no steps had been taken yet in the eastern cities. In the Philadelphia papers, however, obtained in the cars near that city, we learned that the order of Grant had been revoked on Sunday, on presenting the matter to the president by Mr. Kaskel. Still we thought it proper to go to Washington and convince ourselves. We arrived in Washington on Wednesday evening and were introduced to the president the same evening by Mr. Gurley. The interview was of an informal and friendly nature. We had but little chance to say anything, the president having been so splendidly eloquent on this occasion. He assured us in every possible form that neither he nor General Halleck believed that Grant issued so absurd an order, until the official document dispelled every doubt. Furthermore that he entertained no prejudices of any kind against any nationality, and especially against Israelites, to whom he manifested a particular attachment. He spoke like a simple, plain spoken citizen, and tried in various forms to convince us of the sincerity of his words in this matter.[47]

7. THE *NEW YORK TIMES* CRITICIZES THE ORDER'S "BAD WRITING AND WORSE LOGIC"

An editorial from the January 18, 1863, edition of the New York Times *began by reporting on the controversy within the Jewish population over whether "the authorities at Washington" should be thanked for the annulment of Grant's General Orders No. 11.*

The editorial continues with a jocular criticism of the order's grammar and composition but then proceeds, with great conviction, to condemn the order and to marvel over the "humiliating reflection" that "the freest Government on earth" had temporarily revived "the spirit of the medieval ages."

Gen. Grant and the Jews

One of the deepest sensations of the war is that produced among the Israelites of this country by the recent order of Gen. Grant, excluding them, as a class, from his Military Department. The order, to be sure, was promptly set aside by the President, but the affront to the Israelites, conveyed by its issue, was not so easily effaced. It continues to rankle, and is leading to sharp controversies and bitter feuds in the ranks of the Faithful. It seems that a committee of Jews, in this city, took it upon themselves to *thank* the authorities at Washington for so promptly annulling the odious order of Grant. Against the conduct of this committee the bulk of the Jews vehemently protest. They say they have no thanks for an act of simple and imperative justice—but grounds for deep and just complaint against the Government, that Gen. Grant has not been dismissed from the service on account of his unrighteous act. The matter has been made to assume an importance that requires a mention of it in our columns, as constituting an exciting chapter in our current history. We therefore present the order of Gen. Grant, that the public judgment in the premises may rest on a clear perception of the facts;

Headquarters Thirteenth Army Corps

Department of the Tennessee,

Oxford, Miss., Dec. 17, 1862

General Order No. 11.—The Jews, *as a class*, violating every regulation of trade established by the Treasury Department, also Department orders, are hereby expelled from the Department within twenty-four (24) hours from the receipt of this order by Post Commander.

They will see that all this class of people are furnished with passes and required to leave, and *any one* returning after such notification will be arrested and held in confinement until an opportunity occurs of sending *them* out as prisoners, unless furnished with permits from these headquarters.

No pass will be given these people to visit headquarters for the purpose of making personal application for trade permits. By the order of

Maj.-Gen. Grant

John B. Rawlins. A[ssistant] A[djunct] G[eneral]

Official—J. Lovell. Capt. and A[ssistant] A[djunct] G[eneral]

It must be admitted that this order is open to severe criticism in more respects than one. The first and mildest objection we see, is its atrocious disregard of the simplest rules of English composition. To be dealt harshly with is bad enough, but to be vilified in execrable English is cruel, if not unusual, punishment. But if the execrable English of the general excommunication from Grant's attractive Department is very objectionable, the mocker of the allusion to special exemptions is utterly unworthy. "*Any one*" (any Jew) "returning" after a notification to leave, *they* will be sent away as prisoners, "unless furnished with permits from these headquarters." But "no pass will be given these people to visit headquarters for the purpose of getting permits." Such is the substantial and almost literal conclusion of Grant's order. It is mortifying to know that such a jumble of bad writing and worse logic should emanate from the headquarters of a Major-General commanding a Military Department of the United States.

As to the odious principle of Gen. Grant's order, there can be no doubt whatever. To condemn any religious body, as a class, and by wholesale, is contrary to common sense and common justice—contrary to Republicanism and Chris[tianity]. Gen. Grant may have been harassed by hangers-on of his army who were swindlers and extortionists. It was desirable that he should be rid of such. But will he say that all the swindlers that beset him are Jews? We are of opinion that there are degrees of rascality developed by the war that might put the most accomplished Shylocks to the blush. We have native talent that can literally "beat the Jews." Gen. Grant's order has the demerit of stigmatizing a class, without signalizing the criminals. All swindlers are not Jews. All Jews are not swindlers. Gen. Grant assumes that the reverse of this latter proposition is true, and he expels the Jews, "as a class," from the Department. That carries women and children—women at home and children at the breast. A number of Jewish families that had been quiet, orderly and loyal citizens of the town of Paducah for years, hurriedly packed up their goods, and left their home, under this cruel order. They had had nothing whatever to do with Grant or his army, but they belonged to the Jews, "as a class," and were denounced and expelled. Their situation must have revived the history of their unfortunate people during the twelfth, thirteenth and fourteenth centuries, when England, France and Austria successively followed each other in decrees against them of banishment and persecution. And it is a humiliating reflection that after the progress of liberal ideas even the most despotic countries has restored the Jews to civil and social rights, as members of a common humanity, it remained for the freest Government on earth to witness a momentary revival of the spirit of the medieval ages.

If we take a merely selfish view of Grant's treatment of the Jews, it will appear in the highest degree impolitic. Persons "of this class" have come to hold high positions in the leading Governments of Europe, whose good opinions we cannot afford to despise. M. [Achille] Fould, of Louis Napoleon's Cabinet, is a Jew, and his voice might, in the possibilities of things, go far to decide the fate of the American Union. The Rothschilds wield a power in the financial world that is well nigh omnipotent to raise or destroy the credit of any nation. We may find it better to have their friendship than enmity.

But rejecting all such considerations, we rely on the general principles of republican right and justice for the utter reprobation of Grant's order. Men cannot be condemned and punished as a class, without gross violence to our free institutions. The immediate and peremptory abrogation of Grant's order by the President saved the Government from a blot, and redeemed us from the disgrace of a military assault upon a people whose equal rights and immunities are as sacred under the Constitution as those of any other sect, class or race.[48]

8. WISE REFUSES TO VOTE FOR ULYSSES S. GRANT

This excerpt from an article in the "Theological Department" of the February 28, 1868, edition of the Israelite *expresses, with great vehemence, the newspaper's firm opposition to Grant's nomination as a candidate for the presidency. Here, Grant is described as the man who has done the Jews more "injustice than any man in power, in this century . . . in any civilized country."*

This barbarian order caused a general outcry of horror all over this country, in the public press, public meetings and resolutions, in any and every form. In Congress, Mr. Pendelton [*sic*], of Ohio, moved the following resolution:

"Whereas, On the 17th day of December, 1862, Major General Grant, commanding the department of the Tennessee, did publish the following order, to-wit: (here followed the above order *verbatim*). And in pursuance thereof did cause many peaceable citizens of the United States, residents in the said department, to be expelled therefrom within twenty-four hours without allegation of special misconduct on their part, and on no other proof than that they were members of a certain religious denomination; and

"Whereas, The said order in its sweeping condemnation of a whole class of citizens, without discriminating between the guilty and the innocent, is illegal and unjust, and in its executions tyrannical and cruel; therefore

"*Resolved*, That the said order deserves the earnest condemnation of this house, and of the President as Commander-in-Chief."

This was lost in the House, but only because nobody paid any attention to it, and the order had been revoked previously. The vote, after all, was a very close one—56 voted to table and 53 to pass it; two more votes would have done it. Among those voting for the resolution were, besides other republicans, also Mr. [Schuyler] Colfax, the present speaker of the House, Mr. [Frederick] Low, of St. Louis,[49] and other prominent members of that party.

The order No. 11 fell most savagely upon the old Jewish residents in that department; but there was no Senator from those States in Washington, except from Kentucky. Therefore Senator Powell from Kentucky, in behalf of his outraged constituents, introduced in substance the same preamble and resolution in the Senate, where it was defeated in a most shameful manner, where but 7, viz: Messrs. [Garrett] Davis, [Aaron] Harding, [Milton S.] Latham, [James W.] Nesmith, [Lazarus] Powell, [Eli] Saulsbury and [Robert] Wilson of Missouri, had the moral courage and moral rectitude to stand by an outraged class of their fellow-citizens.

President Lincoln could not persuade himself for a long time that General Grant issued that order; but when Mr. Kaskel, of Paducah Ky., succeeded in convincing him of the fact, he immediately revoked it, and expressed his indignation at the outrage in the strongest terms in presence of Messrs. Gurley, Lilienthal and Wise from Cincinnati, and Bijur from Louisville.

There was nobody, at the time, to defend the despotic and barbarous order of General Grant, not a voice was heard in its favor or defence; but plenty, besides President Lincoln, seven Senators and fifty-three members of Congress, in its condemnation. Every free man felt outraged by the lawless ukase of a military chieftain, whom they now want to force upon us as chief magistrate of the country.

We have to say this: As a Jew, we can not and will not vote for a man who has done us a more shameless injustice than any man in power, in this century, has done us in any civilized country. Therefore we hope and expect that the entire Jewish press will come out boldly and justly against the movement to nominate General Grant as President of the United States. Again, as a citizen who loves his country and her free institutions, who considers it his solemn duty to protect justice and freedom as much as it may be in his power, we can not and must not entrust the banner of justice and freedom to the hands of a man who, when possessing the brief power of a commander of a volunteer army (and among them thousands of Jews) abused it so outrageously, and trampled upon his fellow-citizens because they were too weak to resist. That man, in our estimation, is unfit to be the chief of a republic whose citizens claim equal justice and equal freedom. Therefore we hope and expect from all political leaders to drop the scheme of nominating General Grant. As a man, we feel an aversion to every person who disrespects the just claims of humanity and justice, and General Grant by his order No. 11, 1862, is guilty of that disrespect.

That is part of what we have to say on this point, and we will say it over and over again, until the masses shall know and appreciate it; till the feeling of honor shall awake also with those who cry with the millions, laugh or weep by order of their newspaper, cheer or scorn *ad libitum*. When a few scanty and poverty-stricken insurance companies in New York offended the Jews by an order not to insure their property, there was noise, meetings, resolutions, &c.; now when one who outraged the Jew beyond measure or comparison, one who outraged the Jew, the man and the citizen, the laws of the United States and the sacred cause of justice and humanity, is proposed as President of the United States, nobody has the courage or rectitude to talk. Is this principle? Is it manful? Is it honorable? Let cowards be silent for utility's sake; but let men speak out honorably.[50]

5

Lincoln and the Movement to Christianize the U.S. Constitution

During the years that Lincoln was in the White House, a third controversy arose that deeply concerned many leaders in the American Jewish community. This issue began to emerge in the early months of 1861, even before President-elect Lincoln formally took office, when a small religious synod called the "Covenanters"—a Christian denomination that split off from the Presbyterian church in 1809—met in Allegheny County, just outside of Pittsburgh, Pennsylvania. The members of this denomination deplored the fact that the U.S. Constitution did not forbid human slavery. They also decried the absence of any mention of God and Jesus Christ in the foundational law of the United States. The Constitution was a flawed document, they concluded, and "Covenanters" decided to do their best to rectify these errors. Their convictions led them to organize a vigorous religious and political movement that sought to formally amend the Constitution so that the Christian essence of the Republic was made explicit.[1]

The Covenanters' first major success came within days of their meeting, when they persuaded Massachusetts senator Charles Sumner (1811–74), a passionate abolitionist, to submit a "memorial" they had written to the U.S. Congress. The Covenanters called on Congress to see "that provisions be made in the Constitution expressing [firstly] an acknowledgment of the authority of God; secondly, an acknowledgment of the authority of God and Christ; thirdly, a recognition of firm obligations to God's law; fourthly, that the principles be clearly adverse to slavery."[2]

As news of Sumner's action spread, some American Jews took note of this development. Was it possible that the future of the U.S. Constitution, like the Union itself, was in question? If the "American Union [was indeed] tottering to its basis," some American Jewish leaders fretted, the ensuing disorder could indeed result in the dismantling of the Constitution and the rights it guaranteed to all citizens. Isaac Leeser, the prominent Philadelphia rabbi and publisher of the *Occident and American Jewish Advocate*, ominously warned his readers that if a "downfall of the American Republic" occurred, then the chaos that followed might very well become an "excuse for tyranny." Yet, for those who sympathized with the Covenanters and Senator Sumner, the impending collapse of the federal Union and the wicked slave system that triumphed in the American South was the inevitable result of a Republic that exiled God from the nation's founding documents.[3]

U.S. senator Charles Sumner of Massachusetts was a fiery opponent of slavery. Half-length portrait, between 1861 and 1874. Courtesy Library of Congress Prints and Photographs Division, Washington, D.C.

Fanatical abolitionists worried Leeser not because they hoped to abolish slavery by amending the Constitution but because they wanted to demolish Thomas Jefferson's famous "wall of separation between Church & State."[4] In the pages of the *Occident and American Jewish Advocate*, Leeser informed his readers that "should the opportunity be offered again to make a new fundamental law for the whole or part of the confederation, the absolute guarantee of religious liberty would be struck down by the hands of fanatics, even of those who have provoked the bitter hostility which the extreme sections of the country now profess for each other."[5]

The Christian amendment movement continued to build steam during the course of the Civil War. In February 1863, another band of "Christian amendment" advocates, independent of the "Covenanters," came together in Xenia, Ohio. One of the most passionate participants was a young Presbyterian lay leader named John Alexander (1805–94), who delivered a paper asserting that the Civil War and all the accompanying bloodshed was in fact a national punishment. According to Alexander, "by setting up our national government in the name of a new deity, 'we the people,'" the American republic had deeply "dishonored" God. By omitting mention of God and Jesus Christ in the Constitution, the Founders committed "the original sin of the nation." Alexander urged his compatriots to rectify this most serious of flaws by resolving "to amend the Constitution so as to acknowledge God and His authority."[6]

According to Alexander's own memoirs, his appeal did not immediately win the day among those who had convened with him in Xenia. However, he, and others who agreed with him, soon learned about the Presbyterians and Covenanters in Allegheny County, Pennsylvania, and they traveled there in order to collaborate with them. On January 27–28, 1864, this newly formed coalition of advocates held a watershed conference at the First Associate Reformed Presbyterian Church of Allegheny City.[7] The attendees, most of whom represented local Presbyterian churches and seminaries, concluded that America needed to adopt a Christian amendment to the U.S. Constitution as quickly as possible, and they agreed to join forces under a new unified banner. Thus, the National Reform Association (NRA) was born.

The NRA quickly adopted its own mission statement wherein it set forth the essence of its political agenda:

> To maintain existing Christian features in the American Government touching the Sabbath, the Institution of the Family, the Religious Element in Education, the Oath and Public Morality as affected by the liquor traffic and other kindred evils; and to secure such an amendment of the Constitution of the United States as will declare the nation's allegiance to Jesus Christ and its acceptance of the moral laws of the Christian religion, and to indicate that this is a Christian nation, and place all the Christian laws, institutions and usages of our government on an undeniable legal basis in the fundamental law of the land.[8]

A short time later, the NRA moved its headquarters to Philadelphia and began publishing a monthly organ, the *Christian Statesman*.[9]

News of the NRA's establishment worried many American Jews, who feared that the changes this group was proposing posed a severe threat to religious freedom and minority rights in America. Although he admitted that the NRA had not yet become a mass movement, Isaac Leeser warned his readers that if this group ultimately succeeded "in rendering the *faith* of Christians a part of the supreme law of the country, [then] every one who dissents from it might then by a parity of reasoning be justly deprived of having his portion in the benefits conferred by the Constitution."[10]

Only days after the group's organizational meeting was held, on February 11, 1864, a delegation from the NRA traveled to Washington, D.C., to meet with Abraham Lincoln. They read aloud the text of a new preamble to the Constitution that John Alexander had drafted, and they urged Lincoln to support them in their effort to persuade Congress to Christianize the Constitution and permanently abolish slavery.

According to the minutes of this meeting, which were published in 1873, Lincoln asked the NRA delegation to give him ample time to reflect on their proposal. "The work of amending the Constitution," he told them, "should not be done hastily." Lincoln concluded by assuring them that he would act "upon it as my responsibility to our Maker and our country demands."[11]

Before long, news began to spread that a delegation from the NRA had traveled to Washington in order to "win the President of the United States in favor of the [Christian amendment] measure." In a long and passionate essay, Rabbi Isaac M. Wise of Cincinnati disparaged the group's aspirations and activities:

> We do not know how many members of Congress laugh over this joke; but so much we do know, many laughed about it and considered it not

Abraham Lincoln, 1864. Courtesy Library of Congress Prints and Photographs Division, Washington, D.C.

worthwhile to lose a word on it. Its fate is decided, its doom is certain. We, the people of the United States who are no Presbyterians, are not such fools as to place the chains on our own limbs—We, the people of the United States who do acknowledge God as the source of all power, would not allow any body to impose religious dogmas on us contrary or agreeable to our conviction. We claim religious liberty to its full extent and please God we shall maintain it intact and unimpaired as it exists now.[12]

Although the NRA continued to pursue its objectives throughout the remainder of the Lincoln administration, President Lincoln avoided taking any kind of public stance on the matter. Many years later, John Alexander recollected that a few months after the NRA delegation met with Lincoln, the president told an unnamed NRA member, in confidence, that he hoped a Christian amendment would pass during his second administration. "Therefore we believe," Alexander insisted in 1894, "that if Lincoln had lived, he would have recommended the amendment of the Constitution making it Christian."[13]

It is not known whether or not Lincoln actually made such an "off the record" comment, but there can be no doubt that many leading American Jewish personalities disagreed strongly with Alexander's assertion that Lincoln actually supported their cause and wanted to help them pass a Christian amendment during his second term. In the weeks following Lincoln's assassination, many Jewish leaders pointedly described Abraham Lincoln as a man who was always ready to recognize—"in full"—American Jewry's "claims to an equality before the law." Isaac Leeser reminded the members of his congregation that Lincoln "was not guided by sectarian prejudices." Prominent lawyer and Jewish leader Philip J. Joachimsen (1817–90) insisted that Lincoln was the "banner-bearer of the Constitution and of the laws . . . [and he] refused to listen to intimidation." In eulogizing Lincoln, Philadelphia newspaper editor and Jewish communal leader Alfred T. Jones (1822–88) maintained that whenever the minority rights of American Jewry had been impugned, Lincoln "promptly recognized our claims as a religious body to national protection, and acceded unhesitatingly to all our just demands."[14]

As time went on, Jews never tired of reminding the American nation that "there was no room for sectarian narrowness in [Lincoln, who] sought to unite the people at whose head he stood."[15] In 1911, Rabbi Nathan Krass (1880–1949) wrote an essay wherein he insisted that Lincoln was not a partisan of religious denominations but rather "a strong believer in the God of nations and the Providence of the human family."[16] Throughout the late nineteenth and early twentieth centuries, Jewish speakers like Krass repeatedly emphasized Lincoln's universalism. They insisted that as far as Lincoln was concerned, "this is not a government of Christians nor a government of Jews, but a government of the people, for the people, and by the people."[17] For American Jewry, Lincoln was venerated as "the very incarnation of all that was just, true and manly, not only for the Christian, but for the Jew; not only for the white man, but for the negro; not only for the American, but for all men, no matter from what part of the world they came."[18]

For all these reasons, American Jews persistently reassured themselves that the man who asserted that "a government cannot endure, permanently, half slave and half free" would similarly maintain that "liberty and sectarianism [constituted] 'a house divided against itself'—a contradiction in terms."[19]

DOCUMENTS

---

1. The National Reform Association Appeals to President Lincoln
2. Rabbi Wise Comments on the Religious Amendment
3. Isaac Leeser Condemns the Effort to "Engraft Christianity on the Constitution"
4. The Board of Delegates of American Israelites Opposes a Religious Amendment
5. A "Destructive Amendment": Leeser's Concern Intensifies
6. The Board of Delegates of American Israelites Defends
    the Framers of the Constitution

---

1. THE NATIONAL REFORM ASSOCIATION APPEALS TO PRESIDENT LINCOLN

A delegation of prominent Christian clergymen and leaders from the NRA convention met with President Lincoln in Washington on February 11, 1864. The minutes of that meeting were preserved and later published.

What is interesting in the following documents is the language they used in their proposal to Christianize the Constitution as well as the record of Lincoln's response to their appeal. The NRA leaders hoped the president would embrace their cause, and they credited him for having "awakened a hope in the Christian people of this land." Amazingly, they declared themselves opposed to the idea of uniting church and state and clearly believed that a Christian amendment would not lead to this result. As long as the nation did not favor one Christian denomination over any other, they argued, the "wall of separation" endured. A Christian America might very well be tolerant of non-Christians, but if the NRA amendment passed, the Christian character of America would become an unassailable fact.[20]

The Religious Amendment of the Constitution Memorial to Congress

To the Honorable, the Senate and House of Representatives, in Congress assembled:

We, citizens of the United States, respectfully ask your Honorable bodies to adopt measures for amending the Constitution of the United States, so as to read, in substance, as follows:

> We, the people of the United States, [humbly acknowledging Almighty God as the source of all authority and power in civil government, the Lord Jesus Christ as the Ruler among the nations, and His revealed will as the supreme law of the land, in order to constitute a Christian government] and, in order to form a more perfect union, establish justice, insure domestic tranquility, provide for the common defense, promote the general welfare, [and secure the inalienable rights and the blessings of life, liberty, and the pursuit of happiness to ourselves,

our posterity, and all the people,*] do ordain and establish this Constitution for the United States of America.

*And further: that such changes with respect to the oath of office, slavery, and all other matters, should be introduced into the body of the Constitution, as may be necessary to give effect to these amendments in the preamble. And we, your humble petitioners, will ever pray, etc.

Resolved, That a special Committee be appointed to carry the Memorial to Washington, lay it before the President, and endeavor to get a special message to Congress on the subject and to lay said Memorial before Congress.[21]

Address to the President

Mr. President:—The object for which we have taken the liberty of trespassing a moment on your precious time, can be explained in very few words. We are the representatives of a mass Convention of Christian people, without distinction of sect or denomination, which was held in Allegheny City, on the 27th and 28th of January last; and we are instructed to lay before your Excellency the action of that Convention.

We are encouraged, Mr. President, to hope that you will give the great object for which we pray, your cordial and powerful support, because you have already shown, by many significant acts of your administration, that the principle on which it rests is dear to your heart. This principle is our national responsibility to God, which you have expressly and repeatedly recognized. We remember that when, under one of your predecessors, an anti-Christian power had refused to treat with the United States, on the ground that we were a Christian nation, the objection was removed by the authoritative statement that we, as a nation, had no religion; also, that several of your predecessors refused, when earnestly importuned, to appoint days of national fasting and thanksgiving, for the same reason, whilst you, sir, within the space of a single year, have thrice, by solemn proclamation, called us to either national fasting, humiliation and prayer, for our many and grievous sins, especially our sin of forgetting God, or to national thanksgiving for His unspeakable mercies.

You, moreover, as no other of our Chief Magistrates ever did, have solemnly reminded us of the redeeming grace of our blessed Saviour, and of the authority of the Holy Scriptures over us as a people. By such acts as these, you have awakened a hope in the Christian people of this land, that you represent them in feeling and want of a distinct and plain recognition of the Divine authority in the Constitution of the United States. For we hold it most certain truth, that nations, as such, and not individuals alone, are the subjects of God's moral government, are responsible to Him, and by Him are graciously rewarded for their obedience, or justly punished for their disobedience of His divine laws. . . .

We ask for no union of Church and State—that is a thing which we utterly repudiate; we ask for nothing inconsistent with the largest religious liberty, or the rights of conscience in any man. We represent no sectarian or denominational object, but one in which all who bear the Christian name, and all who have any regard for the Christian religion, can cordially agree; and one to secure which we are persuaded that any lawful and wise movement would call forth an overwhelming public sentiment in its support.

We, therefore, do earnestly hope that you, our beloved Chief Magistrate, will not be indifferent in our prayer . . .

The President replied as follows:

Gentlemen:—The general aspect of your movement, I cordially approve. In regard to particulars, I must ask time to deliberate, as the work of amending the Constitution should not be done hastily. I will carefully examine your paper, in order more fully to comprehend its contents than is possible from merely hearing it read, and will take such action upon it as my responsibility to our Maker and our country demands.[22]

2. RABBI WISE COMMENTS ON THE RELIGIOUS AMENDMENT

In his editorial in the Israelite *of June 5, 1863, Isaac M. Wise commented on the movement to amend the Constitution so as to explicitly recognize Christianity as the foundational religion of the United States. Wise points out the contradiction inherent in this proposal, which sought to append an unconstitutional "establishment of religion" on a document that itself prohibits any union of church and state. He also observes that the movement likely had sprung up at this time because "the nation is battling for its life," and "the public mind," being "unsettled and inflamed," is susceptible to "agitation." Wise appeals to his readers to be vigilant: "Who knows but that amid the distractions of the hour the hobby of changing the Constitution might be made a success?"*

The Constitution and Religious Belief

The subject of our caption, so often discussed in our columns, was handled so ably and impartially in the Methodist organ of Pittsburg, Pa., that we must lay it entirely before our readers. The leading points, it will be observed, are precisely like our own, and we republish them in proof of our assertion that the better class of Christian journals are reasonable on this point and contemplate no attack on civil and religious liberty, on the contrary they oppose every violation of rights granted by the constitution. Fanatics and fools think and act otherwise, but their influence reaches not very far.

Our contemporary says: The Convention that framed our National Constitution was composed of different religionists. The Catholic from Maryland, the Puritan from New England, the Episcopalian from Virginia, the Dutch Presbyterian from New York, and Lutheran from Pennsylvania, all assisted in laying this cornerstone of our national edifice. This explains why the great charter of our liberties is wholly unsectarian, since no single class of religionists in the Convention could command a majority of all its votes. To an attentive observer of human events it looks like a providence, which brought about this state of affairs, and launched the nation upon its separate and independent history without sectarian bias and partialism. But from the foundations of the Republic the Constitution has been regarded by some as a godless and infidel document. It has not escaped their anathemas; but they have been so inconsiderable in numbers as to be insufficient for any serious work of agitation in times of peace. The conviction of this has kept them comparatively quiet in former times. But affairs are now changed. The nation is battling for its life. The public mind is unsettled and inflamed. And who knows but that amid the distractions of the hour the hobby of changing the Constitution might be made a success? What if it does increase the public agitation; fomenting dissensions instead of harmony; and by its controversies adding to the perils of the Government. Who would dare to put the national life in a balance against an abstract, sectarian theory. And so it was proposed to take advantage of our national sorrows in order to foist upon the people the scheme of modifying this Constitution. There it is in a nutshell. The time was opportune for agitators.

The Constitution opposes a union of Church and State. It explicitly enjoins that "Congress shall make no law respecting an establishment of religion, or prohibit a free exercise thereof." While this language remains unchanged, the Church and State in America must remain separate. And, who can wish their union. Who would be willing to celebrate their nuptials, or stand sponsor for their good behavior if the bonds of matrimony were cemented? Does not the history of European nations sufficiently demonstrate the sad and desolating effects of such a union? Where has the Church been married to the State and prospered, standing as a light of the nations, moving heaven and earth in regeneration of society? But the idea of uniting Church and State is usually disclaimed by public agitators, who are proposing to amend the Constitution. They know well the repugnance of the mind to such a measure, and avoid providing its heavy opposition.—But the Constitution not only opposes a union of Church and State, it as much establishes the most perfect freedom in religious worship. Now if any religionists are oppressed by the Constitution; or if their religious liberties and immunities are in any just sense curtailed; then indeed should that great national document be amended. But who are so oppressed? In a national history of eighty-five years whose just religious privileges have been restricted or denied? Can the Constitution here be changed for the better? Shall the American people begin to impose restrictions upon the freedom of religious worship? Let him vote aye who will; the sense of the masses will array them, we trust, forever on the negative of the question, and in favor of the largest religious liberty compatible with the public safety.

The Constitution, however, does not once employ the name of God. This, it is thought by some, makes it an infidel document.—They want it to make "a recognition of God," or "a recognition of Christianity." Both these demands appear in the United Presbyterian of this week and since the editor of that paper admits that the Pittsburg agitators have erred in "attempting too much," it is to be presumed that his propositions embrace the most moderate views. Does the simple omission of God's name make an instrument of writing an anti-Christian or infidel document? The Book of Esther does not, we believe, mention the name of God. Is it an infidel document[?] Neither does the Song of Solomon. Is it too an infidel document? Would this justify a revision and amendment of the canon of Scripture? Yet if the reason is valid in one case, it is not less so in the other. But is this advocated amendment of the Constitution possible without restricting the religious freedom of some classes—without imposing restraints upon Jews and Deists? We believe these classes of men in error.—For long years we have taught this publicly and from place to place. But is that any reason why we should restrain their religious freedom and persecute them? Did Christ and the apostles so teach? And would persecution rectify their error and correct their faith? The answer of all history is in the negative. Error persecuted finds sympathy and spreads. It is idle to say that the advocated amendments of the Constitution can be ingrafted upon that instrument without restraining the liberties of any. And the American nation may well pause before it consents to abandon its present liberal policy for a history of persecution and bigotry.

But what do agitators want? Must God and Christianity be explicitly named in order to their substantial recognition? Can they not be recognized by advocating the principles they embody, and represent and teach? And does not the Constitution make this recognition of them? We do not grant what agitators fondly assume, that the Constitution makes no recognition of God and Christianity. It does recognize them. It teaches, as but few human documents ever taught, the principles that God and Christianity embody and underlie. An inspection of the Constitution will show this. And the history of the nation shows it as well. In 1776 the Continental Congress proclaimed a fast—the second ordered by the same authority. Congress then "Resolved, That it becomes the duty of these hitherto free and happy colonies, with true penitence of heart and most reverend devotion, *publicly to acknowledge the overruling providence of God*. Congress therefore earnestly recommends . . . a day of fasting, humiliation and prayer that we may, *by a sincere repentance and amendment of life, through the merit and mediation of Jesus Christ, obtain his pardon; and . . . that he would graciously bless our people, and grant that a spirit of incorruptible patriotism and pure and undefiled religion may universally prevail*." We but recently observed a national fast appointed by very similar language. It was requested by Congress and President Lincoln, in its appointment says: "*That it is the duty of nations, as well as men, to own their dependence on the overruling providence of God . . . and to recognize the sublime truth announced in the Sacred Scriptures, and proven by all history, that those nations only are blessed whose God is the Lord.*" And the President also expresses his sorrow that "we have become too self-sufficient to feel *the necessity of redeeming and preserving grace,*" thus recognizing the atonement in all its untold influences upon man. Has not the nation, without violating the Constitution, thus made public recognition of God, and Christ, and Christianity? What more can agitators want? Would they cast away the substance by grasping a mere shadow? But public agitators are perhaps a necessary evil. If the amendments proposed were granted, others still would be demanded. Restless spirits will always abound. Changes will never cease to be agitated. It will be safe, and pious, and godlike for the American people to conclude that our National Constitution shall never be changed till it is proven an oppressive and illiberal document. This no man can show.[23]

3. ISAAC LEESER CONDEMNS THE EFFORT TO "ENGRAFT CHRISTIANITY ON THE CONSTITUTION"

The Occident and American Jewish Advocate, *a monthly periodical edited by Isaac Leeser, published from 1843 through 1869, was dedicated to informing the Jewish public about issues that pertained to Jewish literature, religion, politics, and culture. In the following selection from the August 1863 issue, Leeser—like his counterpart, Isaac M. Wise—warned his readers about the movement to "Christianize" the Constitution. If the Constitution were to be thus amended, he wrote, all non-Protestant individuals (Catholics, Deists, Unitarians, and Quakers, as well as Jews) could be "crushed under the wheels of the new Juggernaut" and deprived of their civil rights on account of their religious opinions.*

A Ministerial Amendment to the Constitution

We would therefore now draw attention to the present effort to engraft Christianity on the Constitution, by which all who do not admit it as true, may ultimately be excluded from every participation in the government of the country. We trust indeed that the attempt, renewed ever so often, may prove futile, and as nugatory and insignificant as the two meetings in Allegheny and its twin city, Pittsburgh, have as yet proved. But we would warn all who are interested in the maintenance of the Constitution as it was made by the sages of the revolution, who stood a head and shoulder higher than the men of the present age, not to allow such views as now propounded to go abroad without watching closely the progress of things. As in other agitations, the party now small may become gradually the vast majority, and it requires no great stretch of the imagination to conceive the possibility of so powerful a combination of all the protestant sects, that Catholics, Jews, Unitarians, Deists, Quakers, and other dissenters may be crushed under the wheels of the new Juggernaut which is now in the process of erection. It is true that the interests of the various sectarians are apparently not easily reconciled; and that whenever power should be obtained, they may quarrel among themselves over the distribution of the spoils of victory. But this would be no satisfaction at all to those who would have suffered the loss of their political and religious equality; besides which, the re-obtaining of the precious treasure of equal rights would be opposed unanimously by the spoilers, notwithstanding the diversity of sentiment among themselves. Do we not see now the exemplication [sic] in Prussia, where the constitution declares that no citizen shall be deprived of any rights on account of religion, and still the claim of Israelites is constantly evaded by the arbitrary interpretation which ministers of all the various parties, as they obtain office, have contrived to put on the laws of the land? The people are with the Israelites by vast majorities; but the Christian State party understand after all how to avoid doing justice to a large, most intelligent, honorable, influential, and patriotic portion of the community. We do not say that it is *probable* that a similar result may be witnessed in the United States; we rather think, it will take a long while before it can occur, if ever; but we speak of a possibility of the evil developing itself with irresistible force at some day; and we therefore enter our protest now against it in its inception, that should it become a reality at the distant day, it may be known, that honest Israelites were very early cognizant of the conspiracy against human liberty, in the fullest sense of the word.

Now there is no question to our mind, that there are many zealous men, we might call them without offence fanatics in the maintenance of their opinions, who deem Christianity the only safe rule of governing in the State, and who will leave no effort untried to engraft it on the Constitution, from the conviction of the justice of its being done. But we think that the claim to a power of this kind must prove injurious; and hence we trust that all who feel that they may be injured thereby will carefully watch the coming events, and throw their influence in the scale of the opponents of the measure, even if no success should follow, to check the power of the assailants. In this country it is not likely that the Romish faction will obtain an overpowering influence for years to come. We have indeed nothing to expect from them, should they get the superiority; and we would warn Israelites not to be misled by the blandishments which they know so well how to offer, to *entrust their priests and nuns with the education of our children.* But at present they would be as much injured as we, should the religious element be engrafted on the constitution; for they would find it difficult to contend against a united protestant body. We may therefore expect that should the question grow into larger dimensions, we should not be left alone to contend for human rights, but find support no less from our ancient oppressors than from persons indifferent to all religion, not from love for Israelites and those who would be excluded under the new state of things, but from a sense of common danger.

Some readers may deem that we are alarmed without cause. Perhaps it is so. But there is no certainty, we repeat, that the danger is imaginary. It will not hurt us, at least, to be on our guard against surprise; and we have discharged a duty in simply recording, in order to warn the unwary, the second attempt to transfer the idea of the Christian state to American soil, the boast of which has hitherto been that here all men might worship God according to the dictates of their conscience, which right would surely be greatly circumscribed were the messiahship of the man of Nazareth engrafted on the fundamental law of the country. We could easily extend this article to much larger dimensions; we however forbear, content to let our readers form their own conclusions from premises as clear to them as they are to us, especially as their interest in the result cannot be inferior to ours. For it requires no long argument to demonstrate, that, if the agitators should succeed in rendering the *faith* of Christians a part of the supreme law of the country, every one who dissents from it might then by a parity of reasoning be justly deprived of having his portion in the benefits conferred by the Constitution; and thus persecution for opinions' sake would be the next legitimate and inevitable step.[24]

4. THE BOARD OF DELEGATES OF AMERICAN ISRAELITES OPPOSES A RELIGIOUS AMENDMENT

At its December 11, 1864, meeting, the leaders of the Board of Delegates of American Israelites resolved that action must be taken to oppose the movement that sought to Christianize the U.S. Constitution. The BODAI decided that if the National Convention to Secure the Religious Amendment of the Constitution presented a "Memorial" urging the U.S. Congress to adopt such an amendment, then it would prepare and submit a counter-memorial to Congress.

At a meeting of the Executive Committee of the Board of Delegates held on Wednesday, December 11th, 1864.

Present: Rev. I[saac] Leeser, VP in the Chair, Messrs. [Henry] Josephi, [Lawrence] Myers, [Abraham] Hart & [Ellis] Joseph.

The reading of minutes of last meeting was on motion dispensed with.

The Committee on Conference with the Presidents of City Congregations reported progress.

Accepted.

The Chairman stated the object of the meeting to be the taking of proper action with reference to the projected Constitutional amendment recognizing Christianity.

Moved Seconded That the Executive Committee will watch with care and solicitude the proceeding inaugurated at the recent Convention at Philadelphia, looking to an amendment of the U.S. Constitution recognizing Christianity that in the event of a memorial being presented to Congress praying for such Amendment, this Committee will cause a counter-memorial to be prepared & submitted to Congress, with the endorsement of friends of civil religious liberty of whatever denomination.

Carried

Moved & Seconded that Mr. Myers be added to the Committee on Conference with the Presidents of un-represented congregations.

Carried

Moved & Seconded that Mr. Hezekiah Kohn be chosen a member of the Executive Committee in place of Mr. Berlin.

Carried

Letter of Sir Moses Montefiore was received and ordered on file.

The Chairman brought to the attention of the Committee the project for a Jewish College which had been initiated at Philadelphia & also the projects Free Schools at New York.

On motion, adjourned
M[yer] S. Isaacs,
Sec'y[25]

5. A "DESTRUCTIVE AMENDMENT": LEESER'S CONCERN INTENSIFIES

A year after the initial meeting of the National Convention to Secure the Religious Amendment of the Constitution, the movement appeared to be gaining momentum. The proponents met twice more in 1864, and news of their intentions continued to appear in the press.

In January 1865, Isaac Leeser wrote a blistering article in his journal, the Occident and American Jewish Advocate. *Leeser titled this essay "Rishuth,"*[26] *which he defined as "religious intolerance." He asserted that the movement in favor of changing the Constitution had been gaining momentum in large part due to widespread belief that God was so displeased by his having been excluded from the nation's founding documents that he was punishing the nation by prolonging the Civil War and its wanton bloodshed.*

Leeser "grieved" over the emotional enthusiasm of this movement. He insisted that those who advocated this plan—some of whom were his personal acquaintances—were likely "to destroy the liberty of conscience, and to burden the limbs of free America with the shackles which . . . enslaved Europe."

The following excerpt taken from the article's first section concludes with an exhortation to Jews to "defend the cause . . . of Israel" and refrain from thinking that "days of evil can not come in this land of freedom and in this enlightened century."

Rishuth

The day we are commencing this article happens to be the first day of Kislev, coinciding with the 30th of November, and we find in the papers of this morning (we wish to be particular regarding dates and places in quality of a chronicler for future reference,) that a convention of friends for certain proposed amendments to the Constitution of the United States assembled yesterday, November 29, at the West Arch street Presbyterian church. We introduce the subject under a name which is no doubt new to many American Israelites, although sufficiently well known, and alas! too bitterly experienced and remembered by natives of Europe, Asia and Africa, and means, in its general acceptation, the bigoted spirit of intolerance on account of religion displayed by those having different faiths towards the descendants of Abraham. The liberalists of Europe have been in the habit of looking towards America, and with full justice, as the land of free development of the human mind, where the question of belief placed no bar of enmity or exclusion between the various inhabitants, upon all of whom the same sun of equality was shedding his beneficent rays. The Constitution which guarantied this equality still exists on paper; but we grieve to record that there are men, even among our own personal Christian acquaintances, now at work to destroy the liberty of conscience, and to burden the limbs of *free* America with the shackles which the once *enslaved* Europe is fast casting away, guided by the higher development of the human intellect, which acknowledges no arbiter of faith except the Creator, who is great enough and wise enough to punish all offences against his majesty, without invoking the puny aid of fallible mortals. It is humiliating to behold men of influence, and of more than average mortal powers, acting as pioneers in the work of digging the grave of religious liberty and social equality; but it is after all a return to the first principles of the dominant religion on this continent, "that who is not for us is against us," and we are neither surprised nor terrified at this daring attempt to make Protestantism do in America what Romanism has failed to accomplish in the Old World, to wit:—introduce a uniformity of belief, and afterwards of practice, in accordance with what may be deemed by the *conquering* party of the doctrines of Christianity. We use the italicised word with due deliberation; for until one sect, or at least a combination of sects, has made its exposition of Christianity the accepted views by the vast majority of the inhabitants of the country, no serious thought of any amendment to the Constitution can be thought of, and many years must elapse before this contingency will occur; since so many individuals and sects are interested in preserving their right to *free* thought, that the march of the exclusive policy must be more or less slow. At the same time we are free to confess that the success of the new movement is not impossible, nor even improbable. Four years ago it was merely a speck in the political horizon, when one of the numerous branches of the Presbyterian church, sitting at Allegheny city, Pennsylvania, first publicly broached the subject, and sent a memorial to Congress by the hands of Senator Sumner of Massachusetts, of which transaction we took notice in No. 43 of our eighteenth volume, which was issued weekly. But at this day those who sit in the council of the *exclusionists* are members of various evangelical sects, and a former governor of Pennsylvania, and at present director of the U.S. Mint, does not disdain the post of honor to preside over their deliberations. Four years were in olden days but a small portion of time. But at the present period events jostle each other so rapidly, that months suffice to do the work which formerly required years to mature, and it is therefore possible that the movement to Christianizing the Constitution may be speedily brought into Congress, say within a space of fourteen months, with some chance of being favorably received, if the ruling party should choose to consider it compatible with its interests to have the matter there agitated. We will honestly state our impression that the executive himself entertains no opinions in common with the present convention; on the contrary we think ourself justified in supposing that he is liberal in religious matters; but it is still possible on the other hand, that his supporters may not wait for his consent, or rather bring the subject up in Congress for debate against his wishes. We would not hazard a long peep into the arcana of the future as to the result,—we might perchance be deceived; but we do not venture on debatable ground in asserting that religious intolerance, *Rishuth* proper, is increasing in this country on the one hand, while rank infidelity, including the spiritual manifestation madness, is extending with equal rapidity on the other. The present civil war, which has developed the capacity for hateful passions in the people in both sections to an alarming extent, has cast a veil over the beneficent light of sober reason, and the effect on the moral future of the country does not promise to be what a philanthropist might desire, though here too, the calculations of the timid may fail and disappoint him agreeably by an emerging of the republic unscathed from the fiery trial. But there can be no question that the war has a powerful tendency to harmonize the gloomy spirits who regard themselves in every age as the chosen instruments of Providence, and called upon to purge the earth from those evils which they esteem as the cause of the pouring forth of the divine wrath which afflicts the land. It is possible also that the influence of such men over the masses may increase with the augmentation of the sorrows and poverty incident to such a contest, as is now waged in America, which is gradually extending its blighting hand into the family circle of every cottage and palace, so that but few houses will be discoverable, in which some member has not been stricken down, or which has not to mourn the absence of some beloved relative who languishes in prison or hospital; since it is easily conceivable that the gloom felt by the leaders of the people will be transmitted to others not before impressible by serious reflection. Let it be also considered that the Christian sects count their followers by the millions and their churches by the thousands; and that almost daily the ministers have thus the opportunity to come before large audiences in town and country, and expatiate on the sinfulness of the land, which they may aver, as has no doubt been done in the convention in this city, is the absence of the Christian element in the Constitution. Is it not then likely that the people at large, under the state of mental depression which must extend itself gradually, notwithstanding that so many butterflies of fashion whirl along in the mazes of extravagance while hovering on the brink of a volcano, may gradually yield to the united onslaught which will unquestionably be made under the impulse now given by the ministerial phalanx, and demand the amendment to the Constitution, which is all that is needed (so will the agitators say) to reconcile God to the land, and grant it peace, as some may sincerely wish, or the extermination of, or at least a crushing victory over their enemies, as the vast many other desire? The leaders will say, that the Lord is not with the armies of the republic, because the Constitution does not recognise His existence in so many words; that the *mediator*, whom they believe in, has not thought proper to intercede for them, because his name does not head the civil compact under which the people united to form a government, and that no prosperity can be hoped for by armies and fleets, until the sacred Scriptures are made the nominal basis of legislation,—we say nominal, for we have no idea that the agitators honestly mean to be governed by the Ten Commandments even, not to mention the whole "Book of the Law of the Lord," which they declare in their presumption as abrogated and worn out. The people who have no other ideas propounded, who will see nothing in print to counteract them, who are blindly attached to the lead of their teachers, will naturally give their assent to propositions so plausibly laid before them, and to which they are naturally inclined by their early training and all their surroundings. Let it be farther recollected that the representatives in the state and Union legislatures are elected by the kind of constituencies just referred to, that is those under the leadership of the agitating clergy who are perhaps hypocritically, yet actively, engaged in urging the destruction of one of the vital principles of the federal compact, and that such delegates are very apt to share the prejudices of their electors, or at least profess to do so, in order to gain the proper influence, offices and emoluments incident to power: and you have a well-grounded probability that an attempt will be made in Congress, with or without the assent of the chief executive, to engraft Trinitarian Christianity on the Constitution, as an atonement to God for past neglect of the supposed duty.

We have said, that we do not apprehend that the attempted treason will soon succeed; still there is no question but that the number of conspirators will increase every year, as long as the causes which have fostered the rise of the agitation will be operative; and no man is wise enough to fix a period when they will cease. For even if the war should suddenly terminate now, the elements are too much excited to be speedily calmed down, and the stimulus, which has set the springs in motion, will continue to act, though the apparent motive should exist no longer. If we edited a political magazine, we might branch off into details; but religion and its interests are all that we have a legitimate right to handle: we must discuss the subject, and confine ourself to the religious development before us.—In this respect we would call the attention of our readers to a duty which rests upon them, to watch the course of events carefully and cautiously, not to rush into violent excitements on account of the conspiracy which is slowly unrolled before them; but to contribute by their silent, yet energetic action through the ballot, and by pen and speech, to rebuke the sacrilegious attack which ambitious sectarians even now aim at the Constitution, which has protected for nearly eighty years, with a common aegis, the religious liberty of all the inhabitants of the land, so that even the bondmen in the South had freedom of worship, although their bodies were subjected to masters, and their labor exerted for those who claimed them as their own. It is however useless for them to argue with the agitators; they are perfectly aware of their own iniquity; many, we are sure, do not believe in the efficacy of their acts to propitiate the favor of God, as they only labor for an end exceedingly worldly, and this is power. But the whole community is not yet mad; and it is wise therefore to unite with the calm and considerate of all persuasions and modes of thinking, to avert the evil threatening all who differ from the agitators. All however, who love liberty for its own sake, should exert themselves without delay; for possibly the time of trial will come, unless some new direction should be given speedily to public opinion, and divert it from the contemplated movement. We must also be prepared, notwithstanding all honest opposition to the iniquity, to see the *destructive amendment* incorporated into the Constitution, and to find ourselves thus aliens in a land where we had hoped for permanent freedom and equality. But should this be the result of our deceived hopes, we trust that the ancient energy of Israel will show itself again as capable as of old to rise above the trials of the hour, and to glorify the name of the Lord amidst the seclusion of our own firesides, though our lot be again that of humbleness and oppression. In the meantime, while waiting for the full development of the painful drama which it is possible we may have to witness, let all Israelites endeavor to demean themselves so as to give their opponents no cause to charge them with any acts unbecoming their holy ancestry, and to call into being institutions which will dignify their name, and be an honor to their religion, and see to it that they train representative men who will be able to seize the pen in the hour of need and to utter the living word, when occasion calls on us to defend the cause and fair fame of Israel. Much can be done by us if we only will employ earnestly and properly, as well as promptly, the means at our command, and let no one think that it is time enough hereafter to work. Now is the acceptable time, even while our opponents attempt to forge new chains wherewith to bind our conscience,—now let us work, while as yet no restrictions have been contrived to lame our efforts, and let no one in his fancied security think that the days of evil can not come in this land of freedom and in this enlightened century. What has been can be again, and crimes formerly committed are possible again even now. Perhaps there is a providence in all this to wake us out of our lethargy that we may cling closer to God than to worldly things; if so, let us bless the tempest that will purify the atmosphere of our supineness, and kiss reverently the rod that is lifted up to chastise us for our salvation.

6. THE BOARD OF DELEGATES OF AMERICAN ISRAELITES DEFENDS THE FRAMERS OF THE CONSTITUTION

As promised, the BODAI quickly submitted a "counter-memorial" in response to the one Congress received from the proponents of the Christian amendment. The BODAI's "Memorial," dated January 30, 1865, challenged the wisdom of the amendment desired by a "conference of ministers and laymen of various denominations." The memorial points out that the Christian faith is in need of no such bolstering from the Constitution, and it insists that the revolutionary patriots who framed the Constitution deliberately intended to "establish a perfect equality for all modes of belief."

To the Honorable the Senate and House of Representatives of the United States of America in Congress assembled:

The Executive Committee of the Board of Delegates of the American Israelites respectfully show, that your memorialists are a permanent executive committee from a conference representing about forty congregations of Israelites in various parts of the United States, and have been appointed to watch over all occurrences which may interest the Israelites in their social, religious and political concerns. As such your memorialists approach your honorable bodies at this juncture, to protest energetically against the amendments to the preamble of the Constitution of the United States as prayed for in the memorial of the Presbytery of Cincinnati, dated September 20th, 1864, and signed by A. J. Reynolds and twenty-one others, and against any changes in the various articles of the Constitution, to make them agree with the amendments as suggested by a conference of ministers and laymen of various denominations held at Philadelphia, on the 29th and 30th of November, 1864, and which, no doubt, have been or will be presented to Congress at this or the next session.

Your memorialists take this early opportunity to offer their protest, fearing that an entire silence on their part might embolden the persons who seek to deprive them of their *inalienable* rights which they have hitherto enjoyed under the Constitution, as it was made by the fathers of the Republic, to say, that the universal voice of the country demands the amendment to the Constitution, so as to introduce Christianity as the recognized religion of the land, and thus to prejudice the minds of your honorable bodies in favor to the changes, under the impression that no one would be injured by their adoption.

Your memorialists, too, represent many whose fathers and predecessors came to America to enjoy civil and religious liberty. Many of their fathers and friends fought in the war of the revolution, and aided to achieve the independence of the country in the contest the colonies waged against Great Britain. Others of those who profess our religion came to this land, called hither to participate in the religious freedom which they were told in their native countries was the common inheritance of all inhabitants of the Union, let their birthplace be what it may. Many had suffered exclusion from certain rights of man because of their religion, which they cherish as their dearest birthright; as it has been the harbinger of civilization, and has conferred the greatest blessings on the world in sacred books which compose the Bible, and which they have preserved amidst all the trials and banishments which have afflicted them. Your memorialists appeal to their history in this country and challenge comparison with the best of other persuasions as to their morality, frugality, honesty and industry. They contend that, notwithstanding many discouraging circumstances, many a bitter prejudice to which their name and descent have subjected them, they have contributed their full share, according to their numbers, to the prosperity and development of the country. They had trusted that here, where liberty was guaranteed to all by the charter which the people through their highly endowed delegates devised in 1787, they would be left in peace to pursue the course which Providence in His wisdom has marked out for them in history and revelation. But they observe with the deepest regret that they are threatened with a total withdrawal of their precious rights as citizens equal with any others, by introducing a Christian element in the Constitution. They recognize the full right of every man to worship God as his conscience impels him; they claim no right to denounce the Christian, Mahomedan or heathen, for not worshipping the God of Abraham, Isaac and Jacob, or not obeying the laws of Moses as they do. They protest, therefore, against any acts of their fellow citizens calculated to deprive them of their fullest right to pursue their own conscientious convictions.

The Convention which framed the Constitution was composed of men who surely had full faith in the Creator. Their history proves them not to have been without trust in God. Their not reciting their own creed or any creed in the preamble to the Constitution was owing solely, as your memorialists conceive, to their desire to establish a perfect equality for all modes of belief, leaving it to every one to choose for himself what persuasion he might desire to follow. Your memorialists honestly believe, that this omission of a creed has not been hurtful to Christianity, any more than Judaism. For while the people represented by your petitioners are still a very small minority, the Christian sects number hundreds of thousands, and the spire of a village church is seen near the public school in every vale, and near almost every mountain-top. Schools and colleges are everywhere erected, and the press urged by the energetic power of steam distributes Bibles, books, tracts and cards of Christian teaching, not alone over the entire country, but even in savage lands where the enthusiastic missionary endeavors to diffuse the religion which he professes. Your memorialists cannot believe that the land is cursed by God, because He has not been recognized in the Constitution, or else they would respectfully ask why have eighty years of prosperity blessed it on land and sea, in its basket and kneading trough, in the field and city, on going out and coming in? It is in vain to say, that the absence of a *national* creed renders this an atheistical nation; for the deeds of our people prove the contrary; but were it even otherwise, it would be akin to blasphemy to assert that the offended Deity should be appeased by mere words, which a dialectitian can twist to suit his own purposes, and not accept of works which are the true evidences of conviction.

If your memorialists could have the opportunity to appear in person before the proper committees of your honorable bodies, they have no doubt, but that they could offer you many reasons for withholding your assent to the petition from the Cincinnati Presbytery and other similar religious bodies; but they forbear at present, for fear of wearying you, from doing more than presenting their brief protest with a few reasons for it, in the firm hope that you may leave the work of the revolutionary heroes of America unchanged as regards the equality of all citizens of the land under the organic law, no matter what their religious persuasion may be, by not introducing any clause or clauses which could give to any one more prerogatives than others possess, or only permit some to reside here by the sufferance or toleration of others.

And your Memorialists will ever pray.[27]

6

"A Great Man in Israel Has Fallen": American Jewry Mourns Lincoln

On Saturday morning, April 15, 1865, as the American people awoke and began their day, the shocking news of the president's assassination began to spread. Throughout the nation, many Jews were making their way to their synagogues; the day was not only the Jewish Sabbath but also the fifth day of the joyous Passover festival. American Jews had conducted their Passover seders in their homes on the evenings of April 10 and 11, the preceding Monday and Tuesday. More Jews than usual would have planned to attend prayer services on this special Sabbath, which occurred during the eight-day long Passover holiday.[1] Indeed, many American Jews first learned their president had been murdered while they were walking to synagogue or shortly after they had arrived. Like their fellow citizens, they were overcome with grief and sorrow.

Writing only days after the assassination, Rabbi Isaac M. Wise tried to convey a sense of the all-encompassing sorrow that enveloped the streets of Cincinnati: "The old man wept—the old woman wept—the soldier, the statesman, the native and the foreigner—all, all wept. Friends, when grief is universal—when enemies join in the general lamentations—*a great man must have fallen*! And Lincoln was a great man."[2]

In an effort to console their forlorn congregants, American rabbis spontaneously addressed themselves to the shocking event. Some of these unrehearsed comments were captured by newspaper correspondents who published a summary of the extemporaneous remarks the following day. At San Francisco's Congregation Emanu-El, for example, the distressing news stunned Rabbi Elkan Cohn (1820–89) so profoundly that he literally burst into tears and became momentarily "senseless." Once he had pulled himself together, Cohn did his best to break the news to his congregation: "Beloved Brethren! . . . I am scarcely able to command my feelings, and to express before you the sad calamity that has befallen our beloved country. Who might believe it! Our revered President Abraham Lincoln, the twice anointed high priest in the sanctuary of our Republic, has fallen a bloody victim to treason and assassination, and is no more. . . . Oh, the beloved of our heart is fallen . . ."[3]

In New York, Rabbi Samuel Adler (1809–91) of Congregation Emanu-El "attempted to say a few words of consolation to his congregation, but was himself so much overcome with grief that, after an earnest, impressive prayer for the government and the nation, he was compelled to desist."[4]

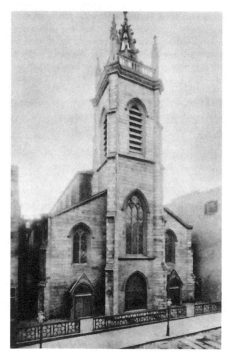

Temple Emanu-El on Twelfth Street in New York City, 1854–66. *Centenary Celebration of Congregation Emanu-El, 1845–1866* (New York: Comet Press, 1945). Courtesy The Jacob Rader Marcus Center of the American Jewish Archives, at the Hebrew Union College–Jewish Institute of Religion, Cincinnati, Ohio.

Rabbi Max Lilienthal left a similarly vivid description of the effect the sad news had on the Jewish community of Cincinnati:

> Oh, on the fatal Saturday morning that brought us such gloomy tidings, when receiving our morning papers, we were only prepared to read the festivities of the nation, and to enjoy once more the jubilee of the past day. We hurried to the telegraphic dispatches—what letters are these? What do they mean? We were unwilling to trust our senses; we thought in the dizziness of yesterday's feast we had forgotten our letters, had unlearned our spelling; we could at first not realize the stern truth. But when we recovered from our first shock—when we became convinced of the terrible reality—then the heart of the nation stood still, breathless, lifeless, paralyzed! And when tears began to relieve our stupefaction, the lips were quivering and shivering with the heart-rending exclamation: O God, our good President has been assassinated![5]

In houses of worship throughout the nation, religious leaders eulogized Abraham Lincoln. An analysis of more than 300 sermons delivered by northern Protestant ministers sheds much light on the sentiments of sorrow and loss that shrouded Christian Americans across the Union in the wake of the assassination. In consoling their parishioners, Protestant ministers expressed a number of common themes. Almost all these church sermons addressed themselves to Lincoln's extraordinary character. Without exception, the ministers praised Lincoln as a heroic leader and an unusually fine human being. They reminded their people that, as the nation's chief magistrate during a grave period of crisis, Lincoln never lost sight of the country's most important values: an insoluble union, a government by the people, a commitment to the inalienable right of freedom for all human beings, and a faithful belief in God Almighty. He was, they preached, a truly honest, forthright, humble, intelligent, and moral human being.[6]

The fact that Lincoln was shot on Good Friday prompted many to compare the martyred president to Jesus Christ. Both pastors and politicians pondered whether Lincoln's death was the final expiation for the nation's sins. The Reverend Cephas Bennett Crane (1833–1917) of South Baptist Church of Hartford, Connecticut, told his people that "Jesus Christ died for the world [and] Abraham Lincoln died for his country." Ohio congressman James A. Garfield, a man who sixteen years later would become the second American president to be assassinated, famously remarked: "It may be almost impious to say it, but it does seem that Lincoln's death parallels that of the son of God."[7]

Like Christian clerics, American rabbis took to their pulpits to eulogize the slain leader. Some of these rabbinic eulogies appeared in local newspapers, and many others were subsequently published separately as monographs. Not surprisingly, Jewish preachers made no mention of Lincoln having died for the nation's sins. Yet many classified his death as a form of martyrdom, and a few rabbis actually referred to Lincoln as the nation's "messiah." The themes these Jewish preachers employed in eulogizing the fallen president had much in common with those used by non-Jewish religious leaders. Above all, they lauded Lincoln's accomplishments as a leader and heaped praise on him as a truly fine human being: "Who was Abraham Lincoln? The first labourer-President! Of his antecedents nothing could be said, but that he had risen by his own energies from the lowest sphere of life. He had battled with all kinds of personal difficulties, and had overcome them; he had struggled against all obstacles, and had conquered them; and by his sagacity, energy and unsophisticated honesty, had succeeded to be elected to fill the greatest office in the hands of the people."[8]

Lincoln, the rabbis resolutely eulogized, was more than a national "hero and patriot." They insisted that Lincoln belonged to the entire nation and was a "friend of the people, the poor and the slave." The fallen president had "a smile for everyone and everything, with the welcoming grasp and winning word." He was "stern to himself [but] lenient towards others." As if with one voice, the rabbis prophesied that Lincoln's name would be as "immortal as the truth of [his] teaching."[9]

In spite of the fact that one can find many commonplaces in the Lincoln eulogies preached by both Jewish and Christian clergy, one cannot help but notice that many of the Jewish obsequies gave voice to a new and significant idea that appeared nowhere in the Protestant funeral sermons. Inside the synagogues of America, the martyred president was also being lauded as a *Jewish* hero. In some instances, this notion was conveyed through the power of suggestion and literary metaphor. Yet some of these Jewish preachers unhesitatingly insisted that Abraham Lincoln was their spiritual kinsman. Rabbi Max Lilienthal expressed the sentiments of many Jews when, quoting directly from the book of Samuel, he stoutly proclaimed: "Indeed, a great man has fallen in Israel! . . . We revered him, we loved him, we regarded him as a man of superior destiny."[10]

Lincoln's responsiveness to the needs of American Jewry during the course of his presidency constituted the basis for the special esteem and affection he merited among Jewish mourners. The rabbis insisted that Lincoln's unswerving commitment to the American ideals of freedom and justice drove him to preserve and enhance the rights of Jews as American citizens. Rabbi Isaac Leeser of Philadelphia, who played an active role in many of the Jewish controversies that came to Lincoln's attention, was so shaken by the assassination that he found it difficult to preach. During the Passover seder that had occurred only a few days earlier, on April 9, 1865, Leeser became so emotionally overwrought when he heard that General Robert E. Lee had surrendered at Appomattox "that he had to stop the Service." Less than a week later, news of Lincoln's assassination upset him so profoundly he found it difficult to organize his thoughts, and he implored his congregation to forgive him for speaking in such a "disconnected manner." Overcome by grief and emotion, Leeser managed to point out that American Jews were particularly indebted to Lincoln because of his efforts to address the injustices of the chaplaincy controversy and General Orders No. 11. "These instances," Leeser declared, "speak loudly for the natural kindness of the late President, which all can cheerfully acknowledge, whatever their political opinions may be."[11]

Like Leeser, Rabbi Henry (Hayyim) Hochheimer (1818–1912) of the Oheb Israel Congregation in Baltimore also noted Lincoln's commitment to protecting and enlarging the rights of Jewish citizens. "More than all others, the 'house of Israel' has cause to mourn this great loss. . . . Need I cite individual cases?" Hochheimer asked rhetorically. Lincoln's unswerving determination to ensure that American Jews received just treatment under the Constitution testified to the fact that Lincoln was a man with no religious prejudice. For this reason, Hochheimer told them, Abraham Lincoln had served as American Jewry's "shield and protection" (*Schutz und Schirm*).[12]

Hochheimer was one of many rabbis who claimed that Lincoln's essential honesty and fair-minded spirit made it possible for him to relate to Jews without bias or ill will. Yet there were some Jewish preachers who insisted that Lincoln's interest in American Jewry was due to something more than his lack of religious prejudice, asserting that Lincoln was a kindred Jewish spirit. They maintained the fallen president had long evidenced a special affinity and respect for the Jewish people and went as far as to suggest that Lincoln was a friend to the Jews because, in many respects, he possessed a Jewish soul!

New York's Rabbi Morris J. Raphall (1798–1868), for example, told his congregation that when he and Lincoln first met, the fallen president treated him as a friend "because he knew [I] was a Jew . . . [and] a true servant of the Lord." Rabbi Benjamin Szold (1829–1902) of Baltimore had once visited Lincoln in the White House, and he spoke of this encounter frequently. The rabbi had accompanied an immigrant Jewish woman to the White House so she could beseech the President to pardon her son, who had been sentenced to death for desertion. The woman, overwrought by the thought of losing her son, became emotional and began pleading with the president in Yiddish. Obviously, Lincoln had no idea what she was saying, but, according to Szold, as he listened to the woman's unintelligible yet piteous appeal, tears began trickling down Lincoln's cheeks. Szold ended the story here, lauding Lincoln's compassion but failing to mention that the young soldier's life was not spared.[13] In his eulogy, Szold told his congregants that spiritually, philosophically, and ethically, Lincoln was a Jew:

> My friends, we should regard Abraham Lincoln, so loyally devoted to [freedom], as a son of Israel. And if many, from a political standpoint, assign him a place in history next to Washington, we, on the other hand, from a higher, from a humanistic standpoint, should place him next to our heroes of virtue and of truth, next to eminent figures of Israelite antiquity. And if, as some will have it, he was not flesh of our flesh or bone of our bone, he was indeed spirit of our spirit and soul of our soul. His spirit and his soul, his heart and mind, his innermost nature and disposition, his fervent enthusiasm for everything noble and lofty, his love for the Fatherland, for Freedom and humanity, everything about him and in him that manifested his nature, his thought and his feeling, down to his way of speaking and the method, all his own, of clarifying lofty ideas by means of analogies in order to make them understood—these were truly Israelitish, in the spirit of ancient Israel. Therefore, just as the old Israelite faith heroes are our eternal exemplars, let us also see in him a lofty and shining exemplar.[14]

Just before noon on Wednesday, April 19, 1865, the long obsequies for President Lincoln began at the White House. Around the country, people flocked to their own houses of worship to mark the occasion locally. At Chicago's Kehilath Anshe Ma'ariv, Rabbi Liebman Adler (1812–92) described Lincoln as a paragon of virtue that Jews should emulate "even though he was a non-Jew." Adler noted that "Lincoln remains for us a glowing example because of his strict honesty, his pure morals and unfeigned faith, his modesty and kindness of heart, and a patriotism aglow with the purest flame. Let us achieve in our modest lives and in a small way what he, in his high position, accomplished on the broadest scale."[15]

In Philadelphia, Rabbi Sabato Morais (1823–97) stood before the historic Mickve Israel Congregation and confessed a profound personal love for Lincoln: "I loved every action, every word of that godly man. I loved him for his patriarchal simplicity; I loved him for his incorruptible character; I loved him for his all-comprehensive ideas, for his generous impulses, his forbearing disposition, his tender compassion for all the oppressed." Then, in offering up a prayer for the president's departed soul, he asked God to "open the portals of eternal bliss" so that Lincoln, "the righteous Abraham of the Western World," could enter into paradise.[16]

David Einhorn (1809–79), a distinguished reformer and probably the nation's most outspoken rabbinic opponent to slavery, elevated Lincoln to an almost saintly status.

Congregation Bene Yeshurun of Cincinnati worshiped in this building on
Lodge Street from 1848 to 1866. Courtesy The Jacob Rader Marcus Center of the American
Jewish Archives, at the Hebrew Union College–Jewish Institute of Religion, Cincinnati, Ohio.

The "High Priest of Freedom" (*des Hohenpriesters der Freiheit*) had been murdered,
Einhorn lamented. Lincoln, he euphuistically proclaimed, was "his people's messiah"
(*Er war der Messias seines Volkes*). Einhorn literally described Lincoln's death as a
form of "*Kiddush Ha-Shem*"—a technical expression in Judaism that refers specifically
to the act of forfeiting one's life for a sacred cause. Just like the holy Jewish martyrs of
old, Einhorn told his listeners, Lincoln gave his life willingly for a sacred cause, and
therefore American Jewry should pay special homage to Lincoln, "who shielded also us
as Israelites and embraced us with a loving heart" (*der uns auch als Israeliten geschützt
und mit liebendem Herzen umschlossen*).[17]

In Cincinnati, Rabbi Isaac M. Wise delivered one of the most remarkable and often quoted of the eulogies. Like Einhorn, Wise—despite his earlier mixed feelings about the president—memorialized Lincoln as an American messiah. "Our very President," he declared, was "the chosen banner-bearer of our people, the Messiah of this country." Embedded in his eulogy, Wise offered up one of the most extraordinary assertions ever made about Lincoln by a Jewish preacher. Not only was Lincoln spiritually aligned with the Jewish people, Wise told his congregation, but the fallen leader had actually told the rabbi he believed he was a descendant of the Jewish people.[18]

Many of the Jewish preachers compared Lincoln to one or another biblical hero. Einhorn observed that Lincoln was like Moses, who was not permitted to set foot in the Promised Land, though he had led the Israelites through a dangerous wilderness. Hochheimer compared Lincoln to his biblical namesake, Abraham, who pleaded with his nephew Lot for familial unity: "Let there be no strife between you and me, we are kinsmen, children of but one land, descendents of one tribe." David was Lincoln, Liebman Adler declared. He was a common shepherd, a man of the people, and a hero who toppled "the Goliath of the Revolution" (namely, the secessionists and rebels) with the smooth stones of "his plain folk morality" (*seine einfache Volks-Moral*).[19]

It is interesting to note that Jewish preachers eulogized Lincoln in cities like Baltimore and Louisville, where some citizens sympathized with the Confederates in spite of the fact that Maryland and Kentucky never seceded from the Union. Even though there may have been Confederate sympathizers in the congregation, Jewish preachers in these regions memorialized Lincoln lovingly. In Louisville, Lincoln was eulogized by Rabbi Bernhard H. Gotthelf (1819–78) of Adas Israel Congregation, who, in 1863, received a commission to serve as a military chaplain. Gotthelf's commission was Lincoln's second such Jewish appointment after Jacob Frankel.[20]

The eulogy that Lewis Naphtali Dembitz delivered to Louisville's Jewish congregation appeared the following day in the *Louisville Daily Journal*. Dembitz's extraordinary oration testified to the fact that Louisville's Jewish citizens not only supported Lincoln during his lifetime but actually referred to him as "Rabbi Abraham," even prior to his death.[21]

In contrast to cities like Baltimore and Louisville, where there may have been southern sympathizers, New Orleans actually belonged to the Confederacy until the Union army occupied that city in April 1862. The Union's first commanding officer, General Benjamin Butler, was thought by some to have cruelly subjugated the city, and consequently many local citizens harbored deep-seated animosity toward the North. Although relations between the occupying forces and the local citizens improved significantly once General Nathaniel P. Banks succeeded Butler, many New Orleanians remained loyal to the South until after the war ended. Interestingly, at least two Jewish orators eulogized Lincoln in New Orleans.

At the Temimi Derech synagogue, Lieutenant Colonel Philip J. Joachimsen, a Union military officer from New York who had been assigned to duty in New Orleans under General Butler, delivered an impassioned sermon that was subsequently published "on request of the congregation." In addition to eulogizing Lincoln, Joachimsen delivered a highly partisan address brimming with disdain for Confederates and the Confederacy. American Jews, he said, "had a distinct ground to love, respect, and esteem" Lincoln because he valiantly protected their civil liberties. According to Joachimsen, the fallen president harbored no bigotry toward Jewish people. Lincoln "appreciated those of our creed who had come forward to sustain him [for] his mind was not subject to the vulgar clamor against Jews."[22]

Another noteworthy Lincoln memorial was delivered by Rabbi Bernard Illowy (1814–71) of Congregation Shangarai Chasset (Shaarei Chesed), also in New Orleans. Although Illowy lived in New Orleans during the Civil War, he was never ideologically aligned with the southerners he served. To begin with, Illowy had been culturally oriented to the North; prior to his move to New Orleans, he held pulpits in New York, Philadelphia, Syracuse, and Baltimore, where he was serving when the Civil War began. Once in New Orleans, Illowy "demonstrated an unwillingness to veer too far from tradition" and found himself at loggerheads with the vociferous liberalizing faction of his congregation. He never adjusted to a city "where rabbis dared to declare oysters kosher for Jews." In fact, by the time of Lincoln's assassination, the congregation was aware of the fact that Illowy's contract had not been renewed.[23]

Since he was about to leave New Orleans anyway, Illowy was able to speak his mind without fear of reprisal by his southern congregants. He eulogized Lincoln as "the dearly beloved father of our country" and emphasized the spiritual connection between Lincoln and the Jews by addressing his listeners with the double entendre "sons of Abraham." The Jews, Illowy preached, were sons of the biblical Abraham as well as of the American Abraham, who "with paternal love and a brave and courageous heart . . . walk[ed] before [the] people, to save their honor, to guard their rights and to restore peace and harmony to their gates." Illowy also reminded his congregation that even though Lincoln conquered New Orleans, he had not subjugated his enemies or "trodden [them] down with rigor." It was Lincoln's desire to transform his enemies into friends, and he largely achieved this goal because so many of his former enemies "now bow down with deference and sincere repentance before our glorious banner of liberty and equality." In an attempt to convey the depth of feeling that Lincoln's memory evoked among so many people, Illowy predicted—only days after the assassination—that Lincoln would occupy a unique place of honor in the pantheon of American heroes.[24]

Finally, it is hard to overlook the prominent role that American Jews played in Lincoln's unprecedented funeral pageant. The New York Times described Lincoln's funeral as one of "the most impressive [spectacles] ever witnessed," and the paper took careful note of how actively the Jews mourned Lincoln. As Lincoln's elaborate funeral train slowly made its way from Washington to Springfield for the president's final burial, Jews all along the way gave vent to "the grief that sorrowed the hearts of the people." A young man named Abraham Abraham (1843–1911), who would later become the founder of the department chain Abraham & Straus, was so distraught by Lincoln's death that he purchased a bust of Lincoln, draped it in black, and displayed it in the window of his store. The editor of the Jewish Messenger took pains to underscore the sincerity with which the Jews in New York and in other cities mourned the president: "It is a singular fact that it was the Israelites' privilege here, as well as elsewhere, to be the first to offer in their places of worship, prayers for the repose of the soul of Mr. Lincoln."[25]

On Tuesday, May 2, 1865, Chicagoans assembled themselves in long lines and waited throughout the day to offer a final farewell to the fallen president. As they entered the chamber of the courthouse where the casket had been placed, they passed under a banner that read: "Illinois clasps to her bosom its slain but glorified son." Upon departing, they passed under another banner emblazoned with a quotation from the Hebrew Bible: "The beauty of Israel is slain upon the high places."[26]

In San Francisco, nearly 700 Jewish citizens participated in the communal funeral assembly that gathered to hear funeral orations and recite prayers on April 20, 1865. Similar displays of sorrow were documented in every Jewish community throughout California. In San Jose, members of the Hebrew Bikur Cholim Society (a group dedicated to visiting the sick) participated in the city's "Grand Funeral Pageant" after adopting a formal resolution wherein they resolved to mourn "the untimely death of our beloved president, as well in his official capacity as in the relation of friend and brother."[27]

In Boston, the Board of Temple Israel voted to decorate the sanctuary with "signs of mourning" and open the synagogue "for mourning services" on Wednesday, April 23. Significantly, the temple's board also decided that for the first month, "a prayer for the soul of the deceased president"—the Kaddish—would be recited on every Sabbath. Temple Israel was not unique in making this religious gesture; Jewish congregations all across the nation followed suit. Traditionally, Jewish mourners recite the Kaddish over their closest relatives—parents, children, siblings, and spouse. The fact that Jews across the land recited this prayer over a non-Jewish president lends powerful testimony to the depth of their affection for Abraham Lincoln.[28]

Two months after Lincoln's death, Rabbi Max Lilienthal of Cincinnati offered his own explanation as to why American Jewry mourned Lincoln so affectionately and piously: "Lincoln's name has become . . . a domestic altar, around which the nation meets with filial affection. No President, not even the father of our country, our immortal Washington, has taken so deep-rooted hold of the nation's sympathy, as plain and unassuming Lincoln did."[29]

DOCUMENTS

EULOGIES

1. "Twice Anointed High Priest in the Sanctuary of Our Republic"
2. "The Goodness of Heart He Displayed"
3. The Whole House of Israel Has Special Cause to Mourn
4. "I Loved Every Action, Every Word of That Godly Man"
5. He Was His People's Messiah
6. The "Dearly Beloved Father of Our Country" Is No More
7. "Bone from Our Bone and Flesh from Our Flesh"
8. You Called Him Rabbi Abraham

MOURNING RITES AND MEMORIAL PRAYERS

9. Minutes of Temple Israel of Boston, April 18, 1865
10. Resolutions to Mourn Lincoln
11. The *New York Times'* Account of the Day of Fasting and Humiliation
12. The *Jewish Record* Describes Lincoln's Funeral Procession

EULOGIES

1. "TWICE ANOINTED HIGH PRIEST IN THE SANCTUARY OF OUR REPUBLIC"

Rabbi Elkan Cohn's stirring and grief-ridden announcement to his congregation was made extemporaneously after he was informed of the assassination just prior to Shabbat morning services on April 15, 1865. A record of the rabbi's remarks appeared the following day in the pages of San Francisco's paper the Daily Alta California.

Abraham Lincoln

Just as the Rev. Elkan Cohn, of the Congregation Emmanuel [*sic*], on Broadway, was ascending his pulpit, on Saturday, to deliver the usual sermon, a copy of the dispatch announcing the assassination of President Lincoln was handed to him, and on reading the same, he was so overcome that, bursting into tears, he sank almost senseless. Recovering, in broken accents he announced the same to the congregation, and it fell upon their ears like a thunderbolt—the whole being moved to tears. The impression created was beyond description. Dr. Cohn made this very impressive and eloquent address on the character of the national calamity, of which the following is the substance, although it does not do justice to the learned Divine:

Beloved Brethren! Overpowered with grief and sorrow at the terrible news which just at this moment was communicated to me, I am scarcely able to command my feelings, and to express before you the sad calamity that has befallen our beloved country. Who might believe it! Our revered President Abraham

Lincoln, the twice anointed high priest in the sanctuary of our Republic, has fallen a bloody victim to treason and assassination, and is no more. He, who by the indomitable power of his energy, stood amidst us like a mighty giant, holding with his hands the tottering columns of our great commonwealth, and planting them secure upon the solid basis of general freedom and humanity; his great mind full of wisdom, his great heart full of love, his whole being, a true type of the American liberal character. Oh, the beloved of our heart is fallen, and is no more amongst the living. And with his soul departed also the soul and spirit of his council, the great statesman who inspired him with wisdom, and stood on his side with the giant intellect of his mind, William H. Seward. Under the burden of this terrible affliction, we can scarcely realize the truth of our bereavement; our feelings quail under the weight of a most intense grief, and we are more inclined to cry than to speak them out. Two great men have fallen. Arise, my brethren, and bow in humble devotion before God! Arise, and honor the memory of the blessed, whose life was a blessing to us, to our country, to the oppressed and afflicted, and to the human race at large. But though they are dead, their noble persons hushed in ethereal silence, their spirits live—live in thousands and millions of American hearts and souls, a sacred inheritance to them of their great dead—never to die out—never, never! The great principles they so nobly and fully represented are the very nerve and essence of our people, and as long as there is upon our soil a mind to think and a heart to feel, these principles will be defended and upheld with the last drop of blood. Glory in heaven will be the celestial reward of our beloved, whom we mourn as children mourn the loss of a father, and we pray to God to receive their souls in love and mercy, and be gracious to these His most faithful servants. Oh, they served God, in their love to man, the most glorious worship upon earth! And we pray that He, in His infinite love, may graciously avert the dreadful consequences of this calamity, calm the passions of the people, so justly aroused at this atrocious crime, soothe the grief and sorrow so deeply cutting in the very heart of our nation, and speak to the Angel of Destruction: "Enough! The noblest victims may be the last. Henceforth, the great work for which they bled stands under my divine protection. They have fulfilled their mission, they have restored the Union, they have rebuilt the great stronghold of humanity and freedom; I will now seal their work with the great blessing of peace!" O God! Thou who hast given victory to Thy people, may it please Thee to bless thy people with peace.[30]

2. "THE GOODNESS OF HEART HE DISPLAYED"

Isaac Leeser's eulogy, delivered to Congregation Beth-El Emeth in Philadelphia on April

15, 1865, powerfully conveys the shock and distress felt by so many upon hearing the report of Lincoln's death. The beginning and the conclusion of Leeser's sermon are included here.

Lincoln's Death

Since we assembled last, yesterday afternoon, in this house for worship of the Almighty God, a frightful and unlooked-for crime has startled the whole land. This morning, when I left my residence, the papers announced that a murderous assault had been made, late in the evening, on the President of the United States, but that at last accounts he was still living, though without hope of recovery; but since the commencement of the morning-service, the president of this congregation has communicated to me that death has closed the scene, and that Mr. Lincoln has been numbered with the dead. The man who was only yesterday, perhaps, the most powerful on earth, who had nearly closed with marked success a war of vast dimensions, which had raged full four years, has been suddenly struck, in the moment of his triumph, by the fatal bullet of the murderer, in the midst of a crowded assembly, by the side of his wife, and has been thus unconsciously hurried into eternity. A week had scarcely elapsed since he entered, as conquerer, the capital of his enemy, where he sat in the chair erst occupied by the chief of the opponents of the government of the Union, and he had returned in safety to the chief city of the country, and the seat of its central power; when the mighty ruler of the republic, to whom the people had confided the government for another term, who had anticipated so much that he had not yet accomplished, was stricken down unawares, unprepared, and now lies low, with none to fear him, with none to do him reverence. For all that will be done hereafter will not affect him; he rests from his toils in the arms of cold death. . . .

Respecting Mr. Lincoln's political career and character it does not become me to speak; politics is not the province into which a minister of religion should enter. You are all familiar with the history of the conflict in which the deceased was engaged as the President of the United States, and it would be useless to enlarge on it at the present moment. But I may fittingly speak of the traits of the goodness of heart he displayed and his sense of justice, of which I have become personally cognizant. I refer to the appointment of a chaplain to the hospitals in this city, about which I wrote to him more than two years ago, as it was deemed a hardship that Jewish soldiers, when sick and wounded, should not have the care and supervision of a minister of their own persuasion, as those of other creeds have. Mr. Lincoln promptly acknowledged the justice of the application, and soon thereafter appointed the Reverend Mr. Frankel to the office of hospital chaplain. And when the Senate of the United States had neglected to act on the nomination, by which means Mr. Frankel's office terminated with the adjournment of the Senate, Mr. Lincoln at once reappointed our worthy colleague as soon as his attention had been called to the case. He thus proved that he recognized in full our claims to an equality before the law, and that he was not guided by sectarian prejudices. So, also, when General Grant banished the Israelites from the military district over which he commanded, it was Mr. Lincoln who at once ordered him to revoke the unjust order, and restored our brothers to their homes and pursuits. These instances have severally come under my own observation, and they speak loudly for the natural kindness of the late President, which all can cheerfully acknowledge, whatever their political opinions may be; and let us hope that all in authority in America may be animated by the same spirit of justice and liberality.

But if we cast a scrutinizing view on the deplorable act of murder which has been committed on the chief magistrate of the republic, we shall discover in it an evidence of the fearful moral deterioration which the desolating civil war has produced. It appears as though the recklessness of strife had loosened the bonds of society, and that men have lost the appreciation of right and wrong. The rights of property have been in many cases not recognized with the nice distinction customary in the times of peace, and also personal security seems to have declined with the habitual scenes of violence which have devastated the land. Formerly the President of the republic needed no armed men to guard him from personal harm, the humblest could freely enter and speak with the head of the executive department, who dreaded no danger from any one. But now, notwithstanding the precaution taken to guard his life, Mr. Lincoln has fallen a victim to the pistol fired by the concealed murderer. O, it is terrible to contrast the two conditions of the republic, the one of safety to all, with the present, when secret danger threatens even those high in authority! It behooves us all to contribute our share to alter this state of things. Every man for himself should endeavour to review his moral character, and apply the corrective of the divine law to cleanse himself from evil, and to counteract the tendency to wrong-doing which is now so universally prevalent. We Israelites, too, have much to answer for; I acknowledge that we are not addicted to slaying a fellow-being, nor to the commission of deeds of violence against the property of others; but for all that, we have awfully transgressed, and swerved in many respects from the path of ancient conformity. We have, in many instances, set the laws of God at defiance, and done deeds which ought to call the mantle of shame over our countenance. Such things ought not to happen among faithful Israelites, who should be distinguished not more for their philanthropic action towards all men, than by a strict conformity to the divine precepts which they have received as the rule for shaping their life.

We can at the same time best promote the welfare of the republic by a close observance of all the moral restrictions which religion imposes on us, and by endeavouring, singly, to stem the torrent of moral delinquency which now is so generally prevalent. We have no separate interest from our fellow-citizens; their weal and their woe are ours likewise. Israelites should therefore labour to identify themselves with all the other inhabitants of the country, and prove the justice of their claims to an equality of rights, by cheerfully sharing all the burdens, and conforming faithfully to the laws enacted for the government of all. When evil befalls the land, let us also share in the grief which afflicts all others; but above all let us cultivate good-will and peace towards our fellow-men of all creeds.

You must excuse me for speaking somewhat in a disconnected manner, more so than is customary with me. The dreadful news and its suddenness have in a great measure overcome my usual composure, and my thoughts refuse to arrange themselves in their wonted order. The crime which has just been consummated is well calculated to appal[l] even the stoutest of hearts. In the midst of a great military success, the director of the national affairs is struck down in a moment; and with the removal of the controlling mind, dark clouds seem to lower over the future of the land. Who will guide safely the ship of state? Who will handle the government with a firm yet merciful hand? Will those who will be intrusted with the settlement of the difficulties, which meet our view everywhere, have the capacity to comprehend the duties which devolve on them, and to fulfill them for the benefit of all? Only by a firm reliance on Providence can they succeed, and not by trusting to their own strength and wisdom. Let us hope that they will choose the right path, and be the means of restoring peace and prosperity to the land so lately heaving under the tumult of civil strife.—As to ourselves, let me exhort you to reflect on the uncertainty of your life. You in general are not exposed to individual acts of violence, for the exalted are more threatened with danger than the humble; the storm will uproot the lofty and branching oak, and leave the lowly herb undisturbed, though torrents of rain have flooded the place where it grows. Still all have to meet their end, and they should be ever ready to obey the dread summons when it is issued by the Lord of our life. Prepare yourselves by obedience to the divine will, that you may be received in favour. And for him who has so untimely fallen, let us ask the divine mercy which we all need to purify us from iniquity: may his spirit be received amidst the blest, and repose in peace after its earthly toils. And as regards the people of the land, let them bow with submission to the evil that has befallen them, and let us all say in the sincerity of devotion: "The Lord gave, and the Lord hath taken; blessed be the name of the Lord!"[31]

3. THE WHOLE HOUSE OF ISRAEL HAS SPECIAL CAUSE TO MOURN

These three paragraphs are taken from the eulogy originally delivered in German by Rabbi Henry Hochheimer before his congregation, Oheb Israel, in Baltimore on April 19, 1865, the day that Lincoln's funeral ceremonies were held at the White House. Hochheimer's remarks emphasize the depth of Lincoln's commitment to freedom and justice and his special kinship to the Jewish people.

Predigt [Sermon]

Frohlockte er über den Fall seiner Gegner? Nein, meine Freunde. . . . Dem gefallenen Feinde reichte er die Hand, er sparte ihm jede Demütigung . . . und, *ein anderer Abraham*, rief er ihm zu: אחים אנחנו אל נא תהי מריבה ביני ובינך כי אנשים "Lass doch keinen Streit mehr sein zwischen mir und dir, wir sind ja Brüder, Kinder eines Landes, Sprossen eines Stammes."[32] . . . Und diesen Mann haben wir verloren . . . als er nach vierjährigen Mühen und Kämpfen seinen Lande einen ehrenvollen Frieden sichern wollte. Ach, nur aus der Ferne war es ihm gegönnt, das Land der Verheißung zu erblicken, betreten sollte er es nicht.

[Did he gloat over the fall of his enemies? No, my friends. He stretched out his hand to his vanquished foe, sparing him humiliation . . . and, like another Abraham, he called out to him: "Let there be no strife between you and me, we are kinsmen, children of but one land, descendants of one tribe."[33] . . . And this man we have lost . . . at a time when, after four years of battles and travail, he wanted to secure for his country an honorable peace. Alas, he was granted to see the Promised Land from afar, he was not to enter it.][34]

Wie jene beiden Priester, Nadab und Abihu, unmittelbar nach ihrer Priesterweihe dahingerafft wurden, so wurde auch er, der als Hohepriester dieses Landes die Urim und Tumim, den Schild des Lichtes und der Gerechtigkeit auf seinem Herzen trug, kurz nach seinem Weihetag dahingerafft. Und es war kein אש זרה kein "fremdes, unheiliges Feuer," das er in das Heiligtum, welches die Nation ihm zum zweitenmale anvertraut, gebracht, nein, es war echtes, heiliges Feuer, das auf dem Altar seines Herzens loderte, das Feuer der Begeisterung für die Freiheit seines Landes, seines Volkes. . . .

Darum "sollen eure Brüder, das ganze Haus Israel, beweinen den Brand, den der Ewige angezündet." Ja, כל בית ישראל "*das ganze Haus Israel*," mehr als alle anderen hat das "Haus Israel" Ursache, diesen großen Verlust zu beklagen; denn in dem Kranz der Tugenden, die Abraham Lincolns Haupt schmückten, war seine Vorurteilslosigkeit in religiösen Angelegenheiten keine der geringsten; sie war so manchem der Unseren—brauch' ich euch erst die einzelnen Fälle aufzuzählen?—Schutz und Schirm.

[As those two priests, Nadab and Abihu, were taken immediately after they were ordained as priests, so was he, who as high priest of this land bore the Urim and Thummim, the shield of light and of justice on his heart, taken from us shortly after his inauguration. And it was not a "strange, unholy fire"[35] that he brought into the sanctum he was entrusted with by the nation for the second time; no, it was an authentic, holy fire ablaze on the altar of his heart, the fire of enthusiasm for the freedom of his country, of his people. . . .

Therefore, "your kinsmen, the whole house of Israel, shall bewail the burning that the Lord has wrought."[36] Yes, *the whole house of Israel*. More than all others, the "house of Israel" has cause to mourn this great loss, because in the wreath of virtues that adorns Lincoln's head, his lack of prejudice in religious matters was not one of the least. For some of us—need I cite individual cases?—it was shield and protection.][37]

4. "I LOVED EVERY ACTION, EVERY WORD OF THAT GODLY MAN"

Profound grief pervades the entirety of this moving sermon by Rabbi Sabato Morais, which he delivered before Congregation Mickve Israel in Philadelphia on April 19, 1865. It is particularly interesting to note that in eulogizing Lincoln, Morais asserted that "many knew not his worth." With rare candor, the rabbi reminds us that prior to Lincoln's death and subsequent apotheosis, Lincoln was bitterly criticized as an "ambitious" politician with a "despotic sway." According to Morais, Lincoln's abilities were underappreciated while Lincoln lived—many "could not see that beneath the crust of apparent dross lay whatsoever is inestimable and precious." The rabbi urged his people to be forgiving and to reunite the nation, thereby paying homage to Lincoln's character as well as to the cause that consumed his life.

The Death of Abraham Lincoln

> Let the priests, the ministers of the Lord, weep
> between the porch and the altar, and let them say,
> "O Eternal God! have mercy upon thy people."
>
> Joel 2:17

The stillness of the grave reigns abroad. Where is the joyous throng that enlivened this city of loyalty? Seek it now, my friends, in the shrines of holiness. There, it lies prostrate; there, it tearfully bemoans an irretrievable loss, Oh! tell it not in the country of the Gauls; publish it not in the streets of Albion, lest the children of iniquity rejoice, lest the sons of Belial triumph. For the heart which abhorred wickedness has ceased to throb; the hand which had stemmed a flood of unrighteousness, is withered in death. How appalling is the change which one week has wrought! The anniversary of the redemption from Egyptian bondage had opened most auspiciously to Israel of America. When your voice, O fellow believers, was attuned to my psalmodical invocation, every fibre in my being thrilled with delightful emotions. For on the eve of the memorable fifteenth of Nissan the arm of the Lord had also been revealed to this people of his love. By its might was the surging tide of adversity driven back. Its Divine strength upraised the standard of universal freedom here unfolded by the purest hands. Grateful to our ears sounded then the roar of cannons which announced the winning of a bloodless victory. We shared not the intemperate zeal of such who laid against our General-in-Chief the charge of excessive leniency. We, with the nation at large, admired the magnanimous hero, and weaved garlands for his noble brow. Praying and longing for the reign of peace, we hailed the messenger of happy tidings advancing towards us with rapid strides. Thus did our attachment to the ancestral faith and to this dear country of our adoption, obtain for us festive enjoyment during four days of our Passover. The fifth day arrived, and with it the Sabbath sanctified to the Creator of the world.

Brethren! If the pulsations of my heart could assume human speech, they would best picture my mental agony upon that never-to-be-forgotten Sabbath. I had never concealed before my love for him who was chosen from among the lowly as a ruler over a great people. Yes, I loved every action, every word of that godly man. I loved him for his patriarchal simplicity; I loved him for his incorruptible character; I loved him for his all-comprehensive ideas, for his generous impulses, his forbearing disposition, his tender compassion for all the oppressed. The ideal of Truth imprinted by nature upon my soul, seemed at length realized in that man of homely mien, but of lofty mind. Alas! that many knew not his worth, and misapprehended his deeds! They called him ambitious; but his ambition was to redeem a pledge he had solemnly taken. They imputed to him a despotic sway; but he exercised power to vindicate the law of the living God. They could not see that beneath the crust of apparent dross lay whatsoever is inestimable and precious. But he who grappled with falsehood, and saved America from ignominious death, needs not my defense. He who removed the burden from every shoulder, and wiped off the mark of degradation from human visage, is far above the encomium offered by one so humble as he who speaks on this melancholy occasion. Verily, my friends, did I possess the eloquence of our lamented Everett,[38] I could not extol in adequate terms a man who knew so admirably to temper justice with mercy, and who, while practicing humility in the highest degree, was so scrupulously chary of the national honor.

But wherefore shall I portray the feelings which pervade my breast, when they are reflected on almost every countenance? The intense grief which I experience is now, alas! our common participation. From each dwelling, from each hovel, throughout the length and breadth of our Union, is a silent tribute of reverence offered to the righteous memory of our martyred President. As my vision rests upon these sable draperies of woe, unbidden tears streak down my cheeks, and with the priests, the ministers of the Lord, I weep between the porch and the altar, and say: "O eternal God! have mercy upon thy people." We all weep for the great and good man that has ruthlessly been torn away from us. The vile agent of a relentless foe, he does not weep. The execrable wretch who has robbed liberty of its staunchest defender, and nature of its noblest creation, he triumphs over his flagitious crime. But the avenging sword is at his heels. It shall never return to its scabbard until it has consumed, with the assassin, his accessories and abettors. "There is no darkness, no shadow of death where the workers of iniquity may hide themselves."[39] The mournful nation shall be avenged; they shall behold the dastardly hand which spilled innocent blood, severed from its venomous body.

But whence shall they derive consolation in their sad bereavement? So long accustomed to identify the lamented President of the United States with the principles he represented; to look for the restoration of peace to his conciliatory and merciful measures, where shall they hopefully turn for the realization of his ardent desires; for the consummation of our happiness?

My friends! It has pleased the Lord sorely to afflict us. But His benign countenance shines yet refulgently upon our holy cause. With almost every vibration of the telegraph wires, He seeks to gladden us with the tidings of fresh victories. Our distress for the irreparable loss sustained, shuts out from our bosom all joyful emotions. Yet, let us be mindful of God's mercies; let us improve them by a grateful demeanor. Confidently relying upon the Director of human events, let us strengthen the hands of the man, who, through a sorrowful incident, has been raised to the highest office in the republic. It is just that our minds cling fast to his immortal predecessor; him we had learned to trust, and upon him we gazed with filial affection. But "the Rock whose all works are perfect,"[40] demands that we submit to His unsearchable will. Let, then, the memory of the upright statesman and ruler be enshrined in the innermost recesses of our soul. But let not the structure which he has founded, remain incomplete for the lack of support. If his paternal voice could reach us from the seat of beatitude, it would exhort us to suffer further privations, to endure hardships, to bear even a temporary defeat, but never to pause until the flag of one reunited people shall wave from Maine to California, from the St. Lawrence to the Gulf of Mexico; for in that event not only our happiness and that of our children is involved, but the cause of human liberty is deeply concerned. If our great Abraham could address us now, he would also beseech us to curb the noble wrath which his murder has aroused within us, lest it may be visited upon the guiltless and the penitent. He would, in his merciful nature, entreat that we prefer magnanimity to severity, forgiveness to vengeance. He would likewise heal our lacerated hearts by the assurance that his mission upon earth was fulfilled, on the day that the supremacy of the Constitution was reasserted, and unspotted hands planted again over the ruins of Fort Sumter the banner which is the symbol of independence and freedom, of justice and humanity. Oh, may his kindly words ever re-echo in our hearts, and incite us to godliness and truth.[41]

5. HE WAS HIS PEOPLE'S MESSIAH

These selections from Rabbi David Einhorn's "Trauer-Rede" (Mourning Sermon), originally delivered in German at Congregation Keneseth Israel in Philadelphia on April 19,

1865, communicate the depth of the loss the Jewish community felt it had suffered and compare Lincoln to an array of biblical figures such as Joseph, Moses, and Elisha. It was Einhorn, one of the nation's most prominent liberal rabbis and a fierce opponent of American slavery, who praised Lincoln as "his people's messiah" (Er war der Messias seines Volkes) whose death, he declared, was comparable to the Jewish concept of holy martyrdom: Kiddush Ha-Shem.

Trauer-Rede [Mourning Sermon]

Nein! Noch ist die Zeit des Trostes nicht gekommen; noch ist die Wunde zu frisch, um vernarben zu können. Haltet Euren Schmerz nicht zurück und lasset Euren Tränen vollen Lauf über den ungeheuren Verlust, den wir erlitten! Lehren ja schon unsere Alten: Man möge niemanden zu trösten versuchen, so lange noch die Leiche des Geliebten vor seinen Augen sich befindet![42]

[No, the time for consolation has not yet arrived; the wound is still too fresh to heal! Do not hold back your grief and let your tears run freely over the tremendous loss which we suffered! Our sages already taught: Do not comfort the bereaved as long as the corpse of his loved one lies before him.][43]

. . . hier ruht Amerikas Stolz und Zierde, er, der—wie Moses—sein Volk durch eine lange öde Wüste bis an die Schwelle Kanaans führte, ohne dieses betreten zu dürfen!

[. . . here rests America's pride and ornament, one who—like Moses—led his people through a long, bleak desert to the border of Canaan, and was not allowed to enter it.]

[Lincoln's death seen as a death of the righteous, according to rabbinic thinking]

Es liegt tiefer Sinn in dem rabbinischen Spruch: der Tod der Gerechten sühne die Sünden ihres Zeitalters.

[There is a profound meaning in the rabbinic saying: The death of the righteous procures atonement for the sins of the age.][44]

Laß, o Gott, seinen Geist auf seinen Nachfolger übergehen, wie einst den Geist des im Sturm entrückten Elias auf Elischah, dass er sein großes Werk glücklich vollende . . .

[O Lord, may his spirit pass on to his successor so that his great work may be happily completed, as was the spirit of Elijah who was gathered into a whirlwind, and whose spirit passed on to Elisha . . .]

Wenn Abraham Lincoln einen Fehler hatte, so war's seine übermäßige Milde gegen die Rebellen, er, den die Demagogen und der Mörder einen Tyrannen schalten! Moses Sünde bestand darin, dass er den Felsen schlug, um Wasser zu geben dem lechzenden Volke, während Gott ihm befohlen, zum Felsen zu reden. Bei Abraham Lincoln verhält sich's umgekehrt. Er glaubte den felsenharten Nacken der Aufrührer durch freundliches Zureden und sanftmütiges

Behandeln zu beugen, uns das Labsal des Friedens zu spenden, während dieser Nacken nur durch Schläge . . . gebeugt werden kann.

[If Abraham Lincoln had one flaw, it was his excessive leniency towards the rebels: he whom the demagogues and the murderer decried as a tyrant! The sin of Moses was to have struck the rock to give water to the thirsting people, whereas God had told him to speak to the rock. The reverse holds true for Abraham Lincoln who believed that, by speaking to the rebels kindly and by treating them gently, he could bend their rock-hard neck in order to bring us the blessing of peace, whereas this neck can be made to yield only with use of force.]

Als Israel aus Ägypten zog, da trug es als entflammendes Siegespanier vor sich her die Bahre mit den Gebeinen Josefs, jenes Gerechten, der unter allen Stürmen nimmer abwich von dem Pfade Gottes . . . und noch in der Todesstunde mit unerschütterlicher Zuversicht die einstige Erlösung seines Stammes verkündete, und sinnig heißt es im Midrasch: "Das Meer, welches Israel trockenen Fußes durchschritt, es wich zurück vor dieser Bahre, vor dieser heiligen Asche, dem Nationalkleinode." Und so wird auch das Meer der Vergänglichkeit nimmer verschlingen können das Andenken an Abraham Lincoln!

[When Israel left Egypt, it was preceded, as by a fiery victory banner, by the coffin containing the remains of Joseph, that righteous man, who, throughout all storms, never veered from God's path . . . and who, even at the hour of his death, proclaimed with unshakable confidence the ultimate redemption of his tribe. The Midrash comments meaningfully: "The sea, which Israel crossed on dry land, parted before this coffin, before the sacred ashes, the national treasure."[45] Similarly, the sea of transitoriness will never succeed in washing away the memory of Abraham Lincoln!]

[Lincoln likened to a Jewish martyr]

Das mosaische Gesetz gebietet: Es solle, wenn die Leiche eines Erschlagenen gefunden wird, ohne dass man des Mörders habhaft werden kann, ein Opfer dargebracht werden, weil die staatliche Gemeinschaft vor der Entdeckung des Mörders sich befleckt fühlt und der Sühne bedarf. Wir befinden uns in demselben Falle, und die Tränen derer zu trocknen, die ihr Blut für uns vergossen—das seien unsere Opfer! So wird denn jeder gern das Seine beitragen; denn es gilt קדוש השם [*Kiddush Ha-Shem*],[46] es gilt *ihn* zu ehren, der uns auch als Israeliten geschützt und mit liebendem Herzen umschlossen.

[Mosaic law requires that when the corpse of a murdered person is found, and the murderer could not be apprehended, a sacrifice be brought because the people feel impure and in need of atonement before the murderer is discovered. We find ourselves in the same situation, in that we need to dry the tears of those who shed their blood for us—let these be our sacrifices! Thus, everyone will gladly contribute his part, because it is a question of *Kiddush Ha-Shem* honoring martyrdom and honoring him who shielded also us as Israelites and embraced us with a loving heart.][47]

6. THE "DEARLY BELOVED FATHER OF OUR COUNTRY" IS NO MORE

Speaking from the pulpit of Shangarai Chasset in New Orleans, Rabbi Bernard Illowy's eulogy, given on April 23, 1865, is particularly remarkable because it was delivered to a congregation of southerners. Illowy was leaving New Orleans, so he spoke from his heart, expressing the enormous admiration he had for the late president. Lincoln was a father figure, the rabbi lamented, and he reminded his listeners that in this way they were all "sons of Abraham."

Abraham Lincoln

Text—II Sam. 3:32–38

And when King David heard that his friend Abner had been as-sassinated by the murderous hand of Joab, he wept at his grave and thus lamented: Must Abner die the death of the wicked?

Thy hands were not bound, nor thy feet put into fetters; as a man falleth before wicked men, so didst thou fall. And all the people wept again over him.

And when all the people came to cause David to eat meat while it was yet day, David sware, saying: So do God unto me, and more, also, if I taste bread or aught else till the sun be down.

And the King said unto his servant: Know ye not that there is a prince and a great man fallen this day in Israel.

My text which I just now read before you, will probably tell you that it must be a melancholy and sad occasion that impels me today to address you with a broken heart, a depressed mind, and an afflicted soul, which on any other occasion, however melancholy it might be, would be regarded as a violation of the sacred hilarity of the Lord's day. But I cannot restrain myself from uttering my feelings of a woe which will tear the hearts of millions at home and abroad, when hearing of the great calamity which befell our country. Sons of Abraham, you have all read the heartrending news which has thrown the whole nation into the deepest depth of sorrow and affliction. Sons of Abraham, you have heard of the most terrible event—that Abraham, the dearly beloved father of our country, is no more. The Great Ruler of the Universe pleased to call him home to the Father's house, and as once, to our patriarch, He said unto him Abram, get thee out of thy country, from thy kindred, from thy people, and go into a land which I will show thee[48]; Abram is gone as the Lord has commanded him to ascend the glorious throne which his hand has erected for his beloved ones, in a land of eternal bliss and perpetual happiness, where the righteous earns the fruits of his righteousness, where the sun never sets, where there is always day and never night. Oh, my friends, how gladly did we listen last Sabbath to the glorious news, to the happy and cheerful tidings which filled our hearts with joy, with overflowing pleasure, and with feelings of gratitude to our Heavenly Father for the gracious favors which He has bestowed upon us, through his faithful servant Abraham, whilst millions who were nearer to the place of calamity were weeping over the great loss of the best of men who ever lived on the American soil. Oh, how short are all earthly pleasures, shorter than a night's dream; they vanish away like a morning cloud; soon and sudden did the Lord convert our joy into sorrow, our tears of pleasure into the tears of deep affliction. Last Sabbath we all cheerfully exclaimed with the pious David, Thank ye the Lord, for He is good, His mercy endureth for ever, and today already we must lament with him, weep with him, and, like him when he mourned for his friend Abner, we must call, Mourn House of Israel; lift up thy clamorous voice House of Judah, for a prince, a great man has fallen today. Like David, when standing at the grave of his assassinated friend, we call after the departed father of our bereaved country, Abraham thy hands were never bound and thy feet were never put in chains. No, thy hands were never bound by the wiles of others, by the ties of flattery or by the galling manacles of fear; thou didst hear nothing but the wishes of thy people, thou didst fear none but God who alone was thy guide and trust, and who was with thee as He had promised on the night of terror, "Fear not, Abram, I am thy shield."[49] Thy hands were always active, always stretched forth to help, when and where thy help was needed. Thy feet were not put in chains, never restrained by selfishness, never checked by ambition, but with self-denial, with noble ardor, with paternal love and a brave and courageous heart didst thou walk before thy people, to save their honor, to guard their rights and to restore peace and harmony to their gates; and thou hast succeeded. Thou hast succeeded and hast achieved glorious victories over enemies whom thou hast not trodden down with rigor, but turned into friends, who now bow down with deference and sincere repentance before our glorious banner of liberty and equality.

Thou hast wound thyself lovingly around the hearts of millions with gentle ties, which even the destructive tooth of time can never loosen. Ages will roll upon ages, but thy memory will still live in the hearts of thy countrymen until the latest generations. Thou hast succeeded to see the full accomplishment of the last work of thy life and the total disappearance of the storm pregnant clouds which were thickly brooding over our country threatening it with ruin. Thou hast succeeded and hast seen before the sunset of thy life, the blissful fruits of the tree which thou hast planted and moistened with the precious blood of thy noble heart—thou wast permitted to see but not to enjoy them, and like unto the great Teacher of mankind, the Redeemer of Israel, did the Lord say unto thee, "Get thee up on this mountain; from there shalt thou see the land which I have given unto thy people, and when thou hast seen it, then shalt thou be gathered unto thy fathers who are gone before thee."[50]

Without any disloyalty to the worthy successor of Abraham Lincoln we may openly avow how deeply and bitterly we deplore his loss, how deeply it has affected us; and the intelligence so sudden and so unexpected, of his having been cut down like a stalk of corn, and fallen under the murderous hand of an infernal fiend, so staggered our belief that we could hardly realize the awful fact, had not the general lamentation confirmed the sad report, that the good and noble-minded father has been called hence by the King of Kings.

He is gone; he is no more; but his spirit will continue to live in the heart of his worthy successor, and his memory will for ever be a blessed one in the hearts of his countrymen, as in the pages of history, for with his name commences a new era in the history of the greatest and most powerful republic that ever existed on earth.

He is gone and is no more. Duly and well prepared he gave up his body to corruption, and his soul he rendered into the hand of the Father of all souls who had given it. His body lies now like once our father Jacob on a cold piece of ground, with a stone pillow under his head, sleeping the sweet sleep of the righteous, but the spirit has ascended the ladder of life on which God's ministering angels are ascending and descending.

And may the stone under his head make his grave, the sacred place where his weary bones rest, a holy temple, in which his latest successors may yet hear with awe and deference the voice of truth and justice, which arises from the grave of Abraham Lincoln, whose memory will forever be, amongst all of us a blessed one. Amen.[51]

7. "BONE FROM OUR BONE AND FLESH FROM OUR FLESH"

Rabbi Isaac M. Wise's "Funeral Address," delivered at the Lodge Street Temple in Cincinnati on April 19, 1865, is well known for its anecdotal assertion that Lincoln had actually admitted to Wise that he was of Jewish descent. But, beyond this piece of sensational information, it is interesting to read the words of a rabbi who had often criticized Lincoln. The erstwhile skeptical Wise praised the fallen president with love and affection. Like Rabbi David Einhorn, Wise also referred to Lincoln as "the Messiah of this country." The rabbi told his congregation that the fallen president had now become a member of the "'covenant of an everlasting priesthood' . . . immortal in his people."

Funeral Address

"And the Lord said unto Abram, Get thee out of thy country; and out of thy birth-place, and from thy father's house, unto the land that I will show thee.

And I will make of thee a great nation, and I will bless thee, and make thy name great; and thou shalt be a blessing. And I will bless those that bless thee, and him that curseth thee will I curse; and in thee shall all families of the earth be blessed. So Abram departed, as the Lord had spoken to him."[52]

Abraham Lincoln departed, as the Lord had spoken to him. Abraham Lincoln, whose biography is too well known to be repeated here, the President of the United States, from March 4, 1861, to the day of his assassination, April 14, 1865; the generous, genial and honest man, who stood at the head of our people in this unprecedented struggle for national existence and popular liberty; whose words and deeds speak alike and aloud of his unsophisticated mind, purity of heart, honesty of purpose, confidence in the great cause, and implicit faith in the justice of Providence, which inspired him to consistency, courage and self-denial; this Abraham Lincoln, who endeared himself to so many millions of hearts, and gained the admiration of other millions of people, both at home and abroad; whom the myriads of freedmen consider their savior, and tens of thousands esteem as high as George Washington, and feel as sincerely and affectionately attached to as Israel to her David, Rome to her Augustus, and France to her Napoleon I; this Abraham Lincoln, whose greatness was in his goodness, and whose might was in his unshaken faith, was assassinated. Blush, humanity!—he was assassinated. This is the lamentable fact which today bends so many stout hearts with sorrow and grief—speaks by the tears of countless myriads, and the dark clouds of mourning which envelop the great Republic. Hark! listen to the voice of grievous lamentation, of woeful complaint, filling the very air of this vast country. "The elders of the daughter of Zion sit upon the ground; they are silent; they have thrown dust upon their heads; they have girt themselves with sackcloth, the virgins of Jerusalem have brought down low their head to the ground. My eyes do fail with tears, my bowels are heated, my liver is poured upon the earth, because of the breach of the daughter of my people. How shall I cheer thee, to whom compare thee, O daughter of Jerusalem?—to what shall I liken thee, to console thee, O virgin daughter of Zion?—for great like the sea is thy breach, who can heal thee?"[53] Hark, listen to the doleful voice of woe, echoing from thousands of hearts: "Fallen is the crown of our head; woe to us, for we have sinned; therefore our heart is woe-stricken; therefore are our eyes dimmed."[54] This is the lamentable cause of our meeting today before God, to weep with the nation, to mourn with our country, to show the last honors to Abraham Lincoln.

Why? Wherefore must it be so? you ask. Silence, mortals! Upon your knees, sons of the dust! "And the Lord said unto Abram, get thee out of thy country, out of thy birthplace, and from thy father's house, unto the land that I will show thee. So Abram departed as the Lord had spoken to him." Who of the finite and perishable creatures will unravel the mysterious ways of infinite and everlasting Providence? The drop comprehends not the seas, the mote understands not the sun; man, whose life is like a passing shadow, can not penetrate the counsels of the eternal and allwise God. Worship with humiliation, look down with awe at the throne of glory, and proclaim anew the sacred words: "The Lord hath given, the Lord hath taken away, the name of the Lord be blessed."[55] We can only look in and about ourselves to find the proper answer to the question: How can we honor best the memory of Abraham Lincoln?

Repent your sins. "Return, Israel, to the Lord thy God, for thou hast stumbled in thine iniquity,"[56] this deplorable event cries, with a loud voice. God has punished us grievously. His mighty hand inflicted a deep and burning wound upon the heart of the nation, and He is just. "The Rock, his work is perfect, for all His ways are just. The God of truth and without iniquity, just and upright is He."[57] The Lord has revealed His powerful arm to remind us of our iniquity, and move us to repentance. Behold the man at whose command the mightiest armies of this world moved, and whose name is associated with the dearest affections of so many millions of men; the man upon whom the whole civilized world looked, and whom, to protect and shield, a great nation was ready, was destroyed by one mad villain. Must not this rouse us from our sinful lethargy to a consciousness of our weakness? All the power, wisdom, goodness and affection of man can not protect us when the Lord decrees to call us hence. Must not this rouse us from our sinful lethargy to a consciousness of our guilt? Abraham Lincoln was a good man; the millions testify, and history, with her impartial pencil will record it. Not in his sins, in ours, he died; "for before wickedness, the righteous is taken away." He is the sin-offering for our iniquities. His death cries aloud, "Repent, repent your sins."

Verily, we need not inquire deeply to find our sins, when we know that an assassin was born and raised in our midst; the assassin of Abraham Lincoln brooded over his diabolic schemes in the very capital of our country. Where shall we begin to speak of the enormity of our sins? Must we speak first of the precepts of revenge which poison so many hearts and pervert so many minds to consider murder and assassination a matter of honor—assassination for offensive words—murder in duels? Or must we mention first the barbarous habit of bearing concealed arms to hide cowardice under the garb of crime? Or must we speak of the mercenary passions, which know of no intrinsic value of either persons or duties, honor or pride, art or science; which weigh or measure all persons and things alike by the standard of the market? Or must we mention the frigid hypocrisy which seeks refuge on the cushioned pews of fashionable churches; the haughtiness of little creatures embellished in costly garments and beglittered with gems, or such other dust; the scorn to which religion is subjected, the smile of pity cast on old-fashioned virtue, or the numerous and costly means to silence the crying conscience? There is no necessity for mentioning either of them, which are the mere fountains of our national sins, when we may look at once upon the broad and mad streams, with their impetuous billows and thousand whirlpools. Remember the frauds which were committed on the nation when hundred thousands of her noblest sons rushed to arms and offered their lives in vindication of her holy cause. Remember the legion of traitors and spies who surrounded our armies and penetrated into the most secret recesses of our Government. Or if that is too vast, too much to be remembered at once, then remember, simply, that our very President, the chosen banner-bearer of our people, the Messiah of this country, was slain by the assassin's hand in the midst of his people; and we must cry with Cain, "Mine iniquity is greater than I can bear."[58]

Repentance is the great lesson which this deplorable event should teach us. Away with your idols of silver and your idols of gold; away with haughtiness, selfishness, delusion, deception and barbarism; prostrate yourselves with humble spirits and contrite hearts before God; confess and repent your sins; be healed of your diseases, distill the Balm of Gilead in the wounds of your conscience; cry for mercy and forgiveness to your God, then rise better men, better citizens, true children of the living God—and you have honored the memory of him who died in our national sins; you have erected a durable and grand monument to that martyr of liberty whose untimely departure we lament. Let him live in your virtues, resurrect in your patriotism; let him glow and shine in your aspirations, for the benefit of humanity, and the triumph of justice and liberty, of light over night, and right over might; and Abraham Lincoln lives as he wished to live—the benefactor of his people; and Abraham Lincoln departed as the Lord had spoken unto him that God might fulfill his divine promise: "And I will make of thee a great nation."[59] So let us do honor to the memory of the departed martyr of liberty.

Honor brethren, honor the deceased President of the United States, by securing to him a perpetual reign, and a dominion everlasting. How? The dead should reign, the deceased one have dominion everlasting? Yes, even so shall you do.

The photographer or lithographer, the painter or sculptor, can not eternize a man; he can not give you more of him than a faint delineation of the outside, shape and features, the most unimportant portion, the mere case of a person. Monuments, however lofty and extensive, crowded with inscriptions and symbols, tell very little, after all, of the man himself, to whose honor they may be erected. The passions, feelings, struggles, victories, motives and thoughts of a great mind, and each of them is a real fraction of his existence, are so innumerably manifold and change so often, that no artist can represent a considerable portion of them. This is the case especially with the deceased, Abraham Lincoln. The best representation of his figure will not tell posterity who he was. His outside appearance bore no resemblance even to his real nature. The most skillful philosopher will fail in describing the man who stood at the head of affairs during this gigantic struggle, his cares and troubles, his sleepless nights and days of anxiety, his thoughts and his schemes, his triumphs and mortifications, his hopes and fears, and ten thousand more sentiments, feelings and thoughts, which moved his mind in the stormy period of his Presidential term. He will be obliged to satisfy himself with the focus in which all these rays of the mind centers, with the actions of the deceased. Let these actions be our political creed, and Lincoln reigns perpetually; his is the "covenant of an everlasting priesthood,"[60] he is immortal in his people.

"I will restore the Union," he promised us, and twice he took the solemn oath to protect and enforce the Constitution of the United States. Let these two points be forever the beginning and end of our political creed. He gave liberty to an oppressed race, "And ye shall proclaim freedom to all the inhabitants of the land." Let us adhere to this great principle. All shall be free, all equal before the law. He was kind, charitable, and lenient towards the enemies of his country, longed and hoped for peace.—Let also these be cardinal points of our creed. Let us not be led astray by blind passions, hatred, a spirit of revenge; let us act entirely and conscientiously in the very spirit of the departed man, and we honor him. He reigns in death, and holds his dominion as though he were living still.

Let us carry into effect and perpetuate the great desires which heaved the breast of Abraham Lincoln; let us be one people, one, free, just and enlightened; let us be the chosen people to perpetuate and promulgate liberty and righteousness, the union and freedom of the human family; let us break asunder, wherever we can, the chains of the bondsman, the fetters of the slave, the iron rod of despotism, the oppressive yoke of tyranny; let us banish strife, discord, hatred, injustice, oppression from the domain of man, as far as our hands do reach, and we secure to Abraham Lincoln a perpetual reign and dominion everlasting; we set him the most durable monument in the hearts of the human family; then he is not dead, not removed even, from our midst, and will live forever. If his person was called from our midst, that we be guarded against the follies of apotheosis, which numerous admirers already approximated, to teach us again the great lesson, "Trust not in the noblest ones, in the son of man with whom there is no salvation,"[61] or as the prophet Isaiah expressed it, "Withdraw yourself from man, whose breath is in his nostrils; because, for what is he to be esteemed?"[62] If God permitted it that we learn the great lesson of the firmness and fitness of our Government, which is the people's Government, depending on no man or party; or to wake us to a sense of duty to our Government, to unite and fraternize us more in mourning and the common sympathy with the deceased President and his mourning family, the abused and ill-treated Secretary of State and his sons; if God has permitted the sudden removal of the person of Abraham Lincoln from our midst, for any or all of these reasons, or for reasons unknown to us, (but just and wise they certainly must be); his personality, his essence and substance, his mind, his soul, his principles, may forever remain with us and be our guiding stars. So we may secure to him a perpetual reign, and a dominion everlasting; for the ideas of union, justice, liberty, peace, kindness, charity, forbearance and goodness are everlasting, like God himself.

Murmur not against the justice and wisdom of Providence. God is just. Abraham Lincoln fought the battles for great ideas, and his enemies, of necessity, must be numerous and violent. He was a man, and where is the mortal one without his measure of faults and infirmities; with a great man, in a great period of time, they only become, with his virtues, more conspicuous. Every man has his mission, his destiny on earth; with men of eminent positions it only becomes more conspicuous. Whenever our mission is fulfilled God calls us hence. Abraham Lincoln fulfilled a great mission; he led the country through this glorious struggle to glorious victory, and bequeathed to us the ideas which, when fully developed and realized, not only will bring upon us the great blessing, "And I will make of thee a great nation," but will also fulfill that sacred and most glorious promise, "And in thee all families of the earth shall be blessed."[63] All families of the earth shall be blessed by freedom, as the chain of the negro was broken; by union, peace, justice, equality, charity and kindness. So Abraham Lincoln shall reign perpetually and have an everlasting dominion. Therefore, "Abram departed, as the Lord had spoken to him."[64]

Brethren, the lamented Abraham Lincoln believed himself to be bone from our bone and flesh from our flesh. He supposed himself to be a descendant of Hebrew parentage. He said so in my presence. And, indeed, he preserved numerous features of the Hebrew race, both in countenance and character.

He was a man of many noble virtues, which may be our heritage; and God may forgive him his sins, and accept his soul in grace among the righteous men of all nations, and the martyrs of every sacred cause. May the Lord send consolation to his bereft widow and children, and heal the burning wound of this country which his departure afflicted on her. Brethren, let us read the funeral service for the soul of departed Abraham Lincoln.[65]

8. YOU CALLED HIM RABBI ABRAHAM

Lewis Naphtali Dembitz, attorney and scholar, had been a Kentucky delegate to the Republican National Convention in 1860, where he had cast his support behind Abraham Lincoln. His strong loyalty for Lincoln made him a natural choice to deliver a eulogy for the president to the members of Adath Jeshurun Congregation on April 23, 1865. Dembitz—the uncle of the first Jew to serve as a justice on the U.S. Supreme Court, Louis Dembitz Brandeis—delivered one of the most eloquent of all the Jewish memorial addresses. From Dembitz, we learn that even while Lincoln was in the Executive Mansion, the Jews of Louisville referred to him as "Rabbi Abraham." Dembitz's moving eulogy, which appeared in the pages of the Louisville Daily Journal, *is reproduced in its entirety below.*

EULOGY ON PRESIDENT LINCOLN—On Wednesday, the 19th Instant, Mr. L. N. Dembitz, being called upon, addressed the congregation of the Green street Synagogue in this city, as follows:

MY FRIENDS: I speak to you on this occasion, not as a preacher—I am not a prophet, nor the son of a prophet—but I stand before you as the chief mourner, thinking, as I do, that, among this congregation, none thought oftener or more than I did of the great dead, whose fate we to-day lament. You often called him, jocosely, Rabbi Abraham, as if he was one of our nation—of the seed of Israel; but, in truth, you might have called him "Abraham, the child of our father Abraham." For, indeed, of all the Israelites throughout the United States, there was none who more thoroughly filled the ideal of what a true descendent of Abraham ought to be than Abraham Lincoln. And, if he was uncircumcised, we are told, "All the nations are uncircumcised in flesh, but all they of Israel are uncircumcised in heart."[66]

The whole duty of Israel was thus comprised in a short compass by the Psalmist King: "Who may go up on the mount of the Lord? Who can stand up in his holy place? He whose hands are clean, whose heart is pure, who did not call up my spirit for falsehood, and did not swear deceitfully."[67] Whose hands, whose heart was purer than his? Who among all our public men was more reverent and more truthful?

The prophet Micah thus comprises man's duty: "What does the Lord ask of thee but the doing of justice and loving kindness, and to walk humbly before thy God?"

Indeed, if the good and great Abraham Lincoln did not always do justice fully, it was only because he loved kindness too much. But who more than he walked humbly before his God? Did he not ascribe all his actions to that overruling Providence which pointed out to him the way he should go?

The prophet Habakuk, however, comprises what is needed for man's salvation in one requisition: "The just shall live in his faith."[68] It was Abraham Lincoln whose faith in the Almighty never wavered, who believed himself but an instrument in His hand, and who was ever ready to give Him honor.

But as mortal man sins, so he, too, did sin. Just as Saul, the first king of Israel, was imperfect in *not sufficiently hating* the Lord's enemies, as he could not say in David's words, *thy enemies I have hated*, and for this the kingdom was taken from him; so it may here have been in the providence of God that an instrument was needed to carry out the stern demands of heavenly justice, while Abraham Lincoln's great duty had been fulfilled.

And as I have compared him with Saul, let me remind you that the most beautiful lamentation over the dead preserved to us is that of David over Saul, and his son Jonathan, who fell together, battling against the Philistines, just as Abraham Lincoln and his sons, not, indeed, in the flesh, but his sons in the good cause, hundreds of thousands of them, and among them many a good Israelite, fell battling together but lately for truth and justice.

"The pleasant and beloved in their lives, even in their deaths, they were not parted; they were fleeter than eagles, stronger than lions."[69] And to this I might add what indeed is not found in the Scriptural lamentation, but in our weekly Sabbath prayer for the souls of the martyrs: "Fleeter than eagles and stronger than lions to do the will of their master, the purpose of their creator;" for we must indeed be no better than unbelievers, than the grossest atheists, not to see in this war the finger, the purpose of God, in obedience to which Abraham Lincoln, and the men who fought under him, laid down their lives.

Let me add from the same prayer: "May God remember them in kindness, with other just men of all ages, and may He avenge before our eyes the blood of his servants that has been spilt."[70]

And I pray myself:

"May my soul die the death of the righteous and may my hereafter be as His." Amen.[71]

MOURNING RITES AND MEMORIAL PRAYERS

American Jews not only eulogized Lincoln as a kindred soul but also, as the following documents illustrate, mourned him with Jewish rites and prayers. In his eulogy, Rabbi Isaac Leeser recited a familiar phrase from Job that is frequently recited at Jewish burials: "The Lord gave, and the Lord hath taken; blessed be the name of the Lord."[72]

We know that in some synagogues the traditional Jewish prayer for the soul's repose, the El Maleh Rahamim, was recited.[73] In memorializing Lincoln on June 1, 1865, Rabbi Jacques Judah Lyons (1813–77) of New York's Shearith Israel Congregation compared the fallen president to the "head of the family [who] has been taken away." As such, the congregation was entitled to pray for "the happiness of his soul." In an excerpt from his sermon, (ch. 7, doc. 1, below) we see that Lyons went on to explain why reciting the Jewish tradition's "prayer for the dead" over Abraham Lincoln would undoubtedly "find favor with an all-merciful God."[74]

9. MINUTES OF TEMPLE ISRAEL OF BOSTON, APRIL 18, 1865

Abraham Lincoln was most likely the first American president whose name was formally mentioned during the recitation of the traditional Jewish mourner's prayer, the Kaddish, in synagogues across the nation. According to the Jewish Messenger, *"at the conclusion of the worship service [that took place on the Sabbath of Passover, April 15, 1865] the whole congregation spontaneously arose and said the 'Kadisch.'" In describing the grief that enveloped the Jewish community of New York, the correspondent informed readers that "in all the synagogues [of New York] the prayer for the dead, the 'Kadisch,' was recited by the entire congregation present." The synagogues were all draped with black shrouds, the article continued, because Lincoln's death was a national calamity that was felt "by none more sincerely and profoundly . . . than the Israelites, who loved the lamented President for his good heart and his devotion to liberty.*[75]

On April 18, 1865, the Board of Temple Israel of Boston met and, according to the minutes, resolved to urge its members to close their businesses the following day out of respect for Lincoln's funeral. The congregation's leaders also decided that, for the coming thirty days of mourning, "a prayer for the soul of the deceased President" would be recited during Sabbath worship in the synagogue.

Mr. President opens the meeting and reports that he is considering it his duty to call this meeting on account of receiving the mournful news of the assassination of the President of the U.S.A. Abraham Lincoln. The whole country was grieved and we give expression of sorrow of the congregation in this general mourning.

By demand of the State and City authorities the April 19th was declared as the day of the funeral of the passed President, it was therefore decided that mourning services should be held in all Churches and Temples and that this day should be considered as the general participation in the mourning of the loss of the nation.

Decided to accede to the demand of the authorities. Wednesday 12:30 PM the Synagogue should be opened for the mourning services for the deceased. Mr. [Joseph] Shoninger[76] was requested to give a speech for this purpose and prayers in English language.

Decided to ask the Shamas to inform all members of the congregation of the above mentioned services and to invite them to take part in them.

Decided that the Synagogue should be decorated outside with signs of mourning for 30 days. Mr. Vice President and Davis Moos were elected as committee for doing this.

Decided that during these 30 days on each Sabbath a prayer for the soul of the deceased President should be said.

Decided that all members of the congregation should close their business establishments on the day of the funeral.

Finally decided above resolutions as well as a short extract of the sermon to be published in the Boston Journal & Herald and the charges to be paid by the congregation.

Meeting closed.

J[oseph] Shoninger[77]

10. RESOLUTIONS TO MOURN LINCOLN

Isaac Leeser published several interesting documents pertaining to the Jewish community's response to Lincoln's death in his paper, the Occident and American Jewish

Advocate. *First, Leeser provided a detailed description of the events in Congregation Beth-El Emeth in Philadelphia on the Sabbath when the horrifying news of Lincoln's assassination was announced to worshipers by the congregation's president, Alfred T. Jones. He simultaneously published the resolutions adopted by Congregation Mikvé Israel, also of Philadelphia, and the Executive Committee of the Board of Delegates of American Israelites. Both resolutions, reproduced here, testify that a grief-stricken Jewish community declared its corporate intention to mourn Lincoln both in their houses of worship and in the community at large.*

Events and Resolutions Published in the *Occident* and *American Jewish Advocate*

The congregation Mikvé Israel have sent us the following proceedings, which we insert as requested:

A Special Meeting of the Trustees of the Synagogue Mikvé Israel, Seventh Street, above Arch, was convened on the 16th instant, to take action in reference to the melancholy tidings announcing the untimely death of the Chief Magistrate of the Union, when the following preamble and resolutions were adopted:

Whereas, The President of the United States having fallen by the hands of a traitorous assassin on the night of the 14th instant; therefore,

Resolved, That this congregation, in common with the whole American nation, mourn the loss of Abraham Lincoln, one of its best and purest Presidents, who, like our own law-giver, Moses, brought a nation to the verge of the haven of peace, and, like him, not allowed to participate in its consummation.

Resolved, That this Synagogue be draped in mourning for the space of thirty days, and that these resolutions be published and entered on the records of the congregation.

On motion adjourned.

L. J. Leberman, Parnas.
A. Hart, Secretary pro tem.
Philadelphia, April 19th, 1865

Resolutions of the Board of Delegates of American Israelites, April 23, 1865

The Executive Committee of the Board of Delegates of American Israelites had a special meeting on Sunday, April 23, for the purpose of taking suitable action with reference to the death of President Lincoln. Mr. Henry Josephi occupied the chair, Mr. M[yer] S. Isaacs acted as Secretary.

The following resolutions were proposed and unanimously adopted:—

Whereas, the Israelites of the United States, in common with their fellow citizens and all mankind, sympathize most profoundly in the nation's grief and desolation at this season of mourning for the lamented President, Abraham Lincoln,

And whereas, it is meet and proper that the Executive Committee should, in behalf of the Board of Delegates of American Israelites and their constituents, record their sense of the nation's loss, and the universal sorrow; be it, therefore,

Resolved, That the national calamity that has befallen our country in the cruel assassination of the good, the amiable, the beloved President, Abraham Lincoln, finds us overwhelmed with sadness and amazement, and prompts us to lift up our hearts to Heaven in humble reliance upon the all-gracious and all-merciful Providence who alone can heal the nation's woe and console a bereaved and lamenting country in the painful affliction of the hour.

Resolved, That the memory of Abraham Lincoln shall be forever cherished as that of an upright man, a zealous and patriotic citizen, a wise and beneficent Chief Magistrate, who, entrusted with the administration of the nation's affairs at a season of unparalleled difficulty, during a long and terrible conflict with a gigantic rebellion, has left an imperishable monument to his virtue, his sagacity, his singleness of purpose in the universal homage paid by an afflicted people, the admiration and reverence of friends of human freedom and progress.

Resolved, That the Israelites of the United States are deeply sensible of the loss humanity has sustained in the painful death of the lamented President; that the trial strikes us with peculiar solemnity and significance at this momentous period of the nation's history when we behold so nigh the end of that unhallowed combination against the government, to the hastening of which consummation the good, the honest Abraham Lincoln contributed so largely, and with all the zeal, the sincerity and the prudence of his kind heart, his clear, practical judgment, his steadfast, unfaltering fidelity to the Union.

Resolved, That as a mark of reverence for his memory, this Executive Committee and all the members of the Board of Delegates now in the city will participate in the obsequies on Tuesday, and that the several Jewish congregations and societies of this city be invited to co-operate with this committee.[78]

11. THE *NEW YORK TIMES*' ACCOUNT OF THE DAY OF FASTING AND HUMILIATION

The New York Times *published a detailed account of the mourning observances that took place in New York City's synagogues on April 19 and 20, 1865. The correspondent recorded an array of fascinating details demonstrating that the entire Jewish community responded to Governor Reuben Fenton's proclamation calling on the citizens of the state to render the day of Lincoln's funeral in Washington D.C. (April 19, 1865), a day of "fasting and humiliation."*[79]

A Day of Fasting and Humiliation in New York, April 19–20, 1865

The Jewish Synagogues throughout the city were well attended yesterday. The American flag was half-masted and the banner itself often enshrouded with folds of crape; long festoons of black and white overhung the entrance-doors; the galleries were draped in black, and the huge tapers almost concealed beneath the somber cloths of mourning. As on Saturday last, when in all the city synagogues the prayers for the dead and dying were repeated by the minister and sorrow-stricken people, so, yesterday, were the buildings crowded with assemblages, whose earnest attention and fervent responses to the supplications of the officiating clergymen, gave evidence of the deep grief that bowed down the hearts of the congregation. As announced in the morning prayer, divine service was held at the various synagogues, appropriate discourses being delivered by the minister or lecturer, and the prayers for the dead and for the welfare and prosperity of the country fervently offered up.

The house of worship of the congregation Shearith Israel, located in West Nineteenth-street, was well filled by a most attentive assemblage. After the singing of some psalms by the choir, the officiating minister, Rev. J[aques] J[udah] Lyons, delivered a short but eloquent address, in which he frequently adverted to the qualities of the man and the unswerving loyalty and honesty of the statesman, whose loss they were thus suddenly called upon to mourn. The kaddisch, or prayer for the dead, was then offered up, and after the recitation of a special prayer for the recovery of Secretary Seward and the future prosperity of the country, the choir chaunted a few additional psalms and the deeply-impressed congregation dispersed.

At the synagogue of the congregation B'nai Jeshurun, situated in West Thirty-fourth-street, after the chaunting of several hymns by Rev. Mr. [Judah] Kramer, minister to the congregation, Rev. Dr. [Morris J.] Raphael [sic], lecturer, ascended the pulpit and delivered a very impressive discourse. After alluding to the mournful events which they had assembled to weep and sorrow over together, he adverted, with much feeling, to the remembrance of the personal acquaintance that had existed between Mr. Lincoln and himself. He reviewed the career of the late Chief Magistrate, expressing the firm conviction that he had been chosen, after four years of ill fate, to save the country from ruin. He spoke of the late President's political errors, and of the spontaneity with which he recognized them, heedless, however, of the perils with which he was constantly surrounded. The speaker, having referred in a feeling manner to the widows and orphans now abandoned to the protection of God, the father of the fatherless, referred to the President elect, in whose steadfastness and loyalty he placed, he said, the utmost confidence, doubting not but that he would punish rebellion and treason as the very exponents of all wickedness. The Rev. Dr. concluded by appealing for mercy to the God of nations, who had ever watched over the destinies of America and sent to us a Washington and a Lincoln, whose memories would remain enshrined in the hearts of the people, and offered up a fervent prayer for the repose of the President's soul and the future welfare and greatness of the country.

At the Broadway Synagogue, the ceremonies were inaugurated by the chaunting of a hymn and psalms by the assistant Minister, Rev. Mr. PHILLIPS. The Echol, or ark, wherein are deposited the scrolls of the law, was then thrown open and the officiating reader offered up the prayer for government, the minister to the congregation, Rev. S[amuel M.] ISAACS, terminating this portion of the service by a special prayer for the soul of the lamented President. After the return of the scrolls of the law to the Ark, Rev. Mr. ISAACS proceeded to deliver an eloquent discourse, taking his text from Genesis, chap. xv, v. 1: "Fear not, Abraham; I am thy shield. Thy reward shall be exceedingly great." At the conclusion of the minister's highly impressive remarks, which were listened to with decided attention, a final prayer and choral ended the ceremonies for the day.

At the minor synagogues, the solemnity of the occasion was celebrated in a becoming manner. German discourses were delivered at the Norfolk-street Synagogue, by Rev. Dr. [Leon] STERNBERGER; at the Poel-Tzedek, by Rev. Dr. [Jonas] BONDI; at the Temple Emanu-El, by Rev. Dr. [Samuel] ADLER, Mr. [Simon] NOOTS, at the Greene-street, and Mr. WALZ, at the Twenty-ninth-street houses of prayer, made remarks suited to the occasion. In a word, the Jewish community fully evidenced its deep appreciation of the loss the nation has sustained, and gave an additional proof of its unfeigned loyalty and devotion.

The neat little synagogue of the Congregation Sheary Berochole,[80] in East Ninth-street, was the scene of very impressive ceremonies. At noon, the building was filled to overflowing with a very respectable audience, mostly dressed in deep mourning, to participate in the services commemorative of the death of Mr. LINCOLN, arranged by the congregation. After reciting Psalms 1, 4, 5, 6, 7 and 10, the Kadish, or prayer for deceased persons, was said, and the Minchah Prayer intoned, at the close of which Rev. H. WASSERMAN delivered the funeral sermon. His text was from Isaiah 44, 7: "For a small moment I have forsaken thee, and all forsook thee." The tenor of his discourse was the necessity of trusting to the goodness of God, however mysterious his providences may seem. He exhorted all to imitate the honesty, charity and good will to all men which had distinguished the life and character of our deceased President. The Hebrew prayer for a deceased father was then said, coupled with an exhortation for the recovery of the Secretary of State and his son was then said, and after the recitation of five psalms, the congregation dispersed.[81]

12. THE *JEWISH RECORD* DESCRIBES LINCOLN'S FUNERAL PROCESSION

A final document, taken from the pages of the Jewish Record *of New York, offers us an interesting and detailed description of Lincoln's funeral procession in New York City and of the "hundreds of Jewish citizens" who participated in the pageant's Fourth Division. This article closes with an impassioned sermon and prayer, delivered by Rabbi Samuel M. Isaacs of New York's Temple Shaarey Tefila.*[82]

Abraham Lincoln's railroad funeral car, 1865. Courtesy Library of Congress Prints and Photographs Division, Washington, D.C.

Jewish Participation in the Lincoln Funeral Pageant, April 25, 1865, at Union Square, New York

With Oriental brightness and warmth did the sun shine down, on Tuesday last, upon crowded house-top and groaning balcony, haughty monument and unpretending dwelling, glorious banners, the emblems of victory, and trailing draperies, somber evidence of woe. Never before had the historian to chronicle so unaffected a display of universal sorrow, so grand a pageant testifying respect for a departed chief. Not in the old world could a monarch, with his unnumbered legion, command the payment of any such tribute of administration even to the memory of a fallen hero. Nor could the new world have beheld such an outpowering [sic] of its masses, had the object of popular recognition been a great conqueror or a great king. It was reserved for the people of this country, through the masses, its true and sole representative, to drop a tear in the yawning grave soon to be closed upon the mortal remains of the late President of the Republic. Everywhere the seemingly silent grief of the people had found utterance in a display of draperies of woe. Everywhere huge banners with bindings of dark crape, forming a strange contrast with the crimson and azure of the stripes and fields, tiny bannerets, with appropriate inscriptions, epitaph-like mottoes of *immortelles*, pendent festoons, golden eagles enshrouded, as it were, by the cloud of gloom, pillars as somber as those of the catafalco itself, badges of mourning, saddened faces and sorrowing hearts.

Artistic skill, the poetry of woe, the tenderness of women were alike brought into requisition to further demonstrate to the eye how solemn was the occasion.

The funeral was a grand pageant. Cavalry that had charged on many a battlefield, artillery-men that had planted their batteries and stared death full in the face, infantry that had shared the forced marches incident to the strategical combinations of war, benevolent and protective association having for object the assisting of the weak, the guarding of the helpless, the healing of mental and physical ills, all professions, all trades and social organizations were hand in hand testifying by their presence in the ranks to the respect they bore the deceased Chief Magistrate. It was a grand, an impressive scene; one which the youngest will remember to the last hour of life, with the recollection of the darkly-brilliant scene undimmed by the lapse of years.

The funeral pageant started from City Hall a few minutes before two o'clock, the military cortege forming the vanguard, followed by the representatives of the City, Country and State governments and of the United States Department. Then came the clergy, the press, the bar and several political organizations. The Fourth Division, in charge of General J. H. Hobart Ward, numbered in its ranks hundreds of Jewish citizens. Foremost of these came the FREEMASONS, in whose ranks were noticeable three organizations numbering none but Jewish members: the Adelphi Lodge, headed by P. M. W. Asheim; Mount Neboh Lodge, in charge of W. Bro. J. Sulzberger, and King Solomon Lodge, under the guidance of Bro. Koch. In direct advanced the INDEPENDENT ORDER OF RED MEN, in whose van there were borne three massive links of a chain, enshrouded with black crape, their banner being also draped in black. The order comprised some eighteen lodges, numbering in all about fifteen hundred members. In direct sequence marched the members of the INDEPENDENT ORDER OF B'NAI B'RITH represented by fifteen lodges and in charge of P. W. Frank, Esq., Grand Marshal, J. Ballin and N. Schainwald, Aids. Each lodge was preceded by its respective officers and all advanced in the following order: New York Lodge, No. 1; Zion, No. 2; Saran, No. 3; Hebron, No. 5; Lebanon, No. 9; Beer-Sheba, No. 11; Jordan, No. 15; Palestine, No. 18; Canaan, No. 29; Rhehoball,[83] No. 38; Arnon, No. 39; Isaiah, No. 41; Mordecai, No. 57; Hillel, No. 28; Tabor, No. 31. The order numbered in all twelve to fourteen hundred members. THE ORDER OF B'NAI ABRAHAM, was represented by Abraham Lodge No. 1, mustering about fifty members. THE ORDER OF B'NAI MOSCHE mustered some four hundred members who bore in front two magnificent banners, bearing the mottoes of the Order, with the brilliancy of the gilding and the brightness of the hue dimmed by the somber shroud that embraces the folds. THE I. O. FREE SONS OF ISRAEL numbered ten lodges under the command of the M. W. Grand Master Bro. Pettenger. In the ranks were the Constitution Grand Lodge; Noah Lodge, No. 1; Reuben, No. 3; Levy, No. 5; Arich, No. 6; Issachar, No. 7; Zebulon, No. 8; Dan, No. 9; Napthali, No. 10, and Gad, No. 11, turning out in all some nine hundred members. THE CHEBRA ANSHE EMUNO numbered about one hundred representatives, headed by Mr. M. Stark, who brought up the rear in the Jewish department of the Fourth Division. In the Seventh Division, the CERES UNION one hundred and twenty-five strong, presented a good appearance, wearing a badge of white satin ribbon, with a heavy black border, bearing the inscription: CERES—[with picture of an] URN—WE MOURN OUR LOSS.

THE NATIONAL GLEE CLUB, a combination of the Henry Clay Debating Society, the Webster Literary Association, made a creditable display, and brought up the rear of the procession, inasmuch as their co-religionists were participants in its grandeur. The dense mass marched onward and upward, the sad music ever and anon swelling in volume and dying away upon the spring breeze and, at length, the lower portions of the city resumed its wonted aspect, no vestiges left of the mighty throng that so recently had invaded every foot of tenable ground. AT UNION SQUARE at four o'clock precisely were assembled at the Nineteenth street Synagogue, delegates from a number of congregations and associations who, in charge of Benj. I. Hart, Esq., marshal, and M. S. Isaac, Esq., aid, marched to Union Square. In the ranks of this large deputation were representatives of the congregation B'nai Jeshurun, Shaary Tefila, Anshi Chesed, Rodef Sholem, B'nai Israel, Ahavas Chesed, Beth Israel Bikur Cholim, Poel Tsedek, Bikur Cholim u Kadisha, Aderath El, Mishkan Israel; of the Hebrew Benevolent Y.M.H.B. Fuel, Hebrew Free School, Hebrew Mutual Benefit, Mutual Benefit and Burial, Jerusalem and Purim associations; and deputies from the Orphan Asylum and Board of American Delegates.[84] In all, the representatives numbered about two hundred; they proceeded through Fifth Avenue to Fifteenth Street, thence to the Maison Doree. The meeting was just being called to order.

On the speakers' platform we noticed the Rev. Drs. [Morris] Raphall, [Jonas] Bondi; the Rev. Mr. [Judah] Kramer; Henry Josephi, Esq., President of the Board of American Delegates, B[enjamin] I. Hart, Esq. and several other co-religionists. After a prayer by the Rev. Dr. [Stephen H.] Tyng, an oration by the Hon. George Bancroft, the reading of the late President Lincoln's last inaugural address, the further reading of a psalm by the Rev. Mr. [William H.] Boole, and the offering up of a fervent prayer by the Rev. Dr. [Ebenezer P.] Rogers, the Rev. S[amuel] M. Isaacs stepped forward and prefaced his prayer to the throne of grace, by the following passage from the scriptures:

"Remember, O Lord, thy tender mercies and thy loving kindness; for they are eternal.[85] Grant us to be among those who die by thy hand, O Lord! those who die by old age, whose lot is eternal life; yea, who enjoy even here Thy hidden treasures. His soul shall dwell at ease, and his seed shall inherit the land.[86] Therefore we will not fear, though the earth be overturned and though the mountains be hurled in the midst of the seas.[87]

"He redeemeth thy life from destruction; He crowneth thee with [loving] kindness and tender mercies.[88] Wherefore doth living [man] complain, he who can master sins?[89] Small and great are there; and the servant is free from his master.[90] For He remembered that they were but flesh; a wind that passeth away and cometh not again.[91] All flesh shall perish together, and man shall return unto dust—who rejoice even to exultation and are glad when they find a grave.[92]

"And such a frail mortal, shall be more just than God? Shall man be more pure than his maker?[93] In God I will praise His Word; in the Lord, I will praise His word.[94] Man is like to vanity; his days are as a shadow of thing that passeth away.[95] Be kind, O Lord, unto those that are good, and unto them that are upright in their hearts.[96] Let the pious exult in glory; let them sing aloud upon their couches.[97] Then shall Thy light break forth as in the morning, and Thy health shall spring forth speedily, and Thy righteousness shall precede Thee; the glory of the Lord shall be thy reward.[98] The Lord shall preserve thee from all evil. He shall preserve thy soul.[99]

"Behold, the keeper of Israel doth neither slumber nor sleep.[100] The Eternal killeth and maketh alive; He bringeth down to the grave and bringeth up.[101] Wilt Thou not turn and revive us, that we may rejoice in Thee?[102] Let us, therefore, trust in the Lord; for with the Lord there is mercy, and with Him is plenteous redemption.[103]

"One generation passeth away and another generation cometh; but the earth abideth forever.[104] For the word of the Lord is upright, and all his works are done in faithfulness.[105] The dust shall return to the earth as it was, and the spirit shall return unto God who gave it.[106] His seed shall be mighty upon earth: the generation of the upright shall be blessed.[107] The Lord gave, and the Lord hath taken away. Blessed be the name of the Lord.[108]

"And as for him, righteousness shall precede him and form steps for his way.

"Ye are blessed of the Eternal, who made heaven and earth."[109]

The reverend gentleman then delivered the following impressive prayer:

"Thou, whose attributes are omnipotence, Thy eye unseen, sees, Thy direction unknown, guides; Thy mercy unbounded, upholds; our God, our Father. From hearts penetrated by grief, we pray; oppressed by the weight of our feelings, bruised in spirit, we most earnestly implore Thee, visit us not in Thine anger, nor chastise us according to our works. Enter not into judgment with us, look not to our iniquities. As frail, erring creatures, in faltering accents we confess our guilt. Who can be justified before Thy immaculate purity? In humble and reverential awe, we approach Thee, invoking Thee to inspire us with a proper spirit and temper of hearts and mind under the powers of Thy providence. God of Abraham, of Isaac, and of Jacob, millions of beings Thy will has created this day fall prostrate at Thy throne, offering the overflowing of their hearts and their resignation to Thy will, as the homage of their adoration. The inhabitants of this land are overburdened with grief. The good being who, like Aaron of old, 'stood between the living and the dead,'[110] so that the war which decimated the land might cease. Alas! he is no more. Thy servant, Abraham Lincoln, has, without a warning, been summoned before Thy august presence. He has served the people of his afflicted land faithfully, zealously, honestly, and, we would fain hope, in accordance with Thy supreme will. O heavenly abode of bliss; that Thy angels of mercy may be commissioned to convey his soul to the spot reserved for martyred saints; that the suddenness with which one of the worst beings deprived him of life may atone for any errors which he may have committed. Almighty God! Every heart is pierced with anguish—every countenance furrowed with grief, at our separation from one we revered and loved. We beseech Thee, in this period of our sorrow and despondency, to sooth our pains and calm our griefs; and, as in days of old, before the sun of Eli went down, Thou didst cause that of Samuel to beam upon Israel, so it may be thy divine will, as the sun of our deeply lamented Abraham Lincoln had scarcely set, and darkness covered the people, that the sun of Andrew Johnson, which has burst upon the gloom, may shed its brilliant rays as sparkling it is borne amid purity and innocence. Our Father, who art in Heaven, show us this kindness, so that our tears may cease to depict our sorrow and give peace to the joyful hope that, through Thy goodness, peace and concord may supersede war and dissension, and our beloved Union, restored to its former tranquility, may be enabled to carry out Thy wish for the benefit and the happiness of humanity. We pray Thee do this; if not for our sake, for the sake of our little ones unsullied by sin, who lisp Thy holy name, with hands uplifted, with the importunity of spotless hearts, they re-echo our supplication. Let the past be the end of our sorrow, the future the harbinger of peace and salvation to all who seek Thee in truth. Amen."[111]

7

Conflicting Obligations: Shavuot and the National Day of Humiliation and Mourning

On April 21, 1865, a nine-car funeral train, draped in the black habiliments of mourning, began a 1,700-mile trip that would carry Abraham Lincoln's remains from Washington, D.C., to the site of his final resting place at Oak Ridge Cemetery in Springfield, Illinois. American clerics, politicians, and communal leaders continued to deliver eulogies and tributes to Lincoln, especially in major cities where the public would be given an opportunity to view the president's body and mark the occasion with a funeral pageant.[1] Even as the funeral train was winding its way across the Old Northwest, a decision was made to schedule a special day of reflection that would help the nation bring the intense mourning period to a close. On April 25, President Andrew Johnson proclaimed that on Thursday, May 25, the citizens of the United States would commemorate a "day of humiliation and mourning." He urged them "to assemble in their respective places of worship, . . . [and] to unite in solemn service to Almighty God, . . . [and to meditate on Lincoln's] memory."[2]

Unfortunately, the day President Johnson and his advisors had selected as the national day of mourning—Thursday, May 25, 1865—coincided with Ascension Day, a day of rejoicing that formally concluded the Easter season. Evidently, the conflict was promptly brought to the administration's attention, and four days later Johnson issued a second proclamation wherein he corrected the faux pas by rescheduling the day of mourning to June 1, 1865. The new date undoubtedly pleased Ascension Day observers, but in changing the date to June 1, Johnson unknowingly created an upsetting dilemma for many American Jews because June 1 corresponded to the second day of the Shavuot festival.

On Shavuot, as on all major Jewish festivals, Jews are commanded to rejoice— mourning and grief are strictly forbidden. American Jews recognized that, in some sense, they were caught on the horns of a dilemma; they wanted to express their allegiance to the nation and their reverence for Lincoln, as well as to properly observe the traditions of their faith. How could American Jews participate in a national colloquium of mourning for their beloved Lincoln and concomitantly participate in a Jewish holy day that literally commanded them to celebrate with "gladness and rejoicing"?[3]

In taking note of this circumstance, the editor of the *Jewish Messenger* expressed his impatience with the Christian clerics who complained about the original scheduling conflict. "It is not to be expected," he wrote, "that President Johnson shall, amid the trying and important duties that devolve upon him at the outset of his administration, keep in memory every festival, fast-day and ceremonial observed by [the various religious traditions]." Ascension Day was far from a major holiday, and by compelling the president to move the date of the day of mourning because of it, the editor suggested the clerics were making a tempest in a teapot. The Jews, the editor predicted, would take the high road; they would find a way to observe the "Feast of Weeks" even while they joined "in a sincere and earnest prayer to God for the repose of the soul of the late President Lincoln, whose memory all revere." Indeed, many of the sermons that American rabbis delivered on Shavuot day—the National Day of Humiliation and Mourning—prove that amid their gladness and rejoicing, most Jews were determined to "spare an earnest moment for communion with God, for heartfelt prayer in memory of the good Abraham Lincoln."[4]

Jacques Judah Lyons, the rabbi of Congregation Shearith Israel in New York, was one of the few Jewish leaders who insisted that even at a time such as this, Jews could not serve two masters. He told his congregants that they had convened on Shavuot to mark the "great festival commemorating the revelation of God on Mt. Sinai," and they were therefore commanded to be glad and rejoice. "Sorrow and dejection, the chief characteristics of a day of humiliation," he told them, "are incompatible with our joy." Lyons quickly added, however, that had it not been a Jewish festival, "we too, in common with our fellow-citizens of all denominations, would have observed this day of humiliation."[5]

In Baltimore, Rabbi Benjamin Szold told his people they would not "lower [themselves] into mournful meditation" on Shavuot. He pointed out that since the traditional

Jacques Judah Lyons, minister of New York's Congregation Shearith Israel, eulogized Lincoln and urged congregants to contribute to the Lincoln Memorial Fund.
Courtesy American Jewish Historical Society, New York, N.Y., and Newton Centre, Mass.

Rabbi Benjamin Szold told his congregation that Lincoln's "thought and his feeling . . . were truly Israelitish." Courtesy The Jacob Rader Marcus Center of the American Jewish Archives, at the Hebrew Union College–Jewish Institute of Religion, Cincinnati, Ohio.

periods of official Jewish mourning for the president, *shivah* and *shloshim*, had elapsed, it would be improper, Jewishly speaking, to perpetuate an official period of lamentation.[6] The period of mourning was over, Szold reassured his congregants, and they had no reason to think they were desecrating the sacred festival. They could participate in the "National Day of Humiliation" not as mourners per se but as loyal Americans who were pausing to reflect on the life of Abraham Lincoln "in love, loyalty and respect."

> We will not shed tears when we remember him but will be seized with silent, holy joy. Let us delight in the thought that such a wonderful man lived in our time and in this country; let us delight in the thought that his name made this nation so much richer; that we not only have a George Washington, but a Lincoln as well, a glorious example of high virtues for us, and all who will come after us. Therefore, my friends, let us think of Lincoln enshrined in beautiful flowers, and let us in spirit visit his grave to admire the blossoms which his virtues made grow out of the dust.[7]

Alfred T. Jones, a newspaper editor, businessman, and community leader, spoke about Lincoln during Shavuot services at Philadelphia's Mickve Israel Congregation. Jones argued that American Jews wanted to participate in the national day of mourning along with their fellow citizens, and this was a duty that was so compelling that it superseded the obligations and duties traditionally associated with the holy festival: "It cannot be improper or inappropriate to recall and reflect upon the great event which sits so heavily upon the nation, thereby evincing to the world that our hearts beat in unison with our fellow-citizens of other denominations; that although a peculiar people in many respects, we feel ourselves a component part of this great community of

States, exulting in their triumphs, deploring their defeats, rejoicing in their joys and partaking in their sorrows."[8]

Worshipers at New York's Bene Israel Congregation may have been a bit surprised to hear Reverend Morris R. Deleeuw (d. 1915)[9] tell them that Shavuot was actually a most fitting day for Jews to mourn the martyred president. It was true, Deleeuw declared, that Shavuot was the day on which Jews rejoiced in remembering that God had given them the Torah. Yet the preacher reminded his congregation that on Shavuot and all other Jewish festivals, it is customary for Jews to recite memorial prayers (*yizkor*) for their deceased relatives. Was it not entirely fitting to count Father Abraham as one of their own departed loved ones? Therefore, Deleeuw concluded, "had the President done so wittingly he could not well have chosen a day more fitting the object of his proclamation."[10]

In the end, the scheduling of the National Day of Humiliation and Mourning for Lincoln on the Jewish festival of Shavuot proved to be a "conflict" that was easily resolved for most American Jews. They instinctively knew they would find a viable way to commemorate their festival as best they could, and, simultaneously, they would "set aside a solemn service in memory of the lamented Abraham Lincoln."[11]

DOCUMENTS

1. "We May Not Raise Our Voice in Lamentation"
2. We Should Regard Abraham Lincoln as a Son of Israel
3. Who Will Refuse to Mingle His Tears with Those Which Flow from a Sorrow-Stricken Nation?
4. "His Kind Nature Cannot So Easily Be Rejected from Our Disturbed Minds"

1. "WE MAY NOT RAISE OUR VOICE IN LAMENTATION"

On Thursday morning, June 1, 1865, Rabbi Jacques Judah Lyons of New York's Congregation Shearith Israel told his people that, much to his deep regret, the Jew was strictly forbidden to mourn on Shavuot. "We can comply but with one direction," he told his congregation, "'Thou shalt rejoice before the Lord thy God.'"[12] Yet the rabbi did offer his people a useful dispensation. During the recitation of the "mourners' prayer"— the Kaddish—which was a regular feature of every Jewish worship service including Shavuot, there should be no objection if Jewish worshipers prayed for "the reception of [Lincoln's] soul into the kingdom of Heaven."[13]

Abraham Lincoln

Yesterday morning the Synagogue of the Congregation "Shearith Israel" on Nineteenth Street, near Fifth Avenue, was crowded with worshipers of the Jewish faith, the especial occasion being with them the commemoration of the Feast of the Pentecost, but also on account of the day being set apart by the President for humiliation and to testify the grief felt at the loss of our late Chief Magistrate.

The discourse was delivered by the minister, the Rev. J. J. Lyons, from the following text: "The Lord is in his holy temple, let all the earth keep silence before him."—Habakuk 2:20.

These are the opening words of the lesson of the prophets of this festival. Throughout the land the court of every shrine is this day frequented; all earthly pursuits and worldly thoughts are set aside and the presence of the Merciful One is sought in his sanctuary by our fellow-citizens, to evince their resignation under the recent calamity that has befallen them, in the murder of their Chief Magistrate. We, as Israelites, however, have come here this day in accordance with our time-honored custom, to complete the celebration of our great festival commemorating the revelation of God on Mount Sinai. Then and there a government was inaugurated, which pointed to God, the Supreme ruler of Heaven and Earth as King, and made all men, of whatever rank, wealth, or learning, equals in the eyes of the law; and well may it be said, it was the occasion from which the world may date with propriety the commencement of its civilization. In the annual commemoration of the great event, during the period of our dispersion, we can comply but with one direction, which is thus recorded in Deuteronomy 6:11: "Thou shalt rejoice before the Lord thy God." Joy, then, my friends, is enjoined upon us as our chief duty upon our present festival. You need scarcely be told that by that joy is meant the emotion excited by a proper appreciation of God's kindness, which excludes all evidence of grief, and is evinced in acts of gratitude and songs of fervent praise. Sorrow and dejection, the chief characteristics of a day of humiliation, are incompatible with our joy. The rules of our ritual prohibit every demonstration of sorrow and all supplicatory invocation on this day of joy. But for this restriction we too, in common with our fellow-citizens of all denominations, would have observed this day of humiliation. Had not the day that was originally appointed for this purpose been changed, we, too, would have mourned "with a great and very sore lamentation" the loss of a true and tried patriot; and like the Egyptians of old, at the death of one of our patriarchs.[14] We could have fulfilled the forty days of embalmment, in the hearts of the people, of that great and good chief, who in the hour of victory had malice for none and charity for all. The Rev. Mr. Lyons then went on to say that as Hebrews we regret that we are prevented by the restriction on our religious rules to give a full response to our feelings. He then went on and eulogized the memory of the President in a beautiful manner, and said that if we may not raise our voice in lamentation, we may as members "of that great house of mourning, where the head of the family has been taken away," avail ourselves of the privilege of praying for the happiness of his soul. The prayer for the dead, which is so well intended to bring consolation to the heart of the mourner, so far from being prohibited, constitutes in some of our congregations a particular feature of the service, this being one of the days designated, whereupon a remembrance of our departed friends is calculated to sanctify our rejoicing, to impress us with the transitoriness of all that is of this earth, and make us aspire to the possession of the eternal joy, reserved for the righteous in a blessed immortality. As we have said from this place on a recent occasion, it is the assurance of our religion. Israel's bondage was broken, and seven weeks after the nation for the first-time was brought in communion with their God to witness the revelation of his power and will. Then and there men's liberty was defined, restraints were placed upon his passions when the all-saving lessons of truth and justice were promulgated, that with the good and with the pious of all creeds it shall be well in the world to come. The religion of Israel, although it comprises the observance of the covenant to the descendants of the patriarchs, does so without any exclusive spirit. The restoration and consequent separation are intended to perpetuate the service, to keep from all possible injury the word of God and his promises to all men. Our holy religion dooms none because of this creed to eternal condemnation. It opens the gates of mercy, of divine knowledge and love to every race, every sect, every person. In this spirit, believing that the merits of our departed President will find favor with an all-merciful God, let us pray for the reception of his soul into the kingdom of Heaven.[15]

2. WE SHOULD REGARD ABRAHAM LINCOLN AS A SON OF ISRAEL

In Baltimore, on the National Day of Humiliation and Mourning, Rabbi Benjamin Szold addressed the members of Ohev Shalom Congregation in German. He told them it was his "solemn duty to dedicate [his] sermon to [the] late President Abraham Lincoln." Like his colleague Jacques Judah Lyons of Shearith Israel in New York, Szold informed his people that, strictly speaking, they were forbidden on Shavuot to lower themselves into a "mournful meditation." Szold quickly pointed out, however, that according to Jewish tradition, the formal periods of intense mourning for the president (shivah and shloshim) had already elapsed. He was therefore free to expound upon Lincoln's extraordinary achievements without fear of fostering an atmosphere of mourning that the Jewish law forbade on holy festivals.[16]

The following excerpts from Szold's lengthy holiday sermon—provided in the German original together with English translations—illustrate the essence of the rabbi's eulogistic message on the National Day of Humiliation and Mourning. He told his people that there are two kinds of flowers by the side of Lincoln's grave, the flower of love and the flower of hope. Sustaining the flower metaphor throughout his sermon, Szold linked it to the Jewish experience, enjoining his congregants to rejoice in Lincoln's love of freedom as well as in the spiritual kinship he had with the Jewish people.

Vaterland und Freiheit [Fatherland and Freedom]

Wir haben heute wieder in Gemäßheit der Proklamation unseres Präsidenten die Aufgabe, unsere gottesdienstliche Betrachtung dem Andenken des verstorbenen Präsidenten Abraham Lincoln zu weihen.—Aber heute wollen wir nicht, wie in unseren früheren, seinem Andenken gewidmeter Reden, das hohe Bild des Verstorbenen in jener blutig schaurigen Gestalt vor uns treten lassen. . . . Wir wollen heute nicht mehr in traurige Betrachtungen uns versenken; denn die von unserer Religion festgesetzten Trauerfristen, Schiwah und Schloschim, in welchen es allein dem Trauernden gestattet ist, mit schmerzvolle Gefühlen und mit blutendem Herzen dem Hingegangenen nachzublicken, sind bereits vorüber.—Außerdem feiern wir ja heute ein Fest, an welchem keine Trauer in israelitischen Gemüten Platz greifen darf, selbst wenn es von dem herbsten Unfallen betroffen wurde; da ja an diesen Feste die Erinnerung gefeiert wird an die Offenbarung am Sinai, welche uns den reichen und frischen Lebens-und Glaubens-quell erschlossen, aus dem wir Trost schöpfen für die herbsten Prüfungen, Linderung für die größten Leiden und Heilung für die blutendsten Wunden des Herzens.

[Today, in accordance with the proclamation of our president, we once more have been assigned the task of dedicating our service to considerations of the memory of our deceased president, Abraham Lincoln.—However, we would not, as we did in our previous sermons devoted to his memory, evoke the noble image of the deceased as a blood-stained and frightful figure, because *shivah* and *shloshim*, the periods of mourning set down by our religion, have already passed, and these are the only times when it is permitted to think back on the deceased with feelings of pain and with bleeding hearts.—Moreover, we are after all celebrating today a festival when no mourning should fill the Jewish mind, even if it has been struck by a most severe disaster. For on this festival, the remembrance of the Revelation at Sinai is being celebrated, an event which opened for us the rich and fresh source of life and creed, from which we draw comfort for most severe tests, solace for greatest suffering, and healing for most heavily wounded hearts.]

... Die Liebesblume, meine Freunde, wurde einst an diesem Feste von dem himmlischen Vater dem Israeliten an den Busen gesteckt mit dem göttlichen Zurufe, der uns da erscholl: "Ehre und liebe deinen Vater und deine Mutter, auf dass du lange in dem Reiche lebest, das Gott dir zum Besitz eingibt."—Diese Liebesblume der Elternehrung schmückte auch den Busen des verstorbenen Abraham Lincoln; denn er ehrte und liebte seinen Vater—er ehrte und liebte das Vaterland! Er ehrte und liebte seine Mutter—er ehrte und liebte die Freiheit, die uns eine liebende und zärtliche Mutter ist.

... Und um dieser Liebe willen, die Lincoln zur Freiheit hegte, ... müssen wir Israeliten das Andenken an Lincoln besonders hochhalten; denn die Freiheit ist ja besonders *unsere* Mutter, die uns zuerst liebend in ihre Arme schloss, die auf ihren Fittichen aus dem ägyptischen Sklavenhause uns zum Sinai hintrug. ...

Israeliten! Wir haben auf unserer großen Wanderung durch die Menschheitsgeschichte manches Vaterland gefunden; aber noch keine Mutter! ... Erst hier in dieser großen Republik haben wir nicht nur ein Vaterland, sondern auch eine Mutter—die Freiheit—gefunden, die alle Kinder des Vaterlandes, ohne Unterschied der Abstammung und des Glaubensbekenntnisses mit gleicher Liebe und Innigkeit in ihre Arme schließt.

[... The flower of love, my friends, was once pinned by the Heavenly Father on the breast of the Israelite, with the divine admonition which resounded: "Honor and love your father and your mother so that you may long live upon the land which God gives you as a possession."—This flower of love, namely honor shown to parents, also adorned the breast of the late Abraham Lincoln, because he honored and loved his father—he honored the Fatherland! He honored and loved his mother—he honored and loved Freedom, our loving and tender mother.

... For the sake of Lincoln's great love of freedom, ... we Israelites in particular must revere his memory because Freedom is in particular *our* mother who took us first into her loving arms and bore us on wings from Egyptian slavery to Sinai. ...

Israelites! On our long travels through the history of humankind we have found many a fatherland, but not yet a mother. . . . Only here, in this great republic, have we found not only a fatherland, but a mother—Freedom—who embraces all children of the Fatherland with equal love and sincerity, regardless of origin and faith.]

Darum, meine Freunde, sollten wir Abraham Lincoln, der unserer Mutter mit solcher Treue ergeben war, als einen Sohn Israels betrachten. Und wenn viele vom politischen Standpunkt aus ihm seinen Platz in der Geschichte neben Washington anweisen, so wollen wir dagegen von einem höheren Standpunkt, vom humanistischen Standpunkt aus, ihm auch seinen Platz anweisen neben *unseren* Tugend-und Wahrheits-helden, neben den Hoch-gestalten *israelitischer* Vorzeit! War er auch nicht, wie manche behaupten, Fleisch von unserem Fleisch und Bein von unserem Bein, so war er doch Geist von unserem Geiste und Seele von unserer Seele. Sein Geist und seine Seele, sein Herz und sein Gemüt, seine ganze innere Natur und Anlage, seine glühende Begeisterung für alles Edle und Hohe, seine Liebe zum Vaterlande, zur Freiheit und zur Menschheit, alles an und in ihm, wodurch sein Wesen, sein Denken und Empfinden sich offenbarten, bis auf seine Redeweise, und die Methode, die ihm eigen war, erhabene Ideen durch Gleichnisse zu erläutern und dem Verständnis näher zu bringen, waren echt israelitisch, von echt alt israelitischem Geiste. Darum wie die alten israelitischen Glaubenshelden uns als ewige Musterbilder gelten, so lasst uns auch in ihm ein hohes und leuchtendes Musterbild erblicken.

[Therefore, my friends, we should regard Abraham Lincoln, so loyally devoted to our mother (= Freedom), as a son of Israel. And if many, from a political standpoint, assign him a place in history next to Washington, we, on the other hand, from a higher, from a humanistic standpoint, should place him next to *our* heroes of virtue and of truth, next to eminent figures of *Israelite* antiquity. And if, as some will have it, he was not flesh of our flesh or bone of our bone, he was indeed spirit of our spirit and soul of our soul. His spirit and his soul, his heart and mind, his innermost nature and disposition, his fervent enthusiasm for everything noble and lofty, his love for the Fatherland, for Freedom and humanity, everything about him and in him that manifested his nature, his thought and his feeling, down to his way of speaking and the method, all his own, of clarifying lofty ideas by means of analogies in order to make them understood—these were truly Israelitish, in the spirit of ancient Israel. Therefore, just as the old Israelite faith heroes are our eternal exemplars, let us also see in him a lofty and shining exemplar.][17]

3. WHO WILL REFUSE TO MINGLE HIS TEARS WITH THOSE
WHICH FLOW FROM A SORROW-STRICKEN NATION?

Although some rabbis admonished their people to preserve their joyful spirit on Shavuot in accordance with Jewish law, there were those who disagreed. Speaking to the members of Mickve Israel Congregation in Philadelphia, Rabbi Sabato Morais explicitly directed the "Hebrews of America" to suppress the spiritual gladness that they would typically be expected to exhibit on the festival of Shavuot. In this excerpt from Morais's "Discourse," delivered on June 1, 1865, the rabbi acknowledged the tremendous grief that had overwhelmed American Jewry in the loss of their "good and great Abraham." Morais enjoined his congregants to acknowledge both their spirit of joy and their expressions of lamentation by vowing to give "unswerving fidelity to the Law of Sinai, and steadfast allegiance to the American Constitution."[18]

A Discourse

> From the uttermost part of the earth we have heard songs, "Glory to the righteous." But I said, Alas! alas! woe unto me! the traitors have dealt treacherously; yea, the traitors have dealt very treacherously."
>
> Isaiah 24:16

Hebrews of America! Repress the joyful emotions that thrill your hearts! Heirs of the fiery law, which from the secret top of Sinai did, at this season, cast forth rays of unquenchable light! dismiss, if it be for a few moments, the pleasurable thoughts that cluster around your minds! True, when the residue of the chosen seed holds a feast to the Lord, you cannot afflict your soul with fasting. Sackcloth and ashes would ill become those who but yesterday came hither adorned with the garment of unfading beauty first donned at Horeb. Yet, the memory of the righteous must, even now, draw from our lips a blessing and a prayer.

We would fain have postponed the discharge of so solemn but mournful a duty. We would have, at least, wished that in this land of equal rights, where the religious tenets of a majority can claim no higher privileges than those revered by a minority, there should not have been found protestants against the first summons of the authorities. But who among us will, this day, let any motives sever him from the community? Who will refuse to mingle his tears with those which, like a swelling stream, flow from a sorrow-stricken nation? . . .

Men of Israel! At the foot of the altar let us vow again this day unswerving fidelity to the Law of Sinai, and steadfast allegiance to the American Constitution, which will henceforth secure to all their inalienable rights—life, liberty, and the pursuit of happiness.

PRAYER

God, who amid myriads of saints didst appear to our fathers on the summit of Horeb! Save this people, and bless their inheritance: sustain them and exalt them for evermore. For the merits of the righteous founders of this Union, who opened for Israel a home of security, forgive the iniquities of their posterity. Remove the heart of stone, which renders them impervious to truth, and vest them with a new spirit and a ductile mind. Then will they know and understand that to uphold the ensign of universal freedom, is to do what is acceptable in Thy presence.

Heavenly Judge! Because of Thy rebuke, the foundations of this land shook, and the pillars thereof threatened to fall, but Mercy stood suppliant before Thy throne, and the disaster was averted. Great is our joy this day, O Lord! at the wondrous deliverance; yet, incomplete, by reason of the dear object so suddenly borne away from our earthly vision. His paternal look and genial smile would have enhanced our happiness. Oh! may the affectionate remembrance of a whole nation be an offering of sweet savor to his undying soul! Sphered in the realms of bliss, may he behold the seed he planted among us blossom like the garden of Eden. Liberty, equality, and fraternity spread throughout the habitable globe. And grant, O Sovereign Maker, the entreaty of the seed of "Abram, the Hebrew": "Spread the fear of Thee upon all Thy creatures, and the reverence of Thee upon all beings, so that they all may form one band to fulfill Thy will with an upright heart. For we, Thy people, know that the rule is Thine; strength and power belong solely to Thee." "Before Thee all knees must bend. All tongues shall swear by Thy Unity."

So may it speedily be; and say ye, Amen![19]

4. "HIS KIND NATURE CANNOT SO EASILY BE REJECTED FROM OUR DISTURBED MINDS"

Perhaps the most radical solution to the conflicting obligations that required American Jews to mourn and rejoice on the same day was proposed by Morris R. Deleeuw of New York's Bene Israel Congregation. On June 1, 1865, Deleeuw not only endorsed the propriety of Jewish mourning on Shavuot but also forcefully insisted that there was "no more fitting day" than the festival of Shavuot for a "National Day of Humiliation and Mourning." Deleeuw based this assertion on the fact that on all Jewish festivals, including Shavuot, memorial prayers for "the souls of departed relatives, friends and prominent men of Israel" are customarily recited during the worship service. For this reason, the preacher assured his people, President Andrew Johnson could not possibly have selected a more appropriate day on the Jewish liturgical calendar to memorialize Lincoln. Deleeuw consoled his listeners by reminding them that the "balmy peace [that] fills the land" testified to the fact that Abraham Lincoln had successfully completed his earthly mission.[20]

Abraham Lincoln

By me kings reign and princes decree justice.

Prov. 8:15

By these words it is clear that obedience to those in authority is a holy duty; this injunction is essential to the existence of government. Had the reverence due it been paid no such thing as rebellion would have found the means to exist, and we would have been spared on this day the solemn task of blending a day of joy with one of humiliation. But emanating as it does from the Chief Magistrate of the nation, we Israelites, as an obedient people, are prepared to observe it. Wanting the proclamation of the President, we have the observance of this particular day enjoined on us by the King of Kings in commemoration of the giving of the law upon Sinai as a day of rejoicing. It is also customary on this day to offer prayers for the repose of the souls of departed relatives, friends and prominent men of Israel. Had the President done so wittingly he could not well have chosen a day more fitting the object of his proclamation. In the words of the prophet:—

"Weep not for the dead, and do not bemoan him."—Jer. 22:10.

The external signs of mourning have disappeared, the earth has closed upon the remains of Abraham Lincoln, and the loud wailing and cry of anguish consequent on the first intimation of the horrid deed have subsided, as it is natural in man that they should. But even if these have disappeared to our hearts the details are yet fresh, as they will ever be, and upon its tablets are deeply and ineffaceably graven a pure and solemn memory; his kind nature cannot so easily be rejected from our disturbed minds, and assuredly by those who loved the man for his principle. It must be clear to all that it was the Divine will to remove Abraham Lincoln from our midst. To his relentless foes his magnanimity was incomprehensible; and, despising it by their crowning wickedness, they have drawn upon themselves the just deserts of their iniquity. A punishment such as no human mind would have devised was meted to the assassin. For three long hours, in the full possession of his clear mind, and yet physically unable to execute its vindictive dictates, beyond all human aid he lay slowly dying, his pangs increased by the sting of his black conscience until he was dead. If we reflect on this the majesty of avenging justice is belittled by the command so literally carried out:

"Vengeance and recompense is mine saith the Lord."[21]

And we know, Oh Lord, Thy judgment is righteous. We have humbled ourselves beneath the stroke of the hand of God, and we prayed to Him, in the midst of our distress, to direct the angel of destruction to stay his hand, and the Lord has heard our supplications.

"I will thank Thee, Oh Lord, that Thou wast angry with me. Thy anger now is turned away and Thou comfortest me."—Isaiah 12:1.

Therefore, war no longer rages in the land. Under the inspiration of our dead President the strife has ceased, and the glory of victory sits proudly on our banners, while balmy peace fills the land. His own life sealed the flow of blood, as it likewise marked the epoch that the task that he assumed at the commencement of his first term had been grandly and successfully accomplished. The successor of our late President has thus far, under Heavenly guidance, fully succeeded. We beseech thee, Oh Lord, not to withhold thy inspiration from him, to enable him to be a successful ruler. And now, my friends, we will pray for the repose of the soul of the illustrious dead.[22]

$\overline{8}$

Criticisms and Commendations: Conflicting Views on the Lincoln Presidency

Toward the end of the nineteenth century, amid the many personal memoirs and reminiscences relating to Lincoln and his career recorded during this era, one finds a small array of noteworthy reflections that indicate that Lincoln's peers did not fully appreciate his importance while he was alive. For example, nearly four decades after Lincoln's death, Carl Christian Schurz—a Republican activist and the first German-born American to serve in the U.S. Senate—took note of the uncomplimentary barbs that had been hurled at Lincoln while he was in the White House. "In vain did journals and speakers represent him as a light-minded trifler, who amused himself with frivolous story-telling and coarse jokes, while the blood of the people were [sic] flowing in streams," but, Schurz continued, "the people knew that the man at the head of affairs, on whose haggard face the twinkle of humor so frequently changed into an expression of the profoundest sadness, was more than any other deeply distressed by the suffering he witnessed."[1]

Julia Ward Howe (1819–1910), the prominent social activist, outspoken abolitionist, and author of the "Battle Hymn of the Republic," agreed completely with Schurz's assessment. In her autobiographical *Reminiscences*, Howe explained that Lincoln was greatly underappreciated and often underrated by many of his contemporaries: "None of us knew then—how could we have known?—how deeply God's wisdom had touched and inspired that devout and patient soul. At the moment few people praised or trusted him. 'Why did he not do this, or that, or the other? He a President, indeed! Look at this war, dragging on so slowly! Look at our many defeats and rare victories!' Such was the talk that one constantly heard regarding him. The most charitable held that he meant well."[2]

Those who delve more deeply into the history of the Civil War are frequently surprised to learn that many of Lincoln's peers did not look upon him as a demigod. To the contrary, the spirit of admiration, respect, and near universal acclaim that has enshrined the memory of Lincoln since the day he was assassinated in 1865 often appears to be in stark contrast to the way he was perceived while he was alive. This phenomenon is particularly true of his years in the White House, when Lincoln had many fierce opponents.

Lincoln's political adversaries not only criticized the way he conducted the nation's affairs but frequently belittled his personal characteristics as well. Lincoln's humble origins, for instance, which today evoke such positive associations, were grist for the critics' mill during his years in office. Political partisans and biting journalists often portrayed Lincoln as a country bumpkin, an ignorant westerner, and a man who lacked the refinements that one would expect to find in the leader of a great nation.

His well-known ability to engage with all types of people, his wit, and the way he loved to hear and tell humorous stories has made him—in America's collective memory—a truly human, accessible leader. This Lincoln is down to earth, one of the people. Yet, especially during his presidency, these same qualities galled his critics. From their perspective, Lincoln was not fit to lead the nation. They insisted he was coarse, undignified, and indecisive.[3]

Between Lincoln's election in November 1860 and his inauguration in March 1861, many southerners had made up their minds that Lincoln planned to abolish slavery as soon as he arrived in Washington. Those in the North who wanted to avoid conflict and war at all cost hoped the president-elect would offer conciliatory statements in an effort to cool tensions. Nevertheless, many in the North and the South held to the firm conviction that Lincoln's election made political compromise impossible, and it was this spirit that fueled a series of events that culminated in the outbreak of the Civil War on April 12, 1861. On December 20, 1860—six weeks after Lincoln was elected and three months before his inauguration—South Carolina seceded from the Union. Six more southern states followed within two months. In summarizing the situation that Lincoln faced as he awaited his inauguration, one writer noted: "The country was divided, hatred was the most prevalent emotion, and there was no effective leadership anywhere in the government."[4]

Even before Lincoln took office, there were those who feared that he was not up to the task. Charles Francis Adams (1807–86), the grandson of John Adams and son of John Quincy Adams, was not impressed with the remarks the president-elect offered on the stops he made during his train trip to Washington in February 1861. Adams concluded that Lincoln's speeches were "rapidly reducing the estimate put upon him." "I am much afraid that in this lottery we may have drawn a blank," Adams wrote. Lincoln's words betrayed "a person unconscious of his own position as well as of the nature of the contest around him. Good natured, kindly, honest, but frivolous and uncertain."[5]

As soon as he took office, Lincoln was subjected to more criticism. For example, his first inaugural address, which today is largely considered an oratorical masterpiece, fell short of some people's expectations. Two weeks after the inauguration, the speech was the subject of a cartoon drawn by a young caricaturist named Thomas Nast (1840–1902). Nast lampooned the fact that Lincoln's words were perceived differently depending on whether one was from the North or the South. For northerners, the first inaugural address appeared to be a plea for peace and conciliation. Yet for southerners, Lincoln seemed a menacing oppressor.[6]

Lincoln's determination to spend many hours each week meeting with office seekers, lobbyists, and constituents exasperated his critics. Editorials excoriated Lincoln for what seemed to be a colossal waste of the president's precious time—particularly at a time of national emergency. Murat Halstead (1829–1908), a prominent newspaper correspondent in Cincinnati during the Civil War, was vexed when Lincoln ignored his recommendation for a friend seeking a patronage position in the new government. Venting his spleen in a letter to a friend, Halstead's disdain for Lincoln was unambiguous: "I use the mildest phrase when I say that Lincoln is a weak, a miserably weak man. . . . He is opposed to stealing, but he can't see the stealing that is done." According to Halstead, Lincoln was "very busy with trifles, and lets everybody do as they please."[7]

Lincoln's most formidable opposition came from a political movement called the Copperhead Democrats. The Copperhead movement was a political coalition composed of different interest groups that shared a common opposition to Lincoln's political agenda. Some of the Copperheads were conservative Democrats who used the rhetoric of Thomas Jefferson and Andrew Jackson to defend states' rights. In addition, they wanted to limit the power of the federal government. Most of the Copperhead Democrats were strict interpreters of the U.S. Constitution. Since the founding document did not explicitly forbid secession, they concluded states had the constitutional right to withdraw from the union. Another faction of the Copperhead movement was composed of German and Irish Catholic immigrants who feared that if the slaves in the South were freed, they would migrate to the North and compete for their jobs. Yet another stream that flowed into this movement carried along those who, for one reason or another, sympathized with the South. These were people who simply wanted to maintain the status quo ante at all costs.[8]

Initially, the Copperheads concentrated on challenging Lincoln's executive actions. In April and May 1861, for example, they opposed his decision to call out the militia, saying that only the U.S. Congress—not the president—was authorized to take such action. At the same time, they contended that Lincoln had exceeded his constitutional authority when he ordered the U.S. Navy to blockade southern ports. Blockading the ports, they thundered, constituted a provocative act of war when the U.S. Congress had not yet declared war. In July 1861, Lincoln asked Congress to pass legislation that would enable the government to raise the funds it needed to put down the rebellion in the South. A month later, he signed the Revenue Act, which, among other things, instituted the nation's first tax on income. Once again, the Copperheads condemned Lincoln's policies as an incursion on the rights of the individual.[9]

One of Lincoln's most controversial decisions occurred in 1862 when he suspended the writ of habeas corpus in order to prosecute the war more vigorously. By suspending habeas corpus, Lincoln hoped to defeat those who were undermining the government's effort to recruit enlistees for the army or who were otherwise aiding the rebel cause. Once the writ of habeas corpus had been suspended, Lincoln could then use the rules of martial law to incarcerate those who were accused of sedition. The decision captured the public's attention and was highly controversial. It rallied and strengthened Lincoln's opponents. The Copperheads called him a tyrant and a despot, and they focused their attention on throwing the Republicans out of office in the elections of 1862.[10]

Yet above all else, it was Lincoln's performance as commander-in-chief of the military that provoked the harshest criticism. Confidence in Lincoln's abilities ebbed and flowed with the battle news from the front. In the summer of 1862, the Union suffered a series of discouraging military defeats, and the public's appetite for the war began to wane. These conditions emboldened Lincoln's critics, and they rallied around a new slogan that would endure for the rest of the war: "The Union as it was and the Constitution as it is." The Copperheads, also called the Peace Democrats, resolved to defeat the Republicans in 1862 and bring the war to a negotiated settlement as soon as possible.[11]

On September 22, 1862, Lincoln issued the preliminary Emancipation Proclamation. As far as Lincoln's opponents were concerned, this decision added insult to injury. The war was going so poorly for the North, and now Lincoln was proposing to abolish slavery in the South—a step that was certain to inflame the southerners and fortify their determination to fight. More and more critics clamored against Lincoln's policies. Henry J. Raymond (1820–69), founding editor of the *New York Times* and a prominent Republican leader, was convinced that in spite of the fact that the people did not care about the emancipation of the slaves, Lincoln was "fighting not for the Union but for the abolition of slavery." Americans, Raymond concluded, were "tired & sick of war." Like Raymond, Thurlow Weed (1797–1882), one of the most prominent Republicans in New York, disagreed with Lincoln's decision to promulgate the Emancipation Proclamation. By issuing it when he did, Weed concluded, Lincoln had made it "impossible" for him to be reelected in 1864. "The people," he said, "are wild for peace."[12]

As the 1864 elections approached, the Union suffered even greater losses on the battlefront, and it seemed unlikely that the Union's military would ever compel the Confederacy to offer an unconditional surrender. From May through the beginning of August 1864, the Union army endured unfathomable losses. Over the course of six short weeks, the Union lost 64,000 men, and 38,000 more died for the Confederacy. One of Lincoln's ardent opponents, Congressman Samuel S. Cox (1824–89)—a Democrat from Ohio—asked a rhetorical question that resonated with an ever increasing number of Americans: "Is it butchery, or—war?" Criticism of Lincoln and his administration reached a crescendo in August 1864, and his prospects for reelection seemed negligible.[13]

Fearing that he might not be returned to office, Lincoln wrote a memorandum saying, "This morning, as for some days past, it seems exceedingly probable that this Administration will not be re-elected. Then it will be my duty to so co-operate with the President elect, as to save the Union between the election and the inauguration; as he will have secured his election on such ground that he can not possibly save it afterwards."[14] Most historians agree that two key factors contributed to Lincoln being able to come from behind and win a second term in 1864. First, news that General William T. Sherman's (1820-91) Union forces took the city of Atlanta on September 2 created a national sensation. Many began to see that this victory meant the end of the war really was on the horizon. Second, Lincoln had the electoral support of the military. Over the course of his presidency, Lincoln constantly visited the Union's troops. The soldiers liked him, and they had come to believe in him. Moreover, once Atlanta had been taken by the Union, those calling for a negotiated peace settlement in order to end to the war at all cost seemed to be denigrating the memory of the thousands of young men who lost their lives in order to preserve the Union. As one Union soldier said, "I do not see how any soldier can vote for such a man [George B. McClellan], nominated on a platform which acknowledges that we are whipped."[15]

After Lincoln's reelection, the news from the war front seemed to reinforce the belief that the war would soon be won. With victory in the air, the bitter attacks on Lincoln's leadership finally began to wane. Richmond was captured on April 3, 1865. Six days later, on April 9, General Robert E. Lee surrendered to General Ulysses S. Grant at Appomattox. The nation rejoiced, and elation dominated in the streets of the North. Lincoln had preserved the Union, and a grateful nation exulted in the moment. These few days were certainly Lincoln's happiest in the White House. "The war is now closed, and we soon will live in peace with the brave men that have been fighting against us," Lincoln told his son Robert on one of the last days of his life. Less than one week later, Lincoln was gone.[16]

Only a few months after Lincoln's assassination, Isaac M. Wise observed that "Lincoln was one of these uncommon men. The longer he was in office, the more we learned to respect him. The more we got acquainted with his homespun virtues the more he won our affections."[17] With these words, Wise was attempting to explain how he had come to speak so highly of Lincoln when he had taken him to task so often while he was president. Indeed, Wise had been one of Lincoln's most outspoken critics.

Wise had long been a partisan of the Democratic Party, and though he was never a supporter of the Copperheads, he had voted for Stephen Douglas in 1860. Wise valued

Rabbi Isaac M. Wise, often a harsh critic of the president, claimed in his eulogy that Lincoln always believed he had Jewish ancestors.
Courtesy The Jacob Rader Marcus Center of the American Jewish Archives, at the Hebrew Union College–Jewish Institute of Religion, Cincinnati, Ohio.

the preservation of the Union over the emancipation of slaves. It was not that he was a supporter of slavery, but he feared that the abolitionists were too radical. Wise agreed with Douglas's "Freeport Doctrine," which maintained that local municipalities could slowly eliminate slavery by adopting laws that made the institution untenable on the local level. Yet Wise also shared Douglas's view that the federal government could not prohibit the establishment of slavery in the territories. To use twentieth-century terminology, Wise was a gradualist when it came to the eradication of slavery. He believed that when the proper conditions were legislated, slavery would ultimately collapse under its own weight.

Wise was a pragmatist. The moralistic and extremist rhetoric of the abolitionists gave him the shivers. As for the "irrepressible conflict," Wise wanted to avoid a civil war at all cost. Like many others, he worried that Lincoln's election might well lead to the Union's collapse. Even before Lincoln took office, Wise expressed his concerns about the president-elect in an editorial. He worried that the Republicans were not attuned to the practical realities of "conciliation and compromise." Their inclination to coerce and crusade was a dangerous instinct, he wrote, and it could spur disastrous consequences:

> Our legislators are forgetting, that the success of a purely Republican government, is not so much the doing the will of the majority, as the protection of the rights of the minority. Greece and Rome were mighty Republics in their time, but, alas! how fallen, and it may be traced to the fact that when the power fell into the hands of certain leaders they tyrannized over their fellow citizens. It is not so much the election of Mr. Lincoln [in itself] that now threatens the destruction of our Common Country, as his individual and the speeches of his colleagues heretofore on the irrepressible conflict doctrine. Another point forgotten by the corrupt politicians of the present day is, that this is a government of conciliation and compromise: not of coercion.[18]

On January 4, 1861, Rabbi Morris J. Raphall composed what would become a frequently cited sermon titled "Bible View of Slavery." The sermon was delivered to his congregation in New York, Bene Yeshurun, to commemorate the "National Day of Humiliation, Fasting, and Prayer" that President James Buchanan had proclaimed. In this widely quoted sermon, Raphall did not mention Lincoln by name, but he explicitly addressed himself to all those who should be concerned about the impending crisis that was facing the nation: "I mean the whole of the people throughout the United States: the President and his Cabinet, the President elect and his advisers, the leaders of public opinion, North and South."[19]

From his pulpit, Raphall urged compromise on both the North and the South. He asked the people of the North and their new leaders to be wary of the "mischief" that moralizing abolitionists had caused. Raphall reminded his listeners that southerners, too, possessed morals. What right did abolitionist radicals have "to insult and exasperate thousands of God-fearing, law-abiding Citizens, whose moral worth and patriotism, whose purity of conscience and of life" were "fully equal" to theirs? Raphall concluded his sermon by urging all northerners—including the newly elected government—to be "content with following the word of God, [and] not insist on being 'righteous overmuch,' or denouncing 'sin' which the Bible knows not."[20]

Like his other critics, Lincoln's Jewish opponents wondered whether the president-elect was the right man for the job. Wise took note of Lincoln's "primitive manner," and he predicted he would look "queer" in the White House.[21] Yet American Jews had their own distinctive grievances when it came to Lincoln. As we have seen, there was widespread concern among Jews over an increasing tendency to assume that America was a Christian nation. Many of the leading abolitionists were Christian pietists, and their commitment to ridding the nation of slavery was inextricably linked to their religious views. There was a great deal of overlap between the Christian abolitionists and the Christians who wanted the nation to adopt a constitutional amendment that would make explicit their belief that America was a Christian nation in both belief and practice.

Wise and many other American Jewish leaders strenuously objected to these views, and they did not appreciate it when Lincoln seemed to embrace this same perspective. Jewish newspaper editors and religious leaders opposed any perceived attempt to render American Jewry a tolerated minority or to suggest that Christianity was more American than Judaism. In 1862, for example, Wise received an angry letter from one of his readers complaining about this very matter and published the note:

> It has often been asserted and now seems to be the opinion of enlightened men in general, that the present distracted and unhappy state of our country is to be . . . attributed in a great measure to the venality and want of patriotism of the majority of the people, by the frequent election to office of mere political tricksters and demagogues and fanatics becoming a darker age.
>
> If any one doubts the truth of the above assertion let him examine and peruse the acts and speeches of our modern law-makers and so-called statesmen; let him read a President's (Lincoln) message, "who trusts to a Christian people," let him travel thro' our Secretary Seward's speeches wherein "Christianity will give the country peace;" or let him read the military bill passed in July last, which owns [sic] its paternity to (Natick Cobbler) Senator Henry Wilson,[22] which reads that for the benefit of the souls of our patriotic soldiers, "Chaplains" should be ordained, they to wear military clothes, but to be of Christianity dress or "Christian denomination," or if one not yet satisfied with the many proofs given and wants more of the stupidity of our leaders, then let him read a speech made on the 31st of Jan., 1862, by Union Senator, Andrew Johnson, of Tennessee in which he says, the Constitution must be upheld at all hazards to save the country, and he ends with the following short and significant sentence: *"Christ first, our country next."*[23]

Wise was not the only Jewish newspaper publisher to insist that in the United States, the American Jew be given equal footing in all matters pertaining to religious practice. Isaac Leeser, a proponent of traditional Jewish practice, disagreed with Isaac Wise on a range of matters. Yet the two men agreed that Judaism was fully entitled to equal recognition with Christianity in the United States. In his newspaper, the *Occident and American Jewish Advocate*, Leeser published a copy of a letter he received from one of his readers. The letter was addressed to Abraham Lincoln, and it was written by the father of a Jewish soldier who recently heard that Lincoln had instructed his generals to make every effort to permit the country's soldiers and sailors to observe a Sabbath on Sunday. The father wanted Lincoln to permit his son—and all non-Christian soldiers—to observe a day of rest that accorded with their own religious practice, in this instance, the seventh day. In addition to publishing the letter, Leeser composed his own lengthy opinion on the topic, which was included as a preface. Leeser insisted that the U.S. Constitution guaranteed equality to Jews as a natural right.

American Jews also took umbrage whenever politicians assumed that the word "prayer" meant *Christian* prayer. Jews wanted to join with their fellow citizens when the government urged them to commemorate a "Day of Humiliation and Fasting," and they took pride in responding to the proclamations even when their Christian neighbors began to grow weary from them.[24] Nevertheless, Isaac Wise did not approve of the government telling its citizens when and why they should pray, and he expressed his annoyance bluntly on the pages of his newspaper: "If President Lincoln can not give everybody a turkey and minze [*sic*] pie, he had better not always trouble us with thanksgiving days, fasts, &c. It is too ridiculous to be always annoyed with those hypocritical demonstrations. The emperor Joseph of Austria saw much trouble in abolishing holidays for the benefit of the operatives, and Mr. Lincoln gives us one every other week. We do not like the religious proclamations, or religion imposed by foolish proclamations."[25]

In the sliver of time that separated the end of the Civil War from the day that Lincoln was assassinated, American Jews shared in the general spirit of jubilee that prevailed throughout the nation. In the pages of his diary, Simon Wolf described the atmosphere in the nation's capital on the day that Richmond surrendered: "Washington in a delirium," Wolf wrote; "men walked the streets as if they were intoxicated." Many of the rabbinical eulogies on Lincoln, as well as the many newspaper accounts describing events that took place in American synagogues after the assassination, begin by noting that the tremendous sense of grief and loss was exacerbated because there had been such rejoicing the week before. A Jewish immigrant named Isaac Goldstein was so overwhelmed with joy by the end of the Civil War that he composed an acrostic prayer in tribute to Lincoln. By the time he submitted it to the Jewish newspapers, however, Goldstein's poem of praise had been transformed into an elegy in memoriam.[26]

Most of the Jews living in the American South left historians no way of assessing how they felt when they first received word that Lincoln had been murdered. Only a few documents of this ilk remain, but the very existence of these rare examples suggests that others must certainly have had similarly harsh reactions—even if they never committed their sentiments to paper.

Ultimately, Lincoln's opponents in the North and the South were silenced by the Confederacy's surrender, and although it is impossible to know precisely how they would have criticized Lincoln and the way in which he might have led the nation through Reconstruction, there can be little doubt that his political detractors would have regrouped and lived to fight another day.

As for Lincoln's most vocal Jewish critics, men like Wise, Leeser, and Raphall joined with the rest of the Union in exalting Lincoln and paying homage to his towering achievements. It is interesting to note, however, that Raphall's lament for Lincoln is distinct in its carefully measured praise. In contrast to almost all of the Lincoln eulogists—including those given by his critics—Raphall reminded his people that for "three-fourths of his term in office [Lincoln] had stumbled, endeavored to advance, and failed in his attempt." While praising Lincoln, Raphall awkwardly rehearsed his shortcomings. Lincoln selected the wrong generals, and he "locked up many a courageous American" when he suspended the writ of habeas corpus. The rabbi even seemed to blame Lincoln for losing his own life. "He had had more than one warning" that there were those who wanted him dead, Raphall told his congregation, yet Lincoln did not take the necessary precautions. It was this "imprudence that hastened on his end." In the end, Raphall conceded that despite his flaws, Lincoln was a "great man" who had "in all his loveliness" perished for the sake of America.[27]

Isaac Leeser reminded his congregation that Lincoln corrected the wrongs that were perpetrated on American Jewry in the chaplaincy controversy and in the revocation of Grant's General Orders No. 11. These acts, Leeser declared, "speak loudly for the natural kindness of the late President, which all can cheerfully acknowledge, whatever their political opinions may be."[28]

In his eulogy on Lincoln, Wise also charged his people to embrace the ambitions of this "generous, genial, and honest man." In doing so, they would succeed in transforming America into a "chosen people."[29]

Wise realized that when Lincoln was taken from America by "the assassin's hand in the midst of his people," the world changed overnight.[30] "The impression of this concluding scene (Lincoln's assassination) [was] so powerful and ineradicable, so moving and profound that no one can forget this great drama of truth. The consequences for history are incalculable."[31]

Wise was correct. As the documents below illustrate, even Lincoln's harshest Jewish critics would soon be transformed into Lincoln admirers and more so. Lincoln's critics as well as his longtime boosters embraced and began the process of memorializing him as an adoptive Jewish brother, as one of their own.

DOCUMENTS

LINCOLN'S JEWISH CRITICS

1. Isaac M. Wise's Editorials Criticizing Lincoln
2. Isaac Leeser Publishes a Letter from a Concerned Jewish Father
3. Rabbi Morris J. Raphall's Critical Thanksgiving Day Prayer
4. An Evaluation of Lincoln's Second Inaugural Address

LINCOLN'S JEWISH COMMENDATIONS

5. Lincoln's Conduct Has Been Invariably Straightforward
6. "I Am Now a Strong Abolitionist"
7. A Hebrew Tribute to Lincoln

REACTIONS TO LINCOLN'S ASSASSINATION

8. "God Grant So May All Our Foes Perish!"
9. Some Southern Sympathizers Cheered
10. "New York Is Literally Clad in Black"
11. Isaac M. Wise's Reflections on Lincoln's Religion

LINCOLN'S JEWISH CRITICS

1. ISAAC M. WISE'S EDITORIALS CRITICIZING LINCOLN

Rabbi Isaac M. Wise of Cincinnati was frequently a harsh critic of Lincoln. While serving as the rabbi of Congregation Bene Yeshurun, a thriving synagogue in Cincinnati, Ohio, Wise simultaneously edited two newspapers—an English paper named the Israelite *and its German language counterpart,* Die Deborah. *In 1875, Wise would found the Hebrew Union College in Cincinnati, a rabbinical seminary for American Jewry.*[32]

Although Jews all across the nation subscribed to Wise's newspapers, his publications had the greatest circulation in the Midwest and the South. Politically, Wise was firmly aligned with the Democrats. He was ready to make concessions to the South in order to avoid war and to preserve the Union. As the documents below illustrate, Wise fulminated in opposition to those whom he considered to be zealots, ideologues, and extremists on both sides of the conflict. These "champions of abstractions," as Wise called them in one editorial, were, in truth, fanatics who were prepared to sacrifice peace and harmony for their own moralistic agenda. It is clear that even before Lincoln took office in 1861, Wise was concerned that his policies would only fan the fire of conflict.

In contrast to the glowing eulogies he famously delivered only days after Lincoln's assassination, while he was in office Wise often criticized Lincoln and his administration in the newspapers he published. Each of the editorials below sheds light on a different facet of Wise's point of view on Lincoln, politics, and the Civil War.

_____

Abraham Lincoln became president-elect on November 6, 1860. Two weeks later, Isaac Wise described the decision to elect Lincoln and place the Republican Party in power as one of the nation's greatest blunders. Decrying fanaticism on both sides of the Mason-Dixon Line, Wise expressed the strong hope that "Mr. Lincoln" would want to avoid war at all cost. To do so, the president-elect would need to placate "Southern demands" vis-à-vis slavery and tone down the inflammatory rhetoric that prevailed during the election. Now that the election of 1860 had been decided, Wise anticipated that uncompromising political positions would "soon give way to the sober and practical schemes."

Above all, Wise wanted to assure his subscribers that he was ready to accept their payment for his paper in any currency they cared to offer!

The People Have Just Committed One of the Greatest Blunders

November 30, 1860

To our Subscribers,

We deem it necessary to inform our subscribers that we take in payment any sort of bills bankable at par in any state of the union, and desire of all friends who are in arrears to this establishment to pay in bills current with them or in any other state of the union, and they will receive full credit for it.

The artificial panic which just now frightens the community is no more than the product of the present state of politics and the cunning contrivance of bankers, brokers, etc. In politics the hottest fanatics will get quiet and cool in quite a short time. The republicans in this section of the country and, it appears also elsewhere, have turned lambkins, tender and innocent, immaculate and bashful. Not one of them ever was an abolitionist, ever talked of "A house divided against itself can not stand," of the "irrepressible conflict," of the "higher law," and such other grandiloquent terms as they usually had on hand. They are as tame and obliging now as the peasant the first time in the city. Hence fanaticism on one hand is gone overboard. The same thing precisely, we have strong reasons to suppose, is the case in the extreme south with fire-eaters, seceders and political circus riders; they have found out by this time that people care very little for abstract ideas, extreme views and false conceptions of honor when their material interests are neglected or even ruined; and if they have not learned yet to appreciate the opinion of the people they will do so in a short time without any civil war, bloodshed or even military maneuvers.

The people of the United States just committed one of the greatest blunders a nation can commit, for which we must pay at once; they permitted extreme fictions to play the hazardous game of the country's welfare and peace for an abstract idea, and the whole issue of the last campaign was an abstract idea and a division of the spoils. Whatever faction was victorious nothing could be gained and the peace of the country lost. Nations have insane moments as well as individuals. In a few short months, however, the champions of abstractions will be taught the Alphabet of politics, viz.: a government is not constituted to protect abstractions, but to protect the material interests of the country. These interests being shaken to their very center, so that every individual throughout the whole land feels its effect, the intoxication of the abstractionists will soon give way to the sober and practical schemes. The reaction has begun already. The republicans already exclaim with the Roman hero: "If we gain one more such victory we are lost,"[33] and the southern abstractionists will say so in less than two months.

In support of what we have said, we cut the following paragraph from the *N.Y. Times*, and let the reader judge they did not give in:

> What are we to concede? Can any of all the opponents of Mr. Lincoln here in the north tell? Of all the issues which have from time to time, since the beginning of the Government, so far as regards the Slavery question, been discussed by the people, there are none of which Mr. Lincoln has not given responses in accordance with former Southern demands. He will comply with the Constitutional requirements to deliver fugitive slaves; he will not oppose the inter-State trade in slaves; he will not oppose the admission of new States applying to be admitted with Slavery; he will not advocate the abolition of Slavery in the District of Columbia unless the owners of slaves themselves desire it, and are compensated; and he abjures all claim on the part of the Federal Government to interfere with Slavery in the States. What more in the name of all that is just, can be asked from a man or party?

> The bankers, stock jobbers and brokers made a mistake. They started the cry of bankruptcy with the intention to make money out of it; but now the flames envelope [*sic*] them on all sides, and they are bankrupt themselves. Now they themselves must quench the fire or they will have the worst part of their hasty transactions.

> Therefore we came to the conclusion to take in payment, all sorts of bills bankable in any state of the union, and request our subscribers to pay without delay in bills as they have them. We also offer all our stock for sale at fair prices and take for it South Carolina, Georgia, Alabama, Virginia, Missouri, Illinois, Baltimore or any other bills bankable anywhere in the union. Nay we even propose to take Massachusetts money notwithstanding Caleb Cushing and Senator Summer. The extremes will soon be cured.[34]

Two weeks prior to Lincoln's first inauguration, Wise published a sarcastic editorial condemning the Lincoln partisans for what he believed to be excesses of public display and an irresponsible use of public money in their celebrations of Lincoln's election. All of this was little more than sycophancy and humbuggery, Wise asserted, insisting that the new president had yet to prove himself and, until he did so, was not worthy of such adulation. He suggested that most of the celebrators were nothing but partisan politicians who were looking for patronage once Lincoln came to power. The rabbi/editor compared these loyalists to the biblical Philistines who worshiped before the false god of "Dagon."[35]

Once again, we see that in spite of the fact that Wise praised Lincoln after his death in 1865, he had criticized him during his presidency. At best, Wise expressed ambivalence about President-elect Lincoln. The rabbi admitted that he seemed to be "an honest man" and "an intelligent man," but he nevertheless had trouble imagining him as the nation's president. "He will look queer, in the white house," Wise concluded, "with his primitive manner."

No Life without Humbug

February 15, 1861

It is strange at the prima vista observation, that the American people, so eminently practical in every respect and living fully up to the rule "time is money," should at the same time be so fond of public spectacles, flimsy demonstrations, noisy processions and all sorts of humbug. Poor old Abe Lincoln, who had the quiet life of a country lawyer, having been elected President of this country, and going now to be inaugurated in his office, the Philistines from all corners of the land congregate around their Dagon and worship him. Here in Cincinnati the post-masters, collectors, judges, marshals, commissioners, *in spe*,[36] begged together about $1,500 to hire some carriages, give a banquet in the evening, drink champaign [*sic*], and sing hymns to Dagon. They disturb the people in their usual occupations, nay even the children in their schools, start an absurd tumult, and the masses run and gaze. Why? Wherefore? To what purpose? None can answer these questions. Why did the patriots not pay for the noise from their own pockets? Why can our big men not entertain the president elect on their own expense? Why all this noise? Nobody can answer.

We can not say what Mr. Lincoln has done for this country in politics, warfares, science or art; being a foreigner we can not be expected to know every man's biography; hence we can not tell why these extraordinary demonstrations, processions, banquets, &c., should be made. Wait till he has done something, then show him the honor due to the man; but even then do not imitate the man-worship of the Philistines; bow not down to Dagon. So we should think; rational men must think. Of course, office-hunters are prompted by other motives. But that the masses should thus blindly be led and confused by the seekers of office, is a poor testimony of the common sense of the multitude.

It strikes us that there is no life without humbug. The multitude must have a spectacle occasionally, and will run whenever and wherever a noisy demonstration is made. There is a tendency in the American people for diversions and spectacles; but it has no great influence upon anybody. Now they run to see and hear Mr. Lincoln. If in two weeks he should say or do anything they dislike, they would drag their own idol into the dust and decry him in the same ratio as they formerly deified him. It is a poor policy to honor a man publicly without knowing by settled precedents what he will do hereafter, just as poor as to decry a man we honored heretofore. Therefore we consider all those man-worshipping demonstrations unprincipled and unbecoming honorable men—of course the office-hunting Philistines always excepted: they must bow down to Dagon. The private citizen should never forget his own dignity as a man, and a republican chief should never accept of any public demonstrations which only degrade the citizen, and do no honor to anybody, especially not to him who knows he has done nothing yet to merit any public demonstrations.

Certain men who are the real benefactors of humanity, such as George Washington, Jefferson, Franklin, or Cromwell, and others in politics; or Bacon, Isaac Newton, Humboldt, and others in science; none of them received honors in advance of the actions; neither of them was fond of public demonstrations. But this is an age of humbug and spectacle, and myriads of thoughtless Philistines are glad when they hear some noise, or see some flimsy display, and must always have some Dagon to worship; because they find not dignity enough in themselves to live without noise; not sense enough to do without humbug. The madness of reckless demagogues having led this country to the brink of destruction, certainly will find pleasure in public demonstrations, to heat up the declining fire of sectionalism, they are excusable. But it would not do for peaceable citizens.

Some of our friends might like to know how the president looks, and we can tell them he looks like *Der Landjunker das erste Mal in der Stadt*, which is in good English, "like a country squire for the first time in the city." He wept on leaving Springfield and invited his friends to pray for him; that is exactly the picture of his looks. We have no doubt he is an honest man and, as much as we can learn, also quite an intelligent man; but he will look queer, in the white house, with his primitive manner.[37]

Lincoln concluded his first inaugural address by appealing to all citizens for peace and tranquillity. "My countrymen," he pleaded, "think calmly and well upon this whole subject." He reminded the nation that the values they shared in common were more powerful than their political divisions: "Intelligence, patriotism, Christianity, and a firm reliance on Him who has never yet forsaken this favored land are still competent to adjust in the best way all our present difficulty."[38]

According to Wise, he received at least a dozen letters expressing dismay over Lincoln's apparent assertion that the nation shared a common bond of "Christianity." Did Lincoln mean to say that American Jews were not part of the nation's social fabric? Lincoln was not the first U.S. president to employ such language in public address. Two decades earlier, for instance, John Tyler issued a proclamation stating that it was the duty of the Christian nation to mourn the death of his predecessor, William Henry Harrison. Many Jews wondered if they should be concerned about Lincoln's choice of words.

Although Wise was known to take notice of such slights, in this specific instance he advised his readers to pay little attention to Lincoln's phrasing. Ironically, Wise—an immigrant who spoke English with a German accent—criticized Lincoln's writing abilities. He explained to his readers that Lincoln, the man who two years later would compose the Gettysburg Address, was a "careless" writer who expressed himself without "either correctness or elegance."

Lincoln Does Not Care for Words

March 15, 1861

Editor's Remarks.—From a dozen letters on the same topic we publish only the above, because it comes from a particular friend. We only have to say for Mr. Lincoln, that his style of writing is so careless and without any successful attempt at either correctness or elegance that he must not be criticized on using this or that word to express an idea. He takes domestic words, as used in Springfield and vicinity to express familiar ideas. In Springfield religion is called Christianity, because people there do not think of any other form of worship, hence Mr. Lincoln uses the same word to express the same sentiment. Mr. Lincoln received the heaviest vote of infidels ever given to any man in this country. We do not believe there is a German infidel, American eccentric, spiritual rapper or atheist in northern states who did not vote for Mr. Lincoln. Let us see how much benefit he will derive from their Christianity, or how he will settle the political troubles with such piety. But his words must not be criticized too closely. He does not care for words. By and by he will learn the precise use and import of terms.[39]

In the context of an editorial on the Jewish holiday of Passover that appeared in the March 26, 1861, edition of the Chicago Tribune, *Rabbis Wise of Cincinnati and Raphall of New York were criticized for their anti-Republican and proslavery views. The unknown writer claimed that these two "pro-slaver divines" were notable exceptions to the vast majority of American Jews "who love freedom."*

In a fiery rejoinder to the Chicago editorial published in the Israelite *on April 5, 1861, the pro-Democrat Wise vigorously denied he was proslavery, but he also insisted that the Republicans were not friends of the Jews. As we have just seen, the rabbi had recently told his readers to ignore Lincoln's allusion to America as a Christian nation. In Wise's editorial response to the* Chicago Tribune, *Wise charges Lincoln with deliberately "forgetting" America's Jewish citizenry by contending that a common faith in "Christianity" could hold the nation together. As further proof of the Republican Party's disrespect for American Jewry, Wise lambastes the new Lincoln administration for failing to give "one single office to an Israelite."[40]*

The Jewish Passover

An editorial from the *Chicago Tribune*

March 26, 1861

Today, the 15th day of Nissan, according to Jewish chronology, the Israelites all over the world celebrate a truly abolition holiday—their Passah, or Passover. This day is kept in memory of the deliverance of the Israelites out of the Egyptian slavery, and though more than 3,000 years have passed since that event, by which the Hebrew nation was born, still today the Israelites praise every year the Lord most fervently for such deliverance; and, on the evenings of these holidays every Jewish family is assembled in its respective house in festive circle, and by hymns and songs express their thanks for being freemen. Taking the history of their people, and considering further, that still, in many parts of our globe, their co-religionists are oppressed, deprived of their natural rights, and looked upon as an inferior race, it is no wonder that the bulk of our Jewish fellow-citizens belong to the anti-slavery party, and fight in the ranks of the Republicans. They consider it their duty to accelerate the arrival of the time when *every* chain of bondage is broken, and *all* mankind celebrate their great Passah. True, the Jewish Synagogue in America is also blessed with some pro-slavery divines, just as well as the Christian churches. But, happily, such abnormalities as Rev. Dr. Wise of Cincinnati, and Rev. Dr. Raphall of New York, are scarce amongst our Israelites, and are the exception to the rule.[41]

Isaac M. Wise's reply to the editorial from the Chicago Tribune

The *Chicago Tribune* of March 26 in an article headed "The Jewish Passover," did not complete the sentence: the antithesis was forgotten altogether, and we must write it down for gentlemen with the expectation to complete that subject. You must continue that article thus: "Therefore Abraham Lincoln in his inaugural said: 'Intelligence, patriotism, Christianity, etc., are still competent to adjust in the best way all our present difficulty,' forgetting altogether his Jewish compatriots.["]—Therefore Senator [Henry] Wilson[42] of Massachusetts said: This country "gives equality of rights EVEN to that race who stoned the prophets and crucified the Redeemer of the world," and did not remember the patriotic supporters of the *Chicago Tribune.*—Therefore the *Boston Transcript* and other Republican organs hurl disgrace on the *Israelite*, forgetting the great devotion of the *Tribune* friends.—Therefore the present government which, as it appears from all transactions, being constituted only to make officers and divide the spoils among the sons of the Philistines has not given one single office to an Israelite, say not to one of all those whom the *Chicago Tribune* compliments.—Therefore "but we shall say no more, we know you and the world knows you.["] Please add this to your article in order to complete it, and do not drag us before the public through your sheet.[43]

In June 1864, the number of lives lost in Civil War battles overwhelmed and appalled the nation. Ulysses S. Grant sacrificed nearly 64,000 lives over the course of a six-week period in May and June 1864. The public had serious doubts that the war could be won, and thousands called on their government to negotiate a peace. Copperhead Democrats were determined to defeat Lincoln in November, and by August of that year, even Lincoln began to believe he was likely to lose his bid for a second term.

The editorial below sheds light on the gloomy atmosphere that prevailed during this time of despair and doubt. Like so many of his contemporaries, Wise had had his fill of "this terrible chaos." He desperately longed for "the blessings of union and peace," but it seemed to so many Americans that their politicians and their government had let them down. Only God, Wise confessed, knew how all of this would end.

This is a powerfully instructive editorial, because it illustrates the inscrutability of the future. In August 1864, Wise deeply resented "the blunders of [the nation's] military leaders" and Abraham Lincoln's "thousand and one demonstrations of imbecility." Eight months later, Wise would memorialize Lincoln as "the chosen banner-bearer of our people [and] the Messiah of this country."[44]

The Situation

August 19, 1864

If God in His infinite mercy should, as once he called into the dark chaos "let there be light," call this chaos of political opinions, pervent [*sic*] passions, horrid bloodshed and devastation, into this chaos of misery and affliction—"Be united!" how the deadly arms would sink from the hands of enraged combatants; how the thunders of cannons would suddenly cease, and the voice of song and joy be heard again; how cheerfully and soothingly the tidings of peace and union would sound from ocean to ocean, re-echo from every hamlet of this large country, and bring gladness home to every heart. How millions of people would shout with joy, if once more the sun should rise over a united country, and the armies beating their swords into plaugh-shares [*sic*], return home, each, to the cheerful hearth of domestic happiness. What a blessing to this country and to the world, it would be, if we should hear of joyous feasts in the place of carnage and conflagrations; if the telegraph informs us daily of the progress of science, art, industry and humanity, in place of the progress of armies! Not even those who, by official positions, family connections, or contract chances are becoming millionaires; not even the dupes of the men in power and legions led by burning passions, dare gainsay the great blessings of union and peace, or the calamity of war, hatred and disunion. All agree on this point; still, unless God in His infinite mercy calls into this terrible chaos "Be united!" no earthly power can heal our wounds, silence our raging passions, or give us back the blessings of union and peace; because we live in the land of extreme factions. God only can help us, no man and no class of men can.

Two factions, the one holding slavery to be a divine institution and the basis of civilized society, and the other considering it intolerable, disgraceful and outrageous—two extremes hurled the country into this abyss of destruction, and both factions are as mad, unscrupulous, reckless and fanatic to day after a million of men were buried or crippled, as they were ten years ago, when either of them was considered as harmless fanatics. The extremes are still as extreme as they were, and sway the scepter of power as they did. A man must either hate every man, woman and child in the rebellious states, or he must worship them as demigods; he must either speak of exterminating them and beg their pardon, in order to belong to the one or the other faction. Either he must rejoice over the defeat of our armies and pray for their destruction, or he must blindly admire the blunders of our military leaders and shout Hosanah to Abraham Lincoln and his thousand and one demonstrations of imbecility, in order to gratify one or the other faction. Either one must believe the Negro was created to be a beast of burden to others, or you must say, he is just as good as you are; in order to gratify your neighbors. Either you must shout the union without slavery or none, or you must say slavery first and liberty then in order to belong to this or that faction. There is no medium way, the factions, the extremes are as mad today as they ever were, the voice of moderate and considerate men is cried down. God alone can heal us of our madness.[45]

2. ISAAC LEESER PUBLISHES A LETTER FROM A CONCERNED JEWISH FATHER

Isaac Leeser, although not formally ordained as a rabbi, functioned in that capacity. He was an extremely knowledgeable lay leader, and he became a pioneering religious leader in Philadelphia. In contrast to Wise, who was an ardent religious reformer, Leeser sought to perpetuate traditional Jewish practice in an American setting. Toward this goal, Leeser worked as an author, translator, editor, and publisher of a journal titled the Occident and American Jewish Advocate.[46]

In January 1863, Leeser published a letter he had received from one of his subscribers, an immigrant Jewish farmer named Bernhard Behrend (1793–1865). Behrend was deeply disturbed about a general order Lincoln promulgated on November 15, 1862, "Respecting the Observance of the Sabbath Day in the Army and Navy." In this order, Lincoln declared that it was the sacred right of "Christian soldiers and sailors" to observe their Sabbath, and as commander-in-chief, he wanted "Sunday labor in the Army and Navy [to] be reduced to the measure of strict necessity."[47] According to Leeser, "Jewish editors throughout the country [took] due notice of the proclamation of the President of the United States."

Behrend, whose son Adajah Behrend (1841–1932) was in the Union army, promptly dashed off a letter of complaint to President Lincoln.[48] Reminding the president that "according to the Declaration of Independence and according to the constitution of the United States, the people of the United States is not a Christian people," the upset father asked Lincoln to issue a subsequent order granting his son—as well as Seventh Day Baptists—the right to observe the Sabbath on the seventh day. "Now I stand before you as your namesake Abraham stood before God Almighty," Behrend emoted; "I do not want [my son] . . . dragged either to the stake or the church to observe the Sunday as a Sabbath."

Although there is no record of Lincoln having responded to Behrend's letter, many years later his son Adajah, who became a highly regarded physician, claimed that in 1863 a general order was issued permitting Jews to be furloughed over the High Holy Days.[49]

Behrend's letter to Lincoln is reproduced below together with most of Leeser's prefatory remarks. Although Leeser noted he did not entirely agree with Behrend's style of expression, he firmly concurred with Behrend's fundamental point: America was not a Christian nation, and the government should not favor the religion of the majority over that of the minority. The editor of the Occident and American Jewish Advocate, *Leeser opined, should not be "placed in a position inferior to that of the Christian."*

Excerpts from "Are We Equals in This Land?"

December 4, 1862

This question obtrudes itself very often on our attention in spite of the most callous indifference to the possession of office by Israelites. Our readers have been often informed incidentally by us that we would look on with perfect equanimity were never a public position conferred on an Israelite in the army, navy, or civil life; for this depends on the relative position as regards numbers and influence, even more than on qualification or talents. Besides which, the men who are called to exercise public trusts think themselves generally absolved from all religious bonds, and transgress the divine precepts as though they had not been written down for the guidance of our conduct. It is moreover notorious that both here and elsewhere no sooner is a Jew dressed up "in little brief authority," than straightways he fancies himself elevated above his fellows, and is taller by a head than all his former companions and relatives: he is a new man and he hardly recognises himself in his new fashion. There now and then have been exceptions, but they only prove the rule; humility is now as always beautiful to Israel.

While therefore we should not utter a complaint if no Jewish names should encumber the lists of the various departments, or offices of whatever kind, save and alone in medical and academical [*sic*] positions: we cannot consent to have any disqualification fastened on us for the sake of our opinions, which do not attach themselves to our fellow citizens of other persuasions for the sake of their respective creeds. Offices may be withheld, though harshly, simply because they who bestow them choose not to confer them on us; it may be against equity and fairness, but it is not against any legal claim which we can set up; yet it is something very different when our personal rights are abridged while we never can have placed them without our consent in the safe keeping of others; wherefore no one has any right, in any conceivable manner, to abridge or to take them away from us.

. . . If for instance it is asserted that the minority of a community must not labor on a certain day in a manner which could confer no possible personal injury on their neighbors, solely because these choose to believe that work on that day is sinful, it says simply that the few who find no wrong in their contemplated action, which is supposed either not injurious or may be even beneficial to others, must forego their purpose, to please the sentiment of those who pay no deference whatever to the convictions of the former. Is this equality?—By what natural right, which only has to yield to the peace of society, can it be made apparent that I am bound to yield to my neighbor in a matter in which he would scout the idea of paying the least deference to my prejudices, convictions, sentiments, opinions, or whatever you may call them? I may yield my possessions from charity to individuals; the State may take my means for its support or defence equally with the possessions of others, because all this is needed for the general good, to which all must contribute as a simple matter of right; but sentiments and acts springing from them cannot be claimed or yielded, as the State cannot have an equitable claim to decide which are proper and which are not.

When therefore the constitution of the United States prohibits the imposition of any religious test, it meant evidently to prevent any part, however large, of the inhabitants of the country to make their religion a concern of the State, by which any one might think himself abridged in his right to think and act in matters which have reference to himself only in his relation to the Creator, but which do not prevent all others to pursue a similar course with respect to their conscientious convictions. It surprises us therefore, that people have by degrees learned to acquiesce in the gradual enforcement of Sunday-laws and similar enactments, as though they were matters which belong to the civil government of the State; when it is evident that Israelites are thereby placed in a position inferior to that of the Christian. We do not say that the latter should not keep the Sunday sacred, if they are so minded, any more than we would find fault with Mahomedans, if there be any in the country, for going to their Mosque on

Friday, and fasting through the month of Ramadan. It is certainly within the limit of their reserved rights; they do no injury to the State thereby, and no one individual has the least pretension to complain that they act differently from him. But with this privilege of doing as they please, their claim to protection for their opinion ceases; they must by the same law under which they take shelter, we mean that of equality, let every other person go his own way unmolested. They have no business to be worried or offended if one or many not sharing their convictions do what they will not practise; for there is no equitable tribunal before whom the parties could appear and have the question settled how far one must abstain from wounding his neighbor's feelings, for which he has no sympathy. The Christian may therefore keep his Sunday without asking the Jew's permission; but so may the latter do with his Sabbath without being justly amenable to the other. And still, every opportunity is seized to gratify the Christian's scruples at the expense of the Jew; a thousand safeguards are thrown around the Sunday to protect those who observe it against all inconvenience liable to arise from their abstaining from work, while everything is done to make the observance of the Seventh day burdensome to the Jew. Is this equality? Or are the rights of the minority of no importance in the eyes of the law-makers and the law-dispensers? But if this be so, we would ask, What use there can be in constitutional guaranties? Were they made to offer to the world a beautiful system in theory, the practice under which should be like that of Europe, which has no written fundamental law springing from the popular will?

The matter is worthy of our earnest attention, and we are pleased to learn that the Jewish editors throughout the country have taken due notice of the proclamation of the President of the United States, wherein he orders the strict observance of the Sunday in the army and navy, while the Sabbath is not even alluded to, in order to dispense thereon Israelites from unnecessary work, such as standing sentinel, while they could exchange their duties with one who felt no scruples for working on that day. For our part we should have passed the matter in silence, had we not received the subjoined from an old correspondent with the request to insert it; we did not think it proper to refuse compliance, although the petition contains a few passages which we do not approve of, and which will strike the reader at first sight. The complaint however is just, and should have met with a prompt redress, of which we have not heard as yet through the usual channels. While thus we present the remonstrance of Mr. Behrend, we thought it proper to append a few remarks of our own, if it be but only to show that we feel a deep interest in the maintenance of the rights of conscience guaranteed in the fundamental law of the land, which are often nevertheless violated, for instance in the late thanksgiving proclamation of the Governor of Pennsylvania, who in recommending that people should "especially pray to God to give to Christian churches the grace to hate the thing which is evil," &c, actually excluded Israelites from participating in the observance of the day. We deemed it useless to complain through the press of this forgetfulness of our presence in the commonwealth, as we had done so on several previous occasions, only to find the offence again and again repeated. But when the same thing strikes others no less than us, we may fairly join our voice to theirs, in the hopes of sooner or later succeeding in having the matter put at rest by acknowledging our equality on all fitting occasions.

To His Excellency the President of the United States

By your order of the 16th day of November, 1862, you recommend that the officers and men of the army shall observe the Sabbath and do no work on Sunday, because we are a Christian people. But according to the Declaration of Independence and according to the constitution of the United States, the people of the United States is not a Christian people, but a free, sovereign people with equal rights, and each and every citizen of the United States has the right and liberty to live according to his own consciousness [sic] in religious matters, and no one religious denomination, be it a majority or minority of the people, can have a privilege before the other under this our beloved constitution.

Now by the order of your Excellency you give the privilege to those officers and men in the army who by their religious creed do observe the Sunday as a holy day and a day of rest; but you make no provision for those officers and men in the army who do not want to observe the Sunday as a holy day, (as for instance those Christians called the Seventh-day Baptists and the Jews, who observe the Saturday as a holy day and a day of rest,) that they may enjoy the same privilege as those who observe the Sunday as a holy day, as well as for the heathen or the so called infidels, who do not want to celebrate either the Sunday or the Saturday as a Sabbath, but choose perhaps some other day as a day of rest.

Now I stand before you as your namesake Abraham stood before God Almighty in days of yore, and asked, "Shall not the Judge of all earth do justice?" so I ask your Excellency, the first man and President of all the United States, Shall you not do justice? Shall you not give the same privilege to a minority of the army that you give to the majority of it? I beseech you to make provision, and to proclaim in another order, that also all those in the army who celebrate another day as the Sunday may be allowed to celebrate that day which they think is the right day according to their own conscience; and this will be exactly lawful, as the Constitution of the United States ordains it, and at the same time it will be exactly according to the teaching of the Bible, as recorded in Leviticus xix. 18: "Thou shalt love thy neighbor as thyself."

I gave my consent to my son, who was yet a minor, that he should enlist in the United States army; I thought it was his duty, and I gave him my advice to fulfill his duty as a good citizen, and he has done so. At the same time I taught him also to observe the Sabbath on Saturday, when it would not hinder him from fulfilling his duty in the army. Now I do not want that he shall be dragged either to the stake or the church to observe the Sunday as a Sabbath. Your Excellency will observe in this my writing that I am not very well versed in the English language, and if there should be found a word which is not right, pardon it, and never such a word shall be construed so as if I would offend your Excellency or the people; for I love my country, the Constitution, and the Union, and I try to be always a loyal citizen.

I remain, respectfully, your most obedient servant and fellow citizen,

B[ernhard] Behrend

Narrowsburg, Sullivan Co. N.Y. Dec. 4, 1862[50]

3. RABBI MORRIS J. RAPHALL'S CRITICAL THANKSGIVING DAY PRAYER

On March 30, 1863, Abraham Lincoln issued yet another proclamation that urged the nation to mark a "Day of National Humiliation, Fasting, and Prayer" thirty days later on April 30.[51] In its coverage of the somber day's activities, the Jewish Messenger *of New York City observed: "It was very evident that less respect was manifested for the recommendation of the Executive, than has heretofore been characteristic of Gothamites. One very large denomination omitted to notice the day; among citizens generally, there was a less cordial and hearty recognition of the necessity of national prayer and humiliation."[52]*

Despite the lack of interest in the general community, the Jewish community of New York dutifully complied with Lincoln's request. The following week, the local Jewish press published a number of the rabbinical addresses that were delivered on the occasion. As we see from the following document, Rabbi Morris J. Raphall of Bene Yeshurun Congregation reflected the cheerless mood that had overtaken a nation weary of bloodshed and strife. His rhetorical question was the same as that of his colleague Isaac M. Wise: When would the bloodletting stop, and when would peace return? There was no answer to this query, because reasonable leaders—"the best men, north and south"—had been "driven" from public service and the reins of power "had fallen into the hands of demagogues, fanatics, and a partisan press."

The prominent Washingtonian Adolphus S. Solomons has recorded that he once helped Raphall obtain a personal audience with Lincoln on a National Day of Humiliation and Fasting—presumably a day other than the one that Lincoln proclaimed on April 30, 1863. Solomons recollected that on that occasion, Raphall wanted Lincoln to promote his son Alfred to the rank of lieutenant. "After Lincoln had heard the Rabbi's request he blurted out, 'As God's minister is it not your first duty to be at home today to pray with your people for the success of our arms, as is being done in every loyal church throughout the North, East and West?'" As Solomons recollected, Raphall was embarrassed by the question, so he assured Lincoln that his assistant was "doing that duty."

"Ah," said Lincoln, "that is different." After agreeing to promote his son, Lincoln supposedly told Raphall—with a smile—"Now doctor, you can go home and do your own praying."[53]

According to the newspaper report reproduced below, on this National Day of Humiliation and Fasting, Raphall was in his pulpit and illustrated his point about the nation's moral decline by noting that the U.S. government had refused to recompense the heirs of a Jew residing in Philadelphia who in the darkest hours of the War of Independence had devoted his vast wealth to the service of his adopted country. Raphall was probably referring to the family of Haym Solomon (1740–85), a Jewish Revolutionary War hero, whose family had been trying to recoup Solomon's personal funds that had been loaned to the fledgling U.S. government.

The National Fast Day

May 8, 1863

The Rev. Dr. Raphall then ascended the pulpit, taking his text from Nehemiah IX:35, which he rendered: "In their dominions, in all the great prosperity Thou didst bestow upon them, and throughout the large and rich land which Thou gavest them, they did not serve Thee, neither turned they from their evil deeds."

> Hitherto the government, in the full pride of national prosperity had deemed one annual day of public thanksgiving a sufficient expression of gratitude; but not that evil times had befallen them, they came again and again, and called upon the people to weary heaven with fruitless professions of a penitence they did not feel, and a humility they did not practice. These proclamation-fast-days, on which no one fasted, were too much like those denounced by the prophet Isaiah. The parallel between the people of Israel and that of the United States was most striking.
>
> All the earthly blessings which as Nehemiah confessed, had been possessed and abused by ancient Israel, had equally, though a more extensive scale, been possessed and perverted by the U.S., for "they served not God." His hearers need not remind him of the many steeple shops,—as the Puritans called them—that every where met the eye. But these brick-and-mortar-witnesses of sectarian rancour, afford no proof that within their precincts God is served. The prophet Hosea tells us that tho' "Israel forgot their Maker, they built temples," and the parallel holds good in the U.S.[54] While in some of these churches the torch of civil war had been kindled; while in others, bloodshed and havoc had been preached; while each church claimed for itself perfection, and consigned all others to perdition, while this world with its sinful passions and vile selfishness reigned paramount in every one of them, it was plain

that God was not served in any of them. The only subject on which the fanatic and ever-rangling teachers in these strongholds of spiritual pride could agree was to hate and revile us, to persecute and falsely to slander the dispersed ones of Israel. If we leave the churches and enter the daily walks of life we shall find that "like priest like people." Every one serves, but not God. It is assumed that the Almighty Creator has, if not quite abdicated, at least delegated a great portion of His power to the almighty dollar. In this service every house is a church, every heart an altar, and every worshipper sincere. Accordingly they do not turn from their evil deeds. The two greatest early blessings Providence has placed within the reach of mankind, education and freedom, had both been perverted by the people on whom they had been so fully bestowed. Education in the U.S. taught neither respect for free institutions nor patriotism nor even common honesty. The simplest precept to the individual, "Honor thy father and mother" was by American education, tested by its priests, perverted into "old fogyism"; the highest duty of the community, a pure administration of justice, was by American education perverted into venal justice, partisan justice, and denial of justice.

As a proof of the latter, we had the action of Congress which evaded the payment of a very large sum of money, long and justly due to the heirs of a Jew residing in Philadelphia who in the darkest hours of the war of independence had devoted his vast wealth to the service of his adopted country.—At the time of his death the country was not yet in a condition to pay him. Since then, it has grown rich and powerful. Millions have been squandered; millions had been pilfered; but tho' the claim of his heirs had been repeatedly examined by committees of both houses of Congress, who reported favorably and recommended immediate payment,—not one cent had ever been repaid.

The abuses of freedom were even worse than those of education. While the best men, north and south, had been driven to stand aloof, public affairs had fallen into the hands of demagogues, fanatics, and a partisan press. The consequence was an atrocious and devastating but needless civil war, at which humanity wept, while we must suppress our sympathy.

Dr. Raphall concluded with a fervent prayer.[55]

4. AN EVALUATION OF LINCOLN'S SECOND INAUGURAL ADDRESS

Some have called Lincoln's second inaugural address his "greatest speech"; Frederick Douglass was deeply moved by Lincoln's words, and he told the president his address was a "a sacred effort." In his autobiography, Douglass said the speech was "more like a sermon than like a state paper."[56]

As we see from the following document, at the time Lincoln's address did not meet with universal acclaim. A Washington, D.C., correspondent with the initials "S. W.,"[57] *writing for the* Jewish Messenger, *described the speech as "decidedly Lincoln, original, terse, and an insinuating desire for a joke all over."*

The President's Inaugural Was as Brief as He Is Long

March 17, 1865

Dear Messenger:—Some months have elapsed since I last had the honor of contributing a moiety of news from the capitol of the nation. This being a pleasant, beautiful day (of which, here, we have few), I feel constrained once again to essay, by informing you that the City of Magnificent Distances is, as in the days of yore, watered by Potomac, that here blatent [*sic*] politicians must do congregate, that Mr. Lincoln, late from the West, was, on the fourth day of March, inaugurated Chief Clerk of the people of the United States, that last night we had an Inauguration Ball, which, by the authority of Jenkins and his tribe, was a "*recherché* affair," visited and enjoyed by the President and lady, Vice-President, Cabinet Officers, Diplomatic Corps, members of Congress, representatives from the Army and Navy, civilians, petroleumites, oilites, shoddyites, and gentlemen about town, with their attendant satellites. Admission was ten dollars, and, from the vast number present, the display of toilettes, diamond, &c., there can be no doubt that greenbacks are plenty, gold on the decline, and glorious peace dawning upon us. Remember, this ball was given to benefit the families of soldiers, and the nett [*sic*] balance will make the anecdote of "catching the tartar" very applicable. . . .

The Re-inauguration, in consequence of bad weather, it having rained incessantly for forty-eight hours, was a small affair, the President's Inaugural was as brief as he is long, and evinced more of the priest than the statesman. It was decidedly Lincoln, original, terse, and an insinnating [*sic*] desire for a joke all over: "The rebels have prayed, so have we, it is yet doubtful whose have been answered." . . .

I am, as ever, truly yours, S. W.[58]

5. LINCOLN'S CONDUCT HAS BEEN INVARIABLY STRAIGHTFORWARD

On January 17, 1862, New York City's Jewish Messenger *began to publish an ongoing series of firsthand accounts of life in the Union army, written by a Jewish soldier. The column, titled "Sketches from the Seat of War," appeared in nine installments, with the last edition of "sketches" appearing on March 14, 1862. The sketches were written by an unidentified Jewish soldier who wanted to give the paper's readers a personalized account of his experiences and thoughts over the first several months of the Civil War.*

In the third installment in the series, the Jewish soldier shared his opinion of President Lincoln, whom he clearly admired. The soldier expressed broad sympathy for Lincoln's political struggles. The president had barely taken up the reins of office when he was confronted with open rebellion and civil war. In spite of these challenges, Lincoln's conduct was genuinely admirable. "Under all these trying circumstances," the soldier opined, lesser men would have resorted to "humiliating concessions . . . duplicity or treachery."

In analyzing why Lincoln became so popular with the enlisted soldiers in the Union army, one historian pointed to the president's remarkable accessibility.[59] The Jewish soldier's testimony lends additional credence to this contention. The writer saw Lincoln with his own eyes when he was reviewing the troops. "You will always find him neat [and] civil," the soldier wrote, "and,—if common report be true—always ready for a joke." These sketches exemplify how Lincoln, through conversation, intelligence, and good humor, earned the support, affection, and admiration of his troops.

Excerpts from "Sketches from the Seat of War"

January 31, 1862

The great issues dependent on this conflict, will give prominent place in History to all those who are now directing the affairs of the nation, and either cover them with glory, or disgrace them in the eyes of posterity, in the same proportion as success or failure will result from their plans and efforts. Foremost among these, is of course, the President Abraham Lincoln, held forth on the one side as the cause of the Rebellion, and on the other as the champion of constitutional government, but in reality representing before his election, nothing more than the principles of a majority in the free states on the subject of slavery, though, after having been constitutionally elected, all loyal citizens of other parties, as well as of his own, look upon him as the chief magistrate of the Republic, whose authority could not be questioned without giving a deathblow to the Union and the Constitution. Having been raised by the whims of fortune from the humble position of a country lawyer, to the most exalted office it is in the power of the American nation to confer, he no sooner hears the gladdening news of his election, than the diabolical spirit of discord and disunion, overshadowing the land, dispels from his mind the pleasing anticipations of a peaceful and harmonious administration. Before he is enabled to wield the power of the government, he sees the national difficulties encouraged and aggravated by a traitorous administration, a rebel government, obeyed by seven states, and enlisting the sympathies of five others,—forts and national vessels freely given up, mints and other public property appropriated by lawless politicians; and when at last, he sets out to assume the reins of government, the assassin's knife is whetted to slay him, whilst a rebel force are lurking in Virginia to seize the capital. Under all these trying circumstances, which a coward would have me[t] with humiliating concessions, and a villain with duplicity or treachery, Mr. Lincoln's conduct, as well as professions, has been uniformly, and invariably straight-forward, exhibiting, on all occasions, an unwavering honesty of purpose, and integrity, earnestness and patriotic devotion, as well as moral courage and firmness, which no failure can ever tarnish nor reverses obliterate from the records of History. His political opponents admit this, and his friends claim nothing more for him.

Like Saul of old, he is head and shoulders taller than his brethren, so that he has actually to stoop when he enters into conversation with ordinary mortals, and it is this, more than his figure, that gives him such an awkward appearance. He is by no means a bad-looking man, nor is his hair uncombed, not his dress disorderly, as most people seems [sic] to infer from the wretched pictures exhibited in the stores. Whether you meet him taking his morning walk, or at a *levee*, you will always find him neat, civil, and,—if common report be true—always ready for a joke. Those that have known him in his social relations, speak of him as a kind father, a too indulgent husband, and a sincere friend.[60]

6. "I AM NOW A STRONG ABOLITIONIST"

Many Union soldiers did not understand the horrors of slavery until they saw the institution with their own eyes while fighting in the South. Such was the case of Colonel Marcus M. Spiegel (1829–64). Spiegel, who served in the 67th and 120th Ohio Volunteer Infantry regiments, wrote detailed letters to his wife, Caroline ("Cary"). More than 150 of these letters survived, and they constitute a rich resource shedding light on the everyday experiences and thoughts of a Union soldier.

In late 1863 and early 1864, when the 120th was stationed near Plaquemine, Louisiana, not too far from Baton Rouge, Spiegel had ample opportunity to observe slavery firsthand. Writing to his wife on January 22, 1864, Spiegel confessed, "I have learned and seen more of what the horrors of Slavery was than I ever knew." After seeing the "peculiar institution"[61] with his own eyes, Spiegel understood Lincoln's decision to emancipate the slaves, and he informed his wife he would never again cast his vote for anyone who supported slavery.[62]

Writing a month later—ironically, on Lincoln's birthday—Spiegel's views on slavery had obviously become more resolute, and he informed his wife, "I am now a strong abolitionist."

Excerpts from Marcus Spiegel's letter to his wife, Caroline

Plaquemine La Feby 12/64
My dear good and kind Cary!

Yesterday I received your very good and loving letter of the 22nd ultimo and I have been joyous ever since; I say like you this is the first real good and lovely letter I have received since I left home; the others all were as blue that they made everything look black to me, but thank God "Richard is himself again."[63]

... I have been to see several large Planters and find them very hospitable; they live like princes, are proud and aristocratic, but exceedingly pleasant and agreeable to the Federal Officers. Slavery has been abolished in Louisiana[64] and they are just as keen to get the negro to work for pay as they used to while slaves, and I am satisfied in twenty five years from now, the negro will be an educated, well to do laborer and the white man none the worse. This you know I see from my own experience; I am now a strong abolitionist, but I want laws and regulations by which the negro must be made to work and educated and the present Master be compelled to do it. Slavery is gone up whether the War ends to day or in a year and there is no use crying over it; it has been an awful institution. I will send you the "black code" of Louisiana[65] some of these days and I am satisfied it will make you shudder.

Now understand me when I say I am a strong abolitionist, I mean that I am not so for party purposes but for humanity sake only, out of my own conviction, for the best Interest of the white man in the south and the black man anywhere.[66] I find some few large slaveholders concur in my opinion; of course the major part of them would prefer the old System. The poor white man, the mechanic and laborer in this country however, find that a new era is dawning for them in this Country (South); herethefore they were almost worse [off] then the negro slave here.

... As long as the war looks so important and call after call for men, it seems as though a soldier and Patriot could have no rest except in the Army. I have an excellent Regiment, my men almost worship me, and if I were to resign to day, one half of my officers would also and perhaps demoralize the Regiment which could be doing the Government more harm then [*sic*] my humble efforts perhaps ever done it good; but never mind, I do not believe you really want me to resign. I think you are really proud of your Soldier man, only you do not like to let on.

Good bye. God bless you, my love to the children and all friends.

Ever your true

Marcus

7. A HEBREW TRIBUTE TO LINCOLN

In 1865, Isaac Goldstein,[67] a Jewish businessman, composed an original Hebrew poem exulting in Lincoln's achievements. The poem is an acrostic; each line of the poem (which is read from right to left) begins with a different Hebrew letter so that the name "Abraham Lincoln"—in Hebrew—appears vertically on the right.

In Jewish liturgical tradition, the acrostic was a popular genre that can be traced back to the biblical era. Goldstein, a Hebrew aficionado, seemed to have modeled his tribute to Lincoln after Psalm 145 (he also borrowed Hebrew verses from Psalms 84, 144,

POEMS

WHO IS LIKE UNTO THEE, O LINCOLN
by ISAAC GOLDSTEIN, *the Levite*

Happy art thou, Lincoln, who is like
    unto thee

Among kings and princes thou art exalted.

Much thou didst with an humble spirit.

Thou art like a unique person in the land.

Who among princes is like Lincoln?

Who shall be praised like him?

Acrostic

ON ABRAHAM LINCOLN, ASSASSINATED NISAN 18th, 5625.

רחם לבי נרבי׳ טוב, אומר אוו מעשי, למלך :

א שריך לינקאלען מי כמוכה
ב ין מלכים ושרים מאור נשאת ׳
ר בות, פעלת בנפש נמוכה ׳
ה נך ליחיד בארץ דמית ׳
מ י בגוזנים כלינקאלען ומי יתהלל כמהו :

ל ך שם גם כגבורים ׳
י מינך עשה חיל ׳
נ גרם, חגרת חרב חללים ׳
ק שתך דרכת יומם וליל ׳
א כ אחד בראנו ׳ אמרת ׳
ל כן דרור השמעת פקודיך ׳
ע ם הכושים לחירות גאלת ׳
נ צח יפארו ויברכו שמיך ׳

מי בחוזנים כלינקאלען ומי יתהלל כמוהו
(אייזיק גאלדשטיין הלוי

The above is a reproduction of a poem, in
its original Hebrew, as it appeared in the
Jewish Messenger, May 26, 1865.

Thou hast also a name among heroes!

Thy right hand has achieved prowess
    against them.

Thou hast girded on the sword of the
    slain.

Thou hast drawn the bow by night
    and by day.

One Father has created us, thou hast said;

Therefore thou hast proclaimed
    Freedom in thy land.

The black people thou hast redeemed
    unto Freedom:

Forever they will praise and bless
    thy name.

Who among princes is like Lincoln and
    who can be praised like him?

(Translated from the Hebrew)

Isaac Goldstein's Hebrew "Acrostic" appeared in the *Jewish Messenger*, May 26, 1865, p. 165, and was republished in Philip Goodman, comp. and ed., *Lincoln's Birthday: Program Material for Jewish Groups* (New York: National Jewish Welfare Board, Jewish Center Division, 1953), 53. The acrostic, probably written prior to Lincoln's assassination, lauds Lincoln for his courage and valor and for freeing the slaves. Courtesy JWB Jewish Chaplains Council.

and 115). Traditional Jews recite Psalm 145 daily, and they would undoubtedly be familiar with Goldstein's allusions in both form and content.

Although it is impossible to date the poem with certainty, the fact that the acrostic makes no reference to Lincoln's death implies that the poem may very well have been written to celebrate the surrender of the Confederacy and the Union's victory. By the time it appeared, however, the president had been assassinated, and Goldstein's poem was published as a postmortem elegy.[68]

REACTIONS TO LINCOLN'S ASSASSINATION

8. "GOD GRANT SO MAY ALL OUR FOES PERISH!"

The year that Lincoln was assassinated, Eleanor H. Cohen (1841–74) was a twenty-six-year-old Jewish woman living in Columbia, South Carolina. Cohen had begun keeping a diary only a few months earlier, in February 1865. On April 30, 1865, Cohen wrote her private thoughts about Lincoln's murder into the pages of her diary. The young woman was an ardent patriot of the Confederacy, and as far as she was concerned, Lincoln deserved the punishment he had received.

It is extremely rare to find such sentiments preserved in writing. In this instance, Cohen was confiding in herself; she assumed no one else would read her words. If Cohen felt as she did about Lincoln, there must have been many others who shared this same point of view. The majority of these people, however, did not preserve such opinions in written form.

Cohen's entry on June 2, 1865, is equally noteworthy. Her slaves had chosen freedom and left her; Cohen still blamed the deceased Lincoln. She believed in the "institution of slavery," and she did not want to see it abolished.

Excerpts from Eleanor Cohen's diary

April 30 and June 2, 1865

April 30th: Politically I have much to say. No peace yet agreed upon, but negociations [*sic*] are being carried on, and people generally think peace will follow. Abram Lincoln was assassinated in the Washington theatre by a man who exclaimed: "Death to traitors; Virginia is avenged!" So our worst enemy is laid low, and [Secretary of State William H.] Seward, the arch fiend, was also stabbed, and today we hear the glorious tidings that the Yankee Congress had a row and [Vice President] Andy Jonson [Johnson] was killed. God grant so

In her diary, Eleanor H. Cohen, from Columbia, South Carolina, expressed satisfaction that Lincoln, the South's "foe," had been assassinated. Courtesy The Jacob Rader Marcus Center of the American Jewish Archives, at the Hebrew Union College–Jewish Institute of Religion, Cincinnati, Ohio.

may all our foes perish! I had a short letter today from Mr. S.,[69] but it told me he was well, and loved me; so I am happy.

June 2d: I cannot but blame myself for my long neglect of this dear old book, but really I have lived in such a whirl that I entirely forgot to note events, important as they are. Peace has come, but, oh, God, what a different peace to the one we prayed for! We are conquered by superior numbers. Sherman and Johns[t]on declared an armistice; since then, the war is over, we know not on what terms.

Slavery is done away with. Our noble [Confederate president] Jeff Davis, as well as all of our great men, are prisoners; even the governors of the several states have been arrested. Confederate money is worthless and greenbacks rule the day. Columbia and all the principal [cities] are garrisoned by Yankees. How it makes my Southern blood boil to see them in our streets! Yes, we are again in the hated Union, and over us again floats the banner that is now a sign of tyranny and oppression. [Andrew] Johnson was not killed and is now President. Sad, sad is the change since the days of [President George] Washington. My brothers are all home after fearful deprivations and hardships. Thank God, they are spared. Poor Josh Moses, the flower of our circle, was killed at Blakely [Alabama, April 1865]. He was a noble man, another martyr to our glorious cause. . . .

Our servants, born and reared in our hands, hitherto devoted to us, freed by Lincoln, left us today. It is a severe trial to mother, and quite a loss to me. Among them went Lavinia, a girl given to me by my grandmother, very handy, and who had promised always to remain with [me] and, when I was married, to go with me. Mr. S. was so pleased; he wrote me to tell her, if she proved faithful, he would take her North and show her [off] as one faithful servant. But she went. She behaved better than most of them; she offered to come to me in town and do anything. She gave me notice and showed regret at parting. This is one of the fruits of war. I, who believe in the institution of slavery, regret deeply its being abolished. I am accustomed to have them to wait on me, and I dislike white servants very much. . . .[70]

9. SOME SOUTHERN SYMPATHIZERS CHEERED

Harris Newmark (1834–1916) was born in Löbau in the province of Saxony. He immigrated to the United States in 1853 and soon settled in Los Angeles. A merchant who later in life began to invest in real estate, Newmark was one of the founders of the Los Angeles Jewish community. Toward the end of his life, Newmark wrote his memoirs, which are an invaluable source of information on the history of Jewish life in Los Angeles during the last half of the nineteenth century.

In the following excerpt from Newmark's memoirs, he recollected how some southern sympathizers cheered when they learned of Lincoln's death. His family physician did so, as did a young German-Jewish immigrant named Henry Baer. Newmark's reminiscences confirm that there were unquestionably some instances of "ill-advised exultation" on the part of southern Jews, but most Jews thought such behavior was improper.

Celebrating Lincoln's Assassination in Los Angeles

On the fifteenth of April, my family physician, Dr. John S. Griffin, paid a professional visit to my house on Main Street, which might have ended disastrously for him. While we were seated together by an open window in the dining-room, a man named Kane ran by on the street, shouting out the momentous news that Abraham Lincoln had been shot! Griffin, who was a staunch Southerner, was on his feet instantly, cheering for Jeff Davis. He gave evidence, indeed, of great mental excitement, and soon seized his hat and rushed for the door, hurrahing for the Confederacy. In a flash, I realized that Griffin would be in awful jeopardy if he reached the street in that unbalanced condition, and by main force I held him back, convincing him at last of his folly. In later years the genial Doctor frankly admitted that I had undoubtedly saved him from certain death.

This incident brings to mind another, associated with Henry Baer, whose father, Abraham, a native of Bavaria and one of the earliest tailors here, had arrived from New Orleans in 1854. When Lincoln's assassination was first known, Henry ran out of the house, singing *Dixie* and shouting for the South; but his father, overtaking him, brought him back and gave him a sound whipping[,] an act nearly breaking up the Baer family, inasmuch as Mrs. Baer was a pronounced Secessionist.

The news of Lincoln's assassination made a profound impression in Los Angeles, though it cannot be denied that some Southern sympathizers, on first impulse, thought that it would be advantageous to the Confederate cause. There was, therefore, for the moment, some ill-advised exultation; but this was promptly suppressed, either by the military or by the firm stand of the more level-headed members of the community. Soon even radically-inclined citizens, in an effort to uphold the fair name of the town, fell into line, and steps were taken fittingly to mourn the nation's loss.[71]

10. "NEW YORK IS LITERALLY CLAD IN BLACK"

The reaction of a young Jewish woman named Josephine Phillips (1814–96) to Lincoln's assassination contrasts sharply with the sentiments expressed by southern partisans like Eleanor Cohen and Henry Baer. Phillips was deeply disturbed by the news of Lincoln's assassination, and in a letter she wrote to her brother-in-law, Adolphus S. Solomons, on April 20, 1865, less than a week after Lincoln was killed, she conveyed a sense of her profound grief as well as the great sorrow that enveloped New York.

Josephine's sister and brother-in-law were prominent citizens in the nation's capital. Lincoln associated with the Solomons, and the family was invited to attend White House receptions and various events together with the president. Adolphus and his wife, Rachel, frequently hosted family members in their home, and some of these familial guests wrote down their memories of these special events.[72]

Having met Lincoln personally, Josephine wrote as though her loss was personal. Citing words written by the poet William Cowper (1731–1800), she memorialized Lincoln "with love & veneration for the man 'whose heart was warm whose hands were pure whose doctrine & whose life coincident exhibit lucid proof that he was honest in the sacred cause & to such are rendered more than mere respect.'"

Dear Adolphus:

I received your letter last Monday & presume you also got mine containing our mutual sorrow & horror at the sad event that has plunged all in profound grief, *never* in history has *any* event in *any* nation brought forth such real regret, & the loyalty of the people high & low rich & poor is seen mingled with love & veneration for the man "whose heart was warm whose hands were pure whose doctrine & whose life coincident exhibit lucid proof that he was honest in the sacred cause & to such are rendered *more* than mere respect." These lines from Cowper are forcibly brought to my recollection as illustrating much of the character of our lamented President. New York is literally clad in black & it is more rare to see a house without it than with it, from the splendid mansion to the smallest Shanty, even the gates of the poorest black or white display their emblem of sorrow; full well I can imagine how badly you feel it was only last week you wrote me about your being at his house & seeing him come out & request the band to play Dixie, & to-day that he appointed to celebrate our victories, his own funeral takes place. I have not yet recovered from the shock of last Saturday. Yesterday we had shool[73] & a very large assemblage, the services were very solemn, the Tabah[74] was covered with black also the pillars & gallery, to-day we have it again at three o'clock nothing is thought or talked of today *no stores* are opened & the poorest person will not work. I see by the paper the body will be here on Monday,[75] his poor wife & children what a sad change for them! I am truly glad Mr. Seward & son will recover[76] & also that his assassin is arrested, but it seems strange Booth has yet eluded the vigilance of the police, his Mother I hear resides in 19th St. N.Y. & is of course in the greatest affliction, what a villain he is!

People already have changed their opinion regarding the new President & seem to think he will carry out the programme in a great measure of Mr. Lincoln.

I trust this will find you all well. Pa has a cold Beck has suffered considerably with Neuralgia.[77] Pa felt very badly about the news, & I dare say all the children from Ida down were grieved, you remember how he noticed them the last visit I was there to see him with you, his likenesses sell like wildfire, the one I bought on the Carte de visit[e][78] one that he sat last for[79] I gave to Isaac[80] when I first came on & he now has it in his window. I may as well leave off for I can write about nothing else, the late victories are not spoken of. I see by this morning paper Mosby & seven hundred guerillas had surrendered.[81] All send much love to dear Rachel, Mary Jane[82] yourself & kisses to the dear children as ever yours most aff—

Josephine[83]

11. ISAAC M. WISE'S REFLECTIONS ON LINCOLN'S RELIGION

In the following document, which appeared in the April 28, 1865, edition of the German language periodical Die Deborah, *Isaac M. Wise provided his readers with his own reflections on "Lincoln's religion." Just days after Lincoln's death, Wise declared that not only he but three other witnesses as well were present when Lincoln announced he had long believed he had "descended from Jewish parents" and, also, that he even looked Jewish!*[84]

In spite of the fact that the rabbi had never hesitated to criticize Lincoln when he was president—even accusing him on one occasion of being an imbecile—Wise nevertheless heaped praise on Lincoln in his eulogies and described the fallen leader as "the most outstanding hero who determined and controlled the conditions."

Wise implies that Lincoln was a Jewish sojourner. Although it is highly doubtful that anyone will be able to validate Wise's story asserting that Lincoln thought he came from Jewish stock, Wise was thoroughly convinced that Lincoln was never a believing Christian. His religious convictions, Wise implied, were spiritually aligned with Judaism's ancient teachings.

Abraham Lincoln's Religion

Honored readers will find in the *Israelite* two speeches delivered in Cincinnati synagogues on the 19th of this month during memorial services for the slain President of the United States. One speech, to appear next week, was by Dr. Lilienthal, the other by the editor of the *Deborah*.

No poet has ever thought up a more magnificent dramatic topic than the Civil War, lasting four years and ending with the most complete victory of freedom and with the death of the most outstanding hero who determined and controlled the conditions. The impression of this concluding scene (Lincoln's assassination) is so powerful and ineradicable, so moving and profound that no one can forget this great drama of truth. The consequences for history are incalculable. Lincoln's murderer has inflamed the heart of this nation. The fire will consume every trace of slavery and oppression, its flame will flash across the seas to rattle the tottering frames of European politics.

The deceased has rendered an important service to the cause of freedom of religion. As I explained in my sermon, Lincoln maintained before four witnesses, I being one of them, that he believed he was descended from

Jewish parents, and he insisted that his face had Jewish features, which was indeed so. In spite of his puritanical piety, which surfaced at times in most poignant expressions, he never in public or in private spoke of a triune God, of a crucified savior, or of anything specifically Christian. He was not baptized, did not belong to any religious denomination and had none of his children baptized or confirmed. The numerous Christian clergymen who, on the 19th of this month, talked about each trait of his character and every action of his life, made no mention of Lincoln's religion. Mr. Chalfant of Cincinnati[85] said in his address: "Of Mr. Lincoln's Christian character, I have said nothing, for I know nothing, but by inference." They all remained silent [on this subject] for the same reason.

A little known clergyman from Illinois, though, recently stated that Lincoln, on being directly asked whether he was a Christian, had replied: "At Gettysburg [after the battle], I was a Christian. I love Jesus," which, in reality, indirectly answers the question in the negative.

There is no need to spell out that this fact will forever stamp the American people with freedom of conscience. The Messrs. Bigoted will do well to refrain from once more asserting one had to be a Christian to be a good human being and a good citizen. On the 19th of this month they all resorted to Old Testament texts, or compared Lincoln to Old Testament heroes like Moses, Joshua, Samuel and others. What they think of his eternal bliss cannot be ascertained; he was not baptized and believed himself to be of Jewish descent. The American people have canonized him and the bigots remain silent.[86]

9

Memorializing and Judaizing Lincoln

The process of memorializing, dignifying, and ultimately transforming Lincoln into a national icon took place incrementally and over the course of many decades. Historians have noted how the American people's perception of Lincoln has steadily evolved in response to the ever-changing needs, interests, and priorities of the nation. Or, as the distinguished American sociologist Charles Horton Cooley famously observed, "present function, not past" shapes the way in which we perceive significant historical personalities and institutions. Analytical interpretations as to how the "Lincoln legend" evolved over time first began to appear in the early decades of the twentieth century, and historians have continued to identify a wide range of factors that influenced the exaltation of Lincoln's reputation over the course of time.[1]

Most scholars agree that it was the shock and grief over Lincoln's horrific murder that "suddenly lifted [him] into the sky as the folk-hero, the deliverer, and the martyr who had come to save his people and to die for them." A very real hysteria engulfed the nation in the wake of the president's assassination and his elaborate funeral, and there arose a "collective impulse" to praise and honor the fallen leader. The historian Merrill Peterson has argued that five large themes have contributed to the apotheosis of Abraham Lincoln over time: Lincoln as the savior of the Union, Lincoln as the Great Emancipator, Lincoln as a man of the people, Lincoln as the first American, and Lincoln as the self-made man.[2]

The memorialization of Lincoln began practically from the moment of his death. As soon as Lincoln drew his final breath, Secretary of War Edwin Stanton declared, "Now he belongs to the ages." As we have already seen, eulogies on Lincoln multiplied, and shortly after the first wave of grief had subsided, the process of memorializing Lincoln's life and career began in earnest. On May 11, 1865—twenty-seven days after the assassination—a National Lincoln Monument Association was formally organized in Springfield, Illinois. The association immediately issued "numerous appeals for aid" and spearheaded a national fundraising drive in order to erect a suitable "Memorial Structure" to honor the memory of the fallen president. The association reached its goal, and in 1874, the Lincoln Memorial in Springfield was dedicated at the Oak Ridge Cemetery.[3]

American Jews participated actively in the fundraising efforts for the Lincoln Memorial Fund, one of the first stages in the ongoing process of Lincoln's beatification. One of Lincoln's Jewish friends, the haberdasher Julius Hammerslough of Springfield,

Illinois, was charged with the responsibility of raising funds from the American Jewish community. On May 29, 1865, Hammerslough distributed a circular that he hoped would reach all of the "Hebrew Congregations, Corporations, Associations, Schools and Colleges in the United States." In his communication to Jewish newspaper publishers like Rabbi Isaac M. Wise of Cincinnati, Hammerslough asked the Jewish community to support what he called "the great and holy work" of the Lincoln Monument Association. It was proper for the Jewish community to contribute to this philanthropic endeavor not merely because it would be a fitting "tribute to the merits of our fallen Chief" but also because it would be seen as an act of "the most grateful remembrance." He wanted American Jews to join with their fellow citizens and contribute a dollar to the cause.[4]

Appeals for contributions were made in synagogues and in various Jewish organizations, and by the beginning of June 1865, the *Jewish Messenger* proudly advertised the fact that in New York, nearly 100 Jews had already donated to the cause. In Cincinnati, Jews voted on this matter during a "general meeting of the Israelites of Cincinnati" and decided to establish a committee that would raise funds for the Lincoln monument from that city's entire Jewish community.[5]

By the tenth anniversary of Lincoln's death in 1875, communities all across America had dedicated a cornucopia of Lincoln monuments, shrines, statues, state portraits, historical paintings, and prints.[6] In Washington, D.C., for example, the sculptor Lot Flannery (1836–1922) won the commission to produce a life-sized sculpture of Lincoln, which was unveiled by President Andrew Johnson on April 15, 1868. In 1869, the *Washington Times* informed its readers that the state of Illinois marked Lincoln's birthday by decorating his tomb with evergreen wreaths.[7]

It was at this same time that the practice of commemorating Lincoln's birthday began to take root. In Buffalo, a well-to-do drug store owner named Julius E. Francis (1822–81) dedicated the remainder of his life to the cause of preserving and promoting the martyred president's memory. Francis initiated numerous Lincoln memorial projects. First, he wanted the nation to establish a national day of memory for the late president, and in 1874 Francis organized, in Buffalo, the first of seven annual observances of Lincoln's birthday. Each year until his death in 1881, Francis rented a hall, underwrote the fees for speakers, poets, musicians, and essayists, and invited the public to attend the occasion free of charge.[8]

The public's enthusiastic response to Francis's commemorations led to the creation of a "Lincoln Birthday Association" in Buffalo, and Francis petitioned the U.S. Congress on two separate occasions for the establishment of a national Lincoln Birthday holiday. Although these petitions failed to rally Congress, the concept of establishing a holiday honoring Lincoln's birthday may be traced to Francis's early and indefatigable efforts in Buffalo. By 1879—the seventieth anniversary of Lincoln's birth—birthday observances were being held in many cities in the nation.[9]

In addition to the work he did to mark Lincoln's birthday, Francis also pioneered in the establishment of Lincoln memorials and the preservation of Lincolniana. Obsessed with the idea of memorializing Lincoln, Francis gathered so many Lincoln

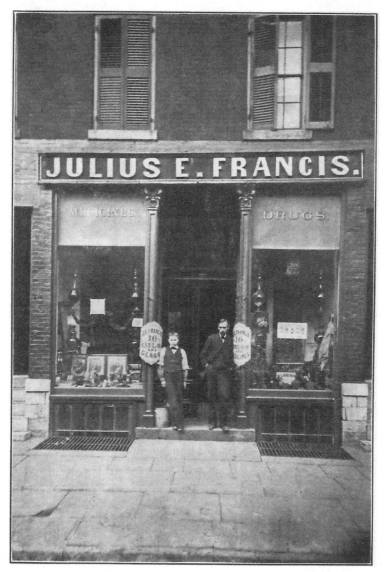

Julius E. Francis, of Buffalo, New York, was dedicated to making Lincoln's birthday a national holiday and founded the Lincoln Birthday Association.
Frank Severance, *The Picture Book of Earlier Buffalo* (Buffalo: Buffalo Historical Society, 1912), 227.

artifacts and relics that, by 1872, a visual display honoring Lincoln's achievements—the "Lincoln Memorial Collection"—was formally dedicated in Buffalo. By the end of the nineteenth century, efforts to collect Lincolniana and Civil War memorabilia intensified. As we will see, many American Jews became prominent collectors of Lincoln memorabilia.[10]

Reconstructing and preserving the story of Lincoln's life went hand in hand with the effort to collect and preserve his personal belongings, his papers, and a record of his life. Soon after Lincoln's death, the first Lincoln biographies began to appear in print. The authors of the earliest such works were more interested in taking financial advantage of the public's preoccupation with Lincoln than in historical accuracy. Lincoln's peers and associates began to publish biographical studies as well. The novelist and journalist Josiah G. Gilbert (1819–81) provided the public with a popular, though flawed, biography in 1866. In 1872, Lincoln's friend and colleague Ward H. Lamon (1827–93) published a more substantial biography of Lincoln that took advantage of a rich collection of primary source documents and irreplaceable oral histories that belonged to William H. Herndon (1818–91). Yet it was Herndon himself, Lincoln's longtime law partner, who published his own very extraordinary biographical study on Lincoln in 1888. Herndon's biography of Lincoln has repeatedly been characterized as "the most influential Lincoln biography ever written because it shaped the public perception of Lincoln in a very profound way."[11]

A decade or so after his death, American schoolchildren began to read about Lincoln in their textbooks. Benson J. Lossing's *A Centennial Edition of the History of the United States* was the first American textbook to discuss Abraham Lincoln. This book portrays him as the Great Emancipator, an equanimous political personality, and a man who was one of the people. Before long, schoolbooks in the North and the South taught pupils about Lincoln, who was described—even in the South—as a noteworthy American figure, a man of strong character, and a successful leader. Reverence for Lincoln continued to burgeon throughout the last half of the nineteenth century, and by the centennial of Lincoln's birth, the sixteenth president had become a national role model and "a man for all seasons."[12]

As the nineteenth century drew to a close and the Civil War generation began to fade from the scene, there arose a pressing interest in documenting the history of the great conflict as well as the many significant personalities who played a leading role in that national drama. In 1886, John G. Nicolay (1832–1901) and John Hay, Lincoln's private secretaries, began publishing their ten-volume study titled *Abraham Lincoln: A History*. Although the work has been consistently criticized for its highly partisan tone, Nicolay and Hay's massive tome was a landmark achievement in that it made extensive use of Robert Todd Lincoln's invaluable documentary collection along with the authors' own documentary resources. Toward the fin de siècle, as the centennial of Lincoln's birth appeared on the horizon, another wave of interest in Lincoln's life swept over the nation.[13]

Not surprisingly, the American Jewish community was keenly interested in participating in the efflorescence of Lincolniana. In 1892, the *American Hebrew* published a long book review describing all of the biographical studies on Lincoln that had recently appeared. "We are just beginning to appreciate the character of the great President who guided the destinies of our nation during the Civil War," the editorial began. "It is a source of great pleasure that poets have found it worthy to sing the praises of so genuine a character as Abraham Lincoln."[14]

Jews participated enthusiastically in all of these efforts to memorialize Lincoln. Like all other American citizens, Jews admired Lincoln and considered him a great American. Yet from the moment Lincoln was assassinated, American Jews regarded the martyred president as a national icon who, though not a Jew by birth, was genuinely imbued with Jewish values and had a "Jewish soul." From the time of his death and through the present day, Jews have cherished the belief that Lincoln was truly a fellow spiritual sojourner whose moral instincts and spiritual impulses were closely aligned with those of the Jewish people.

Toward the end of the nineteenth century, as the eightieth anniversary of Lincoln's birth approached, rabbis, educators, and communal leaders began to deliver special homilies and oratorical lessons in commemoration of Lincoln's birthday. "It is not without significance," the editorial column of the *Jewish Messenger* observed, "that as the years fade the character of Abraham Lincoln shines forth with greater splendor and his name and record acquire a deeper, holier meaning. . . . We Americans need the inspiration of Lincoln's memory."[15] The speeches of the Jewish leaders contained inspiring exhortations based on lessons learned from Lincoln's life. Many of the lessons they derived benefited all Americans, but for many Jewish orators, Lincoln's life served as a particularly valuable model for Jewish living.

For example, on Sunday, February 12, 1888, Simon Wolf delivered the Lincoln Day Address in the nation's capital. It is interesting to note that Wolf began his remarks by explaining why he had agreed to speak on Lincoln's birthday: "I came here as one whose ancestors also were in bondage; . . . not in this, but in other countries, and to whom and for whom Abraham Lincoln achieved as much freedom and liberty as ever the laws of my ancestors have conferred religion and civilization upon mankind." Lincoln's birthday, Wolf declared, provided the nation with an annual opportunity to expose the American people to the life of a man who was an archetypical American. If, as Walt Whitman observed, America was a "teeming nation of nations," then Abraham Lincoln was the embodiment of the loftier ideals such a nation's leader should possess: "[Lincoln was] not only an American [but] in the highest ideal a typical American—the very incarnation of all that was just, true, and manly, not only for the Christian, but for the Jew; not only for the white man, but for the negro; not only for the American, but for all men, no matter from what part of the world they came."[16]

Wolf proceeded to regale his listeners with stories of his own personal encounters with Lincoln, all of which emphasized that Lincoln was the Jew's friend and a man who harbored no bigotry. Wolf stressed the bond that Jews felt for Lincoln as well as the friendship that Lincoln extended to the Jews. Alluding to the social mores of the Gilded Age and, perhaps, the troubling rise in Judeophobia and Jewish social exclusion that typified that era, Wolf expressed his hope that Lincoln's birthday would soon become a national day of education dedicated to teaching "our young men and young women, who perhaps may be falling by the wayside into materialistic views; [that] . . . it is not birth, it is not wealth, that alone accomplishes great things in this country; but it is character and truth, nobility of soul and virtue of example that shall live for all time."[17]

A paradigmatic example of how Jewish leaders embraced Lincoln as an American and as a sojourner among the Jewish people comes from an address that Dr. Herman Baar (1823–1904), superintendent of New York's Hebrew Orphan Society, delivered to the children of the orphanage on the occasion of Lincoln's birthday in 1897. "My children," the headmaster began, "yesterday we celebrated the birthday of one of America's best and greatest sons, Abraham Lincoln. . . . No one deserves more—though he was not of our creed—to be mentioned in our 'Kaddish' prayer today than Abraham Lincoln. Kaddish means holy, and Lincoln's life was a life of holiness. He was a high-priest in the service of humanity; he was a soldier in the battle of human right and liberty; nay he was a champion for the cause of justice and heaven-born freedom! . . . [M]ay he ever inspire us with his lovable and noble heart, with his brave and gentle spirit, and with his kind and generous sentiments!"[18]

As the centenary of Lincoln's birth approached, rabbis were increasingly invited to speak at citywide Lincoln Day festivities. They used these public occasions to emphasize Lincoln's unswerving commitment to the biblical values of justice, liberty, and compassion. During the 1890s, the brilliant rabbinic orator Rabbi Emil G. Hirsch (1852–1923) composed several addresses on Lincoln, whom he described as "the greatest star in the constellation of men [who led the nation] into the glorious path of a larger freedom." Rabbi David Philipson (1862–1949) preached a long sermon on Lincoln to his congregation in Cincinnati in 1898, comparing him to the prophet Amos. Truly great people, Philipson preached, are fighters for justice and righteousness. "Of such was Lincoln's faith," Philipson declared, "an immovable belief in the right." In Philadelphia, Rabbi Joseph Krauskopf (1858–1923) of Rodeph Shalom Congregation frequently preached on Lincoln. Using an effusion of religious allusions, Krauskopf crowned Lincoln "the Nation's Saint, its greatest Master, its holiest Martyr, a people's Messiah and Redeemer, the Talisman and Patron forever of every tyrannized people, of every down-trodden, God-given right."[19]

In one of his Lincoln addresses, Rabbi Hirsch observed that "Abraham Lincoln belongs to no one State." Although he was "in the flesh" an American, Lincoln was

Chicago's Rabbi Emil G. Hirsch frequently paid tribute to Lincoln in sermons that commemorated his birthday. Courtesy The Jacob Rader Marcus Center of the American Jewish Archives, at the Hebrew Union College–Jewish Institute of Religion, Cincinnati, Ohio.

"in the spirit" a model for all humankind. "The whole earth is a pedestal to his fame," Hirsch declared, "and the best and noblest of all nations asks for the privilege to garland afresh every year his memorial in their hearts."[20]

In the 1880s and 1890s, when thousands of East European Jewish immigrants poured onto the American continent, Lincoln served as an American beau ideal. In fact, Lincoln's image and his saga even attracted the interest of Jews who had not yet set foot in the New World. In his autobiography, Ephraim Lisitzky (1885–1962), a highly regarded American Hebraist who spent most of his career working as a Jewish educator in New Orleans, recollected that he and other Jews held Lincoln in special reverence even before they immigrated: "I was fascinated by the emancipation of the slaves and even more so by the personality of Abraham Lincoln, the hero of the event. Lincoln's Jewish name, Abraham, his bearded face with its Jewish expression of sorrow, made him look like a Jewish prophet of old whom Providence raised up for the Americans to free them from the shame of slavery."[21]

One historian has contended that the primary political challenge facing the United States between 1880 and 1920 was "how to assimilate . . . an almost unmanageable influx of people who were not Americans by birth but by immigration. Americans had to be made." During this period, many leaders of the American Jewish community were keenly interested in addressing this same challenge. East European Jewish immigrants

Lincoln often served as an agent of acculturation for the millions of Jews who immigrated to the United States from eastern Europe between 1881 and 1924.
Courtesy The Jacob Rader Marcus Center of the American Jewish Archives, at the Hebrew Union College–Jewish Institute of Religion, Cincinnati, Ohio.

needed to become Americans, and Abraham Lincoln proved to be a catalyst in this endeavor. Native-born Americans were convinced that by compelling immigrants to celebrate the life of Abraham Lincoln, they would succeed in their ambition to give nationhood primacy over ethnicity.[22]

In 1905, the Jewish Chautauqua Society convened a special conference in New York to deliberate on how best to Americanize the Jewish immigrant. Some of the most distinguished Jewish philanthropists and communal leaders of that era participated in this colloquium, including Jacob Schiff (1847–1920), Jacob Gimbel (1850–1922), Simon Wolf, and Rabbis David Philipson and Kaufmann Kohler (1843–1926). Schiff laid out the problem the community faced in the starkest of terms: "The Americanization of the Jewish immigrant well deserves the most earnest consideration of the best minds, for with something like a million newcomers, of which a hundred thousand are of our race, a year, the very foundation upon which the Nation rests, may become displaced, unless we succeed in making Americans in the very highest sense of the word of those, who, year in, year out, flock in such large numbers to these shores; people who come to remain and to make these States the permanent home of their families."[23]

Yet, Rabbi Philipson hastened to urge the leaders of the Jewish community to be careful and strategic in this process lest they unintentionally drove the Jewishness out of the immigrant altogether. "If they can be made to feel they are American and Jewish at the same time," Philipson stated, "then great things can be done." To achieve this objective, Lincoln was one of the most valuable resources because, for the American Jew, Lincoln was not only "the first American" but also a spiritual brother.[24]

In the 1880s, Rabbi David Philipson of Cincinnati began delivering annual sermonic tributes on Lincoln's birthday. Courtesy The Jacob Rader Marcus Center of the American Jewish Archives, at the Hebrew Union College–Jewish Institute of Religion, Cincinnati, Ohio.

Time and again, Lincoln served as a metaphoric nexus that linked Americanism and Judaism together for the East European Jewish immigrant. Rabbi Abba Hillel Silver (1893–1963) crowned Lincoln "a saint of Democracy" and told his people that "Lincoln somehow reminds one of the ancient prophets of Israel. He seems to possess the same colossal height, the same sweep of spirit, and the same outreaching power that we are accustomed to associate with the ancient prophets." Rabbi Samuel Sale (1854–1937) of St. Louis asserted that Lincoln's religion was "the religion of humanity." He was the "best and noblest" because he modeled his life on the teachings of the Hebrew prophet Micah, who compelled us "to do justly, to love mercy, and to walk with [God] in humility." For Jewish settlement houses and immigrant educational institutions, Abraham Lincoln's life served as an enduring proof text that it was possible to be a great American and, concomitantly, a great Jew. In fact, Milwaukee's settlement house for immigrant Jews was actually called the "Abraham Lincoln House." The Hebrew Immigrant Aid Society and the Educational Alliance in New York engaged the renowned Yiddish orator Zvi Hirsch Masliansky (1856–1943) so that he could instruct hundreds of East European Jewish immigrants in their mother tongue about the life of Abraham Lincoln.[25]

In a 1917 article titled "Lincoln and the Immigrant," fiction writer Grace Humphrey (1882–1961) observed that "Lincoln makes the immigrants feel this is their country as well as the country of the native-born far more than any other American." For Jewish children, she continued, "Lincoln was the epic rescuer of the oppressed, the man who freed the slaves." Yet Lincoln also served as a vehicle for Americanization—he was an iconic American who bore the name of the biblical patriarch and first Jew. As a popular song from the era demonstrates, Lincoln made the Jewish name Abraham patriotic:

> You say you're ridiculed by all the boys in school . . .
> But when they call you Abie don't you mind.
> There was a man named Abraham not many years ago,
> A better man you'll never find.
> We didn't have the power to make you look the same,
> The best we could do was to give you his name.[26]

Over the course of the Progressive Era, Lincoln was arguably "the nation's most preeminent historical figure," and there can be little question that the East European Jewish immigrants easily embraced Lincoln as an American Jewish exemplar. In this capacity, Lincoln was sui generis among American icons. As one rabbi observed: "America has given the world many outstanding men. There was Washington, the staid and courtly gentleman whom circumstances made a revolutionist. There was Jefferson, the scholarly and cultured liberal. There was Theodore Roosevelt, the dynamic administrator. There was Woodrow Wilson, the isolated intellectual of exquisite world visions. They were all great men; each had his message and all are revered by mankind. Yet Abraham Lincoln alone is loved. . . . Why? Because in him the world sees itself reflected."[27]

One demonstration of Lincoln's stature as an American Jewish icon may be seen in the custom of naming Jewish children after him. An indeterminate number of American

Jews—those who emigrated from Central and Eastern Europe—eagerly embraced the sixteenth president's legacy with the same honor they might have bestowed on a beloved and lamented parent or grandparent. When one of a set of Jewish triplets in northern California in 1867 was given the name Abraham Lincoln Danziger, it may have been the first documented example of a naming trend that would become a true American Jewish tradition. Twenty years later, particularly for the massive wave of East European immigrants seeking to Americanize, "Abraham Lincoln" became a popular Jewish moniker that authenticated their children's status as both Americans and Jews. Some prominent examples include Abraham Lincoln Fechheimer (1876–1954), a highly regarded Cincinnati architect; Abraham Lincoln Filene (1865–1957), from the famous department store family; Abraham Lincoln Neiman (1875–1970), a founder of Neiman Marcus; Abraham Lincoln Erlanger (1859–1930), a theatrical manager; Abraham Lincoln Polonsky (1910–99); a distinguished American screenwriter; and Abraham Lincoln Marovitz (1905–2001), a well-known Chicago jurist and political activist. Some Lincoln namesakes—such as Abraham Lincoln Feinberg (1899–1986) and Abraham Lincoln Krohn (1893–1958)—became prominent American rabbis.[28]

During the years leading up to the U.S. entry into World War I, Lincoln's legacy was used as a narrative to explain the country's involvement in this overseas conflict. As one scholar noted, after the United States entered the war, "Lincoln and Wilson began to look increasingly alike." In newspapers, magazines, congressional speeches, and sermons, Americans heard that Wilson was following Lincoln's lead in prosecuting his foreign policy. As one newspaper summarized, "Lincoln was the apostle of democracy and before he died he lived to see the whole of America come to him. Today we have a new apostle of democracy: we will live to see the whole world come to him." Speaking from his pulpit in Carnegie Hall, Rabbi Stephen S. Wise (1879–1949) told his listeners that "Lincoln moved cautiously; so does Wilson. Lincoln took the long view; so does Wilson. Lincoln lifted the war to a higher level; so does Wilson. Lincoln won the war and ended slavery; Wilson will win the war and end war."[29]

By the end of World War I, Lincoln had become "part of the substance and continuity of the American soul." Yet for the American Jew, Lincoln's name had become a summons to fulfill a distinctly double obligation. The Lincoln legacy called on Jews to dedicate themselves to the American nation while simultaneously remaining loyal to their Jewish heritage. Speaking to a large Jewish audience at Temple Beth-El in Dorchester, Massachusetts, a future governor, Frank G. Allen (1874–1950), told the state's Jewish community that "a true Jew is a true American." He urged them to emulate the life of Abraham Lincoln by rendering "distinguished service to this great democracy by helping instill the element of spirituality in our life, by showing we are truly our brother's keepers, by practicing the ideals of the Hebrew prophets, and thereby [making] America a blessing for all who are here."[30]

Within months of the date when Allen spoke to his Jewish audience outside of Boston, a New York businessman and Jewish communal leader named Henry M. Toch (1862–1933) was stressing another view about the role Lincoln should play for American

Jewry. "The great prophet and emancipator in America," Toch asserted, should serve as a source of inspiration that would compel Jews to be good Jews, "for good Jews make good citizens, good Americans." After all, Toch declared, Abraham Lincoln was "like Abraham the founder of our faith." Just as the biblical Abraham said, "Here I am," when he was called to duty, so too did Lincoln say, "*Hineni*—Here I am," when he was called to serve the American nation. American Jews, Toch exhorted, must follow Lincoln's example and say, "*Hineni*—Here I am," when they are called upon to strengthen and sustain Jewish life in America.[31]

American Jews shared in the nation's increasing veneration of Lincoln. Yet Lincoln evolved into much more than an American icon for Jewish citizens. He became a unique role model who could teach Jews to be better Americans as he concomitantly inspired them to be better Jews.

DOCUMENTS

JEWS AND LINCOLN MONUMENTS

1. Bear Testimony of Your Love of a Good Man
2. Let Us Vindicate Ourselves by Contributing to This Holy National Work

LINCOLN BIRTHDAY HOMILIES

3. America Is Opportunity
4. He Had Within Him the Spirit of the Ancient Prophets
5. The Savior of His Country
6. Lincoln the *Tsaddik*
7. Lessons from the Life of Lincoln
8. Lincoln's Religion Is My Religion

LINCOLN CENTENNIAL SERMONS

9. Citywide Ceremony Marking the Lincoln Centennial Held at Temple
10. He Pleaded the Law of Justice and the Gospel of Liberty
11. The Personification of the American Nation
12. The Personification of Jewish Values
13. The Realization of the True Spirit of Judaism

JEWS AND LINCOLN MONUMENTS

1. BEAR TESTIMONY OF YOUR LOVE OF A GOOD MAN

Within days after Lincoln's burial, calls for the erection of Lincoln memorials were heard throughout the Union. On May 21, 1865, the New York Times *informed its readers that a "One-Dollar-Lincoln-Memorial-Fund" had been established and had already gathered 119 subscribers.*[32] *The following document testifies to the fact that American Jews actively participated in these early fundraising efforts. In his handwritten announcement to the members of New York's Congregation Shearith Israel, Rabbi Jacques Judah Lyons declared, "A common calamity calls for united and universal sympathy." The rabbi urged his people to support this "noble and commendable" undertaking.*

Subscriptions Announcement in the Handwriting of Reverend Lyons

I have been specially requested by the Committee to call the attention of my Congregation to the project in contemplation to erect a monument in or near one of our public squares, as a lasting tribute of respect of the citizens of New York to the memory of their late beloved and lamented President. A subscription paper has been sent to me, and I can but say I shall be happy to be chosen by you the medium of transmitting your contributions and those of the members of your families to the Committee which has the matter in charge. "A common calamity calls for united and universal sympathy." The amount of subscription is limited to one dollar per person so as to embrace people of all conditions in life, and it is expected that you, my friends, men, women and children, will all avail yourselves of the opportunity to assist in the furtherance of so noble and commendable an undertaking, which will in future bear testimony of your love of a good man, and your appreciation of the services of a faithful officer—peace be unto his memory.[33]

2. LET US VINDICATE OURSELVES BY CONTRIBUTING TO THIS HOLY NATIONAL WORK

One of Lincoln's Jewish friends, the Springfield haberdasher Julius Hammerslough, volunteered to collect funds from the American Jewish community for the National Lincoln Monument Association. As we see from the Israelite *article reproduced below, Hammerslough took his assignment seriously and wrote an appeal to Jewish leaders throughout the nation.*

Rabbi Isaac M. Wise published Hammerslough's written appeal to American Jewry on June 9, 1865. On the basis of this ardent published petition, we know that American Jews contributed to the fundraising effort.[34]

Lincoln National Monument

We received the following circular, which we gladly lay before our readers, and appeal to their sincere attachment to the late and lamented President of the United States:

Springfield, Ill., May 30, 1864

Rev. Dr. I. M. Wise:

Dear Sir:—Benevolence, one of the cardinal principals upon which Judaism is founded, appeals to your kind and noble heart, and solicits your earnest assistance in aiding this great National work. I entrust to your good judgment the annexed Circulars of the national Lincoln Monument Association, and by distributing the same among your Congregation, Schools and Colleges, in your city and surrounding country, you will not only pay tribute to the merits of our fallen Chief, but will also confer a great favor upon me, which shall always have the most grateful remembrance. I would kindly ask you to have the Appeal read in your Synagogue, and impress upon each and every one present the importance of the great and holy work before us.

Trusting your kind assistance and cooperation in the cause for which I appeal to you will bear fruit and meet with success everywhere, I have the honor to remain,

Your obedient servant,
Julius Hammerslough

National Lincoln Monument
Springfield, Ill., May 29, 1864

To the Hebrew Congregations, Corporations, Associations, Schools and Colleges in the United States.

At a meeting of the National Monument Association, held on the 18th last, it was unanimously:

Resolved, That the Hebrew Congregations, Corporations, Associations, Schools and Colleges, throughout the Nation, be requested to contribute to the National Lincoln Monument, at some time in the month of June next; and that Julius Hammerslough, Esq., of Springfield, Ill., be appointed special agent to bring the subject to their notice, and request their favorable action.

In accordance with the above resolution, this is respectfully addressed to the distinguished bodies embraced in it, and it is to be hoped that this appeal will inspire all patriotic hearts, and should insure the liveliest action.

Let the high position that we as Hebrews have ever maintained for generosity and liberality on minor occasions, be still manifested, and let it be evidence to all how highly we, as a race, appreciate freedom and the martyrs of liberty.

It is above all fitting in this land, where the Hebrews have won so proud a name, and are so generally respected and honored that they should thus show their love and veneration for the fallen Chief of the Nation, whose wisdom, honesty and purity of purpose were so highly appreciated by foreign nations, and who was so beloved at home.

Let it be remembered that we have, as a race, despite the advanced and enlightened age, to meet prejudices still existing in the minds of many. Let us quell this feeling, and vindicate ourselves by contributing to this holy national work, in a manner that shall prove that the Hebrews are, as they have ever been, the staunch friends of freedom and liberty, and the foes of all oppression and wrong.

In the responsible position in which I have been placed, I beg the most prompt and heartiest support of one and all of my co-religionists.

It is to be hoped that all patriotic hearts will be moved to show their love and admiration for the character of Abraham Lincoln, and the cause for which he died.

It is to be hoped that we build a monument to such a man—a monument that shall not only be worthy of the immortal dead, but one that shall essay to express the homage of our people for an exalted character, whose greatness is made complete by goodness. Will not such a monument teach all future generations that "he is but half great who is no good," inspiring all with a worthy ambition and the lofty courage which dares to do right for right's sake, while it rebukes and shames the selfish, groveling, politic compromiser? Do we not well to build a monument, to which every parent may point his child and say: "So let it be done to him whom the people delight to honor?" Will not a new era in our national life be marked by such a monument?—will it not still seem grand and worthy, when in the coming centuries, the nation having consummated the policy for which he died, and, become strong and glorious in a Union without a slave, and, appreciate, honor, love and revere, as it cannot now, the sublime character, life and work of her martyred President?

The honor of the State of Illinois is pledged for the faithful application of every dollar contributed to this sacred fund, in accordance with the wishes of the donors.

His Excellency Richard J. Oglesby, the Governor of the State, is President of the Association; Hon. Beveridge, State Treasurer, is Treasurer of the Association, and the other State officers are members. The other corporators are among the most distinguished citizens of the State.

In addition to this the Association is a corporate body; having organized in strict conformity with the forms of law, and the Treasurer is under adequate bonds for the faithful discharge of his duties.

These particulars are given because all who contribute have a right to know to whom the money is paid, and what are the guarantees that it will bear appropriate with scrupulous fidelity and honor.

All contributions should be forwarded to Hon. James H. Beveridge, Treasurer National Lincoln Monument Association, Springfield, Illinois, who will immediately acknowledge receipt. All sums from the largest to the smallest will be accepted and duly acknowledged. Remittances may be made by Letter, draft, or otherwise at the option of the donor.

Any person may become an honorary member of the Association by the payment of ten dollars to its funds, which will entitle him to an appropriate certificate of such membership.

All letters of inquiry should be addressed to me at this place, and will be promptly answered. Each of the different bodies addressed will, of course, adopt its own plan of action, but it is hoped that such action may be had as early in June as possible, and the contributions be immediately forwarded to Hon. James H. Beveridge, as above directed.

The congregation that still adheres to the usual offerings made on Sabbaths and holidays, will thus have excellent opportunities of contributing to aid in this work.

All contributions will be published in the press of the city, and the entire Jewish press of the country.

And now let me appeal to you once more, to manifest your liberal contributions to this great national work that we as Hebrews are not behind the very chiefest in our love for liberty and in our reverence for her *noblest martyr*.

Julius Hammerslough[35]

3. AMERICA IS OPPORTUNITY

Rabbi Emil G. Hirsch, the spiritual leader of Chicago's Sinai Congregation from 1880 to 1922, was a renowned orator and community leader. On February 12, 1892, Hirsch served as the keynote speaker for the city's commemoration of Lincoln's birthday. Central Music Hall held nearly 2,000 people, and the rabbi knew he would be speaking to a general audience.[36] Instead of highlighting the reasons that Lincoln appealed to American Jewry, Hirsch decided to address himself to Lincoln's role as an American moral lodestar. "America has given to the world many a true man," the rabbi told his listeners, but "among them Lincoln is indeed the greatest." Yet even a universalist thinker like Hirsch could not refrain from employing allusions from the Hebrew Bible when speaking of Lincoln's immortality. Lincoln ascended to heaven, Hirsch told his audience, like "the prophet of old, in a golden chariot of fire," and his disciple—the American nation—exclaimed, "Father, father, the chariot of Israel and its horsemen."[37] For Hirsch, Abraham Lincoln was the human embodiment of all that can yet be great in America.

Abraham Lincoln

Lincoln's birthday signifies much more than a mere sentiment. If Washington's birthday opens for us that volume of our history which records what the Eastern colonies, the first states skirting the Atlantic ocean have accomplished; what their spirit contributed to our national wealth; Lincoln's anniversary symbolizes what the West has wrought, how the West has supplemented the productions of the East, yea, given them a wider scope and therefore a truer possibility.

. . . Our Lincoln was tried in the school of disaster. The man loomed up all the higher.

. . . Our Lincoln is not merely our great statesman, the great son of this great land; he types the highest nobility which God has ever given to humanity. . . . Yea, that man, for all his physical affinity with brute worlds, is of higher mold than mere dust, is proclaimed by none more strongly, than by our own Abraham Lincoln. And again, not what he became makes him so illustrious, as what he remained. America is opportunity. We are familiar with the stories of the great men risen from the valleys to the Alps. We are conversant with the career of our generals, our statesmen, our presidents, most of whom in their early youth had to follow avocations which we count menial. None of them remembered the days of his youth so willingly as did Abraham Lincoln. In the White House he was the same man as he was when he split the historic rails. He was without presumption or arrogance; he withheld from none the warm touch of his hand. In his lank and over-grown frame beat a heart as wide as the country that he had sworn to save. He whose official duty it was to send to bloody fray hundreds of thousands of men, had a soul spun of the tenderest chords of sympathy. When the fate of a deserter court-martialed to be shot, waited upon his final decision, sleep would flee from his weary eyes. He, upon whom weighed the concerns of a nation fighting for its very life, found ever time to console the widows or to cheer the wounded in the hospitals. He whom princes addressed as their friend, remained in every detail a man of the people, proud to belong to the people, feeling with the people. President of the United States, master of the tersest English, and the writer of a style so clear and so concise, gifted with an eloquence of which Demosthenes might well have become envious, he was not ashamed to speak the dialect of the backwoods villages, and illustrate, even in the most fateful moments, his arguments by some apt story or other. He remained true to himself, true to his friends. The *man* Lincoln eclipses even the President Lincoln. He will be loved and honored by all who have understanding for the genuine essence of true manhood; he will live in the affections of all true men, when perhaps the greater deeds of the greatest generals on battle-fields will be forgotten; when the glory of many a central sun around which the planet circled will have been clouded in the mists of oblivion. America has given to the world many a true man; among them Lincoln is indeed the greatest. He is a monument to our civilization, which can make of the backwoods boy a president, shaming in his sagacity the kings born to the purple, and vying in renown with the greatest men that ever time did fashion. With the sentiments of the prophets will forever be quoted his words, hallowing the graves of the soldiers who fell on the hotly contested cemetery of Gettysburg, so touching in their appeal and so tender in their simplicity: "with malice toward none, with charity toward all." And when this man fell at his post of duty, the whole world paused and wept. . . . He ascended heavenward as did the prophet of old, in a golden chariot of fire, and his disciple, the nation at large upon whom his mantle fell, looked up to the heights to which he had gone, and exclaimed. "Father, father, the chariot of Israel and its horsemen."[38] He ascended to the realms of immortality, carried upward by a flame of fire, but in his death he sealed a new covenant of love, which today binds together both those that wore the gray and those that wore the blue. Today our flag floats over one country, one union, one freedom. May that flag float on forever. Its stars shine out in the darkness of despotism, beacons of hope wherever human beings are crushed and downtrodden, wherever shackles of slaves are clanking! May its stripes stream out like the forerunner of the rising sun to herald to the world that the mists of slavery are lifted and the day of freedom is here. Lincoln died for this flag, let us live for it. Washington planted it, Lincoln preserved it. Let us be true to the great heritage of the fathers. Each one as far as in him lies in his sphere, must remember that that which the fathers planted and the sons preserved, we the grandsons enjoy, merely to enrich it and to enlarge it, and to become worthy of it. America, land of freedom, washed by the blood of martyred presidents, America, hope of humanity, star of the morning, sing thy song, "Today a child was born unto us, a son was given unto us. Upon him was the dominion, his name was great counselor, mighty in deed, witness of the great Father in heaven; Prince of Peace!"[39] For in this old biblical description of Israel's ideal ruler, America, thou mayest well breathe thine appreciation of thine own son, immortal Abraham Lincoln.[40]

4. HE HAD WITHIN HIM THE SPIRIT OF THE ANCIENT PROPHETS

Rabbi David Philipson's sermon, delivered to Congregation Bene Israel at the Mound Street Temple in Cincinnati, Ohio, on February 12, 1898, exemplifies the stirring encomia that American rabbis used in praising Lincoln to their communities. Philipson described Lincoln as a man whose lips "were touched by the coal of living fire taken from the altar of God" and as a "messenger of the Lord of Hosts . . . , sent unto [the] people." The mere contemplation of Lincoln's life, Philipson effused, would lift one's "soul to the empyrean heights."

Abraham Lincoln

Had, in Lincoln's case, externals been decisive, no man would ever have imagined that his was to be that great, providential career. Gaunt, ungainly and unprepossessing in appearance, the casual onlooker would never for a moment have dreamt that within that homely frame there dwelt one of the greatest souls that ever breathed the breath of life. Yes, yes, again was the old word exemplified, "Men look upon the outward parts, but the Lord looketh upon the heart."[41]

Who has not been thrilled, whose nerves have not been set atingling when reading the plain, unvarnished tale of the life of this masterful man, so wonderfully astute, so wise, simple, sagacious, honest, patient, courageous, humane and tender? There are so many facets to this brilliant diamond, the character of Lincoln, that we can find time to view but few. First of all there was the supreme honesty of the man; he was honest in every fibre of his being, true and straightforward, uncompromising for the right as he saw the right. He had within him the spirit of the ancient prophets; aye; he was a modern prophet in his firm insistence on the right, in his clear view of the external issue between right and wrong. This appeared most strongly in the famous debate with Douglas, when he used the words, so daring in those days of compromise (it was in the year 1858), "A house divided against itself can not stand. I believe this Government can not endure permanently, half slave and half free. I do not expect the Union to be dissolved—I do not expect the house to fall—but I do expect it will cease to be divided. It will become all one thing or the other." When his friends remonstrated and begged him not to use this bold language, urging the plea that it would surely cause his defeat for the Senate, he gave the characteristic answer that he "would rather be defeated with this expression in his speech than to be victorious without it." Time and again he took his firm stand on the pedestal of the right. At the close of a speech in New York he uttered the ringing words: "Men of America! History through the centuries has been teaching us that might makes right. Let it be our mission in this nineteenth century to reverse the thought and to declare that right makes might." It was thought that Amos had come back to earth, as though there was reincarnation of that mighty spirit that twenty-seven hundred years before had declared to the people of Israel, "Let justice flow like water and righteousness like a mighty stream!"[42] The truly great of earth, the prophets, ancient and modern, stand squarely on the moral issue: there is the eternal struggle between right and wrong, the two principles that have stood face to face from the beginning of time; but for the true man there is no question of the final outcome; before the tribunal of the eternal Justice right is right—no half measure, no timid time-serving. Of such was Lincoln's faith, an immovable belief in the right, in the justice of eternal God moved him in his every action. "The purposes of the Almighty are perfect and must prevail, though we erring mortals may fail accurately to perceive them in advance," was another of his winged sentences. Words more deeply religious than these were never spoken by preacher or seer. Truly the lips of this great man were touched by the coal of living fire taken from the altar of God and a messenger of the Lord of Hosts was he, sent unto this people in the most critical time of its existence to lead them by his wisdom, his courage, his prophetic utterances, through the dread years that tried men's souls, he himself burdened with the awful responsibility which seemed too great for any one man, and therefore so often solitary, so pathetically sad, for he was bearing a Nation's woe, his heart was wrung with sympathy for the thousands of firesides made desolate, the tears of widowed mothers, the pains and tortures of brave, sacrificing men.

The contemplation of a life such as Lincoln's lifts the soul to the empyrean heights, and the words that fell from his lips will echo and re-echo in the hearts of men unto latest generations. Many of these words deserve and have found a place in the Bible of humanity. From out the dim vista of the past there looms before us the sad, sad face, furrowed with the lines of care, and there beams upon us the light of the far-seeing eyes, and from his lips we hear fall those great, undying Words, "With malice towards none, with charity for all, with firmness in the right as God gives us to see the right." Aye, truly, we feel, we know, with our great poet that

> Standing like a tower,
> Our children shall behold his fame,
> The kindly, earnest, brave, far-seeing man,
> Sagacious, patient, dreading praise, not blame.
> New birth of our new soil, the first American.[43]

5. THE SAVIOR OF HIS COUNTRY

Rabbi Joseph Krauskopf delivered a memorial sermon marking Lincoln's birthday on February 11, 1906, at Congregation Keneseth Israel in Philadelphia. In this address, Krauskopf asserted that Lincoln's humble roots and simple manner were inexorably linked to his unrivaled purity of character, his honesty, and his spiritual nature. In this markedly religious sermon, Krauskopf encouraged his listeners to accept Lincoln's death as part of God's plan. He compared Lincoln to Moses, Jesus, and Luther and crowned him "the savior of his country, . . . the Chosen of God."

Lincoln, the Chosen of God

It was on February 11, 1861, forty-five years ago this day, that Abraham Lincoln left Springfield, Illinois, to proceed towards the capital of the Nation, as its chosen President. His friends and neighbors came to take leave of him, and, while their hearts rejoiced at the honor that had been conferred upon their fellow-townsman, there were tears in the eyes of many in the hour of parting. Lincoln himself was deeply touched. Had he and they a presentiment that they might never see each other again? "Friends," said he in solemn farewell, "I know not how soon I shall see you again. A duty has devolved upon me greater than that which has devolved upon any other man since Washington. He never would have succeeded except for the aid of Divine Providence, upon which he at all times relied. On the same Almighty Being I place my reliance. Pray that I may receive that Divine assistance, without which I cannot succeed, but with which success is assured."

I have no doubt but that the prayers thus asked for were fervently lifted up for the President-elect, and not by his townspeople alone but also by millions of his supporters throughout the troubled land. Was their prayer answered? Many there are who will at once say *no*, and, in proof, will point to a whole Nation inconsolable, aye, to a civilized world in tears, because of his death of martyrdom, a little more than four years after his leave-taking at Springfield.

As for me, I know of no better instance of prayer answered than the success that attended the supplications that were offered up for Lincoln when he entered upon his perilous office. He did not ask that supplications be offered for his escape from a death of martyrdom; he but asked for prayers that success might attend his labors to save the country from dismemberment and to remove a malignant cancer that threatened the very life of the Nation. In a little more than four years, the Union was saved and slavery was abolished, and, his work being done, the greatest since the days of Washington, martyrdom came as a halo of glory rather than as a sign of failure or as a token of divine disapprobation.

Of course, had mortals had the disposition of it, they would have assigned a far different end to the savior of his Nation and to the emancipator of the slave than death by an assassin's bullet, five short days after General Lee's surrender at Appomattox, on the very day of the rehoisting of Old Glory over Fort Sumter, and but a little more than a month after a grateful people had entrusted itself to his wise and fearless leadership for another term of four years. They would have had him live to a good, old age, they would have had him continue in the full enjoyment of the fruitage of his labors, the idol of his people, the inspiration of all living kind, until a gentle death would have translated him from his field of earthly labor to the regions of his celestial rewards.

But God's ways are not our ways, says the prophet, neither are His thoughts our thoughts. When I consider the wisdom that was manifest in the choice of this peerless leader, I cannot but feel that in his tragic taking-off, when his work was done, there may have been a wisdom no less divine than that which called him when his work was needed. Probably his highest reward lay in having been spared the ingratitude of the Nation he had saved. Many a savior might have died happy had he died when his work was done, had he died before adulation could turn to envy and envy to malice, and malice to calumny, and calumny to base ingratitude.

Every move in this wonderful man's career seems to speak of providential call and guidance. No man was ever more the chosen of God than was Abraham Lincoln, and yet no man ever gave less evidence and promise of it than he. What people, unaided by divine direction, would have dared to select for its leader this untried man of the untrained West, in the crisis in which our Nation found itself prior to the outbreak of the civil war? They would have sought among experienced statesmen, among men of proven executive power, of tried leadership, of great military prowess. They would have inquired among the universities for those of marked attainments and of brilliant records, or among the illustrious families for one whose distinguished name and descent might dazzle the masses and command the largest following of the select. Only the intermixture of the will of Providence with the will of man can explain the daring choice our fathers made when they selected Abraham Lincoln for their chief-executive. The capitol of Washington had never before, and has never since, seen a President like him. Never before had a man received so little training for so exalted a place, never had a man possessed such few graces for a position that was to throw him in contact with the most polished of the land, never had a man had so little schooling for an office that required profound knowledge in many of the most intricate problems of political and economic and military science.

And never before nor since did man master such gigantic problems, within so short a time, as they were mastered by the first of our martyr-presidents. Long before his first term expired, there was no statesman in all the land comparable to him, no master of the English tongue superior to him, no military strategist like unto the chief-commander of the Nation. Read his deliberations with his cabinet, read his consecration of the battlefield of Gettysburg, his second inaugural address, his orders to his generals, or, better, retrace your steps to the wretched log-cabin in the mountain-wilds of Kentucky, where his cradle stood, and then follow his career, step by step, from cabin to capitol, and tell of another like it, in history or in literature, in fiction or in truth.

His father a backwoodsman, unlettered, unmannered, thriftless. His mother an invalid passing into the grave before her boy is yet nine years old. We next see him in the new lands of Indiana but in the midst of the old hardships, differing only from the other in finding here some opportunity for schooling, seven months long in all—the only schooling in all his life. But, if of the school of letters he had little, he had an abundance of the school of life. Life for him, from earliest childhood to manhood's estate, meant hard toil, from early morn till late at night, for little more than the absolute necessities of life. And full of hard toil his life continued to be till his last day, now as farm hand, now as rail-splitter, now as flat-boatman, as shopkeeper, soldier, legislator, lawyer, congressman, and finally as President of the United States.

And while that passage from log-cabin to White House, from farmhand to President was marked by wonderful flashes of intellectual genius and of moral and spiritual greatness, such revelations were vouchsafed only to friends and neighbors or to clients and constituents. To the eastern and southern people from among whom the Presidents and great men had hitherto come, when they first beheld him, he seemed a gnarled, homely-featured, horn-handed, hoosier from the uncultured West, more fit to drive a yoke of oxen than to guide a nation out of a sea of trouble into a haven of rest.

Listen to the impression his appearance made on our own townsman, Mr. Alexander McClure,[44] who had done much toward effecting his election, and who had proceeded to Springfield to confer with him on matters of national importance. "My first sight of him was a deep disappointment. Before me stood a middle-aged man, tall, gaunt, ungainly, homely, ill-clad—slouchy pantaloons, vest held shut by a button or two, tightly fitting sleeves to exaggerate his long, bony arms, all supplemented by an awkwardness that was uncommon among men of intelligence. I confess that my heart sank within me as I remembered that this was the man chosen by a great nation to become its ruler in the gravest period of its history."

It was not long, however, before Mr. McClure discovered, as the Nation discovered later, that it was God who had chosen Lincoln, that, when the people cast their vote for him, they but expressed the will of Providence, which had decreed that the Nation founded by the Colonial Fathers shall not be severed, and that the slave shall be free. They remembered what the Bible said respecting the choice of the shepherd David in preference of other men, who, in external appearance, seemed the better fitted for the kingship: "the Lord seeth not as man seeth; for man looketh on the outward appearance, but the Lord looketh on the heart."[45] They recalled the humble origin of Moses and Jesus and Luther, and recognized that they whom God chooses for his work must have other distinctions than looks or wealth or name or culture. They must have hearts of saints, souls of heroes and martyrs. They must serve as anvils in the smithies of affliction so as to be able to serve as the hammer of God when the hour for striking comes.

It was a critical time in the story of our Nation, the most critical since the days of our conflict with our mother country across the sea. The hand of brother was lifted against brother. The South stood arrayed against the North. The hour called for a great man, for a man wise of heart as well as of mind, for a man of inspired soul and resolute will, for a man whose personalities and family traditions counted as nothing in the balance, for a man who, being of the common people, and the conflict of the hour having the greatest need of the common people, could easiest appeal to them and come in closest touch with them. The hour called for a man all whose labor and ambition were consecrated to his people and all whose purposes accountable to his God.

Such a man was Lincoln. A man more honest than he never lived. Rivals derided him, parties ridiculed him, papers caricatured him but no man was ever able even to breathe the breath of suspicion upon any of his motives. Unlike so many of the schooled diplomats and statesmen, who in their eager development of brain, starve the heart, his brain was all the keener because of its blending with heart, and his heart all the richer because of its blending with brain. An unkind word never passed his lips, an unkind deed never stained his hand, an unworthy thought never polluted his mind. His countenance, rugged and gnarled as it was, was as open as a page of Scriptures; his eye as clear as innocence itself.

Not ambition, not lust of power or wealth, of fame or name, bore him to the heights he occupied. He had never sought an honor or an office, had never thought himself fit for a position of responsibility when it was entrusted to him. Men in public office have been modest, have been unassuming, but never one like Abraham Lincoln. There was no more surprised man in all the land than he when the choice of President fell to him, and it would have been difficult to find one who could have accepted it with greater reluctance. Full forty years long had he yearned for the coming of a man strong and wise enough to rid the Nation of the curse of slavery, without severing its bond of union. Full forty years long had that hope and prayer burnt within him, and would not cease burning, like the vision of the burning bush that Moses saw in the wilderness. And when the call came to him at last, as it had come to Moses, when the voice of God, through the voice of the people, called out to him, saying: "I have seen the afflictions of a people unjustly enslaved; I have heard its cry of anguish by reason of its taskmasters. I know the strife that is tearing the Nation asunder, and I am resolved to deliver it, through thy hand. Get thee to Washington, and inaugurate there the work of redemption and of union," when that call came, he, like Moses, had not the heart to rush upon a work, which the greatest had feared to touch, fearing lest, by unfitness, he overthrow all future chance, all future hope. "Let another and an abler go," he sadly said, "this is a work for giants, not for pigmies, like me."

It was a work for a giant, and for just such a giant as Lincoln was. It required a giant's heart to make an entry into the Capital of the Nation, as President-elect, such as he was obliged to make, in the dead of night, by stealth and by circuitous routes, to escape the assassin's hand. It required a giant's mind to present an inaugural address such as he presented, on the fourth of March, 1861, and to outline a course of action such as he laid before his Secretary of State. The men of his cabinet, proud of their statesmanship and scholarship and polish and influence, had believed that the western hoosier, the accident of the polls, would but be a figurehead, that they themselves would rule and dictate the policies of the land. They soon learned that their chief was a ruler, not only by the grace but also by the call of God, a ruler with the inspiration of a prophet, with the wisdom of a sage, with the will-power of a conqueror. Before a month of his presidential term had elapsed, the Nation marvelled as much as it had doubted, and the South realized that it was a war to the death that it had entered upon.

And a war to the death it continued, four years long, till slavery was abolished and the union was saved. There was no abatement in its vigor, no change in its policy, no quarter to the enemy, until they recognized the stars and stripes as the common flag of all of the United States, until they conceded to the enslaved negro the human rights and political liberties which the white man enjoyed. There had been irresoluteness and vacillation too long, and at too terrible a cost. Had the issue been squarely met, had the voice of God instead of the voice of politics been spoken, had there been whole truths instead of half measures, in short, had their [sic] been a Lincoln in the Presidential chair fifty years earlier, there would have been no need of a civil war, no need of ravaged states, devastated homes, paralyzed industries, impoverished people, no need of brother's hand being raised against brother, no need of six hundred and twenty-five battles being fought, in which blood flowed like water, and which widowed and orphaned and darkened tens of thousands of homes.

Others before him had seen the calamity that threatened the Nation as clearly as he saw it, and had yearned for a redeemer as sincerely as he. Long before him, Patrick Henry had said the slave question "gives a gloomy prospect to future times," and George Mason had written to the legislature of Virginia "the laws of impartial Providence may avenge our injustice upon our posterity," and Jefferson had said: "I tremble for my country when I reflect that God is just, and that His justice cannot sleep for ever," and Madison had said "where slavery exists there the republican theory becomes fallacious"—but, while they saw the danger and despaired, he felt it and acted.

Others dared not risk their political future, he dared to risk even his life. It was his innermost conviction that one nation, under one government, without slavery, had been divinely ordained, and he was resolved that not a State should be struck from the Union by treason. He saw no other assurance for lasting peace than war to the bitter end, no other promise of harmony between the North and South than a decision upon the battlefield whether or not all men are born free and equal politically, whether or not individual states had a right to secede. It was in our old Independence Hall where he solemnly declared that he believed in the Declaration of Independence, that he believed with all his heart that it guaranteed liberty to all, and reaching a climax of eloquence, and speaking as one inspired, he said: "If the country cannot be saved without giving up that principle, I would rather be assassinated on the spot than surrender it."

And well did he see to it that the country did not surrender its principle. And dearly did he pay for it. That of which he had had a presentiment when he spoke in our city came to pass. The assassin's hand struck him down, but not till, by his labors, his country was saved, till the stars and stripes waved again over the North and South, till union and confederate soldier laid down their arms, never to take them up again against each other.

The turf has grown thick over the graves of those who paid with their lives for their country's honor. The bitter enmities of half a century ago are now forgotten. But not forgotten is the name of Abraham Lincoln. Not forgotten is the sacrifice of martyrdom which he laid upon the altar of his country. Annually the still remaining veterans of the long and deadly conflict assemble to do reverence to the memory of their well nigh canonized leader. Annually sons of these veterans assemble to pledge their fealty to the memory of him who led their fathers and their country to victory. Annually, on his natal day, a grateful posterity burnishes into new lustre his crown of glory, and piously resolves that as long as oceans shall beat against our Atlantic and Pacific shores, as long as the Alleghenies and the Rocky Mountains shall lift their heads into the blue empyrean, as long as proud Old Glory shall wave from highest North to furthest South, so long shall the name of Abraham Lincoln live in the loyal American heart as the savior of his country, as the Chosen of God.[46]

6. LINCOLN THE *TSADDIK*

Arthur A. Dembitz (1875–1940) was one of Lewis Naphtali Dembitz's children. Lewis Dembitz was one of Lincoln's earliest supporters, and he helped to nominate Lincoln at the Republican National Convention in 1860. According to a news article in the Jewish Exponent, *Arthur Dembitz, an instructor of Jewish history at Philadelphia's Gratz*

*College and an active member of Philadelphia's "Free Synagogue," delivered a homily on
Lincoln. Employing a familiar Hebrew compliment, Dembitz told his fellow congregants
that Abraham Lincoln was a* tsaddik—*an expression commonly used to describe a person
who is the embodiment of Judaism's highest moral teachings.*[47]

Mr. Dembitz Praises Lincoln

At the Free Synagogue services . . . last Saturday, Mr. Dembitz, after dwelling
for a few minutes on the New Year of Trees, which was to begin Sunday night,
made some comments on the sweetened waters of Marah.[48] The Sedra [Torah
portion] contained the expression "And the Lord showed him a tree," which,
when it was thrown into the water, the water became sweet. In relation to the
water of life being sweetened, the Midrash [rabbinical exposition] gives us a
hint elsewhere as to the meaning of the word "tree." In his exhortation to the
spies, Moses says, investigate (among other things) "whether there be a tree in
it or no,"—by "tree" here is meant a righteous man, under whose shadow and
protecting aegis the inhabitants feel secure. Such a *Tsaddik*, said the speaker,
has been shown by the Almighty to America; Abraham Lincoln, whose birthday this year immediately precedes the New Year of Trees, was indeed such
a "tree," the contemplation of which causes one to say, "Life is not vain; life is
not bitterness; there is a sweetness in life that renders it worth living."

May it never be said of America, "their shadow has departed from them."
Rather be it said that they delight in the shadow of such men as Washington
and Lincoln, whose teachings and noble examples will form abiding elements
of the national character, private and public—insuring perpetuity.[49]

7. LESSONS FROM THE LIFE OF LINCOLN

*Nathan Krass, rabbi of Temple Emanu-El in New York from 1923 until his retirement
in 1933, delivered the sermon from which this excerpt is taken at the Buffalo Ad Club
in Buffalo, New York, on February 12, 1914, on the occasion of Lincoln's 105th birthday.
Rabbi Krass described Lincoln as the epitome of the true universal religious spirit in that
he served as a model for all those who sought to serve God regardless of creed. He was a
man who possessed "an intensely religious soul" wherein "there burned the divine essentials
that make all religions glow." Lincoln was a man who believed that humans could indeed
make their world a better place, and Krass urged his listeners to emulate his idealism.*

Abraham Lincoln

I was asked to draw some lessons from the life of Lincoln for our generation.
Well, one such lesson is this. It is not an essential of greatness to hold one's
self aloof from one's fellowmen. Such is the method of near-greatness. The
greater the man, the more will he love and labor for and live with his fellowmen. The old biblical verses are still true—the first in the old, the second in the

new testaments. "And the oldest shall serve the youngest, the more powerful the weaker." "The greatest among you shall serve the least."[50] This lesson was supremely illustrated in the personality of Lincoln and that is one of many legacies he has left us in our great democracy. He left one more, which I shall mention. It was said that Lincoln was not a churchman. Well, what of it? I can name some others that were not in the technical sense churchmen. And I do this not by way of criticism of the church, but reverently. For there have been great exceptions in the religious world who stood outside the organized church not because they were irreligious, but because they were temperamentally more comfortable outside of the church. Moses was no churchman. Yet, he was profoundly religious. The prophets were not churchmen. Yet, they are the greatest group of religious souls the world has ever seen or heard. Jesus was no churchman. Yet, in the hearts of all these characters, there was that deep, that powerful, that vitalizing sense of spirituality, that absolute feeling of direct communion with God that transcends all externalities. In this sense, Abraham Lincoln was an intensely religious soul. He believed, and that is his other legacy to us, that real religion is spirituality in action, that divine service is service to humanity, and we are learning that lesson as we never learned it before. You are familiar with Churchill's novel, *The Inside of the Cup*. And you recall the description of the church pillars. In Buffalo, as in New York, you will find many church pillars. Pillars are made of stone, and often the human pillars of churches are stony-hearted who lend grace and social status, but no soul and service. They are not religious men. They are not like Lincoln, whose creed was not an oppressive chain around his neck, a contracting gyve around his heart, but whose religion was an open sesame to humanity. And how he loved humanity. "God surely loved the common people, he made so many of them" was one of his familiar sayings. And the religion of democracy, learning its lesson and gaining its inspiration from Lincoln, is none other than the religion without hate and prejudice, that will not cause a tear to flow, but will brush it off the cheek of sorrow and suffering and pain. You may call this religion Judaism. You may name it Christianity. It matters not. Lincoln was so big that every creed claims him. In his soul, there burned the divine essentials that make all religions glow. We would honor Lincoln's memory? Let us emulate him in his idealism. It warmed the souls of millions. We would twine a literary laurel wreath about his name? Remember that in his heart there blossomed the finest flowers that diffused their sweet aroma across a continent and caused stifling, stumbling humanity to inhale a whiff of that which strengthens and uplifts.

With a single verbal alteration, let my final word be a paragraph from Lincoln's eulogy of Washington. "On that name no eulogy is expected. It cannot be. To add brightness to the sun, or glory to the name of Lincoln is alike impossible. Let none attempt it. In solemn awe pronounce the name and in its naked, deathless splendor leave it shining on!"[51]

8. LINCOLN'S RELIGION IS MY RELIGION

Ferdinand M. Isserman (1898–1972), born in Antwerp, Belgium, was ordained at the Hebrew Union College in Cincinnati in 1922. His first served as assistant rabbi at Rodeph Shalom Congregation in Philadelphia. In 1925, Isserman became the senior rabbi of Toronto's Holy Blossom Temple, and in 1929 he assumed the pulpit of Temple Israel in St. Louis, where he remained for the rest of his career.

Isserman earned a national reputation for his many Jewish, civic, and political activities. He was a highly regarded orator, and his weekly radio program in St. Louis made him a prominent regional voice throughout the Midwest for more than thirty years.

In this sermon, delivered on February 9, 1940, Rabbi Isserman told his listeners that "Lincoln's religion" was actually their religion. He asserted his belief that Lincoln's spiritual values were actually one and the same with what he regarded as the essential core of Judaism's message: universalism. Isserman was deeply committed to Reform Judaism's emphasis on a "prophetic Judaism," which stressed the values to which all moral people subscribe—and which was none other than Abraham Lincoln's religion.

Isserman concluded his oration by calling on his listeners to preserve Lincoln's religion, namely, Judaism, "not merely for ourselves but for the Lincolns of the future who will bring to mankind the emancipation that it needs."

The Religion of Lincoln and the Religion of the Synagogue

Abraham Lincoln was not opposed to organized religion nor was he even opposed to denominationalism. He merely could find no organized church, no denomination which would admit him to its fold without any mental reservations. This he made quite clear in a historic utterance[:] "When any church," he said, "will inscribe over its altar as its sole qualification for membership 'Thou shalt love the Lord thy God with all thy heart and all thy soul and all thy might, and love thy neighbor as thyself' that church will I join with all my heart and all my soul." This statement of Lincoln's is based directly on a passage in the New Testament in the Gospel of Matthew (chapter 22, vs. 36[–37]). . . .

Similarly the verse "Thou shalt love thy neighbor as thyself" is found in that great section on holiness in the 19th chapter of the Book of Leviticus which opened with the magnificent words, "Ye shall be holy, for the Lord your God is holy." It then proceeds to define holiness, for in ancient as in modern days, men who sought the religious way of life, to whom immediate revelation with God was denied, were anxious to know what the most sensitive men, the great religious teachers, believed man must do to be holy to approach God. The 19th chapter of Leviticus gives the answer. The holy man must leave the corner of the field for the poor. To be holy men must not curse the deaf nor put a stumbling block in the path of the blind. To be holy every man must revere his parents nor must he steal, nor swear falsely nor oppress his neighbor nor be a tale bearer nor must he hate his brother or cherish vengeance or bear any grudge but he must love his neighbor as himself. This is the heart of the golden rule, "Love thy neighbor as thyself." . . .

Huxley the great scientist said that the religion to which he could subscribe was the religion of the prophets of Israel. Abraham Lincoln, American's great prophet, said that his religion could be summed up in the verses Love the Lord thy God with all thy heart and all thy soul and thy neighbor as thyself.[52] These men [were] stalwarts of the 19th century, leaders of the caravan of mankind, blazers of new trails, who yearned for religion[.] [T]hey yearned for the religion of the synagogue, its monotheism, its conception of God, its emphasis on ethical relationships. That is our religion. It is true that at times ritual and ceremony[—] devised to perpetuate that religion[—]have obscured it, but invariably there have risen within the synagogue new spirits who have brushed away the cobwebs of institutionalism and have revealed the pristine beauty of Israel's faith. Love the Lord thy God with all thy heart, with all thy soul and love thy neighbor as thyself. That is the religion our fathers have proclaimed throughout the ages. That is the religion for which they lived and for which they died. That is the religion for which they bore persecution. That is the religion which inspired Abraham Lincoln to free four million men and gave him the spirit of sacrifice, the heroic temper, the love for mercy which made human immortal spirit. That religion is your religion. It is my religion . . . that we must preserve not merely for ourselves but for the Lincolns of the future who will bring to mankind the emancipation that it needs.[53]

LINCOLN CENTENNIAL SERMONS

9. CITYWIDE CEREMONY MARKING THE LINCOLN CENTENNIAL HELD AT TEMPLE

Many of the ceremonies marking the 100th anniversary of Lincoln's birth reflected a universal spirit as if to honor Lincoln's own commitment to equality. In many cities, the general community filed into Jewish institutions to participate in Lincoln centennial programs. Such was the case in Pittsburgh, where an elaborate commemoration of Lincoln's centennial was held at Temple Rodeph Shalom in February 1909.

Pittsburgh's Jewish newspaper, the Jewish Criterion, *described the event and reproduced the order of the evening's program. Of all the speakers, the* Criterion *gave highest praise to the Episcopal priest, Dr. J. Everist Cathell (d. 1913), who delivered a "hypnotizing" lecture on Lincoln's life.*

Lincoln Services at the Temple

TUESDAY EVENING—DR. CATHELL'S LECTURE

We feel sorry for those subscribers to the Temple Course who failed to attend the lecture of Dr. J. Everist Cathell on "Abraham Lincoln," on Tuesday evening. There have been men of fame on that platform but it is safe to say that no man ever commanded his audience as completely as did Dr. Cathell. [Henry] Watterson and [Jonathan P.] Dolliver and Ward and Mrs. [Agnes] Booth and Gov. [Robert B.] Glenn and all the other eminent public speakers have interested and thrilled our audiences, but it was left to J. Everist Cathell to hypnotize them by his remarkably dramatic and soul-stirring story of Abraham Lincoln. Representatives of the various lecture bureaus located in different parts of the country were of one opinion that the story of Lincoln had never been so graphically or so sympathetically interpreted. It was a revelation to the audience. This man, whose name was not even known to the majority present, who had not been heralded in flambouyant [sic] style, came quietly and unassumingly and completely captured one of the most critical audiences after he had been speaking five minutes. For two hours and five minutes Lincoln the boy, the man, the lawyer, the debator, the slave fighter, the President, the emancipator, the ruling genius of the American people were presented to us in a manner that invited laughter and tears.

Dr. Cathell has the dramatic instinct highly developed and he has the mechanics of public speaking developed to a high degree, and these qualifications, coupled with a beautiful speaking voice, made him master of the audience.

He threw many sidelights on incidents in connection with Lincoln's public life heretofore unknown. And the most interesting and dramatic feature of the entire lecture was the story of his first visit to Mr. Lincoln at the White House. When he had finished everyone was visibly affected by the new light that had been thrown upon the character of the great and good man.

It would be useless to attempt to give even an outline of the lecture.

Only Dr. Cathell's personality and eloquence could lend it the proper charm and interest.

We are happy to have heard this man and count it a rare privilege. In his statement we know that every one who heard the matchless address on Tuesday evening will heartily concur.

Dr. J. Everist Cathell has the right to take the foremost rank on the American platform.

THURSDAY AFTERNOON—SISTERHOOD GIVES EXCELLENT PROGRAM

The Sisterhood of Rodeph Shalom gave one of the most interesting Lincoln programs of the week. Invitations had been extended to all the women of the city and a great throng was present. The rooms were appropriately decorated. Mrs. Josiah Cohen,[54] the president, presided and opened the meeting with a few well chosen remarks, speaking of the great occasion which provoked such inspiring gathering. She was delighted to note the representative character of the assemblage which had gathered to pay homage to the memory of the immortal American. She added that this celebration was in part given over to the hundredth anniversary of the birth of the great Mendelssohn and that the musical program had been arranged with that in view.

The playing of Mr. Edward Tak,[55] the famous Concert-meister of the Pittsburg[h] Orchestra sustained the unusually high reputation enjoyed by this wizard of the violin. The large audience was wildly enthusiastic over his marvelous playing and again and again he was compelled to bow to the plaudits of his hearers. The accompanist, Mr. Carl Bernthaler,[56] needs no encomiums at our hand; his pos[i]tion as a musical artist of the first degree is too well established. The oration on Lincoln by the Rev. Dr. Alfred C. Dieffenbach[57] was a masterly one. Dr. Dieffenbach has all the requirements of the orator, mind, voice and presence, and from start to finish he held completely the attention of the audience as he sympathetically depicted the wonderful character and work of Lincoln. He shed new light on many phases of Lincoln's life and when he had concluded his hearers felt that they knew Lincoln better than ever before.[58]

10. HE PLEADED THE LAW OF JUSTICE AND THE GOSPEL OF LIBERTY

On February 7, 1909, Rabbi J. Leonard Levy (1865–1917) of Congregation Rodeph Shalom in Pittsburgh, Pennsylvania, delivered a centennial birthday sermon titled "Abraham Lincoln's Religion." According to Levy, Abraham Lincoln was a religious man, though he was neither a believing nor a professing Christian. The following excerpts express Levy's assertion that Lincoln was too "broad" or "universal" a soul to have been limited by any one particular religious creed. Remarkably, the rabbi compared Lincoln to Jesus; both men were great souls and chosen of God, both were misunderstood and undervalued during their lifetimes, and both, after meeting their ends, "arose again" to life immortal.

Abraham Lincoln's Religion

He kept the Ten Commandments and realized the Nine Beatitudes. He was great in his goodness.

There is none perfect but God, and Lincoln was not God. He was supremely human, but intensely noble. His was a deeply religious soul. Weighed by human creeds he may be found wanting, but tested by the qualities dear to God, he was one of His chosen. Rejected by sectarian dogmatists, he was, nevertheless, acceptable to the Father of all. Doomed by Articles of Faith, he was saved by the possession of the "clean hands and the pure heart," which entitle their owner to "abide in the hill of the Lord and to dwell in His tabernacle."[59] The opinions of a bitter and bigoted past, which he could not accept, would cast him out from the eternal justice of God, but he felt secure in the Divine Love. He knew that the Divine will is righteousness and that God accepts all who seek Him with all their heart and soul.

If I hold that Lincoln was religious in the best sense of the term, it is because we must differentiate between theology, creed, dogma and religion.

For, what is religion? It is the consciousness of God's overruling Presence, and the performance of duty as done unto Him in His sight. There are many who overburden, who overload religion with ritual and ceremony, as there are many who would have us believe that religion is to be gauged by creeds and Confessions of Faith. Religion bears reference to what a man is, rather than to what a man says he believes. It is the recognition of the immediate, and personal accountability of man to his Maker. Of this the test cannot be the creed, but the life. Religion is a sentiment, deep, holy, all-encompassing, but a sentiment nevertheless; and like every other sentiment it can only be estimated by the life it inspires, by the personality it produces. Let a man be possessed of never so finely-woven a chain of creedal statements; let him hold the most deftly constructed Confession; let him cry aloud with never so earnest a voice, Credo, Credo, "I believe, I believe"; I, nevertheless, hold that conduct and not creed is the measure of religion.

The following lines express my own view, and I think, yours also:

> 'Tis not by prayers loud and long,
> By contrite beating of the breast,
> By psalm, by hymn, by sacred song,
> God's name most truthfully is blest.
>
> 'Tis not by ceremonies vain,
> By antique creed, by ancient rite,
> By customs, which your souls disdain,
> You worship God, the Lord of Right.
>
> But when you aid the righteous meek,
> Bring light unto the darkened mind,
> Support the falling, help the weak,
> You praise the Lord of all mankind.
>
> Love mercy, practice justice true!
> Strive e'er to make injustice fall!
> Assist thy fellow-man, and you
> Will worship God, the Lord of all.[60]

If in these words we find an interpretation, however weak, of the spirit of Israel's Prophets; if they represent, however feebly, the point of view of Isaiah and Micah, and later worthies of the House of Israel; who shall say that Lincoln was not religious? His, too, was a religion of simplicity. "Whenever a church will write over its doors, 'Thou shalt love the Lord thy God with all thy heart and soul and mind and might,' and 'Thou shalt love thy neighbor as thyself,' and impose no other qualifications for membership, that church will I join." In words, such as these, Lincoln asserted the faith that was in him. One whose words bear authority to hundreds of millions of men said that these are the two greatest commandments, as they were always recognized to be in Israel whose prophet wrote them.

But Lincoln, though religious, was not a believing and confessing Christian. He was not a member of a church. Many say that, on this account, he was not religious, and that he is not among "the saved." Some of the noblest souls who ever lived were too broad for the narrow limits of many a church. Some of the crudest, and most unscrupulous of men have been church-members, founders or endowers of churches. I, for one, will take my chances in the after-life with Abraham Lincoln, rather than with Charles IX of France, or Charles I of England, or Tomas Torquemada of Spain. The God who will accept these and cast him out of eternal life is one for whom I have naught but contempt. I shall trust myself to the God Lincoln loved, with much more confidence than the god of recreant kings and persecuting ecclesiastics.

. . . Lincoln's religion was devoid of formalism and ritualism; it was free from soul-cramping dogmatism; it was untainted by bigotry. It was a high expression of those fundamental virtues, those basic qualities that mark the highest manhood. It was expressed by honesty, sincerity, patriotism, malice toward none and charity for all. It was a universal creed, the noble expression of his universal goodness.

. . . Like a Moses, Lincoln cried, "Send away the people that they may be free," for upon his ear there fell the sound of the taskmaster's lash and the hissing of the whip. He led the turbulent people to the foot of a Sinai of duty, and he read to them the law of right and truth. He wandered with them through a wilderness of trial; before him went the pillar of cloud, difficulty, and the pillar of light, faith. He provided his people with manna, the heavenly manna of service. He drank the waters of Marah, and from the flinty rocks of callous hearts and out of the selfishness of brutalized masses, he made the waters of sympathy to flow. He spoke face to face with God. He reached his Nebo. For a few days, he looked over into the Promised Land, and then God gave His beloved sleep.

Like a Jesus, he was born in a manger. There were no angels, however, to announce his birth, but with his coming, there was the assurance of peace on earth and good-will toward men, as well as glory to God in the highest. He was born in poverty, and of him the doubting Nathaniels said, "Can there any good thing come out of Kentucky?" He saw the cause of the downtrodden and the oppressed, and he lived to make men noble, and died to make them free. He pleaded for the law of justice and the gospel of liberty. God called him to be a witness to the truth. The plain people loved him. They heard him gladly. They cried before him, "Master." They accepted him as leader. They, however, placed upon his head the crown of thorns and surrounded him with the halo of martyrdom, because he drove the traffickers in human flesh out of the Temple of the Lord, and scourged with his bitter indignation the money-changers who dealt in human souls. He passed through the Gethsemane of trial. He prayed, "O that this bitter cup might pass away, but if it be Thy will, O Father, Thy will, not mine be done."[61] He met his end on a Calvary, crucified as the truly great have so often been.

Buried, he arose again, and he has since become a spirit immortal.[62]

11. THE PERSONIFICATION OF THE AMERICAN NATION

Edward A. Fischkin (1871–1951), a physician, essayist, and Jewish educator, delivered the main address at the Lincoln Centennial Celebration of the Chicago Hebrew Institute on February 11, 1909. He told his listeners that American Jews identify with the "glorious character of Lincoln." In the excerpts that follow, Fischkin declares that Lincoln's love of liberty and his commitment to social equality enabled Jews to "glory in . . . this nation for its personification of Jewish ideals." It was in America, Fischkin asserts, that Jewish people could earnestly dedicate themselves both to the welfare of their country and to their religion. The love of freedom and the respect for the power of the mind were values that Lincoln and the Jews had in common. Fischkin concluded his oration by yoking these two ideals together in an almost paroxysmal paean to Reason.

Lincoln and the Jewish Spirit

What I intend this evening is to determine our own relation to this national celebration, to ascertain our place at this festival of the American nation. We are part and parcel of this great nation. The joy of this country is our joy, the pride of the nation is our pride. But we are assembled here this evening not only as Americans, but as American Jews. Not only as patriots, but as patriotic units in this great family of races and nationalities. What is our relation to the glorious character of Lincoln, what is our claim to his fame, what our influence on the formation of his great personality?

. . . For if there is any congeniality between the soul of a people and the character of a person, it is the striking similarity between the ideals and aspirations of the Jewish people and those of Abraham Lincoln, it is the feelings, thoughts, and instincts of our people embodied in the personality of this American hero. It is the intellectual affinity of the soul, the "Wahlverwandtschaft der Seelen," which makes the memory of Lincoln adorable and sacred to us as Jews. . . .

What are Jewish ideals? What is the essence of our national soul? What the moving principle of our long historic life? History gives but one answer to these questions: our religion, and it gives but one interpretation to our religion: liberty—liberty and human dignity. Liberty and human dignity are the only ideals which have filled our soul, the only traits which have marked our character, the only motives which have made our history, the only features which have characterized our religion. Judaism and liberty are synonymous. Mosaism and human dignity are equivalent. The Decalogue is the basis of every declaration of the rights of men that has ever been made, and the preface to the Ten Commandments explicitly states that the reason why Israel shall obey them is that it made them free. "You shall not be slaves" is the refrain to every commandment and to every precept given in the Bible. Anti-slavery is the living ideal, the moving spirit, the essence of the Thora; it is a principle, an instinct, a primal energy which has given cause and meaning to every prescription of the Old Testament: be it the rest of the Sabbath, the joy of festivals, the care of the needy or the love for the stranger. . . .

Without liberty, and equality and the pursuit of happiness for all men, America had no attraction for him. "When the know-nothings get control," wrote he in a letter, "it will read, 'All men are created equal, except negroes and foreigners and Catholics.' . . . When it comes to this I shall prefer emigrating to some country where they make no pretense of loving liberty—Russia for instance, where despotism can be taken pure and without the base alloy of hypocrisy." . . .

His ideal of political equality incorporated also the Jewish ideal of social equality. Social justice was for him the basis of a society of equals. "That is the real issue," was his expression, debating with Douglas at Alton, Illinois, in 1858. "It is the eternal struggle between these two principles—right and wrong—throughout the world." . . .

This, ladies and gentlemen, are the traits in Lincoln's character, which make his memory venerable and sacred to us, not only as Americans, but as Jews. . . . In today's celebration, we not only pay tribute to Lincoln as the personification of the American nation, but we glory in our belonging to this nation for its personification of Jewish ideals. This celebration is not only the expression of our American patriotism, but is also the reverberation of accumulated impulses of our Jewish soul. For this is the nation that has built its institutions on the principles of the Old Testament. For this is the land where the lofty sacred Jewish ideals of liberty became the heritage of the people. We celebrate the glorious work of a great American patriot, who sealed his faith in free institutions in his blood and who left us the sacred heritage of liberty and of the free and undisturbed pursuit of our own happiness, but we pay here tribute also to our own glorious past, to the spirit of Israel which revived in this land of liberty. . . .

Let our adherence to our glorious past be combined with the adhesion to our American future. Let the love of American institutions be nourished by the love of Jewish ideals. Let us devote ourselves to the sacred task of keeping alive the identity of these two ideals, that the vision of the greatest visionary shall become realized, that the emancipator's dream of political freedom shall become an actuality, which he expressed in the inimitable, beautiful words: "And what a noble ally this to the cause of political freedom; with such an aid its march cannot fail to be on and on, till every son of earth shall drink in rich fruition the sorrow-quenching draughts of perfect liberty. Happy day when— all appetites controlled, all poisons subdued, all matter subjected—mind, all conquering mind, shall live and move, the monarch of the world. Glorious Consummation! Hail, fall of fury! Reign of reason, all hail!"[63]

12. THE PERSONIFICATION OF JEWISH VALUES

The towering rabbinic scholar Solomon Schechter (1847–1915) adulated Lincoln even before he immigrated to America. On February 12, 1909, Dr. Schechter delivered an address in commemoration of the centennial anniversary of Lincoln's birth to an audience at the Jewish Theological Seminary in New York. Schechter informed his listeners that during his childhood, President Lincoln seemed to him to be the modern-day embodiment of the great Jewish sage and scholar Hillel. While other children studied Lincoln as an American statesman, Schechter "was always studying [Lincoln] from the viewpoint of the student of Jewish literature." In doing so, this distinguished president of a rabbinical seminary delivered a learned discourse that insisted that for the throngs of Jewish immigrants, "Lincoln, his life, his history, his character, his entire personality, with all its wondrous charm and grace, its sobriety, patience, and self-abnegation and sweetness, has come to be the very prototype of a rising humanity."[64]

Abraham Lincoln

It may perhaps not be entirely uninteresting to listen to one whose first acquaintance with Lincoln was made in far-distant Roumania through the medium of Hebrew newspapers some forty-five years ago. There Lincoln was described as originally a wood-chopper (prose for "rail-splitter"), which fired the imagination of the boy to recognize in the President of the United States, a new Hillel, for legend described the latter as having been engaged in the same occupation before he was called by the people to the dignity of Patriarch, or President of the Sanhedrin. Years have come and years have gone, and the imagination of the boy was in many respects corrected by the reading of serious books bearing on the history of the United States, and particularly on that of the Civil War. But this in no way diminished his admiration for his hero, Abraham Lincoln, whom he was always studying, from the viewpoint of the student of Jewish literature; a literature which, in spite of its eastern origin, affords so much in the way of parallel and simile to the elucidation of many a feature in the story of the great Westerner of Westerners.

. . . The greatest human and at the same time religious document, however, left us by Lincoln, for which history hardly affords any model, except perhaps that of the Scriptures is, as is well known, his Second Inaugural: "'The Almighty has His own purpose. Woe unto the world because of offenses; for it must needs be that offenses come; but woe to that man by whom the offense cometh.'[65] If we shall suppose that American slavery is one of those offenses which, in the providence of God must needs come, but which, having continued through his appointed time, he now wills to remove, and that he gives to both North and South this terrible war as the woe due to those by whom the offense came, shall we discern therein any departure from the divine attributes which the believers in a living God always ascribe to him? Fondly do we hope—fervently do we pray—that this mighty scourge of war may speedily pass away. Yet, if God wills that it continue until all the wealth piled by the bondsman's two hundred and fifty years of unrequited toil shall be sunk, and until every drop of blood drawn with the lash shall be paid by another drawn with the sword, as was said three thousand years ago, so still it must be said: 'The Judgments of the Lord are true and righteous altogether.'"[66]

When reading the lines just given, one can hardly believe that they formed a part of a message addressed in the nineteenth century to an assembly composed largely of men of affairs and representatives of a special political party, surrounded by all the pomp and paraphernalia of one of the greatest legislative bodies the world had ever seen. One rather imagines himself transported into a camp of contrite sinners determined to leave the world and its vanities behind them, possessed of no other thought but that of reconciliation with their God, and addressed by their leader when about to set out on a course of penance. Indeed, how little the religious sentiments manifest in this document echoed those of either party is evident from a letter of Lincoln to Thurlow Weed, with reference to the Second Inaugural: ". . . I believe it is not immediately popular. Men are not flattered by being shown that there has been a difference of purpose between the Almighty and them. To deny it, however, in this case, is to deny that there is a God governing the world. It is a truth which I thought needed to be told, and, as whatever of humiliation there is in it falls most directly on myself, I thought others might afford for me to tell it." To take upon one's self the burden of humiliation in which a whole nation should share, is another feature of religious mysticism which realizes in the sphere of morality the unity of humanity and in the realm of history the union of the nation, so that it does not hesitate to suffer and to atone for the sins of the generation.

Nothing is more congenial to the student of Jewish literature than these ingredients in Lincoln's mental make-up which found their expression in his stories, his repartee, his wit and sarcasm, in all of which he was such a consummate master. In this literature, the "mashal" (comparison) or "maaseh" (story) are the most prominent. They were mostly used by way of illustration. The use of the "mashal" (or comparison) in particular, is illustrated by the Rabbis by another "mashal," comparing it to the handle which enables people to take hold of a thing or subject. Occasionally, it forms the introduction to the most solemn discourse. Thus it is recorded of a famous Rabbi that before he commenced his lectures on points of law before his disciples, he would first tell them something humorous to make them laugh, and then, resuming his natural self, commenced in solemn frame of mind his discourse. I need hardly remind you here of the well-known tradition in connection with the President's first reading of the Emancipation Proclamation to the members of his cabinet (September 22, 1862). They met in his office at the White House, and then took their seats in the usual order. Lincoln then took Artemus Ward's book, and read from it the chapter, "High-Handed Outrage at Utica," which he thought very funny, and enjoyed the reading of it greatly, while the members of the cabinet, except Stanton, laughed with him. Then he fell into a grave tone and began the discussion preceding the perusal of this great historical and momentous document.

To give another example: When the Rabbi wanted to impress his audience with the evil consequences of intemperance, he would say, "Story: Once upon a time there was a pious man whose father was addicted to strong drink, which brought great shame upon him. On one occasion, the pious man walked in the street in a pouring rain, when he perceived a drunken man lying in the gutter and exposed to the abuse of the street urchins, who made sport of him. He thereupon thought in his heart, 'I will induce father to come here to show him the humiliation he brings upon himself by his dissipation.' The father came, but the first thing he did was to ask the drunken man for the address of the inn where such good wine was sold."[67]

13. THE REALIZATION OF THE TRUE SPIRIT OF JUDAISM

On February 11, 1909, the New York Times *proudly declared: "The Whole City to Join in Honoring Lincoln." Indeed, in the New York metropolitan area, more than 600 meetings and events had been planned for the upcoming twenty-four hour period.[68] At one of these events, the future president of Yeshiva University, Rabbi Bernard Revel (1885–1940), delivered a centennial oration. Revel, who was in the process of completing his doctoral studies at New York University and Dropsie College, lavishly extolled Lincoln as a modern-day prophet who possessed the embodiment of the Jewish spirit. For most Americans, Lincoln was "the first typical American," but for Revel, Lincoln should "more justly be said to represent the summation of all the noblest qualities of Judaism."*

Lincoln and the Jewish Spirit

Imbued with deep religious feeling and belief in the strength of truth and justice, armed with the Bible, "the Great Book," as he believed, that "God has given to man where all the truth of the saviour of the world is communicated," and having for his motto, "Let us have faith that right makes might, and in that faith as to the end dare to do our duty," he relied upon the assistance of Divine Providence, and during all his life the Lord, our God, was with him as he was with Washington, the Moses of the Union. Through him God emancipated, not only the millions of slaves, but freed the nation as well. Like Joshua, Lincoln lived to see the cause of the nation triumph, to behold the Union victorious and peace and tranquility prevailing in the land. With pride he carried the flag of the people, whom he emancipated and the Union which he saved, until his day of martyrdom.

In the war which Lincoln proclaimed for "Union and Freedom" the Jews were in the front ranks. For they, more than any other nation, had felt the scourge of the task-master and knew the heart of the oppressed. The history of the Jews is one long tragedy of personal sacrifice and heroism, and it is no wonder, therefore, that they were the first to re-echo the cry of abolition and respond to Lincoln's call. During that dark and trying time they took an active part in arousing the sentiments of the people, and throughout the country, North and South, the earnestness of the Jewish character found expression in their devotion to the Union cause. The first official call to organize the abolition movement was signed by four Jews and one gentile, and Jewish editors, writers, rabbis, preachers and men of affairs united in sowing the seeds of liberty. With their blood also the Jews of this country rushed to support the cause of the Union. At the outbreak of the Civil War the number of Jews in this country was less than 150,000. Out of these New York alone furnished 1,996 Jewish soldiers, among them being five brothers from a single family, as well as Col. S. Levy and his three sons. Pennsylvania furnished 527 soldiers, and among their number were the three brothers Emanuel. Moreover, in Lincoln himself were fused all the essential elements of Judaism. If he can justly be called the first typical American he can more justly be said to represent the summation of all the noblest qualities of Judaism.

. . . Lincoln combined the gentlest feeling of the heart with a rigid sense of duty and the perseverance necessary to fulfill that duty. He possessed spiritual insight, moral conviction, solid resolution, undying courage and faith and hope unfailing. He lived in the spirit. God was to him an ever-present, ever-poignant influence. He sympathized with men in the plane of humanity and regarded them in the spirit of philosophy. His fundamental democracy, which was to him a matter more of instinct than of reason, his belief in man's dignity, worth and moral nature gave him faith that on the whole and in the long run man will choose the good and reject the evil. He was convinced that every man should be his own master, should have the right to life, liberty and the pursuit of happiness. An ideal son of the author of the Declaration of Independence and the makers of the Constitution, he was imbued with a spirit of justice, without which freedom is of no avail and is destined to perish. Justice was indeed the breath of his life. Of all the American people, the most humane of any people on earth, Lincoln was the most humane. His great heart throbbed with sympathy for all the unfortunate and shared the pain of every suffering being.

These qualities, which are the brightest gems in the diadem of the greatest American, are they not of Jewish origin? If much of the best that is in the thought and tendencies of progressive life is due to Jewish inspiration, and if all the great social reformers of history have drawn their inspiration from the Jewish prophets, if the Bible is the vade mecum of the Pilgrim fathers from which they received their strength, their hopes and their sustenance, Lincoln was the realization of the true spirit of Judaism. Israel was the first democracy, its religion the first proclamation of freedom. In the very threshold of the Bible, the fatherhood of God, which results in the brotherhood of man, is proclaimed. The dignity of man is the basic conception of Israel's religion. Freedom is to Israel the most sacramental word. It embodied freedom and justice in its commonwealth. Freedom is the underlying motive of Israel's prophecies, hopes, festivals and prayers. Throughout the ages Israel's message to the world was that of freedom and righteousness. It was Judaism that first proclaimed human brotherhood. "Love ye the stranger." It was the Jewish prophet, who, in all the stirring grandeur of indignant rage, cried out, "Have we not all one father? Has not one God created us all?"[69] These were the principles for which Lincoln lived and died. And when the day will come and the American nation following its great prophet, Lincoln will become a model of justice, and through justice a pattern of peace to the world; when the American nation, led by the spirit of its great saviour and preserver, will add its share to the realization of the day which the Jewish prophet's inward vision foresaw thousands of years ago; when there will be universal peace growing out of universal justice and the American nation will show itself worthy of this, its greatest son, then the birthday of Lincoln will be the greatest holiday of a happy, progressive humanity and will represent a milestone in a new era of mankind's history.[70]

10

"His Name Will Ever Be Green in Your Hearts": Jews and the Cultural Preservation of Lincoln's Legacy

As we have seen, rabbis and Jewish leaders joined with their fellow citizens in eulogizing Lincoln after his assassination. Similarly, American Jews played an active role in the renaissance of interest in Lincoln's life, which would ultimately lead to his virtual apotheosis toward the end of the nineteenth century and into the first decades of the twentieth century. During this time, American Jews not only celebrated Lincoln and his Jewish qualities through a wide range of oratorical and literary presentations but also produced a diverse array of fine arts that contributed to the overall national trend of memorializing and exalting Lincoln. Jews lauded Lincoln on canvas, in bronze, in music, in decorative arts, and in belles lettres. American Jews also actively participated in the growing interest in collecting, preserving, and studying Lincolniana, historical material relating to his life and legacy.

Jewish Scholars of Lincoln

In 1894, the publisher Samuel S. McClure (1857–1949) hired a talented reporter named Ida Tarbell (1857–1944) and directed her to find new material on Lincoln, who, in McClure's opinion, was "the most vital factor in [American] life since the Civil War."[1] Tarbell delivered what McClure ordered, and the American public gobbled up her interesting articles on Lincoln that appeared serially in *McClure's Magazine* beginning in 1895. Tarbell's initial research convinced her that McClure had led her to an excellent topic. She realized that there existed a large field of unharvested primary source material on Lincoln, and she decided to begin work on a new Lincoln biography. Tarbell depended on the help of research assistants and also the reading public, who enjoyed her serialized articles on Lincoln and volunteered to assist her. She collected a remarkable array of new data on Lincoln and published a fresh two-volume biography titled *The Life of Abraham Lincoln: Drawn from Original Sources and Containing Many Speeches, Letters and Telegrams Hitherto Unpublished*.

An unassuming and somewhat phlegmatic Jewish newspaper editor named Isaac Markens became one of those who eagerly contributed to Tarbell's research on Lincoln. Markens, a modest businessman and journalist, was a pioneering Lincoln enthusiast and the first Jewish researcher to study Lincoln's relationship with American Jewry. As

Isaac Markens, newspaper correspondent
and prodigious researcher, was the first to
write about Lincoln and American Jewry.
Photographic print ICHi-59748; Chicago History
Museum.

a young man, Markens earned his living by working as a secretary and administrative
assistant. He eventually became an editor for a number of newspapers in New York,
including the *New York Commercial Advertiser*, the *Mail and Express*, and the *New York
Star*. For many years, Markens was also a member of the New York Cotton Exchange.[2]

During the early 1880s, while working as an editor for the *Mail and Express*, Markens
prepared a series of essays titled "Hebrews in America." The positive response of the
paper's readers spurred Markens's interest in writing about the history of Jewish life in
America. By 1888, he had expanded his newspaper series into a significant publication
that became a pioneering comprehensive effort to chronicle the history of American
Jewry: *Hebrews in America: A Series of Historical and Biographical Sketches*. Although
Markens was not a scientifically trained historian, he, like Ida Tarbell, approached his
research with the zeal of an investigative reporter. He delved deeply into published
volumes, state records, and historical societies in order to find his data. To his credit,
Markens also solicited numerous oral histories from prominent contemporaries. Not
surprisingly, the oral memoirs he procured from men like Isaac M. Wise, Bernhard
Felsenthal (1822–1908), Isaac P. Mendes (1854–1904), Benjamin F. Peixotto, Jacob Ezekiel
(1812–99), and many others often include interesting and valuable historical information
that would have been lost had it not been for Markens and his various publications. At
this same time, a small but noteworthy number of university-trained scholars such as
Cyrus Adler (1863–1940) and Jacob H. Hollander (1871–1940) joined together with independent researchers such as Leon Hühner (1871–1957) and Max J. Kohler (1871–1934) to
collect and preserve documentary evidence relating to the history of Jewish life in America as well. In 1892, a group of these scholars established the American Jewish Historical
Society, and Markens participated in the work of the society from its earliest days.[3]

As Markens collected biographical material for his work on the history of American Jewry, he discovered that a number of Jews claimed to have had a personal relationship with Abraham Lincoln, including Dr. Abraham B. Arnold (1820–1904), Leopold J. Blumenberg, Abram J. Dittenhoefer, Henry Greenebaum, Marcus Otterbourg, and Simon Wolf. According to Markens's contemporaries, the information he uncovered while researching his volume on American Jewish history stimulated his interest in gathering material for a full-scale monograph on Lincoln and the Jews. It is likely, in fact, that Markens shared many of his discoveries with Ida Tarbell, as the two investigative reporters were conducting research on Lincoln at the very same time. By the dawn of the twentieth century, Markens had amassed an impressive collection of primary source material relating to Lincoln and the Jews.[4]

As was his investigative custom, Markens corresponded with a wide variety of individuals who seemed likely to possess valuable source material on Lincoln's life, including Robert Todd Lincoln (1843–1926), John Hay, and Helen Nicolay (the daughter of Lincoln's personal secretary, John Nicolay). Although Robert Lincoln's early communications with Markens offered the researcher little hope for meaningful cooperation, the persistent Markens managed to win the reclusive Robert's confidence. The two men developed a remarkable correspondence that lasted more than two decades.[5]

The Markens/Lincoln correspondence sheds a great deal of light on the notoriously private Robert, who overcame his usual reticence, responded patiently to Markens's numerous queries, and helped him with his research. Scholars have relied on the Markens-Lincoln correspondence to unravel some interesting archival mysteries regarding a few famous Lincoln documents. In 1915, for example, Markens informed Lincoln that he had located the missing "original manuscript" of the Gettysburg Address. Eventually, Markens's ongoing communication with Lincoln resulted in bringing that valuable document into the holdings of the Library of Congress. In 1917, Markens posed a number of questions to Robert concerning a letter that Abraham Lincoln had written to a widow named Bixby in 1864. Mrs. Bixby had lost her five sons during the Civil War—all of them killed while fighting for the Union. Many had wondered whether the moving letter of consolation was written by Lincoln or by one of his secretaries. Robert's response to Markens's inquiry has frequently been used by scholars to confirm the authenticity of the Bixby letter.[6]

Markens's historical sleuthing seems to have impressed the only surviving son of the sixteenth president. In 1913, Robert wrote that he had read Markens's volume on the Gettysburg Address titled *Lincoln's Masterpiece* "with great pleasure," and he praised the author for the "labor and zeal" that was evident in the final product. Emboldened by these compliments, Markens sent Lincoln his two earlier publications, which he again claimed to "read with interest." As Markens began collecting material for what he hoped would be a major biography on Lincoln, he intensified his correspondence with Robert Lincoln.[7]

Markens's interest in American Jewish history and Lincoln naturally coalesced as the nation approached the centennial anniversary of Lincoln's birth, February 12,

1909. As early as 1907, the Illinois State Assembly resolved to organize a massive com-memoration of the Lincoln Centennial, and similar celebrations took place throughout the country. As a contribution to the centennial commemorations, Markens wrote a lengthy monograph titled *Abraham Lincoln and the Jews*, which he published in 1909 and, again, in a 1910 edition of the *Publications of the American Jewish Historical Society*. This monograph constituted the first attempt to reconstruct the nature of Lincoln's relationship with American Jewry.

In contrast to other Lincoln scholars who confessed their unending and adoring admiration for Lincoln's humanity and his numerous accomplishments, Markens re-mained mostly detached in his study of Lincoln. He simply observed that despite the "vast amount of interesting material bearing upon [Lincoln's] relations to the Jews," no one had yet attempted to reconstruct the details of this history. Modestly describing himself as a "student of the great war President," Markens suggested that the upcom-ing centennial anniversary of Lincoln's birth provided him with a fitting occasion to provide readers with a history of American Jewry's relationship with "the first of our countrymen to reach the lonely heights of immortal fame."[8]

Those who admired his work insisted that Markens was a true lover of the Great Emancipator: "[Lincoln] was his passion, he was his hobby, he was his cloud by day and pillar of fire by night." Trained as a newspaper correspondent, Markens sought out "old magazines, newspapers, conversations, interviews, and documents, all of which, together with the still surviving actors of the time, were quickly disappearing." Markens was a tireless researcher who relished looking for the proverbial needle in the haystack. Be-cause many of the letters that Markens solicited from those who knew Lincoln seem now to be lost, Markens's *Abraham Lincoln and the Jews* contains source materials that make the work an enduring and especially valuable printed resource filled with primary data.[9]

After *Abraham Lincoln and the Jews* appeared, Markens published three additional studies on Lincoln: *Why Lincoln Spared Three Lives* (1911), *President Lincoln and the Case of John Y. Beall* (1911), and, to commemorate the fiftieth anniversary of the Gettysburg Address, *Lincoln's Masterpiece: A Review of the Gettysburg Address, New in Treatment and Matter* (1913). Markens then began to work on what he hoped would be a major biographical study of Lincoln's life.[10]

Markens's historical contributions to the study of Lincoln have been largely over-looked by scholars. The importance of his efforts, however, did not escape the attention of a New York lawyer named Emanuel Hertz (1870–1940), who succeeded Markens in becoming one of the nation's leading experts on Lincoln in the 1920s and 1930s. Like Markens, Hertz's interest in Lincoln began with a scholarly exploration of Lincoln's relationship with Jews but subsequently led him to become a major collector of Lincol-niana and a highly regarded authority on Lincoln's life and career.[11]

Hertz, the older brother of Rabbi Joseph H. Hertz (1872–1946), chief rabbi of Great Britain, immigrated to New York City from Austria in 1884. Like his brother, Hertz initially studied at the Jewish Theological Seminary. After completing his undergraduate studies at City College of New York in 1892, he earned a master's degree from Columbia

Emanuel Hertz, a lawyer by profession, became one of the nation's leading experts on Lincoln in the 1920s and 1930s. Hertz, ed., *Abraham Lincoln: The Tribute of the Synagogue* (New York: Bloch Publishing, 1927), 516.

University in 1894 and, the following year, upon completing a law degree at Columbia, became an attorney. Toward the end of 1923, Hertz's synagogue, Washington Heights Congregation, invited him to deliver a speech the following February in commemoration of Lincoln's birthday.[12] He went to the public library to research his topic, and according to his own testimony, "from then on he gave all of his spare time to the accumulation of original material [on Lincoln]."[13]

In preparing to speak about Lincoln to the members of his synagogue, Hertz undoubtedly examined a copy of Isaac Markens's *Abraham Lincoln and the Jews*. The title itself certainly would have interested him. He was deeply involved in Jewish life, having served as the president of his synagogue, and, of course, the speech he was preparing would be given to a Jewish audience. The address Hertz produced suggested that one particular section of Markens's monograph especially captured his imagination: "Demonstrations Following the Assassination." Markens had chronicled the expressions of shock and grief that emanated from the Jewish community immediately following Lincoln's tragic death. Although Markens's examination of the sermons was far from exhaustive, Hertz made special mention in his address of the eulogies and synagogal memorial resolutions that Markens cited.

It seems that Hertz's inspiration for his first talk on Lincoln came from the memorial resolution that Philadelphia's Mickve Israel adopted in the wake of Lincoln's murder, in which they declared him "one of the best and purest presidents, who like the law-giver Moses, brought a nation to the verge of the haven of peace, and like him was not allowed to participate in its consummation." The theme that Hertz selected for his first address was "Lincoln the Seer," emphasizing that just as Moses led the children of Israel, so too did Lincoln lead the American nation. Moses and Lincoln, Hertz concluded, were both prophetic figures chosen by God to fulfill a divine mission.[14]

Hertz was inspired by Markens's discoveries and admired his scholarly achievements. When Markens died in 1928, Hertz lavishly praised the unassuming writer's conscientiousness: "[Markens] read more newspapers in his search for Lincoln material than any other man I ever met or heard of." In particular, Hertz lauded Markens's monograph on Lincoln and the Jews:

> Had it not been for his valuable brochure on "Lincoln and the Jews" in which he enumerates Lincoln's Jewish friends some of the most valuable leads in that most neglected phase of Lincoln's life would have been forever lost. . . . [N]o one spoke a word until Markens took up the task and demonstrated that we, the Jewish people, too, stood by the Union. . . . Markens compiled some of the more important events, when the Jewish soldier or private citizen came in contact with Lincoln—and demonstrated once again that Lincoln knew no distinction between creeds or classes—he was indeed Father Abraham to all who made up the great country whose destinies were in his strong but weary hands.[15]

In contrast to Markens, who left scant explanation for his interest in Lincoln and who maintained something of a scientific detachment regarding his Lincoln studies, Hertz literally deified the sixteenth president: "His greatest contemporaries shrink by comparison—and it was really an era of great men. He was, by universal consent, the first American, and was responsible for more epoch-making accomplishments in these four years than had ever been accomplished by another in any other preceding four years. . . . [His soul resides in] the celestial councils where were his kindred spirits of the ages: Hammurabi and Moses, Socrates and Solomon, Plato and Aristotle, Columbus, Galileo and Luther. . . . He stood before the celestial throne of his Maker!"[16]

The study of Lincoln intoxicated Hertz, and he zealously collected thousands of papers, letters, and documents relating to Lincoln's life and career. "Lincoln is a mighty tree," Hertz wrote, and "the shade he cast will endure as long as there is an American history." In a few short years, Hertz had assembled one of the nation's largest private collections of Lincolniana, and in 1931, he began publishing a series of newspaper articles, under the heading "New Light on Lincoln," which were based on a massive number of previously unpublished letters and documents from state archives that he had uncovered and preserved. Hertz's Lincoln collection became so large that he was able to donate 15,000 of his duplicate books to the Lincoln Memorial University near Knoxville, Tennessee, and subsequently, in 1927, he sold a portion of his collection at auction for $43,000. Hertz was widely acknowledged as one of the nation's leading scholars on Lincoln, and in 1936, the Society of Lincoln Authors and Collectors elected him president and Ida Tarbell honorary president.[17]

Although the primary focus of Hertz's work was to reconstruct Lincoln's entire career and personality on the basis of newly discovered documents, he never abandoned the intriguing discovery he made when he had first read Markens's essay on Lincoln and the Jews. Hertz resolved to conduct a thoroughgoing search for Jewish eulogies on Lincoln, thereby enabling him to complete the task that Markens had begun decades earlier. Once Hertz discovered that collections of Lincoln eulogies delivered by Christian preachers had already been published, he decided to do the same for the Lincoln eulogies and addresses that American Jews produced from 1865 forward.[18]

Using Markens's list as a starting point, Hertz set out to find the texts of these eulogies and publish them in a documentary volume that would show that "rabbis and [Jewish] laymen contributed their share in the threnody of lament at [Lincoln's] untimely taking off." Hertz obsessively scoured local newspapers, private libraries, bookstores, and auction houses in search of Jewish eulogies on Lincoln. He also included in his publication about a dozen Lincoln sermons that were delivered on the centennial of Lincoln's birth as well as those that were written up to the point when the book was being prepared. The result of this effort, *Abraham Lincoln: The Tribute of the Synagogue*, constitutes the largest documentary collection of American Jewish eulogies and addresses on Lincoln ever published.[19]

It was during these same tumultuous decades that separated the two world wars—when Lincoln's prestige and reputation reached its zenith in America memory—that a remarkable number of American Jews took an active role in the effort to preserve and promulgate Lincolniana and Lincolnology. The story of Chicago's Abraham Lincoln Book Store and the concomitant proliferation of Civil War Round Table Societies illustrate this trend.

In 1938, Ralph G. Newman (1911–98) established Chicago's highly regarded Abraham Lincoln Book Store, which has become a prominent resource center for those seeking information on Lincoln and the Civil War era. Newman's well-known establishment, at that time located in the building that housed the offices of the *Chicago Daily News* on LaSalle Street, began as a used bookstore in the early 1930s. At the time, two employees of the *Chicago Daily News* were writing books on Lincoln, Carl Sandburg (1878–1967) and Lloyd Lewis (1891–1949). Impressed by Newman's remarkable ability to locate volumes they needed, Sandburg and Lewis urged Newman to abandon his general line of books and concentrate solely on books that dealt with Lincoln and the Civil War. By the early 1940s, the Abraham Lincoln Book Store in Chicago had attracted a loyal following of Lincoln experts and Civil War aficionados. Subsequently, these enthusiasts began organizing Civil War Round Table Societies wherein researchers, scholars, and amateur historians gathered to learn from one another. These societies multiplied, and today there are hundreds of branches throughout the nation.[20]

In addition to Newman, a noteworthy number of Jewish researchers patronized the Abraham Lincoln Book Store and played a founding role in the Civil War Round Table Societies, including the lawyer and well-known civil rights activist Elmer Gertz (1906–2000) and the prominent industrial executive and chemist Otto Eisenschiml (1880–1963). Although they never consciously linked their interest in Lincoln and the Civil War to their Jewish roots, Newman, Gertz, and Eisenschiml—like so many others who were immigrants or children of immigrants—found Lincoln's life and career an inspiration.[21] The phenomenon of American Jewish interest in Lincolniana and Lincolnology continued in the last decades of the twentieth century with the scholarly contributions of Harold Holzer (b. 1949) and the Shapell Manuscript Foundation in

Los Angeles, an independent educational organization dedicated to collecting and researching original manuscripts and historical documents.[22]

In 1936, James G. Randall (1881–1953)—a professor of history at the University of Illinois in Champaign—published a paper he had delivered on Lincoln a few years earlier. Today, this essay is viewed as a watershed event in the historiography of Lincoln studies. In his paper, Randall insisted that although hundreds of books, articles, and essays on Lincoln had been written over the years, it would be a growing cadre of professionally trained historians that would be able to shed new light on Lincoln's life and career.[23]

Bertram Wallace Korn (1918–79) was one of the profusion of scholars and professional historians who responded to Randall's appeal. Korn, a pioneering American Jewish historian and a rabbi, was the leading disciple of the prodigious American Jewish historian Jacob Rader Marcus (1896–1995). Marcus was among the first American-born Jewish historians to use modern critical methodology in studying the history of American Jewry. Korn studied with Marcus, and his research focused primarily on Jewish life in the South during the antebellum and Civil War periods. His first volume, *American Jewry and the Civil War*, based on his doctoral dissertation, included several meticulously documented chapters that uncovered new information on Lincoln's relationship with American Jewry during that time. Korn's painstaking research and his broad familiarity with secondary literature on Lincoln resulted in the first major interpretive analysis of Lincoln's relationship with American Jewry.[24]

After identifying Lincoln's numerous Jewish associates and detailing the crucial role Lincoln played in resolving both the chaplaincy controversy and the calamity provoked by Grant's General Orders No. 11, Korn summarized his findings by asserting that "Lincoln had friendship in his heart for all men—foreign-born and native, Negro and White, Jew and Catholic and Protestant." Korn's carefully documented research proved that Lincoln happily associated with many Jewish citizens and called a few of

Bertram Wallace Korn, rabbi and historian, conducted meticulous research on Lincoln and the Jews for his volume *American Jewry and the Civil War* (1951). Courtesy The Jacob Rader Marcus Center of the American Jewish Archives, at the Hebrew Union College–Jewish Institute of Religion, Cincinnati, Ohio.

those individuals his friends. "A man with Lincoln's broad understanding of human beings," Korn concluded, "could not have been prejudiced against Jews at the first; meeting so many Jews only served to broaden his experience with them."[25]

Brenner and the Lincoln Penny

Victor David Brenner (1871–1924), the man who designed the famous Lincoln penny in 1909, constitutes a remarkable example of how easily the east European Jewish immigrant identified with Lincoln and advanced the conviction that Lincoln was the American spirit incarnate. Brenner, a Lithuanian Jew who immigrated to the United States in 1890, was a talented numismatist whose father taught him to engrave while yet living in Europe. After several years of economic struggle, Brenner gained recognition for his skill and began to receive lucrative commissions to design jewelry for silversmiths as well as a variety of commemorative medals. Once he established himself, Brenner moved to Paris in 1898 and apprenticed with the renowned French medalist Louis Oscar Roty (1846–1911). In 1902, Brenner returned to the United States and began his career. His Amerigo Vespucci medal of 1903 won him broad critical acclaim. In 1908, President Theodore Roosevelt agreed to sit for Brenner so the artist could sketch his profile for a Panama medal. The timing of this sitting proved to be fortuitous for Brenner, because he would come into personal contact with the president at a very advantageous moment.[26]

Roosevelt's fascination with Lincoln has been well documented. His father had been an acquaintance of Lincoln's, and Roosevelt repeatedly recollected how he stood with his father in the streets of New York and watched as Lincoln's funeral cortege passed by. Roosevelt kept a bust of Lincoln on his desk, and an engraving of Lincoln hung next to a portrait of his own father. Lincoln was Roosevelt's beau ideal, and the fact that he nominated John Hay, Lincoln's erstwhile private secretary, to serve as secretary of state in his administration underscored the Lincoln-Roosevelt association. In fact, the day before Roosevelt's inauguration in 1905, Hay gave Roosevelt a Lincoln "mourning ring" which contained a lock of Lincoln's hair. The gift thrilled Roosevelt, who wrote: "Surely no other president, on the eve of his inauguration, has received such a gift. . . . I shall think of it and you as I take the oath tomorrow." As the centennial of Lincoln's birth approached, Roosevelt and Hay took particular interest in the occasion.[27]

The idea of marking the centennial of Lincoln's birth by placing his image on U.S. currency seems to have been an outgrowth of Roosevelt's interest in beautifying American coinage in general. In 1905, Roosevelt contacted the famous American sculptor Augustus Saint-Gaudens (1848–1907) to discuss the idea of entirely redesigning American currency. At the time, Saint-Gaudens was one of the most respected artists in the country, having earned widespread critical acclaim for his sculptures of Civil War heroes such as Admiral David Farragut, Generals William Tecumseh Sherman and John Logan, and Abraham Lincoln himself. Roosevelt gave Saint-Gaudens a commission to redesign American currency, but the only part of the project he completed prior to his death was his beautiful "double-eagle" design for the twenty-dollar gold piece. Saint-Gaudens's death in 1907 compelled Roosevelt to turn to other artists, and good fortune had placed Brenner in the president's company at this very time.[28]

As Brenner sketched Roosevelt for the Panama medal, he had an opportunity to speak about a subject that was important to both men: Abraham Lincoln. Brenner, like many other immigrants, venerated Lincoln and viewed him as a source of hope and inspiration for American newcomers struggling to make this land their home. In 1907, Brenner had created a medallion and an electrotyped plaque of Lincoln based on Mathew Brady's (1822–96) daguerreotype of Lincoln. Showing his work to Roosevelt, Brenner suggested that the penny would be an appropriate coin for honoring Lincoln. The penny, he noted, underscored Lincoln's bond with the everyday citizen: "The smaller the value [of the coin]," he said, "the more people would handle it and come to know him."[29]

Roosevelt had already considered minting a commemorative coin for Lincoln and assumed this project would be developed as part of the commission he had given to Saint-Gaudens. Evidently, Roosevelt immediately embraced both Brenner's design and the concept that inspired it. On January 30, 1909, a note was sent from the Treasury Department to the editor of the Numismatist: "President Roosevelt has given his consent to the placing of the head of Lincoln on one of the popular coins. He conferred today with Director Leach, of the mint, and details are now under advisement. Victor D. Brenner, the New York sculptor, has submitted to the director some models of Lincoln busts, and these have been shown to the president. The head of Lincoln will adorn one side of the coin and the customary coat of arms the other."[30] On August 2, 1909, the first Lincoln cents were released into circulation with Brenner's initials, "V.D.B.," appearing at the bottom of the coin's reverse side, in keeping with longstanding numismatic tradition. Interestingly, a firestorm immediately arose concerning the appearance of Brenner's initials on the coin. Letters were sent to the Department of Treasury with a variety of complaints. Some groused that the recognition was unnecessary because Brenner had been paid for his design, others asserted that Brenner was a craftsman and not an artist, and still others insisted that recognition such as this was excessive and inappropriate. The initials were dropped for the second minting. Brenner was wounded by the decision, but he remained a devout patriot and continued to produce medals and engravings that presented his own vision of "the American type, mixture of all races, conqueror and child of a new continent and a new political order."[31]

Brenner conceived of Lincoln as the embodiment of the American spirit, yet as a Jewish immigrant he also understood how newcomers to these shores looked at Lincoln. For Brenner, Lincoln was the paradigmatic common man who embodied the best of the American spirit. Only Lincoln's image, he observed, could "touch a hardened heart." Brenner would have been pleased to have heard that Carl Sandburg appreciated the essence of his numismatic concept: "The common, homely face of Honest Abe will look good on the penny," Sandburg wrote, "the coin of the common folk from whom he came and to whom he belongs."[32]

Lincoln, Jews, and American Culture

Reflecting on the influence that Abraham Lincoln has had on the development of American culture since his death in 1865, the website of the Abraham Lincoln Bicentennial Commission took care to emphasize the fact that the sixteenth president's "iconic image" has long served as grist for the artist's creative mill. Lincoln's countenance "has inspired professional and amateur artists alike to paint, draw and sculpt for well over a hundred years." Similarly, Lincoln has been the muse for countless musicians who have made him the theme of their songs and symphonies. Poets, too, began paying homage to Lincoln as early as 1865, and as the centennial of his birth approached, a number of poetic anthologies celebrating Lincoln's life and achievements began to appear. Lincoln also become a ubiquitous theme in the realm of American material culture, and innumerable frequently overlooked objects, including decorative arts, toys, and odds and ends, were adorned with Lincoln's image.[33]

As Jews increasingly entered the mainstream of American life during the course of the twentieth century, a growing number made their mark in the world of fine arts and culture. The Jews who contributed to the world of the arts were unquestionably influenced by American culture. Yet, in many instances, it is clear that traditionally Jewish motifs and themes contributed to the development of American culture itself and, in some instances, transformed it. Jews participated in the creation of both high and pop culture in America, and it is often possible to discern their distinctly parochial or particular point of view. As one historian of American Jewish culture noted, "The creativity of American Jewry has also affected and altered [American] culture. Exchanging ideas and images with the larger culture in a network of reciprocity, Jews have borrowed freely but have also expanded the contours of that larger culture—which has itself been protean and fluid." Such a phenomenon reveals itself as we examine the way in which American Jews have memorialized Lincoln in art, song, and in belles lettres.[34]

By creating works of art, poetry, and music as well as artifacts of all sorts that venerated and memorialized Lincoln, American Jews were participating fully in the life of the nation. Loving Lincoln had become a sign of allegiance. Yet, as they participated in this ongoing endeavor, American Jews frequently infused Lincolniana with their own distinctly Jewish culture. As the French-born litterateur Anaïs Nin once observed: "We don't see things as they are, we see things as *we* are."[35]

DOCUMENTS

PERSONAL REMINISCENCES

1. Lincoln Possessed the Noblest Attributes of Human Nature
2. When You Retire, I Will Be the Ugliest Man in the Government:
   Adolphus S. Solomons's Reminiscences of Lincoln

LINCOLN, JEWS, AND THE FINE ARTS

3. Solomon Nuñes Carvalho's Portrait of Lincoln
4. Victor David Brenner and the Lincoln Penny
5. A Southern Jew Memorializes Lincoln: Moses Jacob Ezekiel
6. Lincoln at Gettysburg in the Eyes of an East European Jewish Immigrant
7. An American Jewish Biographer in Bronze

MUSICAL TRIBUTES TO LINCOLN

8. "Washington, Lincoln, and Moishe Rabeiny" by Joseph Rumshinsky
9. The Gettysburg Address in Yiddish
10. "Abraham" by Irving Berlin
11. "Lincoln Portrait" by Aaron Copland

ARCHIVISTS, COLLECTORS, AND HISTORIANS

12. The Pioneering Researcher: Isaac Markens
13. Collector of Lincolniana: Emanuel Hertz
14. The Meticulous Scholar: Bertram W. Korn
15. The Contemporary Authority: Harold Holzer

PERSONAL REMINISCENCES

1. LINCOLN POSSESSED THE NOBLEST ATTRIBUTES OF HUMAN NATURE

On February 13, 1901, the New York Daily Tribune *published the reminiscences of a former Confederate soldier named Goodman L. Mordecai (1829?–1922).*[36] *The Mordecai family of Charleston, South Carolina, was passionately committed to the Confederate cause. Benjamin Mordecai, Goodman's father, donated the handsome sum of $10,000 to the state of South Carolina to facilitate secession.*[37] *Goodman spent four years in the Confederate army and, although he had received an honorable discharge, was apprehended by federal officers in Washington while running a blockade in order to visit Nassau on behalf of southern stockholders who had interests in the island. He spent the winter of 1864 in the Old Capitol Prison in Washington, D.C.*[38] *Friends of the Mordecai family eventually interceded with President Lincoln on Goodman's behalf in order to secure the young man's release. Despite Mordecai's Confederate pedigree, Lincoln approved his release.*

According to Goodman's own reminiscences, his benefactors insisted that the freshly paroled southerner go to the Executive Mansion and convey his personal appreciation to Lincoln for his sympathetic decision. In his published recollection of this meeting written many years later, Goodman Mordecai recalled that Lincoln extended him his hand and, with tongue in cheek, declared, "I am happy to know I am able to serve an enemy." By 1901, Mordecai—the former Confederate soldier and partisan—had become a Lincoln enthusiast who insisted that Abraham Lincoln was "one of the greatest grandest characters in American history."

An Ex-Confederate's Tribute to Lincoln

The Great Emancipator Was Happy to Be Able to Serve an Enemy

To the Editor of The Tribune.

Sir: In the memorable winter of 1864, during the Civil War, one of the most eventful periods in our National history, occurred an incident of more than ordinary interest to every admirer of the martyred and immortal Lincoln. After receiving an honorable discharge from the Confederate army the writer, who had been an occasional contributor to the Southern press, was authorized by an officer of the most prominent blockade company in South Carolina to visit Nassau in behalf of the stockholders, who had large and valuable interests in that island. Immense cargoes of goods shipped from England to this point remained there awaiting a favorable opportunity to run the blockade at Charleston. To facilitate this without further unnecessary delay I left the latter city for Richmond with letters of introduction to the Hon. Judah P. Benjamin, the Secretary of State for the Southern Confederacy. After presenting my credentials and receiving a passport to leave the South I started immediately for Wilmington, N.C., there to embark on a blockade vessel for Nassau. On arrival, to my great amazement and discomfort, I was officially informed by General Whiting, in command of the department, that a conscription order had been issued by the Secretary of War since my departure from Richmond calling on all able-bodied men for active service and a revocation of previous passports to leave the Confederacy. Determined not to be baffled by this unforeseen and unexpected contingency, I returned to Richmond preparatory to running the gauntlet through the confederate and Federal lines. With this in view, I accidentally made the acquaintance of a gentleman whose past experience as an indefatigable blockade runner had been extraordinarily successful. In fact, I was only a novice, while this, his third trip through the lines from Richmond to Washington, had made him strictly a professional. Fortified with two passports, one from the Secretary of State and another from the city authorities, accompanied by my companion, I left Richmond, defiant, but doubtful as to the final result.

Like any young man whose first adventure had made him somewhat egotistical, I felt like proclaiming, "Here the conquering hero comes," but, remembering that absolute reticence and strict secrecy were essential to success, I reluctantly and with great difficulty suppressed my boyish emotions and proceeded on the journey. No soldier ever entered battle with greater emotion than these two weary travellers through the mountains of Virginia. Up hill and down dale, tramping and driving long and short distances, here and there, on the ragged and rugged edge of consternation and danger, these two forlorn wanderers, completely prostrated by fatigue, for a while lost their bearings, not knowing what they were doing nor where they were going. But in time of great doubt and uncertainty, when everything seems lost, there is no safer pilot than determination, pluck and strong presence of mind.

After a long and very monotonous journey we crossed the Potomac at night in the midst of a volley of musketry sharpshooting from sentinels stationed on the banks of the river, and arrived on the outskirts of Port Tobacco, Md., just before the dawn of another day. Completely exhausted, we vainly endeavored to procure accommodations at the only hotel in the town, but were immediately informed that this was no resting place for the suspected rebels, whose presence would surely impugn the loyalty of the proprietor and thus endanger his position and interests in the community. After this rebuff we wandered to the outskirts of the town and there hailed a stage en route from Port Tobacco to Washington. Among the several passengers were furloughed Federal officers and soldiers on their way home. By these we were scrutinized with a peculiar suspicion during the trip, until our arrival at the Potomac Bridge entering Washington. Much to our amazement we were then there arrested and marched by a provost marshal's guard to headquarters for a preliminary examination preparatory to a very long confinement in the Old Capitol Prison.

Picture two forlorn, dejected, dilapidated individuals after such a struggle, on the eve of a most triumphant success, with victory near at hand, to be crushed and crestfallen, and you will thus realize defeat in all its significance. Prompted by conscientious motive we declined to take the oath of allegiance tendered us by the authorities, and as a result were remanded to the Old Capitol Prison for an indefinite period. After an incarceration of several months, while my case was being investigated by General [John H.] Martindale, then acting Secretary of War, interested friends in New-York interceded with President Lincoln in my behalf, among them an influential friend of the President, who visited Washington for the purpose of procuring my release. His call at the White House successfully accomplished this result, and in return for this act of kindness we called at the Executive Chamber to thank President Lincoln for his consideration and magnanimity.

At that time during our Civil War, when the clash of arms resounded throughout the land amid the wails of the wounded and the lamentations of the afflicted, was performed an act of philanthropy characteristic of the true philanthropist. My friend unconsciously informed the President that I had fought against the Government and that my father at that time was prominent in the Confederacy and a liberal contributor to the Southern cause. He grasped my hand, and in response answered: "I am happy to know I am able to serve an enemy."

What a noble contrast to the prevailing bitterness and animosity of that eventful period, a gentle reminder that had he lived the North and South would have been reunited in true brotherly love at a much earlier period, as he desired it, "with charity toward all and malice toward none." Such an act was worthy of example, and reveals a character combining the noblest attributes of human nature.

In the winter of 1865, while at the St. Lawrence Hotel, Montreal, the writer had a conversation with Wilkes Booth, who then claimed he was on his way South to run the blockade for the purpose of entering the Confederate army. A few weeks thereafter this man was an assassin, and Abraham Lincoln was assassinated. On that memorable day I was at the Queen's Hotel, Toronto, when an ex-chaplain of the Confederate army disgraced his clerical robes by exclaiming in the corridor of the hotel that the death of Lincoln was the greatest Southern victory of the war. I then narrated to him Lincoln's kindness to me and recalled to his mind the magnanimity of the illustrious statesman. He immediately acknowledged his error, bowed in submissive silence, and earnestly apologized for the words unconsciously spoken in a moment of great excitement. One of the greatest grandest characters in history was Abraham Lincoln.

I contribute this article as a tribute to his memory on this, the anniversary of his birthday, in honor of that philanthropy and magnanimity which were shining traits in the character of the Nation's martyr and benefactor.

G. L. Mordecai
New-York, Feb. 12, 1901[39]

2. WHEN YOU RETIRE, I WILL BE THE UGLIEST MAN IN THE GOVERNMENT: ADOLPHUS S. SOLOMONS'S REMINISCENCES OF LINCOLN

Adolphus S. Solomons's centennial remembrances of his encounters with Lincoln, which first appeared in the American Hebrew *on February 12, 1909, provided readers with a wonderful bouquet of anecdotes. Solomons, who owned a publishing house and a photography studio during Lincoln's years in Washington, went on to distinguish himself as an activist in both the general and Jewish communities. In 1871, Solomons was elected to Washington's House of Delegates and served as chairman of its Committee on Ways and Means. Perhaps his greatest communal achievement was the role he played in helping Clara Barton to found the American Red Cross. He also contributed to a wide range of Jewish communal causes, including his roles as a founder of Mt. Sinai Hospital in New York City, a supporter of the Jewish Theological Seminary, and a contributor*

to numerous welfare associations dedicated to assisting in the settlement of the east Eu-
ropean Jewish immigrants.[40]

In the following excerpts, Solomons eschews comment on Lincoln's political, per-
sonal, or religious virtues (beyond a closing observation that Lincoln was "one of the
most beloved men God ever created"). Instead, he memorializes Lincoln with a series
of humorous personal reminiscences, which provide a delightful counterpoint to the
many solemn reflections that typified Lincoln encomia on the hundredth anniversary
of his birth.

To know where to begin and where to end in sorting my recollections of our
beloved President Lincoln is a somewhat difficult task. His memory both in
gladness and in sorrow lingers with us all so heartfully, I feel as though treading
on holy ground, lest my words may appear disrespectful to his sacred memory.

Where so much has been collated and written of this great man, it occurs
to me that some little incidents and anecdotes of which I was personally cognizant, might have a greater interest at this time than those facts which have
become matters of history.

It is well known how keen was his sense of humor—a humor so gentle and
kindly that it never wounded the feelings of the most sensitive.

One day while in the White House, awaiting to see the President, I found
myself in line with perhaps fifty others awaiting my turn to come. Immediately
in front of me was a rather tall and stupid appearing fellow, and I wondered
what in the world his mission was. It was soon after these "contrabands" had
begun bringing in information relating to the enemy, and I was not surprised
to hear him say to Mr. Lincoln in answer to his question, "Well my friend, what
can I do for you?" "I see you are rather busy today and I will come in some other
time to tell you about what a 'contraband' told me," and here the President
interrupted him by a slap on the shoulder, and with a steady gaze, beginning
at his muddy boots with his trousers tucked into them and looking upward to
his shaggy red hair exclaimed, "Sit right down here and tell me all you know,"
and winking at me over the stranger's shoulder, added: "and by telling all you
know it certainly cannot take you very long." Evidently the man did not see
the joke, and sitting down told a short story and was soon out of the room.

On another occasion an army officer called upon the President to tender
his resignation, whereupon the President said: "All right, I accept your resignation, but nothing can compensate me for the loss of you, for when you retire I
will then be the ugliest man in the employment of the government":—and yet
Mr. Lincoln was not ugly, for his tall, stooping, ungainly figure was forgotten
in the loving expressions coming from a God-given joy of heart, which became
instantly contagious.

His love for fun served to hide many an inward pang. One day I accepted
an invitation to be present at a review of the First Army Corps of the Potomac

under the command of General [John F.] Reynolds, held near Washington, and the driver of the ambulance in which he rode, becoming angry at his wild team of six mules used some rather original cuss words. Smiling, Mr. Lincoln touched the man on his shoulder and said: "Excuse me, my friend, are you an Episcopalian?"

The man greatly startled looked sheepishly around and replied: "No, Mr. President, I am a Methodist." "Well," said Mr. Lincoln, "I thought you must be an Episcopalian, because you swear just like Governor Seward, who is a very strict church warden."

When Mr. Lincoln returned from his famous trip to Richmond after its surrender I chanced to be in the neighborhood of the White House early one morning, when I saw a detachment on the "route step" with "arms at will." Between their shouts they cheered most lustily. Their wheezy and unmusical band then added to the clamor by injecting snatches of national airs with added cries for "Lincoln, Lincoln." Presently there appeared at the second story window the tall frame of the President, who wore a brown linen duster much wrinkled and spotted with mud. Immediately the band emphasized his presence by a blare of brass instruments, the screaming of fifes and the beating of drums, fearful to hear.

An orderly stepped up to Mr. Lincoln and said: "Mr. President, the band is playing Dixie, shall I order it to stop?" "No," said the President, "let them play; when we captured the Southerners, we captured their tunes." The crowd called, "Speech, speech, speech," until they were speechless themselves, and after much more racket Mr. Lincoln waved his brawny arms for silence and began a speech, which, coming from his manly, good heart, breathed such a loving, kindly feeling toward the South, that had his words been put into cold type, would have incensed the Northern masses, who were still burning with such intense enmity against the South, that he would most surely have been blamed beyond measure for his hasty expressions of forgiveness for the hated enemy of but yesterday. But he was so overjoyed with the prospects of peace that he could not restrain himself and closed by saying, that Dixie, which was the song of the Confederacy, was as much the national air of the republic now as the "Star Spangled Banner" was before the war.

Fortunately the hour was too early for reporters to be present, and I was happy when I saw no mention of the event in the afternoon papers of the day nor in subsequent editions. I afterwards learned that the body of soldiery alluded to came on the same boat from Richmond with the President, who had dodged them after landing, but who were determined to see him once before disbanding to their homes.

On one occasion when business took me to the White House, I had the good fortune to find Mr. Lincoln in one of his most jocular and reminiscent moods. He told me the following story of "How the Reverend Mr. Shofle acquired riches":

"When I first entered upon my duties as President," said Mr. Lincoln, grasping my arm in his peculiar way with one of his long bony hands, while he ran his fingers through and brushed back his shaggy black hair, "I fully made up my mind to appoint to office those only whom I knew to be honest and who had suitable ability. In any event honesty should be the prerequisite, as the lack of a little ability might be easily made up by an honest man endeavoring to do his whole duty conscientiously. While this resolve was fresh upon me there came to visit me a very old friend, a Baptist minister, who had traveled so fast that he had not yet shaken the Illinois real estate off his capacious boots.

"'Why, what brings you here, Mr. Shofle?' (which was not his name, but it will do just as well.)

"'Well,' he replied. 'I came down here firstly to see you and get an old fashioned shake of the hand, and secondly to say that the folks of my congregation are so poor that they can hardly afford me a decent living and I thought maybe you could give me some sort of an office that would pay me better.'

"'Certainly,' I answered, quickly, for I knew he was an honest man and I was looking for stock of that kind. 'Have you in view any particular office?'

"'No,' said the Rev. Mr. Shofle complacently; 'I would not know what to select if you were to hand me a list to choose from.'

"'Nor I what to give you; but I will tell you who will help you out. You know Col. Chootsper of your county. He is now on duty in the Treasury Department. Go and see him; he is a man of resources, and will get you out of your difficulty. Come back to-morrow and report.'

"The next day, according to promise, Shofle put in an appearance, and said that the Colonel had recommended him to apply for a certain position in the Revenue Department.

"'What is the salary?' said I, while signing in a mechanical way a pile of commissions.

"'Two thousand dollars a year.'

"'Well, do you think that enough? I may be able to do better for you,' for I knew he was an honest man and thought he might just as well as not get a place where he could earn more money.

"'Oh, plenty, Uncle Abe, for that is more than double the amount I've been earning for years past.'

"Now I began to think," said our martyr-President, "that I would have to force him in to a place paying a larger salary, and where the government would have a corresponding return for his valuable services, for I was more than ever—if that were possible—convinced that he was an honest man; but I finally concluded to give him his own way, and he was appointed accordingly. Off he went rejoicing but I felt rather mean at my one-horse gift to my good, honest, reverend friend.

"Three years elapsed and the anxieties attending war had completely driven from my mind, for the time being, the incident just related, when my messenger brought me a card bearing the familiar name, 'Rev. Adam Shofle,' and immediately there flashed across my mind all the circumstances attending my appointing him to office. I directed him to be shown in, and in walked, with creaky boots, one of the best and finest dressed men I had seen in many a day. I recognized his countenance at a glance, but it was his marvelous clothes that troubled me. They sat easily enough upon his body, but somehow or other they did not sit so easily on my mind; but wherefore I could not for the life of me tell if I had tried which I didn't.

"'Good morning, Mr. President'—no longer Uncle Abe as before—said he, in a grandiloquent manner; 'I hope you are well and getting on nicely.'

"'Oh, yes,' said I; 'we poor folks eke out a living after a fashion'; intending to give him the bit in his mouth, for I knew what an honest man he was, and how much—I couldn't tell then exactly how much—for I had lost the run of him—we were indebted to him.

"'Mr. President, I have come to resign my office.'

"Feeling somewhat as though I had been struck by lightning I managed to exclaim, 'Indeed!'

"'Yes, I feel that there are many others deserving of the place, and that it is my duty to make way for them.'

"'Was there ever such an honest man as that?' said I to myself, chuckling over my own stupidity on the clothes surprise. 'But,' said I, aloud. 'I'm afraid you are not considering yourself, friend Shofle, and that when you go back to preaching you will be as hard up as when you came here three years ago. Hadn't you better hold on a little longer, say a year more and let us both go out of office together?'

"'No, thank you. I'm going to Europe during that time, but hope to see you here, as President, when I return,' and after a few more kind expressions, off went the Rev. Shofle.

"About a month after, one of the reverend gentleman's neighbors paid me a visit, and among other things remarked casually that I had 'done a pretty good thing for Shofle.' 'Yes,' I replied, 'I gave him a $2,000 a year position for three years.'

"'Besides the balance!' added my visitor. 'Why if he is worth a cent he is worth to-day $200,000, and I can prove it if necessary.'

"What could the idiot mean? To satisfy myself of the falsity of the charge I sent detectives to where he lived and they brought back word that he had made his $6,000 salary in the aggregate yield fully $200,000, but then I knew he was an honest man, and there must be a mistake somewhere!

"By the way," added Mr. Lincoln, with one of his knowing winks, "we have plenty of 'Shofles' left, but, the mischief of it is, it is hard finding them out, and they are not considerate enough to resign, as did our honest friend Shofle."[41]

A native of Charleston, South Carolina, Solomon Nuñes Carvalho was an artist, photographer, diarist, and adventurer. Courtesy The Jacob Rader Marcus Center of the American Jewish Archives, at the Hebrew Union College–Jewish Institute of Religion, Cincinnati, Ohio.

Carvalho's painting *Lincoln and Diogenes* is the only portrait of Lincoln made by an American Jewish contemporary. Gift of John J. and Celia Mack, Maurice and Rose Turner, Justin G. and Gertrude Turner; courtesy The Rose Art Museum of Brandeis University.

LINCOLN, JEWS, AND THE FINE ARTS

3. SOLOMON NUÑES CARVALHO'S PORTRAIT OF LINCOLN

Solomon Nuñes Carvalho's (1815–97) portrait of Lincoln is the only one painted by one of Lincoln's Jewish contemporaries. Carvalho, an artist, photographer, and adventurer, was born in Charleston, South Carolina, but he also lived in Philadelphia, Baltimore, and New York. He is perhaps best known as the diarist and official photographer of John C. Frémont's western expedition of 1853–54. One of the first Jews to travel across the nation to Southern California, Carvalho's published memoirs provide a fascinating account of Frémont's extraordinary exploration.

Carvalho's Lincoln portrait was signed and dated 1865. Since the words "With malice toward none, with charity for all" appear on the scroll in Lincoln's hand, we know that the portrait was painted to serve as a tribute marking Lincoln's second inauguration or, possibly, as a memorial marking his martyred death. Filled with symbolism and metaphor, the portrait conveys a number of powerful messages. Carvalho places Lincoln in front of a draped statue of George Washington, suggesting his loyalty to the ideals of the Father of the Nation. Although Lincoln is seated indoors, the U.S. Capitol Building—symbolizing the Union—appears on the distant horizon. In the foreground, just beyond Lincoln's curtain, the Greek philosopher Diogenes, who always carried a lighted lantern to search for an honest man, has spotted Lincoln. The broken lantern lying next to Diogenes confirms that the philosopher's search has finally come to a successful conclusion. In this Jewish artist's mind, Abraham Lincoln was honesty and patriotism incarnate.[42]

4. VICTOR DAVID BRENNER AND THE LINCOLN PENNY

A noteworthy number of American Jewish artists memorialized Lincoln in every conceivable mode of visual art. Arguably the most famous and widespread image of all is the cast of Lincoln's profile that began gracing one side of the penny in 1909. Victor David Brenner, the man who designed this most famous image of Lincoln, earned this honor by convincing President Roosevelt that he—an east European Jewish immigrant—was uniquely qualified to capture Lincoln's spirit on the face of the coin.

Victor David Brenner with a large plaster model of his design for the Lincoln cent, 1909.
Harper's Weekly, August 21, 1909, 24.

A reproduction of Brenner's Lincoln Medal of 1907.
Courtesy Stack's Bowers Galleries.

Brenner's initials appeared on a small number of Lincoln pennies when
the coin first went into circulation in 1909. The controversial initials were
quickly removed. Courtesy Hyde Park Coin, Cincinnati, Ohio.

*Images of Brenner's designs appear here, along with a reproduction of a poem that
Frank Dempster Sherman (1860–1916), a professor of graphics at Columbia University,
composed to honor both Lincoln as well as Brenner's numismatic talent.*

ON A BRONZE MEDAL OF LINCOLN BY VICTOR D. BRENNER

by Frank Dempster Sherman

This bronze our Lincoln's noble head doth bear.
Behold the strength and splendor of that face,
    So homely-beautiful, with just a trace
    Of humor lightening its look of care!
With bronze indeed his memory doth share,
This martyr who found freedom for a Race;
    Both shall endure beyond the time and place
That knew them first, and brighter grow with wear.

Happy must be the genius here that wrought
    These features of the great American

Whose fame lends so much glory to our past—
    Happy to know the inspiration caught
    From this most human and heroic man
Lives here to honor him while Art shall last.[43]

5. A SOUTHERN JEW MEMORIALIZES LINCOLN: MOSES JACOB EZEKIEL

A recipient of the coveted Prix de Rome in 1873 and an honorary patrician who was knighted at the hands of the Grand Duke of Saxe-Meiningen in 1881, Sir Moses Jacob Ezekiel (1844–1917) was one of the most talented and highly regarded Jewish artists at the fin de siècle. Born in Richmond, Virginia, Ezekiel was a loyal partisan of the South, yet he was willing to overcome his "political scruples" when a New York lawyer offered him a handsome commission to make a bust of Lincoln. In his diary, Ezekiel noted that he wanted to obtain a mask of Lincoln to assist him in producing the likeness. "One day," he wrote, "near Gramercy Place an old grey-bearded man who was very garrulous told me he had known Lincoln, that he had a mask, and that if I would come the next day he would let me have a copy of it, which he did."[44]

*   The following are images of Ezekiel and his art studio in Rome, with the bust of Lincoln in full view, and an excerpt from Ezekiel's memoirs relating to the commission.*

A decorated Confederate veteran who hailed from Richmond, Moses Jacob Ezekiel became one of the most distinguished American sculptors in the last half of the nineteenth century. Courtesy The Jacob Rader Marcus Center of the American Jewish Archives, at the Hebrew Union College–Jewish Institute of Religion, Cincinnati, Ohio.

Ezekiel's studio with his bust of Abraham Lincoln clearly visible.
Courtesy The Jacob Rader Marcus Center of the American Jewish Archives, at the
Hebrew Union College–Jewish Institute of Religion, Cincinnati, Ohio.

Excerpt from *Memoirs from the Baths of Diocletian*

I was invited one evening to a dinner party at the house of Madame Castiglione, Ernesto Nathan's sister. There I also met Alessandro Fortis, Ernesto and Virginia Nathan, and one or two other Roman republicans, myself being the only real republican present. Fortis thought that he would pay me a compliment by drinking to the memory of Abraham Lincoln. I thanked him very much. I had fought against Lincoln and General Grant, I told him, but did not object to drinking to Lincoln's health, although I had not yet quite recovered from the shock of Southern subjugation. They all seemed horrified at the idea of my having fought for slavery and were very much surprised when I explained that we had never fought for slavery, but for states' rights and for free trade. . . .

I went to see the lawyer Nat Myers and his bright, charming wife Josie, who embraced me heartily and made me remain to lunch. After lunch, Nat asked me whether I could overcome my political scruples and do a work for him which he wanted very much. I told him I thought I could and asked him what it was he wanted. To my great surprise, he said he wanted a bust in marble of Abraham Lincoln. I accepted the commission on the condition that I might make either a bust or a relief from the beautiful etching he handed me. So here my dream about Minerva seems to have been verified. How strangely my dream returned to my mind then! [Ezekiel is referring to a "patriotic" dream he had the night before he left Rome and returned to Philadelphia.] The red, white, and blue on the central planet were the American colors; the Minerva had been on the central planet; and here I was to make the War President of America![45]

6. LINCOLN AT GETTYSBURG IN THE EYES OF AN EAST EUROPEAN JEWISH IMMIGRANT

Sculptor Max Kalish (1893–1945) immigrated to the United States from Lithuania together with his family in the late 1800s and settled in Cleveland, Ohio. As a youth, Kalish attended Cleveland public schools and, simultaneously, received an Orthodox Jewish education. At age fifteen, Kalish enrolled at the Cleveland Institute of Art and began studying sculpture. Kalish continued to study sculpture in New York and later in Paris at the École des Beaux-Arts.

In 1923, Cleveland's schoolchildren began to collect small change in an effort to commission a statue of Lincoln for their city. Although he was not a renowned artist, Kalish was awarded the commission because he himself had been a student in the Cleveland public schools. In the course of researching the subject of his sculpture—Lincoln delivering

American sculptor Max Kalish, an immigrant from eastern Europe and a graduate of the Cleveland public schools, was awarded a commission from the Cleveland Board of Education to sculpt Lincoln. Courtesy Peter A. Juley and Son Collection, Smithsonian American Art Museum, J0020817.

the Gettysburg Address—Kalish interviewed Dr. Philip M. Bikle (1844–1934), who at age nineteen had actually been at Gettysburg and heard the president deliver his most famous oration. Bikle described Lincoln as standing erect with his feet apart, "holding the manuscript, sometimes changing it from one hand to the other as he made gestures. He faced the north, and the breeze hit him in the face. His voice was deliberate, and at 'of the people' his hand was working up and down from the shoulder."[46]

The following documents from the Cleveland newspapers relate to Kalish's Lincoln statue. First, a short article from the September 23, 1927, issue of the Cleveland Plain Dealer describes Kalish's search for a tall, gangly man—who could "fill the attenuated coat of Abraham Lincoln"—to serve as a model for his sculpture of the president. Several years later, February 12, 1932, the Cleveland Press described the dedication ceremonies for Kalish's sculpture. On February 21, 1932, the Cleveland Plain Dealer published a photo of the recently unveiled statue in its place on the Mall on the day of the dedicatory festivities.

As can be seen in the image below, Kalish's Lincoln is caught mid-sentence, pronouncing "of the people," with his hair blown by the wind. The statue stands twelve feet high, excluding its base, and stands outside the Cleveland Board of Education building—a fitting location for an artwork purchased by schoolchildren.

Lincoln's Double Wanted as Model

Sculptor Needs Man Who Can Fill Emancipator's Coat

Max Kalish, Cleveland's best known sculptor, is seeking a new model. He wants a bony, work-hardened man, six feet four inches tall, to fill the attenuated coat of Abraham Lincoln.

Kalish has an exact reproduction of the coat Lincoln wore when he delivered the Gettysburg speech. He had it made to order from the original, preserved in the Smithsonian Institution in Washington.

Kalish returned last week from a summer in Europe and is ready to begin his quarter-size model of the Lincoln memorial statue he is creating for erection in Playhouse square.

He is watching crowds and notifying employment agencies in the hope of finding his man with Lincoln's towering figure. He thinks his man will be one from farm stock, his shoulders developed, like Lincoln's, by early years of work with an ax or plow.

In three months Kalish expects to have completed the three-foot plaster cast of his Lincoln. It will be in nearly full detail. If it is entirely satisfactory to him and the committee in charge of erecting the memorial, he will go ahead on the full-size twelve-foot figure, to be in bronze. If not he will scrap the model and start all over. Time is no element of art.

The Lincoln figure Kalish has in mind shows the emancipator on widespread feet, his hands extended, with out-turned palms as in the final gesture of the Gettysburg speech.[47]

Kalish's statue of Lincoln at Gettysburg,
financed by the pennies of Cleveland
schoolchildren, was dedicated in 1932.
Courtesy Bill Nash, abesblogcabin.org.

In Memory of Lincoln

Nine years ago, a group of public-spirited citizens organized the Lincoln Memorial Commission and with the aid of the city's newspapers and school authorities, launched a drive to raise funds for a statue of Abraham Lincoln. No
child was permitted to contribute more than 10 cents, no adult more than $1.

Today, upon Lincoln's birthday, the statue of Abraham Lincoln, the work
of Max Kalish, a Cleveland sculptor, is dedicated.

Kalish's statue, a heroic figure 12 feet high, shows Lincoln in the act of
delivering the Gettysburg address. In one hand, Lincoln holds the manuscript
of the famous address. The wind is ruffling his hair and his clothing. The face
is alive with the light that must have shone upon Lincoln's face when he spoke
his immortal words.

The late Dean Henry Turner Bailey, who was chairman of the commission,
expressed the opinion that Kalish's Lincoln would take its rank with the great
statues of the nation.

Today's dedicatory exercises, appropriately, are chiefly for school children.
An audience of 2500 children, representing the schools of Greater Cleveland,
will attend the ceremony at Public Music Hall.

Max Kalish is to be congratulated upon his splendid work. The Lincoln
Memorial Commission is to be praised for its years of faithful service and for
its wisdom in choosing a Cleveland sculptor. Too often home talent has to go
away from home before it is recognized.[48]

Jo Davidson, an American sculptor of Russian-Jewish descent, was known for creating intensely realistic portrait busts. Courtesy Library of Congress, Prints and Photographs Division, Washington, D.C.

7. AN AMERICAN JEWISH BIOGRAPHER IN BRONZE

Jo Davidson (1883–1952), a well-known American artist who worked mostly in portraiture sculpture, was an immigrant of Russian-Jewish descent. Davidson apprenticed in the studio of the prominent American sculptor Hermon Atkins MacNeil (1866–1947) before moving to Paris to study sculpture at the École des Beaux-Arts in 1907. Best known for his numerous portrait busts of famous twentieth-century American personalities, Lincoln was one of the few nineteenth-century personalities to attract Davidson's interest. The bust of Lincoln was sculpted in 1947 and today is located in the Lincoln Home National Historic Site Visitor Center in Springfield, Illinois. In 2006, the Smithsonian's National Portrait Gallery installed a permanent exhibit featuring many of Davidson's busts. The exhibit labeled the artist "the biographer in bronze."

    A photograph of the artist and his likeness of Lincoln, crafted by memory and without a Lincoln mask or model, are reproduced here.

MUSICAL TRIBUTES TO LINCOLN

8. "WASHINGTON, LINCOLN, AND MOISHE RABEINY" BY JOSEPH RUMSHINSKY

Joseph Rumshinsky (1881–1956)[49] was one of the leading American Jewish composers in the world of the Yiddish musical theater during the first decades of the twentieth century. A professionally trained musician who immigrated to the United States in 1904, Rumshinsky quickly embraced the American theatrical genre, and his compositions reflected this interest. Always aspiring for commercial success, Rumshinsky wrote music for light operetta on the Yiddish stage.

    One of his Yiddish shows, Yente Telebende (1916), featured a popular song titled "Washington, Lincoln, and Moishe Rabeiny" (Washington, Lincoln, and Moses our

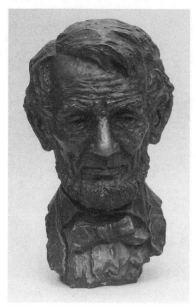

One of Davidson's portrait busts of Lincoln, cast in 1947, stands in the Lincoln Home National Historic Site Visitor Center, Springfield, Illinois. Courtesy Lincoln Home National Historic Site, National Park Service.

teacher), with lyrics written by Louis Gilrod (1879–1930). The song was a duet with lyrics debating who was better, the white or the black man. These lyrics are unquestionably offensive by today's standards, but it is obvious that this piece came from the minstrel tradition of the stage show.[50] *It aimed at bringing a laugh to the audience from the racial stereotyping that typified that era. Was there anyone, the black man asks, who can top Abraham Lincoln as the greatest of the great? Lincoln is great, the lyrics confess, but to the delight of the Yiddish-speaking audience, only Moses is a nobler man:*

> Mir weise menshen steihen auben on mir
> stolziren mit George Washington.
> Der grester man fun alle groise leit is Abraham
> Lincoln wus hot ins fin skalferei befreit.
> Ch'leben ch'leben es is nit shlecht bist doch take oi seier gerecht oi
> Sog mir schwarzer is den bei eich faran a
> moishe rabeiny as a nobler man?
> [We white people stand in a place of honor and
> take pride in George Washington.
> The greatest man among all great men is Abraham
> Lincoln, who freed us from slavery.
> Believe me, believe me it's not bad—you're right indeed . . .
> But tell me black man, is there among you one like
> Moses our teacher—such a noble man?][51]

Cover sheet for *Yente Telebende* with music by J. M. Rumshinsky (New York: The Hebrew Publishing Co., 1916). Rumshinsky's name has been misspelled on the cover. The music for the Yiddish song "Washington, Lincoln, and Moishe Rabeiny" (Washington, Lincoln, and Moses our teacher) was composed by Rumshinsky.

Courtesy John Hay Library, Brown University Library.

9. THE GETTYSBURG ADDRESS IN YIDDISH

Even prior to his arrival in America in 1926, Jacob Weinberg (1879–1956) had already established his credentials as a distinguished composer of both liturgical and secular Jewish works.[52] *In the United States, Weinberg taught for many years at the New York College*

Cover sheet of Jacob Weinberg's score of "The Gettysburg Address," 1954. Jacob Weinberg, a distinguished composer of both liturgical and secular Jewish works, wrote three musical settings for Lincoln's Gettysburg Address. His 1954 version called for the text to be read to the audience in Yiddish translation with musical accompaniment. Copyright © 1954 Transcontinental Music Publications; used by permission.

of Music and at Hunter College, but he continued to compose music aimed primarily at Jewish audiences. In the early 1940s, he organized an annual Jewish cultural arts festival in New York that featured musical and dance performances.

In 1936, Weinberg put the English words of Lincoln's Gettysburg Address to music in a work written for chorus and instruments. This original version was performed at Carnegie Hall on December 13, 1937, by the Dessoff Choir.[53] A few years later, in 1943, Weinberg composed a second variant of the work. This version called for the text to be read to the audience in Yiddish translation with musical accompaniment.[54] In 1954, he created yet a third musical setting for Lincoln's famous address, this one for chorus and orchestra (as shown on the previous page). Weinberg's music and the Yiddish translation place Lincoln's iconic American address into a distinctly Jewish artistic frame.

10. "ABRAHAM" BY IRVING BERLIN

Irving Berlin (1888–1989) is widely regarded as one of the greatest and most prolific song-writers and composers in all of American history. The son of a cantor from Belarus, Russia, Israel Baline (his original name) immigrated to the United States with his family in 1893. As a result of his father's early death, Berlin quit school and tried to make a living on New York's Lower East Side. He began working as a singing waiter, and this job prompted him to compose his own songs. In 1907, he published his first hit: "Marie from Sunny Italy."

Berlin's list of megahits is legendary. His best known songs include "Alexander's Ragtime Band" (1911), "Oh! How I Hate to Get Up in the Morning" (1917), "God Bless America" (1918, rev. 1938), "A Pretty Girl Is Like a Melody" (1919), "Blue Skies" (1926), "Puttin' on the Ritz" (1930), "Easter Parade" (1933), "White Christmas" (1942), "Anything You Can Do I Can Do Better" (1946), "Doin' What Comes Natur'lly" (1946), and "There's No Business Like Show Business" (1946).

In 1942, Berlin composed twelve songs for Holiday Inn, *a film musical starring Bing Crosby and Fred Astaire. The film's runaway hit was "White Christmas." One of the other tunes Berlin composed for the film was titled "Abraham," a song about Abraham Lincoln that "embeds swing-style music-making within a nightclub scene rife with the trappings of minstrelsy." In the film, Crosby and Marjorie Reynolds perform in blackface.[55]*

In addition to the minstrelsy elements of the song's performance, which to the modern listener are offensively stereotyped mannerisms and dialect, Berlin's use of the demeaning term "darky" in his lyrics sparked a controversy. Scholars are quick to remind readers that Berlin used the term in an entirely positive lyrical context, which praises Lincoln as the emancipator of the slaves. Yet even in 1942 the word provoked an immediate outcry of indignation. Berlin promptly instructed his publishers to withdraw the word from the song and replace it with "negroes." "No song is important enough to offend a whole race," Berlin said as he ordered his publisher to change the word. "I should never have released it had I known the epithet was objectionable."[56]

Berlin's lyrics speak positively of Lincoln, reminding the listener that the nation's "united thanks" go to the son of "Nancy Hanks," this land's "finest son."

ABRAHAM

by Irving Berlin

Upon a February morn
A tiny baby boy was born—
Abraham, Abraham.
When he grew up, this tiny babe,
The folks all called him Honest Abe—
Abraham, Abraham.
In eighteen sixty he became
Our sixteenth President,
And now he's in the Hall of Fame,
A most respected gent.
And that is why we celebrate
This blessed February date—
Abraham, Abraham.

When black folks lived in slavery,
Who was it set the negro free?[57]
Abraham, Abraham.
When trouble came down from the shelf,
Whose heart was bigger than himself?
Abraham, Abraham.
"The country's going to the dogs!"
They shouted loud and strong;
Then from a cabin made of logs
The right man come along.
And that is why we celebrate
This blessed February date—
Abraham, Abraham.

The U.S.A.'s united thanks
To one whose name was Nancy Hanks—
Abraham, Abraham.
She gave this land the finest son
Who ever went to Washington—
Abraham, Abraham.
When someone told him Gen'ral Grant
Was drinking ev'ry night

He answered, "Go see if you can't
Get all my gen'rals tight."
And that is why we celebrate
This blessed February date—
Abraham, Abraham.

11. "LINCOLN PORTRAIT" BY AARON COPLAND

Aaron Copland (1900–1990), child of east European immigrants, became one of the most respected American composers of the twentieth century. In 1942, the prominent conductor Andre Kostelanetz (1901–80) commissioned Copland to write a musical tribute to an "eminent American." This request led Copland to compose one of his best-known works, "Lincoln Portrait," which features numerous quotations from Lincoln's own words (see following page).

According to one of his biographers, Copland claimed he had heard Jacob Weinberg's "Gettysburg Address" at an American music festival prior to its having been performed by the Dessoff Choir in Carnegie Hall. This being the case, Copland heard Weinberg's work only a few years before he began composing his famous "Lincoln Portrait" in the early 1940s.[58]

Copland was raised in a Jewish home, and though he was not a practicing Jew, his childhood familiarity with Jewish chant and liturgy continued to influence him throughout his career. It has been noted that one of the most identifiable and emphatic lines in "Lincoln Portrait" is the repetition of the phrase "And this is what he said." These words bear a striking similarity to the sentence "And God said, saying . . . ," which appears frequently in the Hebrew Bible. As one scholar observed, "Surrounded by Copland's text, Lincoln's own words sound both human and divine, pragmatic and idealistic."[59]

ARCHIVISTS, COLLECTORS, AND HISTORIANS

12. THE PIONEERING RESEARCHER: ISAAC MARKENS

Newspaper correspondent and independent researcher Isaac Markens began studying Lincoln's life in the 1890s. His efforts to preserve Lincolniana were extraordinary. By winning the trust of the reclusive Robert Todd Lincoln, Markens obtained a fascinating oral history from Lincoln's only surviving child. Markens also played a pivotal role in retrieving original copies of the Gettysburg Address. His efforts to preserve the history of Lincoln's relationship with his Jewish contemporaries may, however, have been his most noteworthy historical achievement. Without Markens, who literally corresponded with many of Lincoln's Jewish contemporaries or their offspring before they died, much of what we know today would have evaporated into the mist of time.

Two examples of Markens's historical achievements are presented. The first document is an excerpt from his monograph Abraham Lincoln and the Jews, *wherein he reconstructs a crucial meeting between Cesar J. Kaskel and Abraham Lincoln at the Executive Mansion on January 3, 1863. Kaskel had traveled to the nation's capital from Paducah,*

Text of Lincoln Portrait – 1942

A LINCOLN PORTRAIT

SPEAKER:

"Fellow citizens, we cannot escape history."

That is what he said,
That is what Abraham Lincoln said:

"Fellow citizens, we cannot escape history. We of this Congress and this
administration will be remembered in spite of ourselves. No personal
significance or insignificance can spare one or another of us. The
fiery trial through which we pass will light us down, in honor or
dishonor, to the latest generation. We---even we here---hold the
power and bear the responsibility."

He was born in Kentucky, raised in Indiana, and lived in Illinois.
And this is what he said:
This is what Abe Lincoln said:
He said:

"The dogmas of the quiet past are inadequate to the stormy present. The
occasion is piled high with difficulty, and we must rise with the
occasion. As our case is new, so we must think anew and act anew.
We must disenthrall ourselves, and then we shall save our country."

When standing erect he was six feet four inches tall.
And this is what he said:
He said:

"It is the eternal struggle between two principles—right and wrong throughout
the world. .... It is the same spirit that says, "You toil and work and
earn bread and I'll eat it." No matter in what shape it comes, whether
from the mouth of a king who seeks to bestride the people of his own
nation and live by the fruit of their labor, or from one race of men as
an apology for enslaving another race, it is the same tyrannical principle

Aaron Copland's annotated copy of the speaker's part of "Lincoln Portrait," written in 1942.
Courtesy Harry Ransom Humanities Research Center, The University of Texas at Austin.

*Kentucky, to register his outrage over Ulysses S. Grant's infamous General Orders No. 11.
It was during this meeting that Lincoln and Kaskel exchanged their oft-quoted repartee.
Markens implied that the details of this episode were preserved and conveyed to him by
Kaskel's younger brother, Julius, who was still living in Bensonhurst, New Jersey, when
Markens was collecting data for his article.*

A second example of Markens's remarkable historical instinct comes from his correspondence with Robert Todd Lincoln. For nearly two decades, Markens and Lincoln exchanged a cordial and historically significant correspondence. It was Markens who prodded Robert Lincoln to tell him that he had no recollection of either of his parents ever making reference to their having been descendants of Jewish parentage.[60] In the communication that Lincoln sent to Markens on February 13, 1918, we see how Markens—through his interrogative missives—managed to extricate from the president's son remarkably interesting data that may have otherwise been lost.

"And This Protection They Shall Have at Once"

It was determined to send a representative of the Jewish community to Washington to communicate with the President in person, and for that purpose Cesar Kaskel, one of the signers of the appeal, and a vice-president of the Paducah Union League Club, was selected.

Cesar Kaskel was a native of Prussia, in his thirtieth year, and one of the most respected merchants of the town. J[ulius] W. Kaskel, another signer of the appeal, was his brother. A record of the Paducah proceedings was preserved by the latter, now living at Bensonhurst, Brooklyn, N.Y., from which we learn that Cesar Kaskel at once left Paducah by steamer for Cairo. While en route he prepared a full account of the affair which on reaching Cairo was furnished to the agent of the Associated Press, this being the first newspaper report given to the country.

Kaskel, says *The Israelite*, took with him letters from Rabbi Max Lilienthal, and Daniel Wolf, a prominent Cincinnati merchant, to influential parties in Washington and arrived at the National Capital on the evening of January 3, 1863. Accompanied by Representative Gurley of Ohio the two at once sought an audience with the President, reaching the White House at about dusk. Announcing their presence, with an apology for calling at such an hour, the President sent word that he was "always glad to see his friends," and shortly made his appearance. On learning the object of their visit he remarked:

And so the children of Israel were driven from the happy land of Canaan?

Kaskel replied:

Yes, and that is why we have come unto Father Abraham's bosom, asking protection.

Lincoln responded:

And this protection they shall have at once.

Then seating himself at a table the President penned an order to General Halleck requesting his visitors to deliver it at once.

"You may leave for home at once if you wish," said General Halleck to Kaskel on reading Lincoln's instructions, "and before you reach there Grant's order will have been revoked."

Kaskel that same night started back to Paducah, and arriving there was surprised to learn that the order of revocation had not yet been promulgated.

"By whose orders do you return?" demanded the Post Commander, on learning of Kaskel's presence in town.

"By order of the President of the United States," replied Kaskel.

Halleck's instructions to Grant, it appears, had been delayed in transmission and the latter's revocation was not issued until January 7, 1863. Two weeks later, January 21, Halleck wrote to Grant:

> The President has no objection to your expelling traitors and Jew peddlers which I suppose was the object of your order, but as it in terms proscribed an entire religious class, some of whom are fighting in our ranks, the President deems it necessary to revoke it.

Dr. Wise is authority for the statement that Halleck would not believe in the existence of Grant's order until Kaskel showed him the official copy.

Before the result of Kaskel's mission became known Rabbis Wise and Lilienthal, accompanied by Edgar M. Johnson, a lawyer of Cincinnati, Martin Bijur, a lawyer of Louisville, and Abraham Goldsmith, a merchant of Paducah, had gone to Washington. Learning of Kaskel's success on the way they determined nevertheless to complete the journey in order to express their thanks to the President for his prompt action. Rabbi Wise, in *The Israelite*, gave an interesting account of their interview.[61]

1775 N Street, Washington, D.C.
February 13, 1918

My dear Mr. Markens:

It seems to me the simplest way to answer your letter of February 5th is to return it to you with your interrogatories marked and to make the brief answers to them in this way:

1. The proper answer is that he was a total abstainer, but on two or three occasions in my life, not more I have seen him take a sip of a glass of ale and also a glass of champagne. On each occasion he was urged to do this as a tonic. I do not think it ever occurred to him of his own motion to drink anything except water or tea or coffee or milk. As you know, he always was a strong temperance advocate.

2. The Bloomington shipment you refer to is no doubt boxes of papers which Judge [David] Davis took charge of, as administrator of my father's estate, and caused to be removed to Bloomington, his home, where he had a safe storage place for them. They remained unopened until given over to Nicolay and Hay for their work. They are now in my possession.

3. I heard nothing of this while in London, but I have in some way understood that in one of the college libraries, whether in Oxford or in Cambridge I do not know, is hanging framed a lithographed copy of the Bixby Letter. As to the Gettysburg address and opinions of English publications thereon, I have not now any present memory.

4. His methods of office working were simply those of a very busy man who worked at all hours. He never dictated correspondence; he sometimes wrote a document and had his draft copied by either Nicolay or Hay; sometimes he himself copied his corrected draft and retained the draft in his papers; there were no letter press books at all; he never owned such a thing. When he preserved letters to himself, it was ordinarily done by replacing them in their envelopes with the writer's name inscribed; it was not his general habit to keep copies of letters written by himself.

5. I know nothing whatever about this.[62]

6. This letter is in my possession.[63]

7. I never heard of any picture of my grandfather, Thomas Lincoln.

I trust that you are very well and are enjoying some comfort as we are from the change in the dreadful weather of this winter.

Very Truly yours,
Robert T. Lincoln

Isaac Markens, Esq.
545 West 164th St.
New York City[64]

13. COLLECTOR OF LINCOLNIANA: EMANUEL HERTZ

Emanuel Hertz was a lawyer by profession, but studying the life of the sixteenth president became his preoccupying avocation. His family immigrated to the United States from Austria in 1884. He mastered English, earned a baccalaureate degree from New York City College, and studied law at Columbia University. From the earliest years of his legal career, Hertz studied Lincoln's life and devoted himself to acquiring Lincoln documents, pictures, and artifacts. By the 1930s, Hertz was said to have acquired the world's largest privately held collection of Lincolniana.

Like the pioneering researcher Isaac Markens, Hertz was interested in every facet of Lincoln's life but had a special interest in reconstructing the story of Lincoln and the Jews. Building on Markens's groundbreaking research, Hertz assembled an unparalleled collection of Jewish eulogies, homilies, and orations, many of which, without his efforts, might have been lost.

In addition to his interest in Lincoln's Jewish contacts, Hertz produced numerous volumes, articles, and speeches on Lincoln's life. In one of his articles, which first appeared in the American Hebrew *on February 6, 1926, Hertz likened Lincoln to the Bible's towering liberator, the prophet Moses.*

*In 1927, Hertz asked his distinguished brother, Joseph, the chief rabbi of Great Britain,
to write the foreword to his magnum opus on Lincoln and the Jews titled* Abraham Lincoln: The Tribute of the Synagogue. *In this foreword, Joseph Hertz recounted a story he
had heard from one of his teachers, Rabbi Benjamin Szold of Baltimore. The fascinating
anecdote, meant to demonstrate Lincoln's extraordinary compassion, is reproduced below.*

Foreword

by the Very Rev. Dr. J. H. Hertz

Heroic achievement, literary genius or towering personality, each of them
leads to earthly fame. Therefore, the place of Abraham Lincoln who combined all these, and in a pre-eminent degree, is indeed secure in the annals
of man.

He was the protagonist in the greatest war drama of the nineteenth century. He not only preserved unimpaired the heritage of Washington, but made
America truly American. He rolled away the "reproach of Egypt"—negro slavery—from his countrymen. Others had scotched the serpent: he killed it. In
a free land, he felt, it was not the white man who ruled the black, neither was
it the black man who ruled the white: it was justice that ruled. Humanity has
since hailed him "Lincoln the Emancipator."

Few public men possessed his mastery of speech, his wonderful mother-wit
and rare eloquence. Several of his utterances are among the most perfect things
in the language. His Gettysburg Address stands unparalleled since the days of
Pericles; while in his stand for national righteousness and his absolute belief
in the irresistibleness of right, he has the accent of Israel's Prophets.

And Lincoln *the man* is greater than his words or even his world-historic
deeds. He walked in humility with his God, and he never forgot pity. My revered
teacher, Dr. Benjamin Szold (may his memory be a blessing)[,] related to me
the following incident: He had occasion to accompany a poor Jewish woman
to the White House and beseech the President to pardon her wayward son
who had deserted. She told her story in Yiddish, of which the President did
not understand a word. But Abraham Lincoln only saw before him a mother
imploring him for the life of her child; and as he listened to her unintelligible
and yet agonising plea, the tears coursed down his cheeks.

The sublime simplicity and infinite kindliness of this man of the people
who directed and stilled the storm of a titanic fratricidal conflict, have made
his name a benediction far beyond his native land or even the confines of the
English-speaking world. And nowhere has this *anima naturaliter Hebraica*
received more sympathetic understanding, nowhere has his memory been
cherished with more reverential affection, than in the American-Jewish pulpit,
as the following pages amply testify.

London, March 8, 1927—5887[65]

14. THE METICULOUS SCHOLAR: BERTRAM W. KORN

Bertram Wallace Korn, rabbi, scholar, and military chaplain, was one of America's most prominent Reform rabbis during the post–World War II years. Upon receiving his doctor of Hebrew letters degree in 1949 from Hebrew Union College in Cincinnati, Korn assumed the pulpit of Reform Congregation Keneseth Israel in Philadelphia, where he remained for the rest of his career. While ministering to this large congregation, Korn became a noted authority on the history of American Jewry. His first published volume, American Jewry and the Civil War, *based on his doctoral dissertation, appeared in 1951. More than half a century after its publication, this pioneering work remains a valuable and authoritative resource on the subject. Korn devoted an entire chapter to the topic of Lincoln and the Jews.*

The selection below comes from an infrequently cited article titled "Lincoln and the Jews," written by Korn in 1955, four years after his American Jewry and the Civil War. *During the interim, Korn had acquired a remarkable letter that Lincoln had written to Secretary of War Edwin Stanton on November 4, 1862. A copy of this letter, along with Korn's penetrating analysis, sheds light on Lincoln's thoughts about the Jewish minority in the American nation.*

Lincoln and the Jews

A hitherto unknown and unpublished Lincoln letter which I recently had the good fortune to obtain for my collection of Jewish Americana adds one more to the few references to Jews to be found in the writings of Lincoln:

Executive Mansion
Washington, Nov. 4, 1862

Hon. Sec. of War.

Sir

    I believe we have not yet appointed a Hebrew—As Cherie M. Levy, is well vouched, as a capable and faithful man, let him be appointed an Assistant Quarter-Master, with the rank of Captain.

Yours truly
A. Lincoln

This appointment was not a political reward; Levy was the son-in-law of Rabbi Morris J. Raphall of Congregation B'nai Jeshurun of New York City, who was a Democrat and defended slavery. Lincoln was, I believe, living up to his conviction that minority groups ought to be given fitting and fair recognition—and more! He was conscious of the anti-Semitic prejudice which rose to a high point during the tensions and crises of the Civil War and went out of his way to be kind to Jews. Many applicants were "well vouched" as "capable and faithful" men; but the fact that Levy was a Jew apparently made Lincoln eager to fulfill his request.[66]

... The Lincoln who urged a change in the law of Congress to permit the appointment of Jewish chaplains; who ordered the revocation of an anti-Semitic General Order issued by the only Union general who seemed capable of winning battles; and who recommended the appointment of an assistant quartermaster on the grounds of his being "a Hebrew," could not have had any prejudice against the Jews.

On the contrary, he seems to have had an unusual sympathy for them. Perhaps his deep love for the Bible and the tragedies of his own personal life made him feel a kinship with these sons of the prophets. . . .

I believe it to be entirely possible that other as yet undiscovered and unpublished documents will bear out my contention that Lincoln was predisposed to be kind to Jews just because he was conscious of the effects of bigotry and intolerance upon their lives. Is this not what we would expect from the great spirit who spoke of a nation which would live "with malice toward none; with charity for all; with firmness in the right, as God gives us to see the right"?[67]

15. THE CONTEMPORARY AUTHORITY: HAROLD HOLZER

Harold Holzer, a scholar, writer, and lecturer, is a contemporary authority on Abraham Lincoln and the political culture of the Civil War era. By 2013, Holzer had published nearly three dozen volumes exploring various facets of Lincoln's career and the Civil War era.

In 2002, Holzer delivered an address on Lincoln and the Jews at the Skirball Cultural Center in Los Angeles, California. After briefly discussing Lincoln's encounters with his Jewish contemporaries, Holzer described Lincoln's "religion." As the excerpts below emphasize, Holzer avers that it was Lincoln's manifest commitment to liberty and equality, together with his fervent belief in the primacy of the "Golden Rule," that has earned him the admiration of American Jewry, both then and now.

Excerpts from *Lincoln and the Jews: The Last Best Hope of Earth*

The fact is, Lincoln believed deeply in God the Father, but from early adulthood on, notwithstanding twenty years of Sundays in Baptist churches with his family, he seldom mentioned the Son or the Holy Ghost. He did not embrace Jesus as messiah or savior, and opponents occasionally branded him an infidel during his lifetime—often enough that several of his earliest sympathetic biographers took pains to claim that he was a true Christian. But there is scant evidence for it.

Lincoln believed in Divine Will, but of an "Old Testament" variety. As he put it in his Second Inaugural Address, in defense of the enormous sacrifices required by the Civil War: "The judgments of the Lord are true and righteous altogether." That comes right out of Psalm 19, a psalm of David.

Moreover, as Jews knew, Lincoln believed in equal opportunity for all. He had firmly rejected Know-Nothingism, the hateful mid-nineteenth-century Nativist movement opposed to immigration by Catholics and foreigners. As he put it: "How can anyone who abhors the oppression of negroes, be in favor of degrading classes of white people?" Such sentiments put some of his Christian contemporaries ill at ease, but it clearly made Jewish admirers, then and now, comfortable. . . .

As Lincoln had once summed up his faith: "When I do good I feel good, and when I do bad I feel bad, and that's my religion." Perhaps it is no accident that the sentiment is remarkably close to what the sage Hillel had urged in his teachings two millennia earlier: "To forbear doing unto others what would displease us." That deceptively simple but poignant philosophy made Lincoln seem, to Jews of his day, like God's child and America's father at one and the same time. When Lincoln died, many Jews really did feel that "the beauty of Israel was slain upon the high places."[68]

11

"Lincoln! Thou Shouldst Be Living at This Hour!"
Lincoln as a Moral Compass for American Jews

Shortly after the end of World War I, at a time when the nation's love for Lincoln was in full bloom, an interesting poem authored by Kenyon West appeared in an anthology with a title that implied the volume's contents were sacred writings: *The Book of Lincoln*.

> LINCOLN! "Thou shouldst be living at this hour!"
> Thy reach of vision—prophet thou and seer—
> Thy strong and steadfast wisdom, judgment clear,
> Are needed in this stress, thy old-time power
> The ship of state to save from storms that lower
> And threaten to engulf. Dark reefs loom near!
> No "watchful waiting"[1] will avail us here,
> That wind-swept, tossing ship past rocks that tower
> To guide to sunlit waters—calm, serene.
> Oh! for a leader, fearless, strong, and wise,
> Of swift decision, and with insight keen
> To see the dangers; scorn all compromise;
> Restore the honour lost, the faith we prize,
> And bring us back the glory that hath been!

The poem's opening line—"Lincoln! Thou shouldst be living at this hour!"—is highly suggestive of Walt Whitman's famous poetic elegy "O Captain! My Captain!," composed to memorialize Lincoln not long after his death in 1865. Whitman's poem laments a fallen leader who is gone forever: "fallen cold and dead." "O Captain! My Captain!" expressed sentiments of overwhelming loss at the time of Lincoln's death, but in the years following, as the nation commemorated the centennial anniversary of Lincoln's birth, a cry for the return of the great leader appeared, as the nation once again called for its fallen "captain," who now must speak to his people from beyond the grave. By examining Lincoln's life and scrutinizing his human instincts, Americans could depend on him to provide inspiration and guidance as they faced a continual onslaught of social and political challenges. All through the twentieth century, the crises the nation faced inevitably seemed comparable to the tribulations that Lincoln confronted during his own Civil War era.[2]

Throughout the course of the twentieth century, people from all walks of life extracted moral strength and political wisdom from the wellspring of inspiration that flowed from Lincoln's biographical legacy. Republicans and Democrats, northerners and southerners, conservatives and liberals—all wanted to make him the touchstone for their special causes and agendas. Secretary of War William Howard Taft may have been one of the first to pose a famous rhetorical question: What would Lincoln do? Speaking at a dinner marking the ninety-ninth anniversary of Lincoln's birth, Taft averred that "if Lincoln were living today he would be a Republican and a protectionist." Assertions like Taft's were not always plausibly argued. Still, the question became a popular one and was asked again and again throughout the course of the century. What would Lincoln do if he were alive today?[3]

In the "Roaring Twenties," there were those who contended that Lincoln was the avatar of peace, prosperity, and optimism. From this perspective, the sixteenth president would advise the nation to enjoy its prosperity. In his address at the dedication ceremonies for the Lincoln Memorial on May 30, 1922, President Warren G. Harding—ironically speaking to a racially segregated audience—opined that had Lincoln been alive, his heart would have been "aglow" in the knowledge that the nation cherished the same ideals that he, Lincoln, valued. "We are going on," Harding predicted, "always on, holding to constitutional methods, amending to meet the requirements of a progressive civilization, clinging to majority rule, properly restrained, which is 'the only true sovereign of a free people,'[4] and working to the fulfillment of the destiny of the world's greatest republic!" Five years later, to the very day, Harding's successor, Calvin Coolidge, addressed the crowd gathered at Gettysburg in honor of Dedication Day. "The government of the people, by the people, for the people, which Lincoln described in his immortal address," the president told the crowd, "is a government of peace, not of war." He suggested that Lincoln would have wanted the nation "to endeavor by every means within [its] power to prevent the shedding of human blood in the attempted settlement of international controversies."[5]

Once the nation fell into the jaws of the Great Depression, however, Lincoln was drafted to serve as the advocate of another message. Herbert Hoover contended that Lincoln would have wanted the nation to stand fast against those who would use the economic crisis to fortify and centralize the power of the federal government. Lincoln would not have wanted to curtail the individual liberties that all Americans valued. Hoover urged the American people "to show the same commitment, courage, and resourcefulness as they had under Lincoln's leadership." Only a few years later, in 1938, when the dark clouds of worldwide war gathered on the horizon, Lincoln's moral legacy offered the nation wisdom that pertained to an entirely different set of political and economic circumstances. While speaking at the dedication of the memorial on the Gettysburg Battlefield on July 3, 1938, Franklin D. Roosevelt told his audience that, in most situations, comparing oneself to leaders from bygone days is a pointless exercise:

"It seldom helps to wonder how a statesman of one generation would surmount the crisis of another. A statesman deals with concrete difficulties—with things which must be done from day to day. Not often can he frame conscious patterns for the far-off future. But the fullness of the stature of Lincoln's nature and the fundamental conflict which events forced upon his Presidency invite us ever."[6]

Less than a year later, Roosevelt began to prepare the nation for the possibility of war in Europe. He pushed for increased military spending and advocated for the modernization of the country's weaponry. During this time, FDR did not publicly ponder whether Lincoln would have endorsed his administration's policies. Yet a popular Broadway play about Lincoln left little doubt as to what the sixteenth president would want the nation to do. Robert E. Sherwood's *Abe Lincoln in Illinois*, which premiered on October 15, 1938, became an instant sensation. As the play reaches its climax, Lincoln addresses a crowd during his debates with Stephen Douglas. Even though Sherwood's script was built on a foundation of Lincoln's own words, the author shaped Lincoln's soliloquy so as to make the speech "more allusive to the imminent threat of totalitarianism than to the southern slavocracy." The play ends with Lincoln departing Springfield for Washington. He reminds the audience that America must always be willing to fight for liberty and democracy if it hoped to survive in a dangerous world. The play was unambiguous about what Lincoln would do. He would oppose totalitarianism. He would be prepared to fight the dictators.[7]

In the post–World War II era, as the modern civil rights movement began to take shape, Lincoln became a natural and authentic ally for civil rights activists. In 1947, Harry S. Truman became the first American president to address the National Association for the Advancement of Colored People (NAACP), and he did not hesitate to invoke Lincoln's name when he promised African Americans that the federal government under his leadership would move to end discrimination, violence, and racial prejudice in American life:

> The civil rights laws written in the early years of our republic . . . were written to protect the citizen against any possible tyrannical act by the new government in this country . . . [but] we cannot stop there. We must keep moving forward, with new concepts of civil rights to safeguard our heritage. The extension of civil rights today means, not protection of the people against the Government, but protection of the people by the Government. We must make the Federal Government a friendly, vigilant defender of the rights and equalities of all Americans. And again I mean all Americans.

Speaking in front of Daniel Chester French's imposing sculpture, Truman was literally and figuratively standing at Lincoln's feet when he confidently informed the crowd: "Abraham Lincoln understood so well the ideal, which you and I seek today."[8]

Truman's speech at the Lincoln Memorial was neither the first nor the last time the monument served as a commanding backdrop for those who worked to advance the cause of the modern civil rights movement. In 1939, after representatives of the Daughters of the American Revolution informed African American contralto Marian Anderson (1897–1993), a great operatic talent of the period, that she would not be permitted to sing to an integrated audience from the stage of Constitution Hall, the NAACP organized a massive concert in protest. With the help of the Roosevelt administration, the NAACP's concert was held in front of the Lincoln Memorial. Photographers snapped dozens of pictures memorializing what the audience saw: French's lifelike statue of Lincoln watching sympathetically from behind as the performer sang "America the Beautiful."[9]

Those images of Lincoln "watching" Marian Anderson sing flashed across the nation in 1939, and they made an unforgettable impression on thousands of Americans, including a ten-year-old boy named Martin Luther King Jr. Five years later, in the context of a speech he delivered in an oratory contest, King spoke movingly about the past and presciently about the future: "She sang as never before," he said, "with tears in her eyes. When the words of 'America' and 'Nobody Knows de Trouble I Seen' rang out over that great gathering, there was a hush on the sea of uplifted faces, black and white, and a new baptism of liberty, equality, and fraternity. That was a touching tribute, but Miss Anderson may not as yet spend the night in any good hotel in America." Two decades later, King stood on those same steps and delivered his own unforgettable performance as Lincoln watched approvingly, once again, from behind.[10]

Throughout this same period, American Jews joined with the rest of the nation in asking themselves, "What would Lincoln do?" Not surprisingly, Lincoln offered Jews the same political counsel and moral guidance he gave to the general community. Yet American Jews continued to believe that even though Lincoln was speaking to the nation as a whole, his moral legacy was particularly relevant to Jewish causes and concerns.

As part of the festivities marking the 100th anniversary of Lincoln's birth in 1909, Gratz College in Philadelphia invited the distinguished physician, scholar, and civic leader Solomon Solis-Cohen (1857–1948) to deliver the Lincoln Centennial Address. Although Solis-Cohen devoted much of his speech to an analysis of Lincoln's greatness, he used his parting comments to emphasize his conviction that American Jews had good reason to let Lincoln serve as an exemplar of one who tried to make the world better for all humankind:

> And as Americans, as Jews, as men, let us meet the problems of our day in the same spirit of justice and charity wherein Lincoln met the problems of his day. Slavery still exists in our land, though in a subtler form than that which it took in the brick kilns of Pithom and Ramses or the cotton-fields and rice swamps of Mississippi and Carolina. Underneath all the conflicts of races, of nations, of individuals, lies one great problem: that of vindicating the equal right of every human soul to a freedom restricted only by the equal freedom of its fellows. "That which is hateful to thee, do not to any other," said Hillel; and Lincoln, applying the same thought to the conditions of this time and country, spoke words that I would have linger in your memory as the essence of our communion with his spirit

tonight: "Them that deny freedom to others deserve it not for themselves and, under the rule of a just God, cannot long retain it."[11]

At Temple Israel in St. Louis, Rabbi Leon Harrison (1866–1928) used the centennial anniversary of Lincoln's birthday to comment on the great social issues of the day. Harrison informed his congregants that Lincoln, were he alive, would be a "true American" who would fight for the rights of the common man, which were being trammeled by corporate greed. The rabbi's homiletic technique was apparently a success. Newspaper reports appearing the following week noted that Harrison's congregants "loudly cheered" when their rabbi "denounced as traitors the rich men of the city who have monopolized the public utilities."[12]

Stephen S. Wise habitually yoked Lincoln's memory to his views on current events. For example, he compared Lincoln to Woodrow Wilson on a number of occasions both before and after World War I. As Wilson prepared to leave office in March 1921, Wise again likened the ailing president to Lincoln. He told his listeners that both men were unfairly disparaged for no reason other than that they sought to "enhance the greatness" of their country. In 1922, Wise compared the troubling renaissance of the Ku Klux Klan to the vexing social issues that Lincoln had faced during his lifetime "with the problem of slavery and abolition." Calling on America to make the same stand as Lincoln did vis-à-vis slavery during the Civil War, Wise vehemently declared: "Either the Ku Klux Klan has got to go or America will perish."[13]

In the 1930s, Jewish leaders used Lincoln's memory as a prod to agitate against Hitler and Nazi policies. Just weeks before the Germans handed Chancellor Adolf Hitler an electoral endorsement in March 1933, Wise delivered an inflammatory address titled "Germany Chooses Hitler—America Chose Lincoln." Wise was not alone in his effort to enlist Lincoln's memory in service of American opposition to Nazism and Nazi policies. In 1937, for instance, the editors of Philadelphia's *Jewish Exponent* unquestionably had Hitler in mind when telling their readers that Lincoln's birthday should serve as a stark reminder of the dangers the nation faced when he was president and that await all those who blithely acquiesce to tyranny:

> Time in no way lessens the affectionate feeling the American people cherish for the great martyr President Abraham Lincoln. This is a wholesome sign. The outstanding feature in Lincoln's character is his passionate belief in the vindication of the right, his indomitable courage in the face of adversity and his unquenchable confidence in the inherent goodness of human nature. This lesson from the life of this great President is needed at all times and especially in an age when tyranny finds acquiescence among enlightened people, when justice and discrimination are condoned by otherwise moral nations and individuals. Lincoln's life should serve as a potent stimulus to many of us today to continue the struggle for the right, to maintain hope for a revitalized civilization and to stir us to renewed faith in the final victory of the causes of justice and

liberty throughout the world. The anniversary observed today should strengthen us in this critical period and imbue us with courage for better times to come, even though the present appears dark. . . . Viewed in this light, the birthday anniversary of Abraham Lincoln takes on new and timely significance.[14]

Several years later, on Lincoln's birthday in February 1945, the editors of Boston's *Jewish Advocate* pointed out that Hitler's impending demise would be, when all is said and done, a validation of Lincoln's legacy and the moral inheritance he bequeathed to America:

> Once again we celebrate the birthday of Abraham Lincoln, a man who, perhaps above all others, typifies those values for which civilized mankind is now embattled in the fight against Hitlerism.
>
> It was Abraham Lincoln who in the Gettysburg speech gave the definition of democracy which we Americans accept today—"a government of the people, by the people, and for the people."
>
> Hitler had perhaps not realized it, but in taking up the fight against democracy he had to fight "Old Abe," too, for Abraham Lincoln in the spiritual sense, is not dead. The ideals for which he fought have become impregnated in the American people. It may be that here and there, in greater or lesser fashion, there are people in America who have forgotten this lesson but all the Lincoln in the American people cannot be easily rooted out.
>
> This is what Hitler is learning today—the hard way. This is what any of those who eye Hitlerist method must sooner or later find out. Yes, the lesson of democracy which Abraham Lincoln taught has gone deeper in our bones than some of our Fascists realize. Abraham Lincoln taught also another lesson which Hitler is in a position to understand now, the lesson "that you can fool some of the people all of the time, all of the people some of the time, but you can't fool all of the people all of the time."[15]

After World War II, Americans—Jews and non-Jews—slowly began to confront the meaning of the calamitous atrocities the Nazis had perpetrated on European Jewry. These realizations coincided with the beginnings of the modern civil rights movement, and many Jews dedicated themselves anew to the idea that all Americans deserved equal opportunity under the law. For many Americans—and particularly in the Jewish community—the social conditions that made it possible for a government-sanctioned genocide to occur in Germany during the 1930s and 1940s were directly connected to the fight for social justice in America in the 1950s and 1960s. Rabbi Joachim Prinz (1902–88), a refugee from Nazi Germany who immigrated to America and dedicated himself to the cause of civil rights, articulated this very idea in the words he spoke at the March on Washington, August 28, 1963:

When I was the rabbi of the Jewish community in Berlin under the Hitler regime, I learned many things. The most important thing that I learned under those tragic circumstances was that bigotry and hatred are not the most urgent problem. The most urgent, the most disgraceful, the most shameful and the most tragic problem is silence. A great people which had created a great civilization had become a nation of silent onlookers. They remained silent in the face of hate, in the face of brutality and in the face of mass murder. America must not become a nation of onlookers. America must not remain silent.[16]

After World War II, the civil rights movement in America enlisted the support of many American Jews who concluded that, had more German citizens been willing to defend the civil rights of Jews and other oppressed minorities during the 1930s, the Holocaust might well have been averted. The connection between Lincoln and the civil rights movement in the 1950s and 1960s was self-evident to many, but this moral lesson seemed particularly salient to many in the American Jewish community. Lincoln, the man who protected Jewish civil rights during his administration, would want American Jews to continue the fight for social justice. This assertion contributed to a widespread conviction that Jews in the post-Holocaust world must actively support the crusade for civil rights in America. To do anything less would be blasphemous to the memory of the six million Jews who perished in Europe. Commenting on the civil rights legislation that President Truman submitted to the U.S. Congress at the end of January 1949, Cincinnati's *American Israelite* emphasized that Abraham Lincoln had been a civil rights advocate in his era, and he would similarly want all people to support the modern civil rights movement:

> If a modest percentage of the verbal tributes paid annually to Abraham Lincoln were but translated into daily acts of living in the spirit of that great man, the world would be advanced immeasurably along the path to liberty, equality and fraternity. . . .
>
> Nevertheless Lincoln the man and Lincoln the legend continue to serve by firing countless thousands of individuals around the world with a love for democracy that is genuine and irresistible.
>
> In a day when a president has actually "sunk his teeth" into the hard core of the question of civil liberties, we need to study and to take to heart anew the lesson which the emancipator himself learned and taught in another dark and trying day in humanity's long struggle upward.[17]

Even into the 1980s, the annual commemoration of Lincoln's birthday continued to prompt American Jews to anchor their commitment to breaking down walls of prejudice and intolerance in the moral legacy inherited from the sixteenth president. Rabbi Judea B. Miller (1930–95) illustrated this phenomenon when he took note of the fact that, from the 1940s through the 1980s, National Brotherhood Week, sponsored by the

National Conference of Christians and Jews, fell during the third week of February—the week separating Lincoln's and Washington's birthdays. Despite the event's symbolic temporal situation, Miller pointed out that after all the years of commemoration, the idea of brotherhood in America remained "really tentative and fragile." There had been only halting progress, and as far as Miller was concerned, all that National Brotherhood Week had to offer the community was "our unsuccessful efforts for peace today and our frequent crusading attitude of self-righteousness." Yet Miller found strength in the living legacy of Abraham Lincoln, who continued to inspire him to sustain the effort. "Maybe Brotherhood Week and the whole concept of human brotherhood is just a pious hope, a vague dream. But if it is just a dream, it is a wonderful dream. With more people of power who have the spirit of an Abraham Lincoln it may someday become a reality."[18]

In the most famous of all his addresses, the Gettysburg Address, Lincoln said, "It is for us the living, rather, to be dedicated here to the unfinished work which they who fought here have thus far so nobly advanced." Although Lincoln most certainly was referring to the work of preserving the Union, he himself became a moral clarion that called on future generations of Americans to dedicate themselves to the "unfinished work" left by those who preceded them. Thus, in response to the question "What would Lincoln do?," it has been repeatedly asserted that Lincoln would have never tolerated an immoral society. As one politician put it, Lincoln would have worked to abolish the "new slavery" of poverty, homelessness, drugs, and human despair.[19] These ideas were particularly compelling to American Jews, who remembered him as a man who stood up for their constitutional rights.

A week prior to Abraham Lincoln's birthday in February 1956, Autherine Juanita Lucy (b. 1929), the first black student to attend the University of Alabama, was suspended only three days after she began her program in library science. Earlier that same day, a hostile mob had assembled to prevent Lucy from attending classes, and the university maintained it could no longer guarantee her safety. Commenting on this event, the editors of the *Jewish Advocate* of Boston passionately denounced the bigotry that had given the world a "foul impression" of America. "We also know that it is a false impression," the editor added, "created by the worst segment of the population."[20]

The paper then called on its readers to pledge themselves to complete "Lincoln's unfinished business." Why? The editors reminded readers that when Lincoln was coming to power in the late 1850s, thousands of Jewish immigrants from Central Europe were flocking to these shores. At that time, many Americans feared these newcomers and joined the Know Nothing Party. Yet Abraham Lincoln stood up for those Jewish immigrants—he had "better sense." He "both typified and symbolized" a better America. For this very reason, the editors wrote, Jews and all Americans must follow Lincoln's example "in the fight between the forces of light and darkness." For Jews, Lincoln epitomized a moral imperative that called them, as Jews and as Americans, to dare to do their duty as they understood it.[21]

DOCUMENTS

1. I Beseech You in His Name: Love the Oppressed
2. He Would Stand Like a Rock for Human Rights
3. Americanism and Lincoln's Spirit
4. "Love One's Fellowmen without Distinction of Race or Color"
5. A Jewish Lodestar
6. Germany Desperately Needs a Lincoln
7. How Would Lincoln Serve?
8. Faith in Democracy Is as Eternal as Faith in One God
9. Imagining Lincoln in the 1950s
10. The Society of Jewish Science and Lincoln's Ideology
11. Calling the Jewish Community to Action
12. May His Memory Be as a Blessing

1. I BESEECH YOU IN HIS NAME: LOVE THE OPPRESSED

Jacob Salmon Raisin (1878–1946), a scholar and writer, was rabbi of Congregation Beth Elohim in Charleston, South Carolina, for nearly three decades. Raisin was about fourteen years old in 1892, when his parents immigrated to the United States from Russian Poland. Five years later he matriculated at Cincinnati's Hebrew Union College, where he earned his rabbinical diploma. Before coming to Charleston in 1915, he served congregations

in Port Gibson, Mississippi; Butte, Montana; Las Vegas, New Mexico; and Troy, New York.

In 1906, while Raisin was the rabbi of Congregation B'nai Israel in Butte, he delivered a noteworthy sermon on Lincoln's birthday. He exhorted his listeners by saying, "I beseech you by the love you bear his name to love the oppressed." Raisin also told his congregation that Lincoln was "the benefactor not only of the Southern blacks but

In 1906, Jacob Salmon Raisin, rabbi, Hebraist, and scholar, sermonized on Lincoln to his congregation in Butte, Montana. Courtesy The Jacob Rader Marcus Center of the American Jewish Archives, at the Hebrew Union College–Jewish Institute of Religion, Cincinnati, Ohio.

of the whites as well." Nevertheless, Raisin preached, the "white man has sunk into bondage worse than was ever felt in the South." If the American public ever hoped to confront the problems of "political corruption & economic rottenness," they should rely on Lincoln for inspiration. "Emulate his example," the rabbi told his people, and "love the oppressed."22

Less than a decade later, Raisin would accept a call to Charleston, where he would become a firsthand witness to the stratified society he had criticized while he was serving in Butte.

Lincoln, the First American

". . . Every man can say things that are true of Abraham Lincoln, but no man can say anything new of Abraham Lincoln"23—this was the verdict of Frederick Douglas[s] over a quarter of a century ago. And who at this late hour can doubt its veracity? Who, after the manifold eulogies showered upon him since, after having been repeatedly declared by a grateful people as the First American after the best element in the South has united with the universal feeling of the North in doing honor to his memory & singing paeans of praise to his life & canonized as martyr & saint after his death, who now can venture to say anything true & yet new of Abraham Lincoln?

That was a hero such as the world has seldom, if ever, seen before; that was a man for whose like we search but in vain in the voluminous annals of the past. Nor can we justly indulge in the hope of finding his equal in the unwritten records of the future. From the lowliest station in life he rose to the rank of the noblest of the earth; from a shepherd of flocks he grew to be a leader of men, from a rail-splitter he forged his way to the White House & from a humble boatman on the Mississippi he became the captain of the Ship of State. Like most of the great leaders of the people of Israel, like David, like Saul, like Moses himself, he removed all obstacles & hindrances, conquered all opposition & though not only unaided but even decried & derided by blinded dupes or scheming & envious time-servers, he succeeded in inscribing his name & enshrining his fame in the hearts of his countrymen to the remotest generation. . . .

Should only the black man be the friend of Abraham Lincoln? Should the African race alone whom he, like Moses the Jew, had liberated from a worse than Egyptian bondage, celebrate his birthday? Were he even a son of Ham we should have good cause to rejoice upon this contribution to mankind. Had he been born in any other part of the earth we might well be proud of & be grateful for such a specimen of noble manhood. I am thankful for a Booker T. Washington & a Louis [Lajos] Kossuth even [though] the one is not of my race & the other does not belong to my country. But since Lincoln was born on our soil & was flesh of our flesh & time of our time how great must be our joy & how deep our gratitude for the blessing which in him God has bestowed upon our nation.

Nor should this celebration be limited to the North. As one who lived for five years in the South & became more or less identified with their institutions, I claim him for our South land. He was a Southerner of Southerners. A Kentuckian by birth, he later on went to New Orleans & and spent several years as a boatman on the Mississippi: while as President of the United States he, with the great common sense sharpened in the school of adversity, had the good fortune of making real what our noblest Southern gentlemen, what Washington, Jefferson, Patric[k] Henry & Richard Lee were dreaming of, striving for & searching after but could as yet only be as good as an ideal. And when his efforts were crowned with success, when he finally broke the yoke of slavery . . . has he not thereby [been] the benefactor not only of the Southern blacks but of the whites as well? The remover of the heaviest burden of the South as well as the realizer of the fondest hopes of the North? Are we not as much indebted to him for our moral salvation as are the negroes for their bodily emancipation?

Alas that Abraham Lincoln who like Abraham our Patriarch walked in simplicity & integrity before the Lord, was nipped in the very midst of his usefulness. What could he not have accomplished for our country & especially the South, had not the murderous hand of an assassin suddenly removed him from the sphere of his activity? The grave race-problem which still stares us in the face & which God only knows when & how it will be solved might by this time have become a thing of the past. White & colored might now have learned their duties to each other & themselves, have known the requirements of the new era inaugurated by him & knowing them might have lived like brethren together in peace and harmony. But alas God saw fit otherwise. While our nation was Rachel-like bemoaning & finding no consolation for her bravest & best that were lost, while the skirts of Columbia were still crimson with the undried blood of her boys in blue & those in grey, she was suddenly to be bereaved of the greatest of them all, of Abraham Lincoln.

About forty years have now elapsed since his death—as many years as the Children of Israel roamed in the Wilderness of Paran on their way to the Promised Land. What has not our nation endured during that long & dreary period! How often did not we too exclaim, in those gloomy, unsettled years, during the horrible Reconstruction Days, in the reign of the Carpet-bagger, when everyone did as was pleasing in his eyes; Ah, for the days of old, it was better then than now! But thank God, that period of fire and sword, of storm & stress is now nearing its close. Already the South has become a Land of Promise. Already the "New South" foreseen by [Henry W.] Grady,[24] fertilized by the blood of the fathers[,] is rising by the brains of their descendants. More prosperous than ever before, more enlightened than in the dark sixties

& seventies, better days, better years, are awaiting my people; days & years better by far than were ever expected & even most sanguinely hoped for by him whose birthday we recently celebrated, whom we lovingly call our "First American," admire as the greatest of presidents, & cherish as the noblest of our citizens, the good, the brave, the "honest" Abraham Lincoln.

In the dark days of 1862, President Lincoln issued a proclamation asking for three hundred thousand volunteers to fill the stricken ranks of the army. Immediately after the call, Mr. Gibbons,[25] of New York[,] wrote a poem, the first stanza of which read:

> We're coming, Father Abraham,
> Six hundred thousand more,
> From Mississippi's winding stream
> & from New England's Shore.
> We leave our plows & work-shops,
> Our wives & children dear,
> With hearts too full for utterance
> With but one silent tear;
> We dare not look behind us
> But steadfastly before
> We are coming Father Abraham,
> Six hundred thousand more.

It is this cry that should be raised in our times of political corruption & economic rottenness. "We are serving Father Abraham!" We have freed the blacks, but the white man has sunk into bondage worse than was ever felt in the South. I beseech you by the memory of our martyred President to hate slavery of any sort, spiritual as well as physical. I beseech you by the love you bear his name to love the oppressed. I beseech you by the honor which you are willing to show the day of his birth to emulate his example, to try rather to be on the side of God than to expect God to come over on your side. In this way & in this way only, shall we best show our appreciation of & veneration for him who . . .

> Standing like a tower
> Our children shall behold his frame,
> The kindly-hearted,[26] brave, foreseeing man,
> Sagacious, patient, dreading praise, not blame,
> New birth of our soil, the first American.[27]

Amen.

2. HE WOULD STAND LIKE A ROCK FOR HUMAN RIGHTS

In 1898, a Congregationalist minister and Social Gospel activist named Charles Monroe Sheldon (1857–1946) published a volume titled In His Steps: "What Would Jesus Do?"[28] *Nearly a century would pass before Sheldon's question was rediscovered and flourished as a wildly popular American slogan.[29] It was also at the dawn of the twentieth century that a similar question, "What would Lincoln do?," began to be heard. Dozens of speakers and writers wondered aloud how Lincoln might have responded to contemporary social, political, economic, and religious challenges. This rhetorical device reached the height of its popularity during the era of World War I, but the trend, which waxed and waned throughout the twentieth century, included in every decade those who wanted to ponder what Lincoln would do if he were then alive.*

Rabbi Leon Harrison was one of many American rabbis who asked this question, first in February 1909, when he delivered a sermon marking the centennial of Lincoln's birth. On that occasion, Harrison asserted that if Lincoln were still alive, he would be a political Progressive fighting for the rights of labor, children, and women.[30]

Harrison, delivering a very similar message to a group of elderly Jewish Civil War veterans on March 27, 1914, at Temple Israel in St. Louis, expressed confidence that he knew what Lincoln would do were he still alive. According to the rabbi, Lincoln would oppose corruption in government, fight the power of business monopolies, support women's suffrage, prohibit child labor, advance the needs of public education, protect the rights of the "industrial classes," and promote peace among the nations of the world. In short, the rabbi insisted that Lincoln, the first Republican president, would have actually been, in 1914, a Progressive just like the Democrat in the White House, Woodrow Wilson.

What Would Lincoln Do in the White House Now?

If then I ask, what would Lincoln do that has not yet been done by him who now occupies his high place of executive authority, what would the answer be?

He would, I think, do some things to which the hand of his successor is set; and other things, too, that the nation has at heart to execute.

He would stand like a rock, as in his own age, for human rights. He would defend the humble against the powerful; the small trader against the monopolist that seeks to crush and ruin him by legal and immoral tricks. Lincoln always hated monopoly; for he believed absolutely in the equal rights of every man to our common, national inheritance of opportunity. Monopoly, he realized, not only crushes the individual, but corrupts the Commonwealth. It is the invisible government, as illegitimate as it is invisible. It is the hand that soils the whiteness of judicial ermine, whose tainted money contemptuously buys up the country cattle in our legislatures. To regulate and control these great corporations, by making them as amenable to the majesty of the Law as the humblest citizen, would surely be the first task that he would make his own, so that the plain man may not be robbed of his inalienable rights; that he shall not be menaced and overshadowed by a giant competitor against whom he cannot hold his own.

It is a pure accident that we have such a man in the White House today. He might have been a cheap and windy politician; for it is a political machine in this country that lifts up and throws down. It is a few bosses that govern, instead of the whole nation. They select, instead of all of us selecting, by direct vote of the people in the primaries, candidates that are finally to be balloted for at the polls.

You ask what would Lincoln do? This reform in the original choice of candidates is emphatically what he would set himself to bring about. For he believed in a government of all the people, not of a few parasites upon the body politic; uncrowned tyrants, ruling more autocratically than any Czar. There is nothing that would be commended and promoted more zealously by Abraham Lincoln, in the spirit of his life and immortal achievements, than this great and needed change in the political administration of our country.

For he believed in the equal rights of every man, yes, and of every woman. It may not be known to many, that Abraham Lincoln believed in Woman's Suffrage, and publicly declared himself to that effect. He assuredly would have favored national legislation for the protection of women; to regulate their hours of labor; to guarantee them a minimum wage, at least equal to the cost of subsistence.

He would certainly have thrown the whole force of his tremendous personality against the diabolical horrors of Child Labor, as practiced in virtuous New England today, and more especially in the horrible child-working factories of the South, where their life is a hell worse than a convict's jail. This horrible evil he would not long allow to mock at our boasted humanity, to defy with its heartless greed, the best endeavors of patriots and humanitarians.

And the poor and unprivileged have not only economic rights, but also have intellectual rights of opportunity to acquire the traditional heritage of the mind. There are country colleges where many of our lads can work their way through, and gain an education by their own honest toil. But I know of no institution where all who come are furnished with this opportunity. And I am wondering whether it would not be within the scope of the United States government, to establish a great American University; not so much for the uncommon people, as for the common people; to teach not only the Arts and Sciences, but all professions and careers; where the poor boy might come and labor in the spirit of Ezra and Nehemiah, who built the walls of Jerusalem, with a sword in one hand and a trowel in the other; simultaneously building and battling. So our young men could fight the battle of subsistence, while laying stone upon stone of their intellectual structure.

I believe that Abraham Lincoln, who studied by the light of a blazing pine log, and whose books could be counted on the fingers of one hand, would be heart and soul in favor of establishing a great school of learning, where all the children of the poor could not only learn, but labor also for their livelihood.

And I believe further and finally, that this great man, who, all through his early life, was in the dark shadow of impending war, and who was afterwards plunged into its blackest horrors, would have used every resource of his great wisdom, of his remarkable power over men, to bring nearer the peaceful settlement of all burning issues, not only between nation and nation, but between class and class. For the world is entering into a new epoch. Once the world-wide struggle was for political rights. Then came our great war for the equal civil rights of every man. And now the conflict is beginning on the part of millions of workers, for their industrial rights. We have strikes; and the voluntary self-starvation of the poor, as well as the impoverishment of the rich, who will not yield, be it through pride, or principle.

And the public suffers; and the poor suffer vastly more than the rich. The complex life of a civilized community may be suspended and paralyzed by such an industrial crisis. Power and authority must be used by the national government, to promulgate such a law as that of New Zealand, for the compulsory arbitration of industrial disputes. And while the decision of such a tribunal need not be obligatory, it should at least be rendered, and made public, some time before the strike is allowed to be declared, so that public opinion may be informed by an authority in which it has confidence; and may throw its tremendous influence on one side or on the other. I believe this would have been one of the cardinal aims of this man, whose own horny hands had toiled for years for his daily bread; whose whole heart deeply sympathized with and loved the poor; and who loved fair play and justice even more, as manifested in the right way, the short way, the truly American way of settling these terrible conflicts, that sometimes threaten to cleave our entire nation asunder.

Peace between industrial classes would surely have been his aim and end. And peace between the nations. It would be a crowning glory of our generation, if in his spirit we would achieve a peaceful union with all of the great Powers, if we would agree to discontinue, by mutual consent, the present insane race for preeminence in armies and navies, and thus save the millions that are thus squandered in quickly obsolete engines of destruction; and if we would agree to arbitrate all questions whatsoever, not actually vital, to the existence of our nation.

But if we make treaties, we must keep them. And no one would be more insistent than he, who was the soul of justice and honor, that when we enter into an agreement of plain and unmistakable meaning, like our treaty with England with regard to the Panama Canal, that we should keep it to the letter; even if conditions have changed, and it is not to our material profit to keep our plighted national word. Yet, whether it be profitable or not, it is necessary.

About this, there can be no question. It shames us, and lowers our dignity and good repute in the eyes of all civilized nations, that we do not at present propose to live up to our treaty with England, according to the common acceptance of the meaning of its terms by virtually all impartial and qualified witnesses.

What would Lincoln do today, if he were clothed with his pristine power? This is indeed a question replete with interest and charm. But there is a question still more fascinating. It is this—what would Lincoln BE today? What type of man would most nearly represent him in his essence and deeper self, regardless of the surface qualities, due to his origin and environment; in the elements that are of interest to us, as they bespeak the powerful personality behind them all. I cannot help thinking, that to an important extent he would be, in far-flung vision, in the justice and sanity of his views, in the greatness and thoroughly patriotic inspiration of the ends set before him, much like the man we have chosen to be our ruler now. For he illustrates a splendid and characteristic type of American manhood. He is no man's man; he is his own master. He obeys no dictation; he listens to no illicit suggestion. He is swayed and moved only by the divine passion of righteousness that is sovereign in the man. He is a true American. He not only rules us, but represents the best that is in us. . . .

What he was, what he would be, may we strive to be. May that gaunt and shadowy figure still cheer and hearten the wavering line; still be our captain and our chieftain, as he is our hero and national glory.

Soldiers! This text for us, was a reality for you. Our aspirations were your achievements. We imagine the picture; you beheld the original. You knew him as he was. You beheld the mighty frame that enshrined his tender heart. His rugged and kindly face was known to you. You saw him, with eyes of flesh.

And you recall him now, in his spirit and influence. You remember the sturdy virtues that he inspired or deepened in your valiant hearts—the courage, the patriotism, the self-sacrifice that were his, and yours too. Today brings back those great and glorious days. Today you recall once more those fields of honor and of tragedy. You remember your comrades, your companions who will not return, but who are not forgotten, who sleep in glory. And Fame rears their memorial.

Once more you have entered this House of God, with your flag, our flag, borne before you, the flag of our beloved country. This flag was carried in by fewer than before. Time is gathering toll of your bowed frames and gray heads. And more and more, therefore, do we seek to honor you, does the nation wish to manifest its admiration and reverence for the heroes that were its brave defenders. And therefore we have asked our children here to sing the stirring songs of patriotism; and to look upon your venerable faces; and to see you salute the flag, the colors you have fought and bled for. The youngest are here to look upon our oldest and worthiest men. And their presence will console and animate you, and make you feel that you have not toiled and fought in vain. For upon these young hearts your example and your very countenance shall be impressed; and into their young hands you will commit the heritage that you have won for this nation, that there may be under God a new birth of liberty; that the freedom so painfully won by this great American people shall not perish from the earth.[31]

3. AMERICANISM AND LINCOLN'S SPIRIT

The Bureau of Jewish Education in New York City organized an association of high school students called the "League of the Jewish Youth." The league actively sought to attract adolescents who were enrolled in a formal program of Jewish education as well as those who were "unschooled." The league's overarching mission was to strengthen the Jewish identification of these adolescents.[32]

In 1918, the League of the Jewish Youth held a "Lincoln Program" at New York's Central Jewish Institute.[33] The program focused attention on the responsibilities and obligations of American citizenship. The event's organizers reminded their young attendees to imbibe the spirit of freedom, home, and shared values that the United States offered its Jewish citizenry. At the same time, the adolescents were reminded that, as Jews, they had much to offer America. The program as well as the accompanying tableau reproduced from another event which took place in Milwaukee on May 19, 1919, underscored the sought-for ideal of "blending" Jewish heritage and American life.

As we see from the program itself, Rabbi Jacob Kohn (1881–1968) of New York's Ansche Chesed Synagogue delivered a keynote address titled "A Jewish Conception of Lincoln." Unfortunately, the text of Kohn's address on that occasion does not seem to have survived. However, reproduced below are excerpts from another Lincoln address that Kohn gave as they were reported in the New York Times *in February 1923. Speaking before a meeting of the United Synagogue of America, the congregational body of Conservative Judaism, Kohn expressed grave concern over the American government's approach to reconstruction and reconciliation since World War I. He urged his listeners to consider what Lincoln would do if he could advise the nation. Lincoln would call upon America to behave with "charity, . . . love and good-will" toward all the nations of the world.*

What Is Americanism and What Does It Demand of Us?

Can it demand that we deny who we are? Is it possible that it should ask us to become estranged from our fathers and mothers? Shall it ask us to forget the People from whom we are sprung?

No! For Americanism is something positive, not negative; it demands a loyalty, not a disloyalty.

America demands that we give to it what is finest and most profound in our People's life. What these things are we have sought to inscribe on the emblem of our League. "Torah, Avodah, Gemiluth Hasodim,"[34] symbolize for us all of those spiritual ideals and that spirit of service which we have struggled to develop throughout the forty centuries of our history.

But in no less degree does America demand that we also take from it what is finest and most profound in its own life. And we are gathered here tonight for just this purpose—to gain a little deeper insight into the great things for which America stands.

This, then, is the confession of faith of our League of the Jewish Youth.

Not by negation and neglect of our Jewish souls, but by contributing what is finest in us to America and by taking the finest in America unto ourselves can we become loyal to America.

PROGRAM

1. Star Spangled Banner — *Audience*

2. Our Conception of Americanism
   The League of the Jewish Youth, recited by Rose Goldman

3. Introduction of the Chairman — *Daniel Cogan, Pres. Inter-Club Council*

4. Introductory Address — *Abraham A. Silberberg, Chairman, Social Activities Committee*

5. Violin Solo Concerto No 2. — *Leonard Phillip Geller*

6. Recitation: "The Jesters Recantation" — *Mr. Philip Adler*

7. Vocal Solo — *Miss Rose Rabbach*
   - Swanee River
   - Old Black Joe
   - Comin' through the Rye

8. Address: "A Jewish Conception of Lincoln" — *Rabbi Jacob Kohn*

9. Hatikvah — *Audience*

   Miss Sadie Cheifetz at the piano

10. Dancing[35]

Need of Lincoln's Spirit

His Reconstruction Policy Seen as World's Hope

by Rabbi Kohn

Special to the New York Times

Pittsburgh, Feb. 12—The need today for Lincoln's reconstruction policy as outlined in his second inaugural address, was stressed by Rabbi Jacob Kohn

The Wanderer
finds Liberty
in America

AUDITORIUM MAY-18,1919
MILWAUKEE

KUHLI
Photo.

Americanization pageant, Milwaukee, 1919. For thousands of east European Jewish immigrant children, Lincoln epitomized the true American spirit. Courtesy Wisconsin Historical Society, WHS-5348.

of New York at the annual convention of the United Synagogue of America, which is taking place here today.

"His formula was a simple one," said Rabbi Kohn. "He would proceed with 'malice toward none, with charity for all . . . to do all which may achieve and cherish a just and lasting peace among ourselves and with all nations.' He did not live to see the politicians of his day make mock of the sentiment to which he had pledged the nation. In that he was more fortunate than one of his successors in the presidential office.

"The world is still seeking an effective formula for reconstruction. Can we not imagine Lincoln urging upon the nations, America included, the policy which once he offered to our nation alone in the hour of bitter feud? Of charity, of love and good-will there is but little on earth today; of bigotry and of malice there is a heart-breaking abundance. Old national feuds have been revived and intensified, racial hate and suspicion are being fanned into flame; religious intolerance once more unseats men's reason, so that the better world order of which men have dreamed and for which the youth of the world was called upon to spill its blood seems to have been but a mirage of the human soul.

"The wisest political formulae, the most astute economic plans, will remain abortive unless the spirit in which men undertake the task of reconstruction is that which Lincoln foreshadowed."[36]

4. "LOVE ONE'S FELLOWMEN WITHOUT DISTINCTION OF RACE OR COLOR"

Samuel S. Cohon (1888–1958) immigrated to the United States in 1904 and was ordained at Hebrew Union College in Cincinnati in 1912. In 1921, when the sermon quoted here was written, Cohon served as rabbi of Temple Mizpah in Chicago. A few years later, in 1923, he returned to Cincinnati to become a professor of theology at his alma mater, where he remained until his death. Rabbi Cohon was an important figure in Jewish academic life and published numerous books and articles, many of which focus on the relationship between Judaism and Christianity. He also played an influential role in the development of the "newly revised version" of The Union Prayerbook, *which was first published in 1940.[37]*

In the following excerpts from Cohon's sermon of February 11, 1921, titled "The Character of Abraham Lincoln," Cohon took aim at the rise of nativist sentiment that plagued American society during and after World War I. The rabbi had little use for the wave of xenophobia and, especially, the exclusionary nationalism that was termed "100 percent Americanism." It is also interesting to note how, in 1921, Cohon was decrying "all those who seek to strengthen the barriers that stand between the White man and the Negro" as well as those who fostered religious prejudice. Lincoln's religious convictions shaped his "life-mission" and spurred him to expand "human liberty." America and American Jewry, he asserted, should follow Lincoln's personal example in their effort to live religious lives.

The Character of Abraham Lincoln

Lincoln affiliated himself with no Christian denomination, but he was a thoroughly religious man. The Bible was his chief companion through life. He read it as a boy and drew inspiration from its pages as a man. By it he was sustained in his doubts and guided in his difficulties. From it he learned that to believe in a living God, to love God with all heart and soul, and to love one's fellowmen without distinction of race or color, is the whole of religion. His entire outlook upon life and upon the problems of the day, was colored by ideals of the Bible. In his farewell address to his friends at Springfield in 1861, he expressed himself in these words: "I now leave, not knowing when or whether I shall return, with a task before me greater than that which rested upon Washington. Without the assistance of that divine Being who ever attended him, I cannot succeed. With that assistance, I cannot fail. Trusting in Him, who can go with me and remain with you and be everywhere for good, let us confidently hope that all will be well." In approaching the great issues of the day, he ceaselessly sought the light of God. And he gave evidence to his faith, in his public addresses, which are Biblical not only in language but also in spirit. In fact, he appears like a character from the Hebrew Bible. His Inaugural Address and his proclamations display a profound trust in the mercy and justice of God. Like a priest he seeks atonement for the people, and like a prophet he chastises them and leads them to summits of religious aspiration. He pleaded with them: "We have grown in numbers, wealth, and power, as no other nation has grown; but we have forgotten God. . . . We have been the recipients of the choicest bounties of heaven. Intoxicated by unbroken success we have become . . . too proud to pray to the God that made us. We have been preserved these many years in peace and prosperity. It behooves us, then, . . . to confess our national sins, and to pray for clemency and forgiveness." In public as in personal crises, he sought strength and consolation in prayer.

His sterling honesty and firm faith in God and in right, shaped his life-mission of securing the foundations of national Union and of human liberty. . . .

His broad sympathies put to shame our one hundred percenters who are ready to deny their fellow citizen's freedom of thought and of expression, who seek to promote the welfare of our country through jealous intrigues against neighboring lands. His big heart that beat with love for the downtrodden and the disinherited masses, stands out as an eternal warning against those who perpetuate the institution of slavery under changed forms. It warns all those who seek to strengthen the barriers that stand between the White man and the Negro and who sharpen the prejudices of men of one religious denomination against those of another. To all forward-looking men throughout the world, his faith in democracy is like a pillar of fire illumining their way through our trying days of reconstruction. And his simple yet profound faith in and love of God are an inspiration and a benediction to all who seek the Lord and rely upon His guidance.[38]

5. A JEWISH LODESTAR

For some rabbis, Abraham Lincoln served as a Jewish role model. According to Rabbi Philip A. Langh (1895–1946) of Anshe Emes[39] Congregation in Chicago, President Lincoln was "the nearest to the Jewish genius in character, in spirit, in ideals." Langh implied that American Jews would be well served to make Lincoln a Jewish lodestar. The American Jew was "only paying homage to the memory of the greatest [American leader] of them all" when they emulated Lincoln's Jewish ideals: compassion (rachmonos), *humility* (anovos), *and integrity* (t'mimus).

Jewish Ideals in Lincoln

"Lincoln is not a type. He stands alone—no ancestors, no fellows, no successors."

These words uttered about the great emancipator are of particular meaning to the Jew. There is no leading figure in American history whose character so much approximates the genius of the Jew as does that of Abraham Lincoln, whose life so expresses those traits that have ever been held up and idealized by the Jew.

In reading of the life of Lincoln, the student of Jewish literature is immediately reminded of the figure of Hillel, the great rabbi and scholar, who lived in Palestine shortly before the destruction of the second Jewish commonwealth, and who later became its patriarch. A striking parallel can be drawn of the lives of the two men. Both came from poor and lowly homes and both rose to the highest position within the gift of their people. One spent his youthful days pioneering in the unsettled lands of the middle west, clearing woods, building humble log cabins and out of the untamed wilderness endeavoring to eke out a mere existence. The other's early years were passed in Babylonia, regarded at the time by the older Jewish settlement of Palestine as a barbarous land without culture and civilization.

As boys, both labored at the same occupation—Lincoln a rail splitter, Hillel, the wood chopper. Both were thirsty for knowledge; in their love of learning both were typically Jewish. In the country where Lincoln was brought up, there were few books obtainable. Whenever he heard of one anywhere, far or near, he would go on foot to borrow it. "I have read all the books I have ever heard of in the country for a circuit of fifty miles," writes the young Lincoln. And of Hillel, we well know that fascinating story of the lad who, refused admission into the academy because unable to pay the fee, climbed to the skylight over the class rooms, lying there covered by a blanket of snow, yet unmindful of the cold, while drinking in the words of living waters that issued below from the lips of the great teachers, Shmaya and Abtalyon.[40]

Both were known for their infinite patience; for that true humility; for the golden gentleness that the Jews call "anovo." Amid their exalted position they each retained a simplicity that was genuine, a humanness that was touching. Both would mingle unassumingly with everyone, listening to their lowliest wants and attending to their humblest petitions. When Lincoln was asked by his advisors to send away a throng that was tiring him with its petty troubles, he said: "They don't want much and they get so little. Each one considers his business of great importance. I know how I should feel if I were in their place."

And of Hillel similarly, "Be gentle as Hillel" became a common proverb. "My humility is my greatness and my greatness is my humility," was one of his sayings. In the minds of a loving posterity Hillel became the symbol for patience. A man once came to him and, wishing to scoff at religion, challenged him to teach him Judaism while standing on one foot. He had previously gone to Shammai, the contemporary and fellow scholar of Hillel, but who, incensed at the impudence, had thrown the stranger out. But Hillel was gentle and so he said to him: "Do not do unto others what thou wouldst not that others do unto thee. This is the whole of the Torah. The rest is mere commentary." This recalls again Lincoln's summary of religion when he declared: "Whenever any church will inscribe over its altar as qualification of membership the statement, 'Thou shalt love the Lord, thy God, with all thy heart, with all thy soul and with all thy might,' and 'Love thy neighbor as thyself'—that church will I join with all my heart and with all my soul."[41]

Both were given at the hands of an admiring people the highest gift within their power, one the presidency of the Sanhedrin, the other the leadership of a continent. Hillel, when elected over and above many rivals, humbly said to them: "It is not because I am cleverer than you that I have been appointed head of the Sanhedrin." Witness Lincoln's beautiful remark to his compatriots when in February, 1861, leaving Springfield to assume his arduous duties at the national capitol, he said: "Without the assistance of the Divine Being, I cannot succeed: with that assistance I cannot fail."

There are other qualities of character that endear Lincoln to the student of Jewish thought. Lincoln was deeply religious, imbued by a sense of profound piety and feeling the ever-presence of God. For a mind reared in the environs of western America like his, it was unusual to have developed the conception of national sin. Lincoln regarded the Civil War as a punishment of God upon America, both north and south, for the sin of having enslaved a whole people. In his second inaugural he said: "The Almighty has his own purposes. . . . He gives to both north and south this terrible war as the woe due to those by whom the offense came. . . . As was said three thousand years ago, so still it must be said, 'The judgments of the Lord are true and righteous altogether.'"

In the president of the United States to find the consciousness of national sin, of a sin that calls for collective atonement, is to say the least, surprising. It was not the scolding of an Isaiah of old, or of Amos—not the rebuke of rabbi or priest—not the utterance of an evangelist or missionary, nor the fanaticism of a religious zealot, but it was Lincoln the commander-in-chief of the armies of the north, who said: "We have grown in numbers, wealth and power, as no other nation has ever grown. But we have forgotten God. We have been the recipients of the choicest bounties of heaven. Intoxicated by unbroken success we have become too proud to pray to the God that made us. We have been preserved in peace and prosperity. It behooves us then to confess our national sins and to pray for clemency and forgiveness." Nor were these words addressed to a camp of contrite sinners, nor to a church in solemn worship assembled, but it was a national proclamation to the millions of citizenry by the president of their republic. It expresses a "tmimus," a religious piety characteristically Jewish.

As arbiter over the fate and destiny of millions of soldiers, it oft fell to the lot of Lincoln to exercise clemency to condemned men and to grant pardons, a privilege of which he oft availed himself and for which he was much censured. But he could not help it. He had the quality of "rachmonos"—the quality of mercy—in a large measure. Is there a finer story extant of Lincoln than that of the pardon granted to William Scott, the young soldier found asleep while on sentry duty and sentenced to be shot? The president in response to the latter's appeal said: "My boy, you are not going to be shot tomorrow. I am going to send you back to your regiment. But I have been put to a good deal of trouble on your account . . . and what I want to know is, how are you going to pay my bill?" The young soldier answered and spoke of various ways in which he could raise money to pay the president. Then Lincoln put his hands on the lad's shoulders, looked into his face as though sorry and said: "My boy, my bill is a very large one. Your friends cannot pay it, nor your bounty, nor your farm nor all your comrades. There is only one man in all the world who can pay it and his name is William Scott. If from this day William Scott does his duty, so that if I were there when he came to die, he could look me in the face as he does now and say, I have kept my promise, and I have done my duty as a soldier, then my debt will be paid. Will you make that promise and try to keep it?" Some months later the young soldier, while rescuing wounded from the firing line, was shot mortally and thus paid the full measure of devotion that his commander-in-chief had asked of him.

The late lamented Solomon Schechter, who wrote a remarkable essay on Lincoln showing a wonderful insight into the genius of the martyred president, pointed out that Lincoln's inimitable faculty of story telling and using parables is thoroughly akin to the Jewish characteristic of using the "moshol" or "comparison," and the "maaseh" or "story." There have been written volumes of stories and parables attributed to the master story teller, that he uttered—and did not utter—and this aspect of the great emancipator is one of the most attractive.

But whether in his profound religious piety, whether in his quality of "rachmonos," whether in his true "anovo" or humility, whether in his craving for knowledge, whether in his talent for "moshol," whether in a life strangely parallel to that of our own Hillel, the close kinship of Lincoln with Jewish ideals is evident. It is not disrespectful of the other great men of American history; it is only paying homage to the memory of the greatest of them all to say that the nearest to the Jewish genius in character, in spirit, in ideals, was Abraham Lincoln.

And so it is indeed true what has been said of him. "Lincoln is not a type. He stands alone—no ancestors, no fellows, no successors."[42]

6. GERMANY DESPERATELY NEEDS A LINCOLN

In February 14, 1933, the Jewish Advocate *published excerpts from an address Rabbi Stephen S. Wise delivered to mark Lincoln's birthday. He used the occasion to comment on contemporary events—national elections in Germany that were scheduled to take place some two weeks later, on March 5. Adolf Hitler had already been named chancellor of Germany in January 1933, so there was every reason to believe the Germans would vote Hitler and his Nazi Party into office.*

Wise used Lincoln as a foil for Hitler. He began by comparing the values that Lincoln and Hitler espoused, and then the rabbi extended this parallel by comparing the moral fiber of America to that of Germany. The rabbi made it clear that in spite of the fact that Germany desperately needed a Lincoln in 1933, the nation would almost certainly select his moral antipode. Wise concluded by asserting that under crisis and pressure, Americans have always chosen the greatest of leaders to extricate them from the difficulties they faced. On the eve of the German elections, Wise predicted the Germans would turn their backs on their "great and classic tradition of learning and freedom" by handing over their government to the likes of Hitler.

Germany Chooses Hitler—America Chose Lincoln

New York, Feb. 14 (Special Correspondence)—In the course of the address by Rabbi Stephen S. Wise before the Free Synagogue at Carnegie Hall on Lincoln's birthday, Dr. Wise said:

"To marvel at the surrender of Germany to Hitlerism is not to interfere in German policies. Germany is free to choose any sort of government from extreme right to extreme left. Germany may deem it wise and needful, at the behest of its captains of industry, to choose a regime which shall seek to destroy the German Socialist and Communist groups. These are German, not American problems, save as a problem and its solution in one land has its reverberations in every other land.

"If we deal with Hitler, it is not because he is Fascist, or Nazist, not because he is in favor of revision of the Versailles peace treaty or the Polish corridor. These are world problems and our interest in them is that of Americans and humans. But insofar as Hitlerism includes a definitely formulated and activated anti-Jewish policy, we are deeply concerned, and we believe that Americans, irrespective of faith and racial origin, will come to share our concern touching the danger to the German republic of forswearing its enlightened and basic policy of equal and inviolate rights for all its citizens.

"Nor will Americans of faith and race other than our own view with tolerance or equanimity the threatened invasion of Jewish rights and the continuance of assaults upon Jewish life and property by the followers of Hitler. Jews are not strangers nor aliens in Germany. They have lived in Germany for a thousand years, they have been among Germany's builders and creators. Some of Israel's greatest sons have been among the noblest figures in the intellectual and spiritual life of Germany. Jews, wherever they may dwell, whether in Germany or in America, can hardly be expected to learn with unconcern that the fundamental rights of Jews are endangered, Jews whose residence in Germany goes back a thousand years and more, by the leader of a political party whose German citizenship dates back one year.

"Let it not be thought that only Jewish rights are imperiled, though these are most gravely assailed in theory and in substance alike by the Hitlerist party.

"Hitlerism may do unlimited damage to Jews, but it will do still more hurt to the German Republic and the German name. The world is beginning to turn with sympathy and understanding to the German people who have waged a valiant battle for their own rehabilitation and that sympathy will be alienated, that sympathy will be lost if Germany should give carte blanche to a group of men who have boasted that Jews must be degraded to a lower status of citizenship, that Jews must be virtually eliminated from the callings in which they have fruitfully and beneficently served for centuries.

"In saying that America chose Lincoln and Germany is in danger of choosing Hitler, I would not pretend that America has always chosen Lincolns and Germany has always chosen Hitlers. I do, however, maintain that in the time of America's most awful crisis, America chose its greatest son, chose him who alone stands as the peer of the 'father of his country.' America chose Lincoln who, at a time of fratricidal strife and bitterest divisiveness brought to the sundered halves of his country and its people a program of reconciliation, a policy of infinite forbearance. Thus Lincoln said: 'With charity to all and with malice to none.' Germany chooses Hitler, who, whatever the rightfulness or wrongfulness of his political-economic program substitutes for the maxim of Lincoln 'With charity for Nordics and malice to Semites.' Such a principle, such a program, such a policy cannot serve a great nation. A house is never served by him who divides it against itself. A nation can only be served by apostles of forbearance and understanding and conciliation. Lincoln was such an apostle. It were well for Germany, with its great and classic tradition of learning and freedom, to bethink itself before it embarks upon an adventure which will mean that its decisions touching its inner affairs shall be spoken by the sword."[43]

7. HOW WOULD LINCOLN SERVE?

Dr. Samuel H. Goldenson (1878–1962), rabbi of Congregation Emanu-El of New York City, exuded a palpably grim disposition as he spoke from his pulpit on the 130th anniversary of Lincoln's birth, February 12, 1939. He was distressed by world events. During the course of the preceding year, Hitler's behavior had become increasingly ominous. The Anschluss, Germany's annexation of Austria, took place on March 13, 1938. On September 30, 1938, France, Britain, and Italy handed Germany the Sudetenland. The Nazis ransacked more than 1,000 synagogues and broke the windows of more than 7,500 Jewish businesses on

"Kristallnacht" (the "Night of Broken Glass") on November 9–10, 1938. Little wonder why Goldenson began his sermon by observing, "I doubt whether at any time since [Lincoln] passed into the Great Beyond has the anniversary [of his birth] been so significant, has the anniversary been fraught with so much sense of the relevance of his life for our day, as in this year 1939."

What would Lincoln do if he was alive in the year 1939? Goldenson maintained that Lincoln would live by the precepts of "moral reason." Contrasting Lincoln and his manifest respect for reason and for the values of human individualism with the mindless and wanton cruelty of modern dictators, Goldenson viewed Lincoln as an "exemplar of democracy and humanity" in a modern world that stood on the brink of war. "If you and I feel him more," the rabbi concluded, "if you and I live by his nature and his vision more—the world will become a better place to live in."

If Abraham Lincoln Were Alive Today: A Sunday Sermon

We have had many anniversaries since Lincoln died but I doubt whether at any time since he passed into the Great Beyond has the anniversary been so significant, has the anniversary been fraught with so much sense of the relevance of his life for our day, as in this year 1939. And why? Because during recent months especially there has developed for us the full realization of a type of thinking about human beings, about human life, about human society that contrasts itself so completely with Abraham Lincoln and his ways of thinking about man and man's place in the economy of the world. Of all the great figures in history I doubt whether there has ever been a leader of men, aside from Moses himself, who constitutes such an antithesis, such a complete antithesis, between himself and the dictators of our day. He stands at the opposite pole from them. Every aspect in which he may be compared with them—his personal qualities of mind and heart, his conception of the nature of man, his thought about life in general, his philosophy of human welfare, his political policies and program, and his personal commitments—all of them range him upon the opposite side, completely opposed to the men who are known as the dictators in modern society. And this morning let me indicate the major differences between Abraham Lincoln as a leader of men, as a great political spokesman, and the dictators of our day.

To Abraham Lincoln the source of all value was found in the nature and the worth and the dignity of the individual man, the concrete human being without reference to race or creed or color. He loved the individual and all his thinking began with his estimate of the value of the individual, his respect for a human soul because it was a human soul. . . .

You know, friends, this makes me wonder what has happened to society. I often say to myself: How can we explain some of the things that are happening in our day? You know what happens if a sorrow comes into your own family: A child dies, a father or mother dies, a husband or wife dies—how we become grief stricken. Very often the world becomes totally dark for us because of the sorrow through the bereavement of a beloved one. See how precious human life is to us and how much our happiness and our sorrow are bound up with human lives, with men and women that are close to us. How precious they are to us. And I ask myself: What happens in human society that enables men and women, especially men—let me leave out the women—enables men to plan war upon a large scale? It is an enterprise in which one group of men actually try to kill another group of men as if these persons who are killed in war cease to be brothers and sisters, cease to be husbands and wives, cease to be fathers and mothers. And yet that is exactly what is happening in modern society—planning war on a large scale as if human beings cease to be precious.

Now Abraham Lincoln could not think that way. His eye was always fastened upon the concrete person who is the center of a network of relationship. Now, friends, contrast this point of view of vision with the central doctrine of the dictator states. What is the source and seat of value in dictatorships? Not the individual person, not the concrete human being, not the man or the woman as a person, but rather the state, the totality of something that they call the state. See how impersonal it is. See how far-off it is. See what a complete change of attitude there is. The state is the important thing. The state must be served. The state must be saved. The state must be worked for—whatever that is. And the result is that the individual is lost sight of. He becomes merely the means, the tool, an instrument to serve the state itself. That is the first and the first great difference between Lincoln's thinking and the thinking of the dictators. On the one hand you have man the concrete. On the other you have the state, the impersonal and the abstract.

. . . And what is the contrast to Abraham Lincoln at this particular point. How do the dictators serve their cause? Not through rational thinking but through force—the use of sheer power. Not mentality, not morality but sheer physical force. There is here a throwback to the earlier days when men had not achieved the maturity of thoughtful and responsible persons. And let me tell you that that is the reason why there has developed in the recent thinking of the dictators a rather new policy. Or if it is not altogether new it has been developed with greater emphasis than ever. And what is that new policy? It is the public policy of hatred—hatred as a public policy. Why? Because after all the average person, no matter where he lives, whether he lives in England or in America or in France or in Germany or in Italy, the average person has something good in him, something kind, something soft, something lovely in him. The average person is not a brute. He does not like force to be used on him and he does not like to use force on another. And because the average person does not like the use of force and the agency of power, that person has to be indoctrinated so that he will be moved to be something different than he normally is. That is the reason why there is an effort to fill his heart with hatred. It is only when he becomes filled with hatred and fear that he can use force, that he will be willing to use force. So we have in modern society hatred and fear as new public policies.

Oh, how this contrasts itself with Abraham Lincoln. There is no man in the history of our civilization who detested hatred more than Abraham Lincoln. Possibly you recall the utterance that he gave in the very midst of the Civil War. Those that knew him said that he was the unhappiest man in the world during the war because the kindliest of men, the simplest of men, found himself engaged in a business that was so contrasting to his nature. Knowing that he was right in his eagerness to save these common black folk from bondage, knowing all these things yet nothing compensated him for the realization that human beings were hurting one another, even murdering one another. And in the midst of the Civil War during his inaugural address he came forth with one of the noblest utterances of all time: "With malice toward none and charity towards all." Just think of it. "With malice toward none and charity towards all."

When have we heard the word of charity last in the modern world. When has one of these dictators ever spoken of charity or appreciation or things like that. Here is Abraham Lincoln, the gentlest and the kindest of persons. Why. Because force was not in his nature. He would not believe in force. Rather he believed in moralized freedom.

And the next contrast that we find between him and the dictators is in his insistence throughout that the supreme guarantee for human beings living together is that they should live under law—live under law—and to him law was the collective will of the people themselves. No human being is ever secure in a society, who does not live in a society, that believes in law, that has a constitution of mutual understanding and mutual respect. Throughout his period, even during the great war, many a suggestion was made to him to interpret the law differently to gain his advantage or to speed up or accelerate his purposes by changing the basic law. And always he resisted it. He opposed it on the ground that ultimately the sole source and guarantee of the individual is to uphold the law as it is. And if a change is required, that change must come in the regular way—through the provisions made in the basic law.

Compare this with what is happening in the dictator states. Those unhappy people living in Germany or in Italy or in Japan. They do not know from day to day what may happen. A new decree may be made at any time, at any time, by the individual and not through the operation of the regular forces in accordance with a basic law. Here then is another great difference. [In] the law there is the expression of an individual will. It is the expression of an individual purpose. It is the expression of the commitment of a single mind that speaks of itself as the arbiter of the will and the destiny of the people. It is altogether unthinkable for a man of Abraham Lincoln's character to assume such a role. Why?

This brings me to the last aspect of the difference, for after all this includes all the rest: the personal difference. Abraham Lincoln had two major qualities—personal qualities—honesty and humility. You know, friends, very often the complex things of life, the difficult problems in human relations, derive from very simple traits of nature. Abraham Lincoln was an honest person. He was known as honest Abe. And the honesty had to do with two things: his love of facts, his love of reality. He had an eye for things as they were. And then a great passion to state what he saw accurately, honestly. That is a double quality: realism as to the outside; self-criticism within. And so whatever he thought about any problem he stated that problem so simply, so directly, that the commonest man understood. He drew his illustrations, he drew his stories, from the things that everyone can see and understand and feel. And so he was known as "Honest Abe." And then too Abraham Lincoln was one of the humblest of men. It is true he was born in a lowly place, born in a lowly capacity. Why, friends, there are any number of persons who are born in lowly places and are not humble. Abraham Lincoln liked to do two things: He liked to remind himself of his lowly birth and he liked to remind others of his lowly birth. Sometimes we recall our lowly birth but keep it to ourselves. Abraham Lincoln had a way of calling attention to it because of his great honesty, because there was a lesson in it, because he wanted to challenge others to be humble of the lowly state of most people in life. Most people do not occupy the important positions in life. Most people in life are not fitted for them. And Abraham Lincoln felt that it would help him if he reminded himself and others that he was one of them.

With such qualities one cannot become a dictator. Abraham Lincoln would check his utterances and very often with the effect they had upon the lowliest and the commonest. You know, friends, that he was one of the great debaters in American history. He always submitted his point of view, his line of reasoning to others, not only that he might be sure of himself but that they might know exactly how he thought and felt. Now that is a point of view, an aspect of thinking, that is entirely different from the dictators. Here then is Abraham Lincoln. He lives for us again as he should live and I hope he will live throughout the ages. What a great asset he has been. What a great challenge he is. And I hope and pray that the time will come when he will become an influence in the lives of others across the sea as he has been here. And may the time come even here when he shall be more deeply favored, more genuinely loved, than ever before. If you and I understand him more, if you and I feel him more, if you and I live by his nature and his vision more—the world will become a better place to live in, and will become the exemplar of democracy and humanity than which nothing else is more needed in our day.

Amen.[44]

8. FAITH IN DEMOCRACY IS AS ETERNAL AS FAITH IN ONE GOD

Like his colleague Samuel Goldenson, Rabbi Ferdinand M. Isserman of Temple Israel in St. Louis advised his congregation to look to Lincoln as they faced an impending world war. On Friday evening, December 29, 1939, Isserman was inspired to speak about Lincoln after he had seen a local performance of Robert Sherwood's play Abe Lincoln in Illinois.[45] *The theme of the rabbi's sermon was the fate of democracy in a world that was facing a rise of fascism.*

In his conclusion, Isserman compares Lincoln to Moses, Socrates, Jesus, and John Huss, all of whom were reformers who, like Lincoln, were ahead of their times. They all faced bitter opposition during their lifetimes, yet future generations eventually learned to revere their wisdom. "No American is more significant," Isserman asserts, than Lincoln, and he challenged his congregation to do what Lincoln would have done: "preserve and . . . protect that liberty and that democracy" for which Lincoln and so many of their predecessors fought and died.

Robert Sherwood's *Abe Lincoln in Illinois*

It is being urged today that there is no guarantee that democracy is the last word on government. Elemental governmental forms have changed in the past. Why shall we assume that they will not change in the future? Why should we take it for granted that the particular form of government that is ours now, has about it the stamp of eternity. Judaism is now more than twenty centuries old. Its belief in One God and one humanity was created by Moses and the prophets many, many, generations ago. In all the centuries that have passed, there have been many changes in the world. Boundary lines have been changed. Continents have been settled. Peoples have migrated. Languages have appeared and disappeared. Power has been wielded by different empires. Feudalism, nationalism, capitalism have held sway over economic systems. Yet midst all the flux and change of history, the worship of One God, the faith in one humanity, in Judaism, and even in Christianity has remained unchanged. Why? Because there is eternal truth and in eternal truth there is no change. Here are the limits to which man can go in religion. Here are the highest peaks which mortal mind and imagination can ascend. What monotheism is in the field of religion, democracy is in the field of government. The right of every man to govern himself, and the recognition that every man has inalienable rights of life, liberty and the pursuit of happiness, are the highest in government and therefore shall not pass away. Abraham Lincoln sensed that in his age. We must sense that in our age. Changes will come where there are imperfections. Changes may come in methods of government, with regards to proportional representation, with regards to the cabinet form of government, with regards to the tenure of office of president or of judges, but the concept that men have the God-given right to share in the government, there can be no improvement and there will be no change. The faith in democracy is as eternal as the faith in one God. That Lincoln knew. That our generation must know.

In the past few years, we have heard talk that democracy is doomed, that the future belongs to dictatorship. That talk is diminishing. The longer dictatorships endure, the more will they discredit themselves and the more will they indicate the superiority of democracy. Dictatorship both of the left and of the right, have revealed their utter brutality, their lack of moral scruples. Germany with its invasion of Czecho-Slovakia, Austria and Poland. Italy with its invasion of Ethiopia and Albania. Russia with its inhumanitarian attack upon Finland. Dictatorships have brought war. Dictatorships have denied their people fundamental rights. Dictatorships degrade men by treating them like beasts. Dictatorships despise human beings. Dictatorships are inefficient. Dictatorships are indifferent to human life. That we have realized and thus we are more than ever aware of the efficiency, of the superiority and the blessings of democratic form of government. . . .

Lincoln's religion was assailed in his day. When asked by the clergyman with what denomination he was affiliated, Lincoln replied that he was affiliated with no one denomination, although in Washington he did attend the Presbyterian church. He replied, to his questioner, that when he finds as a church whose creed is, "Love the Lord with all thy heart and thy neighbor as thyself," that, that church he would join. This, to the clergyman was atheism. Most clergymen today would recognize that Lincoln was voicing high religion. If Lincoln lived in St. Louis with his religious views he would be welcome in many churches. There are still those in our midst, however, who still believe that only their conception of religion is correct, that only those are religious that believe as they do. They would imprison religion in the cell of one creed, in the jail of one denomination. They would march it in lockstep to the cadence of one melody and would robe it with the vestments of one form of ecclesiasticism. They would still call Lincoln an infidel. Thomas Jefferson's religion was like that of Lincoln's. He too was called atheist and infidel in his generation. The religion of Jefferson and of Lincoln is the religion of the future. They were ahead of the pygmied, ecclesiastics of their own day.

. . . There are those who think that he was fortunate in dying as he did, before he was compelled to confront the difficulties of reconstruction, its havoc, its despair, its confusion, its dishonesty. He died before he was charged with the failure of reconstruction. Though many believed that if Lincoln had lived, many of the evils that still plague the south, would have been eliminated. According to most of his contemporaries, Lincoln was a failure. A man who did not fit in. A man who did not belong. Unhappy at home, unhappy in his career. Hated by his associates and the cabinet, hated by most of the influential men of the day. According to his own lights, he failed. But sometimes, to fail in life is to succeed, and to succeed in life is to fail. Moses, the Hebrew emancipator, was buried in an unknown grave. To his generation he was a failure. Jesus was crucified to the cross. To his generation he seemed a failure. Socrates was executed by the people of Athens. To them he seemed to be a failure. John Huss was burned at the stake. And so on throughout the past. The failures of one age become the martyrs and the hero[e]s of history. Lincoln was a failure in his age, but to posterity, no American is more significant. His whole life is the history of young America, its promise and its hope. His struggle and his martyrdom remain a challenge to America and to the world, to preserve and to protect that liberty and that democracy for all mankind on the altar of which Lincoln's life was offered.[46]

9. IMAGINING LINCOLN IN THE 1950S

After World War II, American Jewish leaders continued to use Lincoln as a moral touch-stone for social action. During the height of the Cold War and McCarthy eras, Rabbi Charles E. Shulman (1900–1968) addressed himself to the question "What would Lincoln have said?," specifically about American politics in the early 1950s. Shulman told his con-gregation that Lincoln would have become a bitter opponent to what Shulman regarded as the degradation of the Republican Party that Lincoln himself had helped to establish. He urged his listeners to speak out in opposition to the same wrongs that Lincoln decried: racial inequality, McCarthyism, the Korean War, and the general climate of fear that had gripped the nation at the century's midpassage. "American superiority," Shulman declared, could not be won through national isolationism or by expansionary military power. It must be achieved "in terms of the spirit" that Abraham Lincoln epitomized. If Lincoln was living in 1951, the rabbi concluded, he would still be fighting for "a new birth of freedom." Americans in every era must take up that same "Lincolnian ideal" that, according to Shulman, has remained our national destiny.

Lincoln's Message for Our Times

February 9, 1951

Four score and seven years ago last November 19th a lean and sad eyed man took a slip of paper from his pocket and stepped forward on a wood platform that had been built in the cemetery [*sic*] at Gettysburg. There were ten thousand people present. They had already listened for two hours to an oration by the noted orator of the time—Edward Everett of Boston. Lincoln wondered whether his remarks would be effective. In a high pitched voice he began his speech, a short speech—two and a half minutes—that ended with the words "that this nation, under God, shall have a new birth of freedom, and that government of the people, by the people and for the people shall not perish from the earth."

With those words the Gettysburg address was history.

History records some curious immediate reactions to that address. Proph-ets are not honored in their lifetime. Few thought much of his words, as few appreciated the man. Had not Lincoln himself said in his speech "the world will little note nor long remember what we say here . . ."?

The Harrisburg Patriot—the newspaper printed nearest to the scene at Gettysburg had this to say about the speech:

"We pass over the silly remarks of the President. For the credit of the nation we are willing that the veil of oblivion shall be dropped over them and that they shall no more be repeated or thought of . . ."

The Venerable London Times across the Atlantic said: "Anything more dull or commonplace it would not be easy to produce."

Time rendered different judgments on that two and a half minute address of Lincoln's. The speech is now cast in bronze on the walls of Oxford College in England as one of the truly great utterances of the English language.

It is more recognizable than the Declaration of Independence.

Anyone in America who has had an elementary school education knows the address.

It is more familiar to Americans than the first stanza of the Star Spangled Banner.

I. Four score years and seven have now passed since Lincoln's famous "Four Score" address. Now as we approach Lincoln's birthday we might ask ourselves the question: How fares it with the land conceived in liberty and dedicated to the proposition that all men are created equal?

The answer is: Some of the things Lincoln had envisaged have come to pass. This nation is united in many things. It is an indissoluble union of States.

It has achieved incredible wealth.

It has assumed leadership of incalculable proportions unwillingly and hesitatingly—leadership greater than [e]ven Lincoln could have for[e]seen during the Civil War.

But the problems that have to do with the angels of our better nature are still unsettled. They still beset us.

Let us list a few:

1. The Negro problem which divided North and South still divides us. In the month of February, Linco[l]n's Birthday, which, incidentally is not recognized in some southern States, the National Association for the Advancement of Colored People protested in vain to the State of Virginia against the execution of seven negroes for rape—stating no white man ever so convicted had ever been executed in the State of Virginia.

2. Freedom is a confused thing in our land when hysteria and fear rule.

We are afraid of the Russians

We are afraid of communism

We are afraid of our own neighbors

We are afraid of ourselves

We are afraid of our own immortal documents of freedom. In a world shrunken as it is our own hearts and minds shrink instead of expanding to meet the challenge.

3. The Great Republican Party whose banner was carried so nobly by Abraham Lincoln, gives frightened counsel of retreat to its adherents. Marquis Childs, able commentator and observer in Washington tells us in this month of Lincoln's birthday that the current optimism of the Republican party for capturing the Presidency in the next election in 1952 and which gives this party leadership confidence is THEIR BELIEF THAT THEY HAVE A GIMMICK WHICH CANNOT FAIL.

The gimmick? Senator [Joseph] McCarthy of Wisconsin and the technique of the big smear. McCarthy received more applause at the Washington Rally starting the Republican campaign than did Mr. Robert Taft.

What is the intent of the gimmick? Childs tells us. IT IS A STOP AT NOTHING technique which seems to ardent Republicans long frustrated in defeat, a heaven-sent answer to their prayer. McCarthy is now in a place of high counsels and invested with power on the senate Sub-committee having charge of appropriations through which he can conduct increasing guerilla warfare against the State Department and American foreign policy.

AND THIS AT A TIME WHEN THE NATIONS OF THE SHRUNKEN WORLD ARE LOOKING TO AMERICA FOR LEADERSHIP AND SEEKING TO FIND FAITH IN THEMSELVES THROUGH FAITH IN THE GREAT DEMOCRACY FATHERED BY WASHINGTON AND BROTHERED BY LINCOLN!

4. And if we would discern the character of the Republican leadership symbolized by Senator McCarthy and the press of the nation behind him which caters to the fears, the prejudices of people, we might, in passing, take note of the remarks of this particular senator as well as the huge one page large type editorial that appeared recently in the Hearst Press.

McCarthy accused everyone and every institution not on his approved list of being communist and did so in terms which fall outside the libel orbit. He added that administration leaders are fighting communism abroad "to disguise their sell out to communism at home."

And the Hearst editorial? I let you judge it under their title: "THE ONE WORLD MIND"

The astonishing capacity for self-deception possessed by the advocates of world government is perfectly demonstrated in Senator [Estes] Kefauver's selection of this particular time to present a "federal Union resolution" in Congress. Senator Kefauver's resolution calls for an international "Federal Convention" to be held this year. IT WOULD AUTHORIZE PRESIDENT TRUMAN TO INVITE THE DEMOCRACIES WHICH SPONSORED THE NORTH ATLANTIC TREATY TO MEET WITH DELEGATES FROM THE UNITED STATES. AND THESE DELEGATES WOULD EXPLORE HOW FAR THEIR PEOPLES AND THE PEOPLES OF SUCH OTHER DEMOCRACIES AS THE CONVENTION MAY INVITE CAN APPLY

THEM WITHIN THE FRAMEWORK OF THE UNITED NATIONS [AND] THE PRINCIPLES OF FREE FEDERAL UNION.

What Senator Kefauver is actually proposing is that THE UNITED STATES SUMMON THE NATIONS OF WESTERN EUROPE AND OFFER TO ABOLISH ITSELF AS A NATION, SURRENDERING ITS SOVEREIGN POWERS TO THOSE NATIONS. As allies of the United States these nations have been weak and unreliable, as friends they have been faithless. Senator Kefauver and 26 of his colleagues in the Senate sponsor a proposal that the people of the United States invite those defaulting nations to govern us.

They would impose their socialism in place of our republican self-government, extract taxes from us as they pleased, draft our men for their armies, our women for their factories, appropriate the bulk of our productive wealth for their own enrichment.

II. WHAT WOULD LINCOLN HAVE SAID TO SUCH UTTERANCES AS those of Hoover, McCarthy, Taft, [William Randolph] Hearst and others who ostensibly are the voices of the Republican Party to which Lincoln belonged?

Here is one of his well known utterances in reply to the question:

"WHAT CONSTITUTES THE BULWARK OF OUR OWN LIBERTY AND INDE-PENDENCE? It is not our army and navy. Our defense is the spirit which prizes liberty and the heritage of all men, in all lands everywhere. Destroy this spirit and you have planted the seeds of despotism at your door. Accustomed to trampling on the rights of others you have lost the genius of your own independence and become the fit subject of the first cunning tyrant who rises among you."

B) When one delves into Lincoln's writings he is immediately struck with the truth that although Americans have not been strong enough to make living the vision of a government by the people and for the people, the ideal is still in evidence in America—in fact it shines all the more brilliantly because of Lincoln who gives it concretion.

C) If Lincoln were living today he would perceive that America's heart must grow bigger as the world grows smaller—that America's destiny must extend spiritually to far flung corners of the earth, that the American blood shed in far away places for justice must be rededicated on an enlarged Gettysburg pattern so that the peoples liberated at the cost of so much suffering cannot perish from our globe.

III. ISSUES THAT LINCOLN WOULD MEET:

1. Communism. The problem involved in Communism is ideological. Americans would resolutely have to see the ideas behind the acts. Linco[l]n's faith in the capacity of the democratic idea to meet the challenge of the other ideas lay clearly in his public utterances.

"Fellow Citizen," he said in his annual message to congress, "We cannot escape history. We of this congress and the administration will be remembered in spite of ourselves. No personal significance or insignificance can spare one or another of us. The fiery trial through which we pass will light us down in honor or dishonor."

In our present international relations we cannot escape history. We will be remembered in spite of ourselves. No isolationism will help us. No fear will help us. No running from the issue that is joined will help us. ONLY THE WILL TO FACE UP TO OUR PROBLEMS SPIRITUALLY AS OUR SOLDIERS ARE FACING UP TO THEM PHYSICALLY IN KOREA CAN AVAIL.

Nor can we desert those who wish to stand at our side in the world any more than Lincoln could have deserted the blacks who stood ready to fight for their freedom in civil war times. Today the people of the yellow, the brown, the black races and the white people of Europe remain in the face of the en-slavement of communism.

Our American superiority must be in terms of the spirit that Lincoln demonstrated if we are to prevail in the world of today.

2. International cooperation. Lincoln's little known letter to the working-men of Manchester[,] England[,] January 19, 1863, shows us his thinking on international affairs. THEY DO NOT SPEAK OF THE PEOPLE OF OTHER NATIONS AS FAITHLESS AND AS READY TO DESPOIL US. Here are his sentiments:

"I have the honor to acknowledge the receipt of the address and resolutions which you sent me on the eve of the new year.

"I know you deeply deplore the sufferings which the workingmen of Man-chester and in all Europe are called to endure in this crisis. It has been often and studiously represented that the attempt to overthrow this government which was built on the foundation of human rights, and to substitute for it one which should rest exclusively on the basis of human slavery was likely to obtain the favor of Europe. Through the action of our disloyal citizens, the workingmen of Europe have been subjected to severe trials, for the purpose of forcing their sanction to that attempt. Under the circumstances, I cannot but regard your decisive utterances upon the question as an instance of sublime Christian heroism which has not been surpassed in any age in any country. It is indeed an energetic and reinspiring assurance of the inherent power of truth, and of the ultimate and universal triumph of justice, humanity and freedom. I do not doubt that the sentiments you have expressed will be sus-tained by your great nation; and on the other hand, I have no hesitation in assuring you that they will excite admiration, esteem and the most reciprocal feelings of friendship among the American people. I hail this interchange of sentiment, therefore, as an augury that whatever else may happen, whatever misfortune may befall your country or my own, the peace and friendship which now exist between the two nations will be, as it shall be my desire to make them, perpetual . . ."

This, mind you, at a time when England was helping the South break the Northern Blockade of Southern ports and trying to get cotton out to Europe!

3. HIS LARGESSE OF SPIRIT . . . in contrast with the smallness of spirit of present leaders who carry the banner of Lincoln's party: Here are significant words from his second inaugural:

"Neither party expected for the war the magnitude or the duration which it has already attained. Neither anticipated that the cause of the conflict might cease with, or even before the conflict itself chouls [sic] cease. Each looked for an easier triumph, and a result less fundamental and astounding. Both read the same Bible, and pray to the same God, and each invokes His aid against the other. It may seem strange that any men should dare to ask a just God's assistance in wringing their bread from the sweat of other men's faces, but let us judge not that we be not judged. The prayers of both could not be answered . . . that of neither has been answered fully.

"With malice toward none, with charity for all, with firmness in the right as God gives us to see the right, let us strive to finish the work we are in; to bind up the nation's wounds; to care for him who shall have borne the battle and for the widow and his orphan—to do all which may achieve and cherish a just and lasting peace among ourselves and with all nations."

CONCLUSION

This sermon is not an attack upon any party. It is devoted to the enhancement of the national ideals. Americans make mistakes these days. They shall probably continue to make mistakes. But the great Americans who have dreamed mighty dreams and have conceived of the greatness of the plan which made and kept us a nation are still the guides to follow in this hour—democrats like Jefferson, Wilson and Franklin Roosevelt, Republicans like Lincoln. Of all the Americans that have come to the high office of President of these United States, Lincoln preeminently had the vision of a united country and a united mankind. To hear Republicans speak in his name in the fashion they do these days is to injure the nobility of their party—the party of Lincoln—but not to injure Lincoln's stature. To have Democratic party members behave in the fashion they do in Virginia and elsewhere in the North and South is to injure the greatness of a party made great by Jefferson and others, but not to injure Jefferson.

The struggle to gain for the nation under God a new birth of freedom still continues. . . . It must in every age. That is a trut[h] to remember on his birthday. We the living of 1951 must again be dedicated to the task yet remaining . . . that our safety as a nation lie[s] with a new birth of freedom everywhere on earth. That is our destiny. Not by running from the task but by meeting it unflinchingly will be worthy of our American heritage—and the Lincolnian ideal.[47]

Tehilla Lichtenstein, spiritual leader of the Society of Jewish Science, preached a sermon on Lincoln and the Cold War in 1950. Photo by Blackstone Studios, 20 West 57th Street, New York; courtesy The Jacob Rader Marcus Center of the American Jewish Archives, at the Hebrew Union College–Jewish Institute of Religion, Cincinnati, Ohio.

10. THE SOCIETY OF JEWISH SCIENCE AND LINCOLN'S IDEOLOGY

Tehilla Lichtenstein (1893–1973) and her husband, Rabbi Morris Lichtenstein (1889–1938), were among the founders, in 1922, of the Society of Jewish Science, a group formed to counteract Christian Science's growing influence upon American Jews. After her husband's death in 1938, Tehilla became the organization's preacher. Over the years and despite the group's diminishing membership, Tehilla became a well-known public speaker, as well as a practitioner and teacher of the "healing methods" of Jewish science. She edited the society's journal, the Jewish Science Interpreter, *and hosted a weekly radio broadcast.*

Speaking during the early years of the Cold War, Tehilla Lichtenstein posed a rhetorical question to her listeners: "Did Lincoln have the answer" to the threat of mass mutual destruction from a nuclear holocaust? Responding to her own question, Lichtenstein concluded, "I think he did." Lincoln's penetrating moral clarity, encapsulated in the admonition "with malice toward none, with charity for all," convinced Lichtenstein that Lincoln's mind was fundamentally aligned with the ideology of Jewish Science. "Oh, that with all our getting we could get us a heart of wisdom!" Lichtenstein wrote. Her antidote for a world standing on the brink of nuclear destruction was to listen deeply to "the kindly voice of our martyred President."

Did Lincoln Have the Answer?

Address delivered at the Jewish Science Forum, New York, 1950

The answer to what? To all the awesome problems which are demanding solution today by a confused and frightened humanity. What shall we do with that dreadful enemy which is threatening to annihilate man, to lay low all the achievements of centuries, to bring to rubble and extinction this now flourishing planet? I am not referring to Russia when I use the phrase "dreadful enemy," I am merely describing man's own diabolical cleverness which has driven him to the discovery of the deepest secrets of God's creation, which has unearthed for him all the laws of matter by which the basic elements of the universe can be taken apart and put together in hitherto unheard of forms, forms of such ferocious power that just a few of them are sufficient to blow little man clear off the planet which he now [believes he] understands so well. Yes, did Lincoln have the answer as to what man should do to avert the threat of the hell-bomb, as it is called by some—the hydrogen bomb—which man is about to construct? Lincoln knew nothing about the advanced mathematical prowess which, less than a hundred and fifty years after his birth, his simple birth in the rude log cabin so dear to those who prize his memory, has enabled us to invent an infernal machine capable of destroying 360 million human beings in one explosion. I can see him smiling sadly, perhaps wryly, at the stupidity of the human race as enormous as its cleverness, perhaps asking drily, "Why go to all that trouble? The lemmings do it much more simply. They commit mass suicide by just jumping off a high cliff into the sea." No doubt his wryness would hide a deep grief at the mad rush towards death which humanity is making. Could he have told us how, can he even now tell us how that same brilliant instrument, that wondrous mind in man's possession, could lead him to life instead of extinction, to rich full living, instead of base dying? . . . Did Lincoln have the answer?

I think he did. He said, in his profoundly simple way, which concealed to the unthinking the depths of his vision, . . . simply, "With malice towards none, and charity towards all." As simply, as it is said in Leviticus, "Thou shalt love thy neighbor as thyself," which, if achieved by the heart of man, in every corner of the earth would lay low all of the barriers to happiness which man has erected against himself. With malice towards none, with charity towards all, there is the answer to man's mortal dilemma today, even the answer to the threat of the Hydrogen bomb. . . .

To avert the war which, to many, seems imminent with communist Russia, we must teach ourselves to look upon Russia and upon the rest of the world with an unjaundiced eye. We must rid ourselves of malice, and partake of the sweet bread of charitableness. Just now we are so full of resentment, so bitter, so ready to put all blame upon the other one, we will not even listen to anyone's side of the story but our own; and towards us, too, is the same blind anger and unwillingness to listen; the Russians are all bitterness towards us as we are towards them. We wonder what has happened to all the sunshine and brotherliness of yesteryear, when Roosevelt and Stalin sat smilingly by each other at a conference table, seeking to work out together a way to bring about the welfare of the world. . . . [Now][48] our newspapers and theirs have only evil things to say, one about the other; we hear of nothing but their base intent, and they learn nothing but of our black and rapacious designs.

... [We] have no other alternative than to listen to the kindly voice of our martyred president, gently bidding us harbor malice toward none and charity for all. It may seem paradoxical to turn to him for an answer to our besetting and frightening troubles, to turn to him to help us avert war, who was himself the leader and commander-in-chief in a war against his own people. But Lincoln fought bitterly, bitterly against that war; he pleaded with north and south to refrain from bloodshed and fratricide. He told his counselors and those who pressed for a declaration of war, for the use of arms, that he would do anything, stop at nothing, to avert such action. Even the freeing of the slaves, which was so dear a goal to his heart, even the emancipation of his black brethren, he was willing to defer; he was willing to let slavery stand for the time being, to leave that in abeyance, rather than plunge the nation into the sin of war. But the war was forced upon him, he took command with a broken and sorrowing heart, only when that way alone was left to him for the saving of his country. It was towards his supposed enemies, towards those against whom he sent his generals to battle, that he uttered his declaration of love and his plea for charity. I am sure he would have asked for charity towards the poor mad actor who brought upon him the untimely death of martyrdom.

We, who are supposedly at peace with all the world, we who supposedly have no enemies, can we not teach ourselves to face the peoples of the world, even those most unlike ourselves, without rancor, without anger, with the charity that begets wisdom? Can we in any other way than that hope to avert the holocaust of World War Three? Oh, that with all our getting we could get us a heart of wisdom! With malice towards none[,] with charity for all, if we do not make that our answer today, the world will be a silent world tomorrow![49]

11. CALLING THE JEWISH COMMUNITY TO ACTION

On February 12, 1960, Rav A. Soloff (b. 1927), a young rabbinic ordinee of the Hebrew Union College in Cincinnati, commemorated Lincoln's birthday by preaching his sermon on the topic of civil rights at the East End Temple in New York City. He told his congregation that Lincoln's birthday was a fitting occasion for calling the American Jewish community to action. Lincoln's legacy should serve to inspire all Americans, and especially Jewish Americans, to oppose racism and be champions of justice for all peoples.

Soloff contended that Lincoln's birthday was important "to all Americans" because the sixteenth president "lives . . . more radiantly than ever before as symbol of these American ideals: unity, equality, brotherhood." Debunking the rationalizations that justify racism's continuing entrenchment in America, Soloff urged his congregants not to "sit by and wait" but actively to work on behalf of the civil rights movement. "Today is the time to rise and act, to stand and be counted among the NAACPers, the ACLUers, the Urban Leaguers, Americans who believe Lincoln must live radiantly in our laws, in our society, in our hearts."

Rabbi Rav A. Soloff characterized Lincoln as a living moral compass in his 1960 sermon on the civil rights movement. Photo by Augusta Berns, Bamberger Studios; courtesy The Jacob Rader Marcus Center of the American Jewish Archives, at the Hebrew Union College–Jewish Institute of Religion, Cincinnati, Ohio.

Lincoln Lives

Exactly one hundred years ago Abraham Lincoln's birthday, his fifty-first, was still a private affair. Mr. Lincoln held no public office, but the taste for what lay ahead was in his mouth. Already an important Republican, in just a fortnight he would deliver "the Cooper Union speech" which so favorably introduced Westerner Lincoln to the political powers of the East. Within the year, thanks to the skill of photographer [Mathew] Brady and the absence of television, ugly Abe Lincoln would be nominated and elected sixteenth president of the United States. And in little over half a decade the immortal Captain would lie dead, having guided his nation through its ordeal by blood and fire.

Today, as has been increasingly true for the past 99 years, Lincoln's Birthday is of moment to *all* Americans. That man, long dead, lives in our generation more radiantly than ever before as symbol of these American ideals: unity, equality, brotherhood.

Lincoln lives alongside us and burns within us now as never before, because at last a ninety-year-old log-jam is breaking up. Perhaps it took two World Wars on top of the murderous Civil War to smash through the massive mud wall of rabid, short-sighted, selfish and self-destructive American racism. Perhaps it took three generations of tireless, often seemingly fruitless effort to set the groundwork. But at last we see genuine emancipation on its way to all Americans.

In the decades since World War II began the Negro has moved at a rate "unmatched by any race—certainly any minority race—in the history of human achievement. Since 1940 the number of Negroes in colleges and professional schools has tripled to more than 200,000. There are ten times as many Negro students of engineering and architecture as two decades ago. . . . The percentage of U.S. Negroes in college is greater than the percentage of all the people of Great Britain in college." And corresponding to this change in the educational picture, have come drastic changes in employment, economic status and political influence.

Of course violent opposition continues: 530 specific, documented acts of racial violence in eleven Southern States over the course of four years—six Negroes killed, 50 bombings and burnings and so on. Of course glaring, unconscionable inequities persist: the Federal Civil Rights Commission reports that "Against the prejudice of registrars and jurors, the United States Government appears under present laws to be helpless to make good the guarantees of the United States Constitution, and almost 4 million out of 5 million potential Negro voters are kept from southern ballot boxes." Of course progress at best is gallingly snail-paced—I mean here in New York, not elsewhere—boys who should become engineers still prepare to push carts in the garment district just because their skin is black.

But the writing hand has left its incontrovertible message on the wall of our nation: Lincoln lives! The unity of America will not again be challenged. The most violent conceivable secessionist movement of 1960 would be an exodus of Southern delegates from the Democratic National Convention, and after the 1948 experience, even *that* seems unlikely.

Lincoln lives! American fact will increasingly accord with our faith in the equality of all men. Congress cannot defer forever, States cannot defy forever, citizens cannot deny forever the clear, clarion demand for moral action.

Lincoln lives! Americans will accept his ideal of hearts bearing malice toward none. Ah, the Lincoln heart—this is the most delicate and the most difficult of our race problems. How?

To cleanse our hearts of malice, and our lips from speaking guile, we must first clear our minds of a great deal of nonsense. We wish to be soft-hearted, but not soft-headed. Let me mention just three items.

First, the problem is primarily objective. One sensitive white American, looking into his society and into his own heart reports the "ubiquitous, demonic intruder is not Jim Crow—symbol of sanctified and legislated segregation, presiding fiend over lynchings . . . [rather][50] call him James Crow, Esquire, a shabby-genteel and soft-voiced demon. . . . [Now][51] James Crow, Esquire—the apostle of genteel apartheid—disowns the cruder and more violent Jim. . . . But, in very real sense, the influence of James is more baleful than Jim's. . . ."

No! The influence of James Crow, of personal prejudice and social pressure may poison the soul of the persecutor, may pain, possibly scar the soul of the victim, but by no hard-headed, cold-eyed standard is its influence "more baleful" than that of "sanctified and legislated segregation."

Give every American the right to vote, the right to any job he can fill, the right to all the education he can stand, the right to any housing he can afford—(colored neighbors, as you know from recent real-estate studies, do *not* automatically lower property values), give him his rights—then go hate him in the secret places of your heart, if you can: the soul that withers will be your own.

Second, it is popular nonsense that you can't alter attitudes by legislation, by law. Attorney General [William P.] Rogers comments, "(The Law) is not a mere abstract body of rules which government officials have imposed upon our society, rather the constitution and the laws of our nation express the conscience and morality of a free people. . . . Because our laws have a moral foundation, they serve to teach, to mold attitudes and outlooks and to crystallize public opinion in support of concepts which are fair and just." The timid soul who would not fight legal segregation now supports legal desegregation; law was his teacher and his pastor.

Third, it is popular nonsense that all self-conscious effort at interracial harmony is vain, that personal attitudes of racial decency and social conditions promoting racial decency cannot be deliberately created. Sociologist Dr. Herbert Blumer concludes otherwise. "There can be no question [that][52] conscious, designed desegregation acts back on and abets natural, unwitting racial desegregation." In other words, *Mitoch shelo l'shmo, bo l'shmo*—right action undertaken even out of mixed motives leads to right action for pure motives.[53]

So Jews have to be reminded of their sacred duty to promote unity, equality, brotherhood? I think that in principle we do not. But there is always the question of what to do, and when. There is a time in human affairs to sit by and wait. Today is the time to rise and act, to stand and be counted among the NAACPers, the ACLUers, the Urban Leaguers, Americans who believe Lincoln must live radiantly in our laws, in our society, in our hearts, Americans who will not see our nation's spiritual maturation put off and will not put off their own spiritual maturation any longer.

By *next* February 12th let us each have a year's personal Lincolnesque accomplishment to review.

Amen.[54]

12. MAY HIS MEMORY BE AS A BLESSING

After World War II, Jewish newspapers frequently used the anniversary of Lincoln's birth as an occasion to remind readers why American Jews cherished the sixteenth president's memory. In an editorial written for Lincoln's birthday in 1970, Albert W. Bloom (1918–90), the editor of Pittsburgh's Jewish Chronicle, *declared that Lincoln was the "President who comes closest to following the character and footsteps of the ancient Hebrew Prophets." Even during the Vietnam War era, when civil dissidence was pervasive and established values routinely challenged, American Jews commemorated Lincoln's life and insisted that his memory was a blessing.*

Abraham Lincoln
(Feb. 12, 1809–April 15, 1865)

February 12, 1970

Abraham Lincoln died on April 15, 1865. He was 56 years old. Not a great deal of time for a once near-illiterate ragged little orphan boy to lift himself up to "belong to the ages." But so he does.

Almost cuttingly brief is the encyclopedic reference:

"On the evening of April 14, 1865, John Wilkes Booth shot Lincoln as he sat in Ford's Theater in Washington, and early the next morning he died."

What tidal waves of history washed over the span of that act and the span of the Lincoln years. Even today, the waves still have not quieted. The constitutional amendments perhaps only hinted at in the first Lincoln Inaugural eventually took form.

But the skeletal thrust of the 13th, 14th, and 15th Amendments (slavery abolished; citizenship rights not to be abridged; equal voting rights for all citizens without regard "of race, color, or previous condition of servitude") have yet to be properly fleshed out.

To this day.

He might have been speaking to all Americans, black and white, this very day when on March 4, 1861 he said:

"In your hands, my dissatisfied fellow countrymen, and not in mine, is the momentous issue of civil war . . . I am loath to close. We are not enemies but friends. We must not be enemies.

"Though passion may have strained, it must not break our bonds of affection. The mystic chords of memory, stretching from every battle-field, and patriot grave, to every living heart and hearthstone, all over this broad land, will yet swell the chorus of Union, when again touched, as surely they will be, by the better angels of our nature."

Abraham Lincoln, the President who comes closest to following the character and footsteps of the ancient Hebrew Prophets—"may his memory be as a blessing" to us all—without regard "of race, color, or previous condition of servitude."[55]

12

Lincoln Miscellany

By paraphrasing the words that the French sociologist Émile Durkheim used in 1883 to describe the heroes of France, a contemporary scholar of sociology summarized Abraham Lincoln's status in the collective memory of the American people. Lincoln is "America's universal man: changing and remaining the same; standing beside the people and above the people; a reflection of and model for them—at once behind, above, and within them." In many respects, this characterization also serves as a useful description of American Jewry's collective memory of Abraham Lincoln. For many American Jews, Lincoln remains a venerable symbol of the best in American life. He endures as an iconic embodiment of America's highest political values as well as its most noble social aspirations. Yet, at the same time, there lingers within the American Jewish experience an ongoing inclination to adopt Lincoln spiritually and to understand him as a fellow American Jewish sojourner—or, to paraphrase Lincoln's own famous turn of phrase, American Jews persistently tend to think of Lincoln as an *almost* chosen person.[1]

In 2011, Ron Paul (b. 1935), a member of the U.S. House of Representatives and three-time presidential candidate, raised many eyebrows by asserting that Abraham Lincoln wanted "to nationalize everything." Paul's glittering generality was certain to vex millions of Americans who considered Lincoln to be republicanism incarnate. Yet, Lincoln's many statements about the role a good government should play in serving the needs of the people, conjoined with his status as the "common man" who rose from humble origins to lead his nation, have convinced many ideologues in the twentieth and twenty-first centuries that had Lincoln been living in their own era, he would have been sympathetic to a liberal or even socialist point of view.

In 1910, a disgruntled ex-Catholic-turned-socialist-activist named Burke McCarty published a pamphlet titled *Little Sermons in Socialism by Abraham Lincoln*. In the pamphlet's preface, McCarty acknowledged that Lincoln was not a socialist, because no such term existed in his day. She also acknowledged that no one could possibly know whether, had Lincoln lived in the twentieth and twenty-first centuries, he would have ever associated himself with socialism or the socialist cause. Having offered those qualifications, McCarty stated her thesis unabashedly: "We do claim, and know, however, that Abraham Lincoln was in spirit to the hour of his death, a class conscious working man, that his sympathies were with that class, that he voiced the great principles of the modern constructive Socialism of today, and that had he lived and been loyal and consistent with these principles which he always professed, he would be found within the ranks of the Socialist Party."[2]

McCarty proceeded to offer readers a host of Lincoln quotations, often wrenched out of context, which validated her thesis. Was it not Lincoln who said, "To secure each laborer the whole product of his labor, or as nearly as possible, is a worthy object of any good government"? Did not Lincoln state that "whatever any one man earns with his hands and by the sweat of his brow, he shall enjoy in peace"? Why did Lincoln proclaim, "Whatever concerns the whole, should be confided to the whole—the general government"? McCarty's ideas about Lincoln were hardly unique; American socialists and communists mustered dozens of Lincoln quotations and bandied them in their newspapers and journals, on Lincoln's birthday, and on a variety of similar occasions.[3]

Thousands of Jewish immigrants from Eastern Europe carried a sympathetic appreciation for socialist principles with them to these shores. Many others who did not come to America with these political tendencies were drawn to them after they had been introduced to the harsh working conditions that characterized the burgeoning American industrialism of the late nineteenth and early twentieth centuries. Just like other socialists in America, Jewish socialists embraced Lincoln and encountered him as a comrade. The Yiddish press became a vehicle for transmitting these ideas to the East European immigrant masses. The fact that "there was little in Lincoln's presidency to warrant his becoming a symbol of economic reform" did not prevent socialists from adopting Lincoln as an exemplar, and the same was true for Jewish socialists.[4]

During the first half of the twentieth century, Yiddish culture was a potent force in America, particularly in New York and other large urban centers. Yiddish newspapers flourished and reached hundreds of thousands of readers on a daily basis. Yiddish theater, schools, and publishing blossomed. It was at this time that Yiddish poetry emerged as one of the most colorful and popular literary genres for the East European Jewish immigrants. Dozens of Yiddish poets aspired to express in Yiddish the best traditions of American poetry. As the introspective poet Aaron Glanz Leyeles (1889–1966) wrote, "Not in vain have we read the American poem / And inhaled, absorbed the Whitman tone" (*Nisht umzist geleyent s'lid amerikaner / un gezapt in zikh dem Vitmaner*). For the American Yiddish poets, Lincoln served as a key symbol of Americanism and of the principles of freedom and justice that they prized. Lincoln appeared in hundreds of Yiddish poems. He suffered with his readers and sympathized with their longings. Leivick Halpern (1888–1962), a leading Yiddish author and poet who wrote under the pen name H. Leivick, explained in his poem "To America" that the Yiddish poet carried within him the "bounty of American freedom, which has been sanctified by the blood of Lincoln," and in one of Reuben Ludwig's (1895–1926) Yiddish poems, "Symposium," Abraham Lincoln, John Brown, and Walt Whitman return from the grave to indict contemporary America.[5]

According to the assessment of at least one scholar, Lincoln was actually the American Jewish left's greatest literary hero. In fact, some Jewish socialists suggested that their love and respect for Abraham Lincoln was even greater than that which was conferred on him by the average American: "Here in America, we socialists celebrate the birthday of the man who brought slavery in America to an end. American capitalists, in contrast, celebrate this day because the end of black slavery ushered in the new lucrative era of wage-salary." Ultimately, Lincoln became an inspirational model for the American Jewish left's deep concern for all downtrodden minorities.[6]

In 1936, this impulse expressed itself in the desire on the part of nearly 3,000 Americans, who joined with thousands of foreign nationals from around the world, to fight in military brigades against Francisco Franco's pro-fascist forces in the Spanish Civil War. Many of these brigades were organized by the Communist International in Moscow. According to some estimates, 10 percent of these foreign fighters were Jews who came from around the globe to fight the Spanish fascists. European and American Jews fought side by side, expressing bitter opposition to the political oppression and program of anti-Semitism that Franco's ally, Nazi Germany, propagated in the mid-1930s. The Jews who fought in the Spanish Civil War from the United States were mostly political leftists, but they were *American* radicals, and they expressed their ideas through the American cultural symbols with which they were familiar. As one historian emphasized, for the American radicals who fought Franco, "the language of the Spanish Civil War was the language of the American Civil War." In particular, this American spirit influenced the naming of the battalions and brigades. The Jewish fighters who went to Spain wanted to project themselves to the world as *American* freedom fighters: "The men voted on a name for the battalion, selecting Abraham Lincoln as the best representative of how they saw themselves—men who would fight to free the oppressed."[7]

In addition to his symbolic significance for Jewish socialists and political radicals, Lincoln continued to serve as a cultural icon for millions of East European immigrants as they moved through the process of Americanization. One of the most prominent examples of Lincoln's status as a cultural icon for the East European immigrants during the twentieth century may be seen in the work of Arthur Szyk (1894–1951), a popular graphic artist, book illuminator, and caricaturist. Born in Łódź, Poland, Szyk immigrated to the United States in 1940. He quickly adapted to his new country, and during World War II, Szyk became what has been referred to as an "artist-activist." Through his distinctive style of illumination and miniature portraitures, Szyk created a body of artwork expressive of American ideals for posters, magazines, and books. He was particularly interested in rendering images of significant American events, personalities, and documents that expressed the ideals that he considered to be core values of American democracy: tolerance and mutual respect. Abraham Lincoln was the subject of two of Szyk's famous illuminations. In 1946, he created a poster that featured a likeness of Lincoln overlooking a framed manuscript that contained the concluding words from Lincoln's second inaugural address ("With malice toward none, with charity for all . . ."). The following year, 1947, Szyk produced a second work, this time for *Coronet* magazine, focusing on an excerpt from Lincoln's "Reply to the New York Workingmen's Democratic Republican Association" ("The strongest bond of human sympathy,

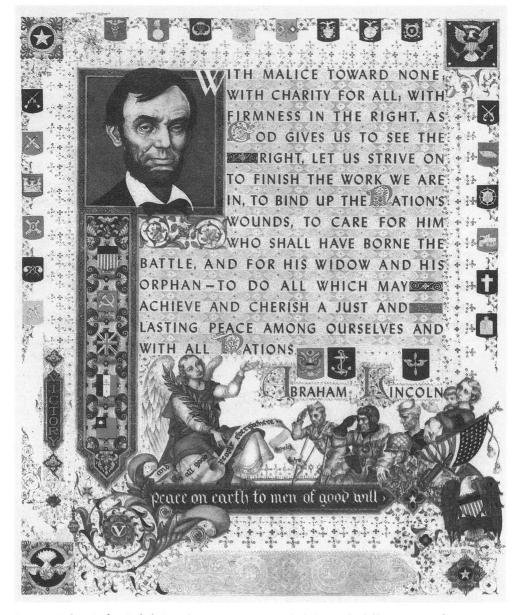

In 1946 Arthur Szyk, a Polish-Jewish immigrant, created a lithographed illumination of Lincoln's second inaugural address. Courtesy the Arthur Szyk Society.

outside of the family relation, should be one uniting all working people, of all nations, and tongues, and kindreds").[8]

The Gettysburg Address has repeatedly been called the greatest speech in American history. Historians continue to offer differing interpretations as to how the speech eventually rose to its current status as American sacred writ. Most scholars agree that by the dawn of the twentieth century and the centennial anniversary of Lincoln's birth, the Gettysburg Address was well on its way to becoming one of the nation's most iconic speeches. As it was with Lincoln himself, Americans consistently interpreted the Gettysburg Address against the context of their own era.[9]

At the turn of the century, for example, when an emphasis on the ideals of national unity intensified and the wounds of the Civil War were healing, Americans became convinced that Lincoln's famous phrase "last full measure of devotion" referred not only to Union soldiers but to the Confederate dead as well. Throughout the course of the twentieth century, the Gettysburg Address was used as an inspirational source that sustained the spirit of America as it endured two world wars, a great economic depression, and the enmities of the Cold War. "If the power of the words shines brightly," one historian recently wrote about the famous speech, then "the uses to which [the words of the Gettysburg Address] have been put, in the United States and around the world, also continue to reverberate."[10]

As we have already seen, American Jews joined together with the rest of the nation in sacralizing the Gettysburg Address. Lincoln scholars and collectors like Isaac Markens and Emanuel Hertz contributed to the archival preservation of the famous document. In Markens's case, he played a pioneering role in reconstructing the history of the various drafts of the famous address. American Jewish leaders adored the address, and it became as revered in Jewish settings as it was in public schools. Its status among many Jewish communal leaders during the early years of the twentieth century may be illustrated by a contribution the financiers Jacob Schiff and Felix Warburg (1871–1937) made when they were donating funds to reinvigorate the Jewish Theological Seminary in New York: Schiff funded the installation of a bronze tablet emblazoned with the words of the Gettysburg Address, not the Holy Scriptures. The tablet was hung on the wall of the school's main auditorium. As far as Schiff as concerned, *this* was the message that American rabbis needed to learn.[11]

It was widely believed that in memorizing and reciting the words of the Gettysburg Address, the children of East European Jewish immigrants would experience acculturation and Americanization. A few famous East European Jewish immigrants put Lincoln's brief but powerful oration in musical settings for the general public's enjoyment, and these early efforts may well have culminated in the iconic composition of Aaron Copland, the child of immigrant Jews, whose "Lincoln Portrait" has become a patriotic mainstay.

At the same time, this same immigrant cohort would offer its own distinctive contributions to the speech's overall exaltation in American life. Rabbi Leo Baeck (1873-1956), widely regarded as one of the most heroic and saintly religious leaders of the twentieth century, venerated Lincoln. From 1933 to 1939, the scholarly Baeck had been president of the Reichsvertretung der Deutschen Juden, an umbrella organization serving the German-Jewish community under the Hitler regime. Even prior to the rise of the Nazis, Baeck studied Lincoln's writings, and he frequently recited lines from the Gettysburg Address. Although he had many opportunities to leave Germany before the outbreak of World War II, Baeck refused to abandon his people. During this dark time, Baeck later recalled how he drew strength from rereading Lincoln's inspirational rhetoric. Corresponding to a friend in 1941, Baeck confessed he had recently "read again the magnificent speech by Abraham Lincoln, on November 19, 1863, in Gettysburg, in which he said '. . . this nation, under God, shall have a new birth of freedom.'" Baeck viewed Lincoln as "a truly religious man," and he was convinced that Lincoln's ideas would ultimately have a beneficial effect on the American people: "Happy is the nation," Baeck wrote, "to which these words could be said by this man."[12]

On February 12, 1948, Baeck—now a survivor of the Nazi Holocaust—was invited to deliver the opening prayer in the U.S. House of Representatives. He used the occasion to praise Lincoln and pray for the welfare of the American nation: "Our Father, our God," Baeck began, "we pray unto Thee on this day on which six score and nineteen years ago was born that man who came to be Thy servant." He told the legislators that Lincoln was the "herald" of God's "command and promise" who had been born for "the sake of this land" in order to serve as "a witness and testimony of humanity." He extolled Lincoln as an "everlasting blessing of this country and of mankind."[13]

In the years following World War II, Jewish folklorists began to examine the concluding paragraph in the address Lincoln delivered before the Wisconsin State Agricultural Society in Milwaukee on September 30, 1859. Lincoln closed this speech by alluding to the story of an "an Eastern monarch" who asked his "wise men" to provide him with a sentence that would be "true and appropriate in all times and situations." The "wise men" fulfilled the monarch's wish by presenting him with this wisdom: "And this, too, shall pass away."[14]

The story Lincoln referenced first began to attract Jewish interest in the mid-1950s, when Israeli anthropologists and scholars of Jewish folklore began collecting oral histories from new immigrants who settled in Israel during that era. In 1955, one of the first legends to be recorded for the newly established Israel Folktale Archives at Haifa University was a story about King Solomon that concluded with the very same phrase, "And this, too, shall pass."

Although the story of the "monarch" was not widely known, the story's key phrase, "This, too, shall pass" (in Hebrew *gam zu ya'avor*), had long been a familiar folk idiom in various Jewish communities around the world. During World War II, for instance, Jewish entrepreneurs sold a "Good Luck Ring" for "Your Boy in the Service" as well as the Hebrew initials gimmel, zayin, and yod, for *gam zu ya'avor*. Ethnologists could not help but wonder how Lincoln obtained this particularly Jewish story. Was it possible that one of Lincoln's Jewish acquaintances related the tale and the legend's distinctive moral appealed to the future president's sensibilities? Perhaps. Yet it is much more likely that Lincoln simply heard the story in a speech or while he was riding the law circuit, or perhaps he read it himself in a book he obtained. In any event, Jews took pleasure in this post–World War II discovery that Lincoln once cited a story that many believed to be of Jewish origin, and this coincidence bolstered the longstanding conviction that Lincoln was intuitively in sympathy with Jewish folk wisdom.[15]

In 1976, the bicentennial anniversary of American independence, Stanley Kunitz (1905–2006), the Pulitzer Prize–winning Poet Laureate Consultant to the Library of Congress, wrote a poem for the library's exhibition of the contents of Lincoln's pockets the night he was assassinated. The poem, "The Lincoln Relics," spoke longingly of Lincoln's "legend and fame," which was "slipping away from us." Kunitz, whose parents were raised in Eastern Europe, mused many years later about the role his Jewish ethical tradition may have had on his poetry. "The people of the Diaspora carry the memory of exile in their blood," Kunitz said. If so, that Diaspora memory, with its longing for a nation that was lost, would have been present when he conceptualized Lincoln as the paradigmatic symbol of the nation's lost glory, of a national greatness that was waning. The poet's words expressed nostalgia for a heroic Lincoln as well as for the nation's ebbing greatness.[16]

In a recent volume that examines the role Abraham Lincoln played in twentieth-century America, sociologist Barry Schwartz offers an explanation as to why Kunitz may have sensed that Lincoln was "slipping away." He notes that in the years following World War II, and particularly after the Korean War, Abraham Lincoln's general prestige and reputation began to diminish. Various national surveys taken between the years 1945 and 2004 indicated that "Lincoln was still the man he had always been, [he] was still admired, but with less fervor than before." To explain this phenomenon, Schwartz offers several theories. First, the onset of a postindustrial society caused dramatic changes in science, technology, and the media, which have influenced cultural norms and resulted in an erosion of American society's "traditional authority structures." Second, the civil rights movement of the late 1950s and 1960s focused almost univocal attention on Lincoln the emancipator. The many other points of relevance that historically had made Lincoln such a vibrant national icon (for example, the savior of the Union, the man of courage, the man of integrity, the general, the First American, and so on) had been displaced. Then, after the intense focus on Lincoln as an emancipator during the civil rights era, the 1970s marked a time when scholars began publishing research that challenged whether Lincoln was genuinely deserving of being called the "Great Emancipator."[17]

Despite the cultural forces that may have dampened Lincoln's iconic status in the last third of the twentieth century, Schwartz notes that Lincoln's prestige cannot fall below a certain threshold because every society must have a "sense of sameness and continuity with what went before." The power of national memory fuels an engine that constantly refits and revises Lincoln's image to meet society's "need for a [stately] past," even as it mitigates the dawning "sense that such a past is no longer relevant." During this period of attenuation, there were still American Jews who provided new ways to make Lincoln relevant to the American mind.[18]

For instance, the psychologist Abraham H. Maslow (1908–70) earned a following by promulgating his now famous "hierarchy of human needs" theory.[19] Maslow, also a child of East European Jewish immigrants, recollected that his own childhood was lonely and unhappy since he felt himself to be "the little Jewish boy in the non-Jewish neighborhood." It is interesting to note Maslow's deep attraction to Lincoln, who became for Maslow an exemplar of the "self-actualized" human being—a person whose life embodies the values of morality, creativity, spontaneity, problem solving, lack of prejudice, and acceptance of facts.[20] From Maslow's point of view, Lincoln "stood for something outside of [his] own skin," and he achieved what Maslow called a "transcendence of time." Even after death, according to Maslow, other human beings can still experience a relationship with self-actualized people like Lincoln in "a very personal and affectionate way."[21]

In his entertaining book *Land of Lincoln*, author Andrew Ferguson describes his encounter with a man named Oscar Esche, who immigrated to Chicago from Thailand in 1973. Not long after arriving in this country, Esche and his wife opened a small restaurant called the Thai Little Home Café in Wicker Park. Having learned about Lincoln while yet living in Thailand, the Esches took a trip to Springfield to visit Lincoln's memorial, and there they purchased a souvenir statue of Lincoln for their restaurant. The Esches became immovably convinced that the Lincoln statue helped their business steadily flourish. In an expression of their gratitude for the sixteenth president's spiritual support, Ferguson reported, every morning the Esches "set out a meal for Lincoln in the restaurant, next to his statue."

> "It's a full meal—everything, entree, dessert, appetizer, drink also," Mr. Esche said. "We change the meal every day, so it's always different. We serve him everything."
> Mrs. Esche interrupted.
> "Yes," Mr. Esche said. "Everything but *no pork*."
> Oh?
> "We do not want to be disrespectful."
> I guess Mr. Esche saw my puzzled look.
> "He is *Abraham* Lincoln, yes?" he said, with special emphasis. "Jewish people, they don't eat pork."[22]

Americans have unquestionably maintained a very personal and affectionate relationship with Abraham Lincoln, long after his death. He occupies a unique place in the collective memory of the American nation, and his enduring rapport with American Jews is one intriguing facet of a much larger Lincoln phenomenon in American culture. It is a fact that Lincoln maintained good relations with many Jews during the course of his lifetime. He also developed real friendships with a select number of Jewish contemporaries. It is similarly true that he exerted himself on a number of occasions in order to protect their constitutional rights—rights that might otherwise have been in jeopardy. Yet beyond all of this, there remains a lingering faith that somehow Abraham

Lincoln was more than a distant friend, more than a fair-minded chief executive. Of the countless ways in which Americans have managed to preserve a meaningful relationship with Lincoln for nearly 150 years, the alluring hope that he was somehow—either by lineage or by legacy—a Jew continues to remain one of the most interesting facets of Lincoln's historical legacy in the American nation.

DOCUMENTS

1. Lincoln's Socialist Leanings
2. Lincoln in Yiddish Poetry
3. Lincoln's Masterpiece: American Jewry and the Gettysburg Address
4. This, Too, Shall Pass
5. Lincoln and Jewish Education
6. Was Abraham Lincoln Jewish?

1. LINCOLN'S SOCIALIST LEANINGS

For Americanized Central European Jews whose families had come to the United States during the 1830s, 1840s, and 1850s, Abraham Lincoln continued to serve as an inspiring exemplar of American patriotism, freedom, and justice. For a noteworthy segment of the East European Jewish immigrant masses, however, who began pouring into this country beginning in the 1880s, Lincoln came to exemplify a somewhat different set of sociopolitical values. Many of the Central European Jews, whose ancestors had settled in the United States prior to the mass migration of Jews from Eastern Europe, believed that Abraham Lincoln's legacy should be used to facilitate the Americanization and cultural indoctrination of their East European immigrant coreligionists. Yet as we can see from the document below, many East European Jewish immigrants began to develop their own distinctive rationale for adulating Lincoln as an American hero. In particular, they identified with Lincoln's role as the Great Emancipator, the man who gave his life so that all Americans could be free and equal regardless of race, color, or religious creed. As we have already seen in previous chapters, East European Jewish immigrants related Lincoln's role in the emancipation of African Americans to their own economic struggles as well as to the immigrant circumstances they encountered in their new country.

Some of the East European Jewish immigrants identified with the values of communism, socialism, and anarchism, and some were actively involved in the American labor movement. These Jews appreciated Lincoln's reputation as an American leader who believed that all peoples, including American slaves, were inherently entitled to equal access under the law. As one historian summarized, "More than any other American hero, Lincoln was embraced in radical Jewish circles."[23]

Lincoln's legacy as a "Common Man" took on special relevance to East European immigrant Jews who were socialists or labor activists. They maintained that if Lincoln— friend of the "common man"—had been alive at the dawn of the twentieth century, he would have been an opponent of capitalism and a firm partisan of labor. Lincoln was, after all, one of the people. As a young man, he had been a laborer—a member of the proletariat—so from this perspective he would have most definitely sympathized with the socialist ideals that meant so much to many of the immigrants.

In the following editorial that appeared in the Yiddish daily newspaper the Forverts *(commonly referred to in English as the* Jewish Daily Forward*) on February 10, 1900, we find one interesting example of how East European Jewish socialists regarded Lincoln as one of their own. According to the editors of the* Forverts, *Lincoln was a comrade in "mankind's larger campaign for freedom." The authors of this Yiddish editorial accuse American capitalists of exploiting Lincoln's legacy in order to convince naive immigrants that the American Horatio Alger story was anything but a pro-capitalist myth.*

In line with the editorial's Marxist point of view, Lincoln did indeed deserve some credit for freeing the slaves. The American slavocracy testified to the fundamentally oppressive nature of capitalism, and by dismantling the slave system Lincoln was contributing to the collapse and ultimate defeat of this corrupt social system. The Yiddish socialists held Lincoln up as a heroic figure in mankind's battle for freedom, and they believed he was a fellow worker in the struggle against America's ruling plutocracy.

In Honor of Lincoln's Birthday

In two days the American nation will mark the birthday of the man whose fate and circumstances placed him at the helm of the great battle for the freedom from slavery of the Negro race—Abraham Lincoln.

This person deserved a better fate than to become the ideal of today's American bourgeoisie. Abraham Lincoln, who despised slavery—and lost a great deal throughout his life—what similarities does he have with today's American oppressors and political corruptionists?! What does Lincoln have in common with today's American land thieves?

Were this honest martyr to come out of his grave today and see the progress the American people have made in the area of freedom and justice, he would not wait for a political adversary to put another bullet in his heart!

What connection does the United States of today have with Abraham Lincoln? Lincoln was not what the ruling class expects from today's American "statesman." In the wild desert of today's American politics there is no such growth as Abraham Lincoln.

How sad does the progress of the United States look in comparison even to the shadow of Abraham Lincoln. How can the likes of [William] McKinley, Mark Hanna and [Theodore] Roosevelt compare with him?

How much credit is due to Lincoln for the liberation of the Negro slaves? Only history can judge this. He was definitely an honest man. He possessed honest convictions, and he loved the American nation from the depths of his heart. These qualities are so far removed from today's politicians—as far as heaven is from earth.

Freeing the Negro slaves was based on a historic economic need, which was inevitable. Therefore, one cannot credit any individual or group of individuals or parties with that achievement. But the feeling against slavery filled many refined souls in the campaign for freedom.

The Lincolns, Greeleys, Wendell Phillipses, John Browns, and Whittiers[24] of the fifties and sixties loved this freedom with all their being and fought for it. Some of them fought for it their entire lives.

Not only did they hate black slavery. Many of them, Horace Greeley for example, were involved in an open battle against the white slave masters. . . . In fact, shortly before his death, Lincoln declared that the greatest danger for the United States was the power of capitalism.

Lincoln's prophecy came true. The American plutocracy burdened the American people with heavy chains, chains like the slaves bore. The desire to enslave the black race has returned today as the desire to enslave entire nations.

Lincoln's battle for emancipation has become McKinley's battle for expansion. From the principle of freedom has developed the principle of slavery.

So—what does today's ruling class in America have to do with Abraham Lincoln?

American capitalists love to use Lincoln as an example for today's youth. Here in America, they say, everyone has the opportunity to become a somebody! The President of the United States was a simple wood-chopping youth!

Do today's American youth really have such opportunities? Is there no Chinese Wall[25] blocking today's working youth? Is not every opportunity occupied by capital and for capital? Does an American working youth have the slightest chance of becoming something other than a slave to capitalism? Is this not exactly what Abraham Lincoln was so fearful of and concerned about?

Abraham Lincoln! The politics of today's bourgeoisie is not a continuation of his battle. His battle is a chapter in the history of mankind's larger campaign for freedom. His inheritors are those who battle for human freedom and against the leadership of the plutocrats![26]

2. LINCOLN IN YIDDISH POETRY

Many poems about life in America were written in Yiddish, and even a simple list of the titles of some of these poems evokes a picture of an earlier time, full of natural beauty, hope, and unexplored opportunity but also, at the same time, of injustice, alienation, and loneliness. As one browses through the index of America in Yiddish Poetry *(1967), selected and translated into English by Jehiel B. and Sarah H. Cooperman, a panorama of the American and the American Jewish experience unfolds. Included in this collection of Yiddish poetry in translation are four poems inspired by Abraham Lincoln.*

The first poem, composed by Reuben Iceland (1884–1955), focuses on Lincoln's famous trip to Richmond on April 3, 1865, less than two weeks prior to his death. Charles Carleton Coffin (1823–96), the well-known war correspondent, had described how former slaves greeted Lincoln as if he were the conquering messiah. "Hallelujah!" and "Bless the Lord!" they cried out, kissing his hands. Reuben Iceland painted a picture, in Yiddish verse,

*of that famous scene that Coffin memorialized in his writings.[27] In the second poem,
"Abraham Lincoln in the White House," Isaac Elhanan Rontch (1899–1985) poetically
conveys how intensely Lincoln worried over the war and the future of his nation. He was
the lonely, sleepless figure walking incessantly through the halls of the White House.[28]
Leonid Feinberg (1907–69), in his poem, recreates in rhyme and verse the thoughts that
may have been running through Lincoln's head during his final moments at Ford's Theater.
The assassin, he writes, set Lincoln free. Finally, the voice of Malka Lee's (1904–76) poem,
"Father Abraham Lincoln," views Lincoln through the rejoicing eyes of a former slave,
expressing how the Yiddish poets identified with the "fellow sufferers," those minorities
who had been oppressed and persecuted like their own forebears.*

LINCOLN IN RICHMOND

by Reuben Iceland[29]

The city in flames. And clusters
Of thick black smoke to the sky curl.
Fat, devouring flames.
And drunken yelling and singing.
Panicky flight of whites;
And just-liberated Negroes,
With garish rags on bodies black,
Stream in waves from place to place,
Screaming and singing,
And carrying devastation in their beastly broad feet.

A mass of black heads, bowed by a storm.

The mob in magnitude is growing and the storm in vehemence,
And painfully he bends his back in shame;
His ears glow red.
Was it this he looked for?
Is not this a mockery,
An affliction from above
For vanity and thirst for power?
He sees devastation, and sees even more,
And with his big, clumsy hand
He wipes the cold sweat off his bony brow.

The mob in magnitude is growing and the storm in vehemence,
And suddenly he stiffens into a wall
Of black heads and deadly silence.

And soon a yell comes through, sharp and fearsome:
"Lincoln!"
And like a wind carries:
"Lincoln!"
And one calls, with eyes staring:
"Lincoln! Jesus's Holy One!"
And, quivering, a voice calls: "Messiah!"
And women their children lift high:
"See the Redeemer!"
And someone shouts wildly:
"The Day of Judgment!"
And wave-like flows over the heads:
"The Judgment Day!
The Judgment Day!
The Judgment Day!"
And thousands fall on their knees in trepidation and awe,
Half singing, half screaming and beating foreheads
On the stones of the pavement.

And he, at whose feet thousands lie,
Stands, humble and meek.
And feels that harder much than scorn is to bear praise,
And lower than dust
Humbles human adoration.
And never before did he crave so much
After rest and quiet and a place
His years to end
With wife and children away from people
And be free of any lust for glory
Vain—and fame.

Abraham Lincoln in the White House

by Isaac Elhanan Rontch[30]

He paces about deeply absorbed, as in the depths of anguish,
Through the hushed parlors of the White House.
It is pitch night, it is deep night,

The long, long hands outstretched
To the Gettysburg battlefield,
To soldier sons of all the states.

The land is all asleep, the citizens rest;
And Washington, the capital, is silent.
Only the President is awake—
Father Abe, great and humble.

He sees young, strong men marching
Off in smoke to suffering and to death.
He hears the drums beating, the trumpets blaring,
Horses taking leave of city stones.

It's now quiet in the White House,
In the lateness of the night, in deep, black night;
But restless is the tall, gloomy President.

He sees ambulances move endlessly,
Like caravans through the desert, crowded with sick.
The town is full of them,
Their throes deafen the sky.
Abe Lincoln covers his face,
Bent with torture and anguish,
And cries and weeps within himself:
"I cannot bear it any longer."
He looks out of the window in the White House,
Abe Lincoln, the President in the Civil War.
It is night, it is black, it is horror.
The land calls, the world calls,
Generations call, long since passed:
"Free the land of shame,
Free the soul of disgrace!"

The land calls you, Abe Lincoln;
Hands of the black slave are outstretched to you,
Prophets of all times are calling upon you.

The blood of the Civil War will be wiped off;
Like the bright sun will truth shine.
United once more will the people be;
And stronger than war, peace is.
In fire and in blood freedom is born
And man must purify himself in torment of battle
To be free.

The city sleeps, the land slumbers.
But in the White House paces lonely,
Deep in thought,
Abe Lincoln, the President.

ABRAHAM LINCOLN

by Leonid Feinberg[31]

The play goes on . . . Honest Abe sits in thought.
His heart is heavy, his face is weary,
He sees how the theater stares cautiously,
But of the play his wakeful ear hears naught.

In his ear echoes still the rumble of artillery . . .
He sees before him so much blood and dust . . .
And suddenly—banging . . . Abe picks himself up
And falls on hands caressed and tenderly.

His dim gaze becomes filled with lead.
On his face spreads the veiled shadow of death:
"I have the slaves from slavery led—
And I swear, by God, I have no regrets.

"And me, today the murderer here set free
From the heavy cross of my daily Golgotha."

FATHER ABRAHAM LINCOLN

by Malka Lee[32]

Of what did my mind become aware—
Lincoln, father of the slaves?
I stand in the fields and look over there
Where the wonders of the world lie engraved.

Where the mountain ranges extend,
On blue mists outspread,
I see there runs a chain of men,
A race with upraised heads.

Father Lincoln, with his hat stiff-crowned,
I see through the mountains he spans;
In its own blood the sun goes down,
The clouds swim by like swans.

For me his lion's voice blares,
For them he freedom decreed.
I stay in the fields and look over there,
How the freed slaves proceed.

The black sons sing,
Their jungle rhythms blare.
And he leads the children to the morning,
Where black and white are brothers there.

The horizon is wrapped in a red firebrand,
The sun goes down in a flaming glow.
I spread over them my motionless hand—
Oh, let us together with him go!

I am the flame of the sunset
That into the valley descended.
Everything stilled in your chansonette,
I am with the mountain and valley blended.

Stars in the roof of the sky ignite,
The quietude sings as with pre-creation;
On a silver horn rides the night
And seeds the valley with stars diamond-spun.

3. LINCOLN'S MASTERPIECE: AMERICAN JEWRY AND THE GETTYSBURG ADDRESS

The first document reproduced below is a copy of a brief address and prayer that Rabbi Sabato Morais delivered on July 4, 1863, in the sanctuary of Philadelphia's Mickve Israel Congregation. Morais was an outspoken supporter of Lincoln's policies, and on Independence Day in 1863, the synagogue hosted members of the Union League of Philadelphia, a local patriotic social society established in 1862, whose purpose was to uphold the Constitution of the United States and support the president's efforts to preserve the Union.[33] The Union League invited the rabbi to speak on a patriotic theme befitting the occasion.

As we can see from the document, Morais was unable to muster much patriotic gasconade. He told his listeners he was deeply despondent over the gruesome loss of life that had just occurred on the Gettysburg battlefield—not far from Philadelphia—on July 1–3, 1863. In the course of Morais's address, he soberly reflected on the profundity of a loss this great, which he linked to the upcoming weeks of penitence preceding the Jewish fast day that occurred on the ninth day of Av (Tisha B'Av).[34]

What is genuinely intriguing about this document, beyond Morais's characteristic eloquence, is the first sentence of the third paragraph, where the rabbi remarks, "I am not indifferent, my dear friends! to the event, which four score and seven years ago, *brought to this new world light and joy" (emphasis added). The following Friday, July 10, 1863, the* Jewish Messenger, *a Jewish newspaper published in New York, printed the entirety of Morais's July 4, 1863 address.*

Most scholars agree that Lincoln's famous turn of phrase "Four score and seven years ago" came from the King James Version of the Bible, with which he was so familiar, and wherein the phrase "three score and ten" appears numerous times. It is nevertheless fascinating to discover that Morais's use of "four score and seven years ago" is arrestingly identical to the immortal words Lincoln employed as he began the Gettysburg Address on November 19, 1863.[35] Is it possible that Lincoln had read Morais's sermon and made mental note of the rabbi's biblical rhetoric? This question has no definitive answer.[36]

The second Gettysburg document comes from a public reception organized by the Hebrew Immigrant Aid Society (HIAS) honoring Moses Alexander (1853–1932), governor of Idaho.[37] The reception was held on Thursday evening, August 26, 1915, in Faneuil Hall in Boston. To bring some humor to the occasion, the highly regarded Hebrew writer Abraham Alpert (1871?–1939), whose nom de plume was "Ish Kovno,"[38] contributed an English parody on the Gettysburg Address lampooning the HIAS. The American Hebraist selected Lincoln's famous oration to serve as the source of a parody that would entertain those who were immersed in the work of immigrant aid. That "Ish Kovno" chose to satirize the "Gettysburg Address"—and not some other familiar Jewish or American text—is a clear indication that Lincoln's speech was already very well known.

It is also interesting to note that many of the Alpert spoofs about the HIAS will still bring a smile to the face of Jewish communal leaders one hundred years after this parody was first published.

Address

יום צרה ותוכחה היום ונאצה הזה

This day is a day of trouble, of rebuke, and derision.[39]

Brethren? You will have recognized in my quotation the words wherewith the messengers of Hezekiah addressed the prophet, Isaiah, in the name of their sorrow-stricken king. The army of Assyria had then invaded the country of Judah and its chief general had added insult to the injury, by public expressions of opprobrium and blasphemy. To avert national dishonor and ruin, the prayer of the inspired servant of God, was at that juncture earnestly solicited.

But the text I have chosen may possibly be deemed too doleful for the occasion I was officially asked to recall to your memory. A stirring oration on political topics may perhaps be anticipated, as the most fitting manner of complying with the request. But with all due deference to the opinion entertained by the influential body of men, who have applied for my services,

I will say,—as the heathen Seer of whom we have read in the section of this morning,—אתו אדבר הדבר אשר ישים אלהים בפי—"The word which God putteth in my mouth, that shall I speak."[40]

I am not indifferent, my dear friends! to the event, which four score and seven years ago, brought to this new world light and joy. I yield to none in feelings of deep reverence for the sages and patriots that labored for its consummation. The principles enunciated in the document unfolded and first read in yonder hall, command still my highest admiration. But the more intently I gaze upon the bright past, the darker does the present appear in my vision.

The murky clouds which have long hovered all over the American horizon, gathered at length menacingly nearer to our homes. The thunder was ready to burst upon our heads, and we,—in our mad security,—neglected to set up the lightning rods, wherewith to blunt its violence. Behold, my hearers! the deplorable consequences and weep. The dust raised by the foot of invasion has tarnished our escutcheon. Havoc and devastation rage in our borders. Verily, I feel humbled to the earth, for, I have heard the reproach of our neighbors—though loyal—whose proffered help we have imperatively needed to shield us from danger. I cannot therefore ignore the present humiliation, and triumph over the past. To evoke joyful feelings in your breasts by description of our former achievements, would be a vain effort; for this day which commemorates them is to us יום צרה ותוכחה ונאצה—"a day of trouble, of rebuke and derision."

But another powerful motive combines to affect us very sadly. Brethren! This day is the opening of the three unpropitious weeks, which preceded the overthrow of Israel's nationality. From the seventeenth of Tamuz, date the aggravation of those evils unparalleled in history, which culminated in the burning of Solomon's temple and the dispersion of our people. The daily sacrifices, which amidst the horrors of a protracted war, had still continued to be offered, ceased upon this day. The Roman sword, reeking with the blood of the brave defenders of the land of their birth, transfixed defenseless women and innocent infants, who had sought refuge beneath the wings of God's dwelling. By the altar whereupon they laid oblations in homage to the Most High, the priests of the Lord fell victims to Roman ruthlessness. The ensign of heathen foes polluted the courts of our Sanctuary. Their carousals were indulged in, even within the holy precincts, which none was suffered to enter but the anointed descendant of Aaron upon יום הכפורים the great day of Atonement. Aye, my Brethren! Upon this inauspicious day, the ravages of famine deadened maternal feelings and robbed nature of its instincts.

Can it be then reasonably expected that I should expatiate upon a joyful theme? Can I delineate in glowing characters the happiness and glory derived, for a period, from the declaration that the colonial states had sundered apart the bonds of dependence, when the effects of a long thralldom and of fraternal strife stare me in the face? No, the times do not warrant it; the melancholy occurrences that befell us, my brothers and sisters in faith, at this season, direct my thoughts to a gloomy subject.

But if I cannot, consistently with the feeling I experience at present, revert to the joyous events of the past, I may and will beseech the Eternal our God the future.

In the communication received officially, I was requested to hold such service as may propitiate the blessing of Heaven upon us and our cause. You will all concur with me in the opinion that I could not more appropriately fulfill the expressed wish than by inviting you to prayer. פנה אל תפלת הערער ולא בזה את תפלתם "God regardeth the entreaty of the forlorn and despiseth not their petition."[41] To it did our fathers betake themselves when suffering tribulations and were relieved. With that armour they protected themselves against heavenly wrath, and the same panoply shall defend us this day from the arrows of a provoked Deity.

PRAYER

Almighty God! Suffer our entreaty to ascend Thy throne and hearken unto it, as Thou didst hearken unto that King Hezekiah and Isaiah the prophet. Our merits cannot, like theirs, intercede for us, but Thy mercy is not measured by human virtues, for alas! we should then have long since been driven from Thy presence.

Behold our confusion by reason of him that reproacheth and derideth. Uplift us from the dust into which our sins have cast us. Raise the horn of our salvation. Encircle Pennsylvania with Thy mighty shield, protect the lives of her inhabitants. Let her adversaries be foiled in their devices; let the fowler's snare be broken, and the souls of Thy suppliants be delivered. Cause the din of war to cease from this our beloved State. But let the sound of Thy praises be heard in her borders, at the tidings of her success. Oh! Return unto us! O God of our salvation, remove from Thy servants Thy fierce anger. Then this day which has brought us trouble, rebuke and derision will henceforth be celebrated with a joyful heart with glory and national happiness. For in Thee alone we trust, O Most High! And through Thy divine aid we shall again walk in enlargement. So may it speedily be, and say ye, Amen.[42]

Gettysburg Address Parody

Four score and seven years ago a score of loyal Jewish citizens brought forth in this community a new organization conceived in necessity and dedicated to the proposition that we "aid, Americanize and naturalize the Jewish immigrants." Now we are engaged in a great civil strife, testing whether this organization or any organization so conceived and so dedicated can long endure. We are met at the crisis of that strife. We have come to dedicate the Hebrew Immigrant Aid Society as a monument for those who gave their energies that this organization might live. It is altogether fitting and proper that we should do this. But in a larger sense we cannot dedicate, we cannot consecrate, we cannot hallow this body. The willing workers here and elsewhere, who have worked here, have consecrated it far above our powers to add or detract.

The world will little note or long remember what we say here, but it can never forget what they did. It is for us, the present members, rather to be dedicated here to the unfinished task which they who labored here have thus far so nobly advanced. It is rather for us to be here dedicated to the great task remaining before us, that from these willing workers we take increased devotion to that cause for which they gave the full measure of devotion; that we here highly resolve that these efforts and sacrifices shall not have been in vain; that this organization, under God, shall have a new birth of freedom, and that the government of this organization by the Jews, and for the Jews, shall not perish from the earth.   A. A. (With apologies to Abraham Lincoln.)[43]

4. THIS, TOO, SHALL PASS

On September 30, 1859, Abraham Lincoln delivered an address to the Wisconsin State Agricultural Society in Milwaukee. Although this speech is not as well known as many others and its rhetoric is not as soaring as that in many of his famous addresses, Lincoln's 1859 Milwaukee speech proved to be a significant and thoughtful oration. He famously told his audience to be wary of politicians who flatter them, since farmers "are neither better nor worse than other people," only "more numerous." In another clever turn of phrase, Lincoln described agriculture as a form of "cultivated thought," saying, "Every blade of grass is a study; and to produce two, where there was but one, is both a profit and a pleasure."[44]

During these agricultural gatherings, "premiums" or prizes were given to farmers who made outstanding contributions to the field of agriculture. Lincoln made reference to this ceremony at the end of his Milwaukee address, and many commented on the concluding paragraphs of the speech, reproduced below. In it, Lincoln quotes an interesting story that was meant to offer a measure of comfort and perspective to those farmers who were destined to experience disappointment in failing to receive a premium from the agricultural society.

The story Lincoln cites is a folk legend that begins, "An Eastern monarch once charged his wise men to invent him a sentence, to be ever in view, and which should be true and appropriate in all times and situations." The wise men presented the monarch with the words "And this, too, shall pass away." Those familiar with Jewish folk literature will recognize this famous apothegm, which is frequently recited in Hebrew, Yiddish, and English and is often mistakenly attributed to the Talmud, though the phrase does

גז״י

‎גם זו יעבור‎
GAM ZU YAAVOR
THIS TOO WILL PASS

$3.95

TRADE MARK
REG. U. S. PAT. OFFICE
NO. 397792

GOOD LUCK RING
FOR YOUR BOY IN THE SERVICE

Through these difficult days, the letters גז״י meaning, "THIS, TOO, WILL PASS" will cheer and comfort everyone who reads it

It is believed that this prophecy of our holy men will bring good luck and peace of mind to all who contemplate it. Your son, sweetheart, brother or friend will be proud to wear this beautiful Sterling Silver Ring and thus carry this inspirational message always with him

World War II "good luck ring" advertisement. In 1859, Lincoln cited a familiar folk legend known as the "This, Too, Shall Pass" story. The expression has endured as a popular Jewish folk saying, "Gam zu ya'avor." See Yehudah Avidah, "Gam Zeh Ya'avor," *Yeda-'Am: Journal of the Israel Folklore Society* 7–8 (May 1951): 14.

not appear as such anywhere in the rabbinic literature. Yet a very similar phrase, "This, too, is for the good" (gam zu l'tovah), does indeed come from the Talmud.[45]

In the Journal of American Folklore, *a distinguished scholar of Jewish folklore, Dov Noy (1920–2013) of Haifa University, noted there exist numerous versions of this story in the folk literature of various Middle Eastern Jewish communities. The Jewish versions of this legend tend to identify the "monarch" as King Solomon.*[46] *During World War II, jewelers and artists began to produce "good luck rings" with the Hebrew acronym "gimmel-zayin-yod" symbolizing this phrase, gam zu ya'avor ("This, too, shall pass"). Later, rings engraved with the entire phrase began to appear, and jewelry of this sort has increased in popularity up to the present day.*[47]

Lincoln's closing observations at the Wisconsin State Agricultural Society, beyond their characteristic kindness, are intriguing because of the legend he chose to quote. Lincoln's use of a folk story that appeared in Jewish literature and that resonated with the spirit of Judaism's ancient wisdom has only served to reinforce a generalized impression that the sixteenth president possessed an intuitive appreciation of Jewish lore and learning.

Concluding Section of an Address by Abraham Lincoln
before the Wisconsin State Agricultural Society

Some of you will be successful, and such will need but little philosophy to take them home in cheerful spirits; others will be disappointed, and will be in a less happy mood. To such, let it be said, "Lay it not too much to heart." Let them adopt the maxim, "Better luck next time"; and then, by renewed exertion, make that better luck for themselves.

And by the successful, and unsuccessful, let it be remembered, that while occasions like the present, bring their sober and durable benefits, the exultations and mortifications of them are but temporary; that the victor shall soon be the vanquished, if he relax in his exertion; and that the vanquished this year, may be victor the next, in spite of all competition.

It is said an Eastern monarch once charged his wise men to invent him a sentence, to be ever in view, and which should be true and appropriate in all times and situations. They presented him the words: *"And this, too, shall pass away."* How much it expresses! How chastening in the hour of pride! How consoling in the depths of affliction! "And this, too, shall pass away." And yet, let us hope, it is not *quite* true. Let us hope, rather, that by the best cultivation of the physical world, beneath and around us, and the intellectual and moral world within us, we shall secure an individual, social, and political prosperity and happiness, whose course shall be onward and upward, and which, while the earth endures, shall not pass away.[48]

5. LINCOLN AND JEWISH EDUCATION

The extent to which Lincoln still serves as an American Jewish exemplar can be seen in the exceptional role he has played in the world of Jewish education. During the last half of the twentieth century, Jewish educators made use of Lincoln's legacy as a curricular tool for Jewish learning. Despite the fact that Lincoln was not a Jew, his life and career have been used to enhance and advance Jewish knowledge. Although three examples of this phenomenon appear below, it will be the task of future researchers to assess the various ways in which Lincoln's persona will have influenced American Jewish educational curricula and program materials over the course of the next half century.

Sadie Rose Weilerstein (1894–1993) became one of the most popular authors of Jewish textbooks from the 1930s to the 1970s. In 1930, she created an imaginary character named K'tonton, a young boy who was always getting into trouble but whose adventures transformed Jewish learning into an exciting experience for generations of American Jewish youth. By the 1970s, Weilerstein had published a dozen textbooks featuring K'tonton and many other lovable characters.[49]

One of Weilerstein's textbooks, Little New Angel, *first published in 1947, featured two young sisters, Ruthie and Debby, and their new baby brother, Michael. In each of* the book's chapters, Ruthie, Debby, baby Michael, and their parents manage to teach readers something new and interesting about Jewish life in America. The chapter reprinted below is titled "A Seder on Lincoln's Birthday." The fact that Weilerstein used the life of Abraham Lincoln as a strategy for teaching Jewish children about Passover is only one noteworthy facet of this chapter. Considering the fact that this work appeared eight years before the Supreme Court rendered its watershed decision in the case of Brown vs. Board of Education, Weilerstein's interest in civil rights for the American black is truly noteworthy. The author wanted her young Jewish readers to recognize that on Passover, Jews should celebrate both the Jewish exodus from Egypt and the emancipation of the Negro slaves in America. Weilerstein's "Lincoln's Birthday Seder" leads seamlessly into the story of George Washington Carver, "one of the little slave children that Abraham Lincoln helped to free." Carver's professional career demonstrated to the readers that Abraham Lincoln, like Moses in the story of the Exodus, had wrought unhemmed good by freeing slaves. "If Abraham Lincoln had not helped to free the slaves," Weilerstein wrote, "George Washington Carver might have stayed a slave all his life."

Rabbi Philip Goodman (1911–2006) joined the program staff of the National Jewish Welfare Board (JWB) in 1942. Until his retirement in 1976, Goodman wrote and coedited a wide range of Jewish educational publications. In 1953, Goodman published a volume titled Lincoln's Birthday: Program Material for Jewish Groups. The book was published by the JWB to assist the Jewish community in commemorating the tercentenary of Jewish settlement in America (1654–1954). The volume's table of contents and especially its introduction—reproduced below—shed light on Goodman's conviction that Lincoln's birthday, a legal holiday in the United States, "may aid in developing an appreciation of the Jewish ideals of democracy that have helped to mold American life [and] create an understanding of the contributions that Jews have made to the growth of America."

In 1992, Benjamin Edidin Scolnic (b. 1953) published an essay in which he presented "a model for the integration of Jewish and secular education" for Jewish parochial schools.[50] Paralleling the dichotomy that separates critical history from memory, Scolnic argued that "Lincoln legends" are just as important in the realm of religious education as "the real-life Lincoln" is to the historian. Rabbinic legends shed light on values and principles that the ancient Jewish sages preserved, but "we can learn a great deal about the values of [America] by examining the process through which the Lincoln legends were developed."

These interesting examples of Jewish educational and program material that appeared in the twentieth century demonstrate that Jewish educators believed that by studying Lincoln's life and legacy, American Jews could ultimately strengthen their Jewish roots.[51] As Philip Goodman pointed out, Lincoln's life offered American Jewry an opportunity to celebrate the values that have been "an integral part of Jewish life for many centuries."

A
Seder on
Lincoln's Birthday

"WHAT are we going to do tomorrow?" asked Debby.

"Tomorrow" was Lincoln's Birthday.

"You'll have a vacation from school," said Mother.

"But what will we *do*, Mother?"

Ruth and Debby were used to doing things on holidays. They lit Hanukkah lights on Hanukkah. They masqueraded on Purim.

91

Sadie Rose Weilerstein's textbook *Little New Angel*, first published in 1947, included a chapter titled "A Seder on Lincoln's Birthday." Reprinted from *Little New Angel* by Sadie Rose Weilerstein by permission of the University of Nebraska Press; copyright 1947 by the Jewish Publication Society.

A Seder on Lincoln's Birthday

by Sadie Rose Weilerstein

"What are we going to do tomorrow?" asked Debby.

"Tomorrow" was Lincoln's Birthday.

"You'll have a vacation from school," said Mother.

"But what will we *do*, Mother?"

Ruth and Debby were used to doing things on holidays. They lit Hanukkah lights on Hanukkah. They masqueraded on Purim. They ate turkey on Thanksgiving day and cherry tarts on Washington's Birthday.

"What would you like to do for Lincoln's Birthday?" Mother asked.

"We could have a Seder or something," Debby answered.

"But a Seder is for Pesach,"[52] said Ruthie.

"We could have a Seder *two* times," Debby insisted. "Abraham Lincoln saved the negro slaves, same as Moses saved us."

So next day the family had a Seder. It wasn't a *Pesach Seder* with *matzah* and the *mahnishtanah* and *Had Gadya*.[53] It was a Lincoln's Birthday Seder.

There was a log cabin for a centerpiece. Ruth and Debby had made it out of their Lincoln logs, and Mother had heaped a pile of peanuts on each side of it. She didn't say why.

"The first thing will be the Four Questions," Daddy said. "Every Seder must begin with four questions. Ask a question, Debby."

But Debby couldn't think of a question to ask. She tried, but not a question came into her mind. Ruth couldn't think of a question either.

"Well," Daddy said, "if you don't ask, you must tell. Tell a story, Debby."

So Debby told the story of Abraham Lincoln. She learned it in school. And now that she didn't *have* to ask a question, a question popped right out of her mouth.

"Was Abraham Lincoln a Jew, Daddy?"

"No," said Daddy, "he was a Christian."

"Then why was his name Abraham?"

"Because his mother loved the Bible stories. She gave her baby the same name as Abraham in the Bible."

"Did the slaves read the Bible stories?" Debby asked.

"They couldn't read," Daddy explained. "They weren't sent to school. But they knew the stories. They sang songs about them."

And Daddy and Mother sang *When Israel Was in Egypt Land*. Ruth and Debby joined in the chorus.

"Go down Moses.

Tell old Pharaoh to let my people go."

After that they sang *Little David Play on Your Harp*, and *Old Black Joe*, and *Way Down upon the Swanee River*.

And that made Debby think of another question.

"Did the negro slaves hide their babies in the Swanee River?"

She was thinking of Baby Moses, whose mother hid him in a basket in the Nile.

"No," Mother said, "they didn't hide their babies in the river. But they loved them very much. That's why they were so happy about Abraham Lincoln. They wanted their babies to grow up to be free and not slaves."

And now Ruthie thought of a question.

"Why are black people black, Mother? Why can't they be white like us?"

"Because God made them black," Mother explained. "He said, 'I must take good care of these children of mine. They live in the middle of Africa where the sun is burning hot. I will put plenty of pigment in their skin. (Pigment is color.) Then the sun won't burn them and they will be comfortable and well.' This was long ago in the beginning of things."

"Any more questions?" asked Daddy.

And Ruthie, who had been looking at the piles of peanuts all through the Seder, asked, "What are the peanuts for, Mother?"

"That's the question I've been waiting for," said Mother. "The peanuts are to eat, after you've heard a story about them."

And mother told the story of [. . .]

GEORGE WASHINGTON CARVER AND THE PEANUTS

The story is about one of the little slave children that Abraham Lincoln helped to free. His name was George Washington Carver. When he was hardly more than a baby, wicked men came and stole his mother away. But a kind farmer's wife looked after him.

Little George was so frightened, it was a long time before he learned to speak to people. He stammered and stuttered whenever he tried. But he talked to the little wild creatures in the wood, and they became his friends. He sang to the flowers and they taught him their secrets. And because he had no father or mother to talk to, he talked to God. He called God, "Mr. Creator."

Little George learned so much from the plants and books, that when he grew up he became a great and wise teacher, a scientist. First he taught the white boys and girls in a university in the north. But he kept thinking about his own people, the ragged, barefooted boys and girls in the south, whose fathers and grandfathers had been slaves just as he had been. They wanted so much to learn, but there was no one to teach them.

"They need me," George Washington Carver said. "I will go down to Tuskegee and teach them to be good farmers."

Tuskegee was a new school for colored people in Alabama.

One day the farmers came to Mr. Carver in great trouble.

"The Boll Weevil has come," they cried. "All our cotton plants are dying. The blossoms are falling to the ground."

The Boll Weevils were tiny bugs with ENORMOUS appetites. The ate and they ate and they ate until every cotton plant was killed.

"What shall we do?" the farmers cried. There were black farmers and white farmers among them. "We have no cotton to sell. Our children will go hungry."

"Plant peanuts," Mr. Carver said to them. "Boll Weevils never hurt peanuts. And peanuts are good for men and good for soil."

So the farmers planted peanuts. The plants grew green and sturdy. The blossoms bent over, burrowed into the ground and turned into plump pods.

But a new trouble came. Nobody wanted to buy the peanuts.

"We have all the bags of peanuts we can sell," said the peanut-stand man.

"What can we do with peanuts? We have all the salted peanuts we need," said the storekeepers.

Again the farmers were sad. But this time they were angry too.

"Why did you tell us to plant peanuts?" they cried. "The peanuts will rot in the ground. We shall grow poor and our children will go hungry."

Then George Washington Carver went off by himself and prayed to God.

"Dear Mr. Creator," he prayed, "please tell me what the peanut was made for. What is it? What can we do with it?"

And he thought God answered: "Go into your laboratory. Take your burners and your pans and your beakers and your chemicals and your microscope. I will show you how to take the peanut apart and put it together again."

Then George Washington Carver took bushel baskets full of peanuts and locked himself into his laboratory. All day long he worked, and all night, and the next day and night, and the next and the next and the next. Then at last he opened his door and called for his pupils. On the table was a long row of things that had not been there before—oil, cheese, milk, stains, ink, soap, flour, cattle feed. All these things George Washington Carver had made—out of PEANUTS.

And he kept on making things out of peanuts—three hundred different things. Now the poor farmers, the white ones and the colored ones, could sell all the peanuts they raised. They weren't poor any more. And it was all because of George Washington Carver.

"And Abraham Lincoln," Debby added.

"True," said Mother. "If Abraham Lincoln had not helped to free the slaves, George Washington Carver might have stayed a slave all his life."

Then they ate their peanuts and the Seder was over.[54]

From *Lincoln's Birthday: Program Material for Jewish Groups*

Compiled and edited by Philip Goodman

Lincoln's Birthday on February 12th is a legal holiday in more than thirty states.

The celebration of Lincoln's Birthday is an inspiring occasion for the people of America. Lincoln's life is studded with gems of toil and perseverance, integrity of purpose, pursuit of justice, humaneness and humbleness, and is crowned with a peculiar genius all his own. From the obscurity of an environment of low social status and dire poverty through conscientious service and devotion to lofty ideals, Abe Lincoln rose to the pinnacle of honor in the United States of America. His achievement is one of the noblest inspirations for modern Americans.

For the Jewish people of our land it has added significance. Not only did Lincoln have Jewish friends but he was a friend of the Jews as well as of all other minority groups. The commemoration of the birthday of the Great Emancipator by Jewish groups should include an exposition of the values exemplified by the celebrant's life which have been an integral part of Jewish life for many centuries as well as a presentation of his biography and his relationships to the Jews. These permanent values—industry, studiousness, honesty, courage, loyalty, love of books, respect for all men and fear of God—are as valid today as they were for Honest Abe a century ago. Lincoln was not perfect. He was human, suffered frailties and overcame many obstacles. Because he was human and yet succeeded in filling an exemplary role in American life, we cherish his memory and strive to learn from his life. Indeed, Lincoln embodied many values that have always been part and parcel of the Jewish heritage.

Appropriate celebrations of Lincoln's Birthday and other uses of the occasion for group programming may aid in developing an appreciation of the Jewish ideals of democracy that have helped to mold American life; create an understanding of the contributions that Jews have made to the growth of America; and promote better relationships among peoples of all faiths on the American scene.

There is an abundance of literature on the life, writings and speeches of Lincoln that is readily available in numerous volumes. . . . This book is primarily although not exclusively limited to the presentation of material for programming concerning Lincoln and the Jews.

Preparation for Lincoln's Birthday may be an integral part of a group's on-going program. Interest may be aroused through any number of the usual means used in group work to stimulate participation. Many aspects of group programming lend themselves to the introduction of the subject. House or club councils may assume the responsibility for initiating suitable projects.

Jewish Community Centers may invite Jewish chaplains, Jewish war veterans, boy scouts and girl scouts to participate in Lincoln's Birthday celebrations.

While such events at Centers may highlight the Jewish interest, they should not preclude the possibility of the Center's cooperating with other civic agencies in sponsoring community-wide celebrations. The observance of Lincoln's Birthday may be combined with that of Brotherhood Week.

The celebration of Lincoln's Birthday offers opportunities for expanding the total Jewish program of the agency. Skillful programming for this occasion involves the integrated use of creative skills—drama, writing, arts and crafts, music—as well as appropriate games, stories, plays and pageants, discussions, trips to points of historical interest, parties, dances and other social activity. . . .

An early publication of the National Jewish Welfare Board on Lincoln's Birthday has been out-of-print for many years. It is hoped that this book will meet the long-felt need to provide program material to aid Jewish groups in the observance of Lincoln's Birthday. Most of the material on Lincoln and his relationships with the Jews is unavailable. This compilation, with the inclusion of much new material hithertofore unpublished, is an effort to present within one binding program suggestions and actual material so as to spare its users the need to refer to sources not generally accessible. A conscious attempt was made to include the most useful material.[55]

Footsteps on the Ceiling and Idols on the Floor: Integrated Study of History and Story in the Conservative Jewish Day School

by Benjamin Edidin Scolnic

YOUNG HONEST ABE: THE FUNERAL OF NANCY HANKS AND "FOOTSTEPS ON THE CEILING"

If we have been raised in the United States we know the stories of Young Abe Lincoln. We heard them as children, and now, as parents, we share them with our own children. We talk about Young Abe walking twenty miles to borrow a book (when we can't get our kids away from the VCR) or of Abe's struggling to read by firelight.

In every book I have read about Lincoln, whether for children or adults, there is at least a passage about the death of Nancy Hanks Lincoln, Abe's mother, when he was only nine years old. There was no funeral as such when they buried her. According to these books, Abe was extremely upset that proper honor was not done to his mother. Some writers maintain that he wrote to a preacher to request a more dignified ceremony at a later date.

The fact is that Lincoln never wrote to a preacher, as "history-legend" has it. Young Abe couldn't have done so; he did not know how to write (he would not learn until five years later). What we know about the culture of his time and place indicates that Lincoln probably wasn't even familiar with the concept of a funeral as we think of it. If he was concerned about such things, he had a strange way of showing it; there would be no monument or marker of any kind over his mother's grave during his lifetime.[56]

This is what history does to meaning. It levels it, often destroys it. There is no history about Nancy Hanks Lincoln's death except that she died. And since that is a terrible fact, it cries out to be cried over, it demands interpretation and analysis. How did young Abe feel? How did he cope? Did he cry? Did this death affect him in lasting ways?

So story fills in the gaps, somewhat like *derash* fills in the *p'shat*.[57] The modern writers superimpose their own feelings about what a funeral should be like and assume that Lincoln must have been terribly disappointed that a proper service was not conducted.

Less than a year after his mother's death, Abe's father left his sister and him totally alone. They were living in an unfinished cabin, without a real ceiling or floor. His father returned with their new stepmother, who immediately insisted that the cabin should be finished. She was especially happy with her new, whitewashed ceiling. Young Abe decided to have a good time. He got his older cousin to lift him upside down so that Abe could make footprints across the clean white ceiling. How would his new stepmother respond? She looked at the footprints and laughed. "Nobody but Abe Lincoln would ever have thought up such a thing," she said. They cleaned up the ceiling together.

What does the story tell us? The new stepmother appreciates Abe. Footprints on the ceiling test her, and a family is created.

The story of the footprints on the ceiling is a cute story, but no cuter than any that most of us have in our own family memory-book. It is only in the context of Abraham Lincoln's life that the story attains historical importance. The roof of the Lincoln cabin was finished because of Abe's stepmother, it was unfinished before she came. She made them turn a hut into a house. Footprints on the ceiling mocked her efforts.

It is not important whether this story is historically true or not. As a written record, it carries the truth of literature or text. It is not a superimposition of meaning which runs counter to the custom of Abe's environment. This cute story becomes important because it represents the new stage of Abe's emotional life with a new mother.

History tells us that Abe never read by firelight. History tells us that Abe Lincoln only went to school for a short while, so he did not walk six miles back and forth for years, as the legends tell it.[58]

But history is not just what happened. History is also what we say happened. History has selected and developed certain stories about Abraham Lincoln's life. That selection process tells us more about American dreams and myths, about the values we want our children to have, than it does about Abraham Lincoln's actual experiences. . . .

We are the stories that we tell about ourselves. Do we really think that the patient on the psychoanalyst's couch is accurately reporting exactly what happened to him? Memory is much more complex than that. In many ways, the patient "creates" his history by interpreting his memory and experiences. The analyst interprets his patient's case-history as story. Even a case-history, then, becomes a literary form. . . .[59]

Each historical figure is a separate case, but the literary traditions about the Biblical Abraham and Abraham Lincoln are fairly typical in the way they develop answers to questions which may never have been asked when the Torah was written or Abraham Lincoln was living. . . .

A story such as "Footsteps on the Ceiling" shows, in a most reassuring way, how human Abraham Lincoln was. The story helps the child to counter the feelings of inferiority. The impact of the story may be that "Abe Lincoln was just a prankster and look how he turned out . . ."

In the separation of levels of meaning, all meanings become clearer. After all is said and done, we are trying to create American Jews who can integrate their religious beliefs with their understanding of the modern world, who are not left with inner dichotomies. In bringing children back to the point where meaning is created, by following the same methodology whether the subject is religious or secular, we will enable the students to achieve their own versions of integration. We are trying to create human beings who understand the implications of history and of classic texts for their own lives. Each child, in his imagination, will achieve his own synthesis of the stories he is told. . . .

CONCLUSIONS

What can we learn about America from the tales it tells about its heroes? Study of Abraham Lincoln would take us back, as William Safire's brilliant novel *Freedom*[60] does, to the real-life Lincoln, with all of the controversy and turbulence associated with his leadership. But what objective history has to say about Lincoln is only part of what America remembers about him. We can learn a great deal about the values of our country by examining the process through which the Lincoln legends were developed. Standing on the verge of the creation of meaning, from the perspective of Lincoln's own time, we can understand not only how but why those legends sprang into existence. The American dream will attain a new and different level of meaning and, thus, a new and different reality.[61]

6. WAS ABRAHAM LINCOLN JEWISH?

It is difficult to determine when American Jews began wondering whether Abraham Lincoln was actually a bone fide Jew. During his presidency, we do know that when

Lincoln lived in the White House, the Jews of Louisville "jocularly" referred to Lincoln as "Rabbi Abraham," and in his oft-quoted eulogy for Lincoln, Rabbi Isaac M. Wise claimed that the president himself told him he had always believed he was a descendant of Jewish parentage. The author of Abraham Lincoln and the Jews, Isaac Markens, asked Lincoln's son Robert if he had ever heard his parents discussing the possibility that the president came from Jewish descent. Robert claimed he had never in his life heard the topic discussed by his parents or by anyone in the family. In 1951, when Bertram W. Korn published his magnum opus, American Jewry and the Civil War, he did not give Wise's assertion any credence, saying, "It is almost incomprehensible that Lincoln should have said the exact words quoted by Wise without having made similar statements to other acquaintances."[62]

In spite of all evidence to the contrary, the belief that Lincoln may actually have been a descendant of Jewish lineage continues to endure. The first document presented below appeared in a publication titled Eden, a monthly publication edited by the Junior Congregation of the Reading Road Temple, Cincinnati, Ohio. To commemorate Lincoln's birthday in February 1929, a student named Morton Reiser[63] composed an eight-verse poem titled "Some Say Lincoln Was a Jew," comparing the sixteenth president to "Moses of old."

The second document, "Was There a Jewish President?," has enjoyed worldwide circulation via the Internet ever since 2006, when the article first appeared. This "urban legend" was attributed to Rabbi Jeff Kahn (b. 1952), then of Temple Har Shalom, Warren, New Jersey. Various versions of this same speculative suggestion have continued to spread, including some anti-Semitic renderings that have even appeared on the websites of white supremacist groups by way of explaining that it was actually Lincoln's "Jewishness" that compelled him to free the slaves![64]

The final document is a sermon written by Rabbi Adam J. Raskin (b. 1974), Beth Torah Congregation, Richardson, Texas. Raskin's sermon, delivered on February 14, 2009, for the bicentennial anniversary of Lincoln's birth, starts by recapitulating the "myth of Lincoln's Jewishness." The rabbi begins by reviewing many of the same ideas that originally appeared in the Kahn document, but he concludes by reminding the congregation of a famous story that the artist Frances B. Carpenter (1830–1900) immortalized. When asked why he never joined a church, Carpenter overheard Lincoln say:

> I have never united myself to any church, because I have found difficulty in giving my assent, without mental reservation, to the long, complicated statements of Christian doctrine which characterize their articles of Belief and Confessions of Faith. When any church will inscribe over its altar, as its sole qualification for membership, the Savior's condensed statement of the substance of both law and gospel: "Thou shalt love the Lord thy God with all thy heart and with all thy soul and with all the mind [sic],"[65] [and also] "love thy neighbor as thyself"[66]—that church will I join with all my heart and all my soul.[67]

Lincoln's decision to cite these particular phrases from the Hebrew scriptures, particularly the admonition that comes from Deuteronomy 6:5—a phrase that traditional Jews recite three times a day—seemed to underscore Lincoln's affinity to the principles that are at the core of Jewish theology. This may be why, the rabbi goes on to suggest, Lincoln was drawn so powerfully toward the path of justice and righteousness during the course of his life.

From the days of Lincoln's presidency, when the Jews of Louisville apparently dubbed him "Rabbi Abraham," to the numerous contemporaneous "urban legends" on the Internet suggesting that Lincoln came from Jewish stock, it is clear that conjectures that Lincoln was a Jew by genealogical descent continue to flourish. Despite the fact that there exists no empirical evidence that Lincoln was a Jew by the standards of traditional Jewish law, it is more than evident that many Americans—both Jews and non-Jews—are fascinated by the possibility, however remote, that Abraham Lincoln may have indeed been a Jew by descent.

As for American Jews, they have long accepted Lincoln as an honorary Jew, or, to paraphrase the president's own famous phrase, American Jews have persistently reconstructed Lincoln into an "almost chosen person."[68]

LINCOLN

by Morton Reiser

Some say Lincoln was a Jew,
For he had all the virtues:
He was kind and loving,
Honest, staunch, and true.
He it was who freed the slaves,
Like Moses did of old.
The Patriarch the Jews did save,
In our history 'tis told.[69]

Was There a Jewish President?

by Rabbi Jeff Kahn

On the twelfth of February, 1809, nearly 200 years ago, a young, poor illiterate woman from Virginia, Nancy Hanks Lincoln, gave birth to a son, in a log cabin, built along the banks of the south fork of Nolin Creek, near what is now Hodgenville, Kentucky. That baby, whom she named Abraham, grew to become one of our greatest, and most tragic, national leaders.

Lincoln was a man of great spiritual conviction. Yet, and I find this fact fascinatingly instructive, Abraham Lincoln was the only American president not to have declared himself a member of any particular religious faith. That fact has given rise to a great deal of interesting speculation. In fact, there are those who believe that Honest Abe was Jewish. After all, his name was

Abraham. His great-grandfather was named Mordechai. Lincoln was the only President not to have a formal religious affiliation. He was neither raised in a church nor did he ever belong to a church.

And there's more . . . the town of Lincoln, in eastern England, whence his ancestors came, has an interesting Jewish history. A Jewish community was established there in 1159. During Crusader riots, the Sheriff of Lincoln saved the Jews by giving them official protection. St. Hugh, the great Bishop of Lincoln, taught love of Jews to his parishioners. His death was marked by an official period of mourning among Lincoln's Jews. Rabbi Joseph of Lincoln was a scholar mentioned in the Talmud; Aaron of Lincoln was a financier whose operations extended all over the country.

In 1255, Lincoln's Jews were accused of ritual murder. Ninety-one Lincoln Jews were sent to London for trial and 18 were executed. Notwithstanding, the Lincoln Jewish community flourished until 1290, when they were forcibly expelled by edict.

Most Jewish historians assume that all the Jews of Lincoln left in 1290. But could it be possible that some remained, practicing their Judaism in secret . . . passing the family secret from generation to generation? The more we learn of the secret life of Spanish Jewry following the Expulsion of 1492, the more we must at least consider the possibility of the same thing occurring elsewhere.

When Abraham Lincoln was assassinated, whole Jewish communities sat shivah. Rabbis all over the country eulogized the fallen President. Rabbi Isaac Mayer Wise, the man who created Reform Judaism in this country, began his eulogy with the words ". . . Brethren, the lamented Abraham Lincoln believed himself to be bone from our bone and flesh from our flesh. He supposed himself to be a descendant of Hebrew parentage. He said so in my presence."

Lincoln was often questioned about his religious beliefs. Time and again, he told of a special passage from Scripture that summed up his theology. It was the twentieth chapter of the Book of Exodus he recommended that every American study, learn and follow. In English it is usually referred to as the Ten Commandments.[70]

Abraham Lincoln and the *Pintele Yid*

By Rabbi Adam J. Raskin

Shabbat Shalom, and Happy President's Day Weekend to all! I'm sure that you all know that Monday is President's Day . . . and this year, President's Day is extra-special because of the bicentennial celebration of the birth of our 16th President, Abraham Lincoln . . . who also of course was the first Jewish president! Surely you've considered the evidence for Lincoln being a Jew. . . . Beyond the fact that he had a beard and wore a black hat . . . he also had a grandfather named Mordechai, worked as an attorney, loved to argue and debate, hated hunting, loved reading, had a tinge of depression, was treated only by Jewish doctors, and had in-laws who didn't think he was good enough for their daughter. Probably because he wasn't a doctor! Sounds *like a Jewish man to me*! Seriously though, Lincoln used to say about Mary Todd's parents that "God made do with one 'd' but the Todds demanded two!" And to top it all off, Lincoln has a street named after him in Jerusalem!

Now you should know that Snopes doesn't totally dismiss the myth of Lincoln's Jewishness. Not so much for the reasons I just listed, but because of other interesting tidbits . . . like the fact that the Jews of Lincoln, England, where the President's family hailed from were famously protected by the Sheriff of Lincoln during the Crusader Riots of 1159. St. Hugh, the bishop of Lincoln, regularly preached of loving Jews, and it was considered a haven of sorts when Jews fled from other places of persecution. Surprisingly, Lincoln never publicly claimed a religious affiliation, an unusual detail for the 19th Century. Surely to publicly claim to be a Jew would have hampered his rise to power in that day and age. Isaac Mayer Wise, the father of Reform Judaism in America who was among several of Lincoln's eulogizers said: "Bretheren [sic], the lamented Abraham Lincoln believed himself to be bone of our bone, flesh of our flesh. He supposed himself to be a descendent of Hebrew parentage. He said so in my presence." How about that for a testimonial! The problem is that we cannot corroborate that Lincoln said that to Rabbi Wise, nor any other suspicions about his ancestry. But there was one detail that Lincoln often mentioned publicly that piqued my interest. Since Lincoln was always so coy about his religious beliefs of affiliation, he was often asked about it by reporters, biographers, and colleagues. His answer was always: "There is one piece of Scripture that sums up my theology . . . the 20th Chapter of the Book of Exodus."

Friends, as we all know certainly this morning, the 20th chapter of the book of Exodus is none other than the thrilling scene at Mt. Sinai, where Moses receives the 10 Commandments. I find it fascinating that Lincoln did not say John 3:16, Matthew 7:3, Mark 10:27, or Luke 18:27 (I didn't make those up, they're all famous, important Christian scriptural citations). . . . No Lincoln chose the most significant, identifiable, transformative moment in Jewish history as the crux of his own theology. Now that's something! The Midrash Tanchuma[71] teaches that all souls of Jews who were living at that time, as well as all the souls of Jews who would ever live in the future were present at Mt. Sinai. People who would be born Jewish, and people who would choose to become Jewish . . . some part of their inanimate life, something of their spiritual matter was present along with the 600,000 Jews who stood together at the base of that Mountain when we went from a band of slaves to a kingdom of priests and a holy nation. Where did the Midrash get this idea? In Deuteronomy 29:14, God says to Moses, I am not making this covenant with you alone, but both with those who are standing here with us this day before the Lord our God . . . and also with those *who are not* with us here this day! The covenant, the mitzvot, Jewish destiny is encoded, not so much in our DNA as deep within in our souls. [Abraham Joshua] Heschel taught us that "every person moves in two domains: in the domain of nature and in the domain of the spirit." Part of us is flesh and bones, and part of us, the nefesh, the neshama,[72] is the intangible yet animating substance that fills our physicality with life. In fact this idea has crystallized into a beautiful, powerful mystical concept known often by its Yiddish name: *dos pintele yid*, or for you Hebraists out there: *Netzotz ha'Yehudi* . . . but I'm sorry it sounds better to me in Yiddish. A *pintele yid*, according to Jewish mysticism[,] is a spark, a little point of light, the innermost quintessence of Jewish identity. "The idea is that all Jews, even if they are unaware of it or have been raised so un-Jewishly that they do not even know they are Jewish, have within them a Jewish essence that can be activated under certain circumstances. To some, this may sound like psychological nonsense. To others, this is a deep spiritual truth (I reckon you know which opinion I subscribe to). If every Jewish soul was at Mt. Sinai, then there is a certain memory of that event imprinted upon our souls. And that imprint is indestructible, and always has the potential— regardless of assimilation or lack of Jewish education—to emerge, and make its presence felt."[73]

Chevrei[74]—I see this all the time. Jews who had little Jewish education as children but something they can't put their finger on draws them back to Jewish life. Jews who spent most of their days unaffiliated, but wake up one day yearning for a connection. People who are not born as Jews, but feel in their soul a growing realization that their lot, their destiny is with the Jewish people. Kids whose parents aren't particularly interested in Judaism but who nevertheless become passionately involved in their own Jewish life (often inspired by Jewish youth groups or summer camps). That mysterious gravitational pull, says the tradition, is the *pintele yid*. I have felt it working in my own life, and I imagine many of you here today—if I asked for a show of hands—could give testimony to it as well.

In 1831, a young Abraham Lincoln was hired along with some other young men to navigate a flat boat down the Mississippi River to New Orleans where the cargo was to be dropped off. It was then that Lincoln encountered his first blush with the cruelty and brutality of slavery. Witnessing a slave auction, Lincoln was horrified by the dehumanization of what he saw. He said to his friends, if I ever have a chance to take on slavery I will do so with a vengeance. I would love to imagine that this disdain for a widespread and globally accepted institution came from a certain *pintele yid*, a spark of Sinai that emerged in his soul and made him revile what he saw. Whether that is true or not, and whether Lincoln was Jewish or not, we are reminded by all the speculation that sometimes someone's Jewishness is not worn on their sleeve or particular obvious or second nature. Sometimes it is buried deep beneath a lot of family, historical, and circumstantial baggage. Wherever it is, let us never forget that this holy spark is the indestructible, ever burning ember of Jewish life. If you feel something deep inside of you, pulling you to learn, to explore, to deepen your Jewish life . . . perhaps that's your *pintele yid* yearning to be unleashed. Don't repress it dear friends . . . let it shine. Let it shine![75]

Epilogue

Toward the end of Philip Roth's blockbuster novel *Portnoy's Complaint*, Alexander Portnoy is reminiscing about a field trip he had taken to the courthouse in Newark, New Jersey, when he was in eighth grade. He recalls that there were two statues near the courthouse, one of George Washington and the other of Abraham Lincoln. Portnoy then offers his thoughts on these two great American presidents: "Washington, I must confess, leaves me cold. Maybe it's the horse, that he's leaning on a horse. At any rate, he is so obviously a *goy*. But Lincoln! I could cry. Look at him sitting there, so *oysgemitchet* [exhausted]. How he labored for the downtrodden—as will I!"[1]

Portnoy's comments about Washington and Lincoln not only are humorous but also possess an element of truth for the American Jew at the end of the twentieth century and the beginning of the twenty-first. It is true that Jews respect George Washington—they may also regard Thomas Jefferson highly and admire Theodore Roosevelt's forceful personality and so forth. Yet Portnoy's observation is indeed a reflection of reality. As Stanley Jerome, the lead character in Neil Simon's play *Brighton Beach Memoirs*, tells his cousin Nora as they plan their dinner conversation: "I'll mention someone like Abraham Lincoln and you look up and say, 'Now there's a man who really stood up for his principles.'"[2] For many American Jews, Lincoln became an American Jewish icon. They related so profoundly to Lincoln and his image that it seemed as though he actually *was* their relative!

On Friday, November 16, 2012, Steven Spielberg's much anticipated film *Lincoln* began playing in theaters all across North America. Spielberg engaged the Pulitzer Prize–winning playwright and screenwriter Tony Kushner to produce a screenplay for the film, which was based, in part, on Doris Kearns Goodwin's best-selling volume *Team of Rivals: The Political Genius of Abraham Lincoln*. Many critics called the film a cinematic triumph. A *New York Times* reviewer, for instance, described *Lincoln* as a "splendid" film and a "noble democratic masterpiece." Another reviewer exclaimed, "'Lincoln' makes politics exciting again," and NBCNews.com insisted that Spielberg's *Lincoln* will "live on long after it leaves theaters."[3]

Even before the film's national release, some commentators took note of the fact that *Lincoln* was written and directed by American Jews. According to one critic, "as imagined by Spielberg and Kushner, *Lincoln*'s Lincoln is the ultimate mensch."[4] Another reviewer wondered whether Spielberg, Kushner, and even Daniel Day-Lewis (who, according to the reviewer, is the son of a Jewish mother) had subconsciously created a movie that offered audiences "a Jewish version of history" by focusing the movie on Lincoln's efforts to persuade the U.S. House of Representatives to pass the Thirteenth Amendment, which would render the institution of slavery unconstitutional. As the reviewer observed, the story of Lincoln's determination to persuade the House of Representatives to pass the amendment was a story of "compassion, charity and the pursuit of justice—these values, which we identify as Jewish values."[5] "Has Spielberg given us a Jewish Lincoln? Or is it that Lincoln was 'Jewish' in his temperament, values and actions: consumed by social justice in his fighting a war to abolish slavery; Moses-like in leading a people to freedom; talmudic in his use of disputation among a 'team of rivals' to lead the nation; alternately morose and jovial . . . ?"[6]

In spite of the thematic focus of this particular documentary history, some may consider it ironic that not a single Jewish character appears in Spielberg's film. That very fact has led some writers to postulate that in this respect, *Lincoln* is "a throwback to the days when Hollywood's moguls, themselves Jewish-Americans, made movies about a seemingly non-Jewish America through the filter of their own very Jewish perspective." Critics will undoubtedly continue to debate whether or not Spielberg's and Kushner's Jewishness pushed them to focus on the story of Lincoln and the Thirteenth Amendment. Yet one fact cannot be disputed: to the present day, there are American Jews who insist that even if he was not a Jew according to *halakhah* (Jewish law), Abraham Lincoln was "most certainly a man with whom we share a common heritage."[7]

In his entertaining and touching book *Land of Lincoln*, Andrew Ferguson takes readers on a trip through contemporary America's world of Lincolniana. The book is filled with dozens of captivating anecdotes Ferguson collected as he visited an array of historical sites and encountered a cornucopia of colorful people, all of whom have some connection to the legacy of Abraham Lincoln. Ferguson concludes his book with a particularly touching encounter he had while visiting Springfield, Illinois, where Lincoln lived and where he is buried.

The story was told to Ferguson by Frank Walker, manager of the Hilton Hotel in Springfield. A few days prior to Ferguson's arrival, an elderly and very feeble man named Henri Dubin had been staying at the hotel. Dubin had difficulty getting around; he was suffering from Parkinson's disease. The old man told Walker that it had taken him nearly forty years to gather the funds he needed to make his trip to Springfield in order to pay his respects to Lincoln. The reader is then told why the aging and ill Dubin had come to Springfield:

> [Dubin] said he'd been in the concentration camp. He pulled up his sleeve when he said this. Every time he mentioned the concentration camp he pulled up his sleeve, and you could see the number there. He said he knew about Abraham Lincoln and George Washington from when he learned about them in school as a boy.

. . . When he was in the concentration camp, and he was all alone in his cell, it was the worst time in his life and he didn't think he could go on anymore. And he said Mr. Lincoln came to him.

Mr. Lincoln stood right in front of him, just like I'm standing here in front of you. And Lincoln said to him, "You never forget: All men are created equal. This is true for all men for all times. And these men who would do this thing to you, who put you here, they're no better than you. You are their equal, because *all men are created equal.* You keep remembering this, and you persevere, you'll be all right!"

Well, from this time onward, the man says he knew he was going to be all right. He knew he was going to persevere. And he vowed if he ever got out of that concentration camp, he would come to Springfield, to thank Mr. Lincoln, he was so grateful. That is what he said.[8]

To say that Lincoln has been a fascinating symbol of courage and leadership to millions of people is to state the obvious. To say that Lincoln has long been a Jewish lodestar is to state a fact. As Henri Dubin's story movingly illustrates, not only have Jews long been inspirited by Lincoln's life and legacy, but they have continuously been steeled by a sense that the idea of Lincoln has the potential to lift the fallen spirits of every generation. This conviction—the belief that Lincoln is the paradigmatic exemplar of America's hope for a better world—may actually be the most enduring of all the bonds that have led American Jews to call Lincoln "Rabbi Abraham."

If Lincoln can justly be called the first typical American he can more justly be said to represent the summation of all the noblest qualities in Judaism.[9]

NOTES
INDEX

Notes

Acknowledgments

1. See, for example, Jacob Rader Marcus, *The American Jew, 1585–1990: A History* (Brooklyn: Carlson Publishing, 1995), vii.
2. Robert Green Ingersoll, *The Works of Robert G. Ingersoll*, Dresden ed., vol. 2 (New York: C. P. Farrell, 1900), 420.

Introduction: Abraham Lincoln and American Jewry

1. *Louisville Daily Journal*, April 23, 1865.
2. William C. Davis, *Lincoln's Men: How President Lincoln Became Father to an Army and a Nation* (New York: Free Press, 1999).
3. See Maxwell Whiteman, "Jews in the Antislavery Movement," in *The Kidnapped and the Ransomed; the Narrative of Peter and Vina Still after Forty Years of Slavery*, by Kate E. R. Pickard (Philadelphia: Jewish Publication Society of America, 1970). For bibliographic sources on Jews and the antislavery movement in America, see Jonathan D. Sarna and Adam D. Mendelsohn, eds., *Jews and the Civil War: A Reader* (New York: New York University Press, 2010), 413–14.
4. Mary Frances Berry, "Lincoln and Civil Rights for Blacks," *Journal of the Abraham Lincoln Association* 2, no. 1 (1980), http://quod.lib.umich.edu/j/jala/2629860.0002.105?rgn=main;view=fulltext (accessed November 19, 2012).
5. Carter G. Woodson, *The Negro in Our History* (Washington, D.C.: Associated Publishers, 1922), 381.
6. Fred C. Ainsworth and Joseph W. Kirkley, eds., *The War of the Rebellion: A Compilation of the Official Records of the Union and Confederate Armies*, series III, vol. 1 (Washington, D.C.: Government Printing Office, 1899), 157.
7. Emanuel Hertz, ed., *Abraham Lincoln: The Tribute of the Synagogue* (New York: Bloch Publishing, 1927), 169.
8. *Israelite*, January 23, 1863, 228.
9. Robert N. Rosen, *The Jewish Confederates* (Columbia: University of South Carolina Press, 2000), 148–53.
10. Pierce Butler, *Judah P. Benjamin* (Philadelphia: G. W. Jacobs, 1907), 193.
11. Rosen, *Jewish Confederates*, 11–12.
12. Butler, *Judah P. Benjamin*, 196.
13. Rosen, *Jewish Confederates*, 11–12.
14. *Louisville Daily Journal*, April 23, 1865.
15. Genesis 3:22 (Judaic Classics version).
16. Hertz, *Tribute*, 45, 111, 98.
17. Ibid., 45.
18. From Rabbi Hyman G. Enelow's prayer delivered at the dedication ceremony for the Abraham Lincoln Memorial at Hodgenville, Kentucky, on November 9, 1911. See the *Israelite*, November 16, 1911, 4.

19. Barry Schwartz, *Abraham Lincoln and the Forge of National Memory* (Chicago: University of Chicago Press, 2000), 195.

20. Ibid., 198.

21. Ainsworth and Kirkley, eds., *War of the Rebellion*, series III, volume 1, 157.

22. Sylvia Barack Fishman, *Jewish Life and American Jewish Culture* (Albany: State University of New York Press, 1999), 15.

23. As quoted in Stephen J. Whitfield, *In Search of American Jewish Culture* (Hanover, N.H.: Brandeis University Press, 1999), 30.

1. Immigrants and the Old Northwest: Lincoln's First Encounters with American Jewry

1. Robert P. Swierenga, "The Settlement of the Old Northwest: Ethnic Pluralism in a Featureless Plain," *Journal of the Early Republic* 9, no. 1 (Spring 1989): 73. For quote, see Emanuel Hertz, *Abraham Lincoln: A New Portrait*, 2 vols. (New York: Horace Liveright, 1931), 1:338.

2. Swierenga, "Settlement," 74, 83.

3. Jacob Rader Marcus, *To Count a People: American Jewish Population Data, 1585-1984* (New York: University Press of America, 1990).

4. Ibid.

5. The best sources for information on Lincoln's Jewish associations are Isaac Markens, *Abraham Lincoln and the Jews* (New York: Isaac Markens, 1909), and the meticulously documented Bertram W. Korn, *American Jewry and the Civil War* (Philadelphia: Jewish Publication Society, 1951).

6. One of Samuel Rosenwald and Augusta Hammerslough Rosenwald's children was Julius Rosenwald (1862-1932), a man who would become a millionaire by transforming the mail-order catalog of Sears, Roebuck & Company into a national corporation.

7. According to Isaac Markens, Hammerslough claimed that he and his brothers "enjoyed very friendly relations with Mr. and Mrs. Lincoln." See Markens, *Abraham Lincoln and the Jews*, 22.

8. Elizabeth Porter Todd was married to the politically controversial Ninian W. Edwards (1809-89), whose father was Ninian Edwards (1775-1833), the man who served as the only governor of the Illinois Territory (1809-18). The senior Edwards was also one of the first two U.S. senators from Illinois (1818-24) and was the third governor of the state of Illinois.

9. Hammerslough also claimed that his firm in Springfield provided the black plumes that ornamented the funeral cortege that carried Lincoln's body to its final resting place in Springfield's Oak Ridge Cemetery. See Markens, *Abraham Lincoln and the Jews*, 22.

10. Ibid., 23.

11. See Rice's obituary, *New York Times*, June 8, 1914. During the Civil War, the military "sutler" was a licensed store owner who was assigned to a regiment or military department of the Union army. The sutlers stocked items such as tobacco, liquor (for the officers), rubber ponchos, and the like for soldiers to purchase. For more on sutlers during the Civil War, see Francis Albert Lord, *Civil War Sutlers and Their Wares* (New York: T. Yoseloff, 1969).

12. Markens, *Abraham Lincoln and the Jews*, 23-24. According to Markens, Rice and Lincoln were such good friends that Rice offered to make a suit of clothing for Lincoln to wear on his inauguration in 1861. Lincoln declined the offer because, according to Rice, Lincoln had previously agreed to accept a suit of clothes from another friend in

Springfield—probably Julius Hammerslough. Markens states that Rice did not receive a government appointment to serve as a sutler, but the existence of a rare 50-cent sutler's coin bearing Rice's name confirms that he did have the post, at least for a brief period of time. To see an image of the Rice sutler's coin, go to the Shapell Manuscript website, http://www.shapell.org/manuscript.aspx?3366078 (accessed August 8, 2012).

13. See Robert S. Frisch, "Salzenstein's Store: Abraham Lincoln Shopped Here," *Chicago Jewish History* 26, no. 1 (Winter 2002): 6-7.

14. Noted Lincoln artist Lloyd Ostendorf created a drawing to commemorate the ax story. To view Salzenstein's store plainly visible in the background of Ostendorf's drawing, see the Abraham Lincoln Collectibles website, http://www.abelincoln.com/orginal/1–12.html (accessed August 8, 2012).

15. On Huttenbauer, see Emilie Jane Levy, "My Family" (history term paper, Vassar College, 1948), GF–411. Courtesy of The Jacob Rader Marcus Center of the American Jewish Archives (hereafter AJA), at the Hebrew Union College–Jewish Institute of Religion, Cincinnati, Ohio.

16. George Harding (1827–1902), a contemporary of Lincoln and a distinguished patent attorney, later recalled how shocked he was when he first set eyes on Lincoln in Cincinnati in 1855: "[He was a] tall, rawly boned, ungainly back woodsman, with coarse, ill-fitting clothing, his trousers hardly reaching his ankles." See Doris Kearns Goodwin, *Team of Rivals: The Political Genius of Abraham Lincoln* (New York: Simon and Schuster, 2005), 174.

17. It is difficult to determine precisely when this incident occurred. According to a fellow lawyer, Henry C. Whitney (1831–1905), who wrote a memoir describing his life with Lincoln on the circuit, the sitting took place in the fall of 1857. Whitney also made mention of another incident in which Lincoln sat for a poor photographer whose identity is not indicated. Although the photograph left Lincoln looking like "a wandering Jew," the photographer displayed it proudly in his "outer showcase." See Henry C. Whitney, *Life on the Circuit with Lincoln* (Caldwell, Idaho: Caxton Printers, 1940), 50. Alschuler's 1860 photograph of Lincoln was taken only two weeks after the election. It is the first in which we see the beginnings of the president's trademark beard.

18. On Jonas and Lincoln, see Korn, *American Jewry*, 189–94. With regard to Jonas's role in the Kentucky state legislature, Korn suggests that he served as a Kentucky legislator, though he subsequently writes that Jonas's first run for elective office was when he ran for the Illinois General Assembly in 1842. For a fine description of Jonas's contributions to the Jewish community of Quincy, Illinois, see David A. Frolick, "From Strangers to Neighbors: The Children of Abraham in Quincy, Illinois," *Journal of Illinois History* 7 (Spring 2004): 2–36.

19. Korn, *American Jewry*, 191.

20. Ibid.

21. Lincoln's name was put into nomination for the vice presidency at the Republican Party's first national convention, which took place in Philadelphia, June 17-19, 1856. See Eric Foner, *Free Soil, Free Labor, Free Men: The Ideology of the Republican Party before the Civil War* (New York: Oxford University Press, 1995), and James D. Bilotta, *Race and the Rise of the Republican Party, 1848-1865* (New York: Peter Lang, 1992).

22. Korn, *American Jewry*, 191; John E. Boos, *Rare Personal Accounts of Abraham Lincoln*, ed. William R. Feeheley and Bill Snack (Cadillac, Mich.: Railsplitter Publishers, 2005), 40.

23. Boos, *Personal Accounts*, 40.

24. Markens, *Abraham Lincoln and the Jews*, 18.

25. Ibid., 191–92.

26. Korn, *American Jewry*, 226–27. On Isaac N. Morris, see the online *Biographical Directory of the United States Congress* (http://bioguide.congress.gov).

27. Korn, *American Jewry*, 228–29. Morris was among those interested in attracting Jewish communal support for political candidates. During the 1868 presidential campaign, Morris tried to reassure Jews that despite his "odious" order (General Orders No. 11), Ulysses S. Grant was a friend of the Jewish community. See Jonathan D. Sarna, *When General Grant Expelled the Jews* (New York: Schocken, 2012), 76–77.

28. A fine summary of this plot to kill Lincoln appears on the website of the Central Intelligence Agency, https://www.cia.gov/library/publications/additional-publications/civil-war/SML.htm (accessed August 30, 2012).

29. Korn, *American Jewry*, 193–94.

30. See Samuel Rose-Carmack, "The Jews of Quincy, Illinois" (term paper, Hebrew Union College–Jewish Institute of Religion), SC–15611, AJA.

31. Frolick, "From Strangers to Neighbors," 22. See also Korn, *American Jewry*, 193–94.

32. For Pinner quote, see Markens, *Abraham Lincoln and the Jews*, 35. On Pinner's antislavery activities, see ibid., 34–36. See also Max J. Kohler, "The Jews and the American Anti-Slavery Movement," *Publications of the American Jewish Historical Society* 5, no. 5 (1897): 152–53. According to Markens, Pinner's name does not appear on the official roll of Missouri delegates to the convention. Pinner subsequently told Markens that his name had been omitted deliberately in retribution for his anti-Bates activity. (He took pride in pointing out that "by preventing the nomination of Bates he paved the way for Lincoln and made his nomination possible and his election probable.") The Houghton Library of Harvard University possesses a collection of ten interesting letters (1860–75) from Moritz Pinner to Wendell Phillips, the well-known lawyer, orator, and abolitionist. These communications prove that Pinner worked against Bates and quickly abandoned Seward in favor of Lincoln. Pinner's affinity for Lincoln as a candidate is apparent in his letters to Phillips. See http://www.math.rutgers.edu/~zeilberg/family/WPLetters.html (accessed August 8, 2012). A letter from Wendell Phillips to fellow abolitionist Cassius Marcellus Clay (1810–1903) confirms that Pinner had been appointed quartermaster on the staff of Major General Kearney. Phillips's letter, dated August 19, 1862, is part of the Cassius Marcellus Clay Collection of the Abraham Lincoln Library and Museum at Lincoln Memorial University. See transcript of the letter at http://www.math.rutgers.edu/~zeilberg/family/phillips.html (accessed August 23, 2012).

33. On Pinner and Dembitz, see Markens, *Abraham Lincoln and the Jews*, 34–36. There is no question that Dembitz attended the Republican Convention of 1860 in Chicago, and it is reasonable to believe that he did cast his vote for Lincoln on the first ballot, while some of his fellow delegates cast their votes for William H. Seward or Benjamin Wade. Although several sources contend that Dembitz was the man who actually placed Lincoln's name in nomination for the presidency, the published minutes of the convention do not verify that claim. See *The Proceedings of the Republican National Convention, Held at Chicago, May 16, 17, 18, 1860* (Chicago, 1860).

34. Markens, *Abraham Lincoln and the Jews*, 27.

35. Simon Wolf, *The Presidents I Have Known from 1860–1918* (Washington, D.C.: Byron S. Adams Press, 1918), 4–5.

36. Ibid., 27.

37. Markens, *Abraham Lincoln and the Jews*, 25. Markens wrote that he received a letter

from Dila Kohn Adler wherein she described her father's impressions of his first meeting with Lincoln. Dila was married to Dankmar Adler (1844–1900), a distinguished architect who was the son of Rabbi Liebman Adler (1812–92). On Kohn, see Hyman L. Meites, *History of the Jews of Chicago* (Chicago: Wellington Publishing, 1924), 44–45. See also Abram Vossen Goodman, "A Jewish Peddler's Diary, 1841–1842," *American Jewish Archives Journal* 3, no. 3 (1951): 81–111.

38. Joshua 1:9. Harold Holzer notes that Kohn's flag was one of several gifts Lincoln received as he prepared to assume office. See *Lincoln President-Elect: Abraham Lincoln and the Great Secession Winter 1860* (New York: Simon and Schuster, 2008), 187. Variants of this phrase appear throughout the Hebrew scriptures, and some historians, like Holzer, believe that Kohn cited Deuteronomy 31:5, while many others contend that Kohn used verses from the book of Joshua (either 1:7 and 9 or 10:25). For example, see Goodman, "Jewish Peddler's Diary," 81. Although an "old glass negative" photograph of the flag survived until the 1980s, the flag itself has apparently been lost. Kohn's daughter Dila spoke about this incident on several occasions. See *American Israelite*, February 13, 1908, 7. On the history of the missing flag, see Joseph Levinson, "Local Man Continues Search for American Flag Presented to Abraham Lincoln," *Chicago Jewish History* 33, no. 1 (Winter 2009): 4-5, 14.

39. For more on Otterbourg's life and career as a diplomat, see Ruth L. Benjamin, "Marcus Otterbourg, United States Minister to Mexico, 1867," *Publications of the American Jewish Historical Society* 1, no. 32 (1931): 65–98. See also *Universal Jewish Encyclopedia*, s.v. "Otterbourg, Marcus."

40. Benjamin, "Marcus Otterbourg," 66.

41. On Schurz, see Rudolf Geiger, *Der deutsche Amerikaner: Carl Schurz—vom deutschen Revolutionär zum amerikanischen Staatsmann* (Gernsbach: Katz, 2007), and Hans L. Trefousse, *Carl Schurz: A Biography; The North's Civil War* (New York: Fordham University Press, 1998).

42. Benjamin, "Marcus Otterbourg," 66. Jonas was probably the first Jew to be appointed by the Lincoln administration. His first day as postmaster in Quincy, Illinois, was May 19, 1861. See the *Quincy Daily Herald*, May 25, 1861, 3.

43. Abram J. Dittenhoefer, *How We Elected Lincoln: Personal Recollections* (1916; repr., Philadelphia: University of Pennsylvania Press, 2005), 15.

44. Ibid., 37.

45. Ibid., 92–94, 97.

46. Ibid., 45–74, for details on Dittenhoefer's visits to the White House during Lincoln's first term in office.

47. Kaufmann immigrated to the United States from Hesse Darmstadt in 1848. A lawyer and an intellectual, Kaufmann quickly became a prominent figure in New York. According to Markens, Lincoln wanted to appoint Kaufmann the U.S. ambassador to Italy, but Kaufmann declined the offer. See Markens, *Abraham Lincoln and the Jews*, 32–33.

48. Dittenhoefer, *How We Elected Lincoln*, 4.

49. *Israelite*, February 15, 1861, 202.

50. Lincoln's inaugural address, March 4, 1861. See www.avalon.law.yale.edu/19th_century/lincoln1.asp (accessed September 10, 2012).

51. *Israelite*, April 5, 1861, 317.

52. One of the most extensive rosters of Lincoln's Jewish friends appeared in a 1940 newspaper article titled "Abraham Lincoln's Many Friends in the B'nai Brith." It is interesting to note that this article also mentions the names of politicians such as

Lorenzo Brentano (1813–91) and Philip Dorscheimer (1797–1868) who may have been members of B'nai B'rith but who did not openly identify themselves as Jews. *Jewish Advocate*, February 9, 1940, 1.

53. On Wolf, see Esther L. Panitz, *Simon Wolf: Private Conscience and Public Image* (Rutherford, London: Fairleigh Dickinson University Press, 1987). See also Sarna, *General Grant*, 50–55. On Wolf's relationships with U.S. presidents, see Wolf, *Presidents I Have Known*.

54. This story comes from a *Champaign News-Gazette* article dated Thursday, February 12, 1959. Courtesy Office of the Publisher, the News-Gazette.

55. Transcription obtained from Champaign, Illinois County Archives/Urbana Free Library, November 19, 2007.

56. The Northern Cross Railroad from Meredosia to Jacksonville, later extended to Springfield, was the first rail route in Illinois over which a locomotive was operated.

57. Anna Paschall Hannum, ed., *A Quaker Forty-Niner: The Adventures of Charles Edward Pancoast in the American Frontier* (Philadelphia: University of Pennsylvania Press, 1930), 46–48.

58. All four letters reproduced here are available at Abraham Lincoln Papers at the Library of Congress, Manuscript Division, http://memory.loc.gov/ammem/alhtml/alhome.html (accessed January 7, 2013).

59. Wolf, *Presidents I Have Known*, 5–7.

60. Markens, *Abraham Lincoln and the Jews*, 33–34.

61. Jonathan Young Scammon was a prominent Chicago lawyer, banker, and newspaperman. Scammon's contact with Lincoln may be traced back to 1839, when there was a legal exchange between the two men. Over the years, Lincoln and Scammon became good friends. Robert Todd, Lincoln's son, apprenticed with Scammon and in 1865 established a legal practice with Scammon's son, Charles. Scammon was one of those selected to serve as a pallbearer for President Lincoln when the funeral cortege arrived in Chicago.

62. Little is known about Abraham S. Cohen. He was evidently a talented correspondent who specialized in reporting on law stories. See obituaries found in the *New York Times*, December 29, 1867, and *New York Evening Express*, December 28, 1867.

63. Markens, *Abraham Lincoln and the Jews*, 25–26.

64. From Philip Goodman, ed., *Lincoln's Birthday: Program Material for Jewish Groups* (New York: National Jewish Welfare Board, 1953), 30–31. Courtesy JWB Jewish Chaplains Council.

65. George Henry Preble, *History of the Flag of the United States of America, and of the Naval and Yacht-Club Signals, Seals, and Arms, and Principal National Songs of the United States, with a Chronicle of the Symbols, Standards, Banners, and Flags of Ancient and Modern Nations* (Boston: A. Williams and Company, 1880), 406.

66. Simon Wolf, *The American Jew as Patriot, Soldier, and Citizen*, ed. Louis Edward Levy (New York: Levytype Company, 1895), 427–28. According to Wolf, the *Reform Advocate* printed excerpts from McKinley's Ottawa speech on July 13, 1895.

67. See Richard S. Lambert, *For the Time Is at Hand: An Account of the Prophesies of Henry Wentworth Monk* (New York: Andrew Melrose, 1947), 81–82.

68. Regarding Mary Todd Lincoln's reference to this matter, see Justin G. Turner and Linda Levitt Turner, *Mary Todd Lincoln: Her Life and Letters* (New York: Alfred A. Knopf, 1972), 218. See also Lester I. Vogel, *To See a Promised Land: Americans and the Holy Land in the Nineteenth Century* (University Park: Pennsylvania State University Press, 1993), 41. In an alternative version of this same recollection, Lincoln whispered

his desire to visit Jerusalem in his wife's ear only moments before John Wilkes Booth entered the presidential box at Ford's Theatre on April 14, 1865. See Dorothy Meserve Kunhardt and Philip B. Kunhardt, Jr., *Twenty Days* (Secaucus, N.J.: Castle Books, 1965), 29. In 1866, Mary Todd Lincoln wrote that her husband "appeared to anticipate much pleasure, from a visit to Palestine," although he was at least now "rejoicing in the presence of his Saviour, and was in the midst of the Heavenly Jerusalem." See Mary Todd Lincoln's letter to James Smith, December 17, 1866, quoted in Turner and Turner, *Mary Todd Lincoln*, 400.

69. Lambert, *For the Time Is at Hand*, 81–82.

70. Solomons's niece, Rachel Rosalie Phillips, lived with her uncle Adolphus during this period, and her diary preserves reminiscences of visiting the White House with Solomons and meeting Lincoln personally. A copy of Rachel Phillips's diary is located in the David M. Klein Collection, MS 695, box 1, folder 2, AJA.

71. On Alexander Gardner, see Mark D. Katz, *Witness to an Era: The Life and Photographs of Alexander Gardner* (New York: Viking Studio, 1990).

72. Although Solomons's partner was a photographer named Franklin Philp (1826–87), the original document does indeed refer to the firm as "Philip and Solomons." We must assume this is a typographical error in the original.

73. Perhaps the most famous poses from that session is the "cracked glass" photograph of Abraham Lincoln. The crack comes from the original negative, which was broken and discarded back in 1865. The "cracked glass" photo with its disturbing flaw has often been said to have betokened the president's impending doom and remains one of most recognizable photographs of the sixteenth president.

74. *American Hebrew* 84, no. 15 (February 12, 1909).

2. "The Most Favored Family Visitor at the White House": The Enigmatic Relationship between Lincoln and Isachar Zacharie, M.D.

1. Zacharie's first name appears with many different spellings in the documents, including Issachar, Issacher, Isaac, Issachor and Isachar.

2. Bertram Korn, *American Jewry and the Civil War* (Philadelphia: Jewish Publication Society, 1951), 194.

3. For the most expansive treatments of Zacharie, see ibid., 194–202, 230–39, and Charles M. Segal, "Isachar Zacharie: Lincoln's Chiropodist," *Publications of the American Jewish Historical Society* 43, no. 2 (December 1953): 71–126.

4. Like countless English children who were born to modest means during the Victorian era, Zacharie had little formal education and was compelled to search for a useful trade at a very young age. For a helpful documentation of Zacharie's apprenticeships in England, see Segal, "Isachar Zacharie," 72–74. Segal notes that Zacharie established a friendship with the distinguished American surgeon Valentine Mott (1785–1865). Zacharie dedicates his book on chiropody to Mott, who taught at Columbia College (which became Columbia University in 1857) and, from 1834 to 1841, studied and taught in Europe. In 1841, Mott returned to Columbia, and the two men might well have become acquainted. See Ira M. Rutkow, *History of Surgery in the United States, 1775–1900* (San Francisco: Norman Publishing, 1988). Segal also notes that in Zacharie's scrapbook there was a letter of introduction attesting to his having studied with the distinguished British surgeon Sir Astley Cooper (1868–1941). See reference to Zacharie's "album," below (n. 7). Segal seems to doubt these references because Zacharie would have been so very young at the time, but children commonly went to work at the unthinkable age of five or six during the Victorian era. See Sally Mitchell,

Daily Life in Victorian England (Westport, Conn.: Greenwood Press, 1996), 43–47. On the history of podiatry and chiropody, see the introductory chapter of David R. Tollafield and Linda M. Merriman, *Clinical Skills in Treating the Foot* (London: Churchill/Livingstone, 1997), 1–6.

5. See Zacharie's advertisement in the *New York Times*, February 11, 1858, wherein it states: "Corns, Bunions, Club Nails, Nails penetrating the flesh, extracted in five minutes, without pain, so that the boot can be worn immediately without the least inconvenience to the patient by Dr. Zacharie, Surgeon Chiropodist. No. 760 Broadway."

6. On Zacharie's peregrinations, see Segal, "Isachar Zacharie," 74–76. Zacharie's letters of reference suggest that the young foot doctor lived in several American cities before opening a New York office for his podiatry business in 1858. In a statement Zacharie made in an 1881 British Census Return, his wife gave birth to a daughter in California in 1855. His name is also found in the records of Congregation Mickve Israel of Savannah, Georgia. See Rabbi Saul J. Rubin, *Third to None: The Saga of Savannah Jewry 1733–1983* (Savannah: Congregation Mickve Israel, 1983), 129. Zacharie may have opened a grocery business in 1857, but this fact does not support the implication that he was a professional charlatan. At the age of twenty-eight or twenty-nine, he would have been a fairly young man, and the many surviving letters of reference from the late 1840s testify to the fact that Zacharie was a skilled practitioner of podiatric technique.

7. An album containing a letter of reference written by President Lincoln and signed by him and Secretary of State William H. Seward (on September 23, 1862) together with other testimonials to Zacharie's professional abilities (dating from 1846 to 1872), with a photograph of Dr. Zacharie, by Turner & Killick, art photographers of Islington, England, n.d., was being advertised online, with a detailed description, by the famed auctioneers Christie's (Sale 9364, Lot 92). See http://www.christies.com/LotFinder/lot_details.aspx?intObjectID=1794852 (accessed May 19, 2011).

8. In a newspaper article detailing Zacharie's proposal, the *New York Herald*'s correspondent could not refrain from making a grimacing pun: Zacharie, he wrote, wanted to provide the Union army with "a corps of corn doctors, or foot soldiers." See *New York Herald*, October 3, 1862, as quoted in Korn, *American Jewry*, 194.

9. *New York Herald*, October 3, 1862.

10. Segal, "Isachar Zacharie," 90. On George S. Denison, see James Marten, "The Making of a Carpetbagger: George S. Denison and the South, 1854–1866," *Louisiana History: The Journal of the Louisiana Historical Association* 34, no. 2 (Spring 1993): 133–60.

11. Korn, *American Jewry*, 231, 235.

12. Ibid., 236–39.

13. For quotes, see ibid., 194, 201.

14. On the Emancipation Proclamation, see John Hope Franklin, *The Emancipation Proclamation* (1963; repr., Wheeling, Ill.: Harlan Davidson, 1995).

15. Korn, *American Jewry*, 195.

16. Evidently, some government figures were discussing the idea of a negotiated peace with the Confederacy at this same time. For more on this subject, see Fred H. Harrington, "A Peace Mission of 1863," *American Historical Review* 46 (1940): 76–86.

17. A copy of Stanton's order was reprinted in the *New York Times*, January 14, 1896.

18. Raymond H. Banks, *The King of Louisiana, 1862–1865, and Other Government Work: A Biography of Major General Nathaniel Prentice Banks* (Las Vegas: R. H. Banks, 2005); Stephen A. Dupree, *Planting the Union Flag in Texas: The Campaigns of Major General*

Nathaniel P. Banks in the West (College Station: Texas A&M University Press, 2008); Fred Harvey Harrington, *Fighting Politician: Major General N. P. Banks* (Philadelphia: University of Pennsylvania Press, 1948); James G. Hollandsworth, *Pretense of Glory: The Life of General Nathaniel P. Banks* (Baton Rouge: Louisiana State University Press, 1998).

19. Isachar Zacharie to William H. Seward, November 24, 1862, SC-13337, American Jewish Archives, Cincinnati, Ohio. Courtesy of The Jacob Rader Marcus Center of the American Jewish Archives (hereafter AJA), at the Hebrew Union College–Jewish Institute of Religion, Cincinnati, Ohio. It may very well have been Banks who first introduced Secretary of State Seward to his capable foot doctor.

20. Nathaniel P. Banks to Isaac Zacharie, January 1, 1863, Bertram W. Korn Collection, MS 99, box 34, folder 9, AJA.

21. Korn, *American Jewry*, 196–97.

22. Isachar Zacharie to Abraham Lincoln, April 25, 1863, appendix C, ibid., 234.

23. Isachar Zacharie to Abraham Lincoln, February 19, 1863, ibid., 231.

24. Segal, "Isachar Zacharie," 118–19.

25. *New York Herald*, October 21, 1863.

26. See Harrington, "Peace Mission of 1863."

27. Korn, *American Jewry*, 233.

28. *New York Herald*, October 21, 1863.

29. See Robert L. Kerby, *The Confederate Invasion of New Mexico and Arizona* (Tucson: Westernlore Press, 1958); Andrew E. Masich, *The Civil War in Arizona: The Story of the California Volunteers, 1861–1865* (Norman: University of Oklahoma Press, 2006); and Andrew Rolle, *The Lost Cause: The Confederate Exodus to Mexico* (Norman: University of Oklahoma Press, 1965).

30. Korn, *American Jewry*, 198.

31. Isachar Zacharie to Nathaniel P. Banks, September 8, 1863, and Isachar Zacharie to Nathaniel P. Banks, July 30, 1863, as cited in Korn, *American Jewry*, 196.

32. That Zacharie was surprised to encounter Benjamin at the meeting can be discerned from the fact that he referred to this encounter as an "unexpected meeting" in the letter he wrote to Benjamin the following day. See Isachar Zacharie to Judah P. Benjamin, September 28, 1863. Original copy of the letter can be found in the domestic correspondence of the Confederate Department of State, box B, file 1, series F, Library of Congress, Washington, D.C.

33. Ibid.

34. Ibid.

35. Ibid.

36. Ibid.

37. Ibid.

38. Ibid.

39. Isachar Zacharie to Nathaniel P. Banks, October 24, 1863, cited in Korn, *American Jewry*, 198.

40. Ibid., 238.

41. Francis Lieber, *Lincoln or McClellan: Appeal to the Germans of America* (New York: Loyal Publication Society, 1864), 4. On Lieber's career, see Lewis R. Harley, *Francis Lieber: His Life and Political Philosophy* (Clark, N.J.: Lawbook Exchange, 2003), and Frank B. Freidel, *Francis Lieber, Nineteenth-Century Liberal* (Clark, N.J.: Lawbook Exchange, 2003).

42. Korn, *American Jewry*, 200. For Lewis quote, see Howard S. Stein, "Samuel A. Lewis:

Nineteenth-Century Jewish American Leader" (term paper, Hebrew Union College–Jewish Institute of Religion, January 7, 2008), 15, SC-15490, AJA.

43. For a helpful summary of the historical evolution of American Jews participating qua Jews in the political arena, see Jonathan D. Sarna, *When General Grant Expelled the Jews* (New York: Schocken, 2012), 69–79.

44. Myer S. Isaacs to Abraham Lincoln, October 26, 1864, cited from "From Haven to Home: 350 Years of Jewish Life in America," Library of Congress, http://www.loc.gov/exhibits/haventohome/haven-home.html (accessed August 18, 2012).

45. Korn, *American Jewry*, 239.

46. Isachar Zacharie to Nathaniel P. Banks, July 31, 1872, in the Nathaniel P. Banks Papers, box 51, Library of Congress, Washington, D.C. This letter also appeared in *The Nation*, August 8, 1872, p. 82, and in the *New York Daily Tribune*, August 2, 1872.

47. *New York Times*, January 14, 1896.

48. According to the website of the Order of the Secret Monitor, Zacharie "joined Bon Accord Mark Lodge in 1882 where he met a number of other brethren who had received the Secret Monitor degree during their travels." On May 5, 1887, a number of brethren met at Dr. Zacharie's house and resolved to form a Conclave of Secret Monitors, to be called the Alfred Meadows Conclave, after the well-known surgeon. Zacharie was nominated as the first Supreme Ruler. A few weeks later, the first Grand Council of the Order was formed on June 17, 1887, with Zacharie nominated as the first Grand Supreme Ruler. It held its first meeting the following month (July 2) when it was resolved that the governing body be styled "*The Grand Council of the Order of the Secret Monitor for the United Kingdom of Great Britain and Ireland and the Colonies and Dependencies of the British Crown.*" See http://www.orderofthesecretmonitor.co.uk/News_27.html (accessed May 19, 2011).

49. With the help of census records, a copy of his death certificate, and a photo of his tombstone, we know that Zacharie died on September 16, 1900, at the age of seventy-three. We may therefore surmise that he was born in 1827. There has been much confusion and misinformation about Zacharie's dates of birth and death. His date of death is often incorrectly said to be 1897. Some sources say he was born in 1820; others say 1825. Perhaps this is because, in 1864, the *New York Times* claimed that Zacharie was between forty and forty-five years old. Although most biographical sketches insist that Zacharie was born in England and immigrated to the United States in the 1840s, one source contends he was born in South Carolina. See the *New York Times*, September 23, 1864.

50. In spite of Zacharie's idiosyncratic personality, it is difficult to believe that so many sophisticated and discerning men like Lincoln, Banks, Seward, and Stanton would have all been taken in by a thoroughgoing charlatan. Clearly the president's podiatrist had a compelling side as well—qualities that Lincoln obviously found trustworthy. See Korn, *American Jewry*, 201–2. See also Segal, "Isachar Zacharie," 126.

51. Isachar Zacharie to Nathaniel P. Banks, December 28, 1863, Bertram W. Korn Collection, MS 99, box 34, folder 9, AJA.

52. Korn, *American Jewry*, 201–2; Isachar Zacharie to Nathaniel P. Banks, December 28, 1863, MS 99, box 34, folder 9, AJA.

53. Korn, *American Jewry*, 195.

54. *New York Herald*, October 3, 1862.

55. William Cornell Jewett (1823–93), also known as "Colorado" Jewett, was a well-known publicist and outspoken peace advocate.

56. This is a reference to Secretary of the Navy Gideon Welles (1802–78).

57. *New York Herald*, October 21, 1863.
58. Korn, *American Jewry*, 194–202, 230–39.
59. David Dixon Porter (1813–91) was a distinguished naval hero. David Glasgow Farragut (1801–70) was the first rear admiral, vice admiral, and admiral in the U.S. Navy. The two men were brothers by adoption—Porter's father had adopted Farragut when he was a young man—and the two brothers fought together during the Civil War.
60. SC-13337, AJA.
61. Zacharie wrote to Benjamin the following day and referred to their encounter as an "unexpected meeting." Isachar Zacharie to Judah P. Benjamin, September 28, 1863, domestic correspondence of the Confederate Department of State, Library of Congress.
62. Isachar Zacharie to Nathaniel P. Banks, October 9, 1863, SC-13335, AJA.
63. Isachar Zacharie to Judah P. Benjamin, September 28, 1863, domestic correspondence of the Confederate Department of State, Library of Congress.
64. Isachar Zacharie to Nathaniel P. Banks, October 9, 1863, SC-13335, AJA. The Willard Hotel, located at 1401–09 Pennsylvania Ave., NW, has had a unique niche in the history of Washington, D.C., and the nation. See "A National Register of Historic Places in Washington, D.C.," http://www.nps.gov/nr/travel/wash/dc36.htm (accessed August 30, 2012).
65. Isachar Zacharie to Nathaniel P. Banks, October 16, 1863, SC-13335, AJA.
66. Korn, *American Jewry*, 237.
67. Abraham Lincoln, *The Collected Works of Abraham Lincoln*, ed. Roy P. Basler, vol. 8 (New Brunswick, N.J.: Rutgers University Press, 1953), 12 (hereafter *Collected Works*).
68. Korn, *American Jewry*, 237.
69. *The World: New York*, Saturday, September 24, 1864.
70. Samuel A. Lewis to Abraham Lincoln, Wednesday, October 26, 1864 (meeting with Jewish committee), Abraham Lincoln Papers, series 1, General Correspondence, 1833–1916, Library of Congress, Washington, D.C.
71. On Myer S. Isaacs, see obituary, *New York Times*, May 25, 1904.
72. Myer Isaacs to Abraham Lincoln, October 26, 1864, available at Abraham Lincoln Papers at the Library of Congress, Manuscript Division, http://memory.loc.gov/ammem/alhtml/alhome.html (accessed January 3, 2012).
73. See Edwin Stanton's response to President Lincoln's January 25, 1865, request, dated the same day, in the Abraham Lincoln Collection at the Library of Congress as cited on "Antietam on the Web," http://aotw.org/officers.php?officer_id=371 (accessed August 30, 2012).
74. Naphtali J. Rubinger, *Abraham Lincoln and the Jews* (New York: Jonathan David Publishers, 1962), 37–38.
75. Abraham Lincoln to Edwin M. Stanton, January 25, 1865, *Collected Works*, 8:238.
76. Rubinger, *Lincoln and the Jews*, 37–38.
77. Kellogg served as a representative from Connecticut in the U.S. House of Representatives from 1869 to 1875.
78. "Freaks of Legislation: Odd Bills and Reports by Congressional Committees," *New York Times*, January 14, 1896, 10.

3. Lincoln and the Chaplaincy Controversy

1. The quote "justice and liberality" comes from Rabbi Isaac Leeser's eulogy on Lincoln. See Emanuel Hertz, ed., *Abraham Lincoln: The Tribute of the Synagogue* (New York: Bloch Publishing, 1927), 135.

2. For the most complete and detailed history of both the "chaplaincy controversy" and General Grant's Orders No. 11 expelling the Jews from the Military Department of Tennessee, see Bertram W. Korn, *American Jewry and the Civil War* (Philadelphia: Jewish Publication Society, 1951), 56–97, 121–55.

3. Ibid., 57.

4. There are many gaps in our knowledge of Allen's activities after he resigned from his role as an army chaplain. After the Civil War, he moved to New York City, where he married Julia Spanier in 1866. Subsequently, Allen became the director of Hebrew studies at the Talmud Torah (Hebrew School) of New York's Congregation Shearith Israel. In 1873, Allen immigrated to Germany in order to be with his wife's family in Hannover, Prussia. A copy of a letter from Allen to a friend in the United States is located in the American Jewish Archives in Cincinnati, Ohio. Allen described his deepening identification with traditional Jewish practice and his satisfaction with the religious devotion of Hannover Jewry. "Our Holy Religion is observed by our people here as it was in times gone by," he wrote, "when no reforms had crept in to mar the observance of our rites and ceremonies." He attributed his religious transformation to the influence of his wife's uncle, the *Landesrabbiner* (chief rabbi) of Hannover Province. Allen kept a journal while he was functioning as a chaplain in September 1861. This diary was transcribed by David de Sola Pool, "The Diary of Chaplain Michael M. Allen, September, 1861," *Publications of the American Jewish Historical Society* 39, no. 2 (December 1949): 177–82. Allen died on May 19, 1907, and is buried at the Jewish cemetery, An der Strangriede, in Hannover. For additional information on the first Jew to serve as a U.S. Army chaplain, see also "Michael Mitchell Allen Chaplain, 'Cameron Dragoons'" on the website of the Jewish-American History Foundation, http://www.jewish-history.com/civilwar/mmallen.htm (accessed August 20, 2012).

5. Korn, *American Jewry*, 58–60. Very little is known about Colonel Max Friedman, who played an important role in this episode. He was born in Nuremberg, immigrated to the United States, and settled in Philadelphia. After the conclusion of the Civil War, Friedman moved to New York, where he worked as a successful Wall Street broker. See obituary, *New York Times*, February 12, 1900, 7. On Friedman and the Sixty-Fifth Regiment, see Samuel P. Bates (Samuel Penniman), *History of Pennsylvania Volunteers, 1861–1865* (Harrisburg: B. Singerly, 1869–71), 568, 577.

6. For the most detailed reconstruction of Fischel's biography, see Jonathan Waxman, "Arnold Fischel: 'Unsung Hero' in American Israel," *American Jewish Historical Quarterly* 60, no. 4 (June 1971): 325–43.

7. Ibid., 325–38.

8. Korn, *American Jewry*, 62–67.

9. For quote, see ibid., 65.

10. *Israelite*, November 29, 1861, 172.

11. Jonathan D. Sarna, *American Judaism: A History* (New Haven, Conn.: Yale University Press, 2004), 119–20.

12. The Board of Delegates of American Israelites, officially organized in 1859, was headquartered in New York. The sensational case of Edgardo Mortara, which first began attracting international attention in 1858, provided an impetus for the establishment of this board. Mortara was an Italian Jewish boy who was forcibly removed from his parents' home by papal authorities after his family's maid announced that she had supervised the child's conversion to Catholicism some years earlier. The Board of Delegates of American Israelites was the first successful attempt to create a national

Jewish organization that would seek to defend the civil and political rights of Jews in America and abroad.

13. Board of Delegates of American Israelites Minute Book, 1859-70, SC-1194, box 952, American Jewish Archives, Cincinnati, Ohio (original at the American Jewish Historical Society, New York). Courtesy of The Jacob Rader Marcus Center of the American Jewish Archives (hereafter AJA), at the Hebrew Union College–Jewish Institute of Religion, Cincinnati, Ohio. A prominent report on the activities of the Board of Delegates appeared in the *New York Times*, December 6, 1861, 5.

14. For quote, see Korn, *American Jewry*, 69.

15. Ibid., 69-70. Although the original copy of Lincoln's memorandum to Fischel dated December 13, 1861, seems to have been lost, Lincoln's note promising he will take steps to correct the problem is quoted in its entirety in the *Jewish Messenger*, December 27, 1861, 101.

16. Korn, *American Jewry*, 70.

17. Isaac M. Wise cites the *Presbyter* in the *Israelite*, March 28, 1862, 308. After quoting the *Presbyter*'s point of view, Wise lambastes the paper's editor with three colorful columns of bitter recriminations condemning the *Presbyter*'s point of view.

18. Waxman, "Arnold Fischel," 341-43.

19. Korn, *American Jewry*, 70-72.

20. Ibid., 341.

21. According to Lance J. Sussman, Leeser's biographer, Leeser was the "Secretary and Founder" of the Philadelphia Board of Rabbis. See Sussman, *Isaac Leeser and the Making of American Judaism* (Detroit: Wayne State University Press, 1995), 224. For an electronic scan and text of Leeser's letter to Lincoln, see http://www .jewishvirtuallibrary.org/jsource/loc/Leeser.html (accessed August 25, 2012).

22. Isaac Leeser to Abraham Lincoln, August 21, 1862, Library of Congress, www.loc.gov/ exhibits/haventohome/haven-challenges.html. One can view the text of this, as well as the written exchange between Hay and Hammond inscribed on the back of the letter, on the website of the Jewish Virtual Library, http://www.jewishvirtuallibrary .org/jsource/loc/Leeser.html (accessed August 25, 2012). For more information on Frankel and his appointment, see Korn, *American Jewry*, 77-80.

23. Even though Jacob Frankel was a cantor (hazan) and did not possess a formal certificate of rabbinical ordination (*hasmakhah*), he did officially hold the office of "rabbi" at Rodeph Shalom Congregation in Philadelphia. Being an occupant of the rabbinical office at the Philadelphia congregation evidently made Frankel a rabbi in the eyes of the federal government. For more information on Frankel and his appointment, see Korn, *American Jewry*, 77-80. For a colorful description of Frankel's funeral and a fine description of his character, see *American Israelite*, January 21, 1887, 9.

24. Fischel's name appears in a variety of spellings, including "Fischell" and "Fishell." Unless citing a direct quotation—as in the case of this document—we will consistently use the commonly accepted spelling: Fischel.

25. This name was commonly spelled "Bene Yeshurun" during the nineteenth century. At some point in the twentieth century, the congregation adopted a variant spelling, "B'nai Yeshurun," which it has used to the present day.

26. Conkling was a member of the U.S. House of Representatives, having been elected to the 37th Congress. He held his seat from March 4, 1861, to March 3, 1863.

27. Board of Delegates of American Israelites Minute Book, 1859-70, SC-1194, box 952, AJA (original at the American Jewish Historical Society, New York).

28. Ibid.

29. Ibid., SC-1194-1195, AJA (original at the American Jewish Historical Society, New York).

30. On E. Delafield Smith, see obituary in the *New York Times*, April 13, 1878.

31. *Lincoln and the Jews, Portfolio No. 1: Facsimiles of Notable Documents in American Jewish History* (Washington: Klutznick Exhibit Hall of B'nai B'rith, 1968), courtesy of the AJA.

32. See http://www.jewish-history.com/civilwar/af121561.html (accessed January 7, 2013). All original letters are at the American Jewish Historical Society, New York. Fischel copied both of these letters verbatim in his December 1861 letter to Henry Hart, president of the Board of Delegates of American Israelites. The original Delafield Smith letter survived, but the text of the Grinnell letter comes from Fischel's letter to Hart. Fischel apparently read Grinnell's signature as "M. A. Grinnell" instead of "M. H. Grinnell."

33. Henry I. Hart was a prominent New York businessman and Jewish communal leader. His premature death at the age of forty-seven may explain why his contributions to Jewish communal life have been so little noted. See obituary in the *Occident and American Jewish Advocate*, 5624/1863, 238-39, 285-86. See also *Publications of the American Jewish Historical Society* 12 (1904): 136.

34. Myer S. Isaacs, an officer of the BODAI, subsequently published a detailed account of Fischel's activities, including the significant wording of Lincoln's memorandum to Fischel dated December 15, 1861, in his paper, the *Jewish Messenger*, December 27, 1861, 101.

35. See http://www.jewish-history.com/civilwar/fischel.htm. All original letters are at the American Jewish Historical Society, New York.

36. Lincoln's personal secretary John Hay expressed these sentiments and assured Leeser that the president would make such an appointment. See John Hay to Isaac Leeser, September 8, 1862, in Korn, *American Jewry*, 77.

37. The Abraham Lincoln Papers at the Library of Congress, series 1, General Correspondence, 1833–1916, http://memory.loc.gov/ammem/malquery.html (accessed September 8, 2012).

38. Adding insult to injury, the BODAI failed to fully recompense Fischel for his efforts, as it had pledged. See Korn, *American Jewry*, 75-77, 80-81. For quote, see p. 72.

39. Copy in SC-4610, AJA. Original found in the Abraham Lincoln Papers at the Library of Congress, series 1, General Correspondence, 1833–1916.

4. Lincoln and the Revocation of General Orders No. 11

1. The famous order is sometimes confusingly labeled "General Orders No. 12." Historian Jonathan D. Sarna has explained the numerical confusion:

   This is the "official text" of the order, issued at Grant's field headquarters in Holly Springs and preserved in the Official Records of the War of the Rebellion, Series I, vol. 17, Part II, 424. Another text, issued from Grant's department headquarters at Oxford, Mississippi, is designated "General Orders No. 12" and carries slightly different wording. Still a third text, with yet other minor differences in wording, was published in the *New York Herald*, January 5, 1863. The discrepancy in numbering was caused by the discovery that a completely unrelated "General Orders No. 11" was issued by the Department of the Tennessee at La Grange, TN on November 26 [1862]. While the text issued at Oxford therefore corrected the numbering and slightly improved the language of the order, "General Orders No. 11" remained the name by which the order was known. For the corrected text issued at Oxford, see John Y. Simon, ed., *The Papers of Ulysses S. Grant*, vol. 7 (Carbondale: Southern Illinois University Press, 1979), 50. Note that the official text properly uses the plural form ("General Orders"), since generals inevitably issued many orders. Unofficially, though, the singular form, "General Order No. 11," was common.

See Sarna, *When General Grant Expelled the Jews* (New York: Schocken, 2012), 7–8.

2. Sarna, *General Grant*, constitutes the most expansive account of this entire incident as well as its effect on Grant's ongoing relationship with the Jewish community. Sarna reproduces the basic text of the order on p. 7. For another fine treatment of this incident, see Stephen V. Ash, "Civil War Exodus: The Jews and Grant's General Order No. 11," *Historian* 44, no. 4 (August 1982): 505–23. See also Bertram W. Korn, *American Jewry and the Civil War* (Philadelphia: Jewish Publication Society, 1951), 121–55. Isaac Markens also provides a variety of primary source material, though regrettably without notation; see *Abraham Lincoln and the Jews* (New York: Isaac Markens, 1909), 10–16. A photograph of one of the actual telegrams containing this order appears in Sarna, *General Grant*, 9.

3. For quote, see Korn, *American Jewry*, 122.

4. On the problem of illegal trade, see Ash, "Civil War Exodus," 505–10. See also Korn, *American Jewry*, 121–22.

5. On the use of the word "Jew" during the Civil War era, see James M. McPherson, *Battle Cry of Freedom: The Civil War Era* (New York: Oxford University Press, 1988), 622 n. 61.

6. For an elucidation of these various explanations, see Sarna, *General Grant*, 45–48. See also Ash, "Civil War Exodus," 508–10. Isaac M. Wise blamed the order on Grant's military colleagues who, he asserted, wanted to rid themselves of Jewish competition as traders. See the *Israelite*, January 2, 1863, 202.

7. Sarna concluded that the "most likely" explanation for the issuance of this order pertains to Grant's displaced anger at his father. See *General Grant*, 47–48. Although there is absolutely no question that Grant drank alcohol throughout his adult life, most modern historians insist that there is no convincing evidence that Grant's drinking was either habitual or problematic. Still, as one historian noted, "there is plenty of evidence that Grant did drink moderately." See Charles G. Ellington, *The Trial of U. S. Grant: The Pacific Coast Years, 1852–1854* (Glendale, Calif.: A.H. Clark, 1987), 35. A historian of bourbon has written, "[Grant] liked liquor and a little whisky showed on him." See Gerald Carson, *The Social History of Bourbon: An Unhurried Account of Our Star-Spangled American Drink* (Lexington: University Press of Kentucky, 1984), 75.

8. General Ulysses S. Grant to Assistant Secretary of War Christopher Parsons Wolcott, December 17, 1862, in Robert N. Scott, ed., *The War of the Rebellion: A Compilation of the Official Records of the Union and Confederate Armies* (hereafter *Official Records*), series I, vol. 17, part 2 (Washington, D.C.: Government Printing Office, 1902), 421–22.

9. The full text of this letter from Ulysses S. Grant to Congressman I. N. Morris of Illinois, September 14, 1868, was published in the *New York Times*, November 30, 1868. For another rare and clearly obsequious comment relating to the Jews by Grant, see also Korn, *American Jewry*, 144. On Grant's relationship with American Jewry, see Sarna, *General Grant*.

10. Sarna, *General Grant*, 8–9, 18–20; *Israelite*, January 23, 1863, 229.

11. *Israelite*, January 2, 1863; *Jewish Messenger*, January 9, 1863; *Jewish Record*, January 13, 1863.

12. For quote, see Ash, "Civil War Exodus," 515.

13. *Jewish Record*, January 13, 1863. Kaskel's name appears in documents under many different spellings, including Ceasar J. Kaskel, Cesar Kaskell, and Cesar F. Kaskell. His brother Julius's name, too, has been misspelled in published documents as J. W. Kaswell. According to their obituaries in the *New York Times*, the names were spelled Cesar J. Kaskel and Julius W. Kaskel.

14. On Cesar J. Kaskel, see Korn, *American Jewry*, 124–25, 128. On Julius W.'s time in Burlington, Iowa, see Augustine M. Antrobus, *History of Des Moines County Iowa and its People* (Chicago: S. J. Clarke Publishing Company, 1915), 115, 191. On the Kaskels in Leadville, see Mitchell A. Levin, *This Day . . . in Jewish History: A Collection of Jewish History and Current Jewish Events*, wherein it says that on May 19, 1882, "the Leadville, CO Jewish community suffered a financial loss when a building owned by New Yorkers Caesar J. Kaskel and Jacob Michaelis burned. The building was the home to a clothing store managed by Julius W. Kaskel." See http://thisdayinjewishhistory .blogspot.com/2012/05/this-day-may-19-in-jewish-history-by.html (accessed August 24, 2012). For an interesting description of their clothing store in New York, see "What Men Will Wear: Masculine Fashions as Exemplified at Kaskel & Kaskel's Store," *New York Times*, October 9, 1885, 8. For notice of Cesar J.'s death, see *New York Times*, April 1, 1892, 5; for Julius W., see *New York Times*, March 9, 1909, 9.

15. See Markens, *Abraham Lincoln and the Jews*, 12.

16. For text of the telegram, see *Official Records*, series I, vol. 17, part 2, 506.

17. This information comes from Isaac M. Wise; see the *Israelite*, January 16, 1863, 218.

18. Daniel Wolf (affectionately known as "Uncle Dan" Wolf) was considered a Jewish pioneer of Cincinnati. He immigrated to Cincinnati from present-day Germany when he was twelve years old, and by the time of the Civil War he was a leader in the Jewish community. He was elected several times to the Cincinnati city council, and he served one term in the Ohio State Legislature (1884–86). For more on Wolf's career, see his obituary in the *Cincinnati Enquirer*, February 14, 1904, A8.

19. Markens, *Abraham Lincoln and the Jews*, 12. On Congressman Gurley, see *Biographical Dictionary of the United States Congress*, http://bioguide.congress.gov (accessed August 28, 2012).

20. According to Isaac M. Wise in an editorial describing Kaskel's trip to Washington, D.C., "Mr. Kaskel arrived in Washington, January 3, and was introduced to the President." See the *Israelite*, January 16, 1863, 218. Isaac Markens, who clearly had been in personal communication with Cesar's brother, Julius W., about this episode, confirms the meeting took place on the eve of January 3—"at dusk." See Markens, *Abraham Lincoln and the Jews*, 12–13. The *Lincoln Log*, however, which chronicles every day in Lincoln's life, contends the visit took place on Sunday morning, January 4. See *The Lincoln Log: A Daily Chronology of the Life of Abraham Lincoln*, http://www .thelincolnlog.org/view (accessed August 30, 2012).

21. Korn, *American Jewry*, 125.

22. Markens, *Abraham Lincoln and the Jews*, 13.

23. Korn, *American Jewry*, 125.

24. Markens, *Abraham Lincoln and the Jews*, 13.

25. Korn, *American Jewry*, 275.

26. Ibid., 126.

27. Sarna, *General Grant*, 24–27.

28. *Israelite*, January 16, 1863, 218.

29. *Israelite*, January 23, 1863, 228.
30. Ash's essay "Civil War Exodus" argues this point persuasively. See pp. 522–23.
31. *Israelite*, January 2, 1863, 202. See also Ash, "Civil War Exodus."
32. *Israelite*, January 16, 1863, 218.
33. "Expulsion of Jews from General Grant's Department—The Circumstances Stated and Documents Quoted," *Jewish Record*, December 30, 1862.
34. Colonel John Van Deusen Du Bois composed an order similar to Grant's General Orders No. 11 several weeks earlier. Wise took note of this incident in his paper. See also Korn, *American Jewry*, 139–40.
35. This is the only known document that refers to Grant's order as No. 29. See n. 1 above for further explanation.
36. William M. Wiles was the provost marshal general, Fourteenth Army Corps, Nashville, Tenn. Rosecrans was his commanding officer.
37. William Starke Rosecrans (1819–98) was a graduate of West Point and rose to prominence during the first years of the Civil War. His military career came to a sudden end following his disastrous defeat at the Battle of Chickamauga in 1863. Rosecrans was known to quarrel with his superiors, including Grant and Secretary of War Edwin M. Stanton. See Peter Cozzens, *This Terrible Sound: The Battle of Chickamauga* (Urbana: University of Illinois Press, 1992).
38. *Israelite*, January 2, 1863, 202.
39. This telegram has the Kaskel brothers' name spelled with two *l*s: Kaskell (see note 13 above). *War of the Rebellion*, series I, vol. 17, part 2, 506.
40. In addition to serving as president of the B'nai B'rith Lodge, Henry Kuttner also served as the rabbi of St. Louis's Beth El Congregation. Hoffman was a local businessman.
41. For a description of this incident, see Korn, *American Jewry*, 126, who aptly reflected, "Was there no one in Washington who objected to an order which 'proscribed an entire religious class' except the President?"
42. St. Louis B'nai B'rith to Abraham Lincoln, Monday, January 5, 1863 (resolution protesting Grant's order expelling Jews), Abraham Lincoln Papers, series 1, General Correspondence, 1833–1916, Library of Congress, Washington, D.C.
43. *New York Times*, January 5, 1863, 5.
44. This name also appears as Goldschmit.
45. *Israelite*, January 9, 1863.
46. *Israelite*, January 16, 1863, 218.
47. *Israelite*, January 23, 1863, 228.
48. *New York Times*, January 18, 1863, 4.
49. Wise errs here. Low was from San Francisco, and he was a member of the U.S. House of Representatives from June 3, 1862, to March 3, 1863.
50. *Israelite*, February 28, 1868, 4.

5. Lincoln and the Movement to Christianize the U.S. Constitution

1. Steven Keith Green, "The National Reform Association and the Religious Amendments to the Constitution, 1864–1876" (master's thesis, University of North Carolina at Chapel Hill, 1987), 14. See also Isaac Kramnick and R. Laurence Moore, *The Godless Constitution: The Case against Religious Correctness* (New York: W. W. Norton, 1997), 145–47.
2. Isaac Leeser read about Sumner's actions on behalf of the Covenanters on January 10, 1861. See the *Occident and American Jewish Advocate* 18, no. 43 (January 17, 1861): 1.

3. Ibid.

4. Jefferson's letter to the Danbury Baptists. See Thomas Jefferson Papers, Library of Congress, http://memory.loc.gov/ammemcollection/jefferson_papers (accessed October 5, 2012).

5. *Occident and American Jewish Advocate* 18, no. 43 (January 17, 1861): 1.

6. Alexander's obituary can be found in J. W. Sproull and D. B. Willson, *The Reformed Presbyterian and Covenanter*, vol. 33 (Pittsburgh: Myer and Shinkle Company, 1895), 92. Toward the end of his life, Alexander reconstructed the early history of the National Reform Association's beginnings. See James Mitchell Foster, *Christ the King* (Boston: James H. Earle, 1894), 15–40. For quotations, see pp. 15 and 20.

7. On this church and its beloved pastor, John Taylor Pressly (1795–1870), see *Allegheny City, 1840–1907* (Charleston, S.C.: Arcadia Pub., 2007), 16.

8. Foster, *Christ the King*, 26.

9. Ibid., 24–26.

10. *Occident and American Jewish Advocate* 21 (August 1863): 222.

11. *Proceedings of the National Convention to Secure the Religious Amendment of the Constitution of the United States: held in New York, Feb. 26 and 27, 1873: with an Account of the Origin and Progress of the Movemen*t (New York: John Polhemus Printer, 1873), viii.

12. *Israelite*, February 19, 1864, 268. Like Leeser, Wise took note of this coalition of advocates and issued a warning to his readers about their agenda. See the *Israelite*, June 5, 1863, 380.

13. Foster, *Christ the King*, 37.

14. Emanuel Hertz, ed., *Abraham Lincoln: The Tribute of the Synagogue* (New York: Bloch Publishing, 1927), 135, 37, 154.

15. *Jewish Exponent* 10 (February 1911): 4.

16. "A Tribute to Lincoln by Rabbi [Nathan] Krass," *American Hebrew & Jewish Messenger*, June 2, 1911, 148.

17. Simon Wolf, *The Presidents I Have Known from 1860–1918* (Washington, D.C.: Byron S. Adams Press, 1918), 29.

18. See "Lincoln's Birthday" by Simon Wolf in the *American Israelite*, April 6, 1888, 5.

19. For a quotation suggesting that the adoption of a Christian amendment would create a "house divided," see Isaac M. Wise's editorial in the *Israelite*, February 19, 1864, 268.

20. *Proceedings of the National Convention*, vi–viii.

21. Ibid.

22. Ibid.

23. *Israelite*, June 5, 1863, 380.

24. *Occident and American Jewish Advocate* 21 (August 1863): 219–22.

25. Board of Delegates of American Israelites Minute Book, 1859–70, SC-1194, box 952, American Jewish Archives, Cincinnati, Ohio (original at the American Jewish Historical Society, New York). Courtesy of The Jacob Rader Marcus Center of the American Jewish Archives (hereafter AJA), at the Hebrew Union College–Jewish Institute of Religion, Cincinnati, Ohio. See also *New York Times*, June 12, 1865.

26. The Hebrew word *rishuth* literally means "wickedness" or "evilness," and for Leeser the term referred to an inveterate injustice brought about by a baseless hatred of the Jew. See the *Occident and American Jewish Advocate* 12, no. 10 (January 1865): 433–41. On "Rishuth," see Jeffrey S. Gurock, *Anti-Semitism in America*, vol. 6 of *American Jewish History* (New York: Routledge, 1998), 189.

27. Board of Delegates of American Israelites Minute Book, 1859–70, SC-1194, AJA (original at the American Jewish Historical Society, New York).

6. "A Great Man in Israel Has Fallen": American Jewry Mourns Lincoln

1. In the Holy Scriptures, Passover was originally established as a seven-day festival. Throughout the Diaspora, Passover has been traditionally celebrated for eight days. Today, a seven-day Passover is celebrated among Reform Jews and also in Israel.
2. *Israelite*, April 21, 1865, 339.
3. Emanuel Hertz, ed., *Abraham Lincoln: The Tribute of the Synagogue* (New York: Bloch Publishing, 1927), 138.
4. *Jewish Messenger*, April 21, 1865, 124.
5. Ibid., 110–11.
6. See David B. Chesebrough, *"No Sorrow Like Our Sorrow"*: *Northern Protestant Ministers and the Assassination of Lincoln* (Kent: Kent State University Press, 1994), 16–40.
7. David R. Goldfield, *America Aflame: How the Civil War Created a Nation* (New York: Bloomsbury Press, 2011), 367.
8. Hertz, *Tribute*, 111.
9. Ibid., 111, 114, 121.
10. Ibid., 111, 113. The phrase "a great man has fallen in Israel" comes from 2 Samuel 3:38 (*Ha-lo teidu ki sar v'gadol nafal ha-yom ha-zeh b'yisrael*).
11. Hertz, *Tribute*, 135.
12. Founded in 1838, Oheb Israel was originally called Fells Point Hebrew Friendship Congregation, Oheb Israel (Eden Street Synagogue). Hochheimer assumed Oheb Israel's pulpit in 1859. See Robert P. Swierenga, *The Forerunners: Dutch Jewry in the North American Diaspora* (Detroit: Wayne State University Press, 1994), 197–98. See Hertz, *Tribute*, 59.
13. Hertz, *Tribute*, xix. Szold's story about the distraught woman may have been essentially true. We know that Szold did in fact meet with Lincoln at the White House and asked him to pardon twenty-two-year-old Private George Kuhn of the 118th Pennsylvania Volunteers. According to newspaper accounts, Lincoln, though sympathetic, declined the appeal (though he agreed to provide Szold with a letter of introduction to General George Meade). There is no mention of Kuhn's mother having accompanied Szold to the White House. Later, Szold attended Kuhn's gruesome execution and, according to one account, fled from the disturbing scene so quickly that he left his purse in the commander's tent. See Bertram W. Korn, *American Jewry and the Civil War* (Philadelphia: Jewish Publication Society, 1951), 109, 270 nn. 68–70. On Szold and the Kuhn execution, see Henry N. Blake, *Three Years in the Army of the Potomac* (Boston: Lee and Shepard, 1865), 238–40.
14. Hertz, *Tribute*, 44–45.
15. Ibid., 144.
16. Ibid., 3, 6. Alluding to the psalmist (110:1), Morais also prayed that "our sainted President" be permitted "to sit at [God's] right hand." In Jewish tradition, the privilege of sitting on the right is a mark of distinction (see 1 Kings 2:19). Morais meant to suggest that just as David enjoyed a privileged relationship with God, so too would Abraham Lincoln now "sit at God's right hand." According to Christian belief, Jesus employs this same phrase to reveal himself as the Messiah (see Luke 22:67–69).
17. Hertz, *Tribute*, 19. The term *"Kiddush Ha-Shem"* literally means "Sanctification of God's Name." For more on the historical meaning of this concept, see Norman Lamm, *"Kiddush haShem and Hillul ha-Shem," Encyclopedia Judaica* (Jerusalem:

Keter Publishing, 1972), vol. 10, col. 977–83. See also Avraham Holtz, *"Kiddush Hashem and Hillul Hashem," Judaism* 10, no. 4 (1961): 360–67.

18. Hertz, *Tribute*, 95.

19. Ibid., 17, 58, 146.

20. Markens mentions Gotthelf's eulogy, though he does not quote from it. See Markens, *Abraham Lincoln and the Jews*, 42. Similarly, Gotthelf's eulogy does not appear in Hertz's *Tribute of the Synagogue*. On Gotthelf, see Julius Herscovici, *Bernhard Henry Gotthelf* (Vicksburg, Miss.: Herscovici, 2001). On the pro-southern sentiment in Louisville and Kentucky, see Henry C. Hubbart, "'Pro-Southern' Influences in the Free West, 1840–1865," *Mississippi Valley Historical Review* 20, no. 1 (June 1933): 45–62.

21. *Louisville Daily Journal*, April 23, 1865. The citation is also noted in Merrill D. Peterson, *Lincoln in American Memory* (New York: Oxford University Press, 1994), 231.

22. Hertz, *Tribute*, 31–32, 35. Shortly after Lincoln's assassination, Joachimsen was thrown from his horse and seriously injured. Receiving an honorable discharge from the military, he returned to New York, where he became a prominent attorney and a leader in the Jewish community. For more on Joachimsen, see especially his obituary in the *New York Times*, January 7, 1890, 5. See also Jacob Rader Marcus and Judith M. Daniels, *The Concise Dictionary of American Jewish Biography* (New York: Carlson Publishing Inc., 1994), s.v. "Joachimsen." On Congregation Temimi (sometimes spelled "Tememe" or "Temime") Derech, see Irwin Lachoff and Catherine C. Kahn, *The Jewish Community of New Orleans* (Charleston, S.C.: Arcadia, 2005), 23–24.

23. Born in Kolin, Bohemia, Illowy studied for the rabbinate in Pressburg, in present-day Hungary. Although he was an ardent defender of traditional Jewish practice in the United States, he was politically liberal and, like many of his Jewish contemporaries, had been a supporter of the liberal revolutions that swept over Europe in the last months of 1848. The conservative backlash that arose in the wake of the failure of these liberal revolts prompted many dejected partisans to abandon the cause in Europe and immigrate to the United States. By June 1865, only a few weeks after Lincoln's death, Illowy had relocated to Cincinnati. On Illowy, see especially Irwin Lachoff, "Rabbi Bernard Illowy: Counter Reformer," *Southern Jewish History* 5 (2002): 43–67. For quote, see p. 53. See also Marcus and Daniels, *American Jewish Biography*, s.v. "Illowy."

24. Lachoff, "Rabbi Bernard Illowy"; Hertz, *Tribute*, 160–63.

25. For quote, see the *New York Times*, April 20, 1865. See also Jonathan D. Sarna, *American Judaism: A History* (New Haven, Conn.: Yale University Press, 2004), 122. For quote, see the *Jewish Messenger*, May 5, 1865, 139.

26. See *New York Times*, May 3, 1865, 1. See also Harold Holzer, *Lincoln and the Jews: The Last Best Hope of Earth* (Los Angeles: Skirball Cultural Center, 2002), 14. For more details concerning the role that Jews played in Lincoln's "funeral pageant," see Korn, *American Jewry*, 240–44. For quotation, see 2 Samuel 1:19.

27. William M. Kramer, "'They Have Killed Our Man But Not Our Cause': The California Jewish Mourners of Abraham Lincoln," *Western States Jewish Historical Quarterly* 2, no. 4 (July 1970): 214–15. See also Ava Kahn, ed., *Jewish Voices of the California Gold Rush: A Documentary History, 1849–1880* (Detroit: Wayne State University Press, 2002), 406, 423–24, 433–34.

28. See Minutes of the Board of Temple Israel, April 18, 1865, Archives of Temple Israel, Boston, Mass. (copy in American Jewish Archives, Cincinnati, Ohio). Courtesy of The Jacob Rader Marcus Center of the American Jewish Archives, at the Hebrew Union College–Jewish Institute of Religion, Cincinnati, Ohio.

29. *Israelite*, June 16, 1865, 404.
30. Hertz, *Tribute*, 138–39.
31. Ibid., 133–37. Hertz incorrectly indicates that Beth-El Emeth was located in New York City. Leeser spent the balance of his rabbinical career in Philadelphia. For quotation, see Job 1:21.
32. Hochheimer's eulogy includes quotations from scripture in both the Hebrew original and the German translation.
33. Genesis 13:8.
34. I wish to express deep gratitude to Professor Elizabeth Petuchowski, former adjunct associate professor in the German department of the University of Cincinnati, for contributing these fine English translations from the German originals.
35. Leviticus 10:1.
36. Leviticus 10:6.
37. Hertz, *Tribute*, 57–62.
38. Morais's reference to "our lamented Everett" refers to Edward Everett (1794–1865), congressman, senator, president of Harvard University, governor of Massachusetts, and secretary of state under Millard Fillmore. Everett, who died on January 15, 1865, was the most prominent American orator of his time and was also an ardent Lincoln supporter. His oration at Gettysburg—over two hours in length—was completely overshadowed by Lincoln's immortal two-minute address.
39. Job 34:22.
40. Deuteronomy 32:4.
41. Hertz, *Tribute*, 1–5.
42. The last line of this excerpt is a citation from Pirke Avot 4:18.
43. I wish again to express deep gratitude to Professor Elizabeth Petuchowski for generously contributing these fine English translations from the German originals.
44. See *Babylonian Talmud Mo'ed Katan* 28a, modified.
45. Einhorn is alluding to a rabbinic legend that suggests that during the exodus from Egypt, the Red Sea parted before the Israelites "for the sake of the bones of Joseph" (see Exodus 13:19). See Jacob Z. Lauterbach, *Mekilta De-Rabbi Ishmael*, 2nd ed., vol. 1 (Philadelphia: Jewish Publication Society, 1976), 220.
46. The Hebrew term "*Kiddush Ha-Shem*" literally means "Sanctification of the Name (of God)." However, in classical Jewish writing, it is commonly used as a euphemism for Jewish martyrdom, when a Jew is prepared to sacrifice his life rather than transgress any of God's cardinal laws. Einhorn is unquestionably expressing the idea of "Jewish martyrdom."
47. Hertz, *Tribute*, 13–19.
48. Genesis 12:1.
49. Genesis 15:1.
50. Deuteronomy 32:49.
51. This version from Hertz, *Tribute*, 160–63. It was also printed in the *New Orleans Times* of April 23, 1865.
52. Genesis 12:1–4.
53. Lamentations 2:10–13.
54. Lamentations 5:16.
55. Job 1:21.
56. Hosea 14:1.
57. Deuteronomy 32:4.

58. Genesis 4:13.
59. Genesis 12:2.
60. Numbers 25:13.
61. Psalm 146:3.
62. Isaiah 2:22.
63. Genesis 22:18.
64. Genesis 12:4.
65. Hertz, *Tribute*, 92–99.
66. Jeremiah 9:26.
67. Psalm 24:3–4.
68. Habakkuk 2:4.
69. 2 Samuel 1:23.
70. Psalm 79:10.
71. *Louisville Daily Journal*, April 23, 1865.
72. Job 1:21. See Hertz, *Tribute*, 137.
73. According to the April 20, 1865, *New York Herald*, the "Al. Mola. Rachamim" [*sic*] was chanted at New York's B'nai Israel Congregation. See Hertz, *Tribute*, 175.
74. Hertz, *Tribute*, 165.
75. *Jewish Messenger*, April 21, 1865, 124.
76. Joseph Shoninger (1829–1910), a talented musician, was the spiritual leader of Temple Israel in Boston from 1856 to 1874. See Meaghan Dwyer-Ryan, Susan L. Porter, and Lisa Fagin Davis, *Becoming American Jews: Temple Israel of Boston* (Hanover, N.H.: Brandeis University Press, 2009), 15.
77. Temple Israel Board Minutes, April 18, 1865 (original located in the Archives of Temple Israel, Boston). According to the document, the German original was translated by a congregant in the 1960s.
78. *Occident and American Jewish Advocate* 23, no. 2 (Nissan 5625/May 1865): 86–88.
79. *New York Times*, April 21, 1865. According to the article, the governor made April 20 the day of mourning, but others felt the governor should have selected April 19, corresponding to the day of Lincoln's funeral in the nation's capital. "[T]he result was that on two consecutive days church services were needed by the people."
80. This obvious misspelling may refer to a small congregation named Shaarey Beracha, established in 1858. See Hyman B. Grinstein, *The Rise of the Jewish Community of New York, 1654–1860* (Philadelphia: Jewish Publication Society of America, 1945), 474.
81. *New York Times*, April 21, 1865. For mention of the various names in this document, see the index in Grinstein, *Rise of the Jewish Community*.
82. This selection first appeared in the *Jewish Record* and subsequently was published in Korn's *American Jewry*.
83. This is probably a typographical error. The name of the lodge would most likely have been "Rehoboth."
84. This probably is a reference to the Board of Delegates of American Israelites.
85. Psalm 25:6.
86. Psalm 25:13.
87. Psalm 46:2.
88. Psalm 103:4.
89. Lamentations 3:39.
90. Job 3:19.
91. Psalm 78:39.

92. Job 34:15.
93. Job 4:17.
94. Psalm 56:10.
95. Psalm 144:4.
96. Psalm 125:4.
97. Psalm 149:5.
98. Isaiah 58:8.
99. Psalm 121:7.
100. Psalm 121:4.
101. 1 Samuel 2:6.
102. Psalm 85:6.
103. Psalm 130:7.
104. Ecclesiastes 1:4.
105. Psalm 33:4.
106. Ecclesiastes 12:7.
107. Psalm 112:2.
108. Job 1:21.
109. Psalm 146:6.
110. Numbers 16:48.
111. This selection first appeared in the *Jewish Record*. This version is from Korn, *American Jewry*, 240–44.

7. Conflicting Obligations: Shavuot and the National Day of Humiliation and Mourning

1. Lincoln's body lay in state in Baltimore, Harrisburg, Philadelphia, New York, Albany, Buffalo, Cleveland, Columbus, Indianapolis, Chicago, and Springfield. For more on Lincoln's funeral, see James L. Swanson, *The Chase for Jefferson Davis and the Death Pageant for Lincoln's Corpse* (New York: HarperCollins, 2010).
2. "Document Archive," webpage of the American Presidency Project, http://www.presidency/ucsb.edu/index_docs.php (accessed September 2, 2012).
3. For more on the various occasions on which Lincoln tributes were delivered, see David B. Chesebrough, *"No Sorrow Like Our Sorrow": Northern Protestant Ministers and the Assassination of Lincoln* (Kent: Kent State University Press, 1994), xiii. For the text of Johnson's proclamations, see the "Document Archive," webpage of the American Presidency Project. The expression "gladness and rejoicing" comes from Psalm 45:15.
4. *Jewish Messenger*, May 5, 1865, 140.
5. Emanuel Hertz, ed., *Abraham Lincoln: The Tribute of the Synagogue* (New York: Bloch Publishing, 1927), 164–65.
6. *Shivah* is a seven-day period of formal mourning that Jews observe after the funeral of a close relative. The first thirty days following the burial (which include the *shivah*) are called *shloshim*.
7. Hertz, *Tribute*, 39–41.
8. Ibid., 151.
9. Very little is known about Morris Deleeuw (whose name was more frequently spelled "De Leeuw"). He seems to have served a number of small New York synagogues in various capacities, including that of the congregation's beadle. A brief notice of his death appeared in the *New York Times*, June 11, 1915, 15.
10. Hertz, *Tribute*, 176.
11. *Jewish Messenger*, May 5, 1865, 140.

12. Deuteronomy 16:11.
13. Lyons's comments appeared the following day, June 2, 1865, in the *New York Herald*. Emanuel Hertz republished that newspaper article in his edited volume, *Abraham Lincoln: The Tribute of the Synagogue* (164–68).
14. Genesis 50:10.
15. Hertz, *Tribute*, 164–68.
16. Ibid., 39.
17. Ibid., 39–47. Translation from the German original by Elizabeth Petuchowski.
18. Ibid., 7, 9, 12.
19. Ibid., 7–12.
20. Deleeuw's remarks appeared the following day, June 2, 1865, in the *New York Tribune*. The *Tribune*'s correspondent introduced the published version of Deleeuw's address by noting, "There was a fine attendance at the Jewish Synagogue, B'nai Israel, corner of Stanton and Forsyth streets, and the ceremonies performed were more than usually solemn." Hertz republished that newspaper article in his edited volume, *Abraham Lincoln: The Tribute of the Synagogue* (176–77).
21. Deuteronomy 32:35.
22. See Hertz, *Tribute*, 176–77.

8. Criticisms and Commendations: Conflicting Views on the Lincoln Presidency

1. *Jewish Messenger*, December 25, 1891, 8. On Schurz, see chapter 1 of this book.
2. Julia Ward Howe, *Reminiscences, 1819–1899* (New York: Houghton, Mifflin, 1899), 153–54. See also *Jewish Messenger*, July 7, 1899, 6.
3. See Jennifer L. Weber, "Lincoln's Critics: The Copperheads," *Journal of the Abraham Lincoln Association* 32, no. 1 (Winter 2011): 33–47, and David Goldfield, "Lincoln's Image in the American Schoolbook," *American Studies Journal* 53 (2009), http://www.asjournal.org/archive/53/166.html (accessed September 15, 2012).
4. Donald T. Phillips, *Lincoln on Leadership: Executive Strategies for Tough Times* (New York: Warner Books, 1992), 8.
5. As quoted in Doris Kearns Goodwin, *Team of Rivals: The Political Genius of Abraham Lincoln* (New York: Simon and Schuster, 2005), 310.
6. For an electronic reproduction of Nast's cartoon, see the website of Illinois Periodicals Online, http://www.lib.niu.edu/2001/iht820129.html (accessed September 20, 2012).
7. Murat Halstead to Timothy C. Day, June 8, July 16, 1861, as quoted in Carl Sandburg, *Abraham Lincoln; the Prairie Years and the War Years* (New York: Harcourt, 1954), 351. See also Sarah J. Day, *The Man on a Hill Top* (Philadelphia: Ware Brothers, 1931), 243, 247.
8. See Weber, "Lincoln's Critics," 33–35. See also Jennifer L. Weber, *Copperheads: The Rise and Fall of Lincoln's Opponents in the North* (New York: Oxford University Press, 2006), 1–42.
9. Weber, "Lincoln's Critics," 33–35. See also Weber, *Copperheads*, 4. Weber's history of the Copperheads asserts that they were powerful opponents obstructing the president's agenda again and again. Weber's thesis challenges historians who argue that the Copperheads were essentially a chimera. See Frank L. Klement and Steven K. Rogstad, *Lincoln's Critics: The Copperheads of the North* (Shippensburg, Pa.: White Mane, 1999).
10. Chester G. Hearn, *Lincoln, the Cabinet, and the Generals* (Baton Rouge: Louisiana State University Press, 2010), 157.
11. Weber, "Lincoln's Critics," 35.

12. Ibid., 42.

13. Charles Bancroft, *The Footprints of Time* (Holmes Beach, Fla.: Gaunt, 2009), 672; Joan Waugh, *U. S. Grant: American Hero, American Myth* (Chapel Hill: University of North Carolina Press, 2009), 87.

14. Weber, "Lincoln's Critics," 44.

15. James M. McPherson, *For Cause and Comrades: Why Men Fought in the Civil War* (New York: Oxford University Press, 1997), 177.

16. Goodwin, *Team of Rivals*, 731.

17. *Israelite*, June 16, 1865, 404.

18. *Israelite*, January 18, 1861, 230.

19. Morris J. Raphall, *Bible View of Slavery: A Discourse, Delivered at the Jewish Synagogue, "Bnai Jeshurum [sic]" New York, on the Day of the National Fast, Jan. 4, 1861* (New York: Rudd & Carleton, 1861), 15.

20. Ibid., 29, 38.

21. *Israelite*, February 15, 1861, 262.

22. Henry Wilson (1812–75), a U.S. senator from Massachusetts from 1855 to 1873, was frequently known as the "Natick Cobbler" because he was a shoemaker in Natick, Massachusetts, before he was sent to the U.S. Senate. In 1872, he was elected vice president of the United States. See Ernest McKay, *Henry Wilson, Practical Radical: Portrait of a Politician* (Port Washington, N.Y.: Kennikat Press, 1971).

23. *Israelite*, February 14, 1862, 260.

24. See newspaper article containing Rabbi Morris Raphall's oration on the "Day of Humiliation and Fasting" observed earlier that year (see next note). The correspondent noted that some large Christian denominations ignored the president's appeal altogether.

25. *Israelite*, August 14, 1863, 49. It should be noted that Wise's complaint about Lincoln's repeatedly calling on the nation to commemorate a Thanksgiving Day precedes Lincoln's historic first proclamation asking the nation "to set apart and observe the last Thursday of November . . . as a day of Thanksgiving and Praise to our beneficent Father who dwelleth in the Heavens." Lincoln's "Proclamation of Thanksgiving" was issued on October 3, 1863. It was essentially a response to an appeal sent to him by the same woman who composed the nursery rhyme "Mary Had a Little Lamb," Sarah Josepha Buell Hale (1788–1879). Hale had been writing annually to the presidents of the United States since the 1840s in the hope of persuading them to create a unified and national thanksgiving celebration. Evidently, Lincoln was the first U.S. president to respond. For the text of Lincoln's "Proclamation of Thanksgiving," written for Lincoln by Secretary of State William H. Seward, see the *Abraham Lincoln Online* website, http://showcase.netins.net/web/creative/lincoln/speeches/thanks.htm (accessed September 12, 2012).

26. Simon Wolf, *The Presidents I Have Known from 1860–1918* (Washington, D.C.: Byron S. Adams Press, 1918), 21.

27. Emanuel Hertz, ed., *Abraham Lincoln: The Tribute of the Synagogue* (New York: Bloch Publishing, 1927), 170–171.

28. Ibid., 135.

29. Ibid., 92, 97.

30. Ibid., 95.

31. *Die Deborah*, April 28, 1865.

32. On Wise, see Sefton D. Temkin, *Isaac Mayer Wise: Shaping American Judaism* (New York: Oxford University Press, 1992).

33. The famous saying of Pyrrhus, king of Epirus, after Greek forces under his command defeated a Roman legion at Asculum in 279 B.C.E.

34. *Israelite*, November 30, 1860.

35. A Philistine deity used here to represent an inappropriate object of veneration.

36. *In spe*, meaning "in the hope" or "future," such as, "She is my mother-in-law, *in spe*." Obviously, Wise is suggesting that all of those who are hoping for a patronage position have gathered to fete Lincoln.

37. *Israelite*, February 15, 1861, 262.

38. See www.avalon.law.yale.edu/19thcentury/lincoln.asp (accessed November 18, 2012).

39. *Israelite*, March 15, 1861.

40. Lincoln would soon dole out some political appointments to Jews. In May 1861, he made his friend Abraham Jonas postmaster of Quincy, Illinois. On August 10, 1861, Lincoln named Marcus Otterbourg the U.S. consul in Mexico.

41. *Chicago Tribune*, March 26, 1861, 1.

42. Wilson was an outspoken opponent to slavery. For more on Wilson, see note 22 above.

43. *Israelite*, April 5, 1861, 317.

44. Hertz, *Tribute*, 95.

45. *Israelite*, August 19, 1864, 60.

46. On Leeser, see Lance J. Sussman, *Isaac Leeser and the Making of American Judaism* (Detroit: Wayne State University Press, 1995).

47. See the website of the American Presidency Project, http://www.presidency.ucsb.edu/ws/?pid=69829 (accessed July 18, 2013).

48. Behrend had two other sons besides Adajah, one of whom fought for the Confederacy while his brother fought for the Union. See "Justice Behrend Eighty Years Old," *Jewish Exponent*, July 16, 1909, 11.

49. Simon Wolf, *The American Jew as Patriot, Soldier, and Citizen*, ed. Louis Edward Levy (New York: Levytype Company, 1895), 4.

50. *Occident and American Jewish Advocate* 20, no. 10 (January 1863): 457–61.

51. See "Presidential Proclamation 97—Appointing a Day of National Humiliation, Fasting, and Prayer" on the website of the American Presidency Project, http://www.presidency.ucsb.edu/ws/index.php?pid=69891 (accessed September 15, 2012).

52. *Jewish Messenger*, May 8, 1863, 154.

53. Isaac Markens, *Abraham Lincoln and the Jews* (New York: Isaac Markens, 1909), 28–29.

54. Hosea 8:14.

55. *Jewish Messenger*, May 8, 1863, 154.

56. John Eaton and Ethel Osgood Mason, *Grant, Lincoln, and the Freedmen; Reminiscences of the Civil War, with Special Reference to the Work for the Contrabands and Freedmen of the Mississippi Valley* (1907; repr. New York: Negro Universities Press, 1969), 174–75; Frederick Douglass, *Life and Times of Frederick Douglass* (Hartford, Conn.: Park Publishing Co., 1881), 441.

57. It is possible that our "correspondent" is Simon Wolf ("S. W.").

58. *Jewish Messenger*, March 17, 1865, 96.

59. See William C. Davis, *Lincoln's Men: How President Lincoln Became Father to an Army and a Nation* (New York: Free Press, 1999).

60. *Jewish Messenger*, January 31, 1862, 31.

61. Although the familiar phrase "our peculiar institution" is typically associated with historian Kenneth M. Stampp's outstanding volume by the same name, the phrase itself was in usage long before the onset of the Civil War. John C. Calhoun was

one of the first to use the phrase when he delivered his "Speech on the Reception of Abolition Petitions: Revised Report" on February 6, 1837. See John C. Calhoun, *Speeches of John C. Calhoun Delivered in the Congress of the United States from 1811 to the Present Time* (New York: Harper & Brothers, 1843), 222.

62. For the complete text of Spiegel's January 22, 1864, letter to his wife, see Jean Powers Soman and Frank L. Byrne, eds., *A Jewish Colonel in the Civil War: Marcus Spiegel of the Ohio Volunteers* (Lincoln: University of Nebraska Press, 1994), 314–17. The original letter (SC-11848) has been deposited at the American Jewish Archives, Cincinnati, Ohio, courtesy of Jean Powers Soman.

63. Colley Cibber, *Richard III*, altered, act 5, scene 3, reprinted in *The Oxford Dictionary of Quotations*, 2nd ed. (London: Oxford University Press, 1959), 144.

64. Though Lincoln had excluded then Union-occupied parishes of Louisiana from the Emancipation Proclamation, General Banks had effectively ended slavery in January 1864 in the entire area under his control. Joe Gray Taylor, *Louisiana Reconstructed, 1863–1877* (Baton Rouge: Louisiana State University Press, 1974), 33.

65. The prewar Slave Code, derived from the French *Code Noir*. Ulrich Bonnell Phillips, *American Negro Slavery: A Survey of the Supply, Employment and Control of the Negro Labor as Determined by the Plantation Regime* (1918; Baton Rouge: Louisiana State University Press, 1966), 493–94.

66. In using the phrase "I am not so for party purposes," Spiegel meant to say that his revised views on slavery had nothing to do with his affiliation with a political party.

67. We do not know the dates of Goldstein's birth and death. Jacob Kabakoff, who studied his life and Hebrew writings carefully, suggested that Goldstein returned to Central Europe after the Civil War. We know nothing more about him from that point. See Kabakoff, "Isaac Goldstein—Pioneer Hebrew Merchant-Author," *Hebrew Studies* 17 (1976): 110–25.

68. Goldstein's "Acrostic" appeared in the *Jewish Messenger*, May 26, 1865, 165. It was republished in Philip Goodman, ed., *Lincoln's Birthday: Program Material for Jewish Groups* (New York: National Jewish Welfare Board, 1953), 53. Courtesy JWB Jewish Chaplain's Council.

69. At the time, Eleanor Cohen was engaged to Benjamin Mendez Seixas (1832–84). She and Seixas married a few weeks later. Eleanor would move to New York with her new husband.

70. Eleanor Cohen's diary appeared in Jacob Rader Marcus, *The American Jewish Woman: A Documentary History* (New York: Ktav Publishing, 1981), 260–67. Courtesy of The Jacob Rader Marcus Center of the American Jewish Archives (hereafter AJA), at the Hebrew Union College–Jewish Institute of Religion, Cincinnati, Ohio.

71. Harris Newmark, Maurice Harris Newmark, Marco Ross Newmark, and James Perry Worden, *Sixty Years in Southern California, 1853–1913, Containing the Reminiscences of Harris Newmark* (New York: Houghton Mifflin, 1930), 337–38. See also William M. Kramer, "'They Have Killed Our Man But Not Our Cause': The California Jewish Mourners of Abraham Lincoln," *Western States Jewish Historical Quarterly* 2, no. 4 (July 1970): 209.

72. For a recollection of one of these occasions, see the typed transcription of the Civil War–era diary of Adolphus and Josephine's teenage niece, Rachel Rosalie Phillips (1846–70), the daughter of Josephine's older brother, Jonas Phillips (1816–90). Josephine's letter to her brother-in-law, Adolphus, proves that she, too, visited the White House and met Lincoln in person. A copy of Rachel Rosalie Phillips's diary is in the David M. Klein Collection, MS-695, AJA.

73. By "shool," Josephine meant "synagogue."

74. Hebrew for "lectern" or "pulpit."

75. The funeral train left Washington, D.C., on April 21; stopped in Baltimore, Harrisburg, Philadelphia, and New York; and then moved on to other cities en route to Springfield, Illinois, the martyred president's final resting place. Philip Van Doren Stern, ed., *The Life and Writings of Abraham Lincoln* (New York: Random House, 1940), 190–91.

76. Josephine was referring to the fact that Secretary of State William H. Seward and his son had been wounded in his home by another conspirator at the same time that Lincoln was shot.

77. Josephine's father was Naphtali Phillips (1773–1870). "Beck" was an older sister, Rebecca.

78. A small photograph patented in Paris.

79. Josephine is referring to the photograph of Lincoln that was taken at Adolphus Solomons's publishing firm, Philp and Solomons. Solomons maintained it was the last photograph of Lincoln.

80. Isaac Franklin Phillips (1854–1929) was Josephine's younger brother.

81. John Singleton Mosby (1833–1916) commanded a battalion in Virginia's First Cavalry known as Mosby's Rangers or Mosby's Raiders. Mosby's battalion became famous for its lightning-quick raids.

82. Rachel Seixas Solomons (1828–81) was Adolphus's wife. Mary Jane Solomons (1819–1905) was Adolphus's older sister.

83. Philip Goodman, "A Personal Tribute to Lincoln by Josephine Phillips," *Publications of the American Jewish Historical Society* 41, no. 2 (December 1951): 204–7. Courtesy American Jewish Historical Society, New York and Newton Centre, Mass.

84. Temkin, *Isaac Mayer Wise*, 124.

85. Reverend James F. Chalfant (1821–84), a Methodist minister in Cincinnati and at one time a presiding elder of the district conference.

86. *Die Deborah*, April 28, 1865.

9. Memorializing and Judaizing Lincoln

1. For Cooley quotation, see Barry Schwartz, "Iconography and Collective Memory: Lincoln's Image in the American Mind," *Sociological Quarterly* 32, no. 3 (Autumn 1991): 302.

2. For quotation, see Roy P. Basler, *The Lincoln Legend: A Study in Changing Conceptions* (1935; repr., New York: Octagon Books, 1969). On the apotheosis of Abraham Lincoln in American history, see Merrill D. Peterson, *Lincoln in American Memory* (New York: Oxford University Press, 1994). See also Lloyd Lewis, *Myths after Lincoln* (New York: Grosset and Dunlap, 1929). Ira D. Cardiff was one of the first to accuse historians of deliberately beatifying Lincoln in order to satisfy the tastes of priests and politicians; see Cardiff, *The Deification of Lincoln* (Boston: Christopher Publishing House, 1943).

3. Peterson, *Lincoln in American Memory*, 53–55; Barry Schwartz, *Abraham Lincoln and the Forge of National Memory* (Chicago: University of Chicago Press, 2000), 67. On the question concerning Stanton's phrase "Now he belongs to the ages" versus "Now he belongs to the angels," see Adam Gopnik, *Angels and Ages: A Short Book about Darwin, Lincoln, and Modern Life* (New York: Vintage Books, 2009).

4. Trying to determine what the comparative value of a $1 contribution would be today depends on the scale of measure one chooses to employ. In terms of the wage index, $1 might be comparable to a $100 donation in 2011. See http://www.measuringworth .com/uscompare/relativevalue.php (accessed August 30, 2012).

5. On Hammerslough, see the *Israelite*, June 9, 1865, 397. For an example of an appeal in a synagogue, see Emanuel Hertz, ed., *Abraham Lincoln: The Tribute of the Synagogue* (New York: Bloch Publishing, 1927), 168. For the roster of Jewish subscribers in New York, see the *Jewish Messenger*, May 19, 1865, 155, and June 2, 1865, 171. For the monument efforts in Cincinnati, see the *Israelite*, July 7, 1865, 5.

6. See Schwartz, *Forge of National Memory*; and Barry Schwartz, *Abraham Lincoln in the Post-Heroic Era: History and Memory in Late Twentieth-Century America* (Chicago: University of Chicago Press, 2008).

7. *Washington Times*, October 7, 2006.

8. Julius E. Francis, *The Lincoln Memorial Collection: Relics of the War of the Rebellion* (Buffalo: Matthews, Northrup & Company, 1887), 25–26. See also James Percoco, *Summers with Lincoln: Looking for the Man in the Monuments* (New York: Fordham University Press, 2008).

9. *New York Times*, February 17, 1869, 1; February 22, 1874, 3; February 17, 1879, 5.

10. *New York Times*, February 17, 1869, 5–6.

11. For quotation, see the online article "Editors Interview on Herndon's Lincoln," *Abraham Lincoln Online*, http://showcase.netins.net/web/creative/lincoln/books/herndon .htm (accessed August 30, 2012). See also William Henry Herndon and Jesse William Weik, *Herndon's Lincoln*, ed. Douglas L. Wilson and Rodney O. Davis (Urbana: University of Illinois Press, 2006).

12. David Goldfield, "Lincoln's Image in the American Schoolbook," *American Studies Journal*, no. 53 (2009): 4, http://www.asjournal.org/archive/53/166.html (accessed on January 8, 2012).

13. Josiah G. Holland, *Life of Abraham Lincoln* (Springfield, Mass.: G. Bill, 1866); Ward H. Lamon and Chauncey F. Black, *The Life Of Abraham Lincoln; From His Birth To His Inauguration As President* (Boston: James R. Osgood and Company, 1872); John G. Nicolay and John Hay, *Abraham Lincoln: A History* (New York, 1886). On Nicolay and Hay, see also Michael Burlingame, *Abraham Lincoln: The Observations of John G. Nicolay and John Hay* (Carbondale: Southern Illinois University Press, 2007). See also Michael Burlingame, "Nicolay and Hay: Court Historians," *Journal of the Abraham Lincoln Association* 19, no. 1 (Winter 1998): 3–19; and William H. Herndon and Jesse W. Weik, *Lincoln; The True Story of a Great Life, The History and Personal Recollections of Abraham Lincoln* (Springfield, Ill.. Herndon Lincoln Publishing Company, 1921).

14. See *American Hebrew*, December 2, 1892, 145; *American Israelite*, October 19, 1893, 4; and *Jewish Messenger*, March 9, 1894, 2.

15. *Jewish Messenger*, February 12, 1892, 4.

16. Hertz, *Tribute*, 187–88.

17. Ibid., 189–90. On the rise of anti-Semitism during this period, see John Higham, "Anti-Semitism in the Gilded Age: A Reinterpretation," *Mississippi Valley Historical Review* 43, no. 4 (March 1957): 559–78.

18. *American Hebrew and Jewish Messenger*, February 19, 1897, 442. On Herman Baar, see obituary in ibid., September 9, 1904, 432.

19. Hertz, *Tribute*, 193–94, 233, 245.

20. Ibid., 208.

21. Ephraim Lisitzky, *In the Grip of Cross-Currents* (New York: Bloch Publishing, 1959), 82.

22. E. J. Hobsbawm and T. O. Ranger, *The Invention of Tradition* (New York: Cambridge University Press, 1983), 279; Schwartz, *Forge of National Memory*, 199–200.

23. *American Hebrew and Jewish Messenger*, July 21, 1905, 213.

24. Ibid.

25. Hertz, *Tribute*, 648, 678; *American Hebrew and Jewish Messenger*, February 15, 1918, 429. The Abraham Lincoln House in Milwaukee was located at the corner of Ninth and Sherman Streets. The house was a predecessor of the Jewish Community Center. For more information on the Lincoln House in Milwaukee, see http://www .jewishmuseummilwaukee.org/history/collections/organizations.php#abraham -lincoln (accessed August 30, 2012).

26. As quoted in Schwartz, *Forge of National Memory*, 195–96.

27. Hertz, *Tribute*, 643.

28. On the triplets, see Ava F. Kahn, ed., *Jewish Voices of the California Gold Rush: A Documentary History, 1849–1880* (Detroit: Wayne State University Press, 2002), 41.

29. For quotation, see Schwartz, *Forge of National Memory*, 230–31. See also *Jewish Exponent*, February 15, 1918.

30. Schwartz, *Forge of National Memory*, 295–96. For the complete text of Allen's address, see the *Jewish Advocate*, October 28, 1926, A7.

31. *American Israelite*, June 16, 1927, 8.

32. *New York Times*, May 21, 1865, 5.

33. Hertz, *Tribute*, 168.

34. Bertram W. Korn, *American Jewry and the Civil War* (Philadelphia: Jewish Publication Society, 1951), 215–16.

35. *Israelite*, June 9, 1865, 396–97; *National Lincoln Monument: Address to the Public* (Springfield, Ill.: National Monument Association, 1868).

36. On Chicago's Central Music Hall, see A. T. Andreas, *The History of Chicago*, vol. 3 (Chicago: Andreas Press, 1885), 652.

37. This is an allusion to Elijah's final departure and the exclamation of his disciple Elisha. See 2 Kings 2:12.

38. 2 Kings 2:12.

39. Isaiah 9:6.

40. Hertz, *Tribute*, 191–207.

41. 1 Samuel 16:7.

42. Amos 5:24.

43. Philipson was quoting from *Ode Recited at the Harvard Commemoration*, by James Russell Lowell (1819–91), written in 1865. Philipson's sermon is found in Hertz, *Tribute*, 232–34.

44. Alexander K. McClure (1828–1909) was a writer, politician, and prominent communal leader in Philadelphia. In 1860, he actively supported Lincoln's candidacy. Later in life, he published a number of volumes containing his reminiscences of Lincoln.

45. 1 Samuel 16:7.

46. Hertz, *Tribute*, 255–62.

47. The "Free Synagogue" was located at 117 North Seventh Street in Philadelphia. This location had been the home of the historic Mickve Israel Congregation from 1860 to 1909. After the congregation sold this property, Dembitz organized a "Free Synagogue," which met in the facility. For necrologies on Dembitz, see the *Jewish Exponent*, June 28, 1940, 7, and the *New York Times*, June 27, 1940, 23.

48. See Exodus 15:23–24 and Numbers 33:8.

49. *Jewish Exponent*, February 17, 1911, 8.

50. Genesis 25:23 and Matthew 23:11.

51. Hertz, *Tribute*, 437–46.

52. Deuteronomy 6:5.

53. Ferdinand M. Isserman Papers, MS-6, box 15, folder 6, American Jewish Archives, Cincinnati, Ohio. Courtesy of The Jacob Rader Marcus Center of the American Jewish Archives, at the Hebrew Union College–Jewish Institute of Religion, Cincinnati, Ohio.

54. Carrie Naumburg Cohen (1849–1947) was one of the most prominent Jewish women in Pittsburgh at this time. She volunteered in numerous Jewish women's charitable organizations. Her father served as a cantor, reader, and teacher for the Rodeph Shalom Congregation. She married Josiah Cohen (1841–1930), Allegheny County's first Jewish judge.

55. Edward Tak (1881–1943) was a highly regarded violinist. He was the concertmaster for the Pittsburgh Symphony Orchestra as well as for the San Francisco Symphony Orchestra. On Tak, see the website of the San Francisco Symphony Orchestra, http://www.stokowski.org/Principal_Musicians_San_Francisco_Symphony.htm#Concert masters Index Point (accessed September 15, 2012).

56. Carl Bernthaler (1879–1925) was a musician and assistant conductor of the Pittsburgh Symphony Orchestra.

57. Alfred C. Dieffenbach was a prominent Unitarian minister.

58. *Jewish Criterion*, February 12, 1909, 4–5. Courtesy Pittsburgh Jewish Newspaper Project–Rodef Shalom Congregation Archives.

59. Psalm 24:3–4.

60. The author of this poem is anonymous.

61. Matthew 26:39.

62. Hertz, *Tribute*, 306–17.

63. Ibid., 349–59.

64. Ibid., 399.

65. Matthew 18:7.

66. Psalm 19:9.

67. Hertz, *Tribute*, 383–400.

68. *New York Times*, February 11, 1909, 5.

69. Malachi 2:10.

70. Hertz, *Tribute*, 360–64.

10. "His Name Will Ever Be Green in Your Hearts": Jews and the Cultural Preservation of Lincoln's Legacy

1. Judith Rice, "Ida M. Tarbell: A Progressive Look at Lincoln," *Journal of the Abraham Lincoln Association* 19, no. 1 (Winter 1998): 57–72.

2. For biographical information on Markens, see Max J. Kohler, "Isaac Markens," *Publications of the American Jewish Historical Society*, no. 32 (1931): 129–32. For additional information, see Jacob Rader Marcus and Judith M. Daniels, *The Concise Dictionary of American Jewish Biography* (New York: Carlson Publishing Inc., 1994), s.v. "Markens, Isaac."

3. Isaac Markens, *Hebrews in America: A Series of Historical and Biographical Sketches* (New York: Isaac Markens, 1888). For the most detailed obituary on Markens, see Kohler, "Isaac Markens," 129–32.

4. Markens, *Hebrews in America*, 131–32, 166, 185, 196, 210, 255, 266. See also Kohler, "Isaac Markens," 131–32.

5. The Chicago Historical Society owns an important collection of Markens-Lincoln letters. A number of these remarkable communications, together with a helpful summary of the Lincoln-Markens relationship, appear in Paul M. Angle, ed., with

the assistance of Richard G. Case, *A Portrait of Abraham Lincoln in Letters by His Oldest Son* (Chicago: Chicago Historical Society, 1968). Courtesy the Chicago History Museum.

6. On Markens and the "original copy" of the Gettysburg Address, see Martin P. Johnson, "Who Stole the Gettysburg Address?" *Journal of the Abraham Lincoln Association* 24, no. 2 (Summer 2003): 1–19. On Markens and the Bixby letter, see Jason Emerson, "America's Most Famous Letter," *American Heritage Magazine* 57, no. 1 (February/ March 2006), reproduced at http://www.americanheritage.com/articles/magazine/ ah/2006/1/2006_1_41.shtml (accessed September 5, 2012).

7. A necrology on Markens indicated that in 1918 he published a monograph titled "Origin of Famous Lincoln Saying," and that in 1917 he issued an article titled "Manassas, an Israelite of Colonial Days." See Kohler, "Isaac Markens," 132.

8. On the resolutions calling for Illinois to mark the centennial of Lincoln's birth, see *Lincoln Centennial: Addresses Delivered at the Memorial Exercises held at Springfield, Illinois, February 12, 1908* (Springfield, Ill.: Journal Company Printers, 1908), 4. See also Isaac Markens, *Abraham Lincoln and the Jews* (New York: Isaac Markens, 1909), 8.

9. Emanuel Hertz, "Lincoln and the Jews: An Appreciation of the Work of the Late Isaac Markens" (delivered over WRNY, Hotel Roosevelt, September 2, 1928), 7, 5. This speech was subsequently published as an offprint and distributed widely. An electronic copy is available on the website of the Internet Archive, http://www28 .us.archive.org/stream/lincolnjews00hert#page/no/mode/2up (accessed September 10, 2012).

10. Evidently Markens completed some thirty chapters of his biographical study on Lincoln. Unfortunately, the manuscript appears to have been lost. See Angle, *Portrait of Abraham Lincoln in Letters*, xii.

11. On Hertz, see obituaries in the *New York Herald Tribune*, May 24, 1940, and the *New York Times*, May 24, 1940.

12. The Washington Heights Synagogue was located on 161st Street in New York City. Hertz was the president of the synagogue in 1915, when the congregation erected its first building. See *American Hebrew and Jewish Messenger*, September 24, 1915, 594.

13. Obituary, *New York Herald Tribune*, May 24, 1940.

14. Hertz, *Address on Abraham Lincoln* (Washington, D.C.: Government Press, 1924).

15. Hertz, "Lincoln and the Jews," 7, 5–6.

16. Emanuel Hertz, *Abraham Lincoln: A New Portrait*, 2 vols. (New York: Horace Liveright, 1931), 1:7.

17. Emanuel Hertz, *Lincoln Talks: An Oral Biography* (New York: Viking Press, 1939), xii; *Who's Who in American Jewry* (New York: Jewish Biographical Bureau, 1926), 262; obituary, *New York Herald Tribune*, May 24, 1940.

18. Emanuel Hertz, ed., *Abraham Lincoln: The Tribute of the Synagogue* (New York: Bloch Publishing, 1927), viii. For Markens's preliminary work, see *Abraham Lincoln and the Jews*, 46–47.

19. Hertz's volume contains more than twenty-five eulogies and sermons written in 1865 alone, and the remainder of the volume contains more than forty additional sermons and addresses written from 1888 to 1927. Recently, two fine collections of nineteenth-century topical Jewish sermons have appeared: Naomi W. Cohen, *What the Rabbis Said: The Public Discourse of Nineteenth-Century American Rabbis* (New York: New York University Press, 2008), contains excerpts of sermons focusing on a variety of issues, and Elliot Gertel, *Jewish Belief and Practice in Nineteenth Century America:*

Seminal Essays by Outstanding Pulpit Rabbis of the Era (Jefferson, N.C.: McFarland, 2006), is an anthology of eighteen essays written by eleven rabbis from 1856 to 1900.

20. On Newman and the history of the Abraham Lincoln Book Store, see Barbara Hughett, *The Civil War Round Table: Fifty Years of Scholarship and Fellowship* (Chicago: Civil War Round Table, 1990), and John Y. Simon, "A Memorial to Ralph G. Newman," *Illinois Heritage* 3, nos. 1–2 (Fall–Winter 2000): 26–28. Daniel Weinberg, the current owner of the Abraham Lincoln Book Store, had been Newman's partner for several years prior to his acquiring total ownership of the store. Weinberg remembered that Newman identified himself as a gastronomic Jew (that is to say, one whose Jewishness comes from enjoying so-called Jewish food).

21. For more on the founders of the Civil War Round Table in Chicago, see Hughett, *Civil War Round Table*. On Gertz, who later in life served as president of the Greater Chicago Council of the American Jewish Congress, see Barbara Hughett, *To Life: The Story of a Chicago Lawyer* (Carbondale: Southern Illinois University Press, 1994). On Eisenschiml, see Otto Eisenschiml, *O. E.: Historian without an Armchair* (Indianapolis: Bobbs-Merrill, 1963), and William Hanchett, "The Historian as Gamesman: Otto Eisenschiml, 1880–1963," *Civil War History* 36 (1990): 5–16. In addition to Gertz and Eisenschiml, other Jewish pioneers of the Civil War Round Table included Seymour J. Frank (1898–1956) and Alexander Isaacs (1907–75). On Frank, see *Chicago Daily Tribune*, September 14, 1956, C11. On Isaacs, see *Chicago Tribune*, February 20, 1975, B18.

22. On Harold Holzer, see Holzer homepage, http://www.haroldholzer.com/hh_2_bio.html (accessed August 30, 2012). On the Shapell Manuscript Foundation, see Shapell homepage, http://www.shapell.org/ (accessed August 30, 2012).

23. James G. Randall, "Has the Lincoln Theme Been Exhausted?" *American Historical Review* 41, no. 2 (January 1936): 270–94.

24. On Korn, see Gary P. Zola, "Bertram Wallace Korn," in *Encyclopedia of American Jewish History*, ed. Stephen H. Norwood and Eunice Pollack (Santa Barbara: ABC-Clio, 2007); and Kerry M. Olitzky, Lance J. Sussman, and Malcolm H. Stern, *Reform Judaism in America: A Biographical Dictionary and Sourcebook* (Westport, Conn.: Greenwood Press, 1993), 112–13. Due to his prodigious scholarship, his work as the rabbi of a large and historic metropolitan congregation, and his distinguished career as a military chaplain, Korn emerged as one of the most prominent Reform rabbis and highly regarded American Jewish historians during the post–World War II years.

25. Bertram W. Korn, *American Jewry and the Civil War* (Philadelphia: Jewish Publication Society, 1951). For quotes, see 206, 203.

26. On Roosevelt's attitude toward Lincoln, see Jason R. Jividen, "Theodore Roosevelt's Use and Abuse of Abraham Lincoln" (unpublished paper prepared for presentation at the Annual Meeting of the Southern Political Science Association, New Orleans, Louisiana, 2007). See also Merrill D. Peterson, *Lincoln in American Memory* (New York: Oxford University Press, 1994); Barry Schwartz, *Abraham Lincoln and the Forge of National Memory* (Chicago: University of Chicago Press, 2000); William F. Hanna, "Theodore Roosevelt and the Lincoln Image," *Lincoln Herald* 94, no. 4 (Spring 1992): 2–9; and David McCullough, *Morningside on Horseback: The Story of an Extraordinary Family, a Vanished Way of Life, and the Unique Child Who Became Theodore Roosevelt* (New York: Simon and Schuster, 2001), 59, 367.

27. For quote, see Hermann Hagedorn, ed., *The Works of Theodore Roosevelt*, vol. 20 (New York: Scribner's, 1926), 375–76.

28. Q. David Bowers, *More Adventures with Rare Coins: Fifty Favorite Numismatic Stories* (Wolfeboro, N.H.: Bowers and Merena Galleries, 2002), 29–30.
29. Schwartz, *Forge of National Memory*, 196.
30. Bowers, *Rare Coins*, 30.
31. Ibid., 31. See also David Margolick, "Foolish Penny," *New York Times*, February 11, 2007. For quote, see the informative obituary on Brenner, *New York Times*, April 6, 1924, 27. In the fall of 1909, Brenner wrote to Farran Zerbe, the president of the American Numismatic Association: "It is mighty hard for me to express my sentiments with regard to the initials on the cent. The name of an artist on the coin is essential for the student of history as it enables him to trace environments and conditions of the time said coin was produced. Much fume has been made about my initials as a means of advertisement; such is not the case. . . . The cent not alone represents in part my art, but represents a type of art of our period." See Bowers, *Rare Coins*, 31.
32. Schwartz, *Forge of National Memory*, 196. For a detailed analysis explicating how Brenner's work is a confluence of his status as an immigrant and his belief in the American ideal, see Paul U. Kellogg, "Two New Worlds and a Sculptor's Clay," *Survey* 35 (October 1915–March 1916): 19–22.
33. On Lincoln in music and the arts, see the website of the Abraham Lincoln Bicentennial Commission, http://abrahamlincoln200.org/lincolns-legacy/music-arts/default.aspx (accessed August 23, 2012). For more on Lincoln and material culture, see Fred Reed, *Abraham Lincoln: The Image of His Greatness* (Atlanta: Whitman, 2009).
34. Stephen J. Whitfield, *In Search of American Jewish Culture* (Hanover, N.H.: Brandeis University Press, 1999), 30.
35. The famous quotation comes from Anaïs Nin, *Seduction of the Minotaur* (Denver, Colo.: A. Swallow, 1961), 124. Coincidentally, Nin uses this phrase in a novel, and her fictional character incorrectly ascribes the phrase's origin to the Talmud. For an interesting discussion on this confusion, see Jonathan K. Crane and Joseph B. Kadane, "Seeing Things: The Internet, The Talmud, and Anaïs Nin," *Review of Rabbinic Judaism* 11, no. 2 (2008): 342–45.
36. See obituary in the *New York Times*, April 27, 1922.
37. See Robert N. Rosen, *Confederate Charleston: An Illustrated History of the City and its People during the Civil War* (Columbia: University of South Carolina Press, 1994), 88.
38. The "Old Capitol Prison" was originally built in 1800 as a tavern and boardinghouse. After the capitol building was burned in the War of 1812, government business took place in the "Old Capitol Prison" until a new capitol building could be built. See William E. Doster, *Lincoln and Episodes of the Civil War* (New York: G. P. Putnam's Sons, 1915), 74–111.
39. *New York Daily Tribune*, February 13, 1901.
40. For more information on Solomons's career and his biography, see "Guide to the Papers of Adolphus Simeon Solomons (1826–1910)" on the website of the American Jewish Historical Society, http://findingaids.cjh.org/?pID=364847 (accessed August 28, 2012).
41. *American Hebrew* 84, no. 15 (February 12, 1909): 386–87, 394.
42. Joan Sturhahn, *Carvalho, Artist-Photographer-Adventurer-Patriot: Portrait of a Forgotten American* (Merrick, N.Y.: Richwood, 1976), esp. 162–65. See also Justin G. Turner, *A Note on Solomon Nuñes Carvalho and His Portrait of Abraham Lincoln* (Los Angeles: Plantin Press, 1960). On Carvalho's life, see Arlene B. Hirschfelder, *Photo Odyssey: Solomon Carvalho's Remarkable Western Adventure, 1853–1854* (New York:

Clarion Books, 2000). See also Bertram W. Korn's introduction to Solomon Nuñes Carvalho, *Incidents of Travel and Adventure in the Far West* (Philadelphia: Jewish Publication Society of America, 1954), 13–52.

43. Frank Dempster Sherman and Clinton Scollard, *The Poems of Frank Dempster Sherman* (New York: Houghton Mifflin, 1917).

44. There is some confusion about Ezekiel's bust of Lincoln. Evidently, Ezekiel produced two bronze busts from his original clay mold. One of these busts is currently located at the Crescent Hill Branch of the Louisville Free Public Library, and a second bust is on display at the Skirball Cultural Center in Los Angeles. Although some histories indicate Ezekiel sculpted the bust in 1880, the artist himself recalls the commission came in 1896. Historians await more accurate and detailed information about the provenance of this piece of art. See Joseph Gutmann and Stanley F. Chyet, eds., *Moses Jacob Ezekiel: Memoirs from the Baths of Diocletian* (Detroit: Wayne State University Press, 1975), 365.

45. Ibid, 272, 365.

46. Alice Kalish, *Max Kalish as I Knew Him* (Los Angeles: Alice Kalish, 1969), 32. While he was a student at Gettysburg College (class of 1866), Bikle attended the dedication of the National Cemetery and heard Abraham Lincoln deliver the Gettysburg Address. See Inventory of Bikle's Papers at Gettysburg College, http://gettysburg.contentdm .oclc.org/cdm/singleitem/collection/p126301c0118/id/95/rec/4 (accessed September 2, 2012).

47. *Cleveland Plain Dealer*, September 23, 1927. © 1927 The Plain Dealer; all rights reserved; used with permission.

48. *Cleveland Press*, February 12, 1932.

49. On Rumshinsky, see Bret Charles Werb, "Rumshinsky's Greatest Hits: A Chronological Survey of Yiddish-American Songs, 1910-1931" (M.A. thesis, University of California, Los Angeles, 1987). See also Joseph Rumshinsky, Milken Archive of Jewish Music, http://www.milkenarchive.org/people/view/all/506/Joseph+ Rumshinsky (accessed September 1, 2012). I would like to express my deep appreciation to Thomas Kernan, a musicology doctoral candidate at the University of Cincinnati's College-Conservatory of Music, for bringing the works of Weinberg and Rumshinsky to my attention and for sharing his fine images of the compositions with me.

50. See Michael Paul Rogin, *Blackface, White Noise: Jewish Immigrants in the Hollywood Melting Pot* (Berkeley: University of California Press, 1996).

51. I would like to express my gratitude to Dr. Gil Ribak, executive director of the Institute on American-Jewish Israeli Relations at American Jewish University, for his assistance with this Yiddish translation.

52. For more on Weinberg, see Milken Archive of Jewish Music, http://www .milkearchive.org/people/view/all/550/Jacob+Weinberg (accessed September 1, 2012).

53. On the history of the Dessoff Choir, see the choir's website at http://www.dessoff .org/new/history/ (accessed September 14, 2012). This same website also confirms the date that Weinberg's "Gettysburg Address" was performed at Carnegie Hall.

54. Aaron Copland had heard the original version of Weinberg's "Gettysburg Address" before he began work on his "Lincoln Portrait." It is difficult to know whether Copland's memorable technique of having quotations from Lincoln's speeches read with musical accompaniment influenced Weinberg's 1943 version of his "Gettysburg Address" or if Copland was actually inspired by Weinberg. See Howard Pollack, *Aaron*

Copland: The Life and Work of an Uncommon Man (New York: Henry Holt, 1999), 358. I am deeply indebted to Thomas Kernan, doctoral student at the College-Conservatory of Music, University of Cincinnati, for generously sharing his research on the Weinberg compositions.

55. Jeffrey Magee, *Irving Berlin's American Musical Theater* (New York: Oxford University Press, 2012), 27.

56. Benjamin Sears, *The Irving Berlin Reader* (New York: Oxford University Press, 2012), 106–7.

57. Originally this couplet read "When black folks lived in slavery / Who was it set the darky free?" Robert Kimball and Linda Emmet, eds., *The Complete Lyrics of Irving Berlin* (New York: Alfred A. Knopf, 2001), 353.

58. See Pollack, *Aaron Copland*, 358.

59. Ibid., 23–28. On the parallel between the phrase "And God said" and "And this is what he said," see Elizabeth Bergman Crist, *Music for the Common Man: Aaron Copland during the Depression and War* (New York: Oxford University Press, 2005), 156–58. See also "Insider's Perspective: Aaron Copland's *Lincoln Portrait*" on the website of the Harry Ransom Center at the University of Texas at Austin, http://www.hrc .utexas.edu/enews/2009/march/insider.html (accessed August 30, 2012).

60. Markens's letter and Lincoln's response, preserved at the Chicago Historical Society, were published in Angle, *Portrait of Abraham Lincoln in Letters*, xi.

61. Markens, *Abraham Lincoln and the Jews*, 12–13.

62. Markens's question: "Can you tell anything more definite than that of Nicolay, on the question of President Lincoln's preference of Andrew Johnson for the Vice Presidency in 1864, or any other facts relating to the matter?"

63. Markens had asked: "Can you tell me the whereabouts of the letter of Queen Victoria to your mother?"

64. February 13, 1918, letter from Robert T. Lincoln to Isaac Markens, from the Robert Todd Lincoln collection at the Chicago History Museum. Published in Angle, *Portrait of Abraham Lincoln in Letters*, 55–56.

65. Hertz, *Tribute*, xix–xx.

66. Bertram W. Korn, *Eventful Years and Experiences* (Cincinnati: American Jewish Archives, 1954), 16–20, 108. General Orders No. 332, AGO, Oct. 9, 1863 (Record Group 94); Special Orders No. 41, Headquarters of the Army, Feb. 18, 1869 (RG 94); Records of Volunteer Officers of the Quartermaster Department, Civil War, 1861–65 (RG 92); War Department Records, National Archives, Washington, D.C. Raphall to Lincoln, March 1, 1864 (in appreciation of a favor done Levy after his discharge), S. F. Chalfin to Levy, July 16, 1864, Robert Todd Lincoln Collection of Papers of Abraham Lincoln, Library of Congress, where "Cherie" M. Levy's name is incorrectly recorded as "Chemie," Abraham Lincoln Papers at the Library of Congress, Manuscript Division, http://memory.loc.gov.

67. *Journal of the Illinois State Historical Society* 48, no. 2 (1955): 187–90.

68. Harold Holzer, *Lincoln and the Jews: The Last Best Hope of Earth* (Los Angeles: Skirball Cultural Center, 2002). For biographical information on Harold Holzer, see his website at http://www.haroldholzer.com/hh_2_bio.html (accessed August 30, 2012). With regard to the "Golden Rule," it was Hillel who said: "What is hateful to thee, do not do unto thy fellow man: this is the whole Law; the rest is mere commentary" (*Babylonian Talmud Shabbat* 31a). Almost the same thing was taught by the Apostle Paul; see Galatians 5:14 and Romans 13:8. The quotation "the beauty of Israel was slain upon the high places" comes from 2 Samuel 1:19.

11. "Lincoln! Thou Shouldst Be Living at This Hour!" Lincoln as a Moral Compass for American Jews

1. President Woodrow Wilson coined the phrase "watchful waiting" in his annual message to Congress on December 2, 1913, when he said: "We shall not, I believe, be obliged to alter our policy of watchful waiting."

2. Mary Wright-Davis, *The Book of Lincoln* (New York: George H. Doran, 1919), 340. For quotation and other poetic appeals for Lincoln's return, see Merrill D. Peterson, *Lincoln in American Memory* (New York: Oxford University Press, 1994), 315.

3. It is difficult to determine who first posed the question "What would Lincoln do?" It seems that Andrew Carnegie made this inquiry in 1898 in a speech he gave comparing Lincoln and McKinley unfavorably. On Taft, see *New York Times*, February 13, 1908, 5. See also Peterson, *Lincoln in American Memory*, 385.

4. This quotation comes from Lincoln's first inaugural address, March 4, 1861. See website of *Abraham Lincoln Online*, http://showcase.netins.net/web/creative/lincoln/speeches/1inaug.htm (accessed September 1, 2012).

5. *President Harding's Address at the Dedication of the Lincoln Memorial* (Washington, D.C.: Government Printing Office, 1922), 8. See also President Calvin Coolidge's "Address at Gettysburg Battlefield," May 30, 1928, on website of the Calvin Coolidge Foundation, http://www.calvin-coolidge.org/address-at-gettysburg-battle-field.html (accessed September 2, 2012).

6. Franklin D. Roosevelt, "Address at the Dedication of the Memorial on the Gettysburg Battlefield, Gettysburg, Pennsylvania," July 3, 1938, on the American Presidency Project website, http://www.presidency.ucsb.edu/ws/index.php?pid=15669 (accessed September 5, 2012).

7. Peterson, *Lincoln in American Memory*, 320–22.

8. Harry S. Truman, "Address to the NAACP at the Lincoln Memorial, June 28, 1947," on the PBS website *The American Experience*, http://www.pbs.org/wgbh/americanexperience/features/primary-resources/truman-naacp47/, (accessed September 1, 2012).

9. Peterson, *Lincoln in American Memory*, 352–53.

10. Alex Ross, "Voice of the Century," *New Yorker*, April 13, 2009, on the *New Yorker* website archive, http://www.newyorker.com/arts/critics/atlarge/2009/04/13/090413crat_atlarge_ross (accessed August 28, 2012). See also Peterson, *Lincoln in American Memory*, 353.

11. *Jewish Exponent*, February 12, 1909. The quote comes from the speech Lincoln delivered at the First Republican State Convention of Illinois in Bloomington, May 29, 1856. See "Lincoln's Lost Speech," *McClure's Magazine*, September 1896, 319–31. The quote is more frequently given as "Those who deny freedom to others deserve it not for themselves; and, under the rule of a just God, cannot long retain it." The Solis-Cohen address also appears in Emanuel Hertz, ed., *Abraham Lincoln: The Tribute of the Synagogue* (New York: Bloch Publishing, 1927), 342–48.

12. *Jewish Exponent*, February 26, 1909, 9. The text of Harrison's 1909 sermon on Lincoln does not seem to have survived, but Harrison gave another address titled "What Would Lincoln Do?" in 1914.

13. *American Israelite*, March 3, 1921, 4; *Jewish Exponent*, December 22, 1922, 10.

14. *Jewish Exponent*, February 12, 1937, 4.

15. *Jewish Advocate*, February 8, 1945, 8.

16. For the full text of this address, see the Joachim Prinz website, http://www.joachimprinz.com/civilrights.htm (accessed September 5, 2012).

17. *American Israelite*, February 10, 1949, 4.

18. *Jewish Advocate*, February 20, 1986, 11. On the NCCJ, see Kevin Michael Schultz, *Tri-Faith America: How Catholics and Jews Held Postwar America to Its Protestant Promise* (New York: Oxford University Press, 2011). On National Brotherhood Week, see ibid., 65.

19. It was Mario Cuomo who delivered an address titled "Abraham Lincoln and Our Unfinished Business." Years earlier, Adlai Stevenson gave similar speeches titled "Unfinished Work of Emancipation" and "The Struggle for Human Liberty." See Waldo Warder Braden, *Building the Myth: Selected Speeches Memorializing Abraham Lincoln* (Urbana: University of Illinois Press, 1990), 218–44.

20. *Jewish Advocate*, February 9, 1956, A2.

21. Ibid.

22. See http://archives.library.cofc.edu/findingaids/mss1075.html (accessed January 6, 2012). I am deeply grateful to Dr. Dale Rosengarten, curator of the Jewish Heritage Collection, Special Collections Department, Addlestone Library at the College of Charleston, Charleston, South Carolina, for bringing this document to my attention and for granting permission to publish its contents. On Raisin, see *CCAR Yearbook* 56 (1946): 267–68.

23. This quote is from Douglass's "Oration in Memory of Abraham Lincoln," delivered at the unveiling of the Freedmen's Monument in Memory of Abraham Lincoln in Lincoln Park, Washington, D.C., April 14, 1876. The precise quotation is: "Any man can say things that are true of Abraham Lincoln, but no man can say anything that is new of Abraham Lincoln." See website of the University of Rochester Frederick Douglass Project, http://www.lib.rochester.edu/index.cfm?PAGE=4402 (accessed September 15, 2012).

24. Henry Woodfin Grady (1850–89), a journalist and orator, distinguished himself as a brilliant and entertaining spokesman for the notion of a "new South." Ironically, Raisin's call for racial reconciliation does not align with Grady's perspective. Grady believed that whites would remain supreme in the "new South." See Harold E. Davis, *Henry Grady's New South: Atlanta, a Brave and Beautiful City* (Tuscaloosa: University of Alabama Press, 1990).

25. James Sloan Gibbons (1810–92), a committed abolitionist, is credited for having written the lyrics to the famous Civil War song "We Are Coming, Father Abraham, 300,000 More." Raisin uses a common variant lyric, wherein the number is 600,000! He was motivated by his determination to assist the nation win a fight that, in his mind, was aimed at bringing slavery to an end. See Helen Kendrick Johnson, Frederic Dean, Reginald De Koven, and Gerrit Smith, *The World's Best Music*, vol. 4 (New York: University Society, 1902), 880–83.

26. In the original verse, this phrase is "kindly-earnest."

27. Raisin is quoting the final verses of James Russell Lowell's (1819–91) famous poem "Commemoration Ode," first delivered at Harvard University on July 21, 1865. Later, he added a strophe on Lincoln.

28. Charles M. Sheldon, *In His Steps: "What Would Jesus Do?"* (Chicago: Advance Publishing, 1898).

29. A youth leader at Calvary Reformed Church in Holland, Michigan, named Janie Tinklenberg owned a copy of Sheldon's book. In 1989, Tinklenberg began asking her students Sheldon's question. Taking note of the popularity of friendship bracelets and "wait until marriage" rings, Tinklenberg approached the Lesco Corporation in Holland to interest them in producing woven bracelets with the letters "WWJD?"—an

acronym for "What would Jesus do?" The acronym and the phrase became an immediate sensation.

30. On Harrison's 1909 address, see note 12.

31. Hertz, *Tribute*, 447–57.

32. For more on the bureau and the Central Jewish Institute, see Alexander M. Dushkin, *Jewish Education in New York* (New York: Bureau of Jewish Education, 1918).

33. The text of the program also appears in Isaac B. Berkson, *Theories of Americanization; A Critical Study, with Special Emphasis on the Jewish Group* (New York: Teachers College, Columbia University, 1920), 217.

34. In English, this familiar quotation from *Pirkei Avot* 1:2 is often rendered: "The world stands on three pillars: on Torah, on worship, and on acts of loving kindness."

35. Berkson, *Theories of Americanization*, 217.

36. *New York Times*, February 13, 1923, 3.

37. The "newly revised" edition of the *Union Prayerbook* for sabbaths, festivals, and weekdays appeared in 1940, and a volume for the High Holy Days appeared in 1945. See Michael A. Meyer, *Response to Modernity: A History of the Reform Movement in Judaism* (New York: Oxford University Press), 321.

38. Samuel Cohon Papers, MS-276, box 21, folder 7, American Jewish Archives, Cincinnati, Ohio. Courtesy of The Jacob Rader Marcus Center of the American Jewish Archives (hereafter AJA), at the Hebrew Union College–Jewish Institute of Religion, Cincinnati, Ohio. Cohon indicated at the top of this sermon that he had composed another sermon on Lincoln the year before, in 1920, titled "In the Light of Lincoln."

39. Today the congregation's name is Anshe Emet.

40. Both Shmaya and Avtalyon ("Abtalyon" in text) were rabbinic sages who lived during the first century B.C.E.

41. Deuteronomy 6:5.

42. Philip A. Langh, "Jewish Ideals in Lincoln," *Sentinel* 58, no. 7 (February 13, 1925): 8, 35. This sermon also appeared in Hertz, *Tribute*, 511–15.

43. *Jewish Advocate*, February 14, 1933, 2.

44. Samuel H. Goldenson Papers, 1918–1947, MS-81, box 2, folder 4, AJA.

45. The American playwright Robert E. Sherwood (1896–1955) wrote *Abe Lincoln in Illinois* in 1938. The three-act play focused on Lincoln's childhood and pre-presidential years and earned Sherwood the Pulitzer Prize for Drama in 1939.

46. Ferdinand M. Isserman Papers, 1870–1971, MS-6, box 15, folder 5, AJA.

47. This draft of the sermon can be found in the Charles E. Shulman Papers, 1917–1969, MS-124, box 6, folder 9, AJA.

48. Brackets are in the original.

49. Tehilla Lichtenstein Papers, 1927–70, MS-22, box 2, folder 1, AJA.

50. Brackets are in the original.

51. Brackets are in the original.

52. Brackets are in the original.

53. Rabbi Soloff is citing a famous quotation that appears numerous times in the classical writings of the ancient rabbis. One famous citation comes from the Talmud, Tractate *Pesachim* 52, where we find the phrase *sh'mitoch sh'lo lishma, ba-lishma* (meaning "for out of [doing something good] with an ulterior motive there comes [something good] for its own sake").

54. A sermon by Rabbi Rav A. Soloff, East End Temple, New York, N.Y., February 12, 1960, Abraham Lincoln Nearprint file, AJA.

55. *Jewish Chronicle*, February 12, 1970, 4. Courtesy Pittsburgh Jewish Newspaper

Project–Rodef Shalom Congregation Archives. The final quote is from the Fifteenth Amendment.

12. Lincoln Miscellany

1. Barry Schwartz, *Abraham Lincoln and the Forge of National Memory* (Chicago: University of Chicago Press, 2000), 312.

2. Burke McCarty, *Little Sermons in Socialism by Abraham Lincoln*, an offprint from the *Chicago Daily Socialist*, 1910, 2. A digital copy of this pamphlet is available on the website of the Internet Archive, http://archive.org/stream/littlesermonsinsoomcca #page/no/mode/2up (accessed September 12, 2012).

3. Schwartz, *Forge of National Memory*, 204–8.

4. Ibid., 204.

5. Julian Levinson, *Exiles on Main Street: Jewish American Writers and American Literary Culture* (Bloomington: Indiana University Press, 2008), 139.

6. Beth S. Wenger, *History Lessons: The Creation of American Jewish Heritage* (Princeton: Princeton University Press, 2010), 91–92; Merle Bachman, *Recovering "Yiddishland": Threshold Moments in American Literature* (Syracuse: Syracuse University Press, 2008), 121.

7. Sarah Sackman, "The Identity Politics of Jews and African-Americans in the Spanish Civil War" (undergraduate prize essay, Queens College, Cambridge, U.K., 2006), 12. A copy of this essay is in the American Jewish Archives (SC-15985d), Cincinnati, Ohio. Courtesy of The Jacob Rader Marcus Center of the American Jewish Archives (hereafter AJA), at the Hebrew Union College–Jewish Institute of Religion, Cincinnati, Ohio. A digitized copy is available on the website of the Abraham Lincoln Brigade Archives, http://www.alba-valb.org/resources/document-library/the-identity-politics-of-jews-and-african-americans-during-the-spanish-civil-war/?searchterm=winner (accessed September 6, 2012). See also Peter N. Carroll, *The Odyssey of the Abraham Lincoln Brigade: Americans in the Spanish Civil War* (Stanford: Stanford University Press, 1994). For quotation, see Marion Merriman and Warren Lerude, *American Commander in Spain: Robert Hale Merriman and the Abraham Lincoln Brigade* (Reno: University of Nevada Press, 1986), 89.

8. The "Reply to the New York Workingmen's Democratic Republican Association" was delivered on March 21, 1864. On Arthur Szyk and his Americana, see the website of the Arthur Szyk Society, http://www.szyk.org/america (accessed September 12, 2012).

9. For two very different interpretations regarding the history of the Gettysburg Address, see Gabor S. Boritt, *The Gettysburg Gospel: The Lincoln Speech That Nobody Knows* (New York: Simon and Schuster, 2006), and Garry Wills, *Lincoln at Gettysburg: The Words That Remade America* (New York: Simon and Schuster, 1992).

10. Boritt, *Gettysburg Gospel*, 201.

11. Ron Chernow, *The Warburgs: The Twentieth-Century Odyssey of a Remarkable Jewish Family* (New York: Random House, 1993), 101.

12. Leonard Baker, *Days of Sorrow and Pain: Leo Baeck and the Berlin Jews* (New York: Macmillan, 1978), 110, 257.

13. Ibid., 326.

14. Dov Noy, "Archiving and Presenting Folk Literature in an Ethnological Museum," *Journal of American Folklore* 75, no. 295 (January–March 1962): 23–28.

15. On the ring, see ibid., 25. For the most detailed overview of the phrase's development, see Archer Taylor, "This Too Will Pass," in *Volksüberlieferung: Festschrift für*

Kurt Ranke, ed. F. Harkort, K. C. Peeters, and R. Wildhaber (Göttingen: Schwartz, 1968), 345–50. It is possible that Lincoln read the story in a book of legends compiled by Edward FitzGerald, *Polonius: A Collection of Wise Saws and Modern Instances* (London: W. Pickering, 1852). On p. 120, there is an anecdote titled "Solomon's Seal": "The Sultan asked Solomon for a Signet motto that should hold good for Adversity or Prosperity. Solomon gave him, 'this also shall pass away.'"

16. On Stanley Kunitz, see obituary, *Jewish Telegraphic Agency*, May 19, 2006. Kunitz shared his thoughts about his Jewishness with Gary Pacernick; see Pacernick, *Meaning and Memory: Interviews with Fourteen Jewish Poets* (Columbus: Ohio State University Press, 2001), 39–47. See also Jeanne Braham, *The Light Within the Light: Portraits of Donald Hall, Richard Wilbur, Maxine Kumin, and Stanley Kunitz* (Boston: David R. Godine, 2007).

17. Schwartz, *Forge of National Memory*, 14–15.

18. Ibid., xi.

19. Maslow hypothesized that psychological fulfillment came in steps. The basic level of fulfillment came from having physical needs met, and the next highest level was the human's desire to have social needs met. He called the highest level of fulfillment "self-actualization," wherein humans managed to fulfill their potentiality.

20. For quote, see website *Biographies of Psychologists*, http://psy.rin.ru/eng/article/48–101 .html (accessed February 17, 2012).

21. For quotes, see Abraham H. Maslow, *The Farther Reaches of Human Nature* (New York: Arkana Books, 1971), 260. See also pp. 229 and 351.

22. Andrew Ferguson, *Land of Lincoln: Adventures in Abe's America* (New York: Atlantic Monthly Press, 2007), 72–76.

23. Wenger, *History Lessons*, 91.

24. The author is obviously referring to a prominent list of abolitionists from the antebellum era: Horace Greeley (1811–72), Wendell Phillips (1811–84), John Brown (1800–1859), and John Greenleaf Whittier (1807–92).

25. This is a reference to the "Great Wall" of China. The writer is stressing that the obstacles obstructing the way for contemporary youth are as formidable as the Great Wall of China.

26. *Forverts*, February 10, 1900. I would like to express my gratitude to Rabbi Sholom Kalmanson of Cincinnati for his generous help in translating this text into English.

27. Charles Carleton Coffin left a famous eyewitness account of Lincoln's visit to Richmond on April 3, 1865. See Coffin, "Late Scenes in Richmond," *Atlantic Monthly*, June 1865, 754. Coffin also wrote about this later in life; see *Freedom Triumphant; the Fourth Period of the War of the Rebellion from September, 1864, to Its Close* (New York: Harper & Brothers, 1891), 436–40.

28. On Lincoln's sleepless nights, see David Herbert Donald, *Lincoln* (New York: Simon and Schuster, 1995), 390.

29. Reuben Iceland, a Yiddish poet and translator, was born in Radomysl Wielki, in present-day Poland. He immigrated to the United States in 1903. All of the English translations for the Yiddish poems in this section come from *America in Yiddish Poetry: An Anthology*, selected and translated by Jehiel B. Cooperman and Sarah H. Cooperman (New York: Exposition Press, 1967). Iceland's poem is on pp. 61–63.

30. Ibid., 398–99. Isaac Elhanan Rontch was a Yiddish writer and frequent contributor to *Jewish Currents* magazine.

31. Ibid., 375. Leonid Feinberg was a Yiddish writer and poet who contributed articles and poems to many Yiddish papers in the United States. Born in the Province of

Podolia, in present-day Ukraine, Feinberg studied in Odessa and subsequently at the University of Moscow. He immigrated to the United States in the 1920s.

32. Ibid., 418–19. Malka Lee, a Yiddish writer who produced numerous volumes of poetry, was born in Monastrishtsh, Galicia. She immigrated to the United States in 1921.

33. The rabbi's outspoken support of President Lincoln during the Civil War resulted in his receiving an honorary membership in the Union League of Philadelphia, despite the fact that Jews were excluded from full membership in that society.

34. Tisha b'Av is a fast day that commemorates the destruction of the First and Second Temples. It has also become a day of general mourning for other major disasters that have befallen the Jewish people.

35. See Robert Alter, *Pen of Iron* (Princeton: Princeton University Press, 2010).

36. We know that Lincoln had once met the rabbi. Morais came to Washington to ask that a Jewish soldier sentenced to death for desertion be given clemency.

37. Alexander was the first Jew to be elected governor in the United States. He served from 1915 to 1919.

38. On Abraham Alpert (1871?–1939), see obituary in the *New York Times*, September 3, 1939, 19. Alpert, a founder of the Boston chapter of HIAS and author of humorous stories, should not be confused with the Hebrew poet Isaac Rabinowitz (1843–1900), who also took the pen name "Ish Kovno."

39. See Isaiah 37:3.

40. See Numbers 22:38.

41. See Psalm 102:17.

42. *Jewish Messenger*, July 10, 1863, 22.

43. English parody on the Gettysburg Address by the Hebraist Abraham Alpert ("Ish Kovno") was delivered at a reception for the governor of Idaho, Moses Alexander, sponsored by the Hebrew Immigrant Aid Society on August 26, 1915, in Faneuil Hall, Boston, Mass. AJA.

44. See www.nal.usda.gov/lincolns-milwaukee-speech (accessed September 5, 2012).

45. See Talmud, *Ta'anit* 21a.

46. Noy, "Archiving and Presenting Folk Literature," 23–28. Noy preserved another story (IFA 126), recorded by Mrs. Heda Jazon from the Turkish storyteller Jehuda Franko. It is told as follows:

King Solomon once searched for a cure against depression. He assembled his wise men together. They meditated for a long time and then gave him the following advice: Make yourself a ring and have hereon engraved the words "This too will pass." The King carried out the advice. He had the ring made and used to wear it. Every time he felt sad and depressed, he looked at the ring, whereon his mood changed and he would feel cheerful.

A folktale hunter who is interested mainly in the plot, type and motifs of the story may ask why King Solomon, the wisest of the wise, needed to assemble his advisors and ask them for help. But our ethnological experience directed us in a quite different way. We asked the narrator: Was there ever such a ring? Has anybody ever seen it? If Solomon's children inherited it, to whom did they leave it? And here comes the answer—the narrator proves the truth of his story by showing a ring. Of course it is not the original ring of King Solomon. But it was copied from a ring, which was copied from a ring, which was copied from a ring, which was copied from the original ring of Solomon. And there is even a specimen of it, a silver ring, engraved with three Hebrew letters GZY, the initials for the three Hebrew words *Gam Zu Ya-avor* "This too will pass."

See p. 25.

47. Noy wrote: "This GZY amulet in the form of a ring is known not only in the Orient. In the 1952 issue of *Yeda-Am*, the journal of the Israel Folklore Society, photographs were published of a 'good-luck ring' sold commercially by a Jewish company in the U.S.A. during World War II. The ring bore an engraved English inscription, 'For Your Boy in the Service,' and three strange Hebrew letters, which are nothing else than GZY, the Hebrew initials of 'This too will pass.'" See ibid., 25.

48. Text comes from the website of the United States Department of Agriculture (USDA), which claims it has been verified against the verbatim copy printed in the *Transactions of the Wisconsin State Agricultural Society, 1858–1859*, 287–99, as reprinted in the *Wisconsin Magazine of History* 10, no. 3 (1926–27). See USDA website, http://www.nal.usda.gov/lincolns-milwaukee-speech (accessed September 5, 2012).

49. On Weilerstein, see Jonathan Krasner, "Sadie Rose Weilerstein through the Looking Glass: K'tonton and the American Jewish Zeitgeist," in *The Women Who Reconstructed American Jewish Education, 1910–1965*, ed. Carol K. Ingall (Hanover, N.H.: Brandeis University Press, 2010), 117–41. See also Paula Hyman and Deborah Dash Moore, eds., *Jewish Women in America: An Historical Encyclopedia* (New York: Routledge, 1997), s.v. "Weilerstein, Sadie."

50. Benjamin Edidin Scolnic, "Footsteps on the Ceiling and Idols on the Floor—Integrated Study of History and Story in the Conservative Jewish Day School," in *Curriculum, Community and Commitment: Views of the American Jewish Day School in Memory of Bennett I. Solomon*, ed. Daniel J. Margolis and Elliot Salo Schoenberg (West Orange, N.J.: Behrman House, 1992), 122–31. © Behrman House., Inc., reprinted with permission, www.behrmanhouse.com.

51. It is hardly uncommon to discover new examples of Lincoln serving as a Jewish educational role model. For example, the Abraham Lincoln Presidential Library and Museum's blog page, "Out of the Top Hat," recently posted a short story about Lincoln written in simple Hebrew for beginners. The story is an undocumented legend wherein a politician visiting the White House finds Lincoln polishing his own boots. The guest was so surprised by this sight that he blurted out, "What! You shine your own shoes?" Lincoln immediately retorted: "Whose shoes would I be shining—someone else's?" See http://www.alplm.org/blog/tag/jewish (accessed on January 15, 2013).

52. *Pesach* is the Hebrew word for Passover. The seder refers to the Passover service and festival meal wherein the story of the Exodus from Egypt is retold in Jewish homes.

53. The *mahnishtanah* is the recitation of the Four Questions that takes place at the beginning of the Passover seder. *Had Gadya* refers to the cumulative song that is sung at the conclusion of the Passover seder.

54. Sadie Rose Weilerstein, *Little New Angel* (Philadelphia: Jewish Publication Society of America, 1947), 91–102. Reprinted by permission of the University of Nebraska Press, copyright 1947 by the Jewish Publication Society.

55. Philip Goodman, comp. and ed., *Lincoln's Birthday: Program Material for Jewish Groups* (New York: National Jewish Welfare Board, Jewish Center Division, 1953), 9–10.

56. For the lack of a stone marking Lincoln's mother's grave, see Albert J. Beveridge, *Abraham Lincoln: 1809–1858*, vol. 1 (Boston: Houghton Mifflin, 1928), 49. On the customs of the Kentucky Baptists, see William E. Barton, *The Life of Abraham Lincoln*, vol. 1 (Brooklyn: Bobbs-Merrill, 1925), 116; Stephen B. Oates, *Abraham Lincoln: The Man*

Behind the Myths (New York: Harper and Row, 1984), 36; and Richard R. Current, *The Lincoln Nobody Knows* (New York: McGraw Hill, 1958), 30.

57. *P'shat* refers to the plain or simple meaning in the exegesis of rabbinical texts, and *d'rash* refers to the applied or interpretive meaning.

58. Counting every day Lincoln had of school in his sporadic education, we get a total of about a year of formal training of any kind. See Oates, *Man Behind the Myths*, 37, and Beveridge, *Abraham Lincoln*, 63. See Oates for why Lincoln could not have read by the fireplace.

59. James Hillman, *Healing Fiction* (Berrytown, N.Y.: Station Hill, 1983), 3–49.

60. William Safire, *Freedom* (Garden City, N.Y.: Doubleday, 1987).

61. Excerpted from *Curriculum, Community and Commitment: Views of the American Jewish Day School in Memory of Bennett I. Solomon*, ed. Daniel J. Margolis and Elliot Salo Schoenberg (West Orange, N.J.: Behrman House, 1992), 124–31.

62. Bertram W. Korn, *American Jewry and the Civil War*, 296 n. 1. See the eulogies delivered by I. M. Wise and Lewis N. Dembitz, reprinted in chapter 6, for more on this topic.

63. After composing his Lincoln poem at age ten, Morton Reiser (1919–87) went on to become a distinguished professor of psychiatry at Yale University School of Medicine and one of the nation's pioneers in the field of neuro-psychoanalysis and psychosomatics.

64. See http://msgboard.snopes.com/cgi-bin/ultimatebb.cgi?ubb=get_topic;f=36; t=000819;p=1; and also http://wiki.answers.com/Q/Was_Abraham_Lincoln_Jewish (accessed August 15, 2012).

65. Although the biblical verse in Deuteronomy 6:5 reads "with all my might," a text that is very familiar to Jews, Carpenter recollected that Lincoln cited the biblical verse as it appears in the Book of Matthew (22:37)—"with all my mind."

66. See Leviticus 19:18.

67. Francis B. Carpenter, *The Inner Life of Abraham Lincoln: Six Months at the White House* (New York: Hurd and Houghton, 1867), 190.

68. Lincoln's address in Trenton, New Jersey, February 21, 1861, www.abrahamlincoln online.org/lincoln/speeches/trenton1.htm (accessed June 29, 2013).

69. *Eden*, February 10, 1929, 2.

70. Rabbi Jeffrey Hahn's Internet essay has literally gone "viral" and can be found on numerous webpages, often under the title "Was There a Jewish President?" My thanks to Rabbi Kahn for granting permission to reprint the essay. Examples included the website of Planet Berry, http://www.planetberries.com/was-there-a-jewish-president. html (accessed September 12, 2012), and the website of Bible Believers, http://www .biblebelievers.org.au/pandora.htm (accessed September 12, 2012). For similar essays on Lincoln's Jewish heritage, see "Abraham Lincoln and the Jews" on AISH.com, http://www.aish.com/j/f/Abraham_Lincoln_and_the_Jews.html (accessed December 31, 2012). See also the website of the *Riverfront Times*, http://www.riverfronttimes. com/2009–02–11/news/abraham-lincoln-was-a-jew-an-unreal-exclusive/ (accessed September 12, 2012). A website titled *USA the Republic* is one of several unsavory web pages that promulgate this theorem in order to foster bigotry and advance stereotyping, The creators of this URL maintain that Lincoln not only was Jewish but was a blood relative of the Rothschilds! See http://www.usa-the-republic.com/items%20 of%20interest/abraham%20lincoln.html (accessed September 12, 2012). A professor in the Business School at Rutgers University, Elizabeth C. Hirschman, has suggested that Lincoln was Jewish, asserting that he was part of an anthropological grouping

called the Melungeons. See Melungeon.com website at http://www.melungeons.com/articles/mar2005.htm (accessed September 12, 2012). Finally, for an unabashedly anti-Semitic twist on Lincoln's Jewishness, see Lyndle J. Gharst, "So You Thought Lincoln Was a Hero: King Lincoln's Reign of Terror" on the website of Israel Elect, http://www.israelect.com/reference/WillieMartin/LINCOLN.htm (accessed September 12, 2012).

71. *Midrash Tanhuma* refers to three separate collections of rabbinic legends drawn largely from the Bible. Scholars generally believe that these collections were redacted and compiled sometime between 400 and 600 C.E.

72. *Nefesh* or *neshama* is Hebrew for "soul."

73. In the written text of this sermon, Raskin indicated that his readers would learn more about the mystical concept of the *pintele yid* by reading an essay titled "An Essential Point" written by an unidentified author, "Philologos." Raskin noted that this essay appeared in the *Forward* on November 24, 2006. It can be read on the online website of the *Forward*, http://forward.com/articles/9020/an-essential-point/ (accessed September 12, 2012).

74. *Chevrei* is Hebrew for "my friends."

75. This sermon is found on the website of Congregation Beth Torah, Richardson, Texas, www.congregationbethtorah.org/congregation/pdf/Abraham_Lincoln_and_the_Pintele_Yid.pdf (accessed September 10, 2012). A copy of this sermon is in the AJA, SC-15983. Courtesy of Rabbi Adam J. Raskin.

Epilogue

1. Philip Roth, *Portnoy's Complaint* (New York: Random House, 1969), 247.

2. Neal Simon, *Brighton Beach Memoirs* (Toronto, Canada: Samuel French, 1984), 37.

3. See A. O. Scott, "Daniel Day-Lewis in Steven Spielberg's film 'Lincoln,'" *New York Times*, November 8, 2012, http://movies.nytimes.com/2012/11/09/movies/lincoln-by-steven-spielberg-stars-daniel-day-lewis.html?pagewanted=all&_r=0 (accessed December 31, 2012); Ty Burr, "'Lincoln' Carries the Weight of History," *Boston Globe*, November 8, 2012, http://www.boston.com/ae/movies/2012/11/08/steven-spielberg-with-tony-kushner-with-help-from-daniel-day-lewis-tell-one-our-country-greatest-stories-using-dialogue-filled/gZo1bEjx4TkCDcmNQBSwZK/story.html (accessed on December 31, 2012); and Gael Fashingbauer Cooper, "Spielberg's 'Lincoln' Forces Movie goers to Care about Backroom Politics" in *NBCNews.com*, November 9, 2012, http://entertainment.nbcnews.com/_news/2012/11/09/15024846-spielbergs-lincoln-forces-moviegoers-to-care-about-backroom-politics?lite (accessed on December 31, 2012).

4. J. Hoberman, "Avraham Lincoln Avinu: Spielberg's Timely New Civil War Biopic Portrays a Man Leading His People to the Gates of the Promised Land," *Tablet Magazine*, November 9, 2012, http://www.tabletmag.com/jewish-arts-and-culture/116078/avraham-linoln-avinu (accessed on December 31, 2012).

5. Tom Teicholz, "The First Jewish President? Lincoln, in the Abrahamic Tradition," *LA Jewish Journal*, JewishJournal.com, November 14, 2012, http://www.jewishjournal.com/cover_story/article/the_first_jewish_president_lincoln_in_the_abrahamic_tradition (accessed on December 31, 2012).

6. Ibid.

7. Ibid. Regarding the "Old Hollywood" tradition of Jews using the movies to redefine American history, see Neal Gabler, *An Empire of Their Own: How the Jews Invented Hollywood* (New York: Crown Publishers, 1988).

8. Andrew Ferguson, *Land of Lincoln: Adventures in Abe's America* (New York: Atlantic Monthly Press, 2007), 267–72.

9. The quote comes from an address of Rabbi Bernard Revel, delivered at the Centenary Celebration of Lincoln's 100th Birthday, New York, February 12, 1909. See Emanuel Hertz, ed., *Abraham Lincoln: The Tribute of the Synagogue* (New York: Bloch Publishing, 1927), 361.

Index

Page numbers in italics indicate illustrations.

Abe Lincoln in Illinois (Sherwood), 311, 339–41, 435*n*45

Abner from Bible, in eulogies of Lincoln, 158, 159

abolitionist movement, 18, 196–97, 265

"About Jews" phrase, Lincoln's letter, 66–68

"Abraham" (song by Irving Berlin), 298–300, 432*n*57

Abraham, Abraham, 145

Abraham from Bible, comparisons, 1, 144, 145, 158–61, 237, 319

"Abraham Lincoln" (Feinberg), 366, 369

Abraham Lincoln: A History (Nicolay and Hay), 230

Abraham Lincoln and the Jews (Markens), 34, 270–71, 300–301

Abraham Lincoln and the Jews (Rubinger), 67

"Abraham Lincoln and the *Pintele Yid*" (Raskin), 386, 388–91, 441*n*73

Abraham Lincoln Bicentennial Commission, 277

Abraham Lincoln Book Store, Chicago, 273, 429*n*20

Abraham Lincoln House, Milwaukee, 235, 426*n*25

"Abraham Lincoln in the White House" (Rontch), 366, 367–69

"Abraham Lincoln's Religion" (Levy), 257–60

Abraham Lincoln: The Tribute of the Synagogue (Hertz), 273, 305, 428*n*19

Abtalyon, 330, 435*n*40

acrostic prayer (Hebrew) praising Lincoln, 198, 219–20, *220*

Adams, Charles Francis, 192

Adelphi Lodge, Freemasons, 174

Adler, Cyrus, 268

Adler, Dankmar, 38, 401*n*37

Adler, Dila Kohn, 20, 37–38, 401*n*37, 401*n*38

Adler, Liebman, 142, 144, 401*n*37

Adler, Samuel, 138, 172

Alexander, John, 118–19, 120, 414*n*6

Alexander, Moses, 371–72, 438*n*37, 438*n*43

Alfred Meadows Conclave, 406*n*48

Allegheny, Pennsylvania, 117, 118–19

Allen, Frank G., 236

Allen, Julia Spanier, 408*n*4

Allen, Michael M., 73, *74*, 408*n*4

Alpert, Abraham (a.k.a. "Ish Kovno"), 371, 373–74, 438*n*38

Alschuler, Samuel G., *13*, 13–14, 26–27, 399*n*17

ambulance driver anecdote (and Lincoln), 283

America in Yiddish Poetry (Cooperman and Cooperman, eds.), 365

American Hebrew, 41–43, 230

American Israelite (a.k.a. *Israelite*), 315

Americanization process, 5–6, 233–36, 325–28, *327*, 356, 358, 363. *See also* assimilation processes; cultural arts

The American Jew as Patriot, Soldier, and Citizen (Wolf), 37

American Jewish Historical Society, 268

American Jewry and the Civil War (Korn), 56, 274, 306, 386

American Red Cross, 281

Amos from Bible, comparison, 232, 245

Anderson, Marian, 312

Arnold, Abraham B., 269

Arnold, Isaac Newton, 20

Asbury, Henry, 16, 17

Ascension Day, conflicts with National Day of Humiliation and Mourning (for Lincoln), 178–79

Asheim, P. M. W. (Freemason), 174

assassination, Lincoln's: celebratory reactions, 221–23, 281; Jerusalem story, 402*n*68; Jonas family warning, 3–4, 17; in

assassination, Lincoln's (*continued*)
Solomons' reminiscences, 43; in Vietnam-era editorial, 353. *See also* eulogies and mourning rites
assimilation processes, 5–6, 233–36, 325–28. *See also* Americanization process; cultural arts
Astaire, Fred, 298
Athens, Illinois, 12–13
Atlanta, Union victory, 194
ax story, 13, 399*n*14

Baar, Herman, 232
Baeck, Leo, 358–59
Baer, Abraham, 223
Baer, Henry, 223
Bailey, Henry Turner, 293
Baltimore, 141, 151–53, 184–86, 415*n*12
Banks, Nathaniel P., 45, 47–49, 50, 52, 54, 57, 60–62, 423*n*64
Barney, Chase, 55
Bates, Edward, 18, 99, 107, 400*n*32
Bayard, James A., 45
Behrend, Adajah, 209
Behrend, Bernhard, 208–9, 212–13, 422*n*48
Belmont, August, 23
Benjamin, Judah P., 4, 49–50, 57, 59–60, 61–62, 405*n*32, 407*n*61
Benton, Thomas Hart (U.S. senator), 45
Berlin, Irving, 298–300, 432*n*57
Berlin, Mr. (on Board of Delegates), 130
Bernthaler, Carl, 257, 427*n*56
Berry, Mary Frances, 2
Beth Israel Synagogue, Louisville, Dembitz's eulogy for Lincoln, 1, 5
Beveridge, James H., 241
Bible story, Kohn-Lincoln meeting, 20
"Bible View of Slavery" (Raphall), 196
Bijur, Martin, 108, 109, 111–12, 303
Bikle, Philip M., 292, 431*n*46
biographies, earliest, 230
Bixby widow, 269, 304
blockade actions, Copperhead response, 193
blockade runner, Lincoln's release, 278–81
Bloom, Albert W., 352–53
Bloomington shipment, 303
Blumenberg, Leopold J., 66–67, 68, 269
Blumer, Herbert, 352
B'nai B'rith, United Order: friendship roster, 401*n*52; Grant's expulsion order, 99, 106–7

B'nai Jeshurun, 79, 409*n*25
Board of Delegates of American Israelites (BODAI): in chaplaincy controversy, 75–76, 77, 79–83; Christian amendment movement, 129–30, 135–37; establishment of, 408*n*12; resolution of mourning, 169–70
Bondi, Jonas, 172
Booth, John Wilkes, 281, 424*n*76
Boston, Board of Temple Israel, 146, 168, 418*n*76
Bowling Green, Kentucky, 111
Boyle, Jeremiah, 111
Brady, Mathew, 276
Brandeis, Louis Dembitz, 165
Breckenridge, John, 22
Brenner, Victor David, 275–76, *287*, 287–89, 430*n*31
Brentano, Lorenzo, 401*n*52
Brighton Beach Memoirs (Simon), 392
Broadway Synagogue, New York City, mourning ceremonies, 172
Brotherhood Week, National, 315–16
Brown, John, 365
Buchanan, James, 17, 196
Buffalo, New York, 228–29, 252–54
Burnside, Ambrose E., 45, 54
Bush, Isador, 24
business owners, Lincoln's encounters, 11–14, 20, 398*n*7
busts of Lincoln, 289–91, *290*, 294, *295*, 431*n*44
Butler, Benjamin, 47, 144
Butte, Montana, Raisin's sermon, 317–20

Cairo, Illinois, 12
Calhoun, John C., 45
Cameron, Simon, 74–75, 79–80
Cameron Dragoons, in chaplaincy controversy, 73–74, 80
Cardiff, Ira D., 424*n*2
Carnegie, Andrew, 433*n*3
Carpenter, Frances B., 386
Carvalho, Solomon Nuñes, *286*, 287
Carver, George Washington, 377, 380–81
Cass, Lewis, 45
casualties, Civil War, 194, 207
Cathell, J. Everist, 255–56
A Centennial Edition of the History of the United States (Lossing), 230

Chalfant, James F., 226, 424*n*85
chaplaincy controversy: overview, 3; BODAI
   actions, 75–76, 77, 79–83; in eulogies of
   Lincoln, 141, 149–50, 199; Fischel's initial
   appeal, 74–75; Lincoln's actions, 76, 77–78,
   85–86, 306–7, 409*n*15; military responses,
   73–74, 82; post-change nomination, 77–78,
   87–89; protests from Jewish community,
   75–76, 409*n*17; role of Congress, 72–73,
   76–77, 80, 82–83; support from Christian
   community, 76–77, 409*n*17
"The Character of Abraham Lincoln" (Cohon), 328–29
"charity toward all" phrase, 243, 281, 337, 348
Charleston, South Carolina, 317
Chase, Salmon P., 45
Chicago: Abraham Lincoln Book Store, 273,
   429*n*20; Centennial Celebration, 260–62;
   eulogies and sermons from, 142, 242–44,
   328–32; funeral cortege, 146; Kohn-Lincoln relationship, 19–20, 36; Republican
   National Convention, 21–22; Scam-
   mon-Lincoln relationship, 36, 402*n*61
Chicago Daily News, 273
Chicago Hebrew Institute, 260–62
Chicago Tribune, 23, 205–7
Childs, Marquis, 343
Christian eulogies, 139–40
Christianity, conflicts about: abolitionist
   perspectives, 197–98; inaugural address
   statement, 23, 204–5; Sabbath observance,
   198, 208–13. *See also* chaplaincy contro-
   versy; Constitution, Christian amend-
   ment movement; religion, Lincoln's
Christian Statesman, 119
Cincinnati, Ohio, 10–11, 97, 108, 112, *143*,
   160–65, 244–45, 412*n*18
civil rights movement, 311–12, 314–15, 349–52
Civil War, casualties, 194, 207. *See also spe-
   cific topics, e.g.,* chaplaincy controversy;
   General Orders No. 11; pardons, soldier;
   Zacharie, Isachar
Civil War Round Table Societies, 273
Clay, Cassius Marcellus, 400*n*32
Clay, Henry, 45
Cleveland Plain Dealer, 292
Cleveland Press, 292–93
coat story, 13–14, 26
Coffin, Charles Carleton, 365–66

Cohen, Abraham S., 402*n*62
Cohen, Carrie Naumburg (Mrs. Josiah),
   256–57, 427*n*54
Cohen, Eleanor H., *221*, 221–22
Cohen, Josiah, 427*n*54
Cohen, M. S., Board of Delegates of Ameri-
   can Israelites, 79–83
Cohn, Elkan, 138, 147–48
Cohon, Samuel S., 328–29, 435*n*38
Cold War era, 341–49
Colfax, Schuyler, 115
common man theme (referring to Lincoln),
   276, 313, 321–24, 354, 363
communism, in Shulman's sermon, 342–45.
   See also McCarthy era
Congregation Adas Israel, Louisville, Gott-
   helf's eulogy, 144
Congregation Adath Jeshurun, Louisville,
   Dembitz's eulogy, 144, 165–67
Congregation Ansche Chesed, New York
   City, rabbi of, 325
Congregation Anshe Emes, Chicago, Langh's
   sermon, 329–32
Congregation Bene Israel (B'nai Israel), New
   York City, Deleeuw's mourning reconcilia-
   tion Shavuot, 181, 188–90, 420*n*20. See also
   Congregation B'nai Israel, New York City
Congregation Bene Israel, Cincinnati, Philip-
   son's sermon, 244–45
Congregation Bene Yeshurun, Cincinnati,
   143, 160–65
Congregation Bene Yeshurun, New York
   City, Raphall's sermon, 196–97
Congregation Beth El, St. Louis, rabbi of, 413*n*40
Congregation Beth-El Emeth, Philadelphia,
   148–51, 169, 417*n*31. *See also* Leeser, Isaac
Congregation Beth Elohim, Charleston,
   rabbi of, 317
Congregation B'nai Abraham, Quincy,
   founder, 15
Congregation B'nai Israel, Butte, Montana,
   Raisin's sermon, 317–20
Congregation B'nai Israel (Bene Israel), New
   York City, mourning service, 171, 418*n*73. See
   also Congregation Bene Israel, New York City
Congregation Emanu-El, New York City, 138,
   139, 147–48, 334
Congregation Emanu-El, San Francisco,
   Cohn's eulogy, 138, 147–48

Congregation Keneseth Israel, Philadelphia, 155–58, 246–51, 306, 417nn45–46
Congregation Mickve Israel, Philadelphia, 142, 153–55, 169, 180–81, 187–88, 271, 415n16, 426n47
Congregation Oheb Israel, Baltimore, 141, 151–53, 415n12
Congregation Ohev Israel, Baltimore, Szold's sermon, 184–86
Congregation Rodeph Shalom, Philadelphia, 232, 254, 409n23
Congregation Rodeph Shalom, Pittsburgh, 257–60, 427n54
Congregation Shaarey Beracha. *See* Congregation Sheary Berochole (Shaarey Beracha), New York City
Congregation Shangarai Chasset, New Orleans, 145, 158–60
Congregation Shearith Israel, New York City, 74, 167, 171, 179, 182–83, 238–39
Congregation Sheary Berochole (Shaarey Beracha), New York City, 172, 418n80
Congregation Sinai, Chicago, Hirsch's sermon, 242–44
Congregation Washington Heights, New York City, 271, 428n12
Congress: in chaplaincy controversy, 72–73, 76–77, 80, 82–83; and Christianizing of Constitution, 117, 122–23, 126–27, 131–32, 135–37; and Grant's expulsion order, 99, 110–11, 115; War Claims actions, 52, 68–71
Conkling, Frederick A., 80, 409n26
Constitution, Christian amendment movement: overview, 3; coalition actions, 118–20, 122–24; Jewish opposition, 117–18, 119–21, 124–37, 414n12; Lincoln's actions, 119, 120–21, 124; origins, 117
contraband anecdote (and Lincoln), 282
Cooley, Charles Horton, 227
Coolidge, Calvin, 310
Cooper, Sir Astley, 403n4
Cooperman, Jehiel B., 365
Cooperman, Sarah H., 365
Cooper Union speech (Lincoln), 21
Copland, Aaron, 300, 301, 431n54
Copperhead movement, 4, 193–94, 420n9
Corwin, Thomas, 33
Covenanters, 117
Cowper, William, 224
Cox, Samuel S., 194

"cracked glass" photograph, 41, 41–43, 403n73
Crane, Cephas Bennett, 140
critics of Lincoln, overview, 3–4, 191–95. *See also* chaplaincy controversy; Leeser, Isaac; Raphall, Morris J.; Wise, Isaac M.
Crosby, Bing, 298
cultural arts: overview, 277; musical tributes, 294–300, 431n54, 432n57; painting, 286, 287; penny design, 275–76, 287, 287–89; sculptures and statues, 289, 289–95, 295, 311–12, 398n9, 431n44, 431n46; Szyk's posters, 356–58; Yiddish poetry, 355, 365–70
Cunningham, Joseph Oscar, 26
currency redesign, Theodore Roosevelt's interest in, 275–76

Dagon (Isaac M. Wise compares Lincoln to), 203–4
Danziger, Abraham Lincoln, 236
Daughters of the American Revolution, 311–12
David, in eulogies/commemorations of Lincoln, 144, 158, 159, 248–49, 318
Davidson, Jo, 294, 294, 295
Davis, David, 303
Davis, Garrett, 115
Davis, Jefferson, 46, 56, 60, 222
Day-Lewis, Daniel, 392–93
debates, Lincoln-Douglas, 4, 15–16, 21, 30, 244–45, 311
Debby character, in Jewish textbook, 376–77, 378–80
Deleeuw, Morris R., 181, 188–90, 419n9, 420n20
Dembitz, Arthur A., 251–52, 426n47
Dembitz, Lewis Naphtali, 1, 5, 18–19, 144, 165–67, 251, 400n33
democracy themes: in Americanization process, 5–6, 233–36, 325–28; in anti-dictatorship sermons, 334–41; in Sherwood's play, 311, 339. *See also* moral compass role, Lincoln's legacy
Denison, George S., 45
Depression Years, Lincoln contention, 310–11
deserters, pardons, 33–34, 141–42, 305, 415n13, 438n36
Deuteronomy verses, 183, 386–87, 389–90, 401n38, 440n65
Die Deborah, 200, 225–26
Dieffenbach, Alfred C., 257, 427n57

Diogenes, in Carvalho's portrait, *286*, 287
Dittenhoefer, Abram J., 21–22, 34, 269
Dix, John A., 69
Dixie anecdote (and Lincoln), 283
Dorchester, Massachusetts, Allen's talk, 236
Dorscheimer, Philip, 401*n*52
Douglas, Stephen, 15, 19, 22–24, 195–96
Douglass, Frederick, 215, 318, 434*n*23
Dropsie, Moses Aaron, 24
Dubin, Henri, 393–94
Du Bois, John Van Deusen, 102, 111

East End Temple, New York City, Soloff's
    sermon, 349–52
Eden (monthly periodical), 386
education, Lincoln's, 384, 440*n*58
Educational Alliance, 235
education curricula, Lincoln portrayals, 230,
    376–85, 439*n*51
Edwards, Elizabeth Porter Todd, 11, 398*n*8
Edwards, Ninian (father), 398*n*8
Edwards, Ninian W. (son), 398*n*8
Einhorn, David, 142–43, 144, 155–58,
    417*nn*45–46
Eisenschiml, Otto, 273
El Maleh Rahamim (prayer for mourners), 167
Emancipation Proclamation, 39–40, 264
Enquirer, 108
Erlanger, Abraham Lincoln, 236
Esche, Oscar, 361
eulogies and mourning rites: overview,
    4–5, 120–21, 138–41, 170–72; Adler's, 142;
    Cohen's, 147–48; Dembitz's, 144, 165–67;
    Einhorn's, 142–43, 155–58; funeral cortege,
    145–46, 170–78, *173*, 224, 398*n*9, 402*n*61,
    424*n*75; Gotthelf's, 144; Hochheimer's,
    141, 144, 151–53; Illowy's, 145, 158–60; in
    Jewish scholarship, 271, 272–73; Joachim-
    sen's, 144–45; Kaddish prayer, 167–68,
    172, 182, 232; Leeser's, 148–51, 167, 199;
    Lilienthal's, 5, 139, 140–41, 146; Morais's,
    142, 153–55, 415*n*16; Raphall's, 141–42;
    resolutions about, 168–70; Wise's, 144,
    160–65, 199. *See also* Shavuot, mourning
    day conflict
Everett, Edward, 154, 417*n*38
Exodus chapter, in Lincoln's religion, 388, 389
expulsion orders. *See* General Orders No. 11
Ezekiel, Jacob, 268
Ezekiel, Moses Jacob, *289*, 289–91, 431*n*44

Farragut, David G., 57, 407*n*59
"Father Abraham Lincoln" (Lee), 366, 369–70
Fechheimer, Abraham Lincoln, 236
Feinberg, Abraham Lincoln, 236
Feinberg, Leonid, 366, 369, 437*n*31
Felsenthal, Bernhard, 268
Fenton, Reuben, 170, 418*n*79
Ferguson, Andrew, 361, 393–94
Fifth Pennsylvania Cavalry, in chaplaincy
    controversy, 73–74, 80
Filene, Abraham Lincoln, 236
Firelands Pioneer Association, 26
first American theme (and Lincoln), 227, 234,
    245, 272, 320
First Army Corps anecdote (and Lincoln),
    282–83
Fischel, Arnold, 74–77, 79–81, *84*, 84–87,
    89–90, 410*n*38
Fischkin, Edward A., 260–62
Fitzgerald, Edward, 436*n*15
flag, Hebrew, Kohn's gift 20, *35*, 35–38, 401*n*38
Flannery, Lot, 228
Footsteps on the Ceiling (Scolnic), 383–85
forgiveness, 283. *See also* Gettysburg Ad-
    dress; pardons, soldier
Fort Monroe, 69
Forverts, 363–65
Foster, John G., 48
Fould, M. Achille, 114
Francis, Julius E., 228–29, *229*
Franco, Francisco, 356
Frankel, Jacob, *78*, 78, 88, 149, 409*n*23
Franko, Jehuda, 438*n*46
Freedman Monument, 434*n*23
Freemasonry, English, 53, 406*n*48
Freeport Doctrine, 196
Free Synagogue, Philadelphia, location,
    426*n*47
Frémont, John C., 15, 24, 287
Friedman, Max, *73*, 73–74, 408*n*5
friends and associates, Lincoln's early
    encounters: overview, 9–11, 25; business
    owners, 11–14, 20, 398*n*7; photographers,
    13, 13–14, 26–27, 399*n*17; political rela-
    tionships, 14–25, 29–37. *See also specific
    individuals*, e.g., Dembitz, Lewis Naph-
    tali; Hammerslough, Julius; Zacharie,
    Isachar
funeral rites/cortege, 145–46, 170–78, 224,
    398*n*9, 402*n*61, 424*n*75

Gardner, Alexander, 41

Garfield, James A., 140

Garrison, William Lloyd, 18

General Orders No. 11: alcohol explanation, 93–94, 411n7; anger explanation, 93, 411n7; as Civil War bigotry example, 100; competition explanation, 93, 103, 104–5, 411n6; congressional support, 99; corruption explanation, 93, 103, 104–5, 411n6; in eulogies of Lincoln, 141, 150, 199; and Grant's presidential campaigns, 94–95, 115–16, 400n27; Kaskel brothers' actions, 96–98, 105–6, 412n20; Lincoln's actions, 97–98, 99–100, 109–10, 112, 412n20; in Markens's scholarship, 302–3; military responses, 95–96, 101–2; motivation for, 91–95; newspaper coverage, 101–5, 107–16; number confusion, 410n1; revocation period, 98–99, 106–7

Germany, Nazism, 311, 313–15, 333–35

Gertz, Elmer, 273

Gettysburg Address: Alpert's parody of, 371, 373–74; in anti-Hitler editorials, 314; and civil rights movement, 316; in Hertz's biography, 305; in Hirsch's commemoration sermon, 243; iconization process, 358–59; Kalish's statue, 292–93, 293, 431n46; in Krauskopf's commemoration sermon, 248; Markens's preservation role, 269, 270, 300, 304, 358; and Morais's sermon, 370–73; in presidential speeches, 310; in Shulman's sermon, 341–42; Szyk's poster, 356–58; Yiddish musical compositions, 296–98 297, 300, 431n54

Gibbons, James Sloan, 320, 434n25

Gilbert, Josiah G., 230

Gilrod, Louis, 295, 296

Gimbel, Jacob, 234

Golden Rule, 307, 432n68

Goldenson, Samuel H., 334–38

Goldschmit, Mr., 111–12

Goldsmith, Abraham, 108, 303

Goldstein, Isaac, 198, 219–20, 423nn67–68

Goodman, Philip, 377, 382–83

Gordon, Martin, 61

Gotthelf, Bernhard H., 144

Grady, Henry W., 319, 434n24

Grant, Ulysses S., 92; Lee's surrender, 195; presidential campaigns, 52, 94–95, 115–16,

400n27. See also General Orders No. 11

Gratz College, 312–13

Greeley, Horace, 16, 52, 55, 365

Green, J. Wesley, 55

Greenebaum, Henry, 19, 269

Griffin, John S., 223

Grinnell, Moses Hicks, 84, 85, 410n32

Gurley, John A., 97–98, 109, 112, 302

Gutheim, James K., 56, 57

habeas corpus, Lincoln's suspension, 193

Had Gadya, 379, 439n53

Hale, Sarah Josepha Buell, 421n25

Halleck, Henry W., 97, 98–99, 107, 109, 302

Halpern, Leivick, 355

Halstead, Murat, 193

Hammerslough, Augusta (later Rosenwald), 11

Hammerslough, Edward, 11

Hammerslough, Julius, 11–12, 227–28, 239–41, 398n9

Hammerslough, Samuel, 11

Hammond, William A., 78

Harding, Aaron, 115

Harding, George, 399n16

Harding, Warren G., 310

Harrisburg Patriot, 342

Harrison, Leon, 313, 321–25, 433n12

Hart, Abraham, 129–30, 169

Hart, B. W., Board of Delegates of American Israelites, 79–83

Hart, Henry I., Board of Delegates of American Israelites, 79–83, 86, 89–90, 410n33

Hay, John: biography of Lincoln, 230; chaplaincy controversy, 77–78, 410n36; Hebrew flag, 36, 37; in Markens's scholarship, 269, 303; pardon of soldier, 34; in Roosevelt administration, 275

Hebrew Bikur Cholim Society, San Jose, funeral assembly, 146

Hebrew flag, Kohn's gift, 20, 35, 35–38, 401n38

Hebrew Immigrant Aid Society (HIAS), 235, 371, 373–74

Hebrew Orphanage Society, 232

Hebrews in America (Markens), 268

Hebrew Union College–Jewish Institute of Religion (HUC-JIR), 200

Henry, Patrick, 250

Herndon, William H., 230

hero themes, and Lincoln, 140–41, 144, 318–19, 355–66

Hertz, Emanuel, 270–73, *271*, 304–5, 428*n*12, 428*n*19

Hertz, Joseph H., 270, 305

Heschel, Abraham Joshua, 390

Hillel comparison, 262, 308, 312, 330–31, 432*n*68

Hirsch, Emil G., *232*, 232–33, 242–44

Hirschman, Elizabeth C., 440*n*70

History of the Flag of the United States (Preble), 37

Hitler, Adolf, 311, 313–15, 333–34

Hochheimer, Henry, 141, 144, 151–53, 415*n*12

Hoffman, Morris, 106–7, 413*n*40

Holiday Inn (film), 298

Hollander, Jacob H., 268

Holly Springs, Mississippi, 95, 103, 111

Holman, William S., 76

Holy Blossom Temple, Toronto, 254

Holzer, Harold, 273–74, 307–8, 401*n*38

honest man anecdote (and Lincoln), 283–85

Hoover, Herbert, 310

House of Representatives. *See* Congress

Howe, Julia Ward, 191

How We Elected Lincoln (Dittenhoefer), 34

Hühner, Leon, 268

humor, Lincoln's, 22–23, 29, 33, 40, 218, 264, 279, 282–85

Humphrey, Grace, 235

Huss, John, 339, 341

Huttenbauer, Samuel, 13

Iceland, Reuben, 365–67, 437*n*29

Illinois General Assembly, 15, 399*n*18

Illinois Senate, 15

Illowy, Bernard, 145, 158–60, 416*n*23

immigrant population, overview, 233; assimilation and Lincoln, 5–6, 233–36, 325–28; in Old Northwest, 9–11; political interests, 2, 51. *See also* friends and associates, Lincoln's early encounters; Wise, Isaac M.

inaugural addresses: criticisms of, 23, 192, 204–5, 216; Douglass's response, 215; in Langh's "Jewish ideal" sermon, 331; in Schechter's memorializing sermon, 263; on Szyk's poster, 356, *357*. *See also* "malice toward none" phrase

inauguration, Lincoln's, 11, 398*n*12

Independent Order of B'nai B'rith, Lincoln's funeral procession, 174

Independent Order of Red Men, Lincoln's funeral procession, 174

In His Steps (Sheldon), 321, 434*n*28

intercession requests of Lincoln: Jonas's family, 18, 32; soldier pardons, 33–34, 141–42, 305, 332, 415*n*13, 438*n*36; Zacharie's family, 50, 52, 59, 66–67

Isaacs, Myer Samuel, 52, 65–66, 79–83, 90, 129–30, 169–70, 410*n*34

Isaacs, Samuel Myer, 65, 95, 172, 175–77

Ish Kovno (Abraham Alpert), 371, 438*n*38

Israel Folktale Archives, 359

Israelite (a.k.a. *American Israelite*), 15. *See also* Wise, Isaac M., *entries*

Isserman, Ferdinand M., 254–55, 339, 341

Jacksonville, Illinois, 12, 28–29, 402*n*56

Jefferson, Thomas, 118, 250, 340, 346

Jerome, Stanley, 392

Jerusalem visit, Lincoln's wish, 38, 402*n*68

Jesus comparisons, 140, 246, 249, 257, 259–60, 339, 340

Jewett, William Cornell, 55, 406*n*55

Jewish Advocate, 314, 316, 333–34

Jewish Chautauqua Society, 234

Jewish Chronicle, 352–53

Jewish community, overview: growth of, 9–11; Lincoln relationship summarized, 1–8; voting arguments, 2, 51, 64–66. *See also* chaplaincy controversy; eulogies and mourning rites; Wise, Isaac M., *entries*

Jewish Criterion, 255–57

Jewish descent claim, 160, 225–26, 385–91, 440*n*70

Jewish Exponent, 251–52, 313–14

Jewish homeland proposal made to Lincoln, 38–40

Jewish Messenger, 65, 95, 145–46, 178–79, 213, 216, 228, 231. *See also* Isaacs, Myer Samuel; Isaacs, Samuel Myer

Jewish Record, 172–77

Jewish Science Interpreter, 347

Jewish Theological Seminary, New York City, 262–64, 358

Joachimsen, Philip J., 121, 144–45, 416*n*22

Johnson, Andrew, 178, 197, 221–22, 224, 228, 432*n*62

Johnson, Edgar M., 112, 303

Jonas, Abraham, 3–4, *14*, 14–18, 21, 29–32, 399*n*18, 401*n*42, 422*n*40
Jonas, Benjamin Franklin, 18
Jonas, Charles Henry, 18, *32*
Jonas, Edward, 15–16, 18
Jonas, Joseph, 15
Jonas, Julian, 18
Jonas, Samuel Alroy, 18
Jones, Alfred T., 121, 169, 180–81
Joseph, Ellis, 81–82, 129–30
Josephi, Henry, 129–30, 169–70
Journal of American Folklore, 375
Judaization process, 5–6, 231–37, 260–66, 329–32, 352–53. *See also* Gettysburg Address; Jewish descent claim; memorialization process

Kabakoff, Jacob, 423*n*67
Kaddish prayer for Lincoln, 167–68, 172, 182, 232
Kahn, Jeff, 386, 387–88, 440*n*70
Kalish, Max, *291*, 291–93, *293*
Kansas-Nebraska Act, 19
Kansas Post, 18
Kaskel, Cesar J., *96*, 96–99, 101–2, 105–6, 109, 300–303
Kaskel, Julius W., 96–97, 103, 301, 412*n*13
Kaufmann, Sigismund, 22–23, 401*n*47
Kearney, Philip, 18
Kefauver, Estes, 343–44
Kehilath Anshe Ma'ariv, Chicago, 20, 36, 142
Kellogg, Stephen W., 68
"*Kiddush Ha-Shem*," in Lincoln eulogy, *143*, 156, 157–58, 417*n*46
King, Martin Luther, Jr., 312
King Solomon Lodge, Freemasons, 174
Know Nothing Party, 16–17, 29, 30–31, 308, 316
Koch, Bro. (Freemason), 174
Kohler, Kaufmann, 234
Kohler, Max J., 268
Kohn, Abraham, 19–20, *35*, 35–38
Kohn, Dila (later Adler), 20, 37–38, 400*n*37
Kohn, Hezekiah, 130
Kohn, Jacob, 325–28
Korn, Bertram Wallace, 56, 67, *274*, 274–75, 306–7, 386, 399*n*18, 429*n*24
Kossuth, Louis, 318
Kostelanetz, Andre, 300
Kramer, Judah, 171
Krass, Nathan, 121, 252–54

Krauskopf, Joseph, 232, 246–51
Krohn, Abraham Lincoln, 236
K'tonton character, in Jewish textbooks, 376
Kuhn, George, 415*n*13
Ku Klux Klan, 313
Kunitz, Stanley, 360
Kushner, Tony, 392–93
Kuttner, Henry, 106–7, 413*n*40

Lamon, Ward H., 230
Land of Lincoln (Ferguson), 361, 393–94
Langh, Philip A., 329–32
Latham, Milton S., 115
Leadville, Colorado, 96, 412*n*14
League of Jewish Youth, 325–28
Leberman, L. J., 169
Lee, Malka, 366, 369–70, 438*n*32
Lee, Robert E., 195
Leeser, Isaac, *88*; in chaplaincy controversy, 77, 87–89, 410*n*36; Christian amendment movement, 117–18, 119, 120, 127–35, 413*n*2, 414*n*26; criticism of war leadership, 4; eulogy of Lincoln, 148–51, 167, 199; Lincoln assassination, 141; mourning resolution, 168–69; on Philadelphia Board of Rabbis, 409*n*21; Sabbath observance controversy, 198, 208–13
Lesco Corporation, 434*n*29
Levinson, Joseph, 36
Levy, Cherie M., 306
Levy, J. Leonard, 257–60
Lewis, Lloyd, 273
Lewis, Samuel A., 52, 64
Leyeles, Aaron, 355
Lichtenstein, Morris, 347
Lichtenstein, Tehilla, *347*, 347–49
Lieber, Francis, 51
The Life of Abraham Lincoln (Tarbell), 267
Lilienthal, Max: eulogizing of Lincoln, 5, 139, 140–41, 146; Grant's expulsion order, 97, 108, 109, 111–12, 116; in Markens's scholarship, 302, 303
Lincoln (Spielberg), 392–93
Lincoln, Abraham: humor of, 22–23, 29, 33, 40, 218, 264, 279, 282–85; Jewish community relationship summarized, 1–8; photographs, *27*, *41*, *42*, *98*, *120*. *See also* cultural arts; eulogies and mourning rites; moral compass role, Lincoln's legacy

Lincoln, England, 388, 389

Lincoln, Mary Todd, 24, 38, 389, 402*n*68

Lincoln, Mordechai, 388

Lincoln, Nancy Hanks, 383–85, 387

Lincoln, Robert Todd, 195, 230, 269, 302, 303–4, 386, 402*n*61

Lincoln, Thomas, 304

Lincoln and Diogenes (Carvalho), *286*, 287

"Lincoln and the Immigrant" (Humphrey), 235

Lincoln and the Jews (Holzer), 307–8

"Lincoln and the Jews" (Korn), 306–7

Lincoln Centennial Celebration, Chicago, 260–62

Lincoln Day Address, Wolf's, 231

Lincoln Day festivities, New York City, 232

Lincoln Home National Historic Site Visitor Center, 294, *295*

"Lincoln in Richmond" (Iceland), 365–67

Lincoln Medal of 1907 (Brenner), *288*

Lincoln Memorial, Oak Ridge Cemetery, 227

Lincoln Memorial, Washington, D.C., 311–12

Lincoln Memorial Collection, 229

Lincoln Memorial University, 272

Lincoln penny, 275–76, 287–89, *288*, 430*n*31

"Lincoln Portrait" (Copland), 300, *301*, 431*n*54

"The Lincoln Relics" (Kunitz), 360

Lincoln's Birthday: Program Material for Jewish Groups (Goodman), 377, 382–83

Lincoln's Masterpiece (Markens), 269, *270*

Lisitzky, Ephraim, 233

literary hero theme and Lincoln, 355–56

Little New Angel (Weilerstein), 376–80, *378*

Little Sermons in Socialism by Abraham Lincoln (McCarty), 354–55

lodestar theme and Lincoln, Langh's sermon, 329–32

London Times, 342

Lossing, Benson J., 230

Lot, in eulogy of Lincoln, 144

Louisiana, slavery abolishment, 219, 423*n*64

Louisville, Kentucky: Dembitz's leadership, 19; eulogies of Lincoln, 1, 5, 144, 165–67, 386; Grant's expulsion order, 108, 109, 111–12, 116, 303; immigrant population growth, 9, 10, 11

Louisville Daily Journal, 144

Lovell, J., 113

Low, Frederick, 115, 413*n*49

Lowell, James Russell, 434*n*27

Lucy, Autherine Juanita, 316

Ludwig, Reuben, 355

Luther, Martin, Lincoln compared to, 246, 249

Lyons, Jacques Judah, 167, 171, *179*, 179, 182–83, 238–39

Mack, Harman, 93

Mack, Henry, 93

Mack, Simon, 93

MacNeil, Hermon Atkins, 294

Madison, James, 250

mahnishtanah, 379, 439*n*53

"malice toward none" phrase: in Americanization, 327; in anti-dictatorship sermon, 337; in anti-McCarthyism sermon, 346; in anti–nuclear war sermon, 349; on Carvalho's painting, 287; in civil rights sermon, 351; in Goodman's reminiscences, 281; in Korn's scholarship, 307; in memorial sermons, 243, 259; Szyk's poster, 356, *357*

Mallory, Stephen R., 49, 57, 61

Manchester letter, Lincoln's, 345–46

Marcus, Jacob Rader, 274

Markens, Isaac, *268*; Dittenhoefer's letter, 34; on Hebrew flag gift, 36; on Kaskel's Washington trip, 412*n*20; on Lincoln friendships, 398*n*7, 398*n*12; Lincoln's Jewish descent claim, 386; questions to Robert Lincoln, 303–4, 432*n*62–63; on Republican Convention activity, 400*n*32; scholarship approach, 267–72, 300–302, 358

Marovitz, Abraham Lincoln, 236

Martindale, John H., 280

Masliansky, Zvi Hirsch, 235

Maslow, Abraham H., 361, 437*n*19

Mason, George, 250

McCarthy era, 341–46

McCarty, Burke, 354–55

McClellan, George B., 22, 45, 54, 195

McClure, Alexander, 248, 426*n*44

McClure, Samuel S., 267

McKinley, William, 37, 38

memorialization process: with birthday commemorations, 228–29, 231–33, 242–55; with centennial sermons, 255–66; with immigrant assimilation, 233–36; with Lincolniana collections, 230, 272–73, 304–5; with monuments, 227–28, 238–41; with scholarship, 230, 267–75, 300–304, 306–8; in school textbooks, 230, 376–85. *See also* cultural arts; Judaization process

memorials and statues, *289*, 289–95, *295*, 311–12, 398*n*9, 431*n*44, 431*n*46
Memphis, Tennessee, 12
Mendes, Isaac P., 268
Meredosia, Illinois, 28–29, 402*n*56
messiah theme, 140, 143–44, 156–58, 160, 163, 232, 246–51, 367
Michael character, in Jewish textbook, 376–77
Michaelis, Jacob, 412*n*14
Midrash Tanchuma, 389, 441*n*71
military support, Lincoln's reelection, 194–95
militia, the calling out of, and the Copperhead response to, 193
Miller, Judea B., 315–16
Milwaukee, Wisconsin, 20–21, 235, 327, 426*n*25
Mississippi, Military Department of. *See* General Orders No. 11
Monk, Henry Wentworth, 38–40
Montefiore, Moses, 130
Morais, Sabato, 142, 153–55, 187–88, 370–73, 415*n*16, 438*n*33, 438*n*36
moral compass role, Lincoln's legacy: overview, 309–10; in Americanization, 325–28; in anti-Hitler arguments, 311, 313–15, 333–41; in civil rights movement, 311–12, 314–20, 349–52; as Jewish ideal, 329–32, 352–53; during McCarthy era, 341–46; in nativism opposition, 328–29; in nuclear holocaust threat, 347–48; in Progressivism issues, 321–25; before World War II, 236–37, 310–11, 312–13
moral reason premise, Goldenson's sermon, 335–38
Mordecai, Benjamin, 278
Mordecai, Goodman L., 278–81
Morris, Isaac N., 16–17, 30, 400*n*27
Mortara, Edgardo, 408*n*12
Mosby, John Singleton, 225, 424*n*81
Moses, Josh, 222
Moses from Bible, comparisons: anti-dictatorship sermon, 335; children's textbook, 377, 379–80; commemorations, 318; eulogies, 144, 157; Hertz's foreword, 305; Isserman's sermon, 339, 340; memorial sermons, 246, 249–50, 253, 259; musical tribute, 294–96, *296*; resolution of mourning, 169, 271
Mott, Valentine, 403*n*4
Mount Neboh Lodge, Freemasons, 174

Mount Sinai story, 389–90
"Mourning Sermon," Einhorn's, 155–58
museum in Athens, Illinois, 12
musical tributes to Lincoln, 294–300, *300*, 431*n*54, 432*n*57
Myers, Gustavus A., 4
Myers, Lawrence, 129–30
Myers, Nat, 290–91

NAACP, 311–12
Nashville, Tennessee, 103–5
Nast, Thomas, 192
Nathan, Ernesto, 290
Nathan, Virginia, 290
Natick Cobbler, 197, 421*n*22
National Brotherhood Week, 315–16
National Day of Humiliation, Fasting, and Prayer, proclamations, 170–72, 196, 198, 213–14, 418*n*79. *See also* Shavuot, mourning day conflict
National Jewish Welfare Board (JWB), 377
National Lincoln Monument Association, 12, 227, 238–41
National Reform Association (NRA), 119–20, 122–24
national sin belief, Lincoln's, 331–32
Nazism, opposition, 311, 313–15, 333–41
Neiman, Abraham Lincoln, 236
Nesmith, James W., 115
Newman, Ralph G., 273, 429*n*20
Newmark, Harris, 222–23
New Mexican Territory, 49, 56
New Orleans, 47–49, 56–57, 70, 144–45, 158–60
new South, 319–20, 434*n*24
New York, Lincoln's reelection campaign, 50–52, 64–66
New York City: coverage of mourning ceremonies, 170–77, 418*n*73, 418*n*80; J. Phillips letter about assassination, 223–25; Jewish Theological Seminary, 262–64; Lincoln Day festivities, 232; sermons from, 181, 188–90, 196–97, 349–52, 420*n*20. *See also* Congregation Emanu-El, New York City; Congregation Shearith Israel, New York City
New York Daily Tribune, 278–81
New York Herald, 45, 46, 49, 54–56, 61, 404*n*8
New York Times, 68, 107–8, 145, 170, 202, 264, 326–28, 418*n*79

New York Tribune, 79–80, 420*n*20
New York World, 63–64
Nicolay, Helen, 269
Nicolay, John G., 230, 269, 304
Nin, Anaïs, 277, 430*n*35
Noots, Simon, 172
Northern Cross Railroad, 402*n*56
Northwest Ordinance, 9–10
Noy, Dov, 375, 438*n*46, 439*n*47
Numismatist, 276

Oak Ridge Cemetery, 227, 398*n*9
"O Captain! My Captain!" (Whitman), 309
Occident and American Jewish Advocate,
    117–18, 127–29, 168–69, 198, 208–9
Oglesby, Richard J., 241
Old Capitol Prison, 278, 280, 430*n*38
Old Northwest, population growth, 9
One-Dollar-Lincoln-Memorial-Fund, 228,
    238–39
Order of the Secret Monitor, 53, 406*n*48
Ostendorf, Lloyd, 27, 399*n*14
Otterbourg, Marcus, 20–21, 269, 422*n*40
Otterbourg, Solomon, 20
"Out of the Top Hat" (title of blog on Lin-
    coln), 439*n*51
Oxford, Mississippi, Grant's expulsion order, 95

Paducah, Kentucky, 95–96, 99, 101–2, 108, 111,
    114
Pancoast, Charles Edward, 28–29
pardons, soldier, 33–34, 141–42, 305, 332,
    415*n*13, 438*n*36
Parker, Theodore, 18
Passover (*Pesach*), 138, 205–6, 377, 378, 381,
    415*n*1, 439*n*53
Paul, Ron, 354
peace negotiations, 47, 48–50, 55–56, 57,
    59–62, 404*n*16, 405*n*32, 407*n*61
peanuts and George Washington Carver,
    story in children's textbook, 380–81
"peculiar institution," the phrase, 218, 422*n*61
Peixotto, Benjamin F., 24, 268
Pendleton, George H., 109, 115
Pennsylvania, Lincoln's reelection campaign,
    50–51
penny, Lincoln, 275–76, 287, 288, 287–89, 430*n*31
Pesach (Passover), 138, 205–6, 337, 378, 381,
    415*n*1, 439*n*53

Peterson, Merrill, 227
Philadelphia, 232, 254, 409*n*21, 409*n*23. *See
    also* Congregation Beth-El Emeth, Phil-
    adelphia; Congregation Keneseth Israel,
    Philadelphia; Congregation Mickve Israel,
    Philadelphia
Philadelphia Board of Ministers of the He-
    brew Congregations, 77–78
Philipson, David, 232, 234, 234, 244–45
Phillips, Beck, 224, 424*n*77
Phillips, Isaac, 224–25, 424*n*80
Phillips, Jonas, 423*n*72
Phillips, Josephine, 223–25, 423*n*72
Phillips, Naphtali, 224, 424*n*77
Phillips, Rachel Rosalie, 403*n*70, 423*n*72
Phillips, Rev., 172
Phillips, Wendell, 18, 365, 400*n*32
Philp, Franklin, 403*n*72
photographers, Lincoln's encounters, 13,
    13–14, 26–27, 399*n*17, 424*n*79
Pinkerton, Allen, 17
Pinner, Mortiz, 18, 400*n*32
pintele yid ("Jewish spark"), 390, 441*n*73
Pirkei Avot, quotation from, 325, 435*n*34
Pittsburgh, 255–60, 427*nn*54–56
Pittsburgh Symphony Orchestra, 257,
    427*nn*55–56
poetry, Yiddish, 355, 365–70
political appointments, Lincoln's, 17, 144,
    193, 401*n*47, 422*n*40. *See also* chaplaincy
    controversy
political relationships, Lincoln's early en-
    counters: associates, 14–18; supporters,
    18–25
Polonius (Fitzgerald), 436*n*15
Polonsky, Abraham Lincoln, 236
population statistics, 9, 10
Porter, David D., 57, 407*n*59
Portnoy's Complaint (Roth), 392
portrait of Lincoln (Carvalho), 286, 287
posters, Szyk's, 356–58
Powell, Lazarus, 110, 115
prayers for Lincoln. *See* eulogies and mourn-
    ing rites
Preble, George H., 37
preliminary Emancipation Proclamation,
    46–47, 194
Presbyter, in chaplaincy controversy, 76–77,
    409*n*17

Presbyterian churches, in Christian amendment movement, 117–19
presidential election, Lincoln's, 16, 18–22, 23, 30, 248, 400*nn*32–33, 426*n*44. *See also* reelection campaign
The Presidents I Have Known (Wolf), 25
Prinz, Joachim, 314–15
profiteers, problem with, during Civil War. *See* General Orders No. 11
Progressivism, 321–24
Prophets, comparing Lincoln to, 353
proprietors, Lincoln's encounters, 11–14, 20, 398*n*7
Psalm 145, 219–20
p'shat (simple or plain meaning in biblical exegesis), 384, 440*n*57
publishers, Philp and Solomons, 25, 41–43, 403*n*72

Quincy, Illinois, 14–18, 31, 401*n*42

Rabinowitz, Isaac, 438*n*38
raccoon story and Lincoln, 13, 399*n*14
railroads, 28, *173*, 402*n*56
Raisin, Jacob Salmon, *317*, 317–20, 434*nn*23–27
Randall, James G., 274
Raphall, Alfred, 213–14
Raphall, Morris J., 3, 141, 171, 196–97, 199, 205, 213–15, 306
Raskin, Adam J., 386–87, 388–91, 441*n*73
Rawlins, John, 99, 113
Raymond, Henry J., 194
Red Sea allusion, in Lincoln eulogy, 157, 417*n*45
reelection campaign, 22, 50–52, 63, 64–66, 194–95
Reform Advocate, 37
Reiser, Morton, 386, 387, 440*n*63
religion, Lincoln's, 226, 257–60, 307–8, 328–29, 331, 340, 386–87
Reminiscences (Howe), 191
Republican Party: Cold War era, 341, 343; formation, 15, 19; national conventions, 16, 18, 19, 21–22, 24, 399*n*21, 400*nn*32–33
Republican State Convention, Illinois, 433*n*11
resolutions of mourning for Lincoln, 168–70, 271
Revel, Bernard, 264–66
Revenue Act, 193

Reynolds, A. J., 135
Reynolds, John E., 283
Reynolds, Marjorie, 298
Rice, Henry, 12, 398*nn*11–12
Richmond, Virginia: Lincoln's trip, 4, 365–67; Union victory, 195, 198; Zacharie's peace negotiations, 49–50, 57, 59, 405*n*32, 407*n*61
ring, good-luck, 359, *375*, *375*, 439*n*47
"Rishuth" (article by Leeser), 130–35, 414*n*26
Roaring Twenties, Lincoln question, 310
Rogers, William P., 352
Rontch, Isaac, 366, 367–69, 437*n*30
Roosevelt, Franklin D., 310–11
Roosevelt, Theodore, 275–76
Rosecrans, William Starke, 104, 413*nn*36–37
Rosenwald, Augusta Hammerslough, 11, 398*n*6
Rosenwald, Julius, 398*nn*6–7
Rosenwald, Samuel, 11, 398*n*6
Roth, Philip, 392
Rubinger, Naphtali J., 67
Rumshinsky, Joseph, 294–96, *296*
Ruskin, John, 38
Russak, B., Board of Delegates of American Israelites, 79–83
Ruthie character, in Jewish textbook, 376–77, 378–80

Sabbath observance, 198, 208–13
Saint-Gaudens, Augustus, 275–76
Sale, Samuel, 235
Salzenstein, Louis, 12–13, 399*n*14
Salzenstein, Myer, 13
Sandburg, Carl, 273, 276
San Francisco, 138, 146, 147–48
Sangamon County, Lincoln's representation, 15
San Jose, communal funeral assembly for Lincoln, 146
Sarna, Jonathan, 410*n*1
Saulsbury, Eli, 115
Savannah, Zacharie's family, 50, 52, 59, 66–67
savior theme, 140, 143–44, 156–58, 160, 163, 232, 246–51, 367
Scammon, Charles, 402*n*61
Scammon, Jonathan Young, 36, 402*n*61
Schechter, Solomon, 262–64, 332
Schiff, Jacob, 234, 358
Schneider, George, 24
Schurz, Carl Christian, 21, 191

Schwartz, Barry, 360

Scolnic, Benjamin Edidin, 377, 383–85

Scott, William, 332

Scripture argument, Christian amendment opposition, 126

sculptures and memorials, *289*, 289–95, *290*, *293*, *295*, 311–12, 398*n*9, 431*n*44, 431*n*46

Sears, Roebuck & Company, 398*n*6

second inaugural address (Lincoln), 215–16, 307, 326–28, 356, *357*

Seddon, James A., 49, 57, 61

"A Seder on Lincoln's Birthday" (Weilerstein), 377, 378–80

Segal, Charles M., 403*n*4

Seixas, Benjamin Mendez (a.k.a. Mr. S.), 222, 423*n*69

self-actualization theory, Maslow's, 361, 437*n*19

Seligman, Joseph, 24

Senate, U.S. *See* Congress

Seward, William H.: in ambulance driver anecdote, 283; assassination attempt, 221, 224, 424*n*76; Christianity perspective, 197; in Lincoln eulogy, 148; presidential aspirations, 18, 400*n*32; Thanksgiving proclamation, 421*n*25

Seward, William H. (Zacharie relationship): Confederate peace negotiations, 49, 50, 60; New Orleans assignments, 47; professional recommendations, 45, 54, 404*n*7; soldier foot care, 68–69

Shammai, 331

Shapell Manuscript Foundation, 273–74

Shavuot, mourning day conflict: overview, 178–79; Deleeuw's reconciliation, 181, 188–89; Jones's response, 180–81; Lyons's regrets, 179, 182–84; Morais's sermon, 187–88; Szold's reconciliation, 179–80, 184–86. *See also* eulogies and mourning rites

Sheldon, Charles Monroe, 321, 434*n*29

Sherman, Frank Dempster, 288

Sherman, William T., 194

Sherwood, Robert E., 311, 339, 435*n*45

shivah, 180, 419*n*6

shloshim, 419*n*6

Shmaya, 330, 435*n*40

shoe shining story (and Lincoln), 439*n*51

Shofle anecdote (and Lincoln), 283–85

Shoninger, Joseph, 168, 418*n*76

Shulman, Charles E., 341–46

Silberman, Mr., 103

silence problem, civil rights, 315

Silver, Abba Hillel, 235

Simon, Neil, 392

Sisterhood of Rodeph Shalom, Pittsburgh, 256–57

Sixty-Fifth Regiment, in chaplaincy controversy, 73–74, 80

"Sketches from the Seat of War," 216–18

slavery: abolitionist movement, 18, 196–97, 265; in anti-McCarthy arguments, 345; in children's textbooks, 379–81; in civil rights arguments, 349, 353; in Cohen's diary, 222; in commemorations of Lincoln, 249–51, 261; Emancipation Proclamation, 39–40, 194, 264, 423*n*64; Northwest Ordinance, 9–10; in *pintele yid* sermon, 390–91; in socialism claims, 356, 364–65; in Union soldier's letter, 218–19, 423*n*62; Wise's expectations about, 196, 202

Smith, E. Delafield, 84–85

smuggling problem. *See* General Orders No. 11

socialism, claims that Lincoln was sympathetic to, 354–56, 363–65

social justice themes. *See* moral compass role, Lincoln's legacy

Society of Jewish Science, 347

Society of Lincoln Authors and Collectors, 272

Socrates, Lincoln compared to, in Isserman's sermon, 339, 340–41

soldier support, Lincoln's conduct, 216–18

Solis-Cohen, Solomon, 312–13

Soloff, Rav A., 349–52, *350*, 435*n*53

Solomon, Haym, 214

Solomon, Jacob P., 75

Solomon, King, 359–60, 374–76, 436*n*15, 438*n*46

Solomons, Adolphus S., 25, 41–43, 213, 223–24, 281–85, 403*n*70, 403*n*72, 424*n*79

Solomons, Mary Jane, 225, 424*n*82

Solomons, Rachel Seixas, 224, 225, 424*n*82

"Some Say Lincoln Was a Jew" (Reiser), 386, 387

Spanier, Julia (later Allen), 408*n*4

Spanish Civil War, 356

Spiegel, Marcus M., 218–19

Spielberg, Steven, 392–93

Springfield, Illinois: Davidson's bust, 294, 295; friends/acquaintances from, 11–12, 15, 21, 246, 398*n*12; funeral train arrival, 145–46; Lincoln's burial site, 178, 227, 398*n*9, 424*n*75; Lincoln's departure from, 19, 23, 204, 246, 311, 328–29, 331; monument fundraising, 227–28, 239–41; twentieth-century visitors to, 361, 393–94

Stanton, Edwin M.: coat story, 14; at Emancipation Proclamation reading, 264; in Korn's research, 306–7; on Lincoln's assassination, 227; soldier pardons, 17, 33; Zacharie relationship with, 45, 47, 52, 68–69

statues and memorials, *289*, 289–95, *290*, *293*, *295*, 311–12, 398*n*9, 431*n*44, 431*n*46

Sternberger, Leon, 172

St. Louis, 254–55, 313, 321–24, 339, 413*n*40

Sullivan, Jeremiah Cutler, 95

Sulzberger, W. J. (Freemason), 174

Sumner, Charles, 117, *118*, 413*n*2

Sussman, Lance J., 409*n*21

sutlers, 12, *93*, 398*nn*11–12. *See also* General Orders No. 11

"Symposium" (Ludwig), 355

Szold, Benjamin, 5, 141–42, 179–80, *180*, 184–86, 305, 415*n*13

Szyk, Arthur, 356–58

Taft, William Howard, 310

Tak, Edward, 257, 427*n*55

Tarbell, Ida, 267–68, 272

taxes, 193, 344

Temimi Derech synagogue, New Orleans, Joachimsen's sermon, 144–45

Temple Beth-El, Dorchester, Massachusetts, Allen's talk, 236

Temple Emanu-El, New York, *139*

Temple Israel, St. Louis, 254–55, 313, 321–24, 339

Temple Mizpah, Chicago, rabbi of, 328

Temple Rodeph Shalom, Pittsburgh, centennial ceremonies, 255–57

Temple Shaarey Tefila, New York City, rabbi of, 172

Ten Commandments, 257, 261, 388, 389–90

textbooks, Lincoln portrayals, 230, 376–77, 378–81

Thai Little Home Cafe, 361

Thanksgiving Day, 198, 421*n*25

Thirteenth Amendment, in Spielberg's *Lincoln*, 393

"this, too, shall pass" phrase, 359–60, 374–76, 436*n*15, 438*n*46, 439*n*47; good-luck ring, 359, 375, 439*n*47

Tinklenberg, Janie, 434*n*29

Tisha b'Av, 370, 438*n*34

"To America" (Halpern), 355

Toch, Henry M., 236–37

Todd, Elizabeth Porter (later Edwards), 11, 398*n*8

trader problem. *See* General Orders No. 11

"Trauer-Rede," Einhorn's, 155–58

Truman, Harry S., 311, 315, 343–44

Tsaddik comparison, 251, 252

ugly man anecdote (and Lincoln), 282

Union League of Philadelphia, 370, 438*n*33

The Union Prayerbook, 328, 435*n*37

United Jewish Charities, 12

United Synagogue of America, Kohn's talk, 325–28

University of Alabama, black student conflict, 316

unprincipled traders problem. *See* General Orders No. 11

Urbana, Illinois, 13–14, 26–27

USA the Republic website, 440*n*70

Vallandigham, Clement L., 72–73

vice-presidential nomination, Lincoln's, 399*n*21

Victoria, Queen, 432*n*63

Volksfreund, 108

Volunteer Bill, 72–73

Waddell, L. J., 95–96, 99, 101–2

wagon travel story, Pancoast's, 28–29

Walker, Frank, 393

Walz, Mr. (delivered eulogy for Lincoln), 172

Warburg, Felix, 358

Ward, Artemus, 264

Ward, J. H. Hobart, 174

Washburne, Elihu B., 99, 110–11

Washington, Booker T., 318

"Washington, Lincoln, and Moishe Rabeiny" (Gilrod), 294–96, *296*

Washington Times, 228

Wasserman, H. (delivered eulogy for Lincoln), 172

"Was There a Jewish President?" (Kahn), 386, 387–88, 440n70

"watchful waiting" phrase, 309, 433n1

Watertown, Wisconsin, 21

"We Are Coming, Father Abraham" (Gibbons), 320, 434n25

Weber, Jennifer L., 420n9

Weed, Chevalier, 55

Weed, Thurlow, 194, 263

Weilerstein, Sadie Rose, 376–77, 378–81

Weinberg, Daniel, 429n20

Weinberg, Jacob, 296–98, 431n54

Welles, Gideon, 55, 406n56

Wentworth, John, 19, 20

West, Kenyon, 309

West End, New Jersey, 12

"What would Jesus do?," slogan origins, 321, 434n29

"What would Lincoln do?," question origins, 310, 321, 433n3. *See also* moral compass role, Lincoln's legacy

Whig Party, 15

Whitman, Walt, 309

Whitney, Henry C., 14, 399n17

Whittier, John Greenleaf, 365

Wikoff, Chevalier, 55

Wiles, William M., 103–4, 413n36

Willard Hotel, 407n64

Williamstown, Kentucky, 15

Wilson, Henry, 197, 206, 421n22

Wilson, Robert, 115

Wilson, Woodrow, 236, 313, 321, 433n1

Wilzinski, S., Board of Delegates of American Israelites, 79–83

Winder, John H., 49, 57, 61

Wisconsin State Agricultural Society, 359, 374–76, 439n48

Wise, Isaac M., 195; on assassination of Lincoln, 138; chaplaincy controversy, 75, 76, 409n17; Christian amendment movement, 119–20, 124–27, 414n12; Douglas support, 195–96; eulogy of Lincoln, 5, 144, 160–65, 199; Grant's expulsion order, 95, 97, 99–100, 101–5, 108–12, 412n20; Hammerslough's Lincoln memorial fund, 239; Lincoln's Jewish descent claim, 160, 225–26, 386, 388, 389; on Lincoln's virtues, 3, 195; in Markens's scholarship, 200, 268, 303; response to Grant's presidential campaign, 115–16

Wise, Isaac M., criticisms of Lincoln: overview, 200; administrative appointments, 205, 206–7; Christianity statement, 197, 204–5; election of, 23, 196, 201–4; military leadership, 207–8; physical appearance, 23, 204; Thanksgiving proclamation, 198, 421n25; writing skills, 205

Wise, Stephen S., 313, 333–34

Wolcott, Christopher Parsons, 94

Wolf, Daniel, 97, 111, 302, 412n18

Wolf, Simon, 19, 24, 24–25, 32–34, 37–38, 198, 231, 234, 269

Wolff, David, 105–6

Wolff brothers, 97

Wolfsohn, M., Board of Delegates of American Israelites, 79–83

Woodson, Carter G., 3

World War II, 310–11, 314–15, 359, 393–94

Xenia, Ohio, Christian amendment movement, 118

Yente Telebende (Rumshinsky), 294–96, 296

Yiddish culture, Lincoln portrayals: overview, 6, 235; musical theater, 294–96, 298; poetry, 355, 365–70

"Young Honest Abe" (Scolnic), 383–85

Zacharie, Isachar, *44, 58*; after Lincoln's assassination, 52–53, 406nn48–49; background, 44–45, 403n4, 404nn5–6; characterized, 45–46, 53, 406n50; diplomatic activities, 46–50, 55–57, 59–62, 407n61; Lincoln relationship, 45, 46, 52, 66–67, 404n7; Lincoln's reelection campaign, 50–52, 63, 64–66; newspaper coverage, 45, 46, 49, 54–56, 63–64; soldier foot care, 45, 47, 52, 58, 68–71, 404n8; testimonials for, 45, 54, 404n7

Zerbe, Farran, 430n31

Gary Phillip Zola is a professor of the American Jewish experience at Hebrew Union College–Jewish Institute of Religion in Cincinnati, Ohio. He also serves as the executive director of The Jacob Rader Marcus Center of the American Jewish Archives and as editor of the *American Jewish Archives Journal*. Zola has written numerous volumes and scholarly articles on the history of American Jewry. From 2006 to 2009 he was a member of the Academic Advisory Council of the U.S. Abraham Lincoln Bicentennial Commission.